Economic Aspects of German Unification

Springer
Berlin
Heidelberg
New York
Barcelona
Budapest
Hong Kong
London
Milan
Paris
Santa Clara
Singapore
Tokyo

Paul J. J. Welfens (Ed.)

Economic Aspects of German Unification

Expectations, Transition Dynamics and International Perspectives

Second, Revised and Enlarged Edition

With 34 Figures
and 110 Tables

Springer

Professor Dr. Paul J. J. Welfens
University of Potsdam
Wirtschafts- und Sozialwissenschaftliche Fakultät
Lehrstuhl Wirtschaftspolitik/Internationale Wirtschaftsbeziehungen
August-Bebel-Straße 89
D-14482 Potsdam, Germany

Pages 514 and 515 of the map of Germany are printed with the kind permission of Westermann Schulbuch-Verlag, Brunswick

Cataloging-in-Publication Data applied for

Die Deutsche Bibliothek - CIP-Einheitsaufnahme

Economic aspects of German unification : expectations, transition dynamics and international perspectives ; with 110 tables / Paul J. J. Welfens (ed.). - 2. ed. - Berlin ; Heidelberg ; New York ; Barcelona ; Budapest ; Hong Kong ; London ; Milan ; Paris ; Santa Clara ; Singapore ; Tokyo : Springer, 1996
ISBN-13:978-3-642-79974-7
NE: Welfens, Paul J. J. [Hrsg.]

ISBN-13: 978-3-642-79974-7 e-ISBN-13: 978-3-642-79972-3
DOI: 10.1007/ 978-3-642-79972-3

43/2202 - 5 4 3 2 1 0 - Printed on acid-free paper

PREFACE TO THE SECOND EDITION

Paul J.J. Welfens

The editor is pleased to present a second edition of Economic Aspects of German Unification which includes new chapters and several postscripts. Almost five years after unification output in the ex-GDR is back to its 1989 level. Due to a massive intra-German resource transfer consumption per capita in eastern Germany has not fallen as much as output and employment which reduced by one-fifth within three years. Given high West German transfers which represented about 5% of West German GDP and more than 50% of East German GDP the fall of industrial output could have been much stronger than had politically been feasible. Hence structural change necessary for productivity growth was dramatic in the ex-GDR where the goods producing sector (manufacturing, mining, energy and construction) strongly changed its proportions; within four years construction almost doubled, and the share of investment goods production reduced by 10 percentage points between 1990 and 1994 and is now down to 21.1%. Mining lost two-thirds of its share in the producing sector which itself was reduced relative to GDP. The share of the services industry increased by 5 percentage points between 1991 and 1994, but with a share of 27.7% in East Germany's GDP it was still about 9 percentage points lower than in western Germany. By contrast, government accounted for 20.9% of GDP in eastern Germany, but for only 13.2% in western Germany. East Germany's labor productivity stood at 29% of western levels in 1989 but will reach about 55% by end-1995 which is a remarkable achievement. Some firms in eastern Germany are even more modern than plants in western Germany; the vintage effect of high investment output ratios in eastern Germany is working in favor of the ex-GDR in the long term. This second edition includes new papers with a focus on structural change by HEILEMANN and LÖBBE as well as by WEGNER; the analysis points to deficits in economic theory with its emphasis on the macro view. The restructuring of the GDR economy within a compressed time frame shows in a nutshell the transformation problems faced by former socialist countries.

Economic growth rates of 7-10 % are feasible in the 1990s in eastern Germany which should help to achieve income parity within Germany within about 15 years. It will take much longer before per capita wealth figures are converging in eastern and western Germany - indeed one may assume that a large wealth gap will remain for decades as many industrial properties and housing stocks have been reclaimed by people from West Germany, including former East Germans who left the GDR during the 40 years of its existence. The restitution of property has created uncertainty and this and the new unemployment risk offset part of the real income gain which is occurring in the course of the transition to a market economy.

There are major economic divergences within eastern Germany where five new Länder (states) were restored; Thuringia and Saxony could become new economic gravity centers in eastern Germany as they benefit from historical economic strengths and traditions while the regional governments are actively promoting new industries and subsidizing high technology investment. The relatively poor state of Brandenburg is expected to merge with the affluent East Berlin/West Berlin which could create an interesting precedent for western Germany's states, too. One cannot overlook that economic divergences are considerable within Berlin and within the whole of Germany. This fact and social conflicts could endanger the stability of Germany. In this situation intragovernmental transfers are particularly important. HENKE, LUTZ and ADE analyze the system of transfers within Germany.

The new Germany could be an economic powerhouse in Europe. However, the united Germany faces major internal and international challenges. While price stability has been regained in 1995 - after a short inflationary development in 1992/93 - unemployment remains a major problem; indeed it will be difficult to remedy while there is an ongoing real appreciation of the DM which is in contrast to a decade of a gradual real depreciation in the period 1979-89 in the European Monetary System. The real DM appreciation also reduces inflows of foreign direct investment such that the overall investment output ratio might decline and offset positive growth effects associated with economies of scale in Germany's nontradables industries. While Germany's influence in economic terms is rising in the EU-15 club there is a relative decline of German and French political power in the EU. It also is unclear which concept the EU and Germany, respectively, will envisage with respect to the eastern enlargement of the EU. WELFENS looks into internal and international problems.

German economic unification shows that massive transfers, radical structural change and modernization of the capital stock quickly can achieve convergence - a strategy which is quite difficult to follow in eastern Europe. It is doubtful that the EU will enjoy sustained prosperity if eastern Europe cannot be reintegrated into Europe and if Russia/the Ukraine cannot be stabilized. To the same extent that socialist statistics created an illusion of economic well-being in eastern Europe and the USSR, there is an underestimation of the difficulties to switch to a market economy in a country in which there is no historical memory of the market economy left. Fifty years of an expanded military industrial complex in the USSR are more difficult to reverse than six years (1939-45) of transitory dominance of the military in Germany's private industry which quickly reoriented itself towards civilian and international markets in the FRG after 1945. These internationalized firms have largely taken over the industry in the ex-GDR where the old elites faced such a sharp shock of currency appreciation and competition that they are unlikely to keep much more than nominal power in industry and government. In the ex-GDR one can already hear Communist nostalgia which argues that it was not really so bad in the GDR; intellectual enlightenment would be needed to correct this biased picture of the GDR which achieved modest economic growth rates by coercion, enormous environmental destruction at the expense of future generations and strict limits on liberty and an omnipotent secret service. German unification offers many insights for international comparisons and is important for international relations and systemic transformation.

Potsdam and Münster, March 1995 *Paul J.J. Welfens*

PREFACE

Robert G. Livingston

Germany's "monetary, economic, and social union" was proclaimed on July 1, 1990 - a decisive step that brought together the liberal, social market economy of West Germany and the centrally planned, communist one of East Germany, the German Democratic Republic. From that day onwards there was no turning back from German unification, and constitutional union followed shortly thereafter, on October 3, 1990.

In truth, however, the union of July 1 was a monetary one only. That was the fait accompli. The West German D-Mark became the official medium of exchange in the GDR. The process of economic and social unification, however, only started to begin. Completing that process, not to speak of political, societal, psychological, and cultural unification, will take many years.

Many of the difficulties that Germany will face in uniting economically became evident quickly in the summer and fall of 1990. Professor Paul J. J. Welfens, who was at that time the John J. McCloy Distinguished Research Fellow in residence at the Institute, foresaw some of these problems and convinced us that the Institute should bring together outstanding economists to analyze them for a wider public.

Professor Welfens succeeded in interesting a broad range of academic scholars, international civil servants, and researchers from business firms and banks to address what were then a completely new set of unanalyzed, even unanticipated, exciting, and important issues. He convened the Institute's conference November 13-14, 1990, less than five months after monetary union. It was held at the University's Paul H. Nitze School of Advanced International Studies, which provided welcome logistical support.

The chapters in this study are the product of the presentations and commentary at that conference. They deal with a range of macroeconomic, microeconomic, national, and international challenges, the dimensions of which have since last November become much more widely recognized. Both the conference and this volume are the product of Professor Welfens's insightful, tireless, and detailed efforts.

The Institute is deeply grateful to Professor Welfens and to the authors and commentators whose work appears in this volume. We are proud to accord it a place in our publication series. Our appreciation is due also to the John M. Olin Foundation, which funds the McCloy fellowship, as well as to the several generous supporters of the conference on "The Economic Aspects of German Unification:" The Dresdner Bank AG, the Lynde and Harry Bradley Foundation, Lufthansa German Airlines, Morgan Guaranty Trust Company, the Representative of German Industry and Trade in Washington, D.C., the Siemens Corporation, and the Fritz Thyssen Foundation.

Robert Gerald Livingston
Director, American Institute for Contemporary German Studies, The Johns Hopkins University

Washington, D.C., July 1991

TABLE OF CONTENTS

Preface to the Second Edition
Paul J.J. Welfens *V*

Preface
Robert G. Livingston, Director of the American Institute for Contemporary German Studies at the Johns Hopkins University *VII*

Introduction: Economic Aspects of German Unification
Paul J.J. Welfens *1*

I. STRUCTURAL AND MACROECONOMIC CHANGES

A. The Structural Renewal of Eastern Germany: Some Initial Observations
Ullrich Heilemann, Klaus Löbbe *9*

1. Introduction: Why Structural Analysis of the East German Economy? 9
2. Determinants of Structural Development 11
   2.1 The Economic Policy Framework 11
   2.2 The Factors of Production and their Prices 13
3. Structural Changes in the Eastern German Economy 14
   3.1 Industrial Structures 14
      3.1.1 Production 14
      3.1.2 Factor Input 16
      3.1.3 Agriculture 18
      3.1.4 Small and Medium-Sized Enterprises 19
      3.1.5 Production and Employment Structures 21
      3.1.6 Economic Structures in East and West Germany - a First Appraisal 24
4. Conclusions 25

B. Integrating the East German States into the German Economy: Opportunities, Burdens and Options
Lutz Hoffmann *39*

1. Introduction 39
2. The Currency Union: Its Genesis and Impact 40
3. Pattern and Extent of Structural Adjustment Needed 45
4. The Starting Position of Individual Industries 50
5. Reconstructing the Capital Stock 53
6. Structural Adjustment Policy 54
7. The Financial Burden on the Public Sector 58
8. Concluding Remarks 59
9. Postscriptum: East Germany in Transition 61
   9.1 Macro-Economic Imbalance 62
   9.2 Structural Adjustment 64
   9.3 External Trade 70
   9.4 Employment and Growth Potential 71

C. Sectoral Shocks and Structural Adjustment in the East German Transformation Process
Manfred Wegner 77

1. Unification Concept and Transformation Shocks 77
2. Past Macroeconomic and Sectoral Performance 78
   2.1 Production and Employment Trends 78
   2.2 Manufacturing 81
   2.3 Small Businesses 84
   2.4 Services 85
3. Investment and Labor Productivity 85
   3.1 Investment Activities 85
   3.2 Labor Productivity 88
4. Regional Developments 89
5. Policy Orientation and Growth Prospects 92
6. Conclusions 95

D. Intergovernmental Fiscal Relations after German Unification: Problems and Solutions
Klaus-Dirk Henke, Peter Lutz, Claudia Ade 99

1. Introduction 99
2. Basic Elements of the System of Intergovernmental Fiscal Relations in Germany 100
   2.1 The Distribution of Public Functions between Levels of Government 100
   2.2 The Structure of Public Revenues 102
   2.3 Primary and Secondary Distribution of Taxes: An Overview 102
   2.4 The Vertical Assignment of Tax-Revenues 106
   2.5 Horizontal Allotment of Local Tax Returns 109
   2.6 Fiscal Equalization Among Länder 111
      2.6.1 Horizontal Turnover Tax Distribution 111
      2.6.2 The Fiscal Equalization Among Länder 112
      2.6.3 The Federal Supplementary Grants and Other Elements of the System of Intergovernmental Fiscal Relations 116
3. Interim Regulations for Unified Germany and their Necessity 117
   3.1 The Political and Economic Framework after Unification: The Development 1990-1994 117
      3.1.1 The Situation in East Germany 117
      3.1.2 The Situation in West Germany 119
      3.1.3 The Necessity for Interim Regulations 122
   3.2 Interim Regulations for the New Länder until 1994 124
      3.2.1 Separated Turnover Tax Distribution 124
      3.2.2 A Separated Fiscal Equalization System Among Länder 124
      3.2.3 The German Unity Fund 125
4. Long-Term Solutions for Newly Formed Germany: The Federal Consolidation Program and Subsequent Measures 127
   4.1 Overview 127
   4.2 Changes in the Turnover Tax Distribution 127
   4.3 Changes in the Horizontal Fiscal Equalization System Among Länder 128
   4.4 New Functions for the Federal Supplementary Grants and the Financial Aids 129
   4.5 Financing the New Regulations 130
5. Conclusion 132

E. Macroeconomic Aspects of German Unification
Hans-Werner Sinn *135*

1. A New Germany 135
2. Unification in International Perspective 136
   2.1 A Comparison With Other Eastern Countries 138
   2.2 Implications for the West 141
3. The Currency Conversion Problem 146
   3.1 Purchasing Power Parity 147
   3.2 The Problem of Two-sided Competitiveness 150
   3.3 The Money Overhang and the Real Asset Overhang 151
   3.4 The Planned and the Actual Money Supply 152
   3.5 Wealth Effects of the Currency Conversion 152
   3.6 The Bundesbank Unification Gain 154
   3.7 Portfolio Reactions 155
   3.8 Demand Reactions 156
4. The Privatization Problem 157
   4.1 The 49 Rule and the Pre-Coasian State 158
   4.2 The Legal Role of the Treuhandanstalt 160
   4.3 Risks of the Privatization Process 161
      4.3.1 Sluggish Privatization 161
      4.3.2 Cross-Subsidization 161
      4.3.3 Competition and Market Concentration 161
      4.3.4 The Erosion of Sales Prices 162
   4.4 Another Method of Privatization 164
5. Structural Unemployment 166
6. Conclusion 169

F. Comments
Rudiger Dornbusch *190*

G. Transforming a Socialist Economy: Currency Unification, Banking Reform and Capital Markets
Karl-Hans Hartwig *199*

1. Socialist Economies and Systemic Transformation 199
2. Money and Banking in a Traditional Socialist Setting 200
   2.1 Banking System 200
   2.2 Active and Passive Money 201
   2.3 Two Distinct Monetary Problems 201
3. Money, Credit and Banking in a Reformed System 202
4. Monetary Problems in the Process of Transition 203
   4.1 German Economic Unification 203
   4.2 Some Lessons from East German Reform 205
   4.3 Elements of a Monetary and Financial Reform 206
5. Perspectives 209

H. Comments
Jürgen Klose *211*

II. National Challenges

I. Labor Markets and Social Security Systems Facing Unification: Systemic Challenges in Germany
Doris Cornelsen *219*

1. Introduction 219
2. Labor Markets 220
   2.1 Facts and Figures 220
   2.2 Perspectives 222
   2.3 The Legal Framework 224
   2.4 The Promotion of Skills, Training 225
3. Social Security Systems: Health Insurance, Old-Age Pensions 226
   3.1 The Systems of Social Security 226
   3.2 Health Insurance 227
   3.3 Old-age Insurance 228
4. Financing of the Social Security Systems 229
5. Conclusions 232

J. Comments
Gerhard Bäcker *233*

K. Environmental Protection: Problems and Prospects in East and West Germany
Günter Streibel *239*

1. Introduction 239
2. Water Management 246
3. Destruction of Areas 246
4. Noise Abatement 246
5. Outlook 255

L. Comments
Peter Palinkas *264*

M. Structural Adjustment and Privatization of the East German Economy
Claus Schnabel *287*

1. Introduction 287
2. Structural Adjustment: Necessity and Perspectives 290
3. Deregulation and Privatization 295
   3.1 Promoting Competition 296
   3.2 Improving Economic Performance 298
   3.3 Improving the Public Finances 298
   3.4 Widening the Ownership of Economic Assets 299
4. The Treuhandanstalt: Organization, Objectives and Problems? 301
5. Privatization Strategies 304
6. Conclusions 306
7. Postscriptum: The Privatization Results 307

N. Comments
Garry J. Schinasi *316*

O. Government Support for Restructuring the East German Economy
Henning Klodt *321*

1. Introduction 321
2. The East German Economy in Transition 322
3. Criteria for Evaluating Different Types of Government Support 331
4. Prospects for Economic Policy 336

P. Comments
George M. von Furstenberg *346*

III. INTERNATIONAL PERSPECTIVES

Q. German Economic Unification and European Integration: Prosperity without Stability?
Paul J.J. Welfens *359*

1. Introduction 359
2. German Economic Unification 361
   2.1 Rapid Progress in East German Economic Restructuring 363
   2.2 Germany's Labor Market Disequilibria 373
   2.3 Supply-Side Changes in Germany and Prospects for a New German Economic Miracle 377
3. European Integration 379
   3.1 The Dynamics of the Single Market 381
   3.2 Problems with EU Enlargements 382
   3.3 Instability in the Political and Economic Sphere? 386

R. External Aspects of German Unification: The Polish View
Andrzej Budziński *391*

1. Introduction 391
2. Short-Term Consequences for Poland of German Unification 392
3. Long-Term Impact of German Unification on the Polish Economy 394
4. Policies Towards Poland's Integration into the United Europe 396

S. Comments
John P. Hardt *402*

T. Economic Reform in the USSR and Prospects for Trade and Economic Relations with Unified Germany
Ruslan S. Grinberg *409*

1. Introduction 409
2. Difficult Reform Situation 409
3. Economic Relations with Germany and Western Europe 413
   3.1 Economic Relations with Germany 414
   3.2 Perspectives 420

U. Comments 422
Angela Stent

V. German Unification as an Incentive for Institutional and Organizational Changes within the EC: A French View 425
Claude Menard

1. Introduction 425
2. New Perceptions and Old Apprehensions 426
   2.1 An Accelerated Process 426
   2.2 Two Attitudes 426
   2.3 Five Problems 428
3. Institutional Changes 429
   3.1 Within Germany 429
   3.2 Within the EC 431
   3.3 The EC and the Rest of the World 433
4. Organizational Effects 434
   4.1 Structural Adjustments 434
   4.2 A More Activist Government 436
   4.3 Effects on Industrial Organization 437
5. Conclusions 437

W. Global Economic Rivalry: New Perspectives on Germany (the EC), Japan and the United States 443
Michael Aho

1. Introduction 443
2. Trade Talks or Trade Tangles 445
   2.1 European Unification and European Preoccupations 446
   2.2 U.S. Policy Responses 450
   2.3 Some Policy Recommendations 453
3. Macroeconomic Coordination and the Coming Global Capital Shortage 455
   3.1 Economic Shock Wave 457
   3.2 Shifting Investment Patterns 458
   3.3 Emerging Monetary Union 460
   3.4 Ebbing Dollar Influence 466
4. Conclusion and Policy Recommendations 467

X. Comments 470
Gary Saxonhouse

Y. EC Integration and Economic Reforms in CMEA Countries: A United Germany as a Bridge Between East and West? 473
Paul J.J. Welfens

1. Introduction 473
2. German Unification from a European Perspective 475
   2.1 The Path to Unification 476
   2.2 The Economic West-East Divide in the Unified Germany 478
   2.3 Major Aspects of Germany's Bridging Function 481
3. EC Problems 483
   3.1 European Opportunities for Trade and Investment 484
   3.2 German Unification and Economic and Monetary Union in the EC 486

3.3 German Unity and the EC's Trade Policy Stance 488
3.3.1 EC Protectionism 489
3.3.2 Restoring Historical Trading Patterns in Central Europe? 490
4. Germany and the CMEA Countries in a Divided Europe 491
4.1 Support for Eastern Europe: EC-Widening? 494
4.2 Germany's Systemic Transformation as a Model for Eastern Europe? 497
5. Global Perspectives and Conclusions 501

Z. Comments
Martin Schrenk *508*

Map of Western and Eastern Germany 514

Appendix: Selected Data on Western German and Eastern Germany 516

List of Authors and Conference Participants *521*

List of Tables and Figures *523*

INTRODUCTION: ECONOMIC ASPECTS OF GERMAN UNIFICATION*

Paul J.J. Welfens

The economic and political unification of Germany in 1990 came unexpectedly. The economic and political collapse of the German Democratic Republic occured after 40 years of a socialist regime which enjoyed only transitory stability and never achieved the proclaimed goal of catching up with West Germany. A unique economic and political challenge emerged for Germany and the Western world when the political division of Germany ended in 1990. What had begun with several hundred people from the GDR seeking asylum in West German embassies in Budapest, Prague and Warsaw quickly became a starting point for a wave of westward migration of East Germans in 1989/90. Starting with the "leak" in the East Germans' favorite tourist country, Hungary (allowing East Germans to cross the border to Austria), the summer of political discontent in the GDR rapidly led to the collapse of the Berlin Wall in November 1989 and, a year later, to the political unification of Germany.

Issues and Problems

The economic unification of Germany raises a host of issues because it not only represents the breakdown of the post-World War II division in Europe, but raises the problem of economic division within a new Germany and a new Europe. It also raises the issue of overcoming income and wealth disparities as well as coping with the international effects of German unification. Many complex and fragile adjustment processes in Germany and the whole of Europe can only be understood if one correctly perceives the national and international impact of German unification. Moreover, the systemic transition of East Germany and the envisaged economic catching-up process lend themselves as unique case studies in institutional change, structural adjustment and economic change. Whether unification is taken as an opportunity not only for changes in the former GDR but also for reforms in the (old) FRG is an open question.

Facing a costly process of unprecedented economic restructuring in eastern Germany and a new regional political balance in Germany and the EC, prosperity and stability in the whole OECD area of Western industrialized nations is at stake. This systemic transformation of the former GDR also serves as a catalyst for changes and reforms in other countries of the Council of Mutual Economic Assistance (CMEA). Without the glasnost-perestroika changes in the USSR, the East German command economy could have survived for some time; however, the stagnation of the socialist countries in eastern Europe and the fact that several newly industrializing countries had surpassed the CMEA countries in terms of per capita income and prosperity in the 1980s was bound to build up pressures for radical reforms in all countries of the CMEA. Moreover, no Wall could prevent modern means of communication - isolation from new technologies to maintain power implied economic stagnation.

** I am immensely indebted to Tim Yarling for his editing talents and for all his other superb assistance.*

Among the CMEA countries East Germany had been perceived as the economically leading country (bolstered by quasi-subsidies from West Germany of some DM 10 bill. annually), but the sudden integration into the West German economy and thus the shift to Western relative price structures plus the full exposure to world market competition quickly revealed the economic weakness of the former GDR. A long adjustment period was not possible for eastern Germany since the collapse of the Berlin Wall - erected in 1961 - established full labor mobility in the all-German territory, and the monetary unification of July 1, 1990 ruled out a currency devaluation as a means of improving price competitiveness. The West German government was eager to seize the political opportunity to unify Germany in 1990, and all initially envisaged gradual steps to overcome Germany's political division were replaced by a fast track approach. The introduction of the West German Deutsche Mark was the first visible step towards (currency) unification, but whether rapid monetary unification and the GDR's rapid adoption of West Germany's complex web of laws, regulations and institutions was the best way to spread Western prosperity to eastern Germany and to maintain the Federal Republic's leading role in the EC integration process remains an open question.

In the first part of this book four authors discuss a subset of economic problems, theoretical aspects and policy issues that are considered to be of general relevance. *Paul Welfens* raises the question to which extent German unity is affecting the EC integration process which had entered a critical stage when German unification occurred. The "EC 1992" (single market) program and the Economic and Monetary Union (EMU) are major steps to an economically unified Western Europe, strongly influenced by West German industry, the Bundesbank's monetary policy and the political cooperation among West Germany and France. The new united Germany - economically divided, financially strained, and politically inward-oriented - is not playing the same role as before. Moreover, the EC partners face new opportunities in as well as new challenges from the greater Germany. East Germany's sudden switch to a market economy on the basis of a functional West German institutional system raises questions for the systemic transition in Eastern Europe, too. Ideas, institutions, investment flows as well as trade flows are changing in the whole of Europe and a united Germany might well play the role of a bridge between a highly dynamic Western Europe and an institutionally disintegrating Eastern Europe. What happens when the rich West German economy embraces the relatively poor GDR? *Lutz Hoffmann* analyzes the economic opportunities, burdens and options of the unification process. The picture painted is relatively bleak and emphasizes the enormous need for structural changes in the East German economy. According to *Hoffmann* intra-German migration of labor is going to play an important role for quite some time. Given the economic divergence of West Germany and East Germany on the one hand, and, on the other hand, the pressure and desire in the former GDR to rapidly catch up with living standards in western Germany, one may expect serious macroeconomic problems of German unification. *Hans*

Werner Sinn gives a theoretically founded assessment of the macroeconomic aspects of German unification. He gives key figures on East Germany and West Germany, raises a host of problems of the currency conversion and thoroughly analyzes the issue of privatizing the formerly `state-owned East German industry. Taking the broader perspective of systemic transformation of socialist economies *Karl-Hans Hartwig* analyzes the role of money and banking in the transition process. The switch to a market-based system implies a host of problems in the monetary and financial sphere for transforming systems. *Martin Schrenk, Thomas Mayer, Rudiger Dornbusch and Jürgen Klose* present remarks on the papers.

Part II of this book focuses on four distinct national challenges of German economic unification. *Doris Cornelsen* presents an overview of the complex problem of merging the West German and East German welfare systems and social policy approaches. The labor markets in the new Germany present particular problems, and it is clear that at least transitorily one can expect a high unemployment rate in East Germany. Based on different institutional arrangements and principles the social security systems of the two Germanies are not easily reconciled along the dominant West German rules of the game. *Günter Streibel* raises the environmental policy issues of German unification. The socialist command economy achieved its modest economic prosperity on the basis of not only mobilizing a very high participation rate of the population and hence a maximum labor force, but will also by radically exploiting the stock of natural resources. Cleaning up East Germany (recently estimated to cost between DM 100-200 bill. in the 1990s) will not only be costly but also translate into an impediment for much-needed private investment.

The structure of the East German economy needs to quickly adjust to new price ratios, the world of market competition and the set of West German and EC laws. *Claus Schnabel* focuses on the comprehensive requirements of structural adjustment in the context of new property right assignments for the formerly state-owned industry. Deregulation and privatization play in his view a key role for the switch to efficiency and the road to economic prosperity. The German state trusteeship Treuhandanstalt - representing some 8000 East German firms - was entrusted to organize the privatization of industry. As emphasized by the chapter's author, the bureaucratic approach to privatization could be costly and time-consuming. What can the West German government do in order to support the restructuring of the East German industry? *Henning Klodt* deals with this controversial question and discusses the alternatives of subsidizing labor or capital in the transition period. The incentive effects of changing economic regimes as well as the fiscal impact and the implications for output, growth and job creation are at the focus of interest in this second section. *Gerhard Bäcker, Peter Palinkas, George M. von Furstenberg and Garry Schinasi* offer comments on these controversial issues.

A final set of papers concerns the international perspectives of German unification. The new economic division line in Europe is between the united Germany and Poland. Poland itself has embarked upon a radical privatization program, and the government has expressed its desire to join the EC in the long term (with negotiations on EC associate membership status taking place in 1991). *Andrzej Budzinski* describes the Polish view of the economic aspects of German unification. Some German-Polish problems are related to geographical aspects, military links and economic exchange of both countries with the USSR. Due to these links the Soviet point of view is of particular interest although the perspectives adopted over time might change in the course of an uncertain reform trajectory. *Ruslan Grinberg* describes the economic reform in the USSR and the prospects for trade and economic relations with Germany. A united Germany is bound to be the most important West European partner country for all East European countries and the USSR. Germany's economic links with Western Europe are likewise gaining in importance, where the special relationship between France and Germany has played a significant role in the formation of the EC. *Claude Menard* raises the question of which institutional and organizational changes one may anticipate in the EC after German unification. For France, the EC has represented not only a welcome market outlet but also a useful political instrument whose significance could be altered by both changing political orientations in Germany, the U.K. and other EC partners as well as by economic shifts within the community and the global system. Japan and West Germany emulated U.S. institutions, gratefully accepted U.S. support for restoring functional market systems and enjoyed growing transatlantic/transpacific trade and investment flows, but with a unified Germany the historically grown international economic structures are likely to change. Relative economic weights are changing, political orientations in Germany and the EC may shift and options to achieve consensus for cooperation in economic policy and questions of international leadership might weaken. *Michael Aho* focuses on global economic rivalry and economic cooperation in an era of changing economic relations and global capital shortage. German unification will contribute to rising real interest rates worldwide and affect trade and investment opportunities in Europe. The EC - strongly influenced by Germany - could become an even more difficult partner for the U.S. as German unification raises conflict-prone issues for the EC member countries. If the EC can gain economic strength in the medium term and successfully achieve monetary union, one may anticipate a declining international role of the U.S. dollar. This in turn impairs the traditional policy approaches of U.S. economic and foreign policy, thereby raising the issue of new options for leadership and cooperation.

Given the complexity of merging two distinct economic systems in the center of Europe it is, of course, not possible to cover all the economic aspects of German unification. However, we hope that the major problems and issues are addressed. At the conference most economists agreed that the problems encountered in the process of German unification will certainly be much more difficult than anticipated by the West German government which in the weeks before the first all-German election had promised not to raise taxes for restructuring East Germany (within weeks after the Kohl government had won the elections, new taxes had to be introduced).

A New German Economic Miracle?

Very optimistic expectations for a quick recovery of the East German industry had, of course, been fueled by the politically popular analogy with the post-1945 West German economic miracle. In mid-1990 a majority of the East German population anticipated reaching West German standards of living within a few years (in the meantime, 10 years is a more realistic representative view). In the 1950s West Germany enjoyed an exceptionally favorable economic environment, wage pressure was moderate; the German currency undervalued for many years; and the market economy memory of managers, workers and (former) institutions well alive. After the currency reform output increased by 14 and 21.5 % in the third and fourth quarter of 1948, and year-on-year growth rates were double digit rates in 1949.IV (11.1 %), 1950.II, 1950.III and 1950.IV (11.5, 10.3 and 13.6 %). In 1950 the inflation rate was -6.3%, in 1951 it reached +7.8%, but in the whole period of 1952-1960 it was in the range of 1-2.6 % p.a. (-1.7 % in 1953). Moreover, the formation of the EC in 1957 supported the expansion of West German industry. In contrast, the integration of East Germany into the EC exposed an outdated industry to the full competitive pressure of a newly contoured single market. After 40 years of a socialist command economy the East German transition situation is different and much more difficult than that in West Germany after World War II. However, one may argue that with West German government transfers to East Germany accounting for 60% of East German incomes, the amount of monetary and real transfers available for the catching-up region are even more favorable than in the West German case with its help from the Marshall program.

West Germany's market economy represents a successful example of a rapid economic catching-up process. Per capita real GNP increased from DM 6,839 in 1950 to 13,199 in 1960, while the unemployment rate rapidly fell from 11.0 % in 1950 to 1.3 % in 1960. Moreover, mainly as a consequence of people migrating from former eastern territories and the GDR, respectively, the labor force in West Germany increased by 3.5 million in the period 1950-60, and more than 5 million new jobs were created. A growing savings rate of private household and high efficient investment contributed to full-employment and high economic growth. In this period the savings ratio increased from 4.2 % of disposable income to 9.4 % in 1959. A relatively high share of output (18.9 % in 1950, 24.3 % in 1960) was devoted to investment which yielded high marginal output effects since World War II had inflicted spots of destroyed private and public capital - much in contrast to the almost general obsolescence of the GDR capital stock after German unification in 1990. The high speed of capital formation was mainly achieved by high profit rates and moderate wage pressure on the one hand, and, on the other hand, by tax incentives for reinvested earnings and anticipated capital gains. Capital income relative to GNP was between 38 and 42 percent in 1950-60, but even more important seems to be the relatively improving wealth position of capital owners as measured by the change of the real value of capital (stock price index/cost of living index). In 1950 the stock price index stood at 10 (1980=100), and the price index at 39.2 (1980=100), but in 1960 the stock price index was at 111 and the price index at 47.2. The real value of capital increased by 822 % in the period 1950-60.[1] By contrast, profit expectations in eastern Germany are moderate and the higher oligopolistic interdependency in industry nowadays will only partly compensate for this; investment by industry leaders can induce parallel investments of rival firms willing to accept low returns on investment in exchange for a minimum market share in eastern Germany.

There is little doubt that East Germany will catch up with its own historical potential in the long run. However, one may expect that it will take more than a decade for the transition process to be completed in East Germany. Economic and political instability in West Germany could result from conflicts over how to finance the adjustment process. Deficit-GNP ratios of 5-6 % imply high interest rates, and increasing value-added tax rates/excise taxes plus higher state-administered prices imply the risk of higher anticipated and actual inflation rates which could reach 4-5 % in 1991/92. Subsidies and welfare benefits in Western Germany have to be cut. Major risks for economic prosperity in the united Germany are the following: distributional conflicts in western Germany; loss of policy credibility of the German government; and high unemployment rates in eastern Germany (partly a consequence of unions which will achieve wage parity for east German workers with those in western Germany by 1994 - way ahead of productivity parity). The socialist experiment in the GDR turned out to be a costly dead end of systemic design that created the illusion of high welfare benefits and full employment at the price of growing economic disruptions, the destruction of nature, a reduced life expectancy (2.5/3 years less than for men/women in western Germany) and the loss of economic and political freedom. Even less favorable conditions in other CMEA countries point to even more complex adjustment trajectories in Eastern Europe and the USSR. In contrast to the former GDR expectations for catching up with the West are certainly more modest. The new Germany can serve as an inspiring example for Eastern Europe and the USSR as regards theoretical considerations, practical failures and the sources of successful recovery. The economics profession, the business community as well as policymakers await new challenges.

Washington, D.C., May 1991, Paul J.J. Welfens

1 Calculations based on Deutsche Bundesbank (1988), 40 Jahre Deutsche Mark. Monetäre Statistiken, 1948-87. In the present east German restructuring one observes rapid privatization. Out of 10,243 firms which were fully or partly owned by the Treuhandanstalt, 2140 (19.8 %) were privatized by end of May 1991. 81 firms had been acquired by 68 foreign investors (of which from Switzerland: 15, France: 10, Sweden: 8, U.S.: 4).

I. STRUCTURAL AND MACROECONOMIC CHANGES

THE STRUCTURAL RENEWAL OF EASTERN GERMANY: SOME INITIAL OBSERVATIONS*

Ullrich Heilemann and Klaus Löbbe

1. Introduction: Why Structural Analysis of the East German Economy?

The economic unification of Germany attracted much attention right from the start (*von Dohnanyi, 1991; Welfens, 1991; Sinn, Sinn, 1991; Priewe, Hickel, 1991*). It is however doubtful whether all the problems which occurred in the course of the political unification process and thereafter have been viewed correctly, and above all whether the recommendations on economic policy were sufficient and accurate (*Heilemann, Jochimsen, 1993, p. 48*). In any case for a long time one deplorable factor was the almost exclusive concentration of the analysis on macroeconomic problems and particularly on fiscal questions, and the corresponding neglect of structural questions - a deficiency, by the way, which for some time also characterized the analysis of the transformation process in eastern Europe (cf., for example, *Kornai, 1990, p. 105*). The idea behind this indifference was that the creation of the proper institutions, regulatory or competition policy and macroeconomic stabilization were sufficient to warrant the catching up, with sectoral and business size policy playing only a complementary part. This kind of thinking had indeed shaped western Germany's economic policy framework since at least the late 1960s - and had proven successful. But it had obviously been forgotten in the intervening period that the assignment and understanding of the roles of economic policy had been different in the course of western Germany's post-war reconstruction (*Heilemann, 1991, p. 144; Wallich, 1955, p. 61; Lehmbruch, 1990*). In the fourth year after unification, these deficiencies and their consequences are, admittedly, only of interest to historians. If the attempt is to be made here at a structural analysis of eastern Germany, the reasons are quite different.

From the point of view of economic policy one has to ask to what extent the findings of structural analysis will necessitate a reorientation or modification of the present economic policy in eastern Germany. Are, for instance, the emerging industrial consequences acceptable? Are corrections in the privatization process required and possible, and can they be implemented against the current economic and fiscal background? What role have subsidies and transfers played? Has regional economic policy achieved its aims? A central question is, finally, that of the further macroeconomic development and its structural differentiation, for it is here, on the supply side, where the competitiveness of the east German economy will be determined.

There are, of course, also cognitive reasons for examining the structural conditions and consequences of the developments in eastern Germany. Looking at eastern Europe, this example will surely be of relatively minor importance given the many and massive involvements of western Germany (*Heilemann, 1991, p. 144*). However without a doubt, the development of eastern Germany sheds - new? - light on previously neglected or ignored factors in the development of modern economies, considering for example the significance of functioning governmental institutions or forms of privatization (*Kreile, 1993, p. 66*).

Interest in the eastern German economic structure does, of course, for the moment run up against a series of obstacles which are hard to overcome, some, completely insurmountable. The purely statistical information base, is extremely thin, with only four observation points (annual data) at best. From a diagnostic point of view it is even more restricted, considering that in many cases market directed processes could only occur after the start of 1991[1]. Even then, the companies in the possession of the privatization agency Treuhand were to a large degree protected from the strong winds of the market economy[2]. A conservative interpretation of the development to date also reveals the major role of the state - indeed, the proportion of transfer payments in 1994 accounts for more than 40 % of private disposable income, and when the indirect effects are taken into account the figure is probably over 60 %. In addition, various delaying factors have surely prevented the direct and complete effect of market economy processes on economic development. Finally, it has to be remembered that even in an established market economy system, current developments are as a rule the result of a host of developments and milestones, some of which reach far back into the past. All this indicates that the picture of the eastern German economy which can be gained at present still reflects to a considerable extent principles other than market economy ones. Put somewhat differently, the current picture can only be transitory in nature, and is extremely limited as a signpost pointing to future structures.

Structural analysis is to a large degree comparative analysis. Because of the regional proximity of the east German economy, its factor endowment, its general economic and policy framework, etc. it appears appropriate to see western Germany as a reference case, probably be corrected for the different levels of income (*Döhrn, Heilemann, 1993, p. 83*). This, however, does not take account of the effects on western Germany's economic structure which have resulted from the foreign trade constellations created by its much larger geographical dimensions, and which cannot be expected for the east. A suitable yardstick for the assessment of eastern Germany would therefore be a region of comparable size, such as the state of North Rhine-Westphalia (*Hamm, Heilemann, 1991*), which however entails different problems. This touches upon a further difficulty: Can the development of eastern Germany be regarded as so homogeneous that an analysis *in toto* is justified, or does the aggregation this implies has to be regarded as impermissible, especially as it loses sight of the development of the "islands and lighthouses"?

The following analysis is divided into three sections. In the next section (2), the determinants of structural development - the initial situation, availability and prices of the factors of production, and economic policy - are examined. This is followed by an analysis of the structures and structural developments for production, employment, income and demand (3). On the basis of these findings, the consequences for eastern and western Germany are addressed (4). A summary and assessment of the results conclude the analysis.

2. Determinants of Structural Development

2.1 The Economic Policy Framework

With German unity, the conditions were created for sectoral structural change to take place in the former GDR according to the rules and principles applying in the west. The factors determining structures are on the one hand the preferences of consumers, expressed in the market demand for goods and services, and on the other hand the level of technology, indicated by the quantity and structure of fixed assets and the nature of production processes. Possible differences between the (sectoral) supply and demand structures should be revealed and overcome by the free movement of prices for goods and the factors of production on the markets - without overlooking the fact that markets are not always perfect and prices are also the result of collective actions and manifold governmental interventions. Sectoral structure formation finds its concrete manifestation in factor input ratios, i.e. the distribution of the workforce among the branches of the economy. But government intervenes at this level too, in order to cushion the social effects of temporary disequilibrium on the job market, to avoid regional disparities or ecological distortions, or to remove deficits in markets which are actually or possibly to be of great future potential (*Löbbe, Döhrn, von Loeffelholz, 1993, p. 29*). In the course of unification and thereafter the social security systems, and also the rich variety of promotional tools - investment grants and tax concessions, regional aid and information programs, programs aimed at medium-sized enterprises and export aids - were applied to east Germany (*Bundesministerium für Wirtschaft, 1993; Kreditanstalt für*

Wiederaufbau, 1993); in addition, there are subsidy programs from state governments, which in some cases are considerably more extensive than in the western *Länder*.

It is now almost a truism that the establishment of this social, legal and institutional environment which is the necessary condition for rapid and (where possible) smooth structural change is taking much more time than had at first been assumed. The bottlenecks in public administration in the eastern states which have been pointed out unfavorably again and again in the last few years, the long, drawn-out planning and permit proceedings and the unclarified questions of property ownership are for the most part an expression of the fact that fundamental transformation of an economic and social system is a time-consuming process, with these systems having in the short run only a limited capacity for absorption and adaptation[3].

At the same time, the GDR-economy was exposed to the western conditions of free competition without any preparation: the state monopoly on foreign trade was replaced by free movement of goods, and the freedom to conclude contracts, take up a trade, practice a profession and live where one wished was realized; and above all, the DM was introduced. From one day to the next, the old production structures were called into question and measured against the efficiency criteria of the market system - with the result that the existing deficiencies in production range, in management and marketing, and also in the governmental infrastructure became apparent. Material and human capital were devalued to a dramatic extent and at a stroke.

As with the reorganization of the institutional framework, the overcoming of these supply side weaknesses is a time-consuming process: the absorption capacity of an economic system, its ability to implement new production and organization concepts and - not least - transforming financial means into real capital, depends on the time available. And for political reasons time was obviously extremely short. The objection that this reorganization could have been completed more rapidly and smoothly - pointing to the post-war experience of the FRG and to the massive fiscal transfers to east Germany - fails to recognize that at the time the competitiveness of western Germany was supported by an undervalued Deutschmark, and also by a carefully balanced system of internal price controls and free world market prices (*Rheinisch-Westfälisches Institut für Wirtschaftsforschung, ed., 1980, p. 4.; Schlecht, 1991, p. 13; Heilemann, Jochimsen, 1993, p. 37*).

2.2 The Factors of Production and their Prices

The rapid catching up of eastern German wages and salaries with western levels is believed by many to have been an extremely serious handicap to the transformation process. The two sides of industry had agreed on drastic wage rises for as early as 1990, not least to compensate for the strain resulting from the introduction of the western German tax and social insurance system (*Sachverständigenrat zur Begutachtung der gesamtwirtschaftlichen Entwicklung, 1990, p. 70*). For the following years too, under the impression of a (real or imagined) threat of massive emigration from eastern Germany, and being convinced that the creation of a low wage region inside a common economic area is neither possible nor desirable, the parties agreed on further large increases in wage scales in staggered collective bargaining agreements. As a consequence, effective earnings in the new *Länder* in mid 1992 amounted to 50 to 60 % of western German wage levels - and thus widely out of proportion with sales or productivity (Table 5; *Löbbe, 1993, p. 142*).

In contrast, and not least as a consequence of the massive subsidies (investment grants and preferential interest rates, special depreciation), capital is a relatively "cheap" production factor - and this was the case even though the existing stock of fixed assets had been devalued and revealed an extremely high demand for real capital.

Doubtless, the workforce potential is one of the most important locational factors in the eastern German economy; in this connection one has to consider the high propensity to purchase, the relatively favourable age structure and the comparable high level of qualifications (cf. *Scheuer, 1990, p. 67*). This still applies in principle today, even if a number of skills have in the meantime become obsolete and others have not yet been acquired to the necessary extent. The relatively high wage levels in eastern Germany thus represent an extremely important course-setting factor for the direction and intensity of structural change. Despite these policies, however, east Germany experienced a net migration loss of more than 1 million people, although with west Germany entering the recession in 1992/93 east-west migration came to a standstill.

The consequences of the wage policy were predictable (e.g. *Sinn, Sinn, 1991, p. 193*): businesses and industries which did not succeed within a short time in achieving a corresponding level of productivity by restructuring their production ranges and/or intensifying their capital were forced to cease production and to experience massive lay-offs. In addition, the sectoral wage differences in the *Länder* are still significantly less pronounced than in west Germany, and obviously take too little account of differences in productivity.

Wages well above average continue to be paid in the construction and printing industries (with their relatively full order books), but also in the mining industry and in shipbuilding. The sectoral spread of wages and salaries, measured in terms of the standard deviation from the unweighted average wages, has admittedly continuously increased since July 1992, but still remains well behind western German wage differentials.

All in all, the eastern German economy embarked upon the process of German re-unification with serious handicaps on the supply side. The changes in the industrial structure in the statistically covered period are characterized above all by the dismantling of obsolete production capacities and by the frictions associated with system transformation.

3. Structural Changes in the Eastern German Economy

3.1 Industrial Structures

3.1.1 Production

Immediately after unification, the disturbances described led to a dramatic drop in production and in value added, above all in the manufacturing industry, which only few people had considered possible (cf. as one of the few exceptions *von Dohnanyi, 1993, p. 270*). Only gradually are signs of stabilization, and here and there a hesitant recovery, appearing.

The branches of industry which have experienced relatively favorable developments predominantly include those areas which are dependent on regional demand, especially private consumption and construction investments and are thus fed to a great extent by governmental transfers or investment promotion. The first such sector is the food and beverage industry, which has been able to increase its share of manufacturing industry production significantly in the wake of a "return" by consumers to eastern German products (cf. Table 1). The building industry has also benefited, particularly in those areas where there is hardly any competition from west German suppliers due to high transport costs (e.g. the non-ferrous metal and wood-working industries); in a number of areas, demand appears increasingly to be approaching the limits of capacity. In this connection, however, attention also has to be drawn to a number of the problems of the eastern German construction industry. These include the fact that in industrial pre-fabricated construction (i.e. reinforced concrete skeleton and large scale panel construction), which is once again becoming important in eastern Germany, ever-increasing shares of supplies are coming from western German companies. The eastern German capacities in the pre-fabricated construction sector were shut down after the reforms - partly because the business units were too large, and partly because the quality of their products was deficient. In addition, eastern German firms are often incapable of solving complex construction problems, because they no longer have sufficiently qualified staff in the wake of the slimming down process (*Deutsches Institut für Wirtschaftsforschung, Institut für Weltwirtschaft (eds.), 1993, p. 139*). Apart from these product sectors dependent on local demand, relatively good production performance can also be found in the steel and lightweight metal-working industry (particularly rail car building), shipbuilding, precision mechanics and optics. This is due in part to governmental aid, in some cases extensive, which has been received for the completion of existing orders and for reasons of regional policy. As a further plus - for the development of the labor market, and also as a sign of a stronger permeation of the industry's structure by legally and economically independent, modern service enterprises - there is also the expansion of banks, insurance companies and other financial institutions, and of services for households and businesses.

In contrast, the capital goods manufacturers, and above all mechanical engineering as eastern Germany's formerly most important sector of industry, have been faced with serious decline. Their production program had been strongly oriented towards the needs of the eastern markets, and they faced massive drops in production following the reforms there - and the expiration of the transfer rouble arrangement at the end of 1990 - for example for metal-working machines, textile machines and mining materials (cf. Table 2). The move into western markets was recognizably difficult, as the companies were not yet able to react to the changed product requirements or to establish new sales organizations. The demise of industrial research also frequently appears to play a part here[4]. In many cases, however, the potential customers also appear to doubt the businesses' (future) capability to deliver, and fear a lack of after-sales service and spare parts supplies - as would happen if the eastern German enterprises were liquidated (*Sachverständigenrat, 1992, p. 87*). The same applies - partly in a less pronounced form - to electrical engineering. The production range of that industry was also determined by the division of labor within COMECON; the focus was discernibly on machinery and equipment for electricity generation and distribution. (A more precise analysis of the product structure presented in Table 3 is however impeded by considerations of data protection.)

The chemical industry is continuing to face particular difficulties. In the GDR, the industry was raw material-oriented, and to a great extent concerned with the processing and finishing of the primary energy sources (crude oil and natural gas) supplied cheaply by the former USSR (cf. Table 4). As the majority of its customers were also in that region, the eastern German chemical sector was hit particularly hard by the political changes in eastern Europe. It will now have to move towards a comprehensive renewal of its production capacities, and in particular change its basic raw materials, but is handicapped in doing so by numerous ecological burdens from the past.

In comparison with its size in the GDR, the iron and steel industry has also shrunk considerably (*Wienert, 1992*), down to around a third, and as measured by the number of jobs to around a quarter. The process of lay-offs will continue, as labor productivity is still significantly lower than in the west. A stabilization is taking shape in production levels, but the structure of the industry will have to undergo further changes. On the sales side, the previous eastern orientation will decrease, and on the production side electric furnaces will surely totally displace the current processes. At least, the lack of economies of scale and considerations of transport costs militate against steel production by blast furnace, oxygen converter and hot wide strip rolling. As electric furnace steel mills are relatively compact and achieve high labor productivity, they play a relatively minor role as creators of regional employment; in contrast to integrated large-scale mills, they also have hardly any spill-overs on other industries, and therefore intervention in steel policy motivated by regional economic considerations would not be appropriate.

In the remaining areas of manufacturing industry, the major decline in the textile and clothing industry, is also worth mentioning. It is suffering on the one hand from the fierce competition from low wage suppliers in eastern Europe and Asia, and on the other hand from the increased quality requirements of customers.

All in all, the industrial structure of eastern Germany - comparable production figures are available to date only for this sector - continues to be characterized by a considerable differentiation (cf. Table 1). This reflects the fact that the Länder grouped together here - in terms of area and population - reach a size equivalent to North Rhine-Westphalia or Bavaria, and therefore (have to) have a differentiated structure for obvious reasons. They can however also be regarded as the heirs to the GDR period, in which - despite a totally committed integration into the eastern European division of labor - there was nevertheless a noticeable desire to come into line with the west in as many areas as possible[5].

3.1.2 Factor Input

To adjust the labor input to the greatly reduced production, eastern German businesses were able to take advantage of a special ruling on short-time working up to the end of 1991 , and many obviously did so. In 1991, as a consequence of the short-time working arrangements in manufacturing (including mining), the average working hours per employee were one fifth below the average of the western German figure (cf. Table 5)[6]. This was sufficient, at least temporarily, to put a brake on the loss of jobs, and it was only in 1992 and (less rigorously) in 1993 that the number of employees had to be cut, with Treuhand's departure from involvement in job-creation companies also playing a role. In total, around 3.7 million or 37 % of all jobs were lost in the years from 1989 to 1993. As a background to this negative balance there are - illustrating the particularly dramatic nature of this structural change - both drastic cuts in some sectors (especially agriculture, mechanical engineering, electrical engineering, textiles and clothing and the public sector), but also major gains in jobs in the service sectors (cf. Table 6).

Nevertheless, it was possible to achieve a significant increase in labor productivity with the temporary short-time working (sometimes reduced to zero working hours) and a reduction in jobs; turnover in manufacturing industry per employee and per hour - as an approximation of labor productivity[7] - has increased significantly, from 25 % of the national average (based on employees) and 30 % (based on hours) in 1991 to a full 50 % of the total German average in the first eleven months of 1993. At the same time, gross wages and salaries - in total and per capita - were indeed increased (to 60 % of the comparison figure of the latest survey), but fell in relation to unit of turnover by around 10 % in both years. The unit labor costs - gross wages and salaries per unit of turnover - of DM 24.62 for the 1993 average are thus now "only" 12 % above the average for Germany as a whole (cf. Table 5).

It is precisely these "unit labor costs" which, in sectoral differentiation, not only reveal persistent problems predominantly in the traditional fields of east German production (mining, petroleum processing, the leather, textile and clothing industries), but also provide the first indications of new, competitive structures (cf. Table 7). Gross wages and salaries per unit of turnover were thus in 1993 significantly below the comparable level for Germany as a whole in the automobile industry where production facilities newly established by western German enterprises have started production. A similar picture is found in the ship building and synthetic processing industries. For the rest, the positive influence of regional demand and the benefit of governmental sales assistance are also becoming visible in the development of unit labor costs - for example in the non-ferrous metal industry, in the foodstuffs, trade, and in shipbuilding. For the remaining sectors, there are more or less significant cost disadvantages in relation to western German suppliers, and this - with the existing limits for price increases - is causing a continuing pressure for lay-offs.

To sum up, a rapid recovery in the level of employment in eastern Germany does not yet appear to be in sight, and stagnation is rather to be expected in the foreseeable future. A number of product areas do, however, seem to be quite able to keep up with western German enterprises, in terms of (wage) costs and thus competitive pricing, and also in terms of quality of the products.

3.1.3 Agriculture

The sector agriculture, forestry and fishing is an impressive example of the dramatic changes which have occurred outside the sectors of industry. By 1993, the 4,500 agricultural production co-operatives, 580 state-owned farms and 3,600 private businesses were transformed or broken up into new companies and new legal forms. The result was around 20,500 individual farmers (both full and part-time), 1,900 partnerships, 1,400 registered co-operatives, 1,300 limited companies and 200 other legal entities (data for 1993 from *AGRA-EUROPE, 1994, p. 8*).

The corporate entities - successors to the agricultural production co-operatives in the GDR - are noticeably losing ground to the partnerships (averaging 511 ha per business) and individual farmers (45 ha per business), who enjoy unusually large areas of land in comparison with the western German situation. The share of agriculturally used land held by individuals was already 35.7 % in 1993, having increased by 8.7 % relative to the previous year. This took place above all at the expense of the registered co-operatives, whose share of total area dropped by 6 % to 38.8 % although there was no major reduction in the number of co-operatives.

The previously highly excessive labor force in eastern German agriculture experienced a radical cut from 850,000 workers in 1989 to 180,000 in 1993. The manpower ratio in eastern German agriculture, now 2.8 manpower units/100 ha, is significantly below the western German figure of 4.6 manpower units/100 ha. By European standards, the unusually low manpower ratio in the east can be partly explained by the major reduction in livestock quantities in recent years.

The earnings positions of agricultural businesses in eastern Germany continue to be highly divergent: in a comparison of corporate forms, the partnerships perform best. These businesses are generally highly specialized, and exhibit extremely low staffing ratios with large areas of land. The profits made in the partnerships, and also by the individual farmers among the Agriculture Ministry's accountancy review businesses, were significantly above the relevant figures from the full-time western German businesses reviewed. In comparison, the earnings and output levels of the corporate entities are still very low. On assessing the economic development of the sole traders - and the partnerships - it has to be remembered that the establishment of these businesses is not yet complete: above all, a considerable increase in livestock and a further increase in area by renting of additional land are to be expected.

Developments in productivity have to be assessed in a highly differentiated form. "Oil productivity" on both sides is becoming less and less comparable due to the divergence in the relevant factor relationships (tendency towards more extensive farming in the east). In the development of animal husbandry performance, a close approximation to the western German level can be noted. Labor productivity is however surely - above all because of the poor performance of the corporate entities - significantly below that of western German agriculture.

All in all, eastern German agriculture has made great strides towards the implementation of efficient structures. It is becoming more and more apparent that agrarian structures which differ greatly from their western German counterparts with regard to factor input ratios, business sizes, and ownership conditions (proportion of additional land leased) will prevail in eastern Germany in the long term. The successors to the agricultural production co-operatives are threatened by a process of decay, which will most likely end with the establishment of very large family businesses (individual farmers or partnerships). In the longer term, the creation of a highly efficient agricultural sector in eastern Germany could exert a considerable pressure to adapt, above all on the agriculture in the south-west of the former West Germany with its host of small businesses. The decisions of the European Union on agricultural policy in the last two years - for instance *not* to adopt the planned area limitations on income transfers - have shown that the status of large-scale business elements has been enhanced in European agricultural policy by the east German *Länder*.

3.1.4 Small and Medium-Sized Enterprises

In contrast to the export-oriented manufacturing sectors with their large-scale business structures, medium-sized enterprises have experienced a remarkable upswing since 1990. This has predominantly been oriented towards the supply of local and regional markets. The small and medium-sized enterprises have thus profited from a development constellation in which - supported by massive transfer flows - growth impetus has been derived predominantly from regional consumption and from construction. In addition, with the fundamental change in the conditions for entrepreneurial activity, private enterprises have now been able to fill attractive market gaps once again in fields previously barred to them.

The information available restricts the analysis to the quotation of a few basic parameters to indicate the relevant orders of magnitude. In 1989, there were around 100,000 small private businesses in the GDR - including 80,000 enterprises in the craft trades. At the end of 1992, the number of small and medium-sized enterprises was estimated by the Institut für Mittelstandsforschung to be 394,800 (*Bundesministerium für Wirtschaft, 1993, p. 287*). In 1993, the number of small and medium-sized enterprises active on the market should have risen to around 440,000.

The increase in the number of self-employed persons in the total workforce is to be regarded as the expression of the eastern German economic structure moving closer to that of the former West Germany. The proportion of self-employed has risen in eastern Germany from around 1.9 % in 1989 to around 7.4 % at the end of 1993. At that level, it is still significantly below the comparable figure of approximately 9.0 % for western Germany. Excluding the agricultural sector, the structure of which as mentioned above differs strongly from east to west, the proportions of self-employed persons in the new and old *Länder* are now virtually equal: in 1993, they must have been around 7.3 % in the east and 7.4 % in the west of Germany. The western German self-employment rate in sectors other than agriculture was already around 7.3 % in 1970, dropped slightly in the seventies, and reached its lowest level of 6.8 % in 1981. Since then, a slight rise can again be observed.

Employment in the small and medium-sized enterprises was around 3 million at the end of 1993. According to that figure, every second job in the new federal states is already provided by a small or a medium-sized enterprise. On balance, this sector has not been able to meet the high expectations of some observers and absorb the workers made redundant in the former nationalized industries, and in the overstaffed civil service and agriculture sector. Nevertheless, the development as a whole is far better than sceptical observers had assumed.

Medium-sized enterprises have experienced different developments in the various sectors of the economy (1992 data from *Bundesministerium für Wirtschaft, 1993, p. 287*). In the craft trades, there has been a pronounced increase in employment in the last three years. According to estimates, the number of employees in the craft trades - including similar trades - passed the million mark at the end of 1993 (*Zentralverband des Deutschen Handwerks*, 1994, p. 35). The number of businesses at the end of 1993 was, according to this source (Chambers of the Craft Trades), around 121,000 for "true" crafts (as defined in Annex A of the German Craft Trades Law - "Handwerksordnung") and around 17,000 for "related" trades (as defined in Annex B of the German Craft Trades Law). The craftsman quota of 62 employees per 1,000 head of population in eastern Germany was only slightly behind the western German level of 64.

Restitution, privatization and the foundation of new enterprises in eastern Germany have created a new small and medium-sized industry which, according to calculations by the Institut für Mittelstandsforschung, comprised 8,500 enterprises by the end of 1992, in which around 374,000 people were employed. In 1993 - following the business registration statistics - the number of small and medium-sized industrial enterprises should have risen significantly (by around 2,500 enterprises). The number of Treuhand-owned enterprises which can still be reprivatized or privatized by management buy-outs is hardly likely to exceed 1,000. In contrast, newly founded enterprises are providing a strong impetus. The chances of survival of these medium-sized industrial enterprises are however highly divergent. While part of the medium-sized industrial enterprises have made considerable progress in terms of productivity and sell a growing proportion of their production to western Germany and abroad, the commercial survival of many other small and medium-sized industrial enterprises is questionable.

The establishment of offices by professionals has developed very rapidly since 1990, particularly where suppliers of household-related services are concerned. The wave of new doctors' and dentists' surgeries, taking on the inheritance of the polyclinics of the GDR era deserves special mention. The deficit in the legal profession inherited from the old regime has also been at least partly made up in recent years by the foundation of law firms. The number of offices and firms in the professions was 65,000 at the end of 1992, and is likely to have risen to 75,000 in 1993.

According to current estimates, there were a total of around 190,000 small and medium-sized trading and service enterprises (not counting the professions) at the end of 1992. These enterprises provided employment for approximately 885,000 people. This sector of the economy continued to enjoy a positive development in 1993, and the totals can be assumed to be around 210,000 enterprises with 950,000 employees. Enterprises supplying production-oriented services mostly arose from the splitting off of divisions and departments in nationalized industries. In comparison with western Germany, however, this sector is still relatively poorly developed. In the trading sector, there has only been a modest expansion in the number of small retail enterprises, while commerce in total has ranked among the most dynamic sectors of the economy.

3.1.5 Production and Employment Structures

The shifts in the sectoral production structure reflect not only the reactions to demand outlined above, but also changes in production processes and market structures. To make these changes transparent and to characterize them, the sectors of industry are assigned below to various groups and the relative gain or loss in significance of those groups is determined. For example,

the question is thus, raised as to how great the share of those sectors is which in general are regarded as particularly research-intensive or internationally oriented and how their share in gross value added and employment in the economy has changed since 1989.

A warning of possible misinterpretation is, however, necessary. On the one hand, the sectors of industry are - in the absence of specific data for eastern Germany - assigned to groups defined by western German experience. Of course there is at least a theoretical possibility that a particular sector in eastern Germany will be more capital-intensive in production, emit greater quantities of pollutants per product unit, or be more closely incorporated in world trade than its western German counterpart. On the other hand, - also because of lack of data - changes in the sector characteristics in the course of time are neglected. A rising or falling share of a sectoral group - for instance those areas of the economy classified as research-intensive - therefore in no way reveals whether the intensity of research and development in the individual sectors or businesses has increased or decreased in the period covered; it is merely the result of a relatively simple grouping of sectors in which all 58 sectors of the economy - between which distinctions are made in sectoral structural reporting - are assessed against certain criteria. Finally, multiple assignments are possible; the chemical industry, for example, is classified as research-intensive, but also as service-intensive and environmental-intensive. Accordingly, it is included in several of the sectoral groups separated here (*Löbbe, Döhrn, von Loeffelholz, 1993, p. 180*).

The results presented in Figure 1 reveal a number of the central weaknesses of the eastern German economy; they result primarily from the sales structures of the businesses, i.e. in the extensive collapse of the "world market oriented" industries - those industries which were formerly able to supply the eastern European countries in specified sales channels and at set terms and conditions, but which now have to gain a foothold on new markets (predominantly in the west). In this new price and quality competition, the high unit labor costs above all are proving to be a severe handicap. The results show that what in public discussions is often referred to as "de-industrialization" is a much more complex phenomenon: a decline of the world market-oriented, large-scale industries and of the secondary industries, i.e. those to be assigned to the sector of trade. By definition, this also reveals that the preponderance of the primary sector, just as typical of the GDR economy as its deficit in small businesses of the tertiary sector, has already been decisively corrected in the last three years.

The changes in the sectoral structure of the economy observed since 1989 have also permanently altered the factor input ratios in the new Länder. It will be remembered that stagnating industries with a high factor demand - i.e. with considerably higher specific labor input than in western Germany, but with just as high a capital coefficient at least - were numerous. In addition, the proportion of environmental-polluting industries was much higher (*Halstrick-Schwenk, Löbbe, Wenke, 1990, p. 26*). The changes occurring in the wake of German unity also become clear in Figure 1. There, the decline in the capital-intensive and environmental-polluting sectors and the growing importance of interindustrial and intraindustrial services are particularly striking. Figure 1 also shows that the widely bemoaned collapse of industrial research also has sectoral causes: the proportion of research- and technology-intensive industries has noticeably dropped.

These findings on the present sectoral structure of the eastern German economy can be summarized as follows:

- It is still characterized by a relatively high proportion of low growth industries even if these sectors in particular have been reduced considerably since 1989.
- The deficit in the sectors of the economy characterized by small medium-sized enterprises (i.e. particularly trade and services) has been extensively reduced.
- The losers from structural change in eastern Germany include the supposedly world market-oriented industries. This result is immediately understandable when one considers the collapse of east German foreign trade, coupled with the growing importance of product sectors which serve local demand.
- There are still a great number of environmental-polluting and capital-intensive industries, and also sectors intensive in human resources and wage costs. This is in line with the thesis that the GDR economy made extensive use of the factors of production (*Halstrick-Schwenk, Löbbe, Wenke, 1990, p. 26*).
- It is characterized by a decisively low proportion of research and development intensive industries. This is very much reflected in the disproportionately great decline of the capital goods sector.

It may, however, be assumed that the current industrial structures reflect the future sectoral specialization pattern of the eastern German economy only to a limited extent. The influence of intraregional demand based on consumption, and the need for redevelopment and re-establishment of the infrastructure, and of subsidies, is very clear. It is necessary for these structures to be crystallized out in the medium and long term, not least by their effects on other sectors through backward and forward linkages. In this way, new growth centers could be created, which would then be able to attract demand and incomes from other regions. Rapid success is not, however, to be reckoned with on the way to these "final" structures; and it is to be expected that this "second structural blow" in the eastern German economy will make great demands on the formation of financial, material and human capital in the FRG or at least its western half. A conflict of aims with the continuing high demand for capital of western German businesses and the government seems unavoidable.

3.1.6 Economic Structures in East and West Germany - a First Appraisal

It is suggestive to attempt on the basis of the criteria established here - the classification of sectors by particular input and output characteristics - a first appraisal of the eastern German and western German economies. In concrete terms, the issue is

- whether the economic structures in east and west are to become characterized by substitutional relationships. This would mean that the structures would move closer together, and that eastern and western German businesses would compete on their internal and external markets with extensively similar products, or
- whether they are to become complementary to one another, each then specializing in those products which can be manufactured especially well or cost-effectively in eastern or western Germany respectively, or which enjoy regionally concentrated demand (*Heilemann, Jochimsen, 1993, p. 54*).

Current findings tend to be more in favor of a convergence than a divergence of the two economic structures. Measured against the criteria employed here - the sales and business size structures, the input factors required and factor qualities - a relatively high degree of harmony is already apparent in the distribution of the workforce among the various sectors of the economy (Figure 2).

The conjecture that a mutual adjustment of the economic structures is to be expected rather than a specialization appears plausible when one considers that the basic economic conditions are already very similar by now. This is revealed by

- the almost complete application of western Germany's legal and institutional framework to the new Länder,
- the shift to a uniform rate of exchange with the introduction of the DM,

- the harmonization of the relative prices of factors of production - on the one hand resulting from rapid progress in bringing wages into line, and on the other hand from fundamentally uniform capital market rates[8],
- and the expected removal in the long term of differences which still exist, for instance in the structure and quality of the education system or of the infrastructure.

As a consequence, eastern German enterprises will in the long run be found on the same markets and with the same or similar products as west German businesses, i.e. there will be increased competition on the national and international (particularly European) markets. This development is all the more significant in that the (western) German economy is characterized on the international stage by relatively high export shares and a (still) relatively high share of total added value attributable to the importance of its manufacturing industry. It is highly oriented towards the world market, and it is "overindustrialized"[9]. One direct consequence could be an increased shift of certain production processes (with low requirements for the quality of material and human capital, and with low sensitivity to transport costs) into the eastern European countries. Under certain conditions, however this could also give rise to demands for protection of domestic markets or promotion of exports - for instance by means of low interest loans, export guarantees, or managed exchange rates.

4. Conclusions

The unification of the two German states and the collapse of the eastern European markets in addition to inadequate governmental framework conditions and disfunctional developments, for instance in the wage sector, have made large sections of the eastern German production structures obsolete. The social consequences of this decline, the ecological problems, and a number of other problems in eastern Germany represent a secular challenge to the "new" FRG. It will take considerable time and resources - official estimates expect transfers of 5 % of GDP to east Germany for at least the rest of the decade to master it (*Bundesministerium der Finanzen, 1993, p. 11*).

Starting from the findings of the present analysis of the east German economy - what can and must be done from a sectoral point of view? First of al it should be indisputable that for some years to come east Germany's development will be determined directly (production links) and indirectly (investment, fiscal transfers etc.) by west Germany's economic performance.

Secondly, direct governmental assistance for individual enterprises in east Germany - whether with the aim of preserving inherited structures or shaping future structures - is economically counter-productive. The massive distortion of competition on the eastern German goods and factor markets brought about by the manifold allocative competences of the Treuhand and "their" companies, to the detriment of small and medium-sized enterprises and new businesses, cannot, of course, be overlooked. But this is not sufficient to necessitate a call for an "active industrial policy" and conscious shaping of the future economic structures in eastern Germany, notwithstanding the fact that in most cases the Treuhand umbrella very much delayed a quick and proper adjustment to the new conditions of production. Where the sectoral and regional strengths of the eastern German economy will lie cannot be predicted with the necessary accuracy either analytically or empirically. The paramount function of government in a market economy is to establish an appropriate framework and functioning institutions, so as to promote economic growth and (sectoral) structural change and to shape them in a socially agreeable manner. In the present context, the following points deserve special attention (*Wissenschaftlicher Beirat, 1991, p. 39*):

- a rapid and thorough renewal of the infrastructure,
- further increases in the efficiency of public administration,
- removal of the remaining obstacles to investment by rapid, obligatory planning and permit procedures,
- a wider opening up of the markets and a rapid completion of privatization.

Above and beyond this, federal, state and local governments are sponsoring structural change in eastern Germany with a broadly based and richly varied range of promotional tools; investment grants and special depreciation allowances, measures to preserve jobs which at least come very close to wage subsidies, and specific assistance to sales (guarantees) have doubtlessly made the unavoidable reduction in employment levels easier to bear and created incentives for restructuring and for the founding of new businesses. No new, as yet untried, instruments - apart from a so-called added value preference - are in sight. It does, however, appear necessary to conduct a critical examination of these measures from the point of view of efficiency. This could reveal that in the given situation capital subsidies to enterprises are still the most acceptable method: The time limits always to be set for subsidies appear very easily implementable here, and private capital is the relatively scarce factor in the new *Länder*. From this point of view, wage subsidies are to be assessed much more critically: for the rest, all that has been said for and against wage restraint also applies to wage subsidies (*Heilemann, Jochimsen, 1993, p. 34; Löbbe, 1993, p. 148*). Objections to government aid to promote sales of eastern German products (perhaps in the form of preferential value added tax treatment) could be raised in that such arrangements leave businesses with a large amount of room for manipulation which cannot be effectively limited even by extensive bureaucratic control. Sales promotion for eastern German products on a "voluntary" basis - perhaps in the form of purchasing quotas for western German businesses and authorities - is, as has been seen, a relatively harmless instrument but also one of limited effectiveness. Anyway, the east German economy is already structurally diversifying so much that time has rendered most of these proposals obsolete.

Thirdly, what still seems necessary to stimulate and accelerate structural change in the new *Länder* is a change in wage policy. On the macroeconomic level wage increases should be limited to a level which approximately secures real incomes. On the sectoral/regional/occupational level a further spreading out of wage structures is also necessary. Whether this will make changes in the regulatory framework of labor markets of eastern and possibly western Germany necessary (perhaps in the form of relaxation clauses in collective bargaining agreements or in law, or the involvement of non-organized entrepreneurs in collective bargaining), or whether a process of inflation will force this restraint on real incomes (*Teschner, 1992, p. 148*), remains to be seen. The extent to which the social security nets are still capable of cushioning the consequences for the income position to the desired extent will, however, have to be examined. This addresses in particular the financial capabilities of the unemployment and pension insurance schemes, and also those of the *Länder* governments (and thus also the financial compensation mechanism between the Länder).

Appendix

Table 1: Gross Outputs of Manufacturing Industry (including Mining) in Eastern Germany by Kinds of Products

	in Mil. DM	Shares in % all kinds of products = 100			D = 100[a]	
	1993	2nd half-year 1990	1991	1994[b]	1991	1994[b]
Mining products	3 991	11,7	8,8	3,5	22,3	13,2
Oil products	2 031	2,8	4,0	2,1	12,8	9,2
Stones, earth	5 649	2,9	3,0	9,1	6,5	17,0
Iron and steel	2 316	3,0	6,9	2,7	6,1	6,2
Non-ferrous metals	1 167	1,9	1,7	1,4	5,6	5,5
Casting products	571	1,2	1,3	0,9	6,3	6,6
Drawing, cold rolling mills and steel forming	1 171	1,1	1,1	1,6	2,4	4,4
Steel construction products	6 223	4,0	7,1	6,9	15,3	18,1
Mechanical engineering products	7 858	15,3	13,1	8,7	5,2	4,6
Road vehicles	5 334	10,6	2,7	8,2	0,9	3,4
Watercraft	1 653	1,6	1,6	2,3	19,5	32,8
Aircraft	15	0,0	0,0	0,0	-	-
Electrotechnical products	7 012	9,9	8,5	9,1	4,1	5,3
Precision engineering, optics	464	0,8	0,5	0,7	2,1	3,7
Metal products	1 956	1,4	1,6	2,5	2,1	3,8
Musical instruments, toys and sundries	299	0,5	0,3	0,4	2,9	4,3
Chemical products	5 326	7,0	9,1	6,7	4,3	3,7
Office machines, EDP-products	305	0,6	0,4	0,5	1,7	3,2
Fine ceramic products	397	0,4	0,5	0,5	6,9	9,0
Glass and glass products	837	0,7	1,0	1,1	5,9	7,8
Wood	320	0,5	0,5	0,5	3,3	4,2
Wooden products	2 531	1,8	2,4	3,1	4,5	6,5
Pulp and paper production	499	0,7	1,0	0,8	4,3	4,4
Paper products	648	0,6	0,7	0,9	2,0	3,3
Printing products	1 236	0,8	1,5	1,6	3,4	4,4
Synthetic products	1 901	0,7	0,9	3,2	1,2	4,8
Rubber products	412	0,6	0,6	0,6	3,0	3,9
Leathers and leather products	268	1,0	0,7	0,3	8,1	6,0
Textiles	1 322	3,1	2,2	1,7	4,6	5,3
Clothing	557	1,4	0,9	0,7	4,2	4,7
Foodstuffs	14 490	11,4	15,2	17,7	7,2	9,6
Tobacco	0	0,3	0,4	0,0	4,0	-
Pre-fabricated construction parts in structural engineering	56	0,1	0,1	0,1	2,6	1,7
Total, all products	78 814	100,0	100,0	100,0	4,9	6,1

Source: Statistisches Bundesamt; authors' calculations and estimates. - [a]D = Federal Republic of Germany after unification. - b = January till September.

Table 2: Composition of Mechanical Engineering in Eastern Germany
1992

	in Mil. DM	Percentage change from previous year	Shares in % all kinds of products = 100	D = 100[a]
Agricultural machinery, tractors	614	-34,3	8,1	7,1
Mining machinery and facilities	234	-56,9	3,1	10,9
Smelter, rolling mill facilities, and sundries	152	-24,4	2,0	3,3
Chemical and synthetic processing machinery	587	3,5	7,8	4,8
Paper and printing machinery	300	-38,9	4,0	2,6
Machinery for leather, textile, and clothing	277	-44,1	3,7	3,0
Machinery for foodstuffs and others	310	-6,9	4,1	2,8
Construction, building material, and similar machinery	386	5,2	5,1	2,9
Metal-working machinery	620	-54,1	8,2	4,4
Tools for metal working	302	-0,7	4,0	4,1
Internal-combustion engines, pumps	518	-36,2	6,8	4,3
Mining and extraction technology	614	-14,0	8,1	4,0
Fittings, oil hydraulics, and pneumatics	333	-21,4	4,4	2,2
Other mechanical engineering products	2 325	-17,3	30,7	4,2
Total	7 572	-26,8	100,0	3,9

Source: Statistisches Bundesamt; authors' calculations. - [a]D = Federal Republic of Germany after unification.

Table 3: Composition of Electrotechnical Industry in Eastern Germany - 1992

	in Mil. DM	Percentage change from previous year	Shares in % all kinds of products = 100	D = 100[a]
Devices and installations				
for electricity generation and transformation	669	-17,6	10,4	4,1
for electricity allocation	1 232	0,6	19,2	4,4
for industry and household	424	-16,0	6,6	1,9
Electric lights and lamps	193	-2,2	3,0	2,6
Telecommunication devices and facilities	355	-34,5	5,5	2,0
Broadcasting, television, and record-player facilities	411	-44,8	6,4	2,2
Electric measuring, testing and controlling devices	288	9,5	4,5	1,7
Other electrotechnical products	2 837	16,5	44,3	7,8
Total	6 409	-4,7	100,0	3,9

Source: Statistisches Bundesamt; authors' calculations. - [a]D = Federal Republic of Germany after unification.

Table 4: The Chemical Industry in Eastern Germany -1992

	in Mil. DM	Percentage change from previous year	Shares in % all kinds of activities = 100	Shares in % D = 100[a]
Inorganic basic substances and chemicals	585	-17,7	9,9	5,7
Organic basic substances and chemicals	956	-25,8	16,3	4,0
Fertilizers, pesticides	332	-36,2	5,6	8,2
Synthetics and synthetic india rubber	1 076	-20,0	18,3	4,0
Synthetic fibres	315	1,9	5,4	6,3
Dyestuffs, paints, varnishes and sundries	315	7,8	5,4	1,7
Pharmaceutical products	1 555	-18,7	26,5	4,7
Other chemical products	740	-7,0	12,6	1,8
Remaining chemical products	4	-32,9	0,1	0,2
Total	5 878	-18,1	100,0	3,6

Source: Statistisches Bundesamt; authors' calculations. - [a]D = Federal Republic of Germany after unification.

Table 5: Turnover and Wage Costs in the Manufacturing and Mining Industry in Eastern Germany
1991 and 1993

	Year 1991	Year 1992	Year 1993	Change in % 91/92	Change in % 92/93	Germany=100[a] 1991	Germany=100[a] 1992	Germany=100[a] 1993
Turnover								
in bill. DM	96,62	92,97	98,11	-3,8	5,5	4,7	4,5	5,1
per employee, in DM	54 930	98 640	133 290	79,6	35,1	24,9	39,8	52,0
per working hour, in DM	44,30	64,20	86,00	45,0	33,9	30,3	40,6	.
Gross wages and salaries								
in bill. DM	29,60	25,61	24,18	-13,5	-5,6	6,9	5,8	5,7
per employee, in DM	16 828	27 172	32 844	61,5	20,9	36,2	51,0	58,7
per working hour, in DM	13,60	17,70	21,20	30,3	19,8	44,1	52,0	.
per unit turnover, in DM	30,63	27,55	24,64	-10,1	-10,6	145,6	128,1	113,0
Memorandum items:								
Employees, in 1 000	1 758,8	942,5	736,1	-46,4	-22,3	23,4	12,9	10,8
Total workvol. (bill. h)	2 183	1 449	1141	-33,6	-21,3	.	.	.
Working time per employee, in h	1 241	1 537	1550	23,8	0,8	.	.	.

Source: Statistisches Bundesamt; authors' calculations. - [a]D = Federal Republic of Germany after unification.

Table 6: Sectoral Employment in Eastern Germany[1]
1989 and 1992

	in 1,000		Shares in %		D = 100[a]	
	1989	1992	1989	1992	1989	1992
Agriculture, forestry and fishing	1 050	330	10,6	5,2	50,5	26,3
Energy and water supply	180	100	1,8	1,6	39,0	25,8
Mining	215	120	2,2	1,9	53,1	42,4
Manufacturing industry	3 025	1 315	30,7	20,6	25,8	12,8
of which						
Chemical industry	220	90	2,2	1,4	25,6	12,3
Steel and light metal Engineering	115	84	1,2	1,3	38,6	29,9
Mechanical engineering	530	221	5,4	3,5	31,4	15,7
Road vehicle engineering	130	68	1,3	1,1	11,4	6,1
Shipbuilding	50	20	0,5	0,3	58,8	37,5
Electrical engineering	380	160	3,9	2,5	23,8	11,7
Textile industry	210	42	2,1	0,7	46,3	16,3
Clothing industry	180	37	1,8	0,6	43,2	14,9
Food and beverage industry	275	169	2,8	2,6	25,7	16,2
Construction	780	750	7,9	11,8	29,9	28,0
Trade	860	660	8,7	10,3	19,3	14,2
Transport and tele-communications	700	545	7,1	8,5	31,0	24,7
Banking and insurance	80	150	0,8	2,4	8,6	13,7
Other services	470	1 020	4,8	16,0	10,6	17,9
Government, Non-profit-making organisations[2]	2 500	1 390	25,4	21,8	31,3	19,8
All sectors	9 860	6 380	100,0	100,0	26,3	17,8

Sources: Statistisches Bundesamt, Institut für Arbeitsmarkt- und Berufsforschung, and Deutsches Institut für Wirtschaftsforschung; authors' calculations and estimates. - [1]Work-place concept. - [2]Including employees in job-creation schemes. - [a]D = Federal Republic of Germany after unification.

Table 7: Labor Cost in the Manufacturing Sector in Eastern Germany
1993

	Gross wages and salaries per employee		Turnover per employee		Gross wages and salaries per unit of turnover	
	in 1,000 DM	Germany = 100[a]	in 1,000 DM	Germany = 100[a]	in 1,000 DM	Germany = 100[a]
Mining	47,7	80,9	114,6	66,6	41,6	121,5
Oil processing	35,2	48,2	386,4	11,0	9,1	440,7
Stones, earth	36,3	66,8	197,0	73,5	18,4	90,9
Iron and steel industry	29,8	55,5	179,9	74,9	16,6	74,1
Non-ferrous metal production and processing	34,5	57,5	286,7	85,8	12,0	67,0
Casting mills	29,7	57,7	62,8	43,3	47,3	133,2
Drawing and cold rolling mills	32,1	230,7	117,4	190,3	27,3	121,3
Chemical industry	33,8	49,4	127,9	38,8	26,5	127,3
Wood-working	28,4	57,8	117,0	1 300,6	24,3	4,5
Pulp and paper production	30,2	51,9	124,8	39,1	24,2	132,8
Rubber processing	29,1	53,0	94,0	46,8	31,0	113,1
Steel and light metal engineering	33,4	65,9	84,4	51,5	40,0	128,0
Mechanical engineering	32,3	55,7	91,0	47,3	35,5	117,6
Road vehicle engineering	30,6	48,9	193,2	65,9	15,9	74,3
Shipbuilding	32,3	63,2	128,4	66,0	25,1	95,6
Electrical engineering	34,2	57,9	113,7	53,1	30,1	109,1
Precision engineering, optics	28,8	55,9	59,3	35,2	48,5	158,8
Metal products	30,0	59,3	116,9	57,4	25,7	103,4
Musical instruments, toys and others	25,4	59,9	60,8	38,3	41,8	156,5
Office machines, EDP	27,6	36,3	121,0	31,6	22,8	114,7
Fine ceramics	26,6	66,2	52,5	48,2	50,7	137,2
Glass	30,0	58,7	99,7	52,0	30,1	112,9
Wood-processing	28,6	59,8	114,1	56,0	25,1	106,6
Paper processing	28,8	57,5	122,3	51,6	23,6	111,5
Printing	49,9	73,9	121,6	64,2	36,1	115,2
Synthetics	31,3	62,9	154,5	74,6	20,3	84,4
Leather production	25,6	59,5	85,6	36,1	30,0	165,0
Leather processing	23,3	61,3	60,2	29,9	38,8	205,3
Textile industry	24,7	57,4	75,1	38,3	32,9	149,8
Clothing industry	21,3	60,3	56,0	29,2	38,1	206,7
Repair of consumer durables	25,6	79,7	66,4	80,3	38,5	99,3
Food industry	29,3	64,3	261,2	66,0	11,2	97,4
Tobacco processing	40,0	59,1	1158,4	62,7	3,5	94,3
Others	30,5	.	88,6	.	34,4	137,7
Total	32,8	58,8	133,3	52,4	24,6	112,4

Source: Statistisches Bundesamt; authors' calculations. - [a]D = Federal Republic of Germany after unification.

Figure 1: Employed in Eastern Germany by aggregated sectors

Employed in Eastern Germany by aggregated sectors

Shares in the sum of all sectors in %

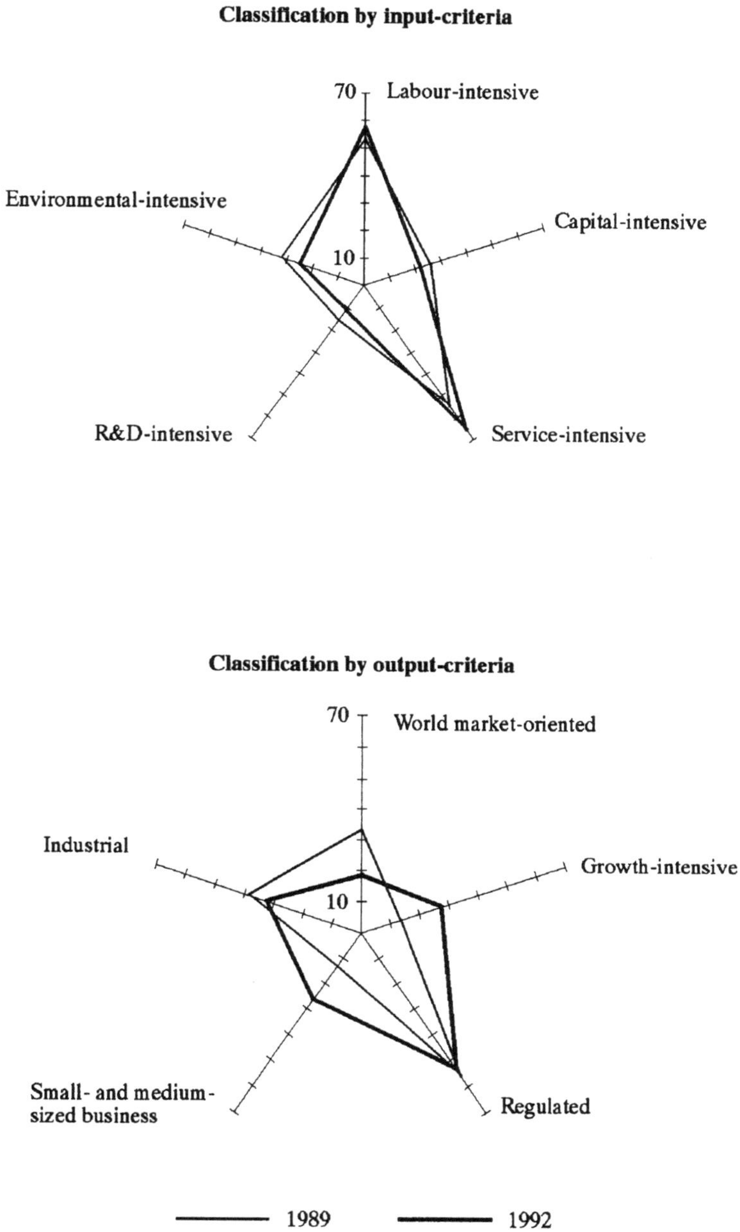

Authors' calculations.

Figure 2: Employed in Eastern and Western Germany by aggregated sectors

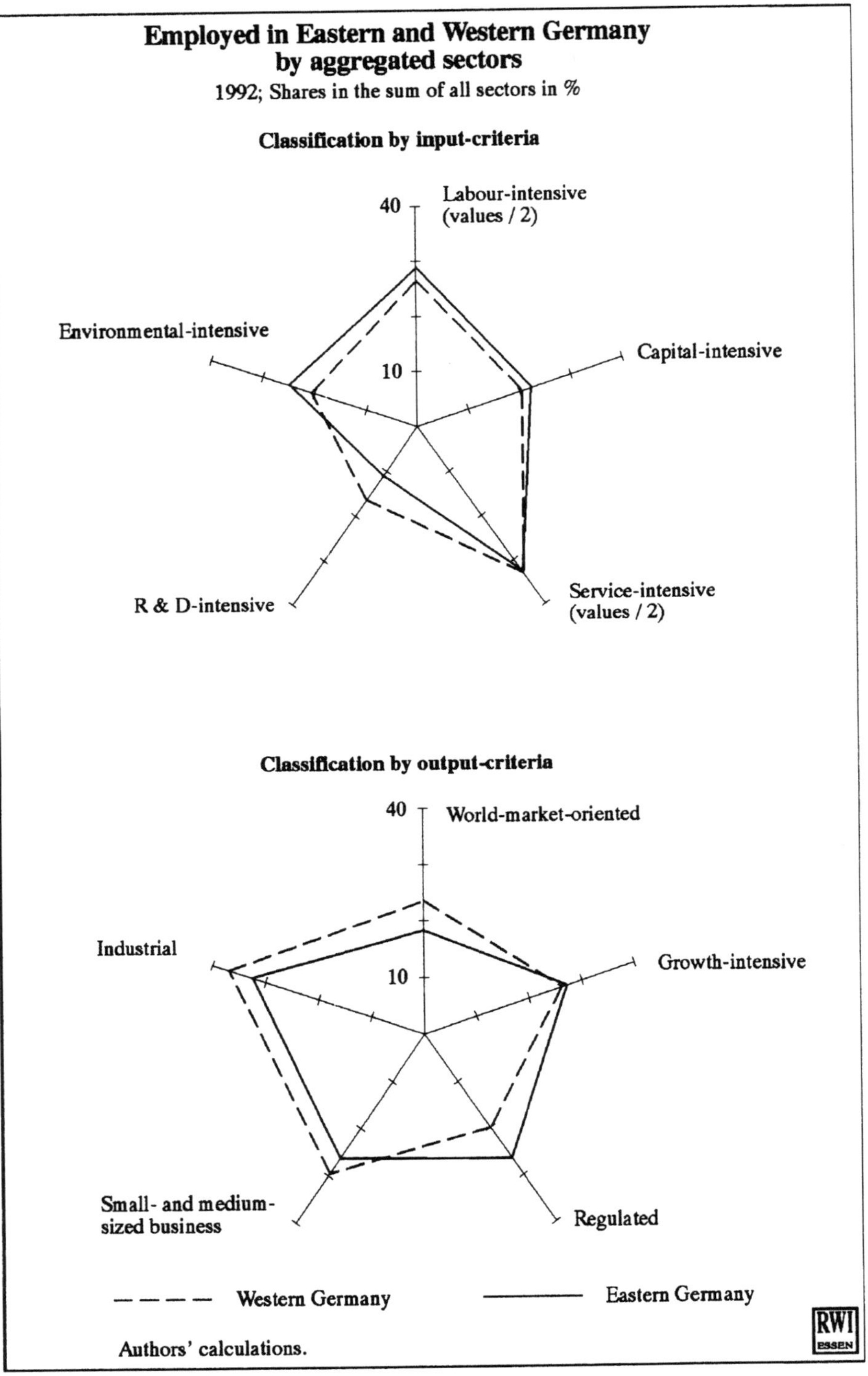

Endnotes

* *The authors are very grateful to Rainer Graskamp (RWI) for his assistance.*

1 For a detailed chronology of the policies and events of German unification see Heilemann, Jochimsen, 1993, Appendix.

2 A final assessment of the Treuhand policy is still to be made. In 1990 the Treuhand Agency had about 2.9 mill employed or nearly 40 % of the east German labor force under its umbrella. This share will be reduced to about 3 % or 170 000 by the end of 1994.

3 The concept of absorption capacity refers to the ability of an economy to transform a certain investment amount into real economic assets (Adler, 1965). It is used in this sense in the further course of this document. In connection with the "sudden and comprehensive change in elementary conditions of action for the people in the new federal states", Hüther identifies a "minimum of structural continuity ... as the expression of a limited capacity of people to adapt" (Hüther, 1993, pp. 32f.).

4 In contrast to western Germany, where joint industrial research plays a special role, research and product development were predominantly the province of the combines. The adoption of modern technologies - for instance by way of licences - frequently ran up against insurmountable revenue or liquidity problems.

5 For a comparative analysis of the eastern and western economic structures "on the eve of German unification", see for example Halstrick-Schwenk, Löbbe, Wenke, 1990 and the references listed there.

6 These data include our own estimates of the working hours of white collar workers, and it is assumed that white collar workers were significantly less affected by the short-time working arrangements than blue collar workers.

7 A sectoral grouping of gross value added (i.e. production values or sales less input amounts) is not available.

8 The latter are indeed being modified, not least by the loan cost reduction programs, e.g. that implemented by the Kreditanstalt für Wiederaufbau (Reconstruction Loan Corporation), in the context of regional policy. In this connection, the extensive promotional programs of the federal states themselves should not be forgotten although their actual effects are hardly possible to assess.

9 The thesis of the "overindustrialization" of west Germany goes back to Fels, Schatz, Wolter, 1971. For a critical evaluation see Löbbe, 1986/87.

References

ADLER, JOHN H. (1965), Absorptive Capacity. The Concept and Its Determinants. (Brookings Staff Paper.) Washington, D.C.

AGRA-EUROPE (1994), Agrarbericht 1994, vol. 35, Bonn, Nr. 8, Dokumentation.

BUNDESMINISTERIUM FÜR FINANZEN (1993), Finanzbericht 1994. Bonn.

BUNDESMINISTERIUM FÜR WIRTSCHAFT (1993), Unternehmensgrößenstatistik 1992/1993. Daten und Fakten. (BMWI-Studienreihe, Nr. 80.) Bonn.

BUNDESMINISTERIUM FÜR WIRTSCHAFT, Referat für Öffentlichkeitsarbeit (ed.) (1993), Wirtschaftliche Förderung in den neuen Bundesländern. Stand August 1993. Bonn.

DEUTSCHES INSTITUT FÜR WIRTSCHAFTSFORSCHUNG und INSTITUT FÜR WELTWIRTSCHAFT AN DER UNIVERSITÄT KIEL unter Mitarbeit des INSTITUTS FÜR WIRTSCHAFTSFORSCHUNG HALLE (eds.) (1993), Gesamtwirtschaftliche und unternehmerische Anpassungsfortschritte in Ostdeutschland. Achter Bericht. DIW-Wochenbericht, Berlin, vol. 60, pp. 131-158.

DÖHRN, ROLAND and HEILEMANN, ULLRICH (1993), Structural change in Eastern Europe. In: Bernhard Heitger and Leonard Waverman (eds.), German unification and the international economy. London: Routledge, pp. 83- 113.

FELS, GERHARD, SCHATZ, KLAUS-WERNER und WOLTER, FRANK (1971), Der Zusammenhang zwischen Produktionsstruktur und Entwicklungsniveau. Weltwirtschaftliches Archiv, Tübingen, vol. 106, pp. 240-278.

GAHLEN, BERNHARD, HESSE, HELMUT und RAMSER, HANS -JÜRGEN (eds.) (1992), Von der Plan- zur Marktwirtschaft. Eine Zwischenbilanz. (Schriften des Ottobeuroner Seminars, vol. 2). Tübingen: Mohr und Siebeck.

HALSTRICK-SCHWENK, MARIANNE, LÖBBE, KLAUS und WENKE, MARTIN (1990), Die sektoralen Wirtschaftsstrukturen in der Bundesrepublik und der DDR. RWI-Mitteilungen, Berlin, vol. 41, pp. 11-28.

HAMM, RÜDIGER, HEILEMANN, ULLRICH (1991), Folgen der deutschen Vereinigung für die nordrhein-westfälische Wirtschaft. (RWI-Papiere, 21.) Essen.

HEILEMANN, ULLRICH (1991), The Economics of German Unification - a First Appraisal. Konjunkturpolitik, Berlin, vol. 37, 127-155.

HEILEMANN, ULLRICH and JOCHIMSEN, REIMUT (1993), Christmas in July - The Political Economy of German Unification Reconsidered. Brookings Occasional Papers. Washington, D.C.: Brookings Institution.

HÜTHER, MICHAEL (1993), Integration der Transformation. Überlegungen zur Wirtschaftspolitik für das vereinigte Deutschland. Jahrbuch für Sozialwissenschaft, vol. 44, Göttingen, pp. 31-52.

KORNAI, JANOS (1990), The Road to a Free Economy. Shifting from a Socialist System - The Example of Hungary. New York: Norton.

KREDITANSTALT FÜR WIEDERAUFBAU (ed.) (1993), Geschäftsbericht 1993. Frankfurt.

KREILE, MICHAEL (1992), The Political Economy of the New Germany. In: Paul Stares (ed.), The New Germany and the New Europe. Washington, D.C.: Brookings Institution, pp. 55 - 92.

LEHMBRUCH, GERHARD (1990), Die improvisierte Vereinigung. Leviathan, Opladen, vol. 15, pp. 462-486.

LÖBBE, KLAUS (1986/1987), 10 Jahre Strukturberichterstattung - eine Zwischenbilanz. RWI-Mitteilungen, vol. 37/38, pp. 455-474.

LÖBBE, KLAUS (1993), Tarifpolitik im vereinten Deutschland: Gratwanderung zwischen Einkommens- und Beschäftigungsziel. In: Horst Siebert (ed.), Die zweifache Integration: Deutschland und Europa. Workshop zur Strukturberichterstattung. Tübingen: Mohr und Siebeck, pp. 135-161.

LÖBBE, KLAUS, DÖHRN, ROLAND, VON LOEFFELHOLZ, HANS DIETRICH U.A. (1993), Strukturwandel in der Krise. (Untersuchungen des Rheinisch-Westfälisches Institut für Wirtschaftsforschung, Heft 9.) Essen: RWI.

PRIEWE, JAN und HICKEL, RUDOLF (1991), Der Preis der Einheit. Frankfurt a. M.: Fischer.

RHEINISCH-WESTFÄLISCHES INSTITUT FÜR WIRTSCHAFTSFORSCHUNG (ed.) (1980), Analyse der strukturellen Entwicklung der deutschen Wirtschaft - RWI-Strukturberichterstattung 1980. Gutachten im Auftrag des Bundesministers für Wirtschaft. Band 2: Wirtschaftspolitik und Strukturwandel - Einzeldarstellungen. Essen: RWI.

RHEINISCH-WESTFÄLISCHES INSTITUT FÜR WIRTSCHAFTSFORSCHUNG und WSF WIRTSCHAFTS- UND SOZIALFORSCHUNG (eds.), Beruflicher Fortbildungsbedarf von Facharbeitern in den neuen Bundesländern - Am Beispiel von Industriemechanikern und Zerspanungsmechanikern. Gutachten im Auftrag des Bundesministeriums für Bildung und Wissenschaft. Essen und Kerpen 1993.

SACHVERSTÄNDIGENRAT ZUR BEGUTACHTUNG DER GESAMTWIRTSCHAFTLICHEN ENTWICKLUNG (1990), Auf dem Wege zur wirtschaftlichen Einheit Deutschlands. Jahresgutachten 1990/91. Stuttgart: Metzler-Poeschel, 1990.

SACHVERSTÄNDIGENRAT ZUR BEGUTACHTUNG DER GESAMTWIRTSCHAFTLICHEN ENTWICKLUNG (1992), Für Wachstumsorientierung - gegen lähmenden Verteilungsstreit. Jahresgutachten 1992/93. Stuttgart und Mainz: Metzler-Poeschel.

SCHEUER, MARKUS (1990), Ausbildung und Qualifikation der Arbeitskräfte in der DDR. RWI-Mitteilungen, Berlin, vol. 41, pp. 67-79.

SCHEUER, MARKUS, RAPPEN, HERMANN, WALTER, JOHANN und WENKE, MARTIN (1992), Ein Beitrag zur Beurteilung der in der DDR erworbenen beruflichen Qualifikationen in den Bereichen Metall und Elektro. Mitteilungen aus der Arbeitmarkt- und Berufsforschung, Stuttgart, vol. 25, pp. 553-582.

SCHLECHT, OTTO (1991), Die deutsche Einheit als Herausforderung an die Ordnungspolitik. In: Helmut Gröner, Eberhard Kantzenbach, und Otto G. Mayer (eds.), Wirtschaftspolitische Probleme der Integration der ehemaligen DDR in die Bundesrepublik. (Schriften des Vereins für Socialpolitik, N.F. vol. 212.) pp. 9-24.

SINN, GERLINDE und SINN, HANS-WERNER (1991), Kaltstart. Volkswirtschaftliche Aspekte der Deutschen Vereinigung. Tübingen: Mohr und Siebeck.

TESCHNER, MANFRED (1992), Stärkere Lohnzurückhaltung - Voraussetzung für einen Wirtschaftsaufschwung in Ostdeutschland? Konjunkturpolitik, vol. 38, pp. 148-151.

VON DOHNANYI, KLAUS (1991), Das Deutsche Wagnis. Über die wirtschaftlichen und sozialen Folgen der Einheit. München: Knaur.

WAGENER, HANS-JÜRGEN, (ed.) (1991), Anpassung durch Wandel. Evolution und Transformation von Wirtschaftssystemen. (Schriften des Vereins für Socialpolitik, N.F. vol. 206.). Berlin: Duncker und Humblot.

WALLICH, HENRY C. (1955), Triebkräfte des deutschen Wiederaufstiegs [Mainsprings of the German Revival]. Frankfurt a.M.: Knapp [New Haven: Yale].

WELFENS, PAUL J.J. (ed.) (1990), Economic Aspects of German Unification. National and International Perspectives. Berlin: Springer.

WIENERT, HELMUT (1992), Die Stahlindustrie in der DDR. (Schriftenreihe des Rheinisch-Westfälischen Instituts für Wirtschaftsforschung, N.F. vol. 52.) Berlin: Duncker und Humblot.

WISSENSCHAFTLICHER BEIRAT BEIM BUNDESMINISTERIUM FÜR WIRTSCHAFT (1991), Lohn- und Arbeitsmarktprobleme in den neuen Bundesländern. Gutachten vom 15. Juli 1991. (BMWi-Studienreihe, 75.) Bonn.

ZENTRALVERBAND DES DEUTSCHEN HANDWERKS (1994), "zdh-intern", Bonn, vol. 1994, Nr. 4.

INTEGRATING THE EAST GERMAN STATES INTO THE GERMAN ECONOMY: OPPORTUNITIES, BURDENS AND OPTIONS

Lutz Hoffmann

1. Introduction

There was rarely ever such a wide range of opinions and forecasts on the future development of a country or a region as one can presently observe for the former GDR. Some people argue that, after a period of transition, output will grow at high rates, repeating, if not exceeding West Germany's so-called "Wirtschaftswunder" during the years following the currency reform in 1948. Others fear that the enormous structural distortions of East Germany's industry, the rotten infrastructure, a labor force not used to working efficiently and a largely incompetent or uncooperative local administration will assign to this part of Germany the role of a depressed region for a long time to come, if not permanently. They point to other backward areas in Europe, such as northern England or southern Italy, which despite considerable financial transfers have not managed to catch up with the rest of the respective economy. The Italian government, for instance, has invested into its "Mezzogiorno" an estimated 100 bill. dollars between 1950 and 1984 and has scheduled for the period 1985 to 1993 another 115 bill. dollars. Nevertheless, economic growth rates of southern Italy are below the average of the country, per capita income is only half as high as in northern Italy, unemployment is four times as high and outmigration of qualified labor continues (*Bender, 1990*).

Of course, East Germany, unlike the "Mezzogiorno", is not an area with a basically rural tradition. In the pre-war years, its southern part was a thriving industrial area where many of Germany's technologically advanced industries were located. However, industrial tradition does not guarantee the success of a restructuring policy, once a region has fallen behind.

The old industrial centers in France and the United Kingdom with the iron and steel industry as focal points have not managed to regain a leading position in their economies, despite large-scale subsidies. Hence, past experience does not support exaggerated optimism. The road to success in East Germany will be full of pits and snares. It will require an outstanding effort by both the private and the public sector and will be very demanding on the skills and the courage of the politicians to adopt sound economic policies rather than populist solutions.

2. The Currency Union: Its Genesis and Impact

The organizers of this conference have asked me to discuss options, burdens and opportunities of the German integration process. If I had dealt with this topic a year ago, the analysis and conclusions would have been very different from what they will be today. With the announcement by Chancellor Kohl on the 7th of February this year to offer to the GDR the introduction of the Deutschmark, the range of options has very much narrowed down. This decision was quite at odds with what leading economists in Germany considered as sensible, and it also was in stark contrast with statements by the President of the Bundesbank, the Minister of Economics and the chairman of the Council of Economic Experts only days before the announcement. The chairman of the advisory council to the Ministry of Economics, Christian Watrin, characterized this policy move aiming at rapid economic integration as an attempt "to climb the Eiger north face in winter" and others added "at night".

The Chancellor clearly made his decision from a political and not an economic perspective. It was obvious that the East German electorate would greatly welcome the currency union because the Deutschmark was considered as the symbol of freedom and economic prosperity. With elections forthcoming on the 18th of March, the announcement was an ingenuous political step. Once announced, there was no way of reversing it. A fact had been established which from then on was decisive for what developed thereafter. To be fair, it ought to be mentioned that obviously the Chancellor not only had the elections in mind but was also concerned about the persistence of a political climate in the Soviet Union which was conducive to German unification. By extending the circulation of the Deutschmark to the whole of Germany, economic unification progressed to an extent, which would have made it rather difficult to uphold political unification for much longer. In that sense, the move could also be understood as a hedge against a sudden deterioration of the political climate within the Soviet Union.

When the present author published an article in the Frankfurter Allgemeine Zeitung on February 10th (*Hoffmann, 1990, p. 15*), arguing that the German currency union would lead to massive unemployment which could be in the order of magnitude of 2.5 million, it was heavily criticized both by politicians who simply did not like that message in an election year and by fellow economists who thought that such a figure was highly exaggerating the problem. The figures circulating then were putting an upper limit for the number of unemployed at 800 000 or roughly 9 per cent of the labor force.

Although it was well-known that most of East German industry produced at considerably higher costs than West German producers with whom they would compete on a one-to-one level in a currency union, much hope was placed on the possibility of maintaining wage differences in line with productivity differences and on cost reductions due to more efficient organization of work, lower priced inputs from West German and foreign sources as well as the abolition of the confiscatory GDR tax system. What most people apparently underestimated was, first, that in a currency union two levels of wage rates for the same type of work cannot be maintained for long and, second, that quality differences may have an even greater impact on competitiveness and employment than price differences.

Both factors probably played a significant role in the disaster which followed the establishment of the currency union on July 1. Wages rose rapidly during the first half of 1990. Towards the end of the year they will be almost 40% higher than the year before (37% including public administration and 45% without). Next year, another 20 to 25% increase is expected. The inferior quality of East German products, as perceived by the consumers, made many products unsalable once supplies from West Germany became available. There may have been some over-reaction on the side of East German consumers due to the fact that they were fenced off for such a long time from Western products. But there is little doubt that if one understands under quality not only the product as such but also its design and packaging, most East German products were and are indeed inferior to supplies from the West.

The collapse in industrial production which followed went beyond almost anything that hitherto has been observed anywhere in the world. Output dropped in a free fall by 35% in July and another 15% in August. As a consequence, industrial production was by the end of August on average roughly half of what it was during the first half of 1990; and even the latter output was already lower than the 1989 figure because the political unrests and the heavy outmigration during the first quarter of 1990 had negatively affected production.

The disruption of output differed from industry to industry. The strongest decline occurred in the basic metal industry and in food production where output reached in August only one-third of the level a year ago, indicating the severe competitive disadvantage these industries have vis-à-vis Western suppliers. There were a few industries, primarily in the machinery and transport equipment sector, which did significantly better than the average. Machinery and transport equipment, such as rolling stock for the railways have always been important earners of foreign exchange for the GDR. Within certain product categories they have proven to be quality-wise competitive. However, past experience permits no judgement on cost competitiveness because the GDR foreign trade authorities used to fix export prices independent of costs.

FIGURE 1: DAILY INDUSTRIAL PRODUCTION OF THE ECONOMY
ANNUAL AVERAGE 1985 = 100

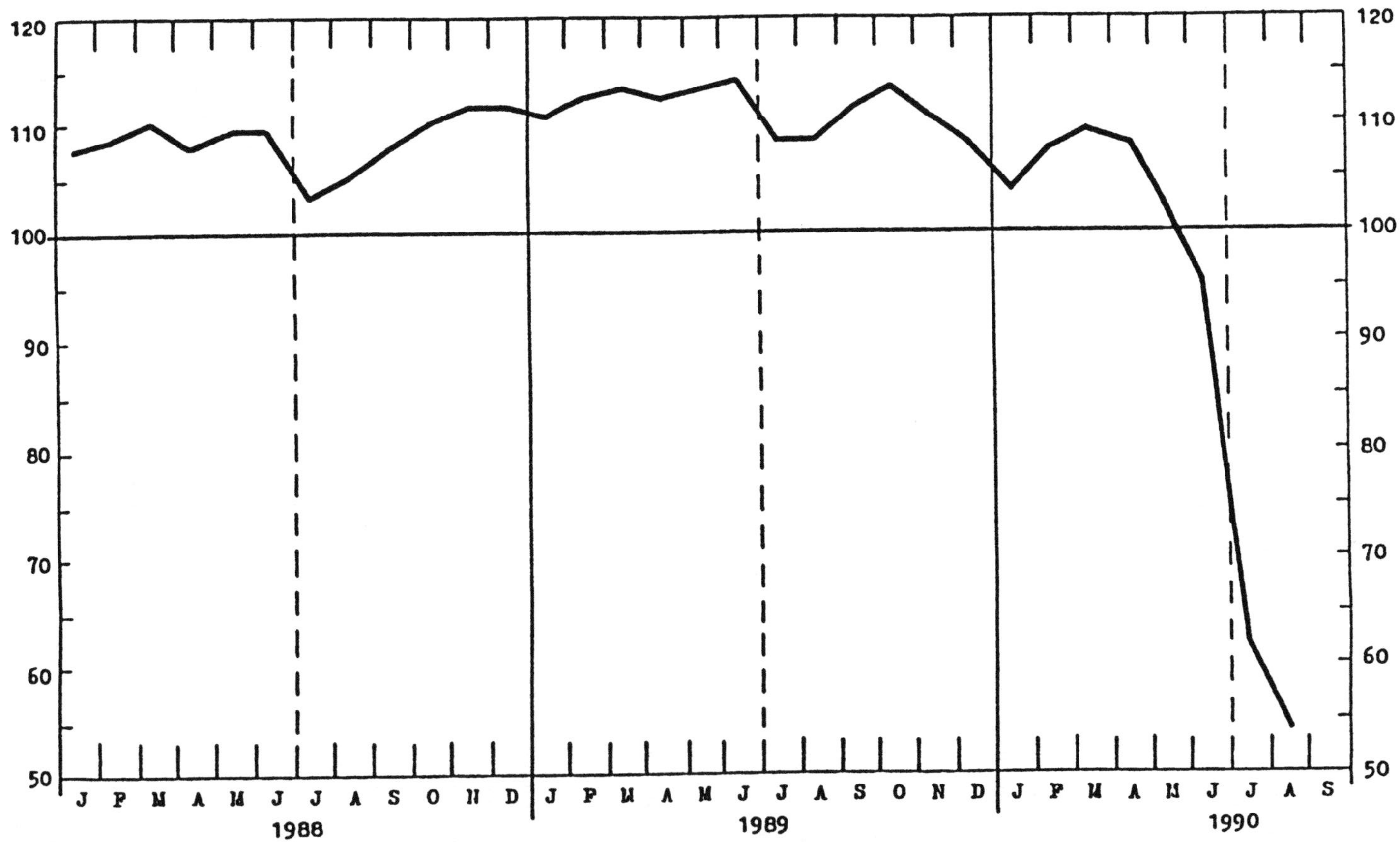

Statistical Office of the GDR 1990

Figure 2: Unemployed

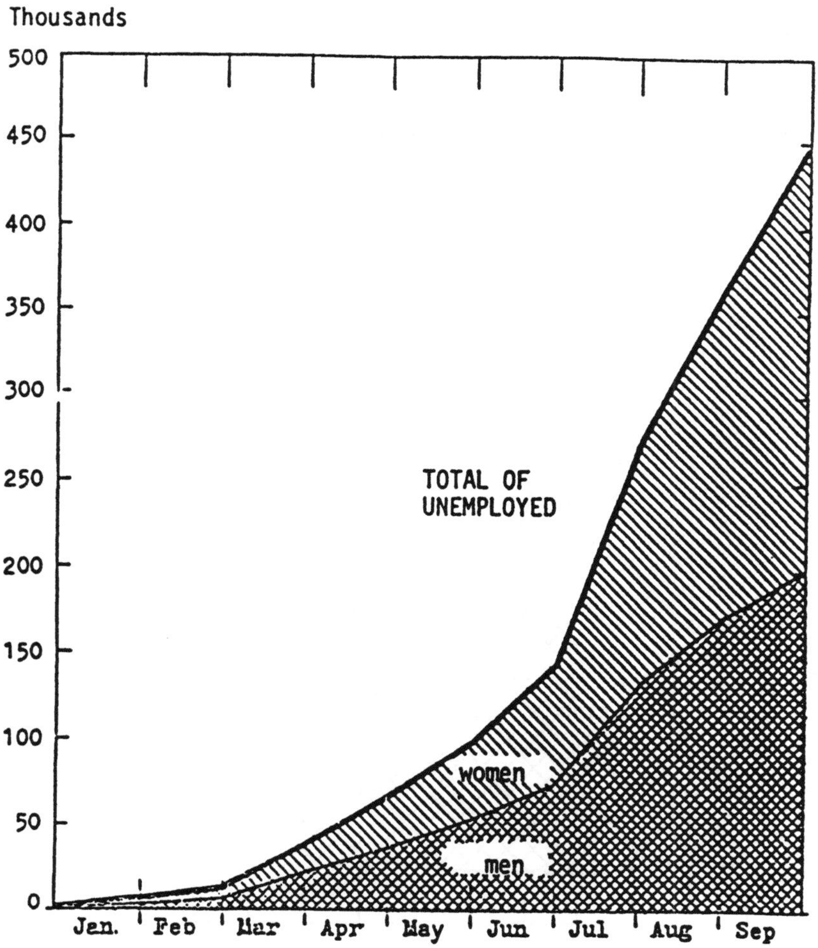

Source: Statistical Office of the GDR

Figure 3: Immigration and Outmigration Across the Borders of the Former GDR

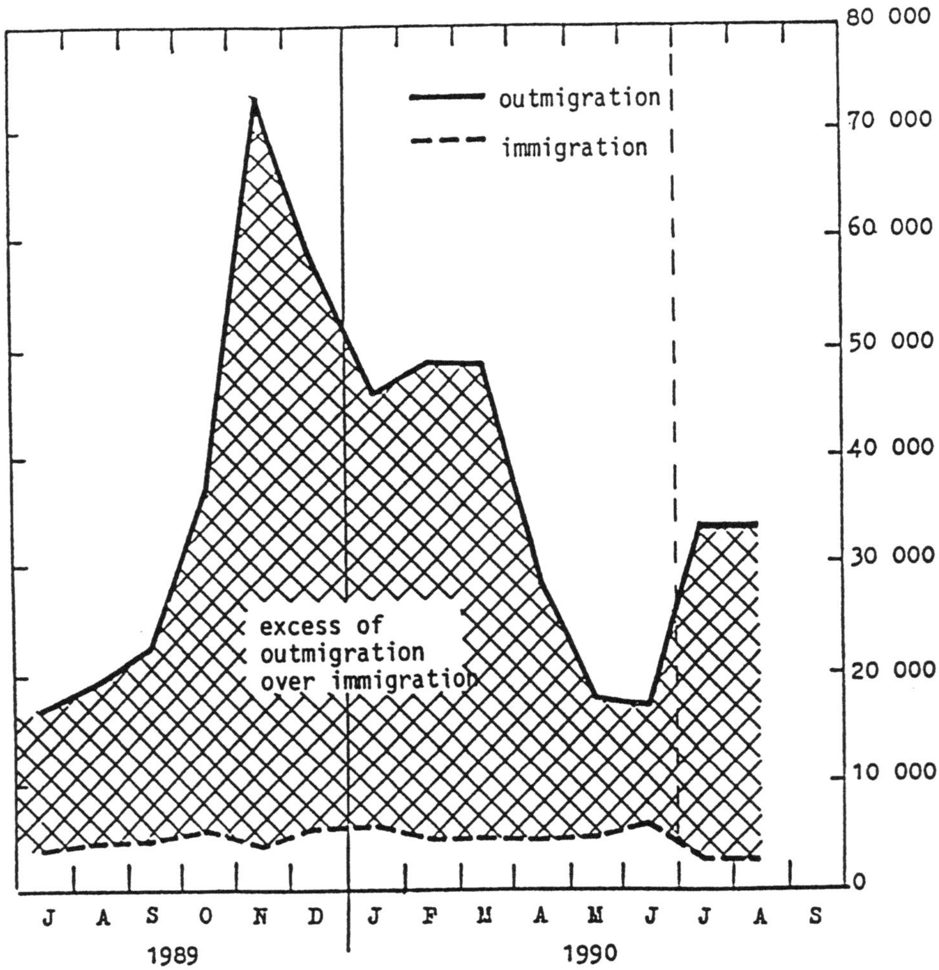

Source: Statistical Office of GDR, 1990

Employment declined in parallel to production, but at a lower rate, with the consequence that productivity fell significantly. In conjunction with the increase in wages, this was an enormous push in unit labor cost which in a vicious circle contributes to the decline in production and employment. The number of unemployed, which stood at 140 000 before the currency union in June, almost quadrupled to 540 000 in October. The number of part-time workers reached 650 000 in July and almost 1.8 million in October. Only one-third of the part-time workers were engaged for 50% or more of the normal working time. As this is not cyclical part-time work but low utilization of labor due to basic structural deficiencies, many of the part-time workers will become unemployed sooner or later. Together the unemployed and part-time workers amount to almost a quarter of the labor force. The five leading economic research institutes expressed the expectation in their recent forecast for the German economy that the number of unemployed will peak at 1.7 million next year and the number of part-time workers at 2 million, which together would be 40% of the labor force (*DIW, 1990a, p. 616*). These figures still underrate the actual decline in employment, as a considerable number of the population has left East Germany since the opening of the border in November 1989 and some left even earlier to other socialist countries because they hoped that somehow they would be able to move further to the West, as it then actually happened.

Altogether outmigration amounted to around 300 000 people in 1989. Almost half as many left the country during the first three months of 1990. The expectation that the announcement of the currency union would put a brake on migration did not materialize. Migration slowed down only after the election, suggesting that it was not so much the prospect of getting the currency union but the assurance that the old regime was definitely over which instilled confidence into a better future. Migration reached its lowest level in June but then jumped up again by almost 100% in July after the currency union had been introduced and made its first impact on output and employment. With about 275 000 migrants in 1990 up to the end of August, total migration this year could easily exceed 400 000.

3. Pattern and Extent of Structural Adjustment Needed

As regrettable as the enormous reduction in employment may be from a social point of view, it is absolutely necessary for economic reasons. If jobs would artificially be maintained in industries which have become uncompetitive - which is actually taking place to the extent of subsidized part-time work and other subsidies - the process of structural adjustment is hampered and the recovery process delayed. In order to better understand what the restructuring process might lead to, the *DIW (1990b, p. 241)* has assessed the two steps of the adjustment process: the structural change generated by the transition from the planned system to the market system and the structural change required in order to lift East Germany to the productivity and income level of West Germany.

Methodically, the estimation can be related to the analysis of patterns of structural change as pioneered by Colin Clark and Simon Kuznets and later expanded as well as refined by Hollis Chenery and his research group at the World Bank. Assuming that there exists a distinct pattern of structural change related primarily to per capita income or labor productivity and that West Germany as a fairly open economy conforms relatively well with the "normal" pattern, one could use the structure of the West German economy as a yardstick against which the structure of the GDR economy is compared.

This hypothesis led to the following estimation procedure. At first, the year was identified in which the West German productivity level was roughly the same as today's productivity in East Germany. This was the year 1970. Since the overall labor force participation rate in East Germany was considerably higher than in West Germany - mainly due to a higher participation rate of women - the observed number of employees and self-employed in East Germany was adjusted according to the participation rate in West Germany. This employment figure was then distributed over the various industries according to the structure of employment prevailing in West Germany in 1970.

The result of the calculation is presented in the second column of *Table 1*. It can be interpreted as follows. If the GDR had been a market economy exposed to international competition, the overall productivity level achieved and the scarcity of resources it represents would have led to a structure of output and productivity which in turn would have produced the estimated structure of employment. A comparison of the observed employment structure in East Germany and the calculated one indicates in which direction structural change is likely to take place during the transition from a planned economy to a competitive market economy.

Column 4 of *Table 1* shows that this transition process would already induce considerable structural change. The magnitude of change within individual industries should not be taken at its face value because these figures are, among others, affected by the adjustment in the participation rate. More important are the directions of change. They partly confirm and partly conflict with expectations voiced in the recent discussion in Germany. However, one should emphasize that these changes only reflect the transition process and not the adjustment to the higher productivity level as prevailing in West Germany.

Hence, if one looks at the transition process in isolation one observes the strongest decline in the services sector, whereas most hopes for a recovery in employment are placed exactly on

Table 1
Employment Potential in the GDR by Sector

ches	Employees[1] 1989	Model calculations conditions as in FRG: as of 1970	as of 1987	Differences against model calculations 1970	1987	Estimate of changes in the GDR after initial consolidation phase: Differences against 1989		Employees
		in 1000					in per cent of employees	in 000s
:ulture, forestry, fishing	920	700	403	−220	−517	−250	−27	670
gy and mining	295	150	117	−145	−178	−100	−34	195
ergy and water supply	120	63	65	−57	−55	−20	−17	100
ning[2]	175	88	52	−87	−123	−80	−46	95
ufacturing industry	3168	3027	2417	−141	−751	−820	−26	2348
emical ind.	152	183	164	31	12	−80	−53	72
ude oil refining	58	10	5	−48	−53	−30	−52	28
ıbber products, plastics	97	103	114	6	17	−20	−21	77
arrying	96	94	56	−2	−40	10	10	106
ne ceramics, glass	66	56	40	−10	−26	0	0	66
etal production/working	183	276	192	93	9	−40	−22	143
eel and light metal construction	109	97	56	−12	−53	10	9	119
gineering	548	368	318	−180	−230	−130	−24	418
tomobile ind.	208	268	321	60	113	−50	−24	158
ectrical engineering	398	340	306	−58	−92	−150	−38	248
fice machinery	56	28	29	−28	−27	−20	−36	36
ecision mechanics, optics	57	63	64	6	7	−10	−18	47
etal bars and sheets	115	146	97	31	−18	−25	−22	90
ood industry	145	159	116	14	−29	−5	−3	140
per industry	51	69	47	18	−4	0	0	51
inting	13	89	75	76	62	20	154	33
usical instruments, toys	66	24	25	−42	−41	0	0	66
othing, leather	197	211	110	14	−87	−80	−41	117
extiles	217	158	69	−59	−148	−120	−55	97
ood processing	336	284	214	−52	−122	−100	−30	236
struction	563	621	520	58	−43	100	18	663
e[3]	721	1059	1167	338	446	230	32	951
holesale	258	421	420	163	162	90	35	348
etail	463	638	747	175	284	140	30	603
sport	628	442	460	−186	−168	−30	−5	598
ail[4]	245	126	82	−119	−163	−50	−20	195
ipping, ports	33	28	14	−5	−19	0	0	33
her transport	223	152	211	−71	−12	10	4	233
lecommunications	127	136	154	9	27	10	8	137
ices, non-commercial state organisations	2615	1841	3100	−774	485	40	2	2655
anking, insurance[5]	63	230	346	167	283	120	190	183
otel and catering	180	212	283	32	103	50	28	230
ealth and veterinary services[6]	381	218	377	−163	−4	0	0	381
dvisory services	133	122	394	−11	261	80	60	213
her services	284	240	398	−44	114	50	18	334
lucation, science	629	228	457	−401	−172	−70	−11	559
ocial services	155	54	77	−101	−78	−20	−13	135
ılture, media, sport	134	57	134	−77	0	−30	−22	104
ıblic administration[7]	473	416	517	−57	44	−50	−11	423
ıurches, para-state organisations, political parties[8]	183	64	117	−119	−66	−90	−49	93
	8910	7841	8184	−1069	−726	−830	−9	8080
r state activities	390					−170	−44	220
l	9300					−1000	−11	8300

ıs: 1) Excl. apprentices. – 2) Incl. uranium mining. – 3) Incl. foreign trade: excl. HO (state-run) restaurants. – 4) Incl. Reichsbahn (railway) ngs Bank. – 5) Incl. social insurance. – 6) Incl. university and college clinics. – 7) Incl. police, state security apparatus; excl. armed forces. Incl. the so-called mass organisations in the GDR.

rces: GDR's Statistical Office: Federal Statistical Office, National Accounts 1988: DIW calculations and estimates

urce: DIW Economic Bulletin, Volume 27 Number 5, July 1990, p. 19

this sector. It is, of course, correct that many services, such as trade, financing and the hotel and catering business are highly underdeveloped and therefore will register considerable increases in employment, but there are also other services in the GDR which had relatively much higher employment than in West Germany. This holds for the transport sector - in particular the railways - as well as for education and research and health and social services. The transition process as such, therefore, implies that half of the overall reduction in employment, due to the adjustment of the participation rate, is accounted for by the services sector with the rest accounted for by a 20% fall in agriculture and 15% each in the sectors energy and mining and manufacturing. Employment increases are expected, apart from the services mentioned, in construction, the transport sector, metal manufacturing and printing, to mention only a few.

A transformation process along this pattern is likely to take place in countries such as Czechoslovakia, Hungary and Poland which probably will not experience rapid increases in overall productivity levels. East Germany is in a rather different situation. The currency union puts the former GDR under an enormous pressure for productivity adjustment which cannot be compared to any historical experience. This adjustment pressure results from three factors:

- The overall productivity level of East German industry is at best only half as high as that of West Germany,

- the difference in wages, which initially was roughly in conformity with productivity differences, is rapidly narrowing down and

- the quality of products made in East Germany is significantly below that of West German products.

The adjustment pressure arises from the fact that due to the currency union lower quality and higher costs cannot be compensated for by exchange rate adjustments, whereas this option is available to the Eastern European countries. Poland, for instance, has drastically devalued its currency to an extent that the trade balance is now in a comfortable surplus position, whereas East Germany has a trade deficit of about 10 billion DM (including direct purchases of East German consumers in West Germany) or 20% of its GDP in the third quarter of 1990.

With the exchange rate mechanism being abolished, the burden of adjustment would have to be carried by the wage mechanism. However, it has become evident that in a currency union a limitation of wage increases to productivity increases is not possible. Neither can the trade unions afford to accept large differences in wages for the same type of work in different regions without risking major losses in membership, nor can employers prevent labor unrest and outmigration if they refuse to pay more to labor than productivity justifies. Hence, one has to assume that the wage level differences between East Germany and West Germany will rapidly be evened out and that productivity growth has to catch up with wage development if continuing unemployment is to be avoided.

In order to estimate the structural change implied by productivity adjustment, the 1987 employment structure of West Germany was applied to the East German overall employment level as adjusted by the West German labor force participation rate in 1987. The 5th column of *Table 1* shows that the structural change induced by the catch-up effect partly reinforces and partly offsets the transition effect.

In agriculture, the decline in employment is now much higher because there are large productivity differences between the two regions, but no equivalent differences in agricultural output shares. Both regions have followed for different reasons a policy of being largely self-supporting in agricultural production - West Germany by production-stimulating price subsidies and the GDR by allocating through the planning system the resources required to achieve the autarky target independent of cost. In West Germany 2% of GDP is produced in the agricultural sector by 5% of the labor force, whereas in East Germany agriculture still absorbs 10% of the labor force.

While in mining the adjustment process would also reduce employment somewhat, primarily in the exploitation of lignite, manufacturing would be very heavily affected. By far too many are employed in the production of machinery, textiles and clothing, and food and beverages, whereas the transport equipment industry could employ more than at present. These results are surprisingly well in conformity with what presently is observed with respect to the structure of unemployment and part-time work as well as planned new investments. However, the decline in employment by far outweighs the increases.

In the services sector the productivity adjustment effect is partly offsetting the transition effect. This is due to the fact that the employment structure of West Germany has followed the "normal" pattern during the last two decades, i.e. a decline in the share of employment in manufacturing and an increase in the share of employment in services. If East Germany is going to achieve the productivity level of West Germany, it has to catch up on this development. Hence, the second adjustment step, which along the time dimension overlaps with the first, not only aggravates the adjustment pressure, such as in agriculture or manufacturing, but also eases it in services. At a higher productivity level, there is more room for employment in education and research, in health services or in social services than there would be if adjustment took place at productivity levels presently prevailing in East Germany. Altogether, the employment increases in services largely outweigh the employment decreases in manufacturing.

Whether these structural changes will in the long-run affect overall employment negatively and whether this would lead to unemployment depends on several factors. One aspect is whether or not structural change in West Germany will be job-creating as in the past. Since the middle of 1988 employment rose in West Germany by 1 million and since spring 1985 by 2 million. In spite of this, the unemployment rate came down only slowly. This was due to the strong rise in the labor force participation rate during the 1980s, whereas it remained fairly stable during the 1970s. Most projections suggest that the direction of structural change will continue and that, as a consequence, employment will increase further. The increase in the participation rate, on the other hand, is likely to level off, suggesting that as a result of both factors unemployment will decline.

East Germany also will benefit from this job-creating structural change. Whether it suffices to bring down unemployment to a low level will, among others, depend on the development of the East German participation rate. If the presently very high participation rate in East Germany declines, labor supply will also come down and the unemployment rate will be reduced. The closing scissors of a declining participation rate and a job-creating structural change would produce the desired result of a low unemployment rate. If, on the other hand, the participation rate remains high the decline in the unemployment rate will be delayed.

It is to be emphasized that the figures presented here should not be considered as a forecast. How structural change will actually proceed over time depends on the one hand on the present situation in different industries and on the other on the course of economic policy and its impact.

4. The Starting Position of Individual Industries

Agriculture: East German agriculture is in a rather difficult situation due to high costs of production. In 1988, producer prices for cereals were 75% and for live stock 160% higher than in West Germany (*DIW, 1990c, p. 469*). These high prices made it possible to equalize income from rural and industrial sources. The high cost level of East German agricultural production was due to expensive inputs, an excessive number of employees, inefficient organization of production and a largely outdated and defective capital stock. Employment could be reduced considerably without impairing production.

Energy: The main problem of the energy sector is outdated power stations and transmission lines, which in the past repeatedly led to electricity blackouts. With 20 to 25% efficiency, East German power stations are not viable anymore, both from an economic and an ecological perspective. Environmental considerations also require that lignite, now the predominant fuel, be substituted for by other fuels. Nuclear power stations have been shut off for safety reasons. Required annual investment will be on the two-digit-billion level for the coming three years.

Mining: There is not much to restructure in this sector, but rather to close down most of lignite and potash production. Here again, economic and ecological reasons make these production processes unviable in the future.

Chemicals: Also in the chemical industry, most existing plants have to close down. However, new plants will be constructed. The East German chemical industry is too much biased towards basic chemicals and lignite as well as potash and raw material inputs. The erection of a new chemical industry will require much capital that has to come largely from West German investors. A major problem is posed by the existing soil contamination, for which according to the Second State Treaty the government can accept the responsibility as far as public law is concerned, but not for claims under civil law.

Basic Metals: Production equipment in the iron and steel industry is at least 15 years behind the technology presently employed in Western countries. Production costs are therefore high, and the profile of output does not correspond to what is demanded on Western markets. Major parts of the iron and steel industry were geared towards low quality steel of which a substantial proportion was supplied to the Soviet market. The world steel cycle seems to have reached its peak. When it turns downward a large part of the East German steel industry in Brandenburg, Henningsdorf, Riesa and Unterwellenborn will have to close down. Here again, the ecological problems are serious.

Electrical Equipment and Machinery: This industry is technologically relatively up-to-date, but produces the wrong products. With the integration into the German and European market, the industry will face fierce competition from the Far East and other European countries. However, in light of the rapid expansion of demand which can be expected as a result of reconstruction in East Germany, the industry has a good chance to survive as an important supplier if it adjusts its output profile.

Machinery: Most experts agree that the East German machinery industry has the best prospects of all East German industry to reach a high level of international competitiveness fairly soon. Up to now, labor productivity is still low, due to redundant employment and also partly outdated equipment. The production profile is by far too broad. Here, as in many other industries, companies preferred to produce a wide range of products because the planned economy was riddled by notorious shortages of supply. It has been estimated that the machinery industry in East Germany produced 50% of the world steel assortment as compared to 17% in West Germany.

While the overall position of the machinery industry looks relatively good, certain parts of it will face problems of survival, partly because they were largely dependent on the Eastern European market and in particular the Soviet Union. This holds for agricultural machinery and parts of the heavy machinery industry. If beginning next year trade with Eastern Europe and the Soviet Union will not be based anymore on payments in transferable rubels but in convertible currency, East Germany automatically also competes on these markets with highly efficient suppliers from the Far East and other Western European countries. That will put great pressure on this industry to modernize and to specialize in order to survive in this competition.

Transport Equipment: The East German car industry has almost entirely lost its domestic market. However, with the realization of investment plans announced by Volkswagen, Daimler-Benz, Opel and BMW the recovery of the industry seems to be assured. The production of equipment for the railways has reached a high degree of efficiency and is for the most part internationally competitive. A problem is again the Soviet market, not because of more efficient competitors, but simply due to a threatening illiquidity of the Soviet Union. The shipbuilding industry has in the past been very dependent on the Soviet market. It has for the same reasons an uncertain future. Beyond the Soviet market it will hardly be competitive against suppliers from the Far East.

Food and beverages: The food industry has to be completely reconstructed. Present plants and equipment are so outdated that there is little chance of survival.

Textiles and Clothing: This industry could only exist in its present structure due to the absence of international competition. It produces in the lower quality range and is by far too large for a country like the former GDR. Employment in East Germany, which has only one quarter of the population of West Germany, is larger than in West Germany, even in absolute numbers.

Services: This is a very heterogeneous sector. Some parts which require no specific skills, such as the hotel and catering industry, could expand relatively fast. There is a tremendous shortage of restaurants and general tourist facilities. Other services, like lawyers, accountants, education and research, will require a longer learning period.

5. Reconstructing the Capital Stock

The analysis of the present situation of East Germany's industry reveals that the reconstruction of the capital stock, both in industry and in infrastructure, is a key problem. This raises two questions: What are the orders of magnitude involved and how could private capital be attracted to East Germany?

Estimation of investment requirements during the 1990s range from 1 to 2.7 trillion DM. If one assumes that by the year 2000 East Germany should reach at least the capital intensity of West Germany at present - 1989: 320 000 DM per employee (*Statistisches Bundesamt 1989, p. 107*) -, a complete renewal of the capital stock would imply investment of 2.4 trillion DM for a labor force of 7.5 million. That would require an average annual investment volume of 240 billion DM, as compared to 63 billion at present and an estimated 75 billion in 1991. To achieve this, annual investment would have to grow at a rate of more than 20% over the next ten years. This is a formidable task which would require a high attractiveness of East Germany for private capital.

This raises the question what the locational advantage of East Germany is in comparison to West Germany or foreign countries inside and outside of Europe. What originally was considered as a major advantage, low costs for skilled labor, is rapidly losing significance as East German wages approach those in West Germany. Another point of attraction could be the availability of production sites at low costs as the population density in East Germany is much lower than in West Germany. However, up to now this is not yet the case. There are, first of all, unsettled questions about property rights. Unfortunately the State Treaty stipulates that former owners who were expropriated by the communists have the right to be reinstated into their former position, whereas, for instance, the Hungarian government only grants the right to obtain compensation. It is likely that this issue will occupy lawyers for a couple of years and will unnecessarily discourage potential investors, in particular smaller ones. Another problem is that the Treuhandanstalt (state trust) does not see itself in the position to fix definite prices for land on sale. How should a manager go before his board and say that he bought a piece of land without knowing the final price? And there is, finally, the problem that land use planning is just in its beginning and that municipalities therefore are reluctant to let investors proceed with construction in areas of which the final use is not yet clear. Some of these problems are, of course, of a short-term nature. The problem is that they impede investment during this initial period when unemployment is growing rapidly and job creation through new investment therefore needed most.

The availability of skilled labor is clearly a positive factor, even if its cost would not be low anymore. This may turn out to be the most important asset upon which hopes can be built. In this context, language skills for trade with Eastern Europe are also often mentioned. One may wonder whether this could really be an important factor because the few employees needed for undertaking negotiations with Eastern European partners could easily be hired from any place in West Germany or Western Europe.

There is finally the aspect of closeness to the Eastern European market. Taken by itself, this is probably not an important factor because transport costs are not of much significance anymore for international trade. Therefore, most exports to Eastern Europe could be made from West Germany as easily as from East Germany.

The attractiveness of the East European market could be high in the long run but is unlikely to be significant in the short to medium-run. In terms of population, the market is large, but purchasing power is low and so is the availability of foreign exchange. As long as these countries have not redeveloped their export base in line with their comparative advantage, they are unlikely to export much more than at present to the West and therefore will also not be able to import more. Large loans from western countries, like the ones recently agreed on between the Soviet Union on the one hand and Germany, Italy and France on the other, could only temporarily raise the purchasing power of these countries.

An indication of the problems to be expected for trade with Eastern Europe are the most recent developments shown in *Tables 2 and 3*. According to these figures, the decline in exports during the first half of 1990 accelerated considerably in July and August. The reduction in imports was even more pronounced. With a decline by about 77% in August this comes close to a complete break-down. The lack of foreign exchange in most of these countries makes an early recovery of imports unlikely. According to recent press reports, the debt of the Soviet Union resulting from trade deficits with East Germany is estimated to reach 5 billion transferable rubels by the end of 1990 (*FAZ, November 1, 1990, p. 15*). The reason for the relatively small decline of exports to the USSR are the heavy subsidies granted for these supplies by the Treuhandanstalt, which accumulated to DM 6.5 billion by the middle of September this year.

6. Structural Adjustment Policy

Economists are rather ambiguous about the necessity of a structural policy which goes beyond competition policy. Liberal economists would argue that every region has its comparative

Table 2: GDR Exports to Eastern European Countries

	Millions of DM			Percentage Change Vis-A-Vis Same Period of Previous Year		
	1st Half 1990	July 1990	August 1990	1st Half 1990	July 1990	August 1990
USSR	8052.5	1262.2	1296.6	-2.7	-2.6	-4.4
Poland	1069.1	211.2	251.9	-33.9	-14.3	-2.9
CSFR	2056.2	235.8	240.4	+10.5	-26.3	-31.1
Hungary	1262.7	307.5	184.3	-4.6	+34.5	-28.1
Rumania	784.6	101.4	103.7	+17.1	-19.1	-21.9
Bulgaria	819.4	89.0	86.8	-21.2	-17.1	-21.7
Total	14,008.5	2207.1	2163.7	-2.6	-5.0	-12.6

Source: Statistical Office of GDR; IAW, Berlin

Table 3: GDR Imports from Eastern European Countries

	Millions of DM			Percentage Change Vis-A-Vis Same Period of Previous Year		
	1st Half 1990	July 1990	August 1990	1st Half 1990	July 1990	August 1990
USSR	6526.1	458.5	356.0	-14.0	-61.3	-72.6
Poland	1366.8	32.6	41.2	+8.9	-85.7	-82.7
CSFR	1350.2	34.3	52.2	-12.0	-87.7	-75.3
Hungary	954.4	38.2	33.9	-14.4	-80.7	-82.4
Rumania	351.2	6.5	6.9	-52.5	-94.9	-93.8
Bulgaria	500.1	13.7	2.2	-22.4	-77.9	-98.3
Total	11,048.8	583.8	492.4	-14.2	-72.6	-77.4

Source: Statistical Office of GDR; IAW, Berlin

advantages and disadvantages and will develop its pattern of specialization according to its endowment with resources. This statement can, by and large, be considered as valid if there is competition on all markets and price flexibility. However, these conditions are not guaranteed. Agriculture, for instance, in which East Germany could develop a comparative advantage due to its favorable land-population ratio, is a highly regulated sector. In the labor market, the assumption of price flexibility is unrealistic as was pointed out above. A specialization in labor-intensive lines of production is therefore not feasible. Given these circumstances, the labor-capital ratio is above its equilibrium level. Therefore, labor outmigration or capital immigration would be the required forms of adjustment. Since the government is not willing to accept the option of labor outmigration, it is confronted with the question how it could achieve capital immigration.

A recent survey by the Ifo Institute about investment impediments, as seen by West German companies, suggests that the government would have to act on three fronts: first, to settle as fast as possible the property issue; second, to improve the infrastructure; and third, to establish a functioning administration and to abolish red tape (*Ifo, 1990, p. 11*). It is interesting that a survey among East German companies revealed slightly different priorities (*IAW, 1990, p. 33*). The property question also ranked very high, but second came financial obligations to the banking system which the companies inherited from the former government. The survey also indicates that initiated cooperative agreements between East and West German companies are concentrated in the construction sector and in services, such as banking and insurance, tourism and trade. Only few cooperative agreements have been signed for industrial production. This holds particularly for capital-intensive lines of production where investors from the West consider a significant improvement of the infrastructure and the freeing from obligations resulting from environmental contamination as preconditions for major investments.

Most of what has been said up to now points into the direction that private capital flows into East Germany are not spontaneously forthcoming. Apart from administrative and legal problems, market and cost factors as such do not appear to be highly attractive to companies with a short to medium term profit perspective. That is why most investment up to now goes into distribution networks and is coming from large companies who can afford to forego short-term profits for the expectation of long-term profits. If companies like major car producers or a leading chemical company such as BASF are investing in East Germany they have in mind an early positioning in a growing market which in the long run is likely to be also highly profitable.

Different from several other backward areas in Europe, East Germany has an important asset with its skilled labor and the basic framework of an industrial infrastructure. Of course, presently the infrastructure is absolutely insufficient. But one can expect that there will be enormous pressure on the German government to accelerate and substantially enlarge its efforts to reconstruct the infrastructure. The financial burden for public investment would, of course, be substantial. This burden could significantly be eased if institutional barriers to private investment in infrastructure are abolished. For instance, the offer by a consortium from the United States to construct a highway between the cities of Dresden and Görlitz is presently conflicting with legal provisions which stipulate that such investments come under the authority of the federal government alone. Similarly, for reconstructing the telecommunication network the newly established public company "Telekom" is exclusively responsible. Competing telecommunication companies, such as in the United States, are not known in most European countries. It is hoped that under the pressure of the task ahead, initiatives to liberalize the public infrastructure sector will be undertaken.

It has repeatedly been argued in Germany that due to capacity limitations of West German companies and the unavailability of efficient suppliers in East Germany infrastructural development cannot proceed as fast as desired. This again is more a problem of regulation than insufficient capacities. Public procurement is still a national affair in Europe and as long as it prevails a capacity problem indeed exists. However, by first January 1993 this area is supposed to be liberalized within the European Community. From that date on, the entire capacity of the Community would be, in principle, available for such activities and there is no question that it would be sufficient. It would, of course, be highly preferable if the German government already went ahead with this liberalization, instead of waiting another two years, and extend it to suppliers from Eastern Europe. If the government would act on all fronts together, reducing administrative barriers, liberalizing institutional barriers to private investment in infrastructure and liberalizing public procurement, there is little doubt that the worst infrastructural deficiencies of East Germany could be overcome in, let's say, 3 to 4 years and that such investment activity would act as an important stimulant for private productive investment and would, at the same time, help to create jobs for now released employees of companies going bankrupt.

The government is presently granting a general subsidy for private investment in East Germany of 12%. Under specified conditions, this can be increased up to 33%. The Minister of Economics and his party have also proposed generous tax reductions for all investment in East Germany. The advantage of the first type of measures is that it provides an immediate incentive, even before profits arise. Its disadvantage is that it subsidizes not only profitable investments but also those which finally turn out to be unprofitable. The risk of private investment, which should entirely lie with the entrepreneur, is thus partly transferred to the government, whereas profit tax reductions would only materialize if profits are made.

However, this argument does not hold if West German investors could balance their investment outlays in East Germany against their profits in West Germany. It is also well-known that such tax holidays lead to all kinds of circumventions without positively affecting investment where needed. In any case, several studies for developing countries have demonstrated that tax holidays and also investment subsidies are often only taken advantage of without having a decisive impact on investment decisions. They cannot compensate for the absence of basic economic factors, such as low-cost inputs or a sufficient market. They can also be highly expensive in terms of expenditures, in the case of subsidies, or taxes forgone, in the case of tax holidays. They distort investment decisions by indicating a too high post-tax profitability and, once established, they are very difficult to abolish. The special subsidies and tax preferences for Berlin, which have prevailed over decades, have highlighted the conclusion that the distortive effect can be substantial and lead to a fragile and hardly growth-oriented structure of production.

7. The Financial Burden on the Public Sector

There is no economic issue which has excited public opinion more than the question of how much the public sector would have to spend for German unity. Unfortunately, the government has maneuvered itself into a back-to-the-wall position by arguing right from the beginning that, first, public expenditures would not be largely increased, second, the rapid growth of West Germany would generate sufficient additional revenue to finance whatever may be needed and, third, that expenditures would be cut in other areas in order to make room for additional expenditures which may be needed beyond the increase in tax revenue.

When this position became questionable, the government argued that it would finance any further expenditures by raising loans. It therefore established the fund "German Unity" with a total amount of DM 115 billion to be distributed over the years 1990 to 1994. 20 billion were scheduled to be financed by expenditure cuts and 95 billion to be raised as loans by the Federal government, the states and the communities.

Since then it has become apparent that these means will not be sufficient. The government still insisted that it would not increase taxes - because elections were due in a few weeks - but would seek even more loans. This is justified by the argument that these loans were an investment into the future growth of East Germany and would easily be recuperated by rapidly rising tax revenues in this part of the country. The Bundesbank recently has warned that excessive loan financing may imply a stability problem and force the Bundesbank to take restrictive measures and that the shifting of the financing burden to future generations might also be not very sensible. Although the Bundesbank cannot officially say so, it now seems clear that it would favor at least some tax increases if the government does not succeed with sufficiently deep expenditure cuts.

For this year alone, financial assistance to the East German public budget amounts to DM 46 billion, of which 22 are financed through the fund "German Unity", 5, 3, and 15 billion by three budgetary supplements and 1 billion from other sources. The German public sector as a whole will run a deficit of almost DM 100 billion this year.

Next year, the overall deficit is projected to grow to DM 120 to 140 billion, of which DM 80 billion alone are accounted for by East Germany. Tax income is still relatively low in East Germany - this year over 30 billion and next year about 42 billion. The large deficit mainly comes from various support measures, such as the social security system and various subsidies. Public investment is still low, with about six billion during the second half of 1990 and an estimated 16 billion in 1991. This is by far too little investment as compared to what is needed. A significant amount in the range of 15 billion is expected to be needed for subsidizing companies. If this amount would be reduced, public investment could be correspondingly higher.

The Vice President of the Bundesbank, Mr. Schlesinger, has recently proposed utilizing revenue from privatization as an additional source of finance. Another source could be the revenue the Treuhandanstalt will generate by selling companies. It now seems rather doubtful whether this will lead to substantial amounts in the near future, as privatization is proceeding rather slow. However, Mr. Schlesinger also has proposed more privatization in West Germany. The amount that, according to his estimates, could be obtained would exceed DM 300 billion. This would indeed be a remarkable amount. However, the experience Mrs. Thatcher has made with privatization in the United Kingdom suggests that such efforts are taking time, more time than the present government has to solve the financing problems of East Germany.

8. Concluding Remarks

Once the early creation of a currency union between East and West Germany was agreed upon, there remained only two options for adjustment in East Germany: labor outmigration or capital immigration. As the first option was politically unacceptable, the adjustment burden had to be born by capital immigration. The government's hope that private capital would move spontaneously and in great quantities, once the planning system had been abolished, did not materialize. Various institutional impediments and the lack of adequate infrastructural facilities made investment in East Germany up to now rather unattractive, in particular for small and medium-sized companies.

A head-on attack on the property issue, the establishment of an efficient public administration, broad based deregulation and a big push in infrastructural investment are the tasks for the new government after the elections on the December 2nd of this year. Populist policies, like the permissive attitude towards large and undifferentiated wage increases, high direct subsidies to private companies, a hesitant policy on privatization and property rights, as well as hiding from the electorate the financial implications of a reconstruction of the infrastructure, are to be avoided. If such a policy is pursued courageously, the opportunities for rapid growth of output and employment, after a transition period, should be there.

9. Postscriptum: East Germany in Transition

East Germany's share in German territory ist 30 %, in the labour force 21 % and in GDP 9 % (*Table 4*). Real output of the East German economy declined in the year of the currency union (1990) by 15,5 % and in the year thereafter nearly 30 %. In 1992, East Germany staged a strong recovery with a growth rate of over 9 %. Since then economic growth ranges between 6 and 7 %.

Table 4: Key-Economic Indicators of East Germany in current prices

	1993 Values	% of total Germany
Area (km2)	108331,8	30,3
Population	15668,8	19,3
Labour force *)	7866,0	21,4
Employment	5683,0	18,0
GDP	275,5	8,9
Manufacturing	44,7	5,4
Services	60,2	6,1
Consumption	232,3	13,0
Investment	139,2	19,7
Exports	76,1	6,9
Imports	277,2	25,3
*) Labour force data only for 1992.		DIW 6/94

Source: German Institute for Economic Research (DIW), Berlin

It is now widely acknowledged that the initial economic breakdown of East Germany resulted from the supply shocks of the currency union and the wage explosion. The alternative interpretation that there was a lack of demand due to reduced purchasing power in the region and the collapse of export markets in Central and Eastern Europe cannot be maintained. Over the entire period since the introduction of the D-Mark as legal tender in East Germany aggregate demand was far in excess of aggregate supply. Demand was not only maintained, but even increased due to the rapid build-up of a large transfer flow from West to East Germany. The currency union and the transfers distinguish East Germany from other formerly Socialist countries and make the adjustment pattern of East Germany unique. In the subsequent discussion I will focus on four issues: macro-economic imbalance, structural distortions and adjustment, external trade and East Germany's growth potential in the years to come.

9.1 Macro-Economic Imbalance

The overall macro-economic imbalance is illustrated in *Figure 4*. It is seen that over the entire period not only total demand, but also domestic demand exceeded domestic supply. In 1992, domestic demand surpassed supply by 85 % and in 1994 it will still be almost 70 % higher. Even though investment is substantial, it is mainly consumption which accounts for this huge demand overhang. The high disposable income which makes this consumption demand possible results from high wages which rapidly approach the West German level on the one hand, and from large income transfers for unemployed, public work programs and retired persons on the other.

Whereas at the start of the currency union East German effective wages amounted to 40 % of the West German average, they will stand at 80 % in 1994. Overall net transfers from West Germany to East Germany rose from 45 billion in 1990 to over 160 billion in 1993, which is three quarter of East Germany's GDP. It is estimated that about two thirds of these transfers went into consumption and the remainder into investment. This rapid increase of transfers has been the basic source of recovery in 1992 and 1993. It therefore is appropriate to speak of transfer-led growth rather than self-sustained growth.

As a consequence of the large disposable income as compared to domestic output, the wage share in GDP is extraordinarily high. It has been larger than 100 % over the last three years and will touch the 100 % line only this year. That means that the enterprise sector as a whole was unable to make profits up to now. This is the main raison why private investment almost entirely relied on West German sources.

Another implication of the large macro-economic imbalances was a high negative external balance of the East German region (*Figure 5*). The deficit on current account was in 1991 almost as high as GDP and is expected for 1994 to just fall short of 70 % of GDP. This is, actually, what explains the swing in the external account position of Germany as a whole. Whereas in 1989 Germany's current account surplus was over 100 billion D-Mark, it turned into a deficit after unification which now stands at about 40 billion D-Mark. Contrary to the impression prevalent in public discussion, the West German external account position has not worsened, but rather improved.

Figure 4: Supply and Demand in East Germany (Million DM, in constant 1991 prices)

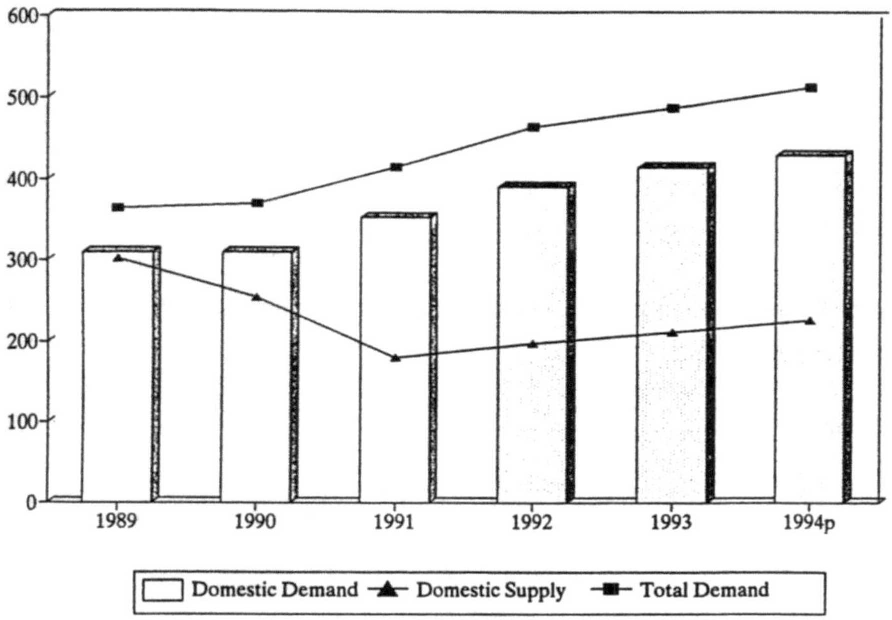

Source: German Institute for Economic Research (DIW), Berlin.

Figure 5: External Balance (Billion DM, in constant 1991 prices)

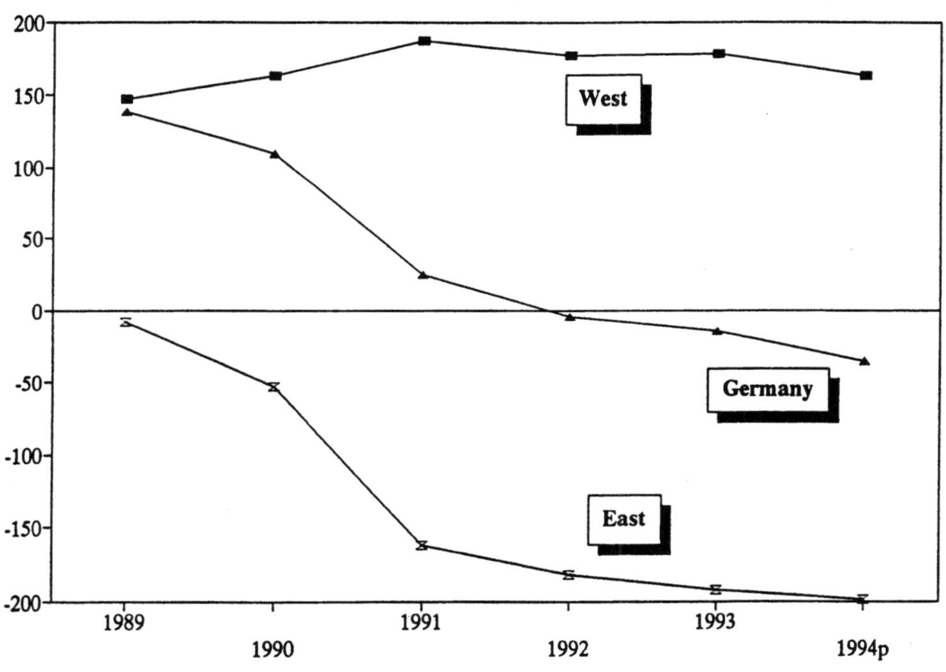

Source: German Institute for Economic Research (DIW), Berlin.

9.2 Structural Adjustment

High aggregate demand and falling supply led to major structural distortions both on the demand side as on the supply side. The East German consumption ratio, which in 1989 was almost equal to that of West Germany shot up to roughly 140 % in 1991 and is only gradually declining since then (*Figure 6*). The investment ratio increased continuously since the currency union. In constant 1991 prices the investment ratio overshot the 50 % mark in 1993. This is the result of rapidly rising private as well as public investment.

Figure 6: Ratio of Consumption to GNP (1) and Ratio of Investment to GNP (2) in East and West Germany

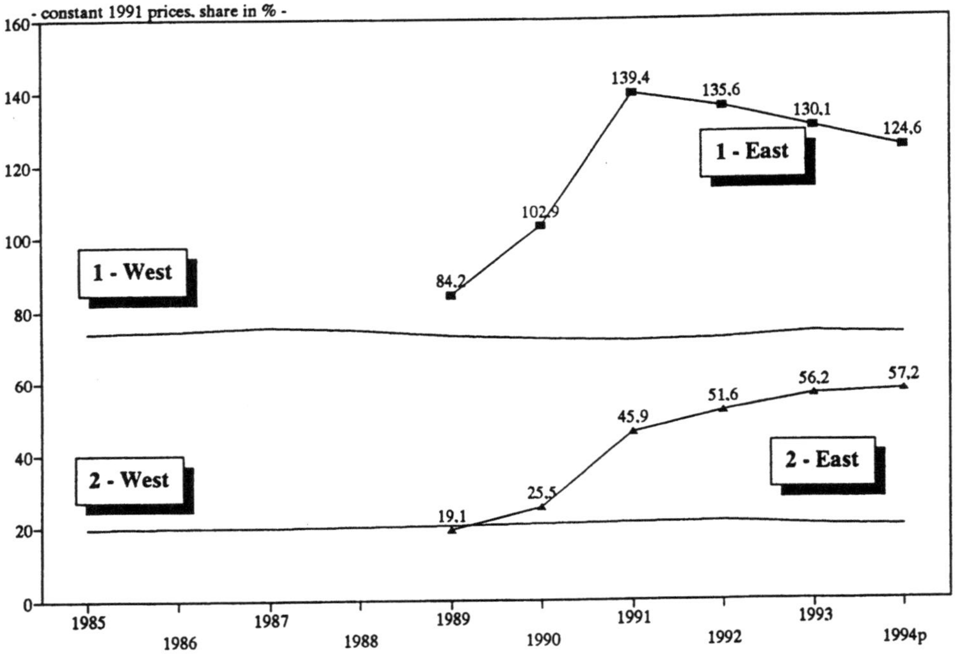

Source: German Institute for Economic Research (DIW), Berlin.

On a per capita basis public investment is now considerably higher in East Germany than in West Germany, while private investment is almost on the same level. Whereas the rise in public investment is due to the political commitment to rebuild the East German infrastructure, private investment was stimulated by very high investment subsidies. A large part of investment went into services, partly to build up the retail system for products delivered from

West Germany, but also into banking, insurance and other service activities which were non-existent or underdeveloped in the GDR (*Table 5*). However, also manufacturing and construction attracted substantial investment. The construction industry, actually, experienced a boom fuelled by large public construction contracts. Investment in manufacturing was largely associated with the privatization activity of the Treuhand (the state trust company in charge of privatizing the formerly state-owned companies). With the privatization process now coming to an end and the build-up of a viable service sector tapering off, the investment ratio is unlikely to maintain its high level.

Table 5: Investment in East Germany by Industry - in billion DM[a)]

Industry	Investment			
	1991	1992	1993	1994
Agriculture/Foresty/Fishing	1.5	1.4	1.5	1.6
Producing industries	29.7	37.2	42.3	45.5
- Energy, water, mining	8.9	10.4	12.0	14.2
- Manufacturing	17.2	22.3	24.3	24.3
- Construction	3.6	4.5	6.0	7.0
Trade	4.4	5.2	5.2	4.7
Transport and telecommunication	16.2	21.9	23.8	26.3
Other services	22.4	32.8	46.2	58.4
- Residential housing	15.0	23.0	33.0	42.0
Total industry	74.2	98.5	119.0	136.5
Government and non-profit organisations	14.3	20.5	23.0	25.5
Overall total	88.5	119.0	142.0	162.0
Industry without residential housing	59.2	75.5	86.0	94.5

a) Estimates of ifo institute, Munich

Source: ifo institute, Munich; Federal Statistical Office, Wiesbaden.

The structural distortions on the supply side were even more severe than on the demand side. The share of manufacturing in GDP halved between 1989 and 1991 and is since then only slightly increasing. The share of construction trebled due to the building boom, nourished first by public and later on also by private investment. Also services increased their share significantly (*Figure 7*).

Figure 7: Share of Manufacturing (1), Services (2) and Construction (3) in GDP in East and West Germany

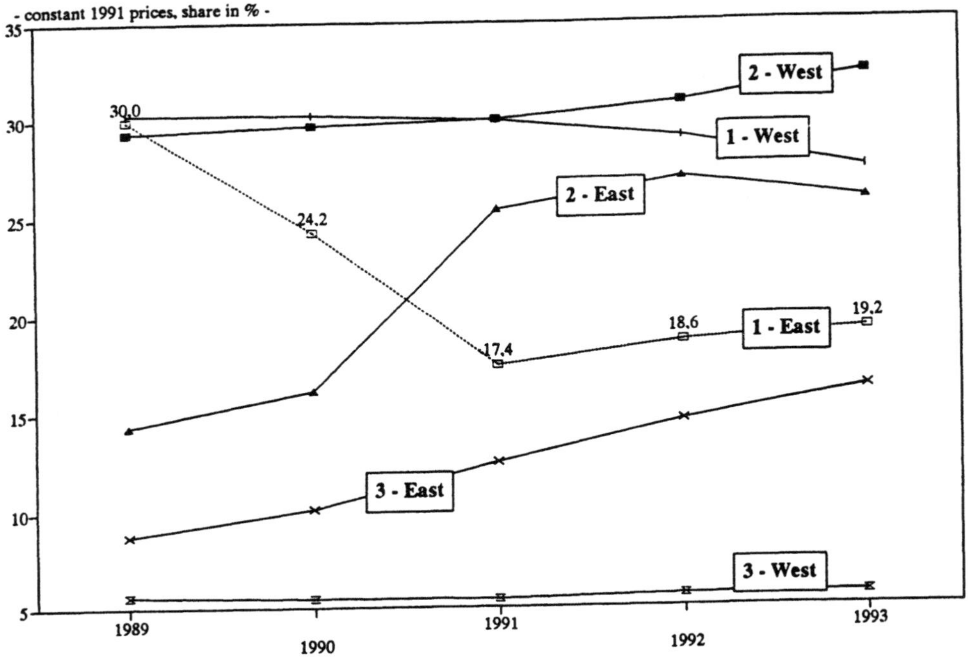

Source: German Institute for Economic Research (DIW), Berlin.

If one looks at what had happened within major sectors, the following picture emerges for manufacturing. In the former GDR 'investment goods', in particular machinery, had a relatively high share in production (*Table 6*). The earlier hopes that the strength in investment goods could be maintained did not materialize. All tradeable investment goods witnessed dramatic declines in output. The machinery industry saw its share in manufacturing output falling from almost 25 % at the time of the currency union to 12 % by the end of 1993. A recovery is not yet in sight. Also industries which survived in East Germany only because they were sheltered from foreign competition, such as clothing manufacturing, textiles and leather products shrunk much more than the rest of manufacturing.

Table 6: Production in Manufacturing in East Germany - Structure 1990 - 1993 (share in %)

	2.Hj. 1990	1991	1992	1993
Total manufacturing	100	100	100	100
Basic and production goods industries	19,2	22,0	23,4	23,4
Petroleum refining	2,1	4,0	4,3	4,0
Quarrying	4,2	3,9	6,3	8,2
Iron and steel products	1,3	1,3	1,2	1,1
Non-ferrous metals	1,3	1,6	1,8	1,7
Foundries	1,8	1,5	1,2	0,9
Drawing plants, cold rolling mills	0,4	0,4	0,3	0,2
Chemical products	6,7	8,0	6,9	5,5
Sawmills and timber processing	0,4	0,3	0,2	0,2
Pulp and paper processing	0,0	0,0	0,0	0,0
Rubber products	1,0	0,9	0,7	0,7
Capital goods industries	54,9	46,7	43,3	43,5
Structural metal products	4,9	8,1	10,7	11,4
Mechanical engineering	25,4	19,9	12,9	11,5
Road vehicles	4,5	3,4	3,9	5,4
Shipbuilding	0,4	0,3	0,2	0,2
Electrical engineering	14,2	10,3	10,5	10,1
Precision an optical instruments	1,8	0,6	0,8	0,5
Tools, fabricated metal products	1,8	2,9	3,3	3,2
Office machinery, data proc. equip.	1,5	0,8	0,5	0,4
Consumer goods industries	12,0	12,6	13,4	13,8
Musical instruments, toys, etc.	0,7	0,4	0,4	0,4
Ceramic products	0,4	0,3	0,3	0,3
Glass products	0,5	0,7	0,7	0,7
Wood processing	2,6	2,9	3,1	3,5
Paper products	0,5	0,6	0,7	0,7
Printing and publishing	2,2	3,8	4,4	4,0
Plastic products	0,8	0,8	1,3	2,1
Leather and leather products	0,9	0,4	0,3	0,2
Textiles	2,8	1,8	1,4	1,2
Wearing apparel	0,7	0,4	0,3	0,3
Food, beverages and tobacco	13,9	19,1	20,4	19,7
Food and beverages	11,5	14,8	17,0	16,9
Tobacco	2,4	4,1	3,3	2,8

Source: Federal Statistical Office; DIW. DIW 6/94

Source: German Institute for Economic Research (DIW), Berlin.

If one compares the performance in production industry by industry, the following general pattern emerges. Relatively well did industries which benefitted from the high consumer demand and which were not exposed too much to transregional competition. Food products as well as printing and publishing are cases in question. Industries related to the booming construction activity also showed a good performance. To these belong the stones and quarrying industry, the manufacturing of steel and metal structures, sheetglass production and in particular all crafts engaged in construction activities.

Until mid-1993 manufacturing as a whole did not recover from the shock of the currency union. Since then, however, significant output increases are visible in a number of activities, whereas in others the decline has been stopped. The output increases largely reflect the going into production of earlier investments. Given the low base of output, any new production unit which starts operation makes a significant impact on the growth rate. Although it is a great relief that the decline has reversed into an upswing, one has to realize that this is not yet a self-sustained growth emanating from indigenous investment and entrepreneurship. The competitiveness of East Germany's industries is still highly fragile. Wages are high and profits low or negative. Without special efforts from the West German private sector, such as the "buy East German" initiative, the performance of the East German industry would probably be much less satisfactory.

The partial recovery in output did not improve the employment situation. On the contrary, even in those industries where output stagnated or increased, employment continued to decline. The pattern of employment development is remarkably similar among industries, almost independent from the fact whether output fell or rose. This suggests that not only economic factors were responsible for employment development, but also the various public support programs and the policy of the Treuhand to maintain companies and jobs even though they were not economically viable any more.

The consequence of the diverging output and employment developments are widely differing productivity changes. With fairly similar increases in wages, this implies very different unit wage cost developments. In some industries, such as plastic products, competitiveness improved as unit wage costs fell, whereas in others, such as ship-building, machinery industry and steel making, unit wage costs rose and competitiveness deteriorated. One may conclude that there are positive signs of recovery and improving competitiveness in some industries, but negative ones in others. The de-industrialization which began with the currency union has not yet been overcome. The new industry structure which emerges is likely to look rather different from the previous one and from that of West Germany. Earlier expectations that after a period of adjustment the industrial structures of the two parts of Germany would again look relatively similar are now less likely to be fulfilled.

The output decline in the construction industry was much less severe than in manufacturing. Part of the explanation is that prior to the currency union West German construction companies were already active in East Germany in anticipation of the coming construction boom. Only housing construction fell considerably because the first construction contracts came from the public sector and went into infrastructure projects. Investment into housing construction was hampered by unsettled property disputes and the initially very low rents which made investment into housing unprofitable. In the meantime, some progress has been made in clearing property rights and rents have gone up considerably in East Germany. They now roughly stand at the level of West Germany in the early 1980s. Housing construction therefore has strongly picked up and is likely to further accelerate in the coming years. The shortage is substantial, a fact which partly explains the steep rise in rents.

In most of the service sector, the competitive environment is fundamentally different from that in manufacturing. Transregional competition is of rather limited significance. Production takes place where there is a demand. The type of services being supplied therefore largely depends on the type of demand that exists on the spot. The high and rising consumer demand as a result of large income transfers from West Germany generated a wide and growing range of consumer services. Also producer services began to develop initially, but when manufacturing production collapsed, many producer services lost their base of existence.

The dramatic structural change that took place in services can best be illustrated by the developments of the transport sector. Due to the decline in production, the transport of goods also fell significantly. However, whereas road transport began to increase again in 1991, rail transport continued to decline strongly. The railway system was unable to adjust itself fast enough to the change in transport direction, now mainly West-East, whereas formerly mainly North-South. In addition, many West German transport companies greatly benefitted from the investment subsidies available in East Germany by registrating their new trucks at an East German location. Once being established there, they successfully tried to capture a major share of the transport market. East German transport companies had a very difficult stance vis-à-vis experienced and large West German transport suppliers. They also were at a disadvantage due to the fact that in line with trade flows much more was transported in the West-East direction rather than the East-West direction.

In passenger transport, the development was similar. Rail transport declined whereas road transport increased. The number of passenger cars per capita rapidly rose since 1989. Also local public transport companies suffered substantially, whereas private transport increased, both transport by bus as well as by passenger car. It is quite obvious that East Germans had the desire to make up for the long period of deprivation of the freedom to move individually by car within and outside of East Germany.

9.3 External Trade

During the times of the GDR, East German industry was fully integrated into the Socialist trading block. Nevertheless, East Germany also maintained substantial trading relations with Western Europe, in particular West Germany. Its "revealed comparative advantage" as expressed by the trade balance in various commodity categories, lied in trade with the East by investment goods and in trade with the West by consumer goods and basic products. That may partly explain why the shock of the currency union affected more severely investment goods as compared to consumer goods and basic products. If one examines the trade performance of individual industries it becomes apparent that East Germany was quite competitive in a number of lines of production under the old trade regime. For these industries it was the cost shock associated with the currency union and the wage equalization which threw them out of the market. One may conclude that if an own currency for East Germany had been maintained and wage levels only gradually increased, the East German market would not have been swamped by products from West Germany to the extent as it actually happened and East German exporters would have been able to maintain some of their exports.

Of course, the developments in the former Soviet Union and its satellites also contributed to the breakdown of export activity. In the first half year of 1991 these exports fell to about one third of their value a year before. Also exports to Western countries declined. Only deliveries to West Germany increased by about 20 %.

The government tried to counteract the loss of the Eastern European market by providing export guarantees for a wide range of products. A 100 % export guarantee was granted for deliveries to the former Soviet Union. Preference was given to supplies from East Germany. In 1991 alone, these amounted to almost 10 billion D-Mark. These guarantees were continued at a lower level over the subsequent years. The exposure of the government resulting from these guarentees accumulated to over 30 billion D-Mark by the end of 1993. Although important for the survival of a number of companies administered by the Treuhand, the guarentees could not prevent a further continuing decline of exports to the East.

On the import side, deliveries from the East also declined. So did direct deliveries from Western European countries. But deliveries from the West via West Germany increased very substantially. They were only surpassed by the virtual explosion of supplies from West Germany.

9.4 Employment and Growth Potential

The economic performance of a country or a region depends, according to economic theory, on its endowment with resources, such as raw materials, labor and capital, and the productivity of these resources. East Germany is basically a resource-poor region. The economy depends on the availability of labor, its qualification, on capital and its technological standard.

The economic decline after the currency union was accompanied by a large flow of people who migrated from East Germany to West Germany. Of a population of 16 million, almost 1 million have left the region. On top of this, nearly 400 000 East Germans work as daily commuters in West Germany. More than 800 000 went into early retirement and 350 000 are engaged in government-financed work or training programs. About 1.2 million are unemployed. Of the earlier work force of almost 10 million, barely 6 million are still actively working in the region. This means a tremendous loss of resources. It is not only the sheer numbers that count, but also the fact that a lot of human capital has either left the country, taken out of the labor market or become obsolete.

Those who left the country or were taken out of the labor force cannot be reactivated for future growth. They are definitely a permanent loss of valuable human resources for the region. The total future labor force potentially available for production is likely to be closer to 8 million rather than the previous 10 million.

The GDR's endowment with capital in the form of infrastructure and machinery and equipment was poor in terms of quality, not quantity. The capital stock was run down and technologically outdated. The currency union and the rapid rise in wages made more capital economically unviable, even if it was still operative from a technical point of view. Under these circumstances it was fortunate for East Germany that both public and private investment from West Germany were rapidly forthcoming. The build-up of a modern capital stock which the investment figures reflect is one of the major sources of future growth of the East German region. As economic growth can be defined as the product of the investment ratio and the marginal productivity of capital (MPC, the inverse of the marginal capital-output ratio), the future growth potential will depend on whether the present high investment ratio can be maintained and how the MPC might develop. With an investment ratio of 58,8 % and a measured growth rate of 7,1 % in 1993 the implied MPC is 12,1 % (*Figure 8*). An acceleration of economic growth would require a further increase of either the investment ratio or the MPC or both.

Figure 8: Marginal Productivity of Capital (MPK), Ratio of Gross Investment to GDP (IQ), Rate of Growth (GDP % p. a.) in East Germany

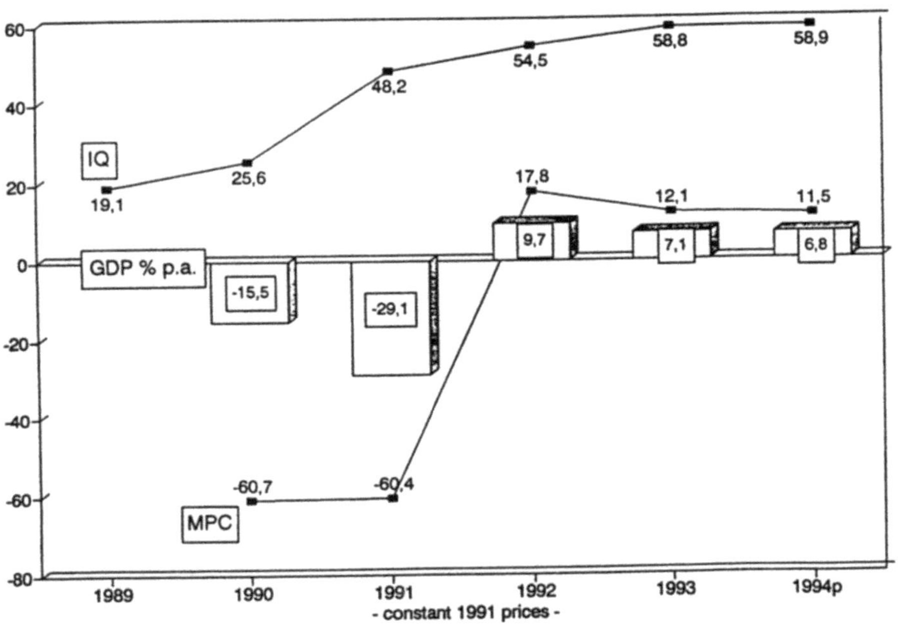

Source: German Institute for Economic Research (DIW), Berlin.

The present high investment ratio is not only due to a large flow of investment, but also the result of depressed output. To the extent that output grows and investment does not increase even faster, the investment ratio is bound to come down. This is suggested by international comparisons of investment ratios in high-growth countries. Even the rapidly growing little "tigers" in South-East Asia, such as Singapore, Taiwan or South Korea never have realized investment ratios as presently observed in East Germany. Although their investment ratio was high - in the range of 35 to 40 % - their rapid growth primarily resulted from a high MPC. This raises the question whether East Germany equally could achieve a substantial higher MPC than the present one.

Since 1992 the MPC has been on a level which is quite comparable with values observed for West Germany over the last two decades. To argue for a higher rate, one would have to reason why East Germany's MPC should be higher than that of West Germany. That is not easy because there is little information available on the MPC of various lines of production.

For industrial output, a significantly higher MPC is not very plausible. The new plants which are now being built in East Germany are highly capital intensive and of the most advanced technology. Labor productivity is likely to be high, but capital productivity will not be more than normal. The old labour intensive lines of production have or are being phased out. Therefore, the output structure is shifting towards a higher average capital intensity. At least in the medium to longer run the capital intensity will not differ very much in industry from that in West Germany and the marginal productivity of capital therefore is also unlikely to be much higher.

The service sector in East Germany has a significantly higher share in output and employment than in West Germany. Because of the high rate of unemployment many job seekers get engaged in services where they try to make a living in trades with low capital equipment. This phenomenon was observed in the United States in the 1980s and could well become significant for East Germany in the 1990s. The low capital equipment may mean a high capital productivity, higher than in manufacturing. If that is the case, the different sectoral structures could, indeed, imply that the overall MPC in East Germany turns out to be higher than in West Germany.

One may conclude that a somewhat higher marginal productivity in East Germany as compared to West Germany is quite possible. However, it will never reach the levels achieved in the newly industrializing countries in South-East Asia. If we assume a margin of 25 to 30 % between the East German and the West German MPC - what would correspond to the MPC of West Germany in the 1960s - and if we further assume that the investment ratio "normalizes" to a level of 40 % a 7 % medium-term growth rate for East Germany appears to be feasible.

One may well question why the earlier expectations of double-digit growth rates which would imply a rapid catch-up to West-German income and production levels is not feasible. After all, the South-East Asian countries and more recently China have demonstrated that this is possible in principle. The answer is relatively simple. East Asia produces much more labor intensive with lower wages and longer working times than East Germany. If capital is combined with large amounts of other resources, such as labor, a high MPC is no miracle. With unification,

East Germany reaped all the benefits of the West German welfare state, such as high income and low working times. Applying the same amount of labor in terms of working hours to capital as in East Asia would make production in East Germany unviable, because labor is too expensive. Economic growth in the two-digit range is simply not feasible under these circumstances. This is one of the major lessons from German unification. If consumption and social benefits rank high before productivity and efficiency, economic growth is bound to be slow. Only extraordinarily high investment ratios can compensate for a relatively low marginal productivity of capital. But that cannot be sustained for long.

References

BENDER, KLAUS W. (1990), Private sollen beim Aufbau des italienischen "mezzogiorno" helfen, Frankfurter Allgemeine Zeitung, October 31, 1990, p. 19.
DIW (1990a), Deutsches Institut für Wirtschaftsforschung, Wochenbericht 43-44, Berlin: Duncker & Humblodt.
DIW (1990b), Deutsches Institut für Wirtschaftsforschung, Wochenbericht 17, Berlin: Duncker & Humblodt.
DIW (1990c), Deutsches Institut für Wirtschaftsforschung, Wochenbericht 33, Berlin: Duncker & Humblodt.
HOFFMANN, LUTZ (1990), Wider die ökonomische Vernunft: Frankfurter Allgemeine Zeitung, February 10, 1990.
IAW (1990), Institut für angewandte Wirtschaftsforschung, Die ostdeutsche Wirtschaft 1990/1991 - Trends und Perspektiven, Berlin, October 22, 1990.
IFO (1990), Ifo-Institut für Wirtschaftsforschung, Ifo-Schnelldienst 26-27, München.
STATISTISCHES BUNDESAMT (1989), Fachserie 18, Reihe 1.2, Wiesbaden.

SECTORAL SHOCKS AND STRUCTURAL ADJUSTMENT IN THE EAST GERMAN TRANSFORMATION PROCESS

Manfred Wegner

1. Unification Concept and Transformation Shocks

The breakdown of the political regime of the German Democratic Republic and the ensuing German unification have been completely unexpected. The sudden regime change and the design of transformation policies profited neither from a coherent theoretical blueprint nor from concrete preparations in specific policy areas. Thus, it has been tempting to revert to the experience of the "economic miracle" of postwar Germany in the early 1950s as guidance for practical policies. But the hope for repeating the former rapid and self-sustained growth performance was based on false assumptions and analogies and led to unrealistic expectations. The political promise to create "blooming landscapes" within a few years could not be realized. Today, the initial euphoric expectations have been replaced by disillusion and sometimes even by resignation, at least in East Germany.

For political reasons and in contrast to the advice of most economists the great "Big Bang", a super shock therapy, was chosen as unification concept. The wholesale take-over of the institutional infrastructure, legal order, social and economic regulations from Western Germany, as well as the introduction of the Deutschmark as the new and common currency was accomplished in one stroke. In addition, the complete and abrupt liberalization of prices, markets and trade relations exposed the Eastern economy to international competitive pressures without any delay and transitional arrangements. One central part of the unification strategy consisted in the rapid privatization of previously state-owned firms and combinates through the *Treuhand* agency, which will be almost completed at the end of 1994. Finally, large-scale public transfer payments in favor of infrastructure investments and social and labor market measures, massive subsidies for private investment projects and the establishment of new firms were part of the government support for promoting the adjustment process in the East German economy. The financial burden was mainly imposed on the Federal budget and resulted in a rapid increase of public debts and some tax increases.

The principal objective of the transformation concept, partly formed by "trial and error", was based on policies for mobilizing private and public capital, thus promoting the structural change and reconstruction of a modern infrastructure and the private capital stock as quickly as possible.

The following paper focusses on sectoral and regional change and the perspectives of the transformation process in East Germany. Where does the East German economy stand after four years? How quickly will Eastern Germany`s economy adjust to the productivity and income standards of West Germany? Is there a chance for a self-sustained growth process in the near future, or will East Germany remain a lagging region requiring permanent subsidies and government support? What are the lessons from the Eastern German restructuring efforts for reform countries such as Poland, Hungary and the Czech and Slovak Republics?

2. Past Macroeconomic and Sectoral Performance

At first, the transformation the isolated East German command economy into a decentralized and open market-economy had disastrous consequences. The degree and the reasons for the dramatic collapse have been described elsewhere[1]. Yet, the general progress of the reconstruction of the East German economy cannot be overlooked. After the steep fall of production and employment in 1990 and 1991, the real Gross Domestic Product (GDP) has grown for the first time in 1992 by almost 8 percent and by 6 percent in 1993. Macroeconomic growth rates between 8 and 9 percent can be expected in 1994 and 1995. By 1995, the cumulative growth of real GDP over the last four years will have compensated for about three quarters of the former losses. Although the global growth performance is mainly based on construction, construction-related suppliers and some service sectors, the production in manufacturing increased markedly since 1993. Apparently, the overall recovery in the new Länder is broadening and justifies the hope that the growth trend will continue if structural change and the modernisation and reconstruction of the the capital stock is not hindered. A number of facts also indicate that the decline of overall employment is slowing down and will peter out in 1994 (Figure 1).

2.1 Production and Employment Trends

Nevertheless, there are still reasons for concern. The three economic research institutes concluded in their report from September 1993: "In fact the constitution is still weak. The East German economy is yet dependent on high transfers and many firms are only surviving with public support...... But the Eastern economy needs a healthy industrial base for becoming independent from western transfers. There is still no convincing answer available for solving this problem." The same institutes confirmed in March 1994 that the restructuring process has made some big progress but is still lacking a broad industrial base.[2]

**Figure 1: Real Growth in the New Länder, 1992 - 1995
(Annual percentage changes, at prices of 1991)**

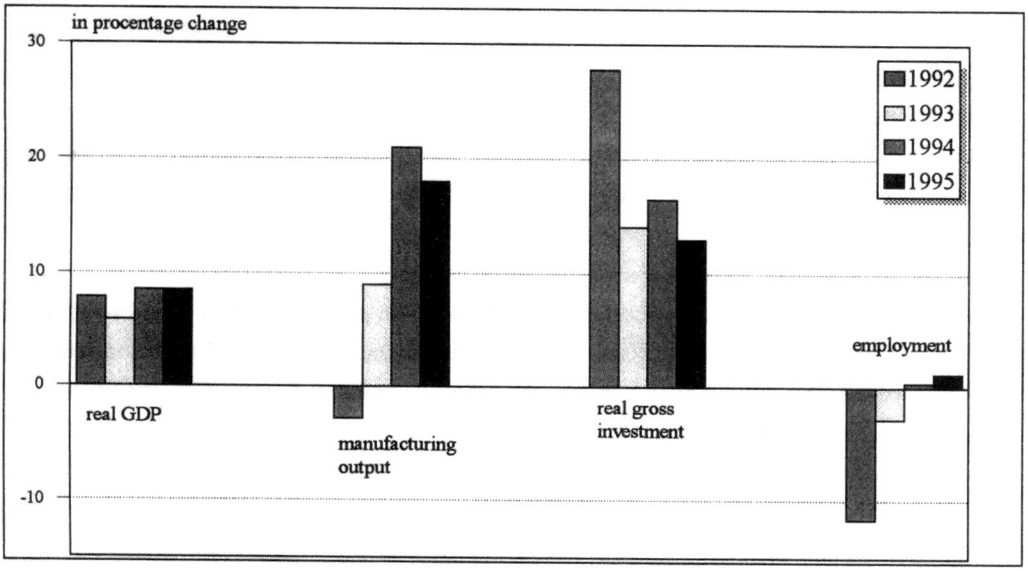

Sources: Federal Statistical Office (Sept. 1994), Forecast of the German Research Institutes (Oct. 1994).

The substantial progress made toward the reconstruction of the East German economy is based on the success in transforming East Germany into to a market economy, and an impressive investment performance - the decisive variable for the growth and reconstruction process. Until now structural change proceeded in an unbalanced and mainly transfer-led way. Detailed analysis and surveys have shown the usefulness of public promotion measures during the last three years.[3] But growing budget constraints give rise to the question wether these programs should continue under the existing conditions or be applied in a more coordinated and streamlined fashion, avoiding the efficiency losses of widespread "across the board" interventions and the formation of a dangerous mentality of permanent subsidies.

The global investment ratio - the share of gross capital formation in total domestic demand, currently more than 30 percent - remains exceptionally high. Total investment is dominated by construction - comprising more than two thirds - thus mainly favoring the reconstruction of the East German infrastructur (including housing, energy, transport and telecommunication). Total real gross capital formation has increased from 1991 to 1993 by roughly 20 percent per year and so overtaken the West German level per capita already in 1993. But the investment boom seems to have moderated recently. Real investment in machinery and equipment, the driving force for industrial modernisation, has grown only by 7 percent in 1993.

The real growth rates of overall output reflect the extremely low initial levels after the steep fall of production in 1990 and 1991 (by a combined 45 percent for real GDP and 65 percent for net production in manufacturing) on the one hand, and are the result of massive transfer payments and public promotion programs on the other hand. The reconstruction of the East German economy is mainly alimented from outside and is not yet led by a self-sustained growth performance.

The structural change of the East German economy has been profound. The upward movement of sectoral production since 1992 proceeded in a differentiated way. Overall expansion in East Germany is driven by the boom in construction which is gradually loosing its dynamism, by some service sectors, only recently by the increase in manufacturing (Table 1). The fall of total employment corresponded with the output decline. From the initial 9.7 million employed persons only 5.8 million regular jobs remained until the end of 1993. More than half of the total loss fell to the industry.

Table 1: Real Gross Value-Added in East Germany, 1991-1994
(Annual percentage changes, at prices of 1991)

Sectors	1992	1993	1994(1)
Agriculture, forestry and fishery	6.5	3.7	-26.3
Goods producing sector	10.2	9.2	15.2
Trade and transportation	3.0	11.4	6.4
Other services	16.8	4.6	7.3
Government, non-profit organisations	-1.2	-1.9	-1.2
Total gross value added	7.8	5.8	8.9

(1) First half of 1994.

Source: Federal Statistical Office, September 1994.

2.2 Manufacturing

In East Germany the concern therefore still prevails, that the ongoing adjustment crisis could lead to a devastation of the industrial base which would be reversible only in the long run and at high costs. At the end of 1993 industrial production in East Germany amounted only to 5 percent of production in total Germany. The share of manufacturing value added respresented more than half of the whole economy in former years and was lowered to 15 percent in 1993. Global output is dominated by services. The value added of government and private non-profit organisations alone accounted for more than 22 percent; this is much higher than in West Germany (Table 2).

Table 2: Gross Value-Added and Employment in the New and Old *Länder*, 1989-1993 (Shares in percentage of total economy)

Sectors	New Länder (including Berlin-East)				Old Länder	
	Gross value added formation (1)		Employed persons (without commuters)		Value added (1)	Employ-ment
	1991	1993	1989	1993	1993	1993
Agriculture, forestry, fishing	3.4	2.2	10.0	3.9	1.1	3.0
Goods producing industries	36.8	34.7	45.0	35.4	35.6	37.3
Trade and transportation	14.3	12.8	15.5	18.4	14.7	19.3
Other services	22.0	27.8	6.3	17.0	35.0	20.6
Government, non-profit org.	23.6	22.5	23.1	25.3	13.6	19.8
Total economy	100	100	100	100	100	100

(1) in current prices.

Source: Federal Statistical Office, September 1994.

The de-industrialization process of the East German economy is mainly reflected in the decline of industrial employment. In manufacturing (including small enterprises) the number of employed persons has been reduced by more than 2.1 million between 1989 and 1993, i.e. almost by two thirds. In 1993 the share of manufacturing in total employment has been only 21 percent (in contrast to 35 percent in 1989) and is falling also in 1994. The number of employed persons in manufacturing per 1000 inhabitants was 72 in 1993, in West Germany around 124. In addition, the shedding of labor continues in agriculture (which formerly presented a share around 10 percent, yet in 1993 only 4 percent), in the transport and government sector.

Industrial firms with more than 20 employees employed roughly 635 000 persons in June 1994. This number will come down to almost 600 000 at the end of 1994, but underestimates total employment in manufacturing. In mid 1993, approximately 1.13 million people were employed in manufacturing with 40 percent in small firms with less than 20 employees. Nonetheless, the industrial density is very low in East Germany reaching only 60 percent of the level in West Germany. Investment goods producing industries such as machinery, electrical engineering, chemical industry and oil refining will suffer most from the expected job losses. The main reductions will be in the area of administrative functions. Positive employment effects will be realised in the construction sector especially in smaller firms.[4]

Between the second half of 1991 and 1993, net production of manufacturing has risen by 11 percent, and in June 1994 by 21.5 percent compared to the previous year. A more detailed analysis reveals some interesting insights into the process of industrial reconstruction (Figure 2 and Table 3). Industrial expansion is concentrated in branches which profit from the construction boom: light metal construction, stone and quarrying, wood processing or from local consumer demand like printing and publishing, and food and beverages. The latter industry responded to the return of East German consumers to home products, but has big difficulties in penetrating West German markets. The private initiative of "buying Eastern products" and some preferential treatment of public procurement contracts for industries in Eastern Germany have been helpful but of limited scope due the recessionary environment in West Germany.

Table 3: Net Production in the Goods Producing Industries, 1991 to 1994 (Indices, second half year 1990=100, corrected by working days)

	Second half of year		June
	1992	1993	1994
Goods producing industries, total	82.1	92.5	103.7
Energy and water supply	98.1	104.0	98.3
Mining	48.9	36.9	33.1
Manufacturing industries	66.4	75.4	88.1
Basic and intermediate goods	77.9	91.4	117.3
Investment goods	53.9	60.8	69.2
Consumer goods	71.9	85.3	98.5
Food and beverages	96.9	104.5	115.3
Construction industry	139.7	170.1	196.2

Source: Federal Statistical Office, Produzierendes Gewerbe, Fachserie 4, Reihe 2.1, July 1992 and 1994.

All industries which trade their goods in international markets and which are exposed to foreign competition - such as clothing, textiles, leather and shoes, mechanical and electrical engineering - have not yet recovered from the heavy losses and knock-outs in previous years. An exception are road vehicles where large new investments in "green fields" (VW, Opel) are now starting to produce. In June 1994 the road vehicle production has increased by 73 percent when compared to the previous year.

Figure 2: East German Industrial Production in Important Branches, 1990-1994 (Index of net production; second half year 1990 = 100)

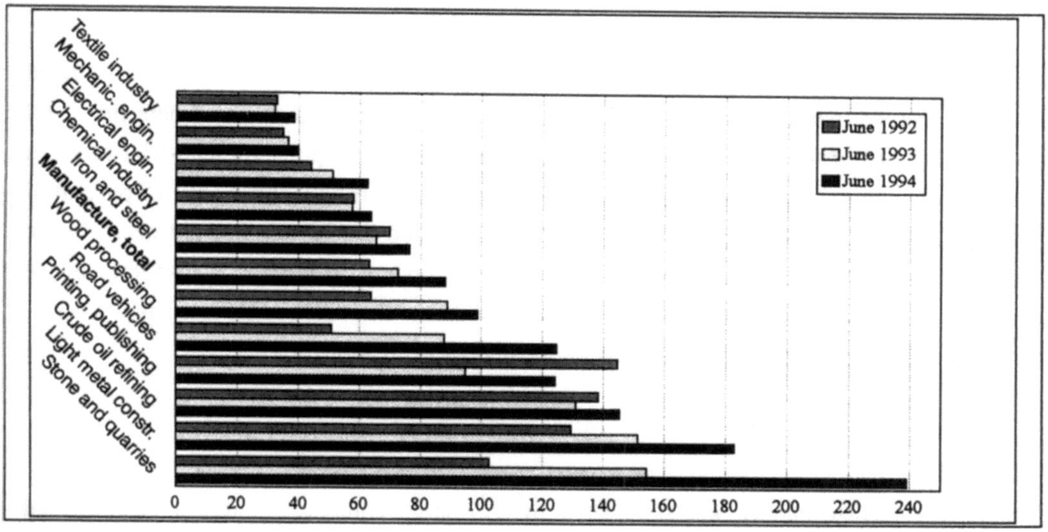

Source: Federal Statistical Office, Produzierendes Gewerbe, Fachserie 4, Reihe 2.1, July 1992 and 1994.

In former times the machinery and chemical industry belonged to the show cases of the GDR-industry supplying large parts in Central and Eastern Europe. Both industries are still depressed and employ perhaps only a quarter of the initial jobs. After four years of unification only 40 000 jobs (often only due to short time work) remained in the Eastern chemical industry out of initially 180 000 employed persons (without the mineral oil industry). Large numbers of the employees found work in semi-public enterprises for work-promotion, employment and structural change, which have been established in the new Länder in order to restructure ailing state enterprises and improve environmental conditions. A relatively large number of firms in the machinery and chemical industry are still owned by the Treuhand agency.

The general weakness in competitiveness in the East German industry is manifested in the export performance. Since their decline in 1990 and 1991 by two thirds, East German exports are stagnant. The share of East German exports (excluding intra-German trade) in total German manufacturing exports amounted to two percent in 1993. The fall of exports has hit mainly the investment goods industry. The export of East German railway-waggons, for example, depends heavily on important government (Hermes) guarantees. The reasons for the weak export performance are the previous one-sided supply orientation towards Central and Eastern Europe and even more the insufficient competitiveness of East German products, the lack of marketing knowledge and reputed brand names, as well as the non-agressive export strategy of East German firms.

One of the important handicaps for modernising East German firms and products is the rapid disappearance of industrial research capacites. Currently, only 13 000 researchers have still got jobs out of the former 75 000 persons in industry. The low point of industrial research corresponds with the sudden crash in patent activities which currently cover only 15 percent of the level in 1989. The research promotion by the *Bund* and the *Länder* has not been able to improve the innovative weakness of the East German economy. A further disadvantage of the excessive wage demands is the pressure of rationalization through capital-intensive process-innovations, instead of product-innovations supporting job-creation.

2.3 Small Businesses

The former GDR-economy was dominated by 127 large combinates, almost autarkic and monopolistic conglomerates managed by the state and political hierarchy. In general, the former dinosaurs would not have been able to survive in the new competitive environment. Therefore, their decomposition by the *Treuhand* agency was inevitable. Independent small and medium scale enterprises did not exist anymore in the GDR with the exception of some small handicraft. The German unification process created new small business firms whose dynamism and flexibility will contribute to the reconstruction of the East German economy. Small and medium-sized business will also be the most important area in creating new jobs.

Currently, there are approximately 450 000 small and medium firms in the new *Länder* (including liberal professions). The total number of employed persons in the small and medium sector is estimated at 3 million by the *Institut für Mittelstandsforschung* (Bonn). Handicraft and small trade businesses developed quickly. But the formation of small industrial business is lagging behind. The number of small and medium firms in industry has been estimated at 11 000 at the end of 1993 (in the old *Länder* at around 100 000) with some

550 000 employed persons. It may be that the industrial base is still too fragile and uncertain or the governmental promotion for industrial small firms remained insufficient..

2.4 Services

In recent years services (including trade, transport, other services and government) have made rapid progress. The supply of services has been improved markedly through large investments of DM 100 billion (excluding government and housing) from 1991 to 1993. Service expansion has mainly been based in banking and insurance, retail and wholesale trade, telecommunication, hotels and restaurants including tourism. In some regions already overcapacitities in retail trade are emerging.

By the end of 1993 the number of self-employed has increased at 350 000 reaching thus three quarters of the West German level per inhabitant. However, the surge of new service establishments and liberal professions (restaurants, education, culture and entertainment, health and other services) may have passed its peak. Currently, the catching-up of demand for professional services is retarded by the weakness of the industrial base and their easy external supply from West German firms.

From 1989 to 1993, about 382 000 jobs have disappeared in reatail and wholesale trade and in transportation and communication. At the same time, 450 000 jobs have been created in other services, including liberal professions, resulting in a net creation of 66 000 private service jobs. This gains have to be contrasted with job losses in the public sector, where the potential for labor-shedding is not yet exhausted. A further increase of service jobs will depend on growing incomes of private households and on broadening the industrial base in East Germany.

3. Investment and Labor Productivity

The progress in modernising and reconstructing East Germany´s economy can be described most easily by the increase of investment and labor productivity.

3.1 Investment Activities

In 1992 and 1993, total real gross capital formation increased with unuasual speed, and has overtaken the West German level per capita and per person employed in 1993. Apparently, business investment (excluding residential construction and the public sector) advanced at a slower rate than total investment. The speed of real capital formation is illustrated in Table 4.

Table 4: Real Gross Capital Formation, 1992-1995
(Annual percentage changes, at 1991 prices)

	1992	1993	1994	1995
Gross capital formation, total	27.8	24.0	15.6	8.5
-- equipment	9.0	10.8	8.2	8.0
-- construction	43.3	36.2	21.2	9.0
Investment ratio (1)				
in percent of domestic demand	28.6	30.9	33.4	35.9
in percent of GDP	53.0	57.1	61.3	63.9

(1) in current prices

Sources: Federal Statistical Office (Sept. 1994), German Research Institutes (Oct. 1994).

The infrastructure for transportation and telecommunication has improved quickly. From 1990 to 1993 the East German railway *(Reichsbahn)* has invested almost 20 billion DM. The number of telephones per 1000 inhabitants in East Germany reached two thirds of the Western level. The difference will be absorbed in 1997. Up to now investment in the telecommunication sector amounts to DM 30 billion, providing 3 million new telephone connexions. There are also improvements in environmental protection especially by reduced emissions. Mega-projects like the new Berlin airport are in preparation.

In 1993, total investment in manufacturing covered less than a fifth of total capital formation. The main emphasis of the investment activities was located in branches like stone and quarries, chemical and electrical goods and food and beverages absorbing almost two thirds of the total. The capital intensity in industry (investment per employee) was more than two times higher than in West Germany and has advanced in 1993 by almost 16 percent in nominal terms (Table 5). In 1994 the share of investment from West German firms will stagnate because of falling engagements in manufacturing due to the recession.

Recently, the initial investment boom in 1991 and 1992 has given way to a more modest growth in manufacturing. IWH-surveys indicate a reduced investment propensity of West German entrepreneurs which will be compensated only partly by higher foreign investment. Western sources (including railroad) amount to more than 60 percent of total investment in manufacturing. The most recent Ifo-survey (excluding firms with more than 20 employees) indicates continued investment with strong sectoral pattern favoring basic goods industries where it will rise by 20 percent in 1994.[5]

Table 5: Investment per Employee in Manufacturing - in DM

	1992	1993	1994 (1)
Industrial firms	24 800	28 700	31 100
of which: firms with 1-9 employees	33 200	43 000	53 800
- - firms with 500 employees and more	20 000	28 500	34 000
- - Treuhand firms	14 500	16 500	24 200
- - private firms	28 400	33 000	33 500
- - newly established firms	46 200	52 000	54 000
Handicraft	20 500	18 100	26 500

(1) planned

Source: DIW-Survey (in winter 1993/94), cited in: DIW/ IFW/ IWH (1994) (Tenth Report), March 1994.

Table 6: Gross Capital Formation by Sectors, 1991-1994
(At current prices and shares in precentage)

	In billion DM			Index	Shares in %	
	1991	1993	1994	1994/90	1991	1994
Agriculture, forestry, fishing	1.5	1.5	1.6	107	1.7	0.9
Goods producing sector	29.7	42.3	45.5	153	33.6	28.1
-- Energy and mining	8.9	12.0	14.2	160	10.1	8.8
-- Manufacturing	17.2	24.3	24.3	141	19.4	15.0
-- Construction	3.6	6.0	7.0	194	4.1	4.3
Retail and wholesale trade	4.4	5.2	4.7	107	5.0	2.9
Transport and telecommunication	16.2	23.8	26.3	162	18.3	16.2
Other services	7.4	13.2	10.6	222	8.4	10.1
Housing	15.0	33.0	42.0	280	16.9	25.9
Government, non-profit organisat.	14.3	23.0	25.5	178	16.1	15.7
Total economy	88.5	142.0	162.0	183	100	100

Source: Ifo Institut für Wirtschaftsforschung München, Ifo-Schnelldienst 6/1994, February 1994.

The capital formation (in nominal terms) has increased differently by sectors (Table 6). The most rapid increase experienced the housing sector, along with construction (finishing branches) and energy, where the lagged performance will be reversed after the end of the legal dispute between large energy firms and municipalities.

3.2 Labor Productivity

Labor productivity has increased quickly in recent years because of the rapid decline of employment, which was accelerated by the excessive rise of wages and the once-for-all improvements in industrial organisation and management. The progress of aggregate and sectoral productivity in manufacturing shows jump increases which are not necessarily linked to internal capital formation (Burda and Funke 1994). The overall productivity gap compared to West Germany, measured as real GDP per employed person, still amounts to almost 60 percent. Even more pertinent is the labor cost gap, the difference between gross wages per head and productivity. The overall unit labor costs in East Germany are still more than 30 percent higher than in West Germany and are decreasing slowly.

Measuring labor productivity poses difficult problems of definition (degree of capacity utilization, labor input a.o.). The use of different labor inputs results in diverging growth rates (Table 7)

Table 7: Macroeconomic Labor Productivity in East Germany, 1992 - 1995
(Annual percentage changes)

	1992	1993	1994	1995
Employed persons (domestic concept)	-11.7	-2.9	0.4	1.2
Employed full time equivalents 1)	-2.3	-1.2	0.6	1.4
Gross domestic product (prices of 1991)	7.8	5.8	8.5	8.5
per employed person	20.4	9.0	8.5	7.2
per full time equivalent	10.3	7.1	7.8	7.0
per working hour	8.9	6.5	8.5	8.0
Labor productivity 2) in percent of West Germany	37.6	41.0	42.8	44.8

1) Employed persons excluding the estimated work losses due to short-time work.

2) Real GDP per employed person.

Sources: Federal Statistical Office (Sept.1994), Forecast of the German Research Institutes (October 1994).

The first labor cost survey of the Federal Statistical Office for East Germany reveals that the value added per worker in mining and manufacturing in 1991 was down at 20 percent of the West German level. In the current phase of transformation, a large part of industrial firms also suffers from losses, while only 20 percent of Eastern firms experienced profits at the beginning of 1993.

The catching-up in industry when compared to West Germany can be observed by the difference in the performance of manufacturing output per worker in *Treuhand* and ex-*Treuhand* firms. Measured by that productivity standard indicates that *Treuhand* firms are situated 10 percentage points below ex-*Treuhand* firms which attained only 55 percent of the West German level in 1993 (compared with 36 percent in 1991). The most rapid increase in productivity in 1993 has been observed (based on surveys) in the food sector (75 percent), the most lagging sector was the intermediate goods sector.[6] According to some recent surveys real value productivity in Treuhand firms amounted only to one third of that in West Germany, whereas Ex-Treuhand firms expect to reach two thirds of West Germany's productivity level in 1994.[7]

Aggregate labor productivity data belie considerable sectoral dispersion. This heterogeneity can be illustrated in manufacturing (Burda and Funke 1994). Here, net production per employed person increased from January 1991 to December 1993 between 26 percent (shipbuilding), and 850 percent (office machinery).

4. Regional Developments

Because of the disastrous breakdown of production in 1990 and 1991, East Germany became an economic region whose domestic output per head was lower than in all other European countries. In 1991 GDP per head in East Germany amounted to 35 percent of the average of the European Community.[8] Up to now the regional development of the new *Länder* proceeded at a different pace and is lead by Thuringia whose real GDP per capita advanced by almost 12 percent in 1993 (Table 8).

The first phase of the adjustment process has hit most regions in East Germany with similar intensity. Only recently some more pronounced sectoral adjustment crises - for example in the lignite and potash mining branch, the mechanical engineering or the chemical industry - resulted in growing regional divergences and competitive problems of specific regions. Today, spatial disparities manifest itself in underemployment ratios (unemployed, short time worker, participants in work creation (*ABM*), training and early retirement measures in percentage of working population) of local work office districts. In autumn 1993, these ratios spread between 30 (Berlin-East, Potsdam) and 50 percent (Neckarmünde). Crisis regions are either mainly agricultural areas in peripheric locations or old industrial regions with monostructures and, in part, serious environmental burdens (like the chemical triangle Halle-Bitterfeld-Merseburg). Crisis regions are generated by various factors. One of them is the limited wage flexibility. Scattered information for the Treuhand and Ex-Treuhand firms and regional date for 1992 illustrate that regional wage differentials are small. The cofficient of variation for the regions in East Germany was 4.5 percent, compared to 8.7 percent for the regions in West Germany. The main bottlenecks of regional development are still the insufficient transportation infrastructure, the obstacles in labor mobility, the deficiencies of housing, the low environment and life quality and the administrative and planning deficits of municipalities.

Table 8: Regional Divergence and Growth Performance in East Germany

	GDP per head* EC-level=100	Real GDP growth		Real GDP growth per capita	
	1991	1992	1993	1992	1993
Berlin-East	42	11.3	12.1	10.3	1.3
Brandenburg	38	4.4	5.6	6.6	5.3
Saxony Anhalt	35	10.9	6.3	12.2	6.2
Saxony	35	10.0	8.0	10.6	7.2
Mecklenburg-West Pommerania	33	10.0	6.7	12.0	5.8
Thuringia	30	12.9	11.8	15.5	11.6
Eastern Germany	35	9.7	7.1	10.5	7.1
Western Germany	123	1.6	-1.9	0.4	1.5
Portugal	61	1.1	-0.5	1.4	-0.5
Greece	50	1.3	-0.2	0.5	-0.8
European Community (12)	100	1.0	-0.5	0.5	-0.9

*in Purchasing Power Parities.

Sources: eurostat 1993; Statistical Offices of the New Länder, *March 1994.*

The long list of comperative disadvantages is evidence for the concern that regional disparities in East Germany will be much larger than in West Germany, to be only slowly reduced through regional policy efforts. The most costly prescription would be the lump sum "maintenance of industrial cores", which is frequently demanded, and will slow down structural change and the reconstrution of industrial firms. Nevertheless, more efforts are necessary to abolish the still existing obstacles for investments, to provide more efficient administrations and to promote efficient industrial innovation and research. Labor mobility within Eastern Germany is still very limited (with the exception of commuters) and mainly impaired by the lack of sufficient housing, the large rent difference between cheap local and newly constructed housing and the insufficient wage differentials.

The regional indicators of labor productivity and industrial wages between the new *Länder* do not reveal growing disparities (Table 9). Similar patterns can be observed by comparing the average monthly wage developments since the beginning of 1991 between industrial branches.

In the long run, the old industrial centers between Chemnitz, Leipzig, Jena and Halle may be re-established in the South of the new Länder. Metropolitan Berlin could serve again as a dynamic service, telecommunication and cultural center, acting also as bridge between Western and Eastern Europe. Berlin, as the "new" capital, will attract human capital and help to establish linkage effects in the Eastern parts of Germany, based on its modern infrastructure and cultural environment. In contrast, border regions in Branden-burg and Mecklenburg-West Pommerania will face serious difficulties to reduce their regional disparities and unemployment rates. It is to be feared that a double regional gap from North to South and from West to East will be generated in East Germany.

Table 9: Productivity and Wage Levels in the New *Länder* (Total New *Länder* = 100)

	Labor productivity (1)		Gross wages (2)	
	1991	1992	July 1992	July 1993
Berlin-East	110.4	106.1	100.9	111.9
Brandenburg	106.4	101.4	110.9	107.2
Saxony Anhalt	98.8	98.4	98.5	101.0
Saxony	101.6	102.7	98.6	96.2
Mecklenburg-West Pommerania	97.2	98.9	100.4	99.8
Thuringia	86.9	92.4	91.1	94.8

(1) Nominal GDP per employed person.

(2) Gross monthly wages per worker in industry (excluding construction).

Source: Federal Statistical Office, March 1994.

5. Policy Orientation and Growth Prospects

A self-sustained growth process has not yet begun. The degree of dependence on external savings and resources in East Germany is displayed by the gap between aggregate domestic demand (total of consumer and investment expenditures) and the Gross Domestic Product. This gap, the East German "trade deficit", i.e. net imports (including services), increased in nominal terms from DM 52 billion in 1990 to DM 212 billion in 1993 and is forecast at DM 218 and 223 billion in 1994 and 1995, respectively (see figure 3).

Figure 3: "Trade Deficits" in East Germany, 1990 - 1995
(In billion DM and in percentage of total domestic demand)

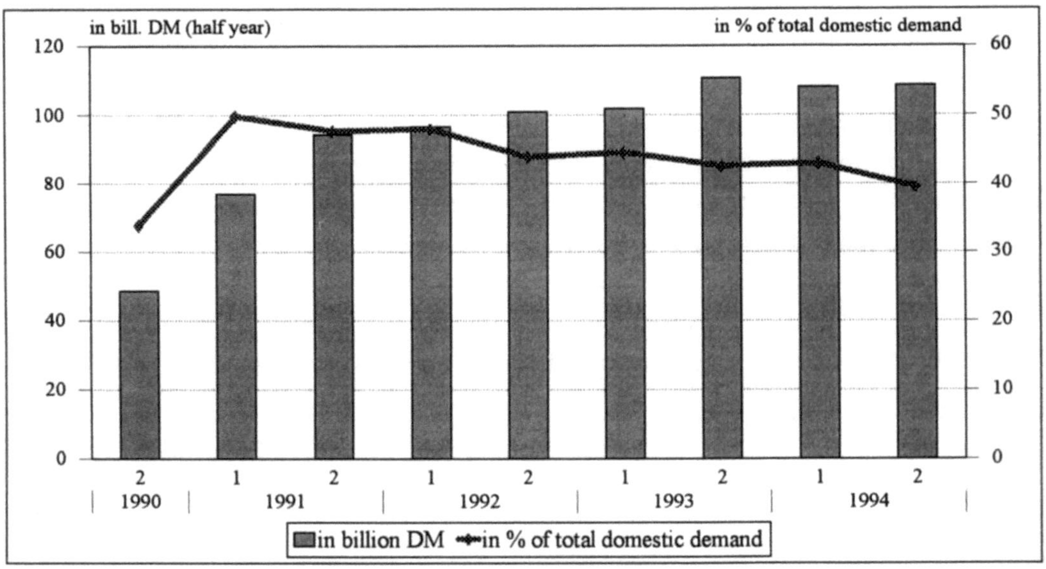

Sources: Federal Statistical Office (Sept. 1994), German Economic Research Institutes (Oct. 1994).

The slow reduction of the internal resource gap expressed as percentage of domestic demand indicates the difficulties to finance the reconstruction of East Germany out of own efforts and savings by higher exports or/and slower consumption growth. Because of the wide initial gap the reduction of the "foreign" deficit will take a long time.

The deficit is "financed" by public transfers, estimated at DM 190 billion (including Treuhand), and by private capital flows. Both external sources depend on a strong and growing West German economy and on external capital imports. It can not be excluded that the long-term burden of unification will temporarily reduce the growth rate and certainly delay some infrastructure investments in West Germany.

A broad export basis and the access to new international markets have not yet been established. The need for and implications of governmental industrial policies in form of a more horizontal growth policy or of more target- and industry-oriented interventions are therefore still being debated in Germany. Supporters of industrial policies favoring the "maintenance of industrial cores" have asked for long-term structural adjustment programs; these are to focus on the reconstruction of an industrial base and integration of the various global and regional support instruments by the government and Treuhand agency. Opponents of industrial policies fear structural conservation und misallocations through the politization of economic decisions. Regional policies, concentrating on the creation of a framework for promoting growth, were assigned to the *Länder* governments and based on the already well-established regional community program "Improvement of the regional economic structure". These programs were set in motion only reluctantly in East Germany, however, because of numerous obstacles and deficiencies. But it remains doubtful whether regional policies alone are a sufficient vehicle for avoiding the aggravation of regional disparities or for repairing the damage created by the excessive and rigid wage adjustment.

The list of obstacles of the adjustment process in East Germany has not changed substantially in the last years. Recent surveys presented the following ranking of the most important deterrents to investment in industrial firms:

- excessive rise of labor costs,
- growing problems in penetrating new markets due to the recession in West Germany,
- short-term liquidity constraints and lacking financial resources,
- crowding out of East German products by less expansive competitors from Eastern Europe,
- insufficient infrastructure and slow-functioning administrations.

The obstacles and insufficiencies in East Germany are an outline for the policy orientation of the next years.

How quickly will the new *Länder* converge to the welfare standards and per capita production levels of West Germany? The debate about the regional convergence of East and West Germany has been stimulated by recent studies,[9] which foresee a catching-up period of more than a generation. Burda and Funke (1994) have argued that this extreme pessimism is not justified in view of specific advantages in the German transformation process (initial efficiency gains, strong investment growth, high capital mobility a.o.), which allow the closing of the gap in productivity and living standards between East and West Germany much sooner.[10]

This more optimistic assessment is based, at least, on two policy implications:

- the sustained preference for efficiency in contrast to conservationist and protective measures, i.e. accepting a supply-oriented approach and the trade-off between high (open and disguised) unemployment today in expecting more rapid job creation potentials for tomorrow;

- the capacity of West Germany´s economy to finance the longer-term burden of large transfer payments for investment and social purposes (capital subsidies, infrastructure, income support and labor market actions) without a substantial decline of its potential growth rate.

In 1993, total gross capital formation per employed person in East Germany amounted to 22 700 DM (in nominal terms); thus overtaking the level in West Germany (19 500 DM). The corresponding marginal capital productivity in East Germany was 12 percent.[11] An acceleration of GDP growth implies either a further rise of the investment ratio or an increase of the marginal productivity of capital. Applying the Western marginal productivity (of 15 percent) to an investment ratio of 50 percent results in an annual real GDP growth rate of 7.5 percent which indicates perhaps the upper limit of the feasible long-term growth performance of East Germany.

In East Germany GDP per capita rose from 31 percent of the West German level in 1991 to 49 percent in 1994. From 1992 to 1995 the average growth differential of real GDP per capita was alsmost 8 percentage points per year and 5 to 6 percentage points for labor productivity. If the excess growth in East Germany could be sustained at 5 percentage points per year above the West German growth rate the aggregate level of per capita GDP in the year 2000 would attain almost 70 percent of the average West German level and more than 90 percent in the year 2005.[12] An 80 percent convergence goal of output per capita corresponds with the level reached by some poorer West German states (Lower Saxony and Schleswig-Holstein) in relation to the West German average. Therefore, the completion of a reasonable convergence path may require 10 to 15 years. Yet, this convergence is by no means a guarantee for a full-fledged self-sustained growth process.

In view of the vast infrastructure programs (roads, railways, communication) and the housing needs, the construction sector will remain an important factor for expansion in Eastern

Germany for a long time. Recent estimates assume that at least two million houses will have to be modernised, and that one million lodgings are lacking in Eastern Germany.[13] East Germany will remain for long years and probably beyond the year 2000 the largest building site of Europe.

6. Conclusions

Up to now German policymakers have steered a middle course and favored massive income and welfare support schemes in East Germany, thus risking the re-implementation of the deep-rooted mentality of subsidies and interventions, which had been one of the heritages of the former GDR. The Bonn government has failed to abolish more radically the multitude of perfectionist regulations in the field of social, regional, labor market and tax policies, and to design more simplified procedures.

Since 1992 the transformation of the East German economy has made substantial progress, but there are still concerns about the creation of a viable industrial structure and a sufficient number of new jobs. In general the main policy emphasis still has to be placed on providing an efficient framework for rapid growth conditions and efficient resource allocation. The government incentives and programs for attracting private capital and for improving the human capital formation have to be sustained, but capital subsidy schemes should be phased out gradually and be abolished at the end of this decade..

The risks that government support is becoming permanent must be avoided. Economic development in East Germany has to be financed by her own resources of households and enterprises. Self-sustained growth, however, has to be based on a viable export and industrial base, thus justifying a more concentrated and streamlined government support of tradables goods industries and small businesses. Two central problems have to find policy solutions: more modest wage increases linked to a much stronger flexibility, and dispersion of effective wages and more efficient regional policies. No ready-made answers are available for these challenges. The creation of new jobs will be a long-term task for social partners and governments alike; it could be made easier by wage agreements linked to productivity and investment performance of firms. A more equitable wealth distribution of the new regional wealth created in East Germany could improve the social and political climate, as well as the acceptance of inevitable market-oriented adjustments.

After some painful lessons, it is gradually being recognized that German unification is not a temporary deviation from normalcy, but a fundamental chance to break up a number of rigid attitudes and to reshape the institutional and locational conditions in favor of a more dynamic Germany as a whole. If Germany were to lose this chance, it would be faced with large and multiple problems which could lead to difficult distributional struggles and jeopardize the long-standing political and social stability. At the same time, external pressures and new challenges are an opportunity for accelerating structural change and for improving the conditions of economic growth.

The successful transformation of East Germany will cause serious repercussions in the competitiveness and attractiveness of Germany as a whole. In the coming years neither the agressive wage policies nor the over-regulative framework can be sustained. The growing pressure to reduce public spending will have beneficial effects on the behavior of public institutions, resulting in the rationalization and privatization of public activities; it will furthermore lead to the simplification of the burdensome regulations and procedures which have hindered severely structural change and potential growth.

The economic and social transformation of East German has benefited from special circumstances and suffered from difficult conditions and policy errors. The unique experience of German unification can therefore not be replicated elsewhere. Nevertheless, some lessons can be drawn from the longer adjustment process underlying most tranformations of centrally planned economies toward competitive market economies. First, the adjustment and learning process must be facilitated by modest wage increases below productivity growth, giving room to higher profits and investments. Second, important elements of the transformation process include rapid privatization and clear property rights as strong market signals for private investors. Third, a stable macroeconomic environment and credible monetary framework are the prerequisite for efficient microeconomic policy making. Finally, the transformation and adjustment process should be accompanied by long-term qualification programs and a solid social network for absorbing the painful social consequences.

For Germany, the unification shock is a financial burden in the medium run. Yet it is also a long-term investment and a unique opportunity for revitalizing the private as well as the public sector. In fact, Germany has the potential capacity and strength to solve most of the problems within a decade if the policy framework becomes more growth-oriented, and if the external conditions in Western and Eastern Europe remain favorable.

Endnotes

1 Gerlinde and Hans-Werner Sinn (1993), Jumpstart, The Economic Reunification of Germany, MIT Press; Lutz Hoffmann (1994), Warten auf den Aufschwung- eine ostdeutsche Bilanz, Regensburg.

2 Deutsches Institut für Wirtschaftsforschung Berlin, Institut für Weltwirtschaft Kiel and Institut für Wirtschaftsforschung Halle, Gesamtwirtschaftliche und unternehmerische Anpassungsfortschritte in Ostdeutschland (Ninth and Tenth Report), Berlin and Kiel, September 1993 and March 1994.

3 Ifo-Institut für Wirtschaftsforschung und Institut für Wirtschaftsforschung Halle (1994), Die Effizienz der finanzpolitischen Fördermaßnahmen in den neuen Bundesländern, Ifo studien zur Finanzpolitik 53, München.

4 Gürtler, J. (1994), Neue Bundesländer: Beschäftigungserwartungen in der Industrie, im Baugewerbe und im Handel, in: ifo Schnelldienst, 14/1994, München.

5 Jäckel, P. (1994), Neue Bundesländer: Weiterer Anstieg der Industrieinvestitionen, in: Ifo-Schnell-dienst 24/94, München.

6 See the regular surveys of *SÖSTRA* (*Sozialökonomische Strukturanalysen*) and the *Institut für Arbeitsmarkt- und Berufsforschung*, Beschäftigungsperspektiven von Treuhandunternehmen und Ex-Treuhandunternehmen - Befragung April 1993, Berlin, October 1993.

7 Wahse, Dahms and Schäfer (1994), Beschäftigungsperspektiven von Treuhandunternehmen und Ex-Treuhandfirmen im Vergleich (SÖSTRA-Befragung April 1994), Berlin.

8 The income and consumption level per head in East Germany are much higher because of massive public transfer payments which represented about 55 percent of East German GDP in 1993.

9 Barro, Robert and Xavier Sala-i-Martin (1991), Convergence across States and Regions, in: Brookings Papers on Economic Actitivity, 1:1991, Washington, D.C.; Dornbusch, Rüdiger and Holger Wolf (1992), Economic Transition in Eastern Germany, in: Brookings Papers on Economic Actitivity 1:1992, Washington, D.C.

10 Burda, Michael and Michael Funke (1994), Eastern Germany: Can`t We Be More Optimistic? mimeographed paper, Humboldt University, August 1994, Berlin.

11 Per definition the increase of real GDP (y) corresponds with the product from the investment ratio (IR) and the marginal productivity of capital (mpc), i.e. y = IR * mpc. From 1982 to 1993 the capital productivity in West German has attained 15 percent (investment ratio: 20.5 percent, real GDP growth: 3.0 per year).

12 The results take into account a substantial decrease of population in East Germany due to further immigration and declining birth rates and a corresponding increase in West Germany.

13 In 1992, the Ifo-Institute for Economic Research has quantified the financial requirements for construction up to 2005 (assuming the equalization of social and life standards with West Germany) which amounts to the total of 2 400 billion DM (in prices of 1991) of which approximately one trillion DM is accounted for the housing sector.

References

BARRO, ROBERT AND XAVIER SALA-I-MARTIN (1991), Convergence across States and Regions, in: Brookings Papers on Economic Actitivity, 1:1991, Washington, D.C.

BURDA, MICHAEL AND MICHAEL FUNKE (1994), Eastern Germany: Can`t We Be More Optimistic? mimeographed paper, Humboldt University, August 1994, Berlin.

DEUTSCHES INSTITUT FÜR WIRTSCHAFTSFORSCHUNG BERLIN, INSTITUT FÜR WELTWIRTSCHAFT KIEL AND INSTITUT FÜR WIRTSCHAFTSFORSCHUNG HALLE, Gesamtwirtschaftliche und unternehmerische Anpassungsfortschritte in Ostdeutschland (Ninth and Tenth Report), Berlin and Kiel, September 1993 and March 1994

DORNBUSCH, RÜDIGER AND HOLGER WOLF (1992), Economic Transition in Eastern Germany, in: Brookings Papers on Economic Actitivity 1:1992, Washington, D.C.

GÜRTLER, J. (1994), Neue Bundesländer: Beschäftigungserwartungen in der Industrie, im Baugewerbe und im Handel, in: ifo Schnelldienst, 14/1994, München

HOFFMANN, LUTZ (1994), Warten auf den Aufschwung- eine ostdeutsche Bilanz, Regensburg

IFO-INSTITUT FÜR WIRTSCHAFTSFORSCHUNG UND INSTITUT FÜR WIRTSCHAFTSFORSCHUNG HALLE (1994), Die Effizienz der finanzpolitischen Fördermaßnahmen in den neuen Bundesländern, Ifo studien zur Finanzpolitik 53, München

JÄCKEL, P. (1994), Neue Bundesländer: Weiterer Anstieg der Industrieinvestitionen, in: Ifo-Schnell-dienst 24/94, München

SINN, GERLINDE AND HANS-WERNER (1993), Jumpstart, The Economic Reunification of Germany, MIT Press

SÖSTRA (SOZIALÖKONOMISCHE STRUKTURANALYSEN) AND THE INSTITUT FÜR ARBEITSMARKT- UND BERUFSFORSCHUNG, Beschäftigungsperspektiven von Treuhandunternehmen und Ex-Treuhandunternehmen - Befragung April 1993, Berlin, October 1993.

WAHSE, DAHMS AND SCHÄFER (1994), Beschäftigungsperspektiven von Treuhandunternehmen und Ex-Treuhandfirmen im Vergleich (SÖSTRA-Befragung April 1994), Berlin

INTERGOVERNMENTAL FISCAL RELATIONS AFTER GERMAN UNIFICATION: PROBLEMS AND SOLUTIONS

Klaus-Dirk Henke, Peter Lutz and Claudia Ade

1. Introduction

During the negotiations on the Unification Act in 1990 a serious problem occurred: The system of intergovernmental fiscal relations would have been overstrained in a non manageable degree, if the new East German Länder were included. This system was constructed for a quite homogenous federal state and not for managing the extreme differences between the West German and the new East German Länder. It was therefore not possible to immediately integrate the new Länder into the current system. Since restructuring the system within a short period of time was also out of the question, flexible and provisional interim regulations had to be worked out. After about three years, when sufficient data for the new Länder was available, the system of intergovernmental fiscal relations was restructured; this common effort considered the problems of unified Germany up to the year 2000 and beyond. Thus the German system of intergovernmental fiscal relations has changed from an obstacle for unification to the major element in the completion of economic and social unification.

In Chapter 2 we describe and analyze the current system of fiscal relations, which will show the problems that occurred in the unification process. These explanations are necessary to comprehend the restructured system that will be in force from 1995 onwards, because it is based on the former system. The interim regulations, which substitute the system of intergovernmental fiscal relations on the territory of the new Länder up to 1995, will be explained in Chapter 3. These regulations especially serve to temporarily compensate the low fiscal capacity of the new Länder. The restructured system of intergovernmental fiscal relations described in Chapter 4 contains many new instruments for building up the new Länder in the long term. Finally, we give an impression of future challenges for the German fiscal relations system, e.g. the mastering of European Unification.

2. Basic Elements of the System of Intergovernmental Fiscal Relations in Germany

2.1 The Distribution of Public Functions between Levels of Government

The intergovernmental fiscal relations not only include the distribution of public revenues among the different levels of government, but also the assignment of public functions. To assess the distribution of revenues and its problems in a proper way, it is necessary to first study the distribution of public functions which determine the fiscal needs. It is a basic principle of German federalism for each level of government to carry the costs that are generated by the performance of its functions (Art. 104a, Basic Law).

Firstly, we look at the functions of German communes. Art. 28 Basic Law prescribes that the communes regulate all local affairs in their own responsibility. In practice, the communes have responsibilities for schools, cultural affairs, traffic, local energy provision, garbage disposal, and waste water. Important competences regarding youth and social care also belong to the communes.

The functions of the Länder are mainly regulated in Art. 30 Basic Law. De jure the Länder do have the competence for all tasks, except when they are explicitly assigned to the Federation. Through Art. 72 Basic Law, which regulates the so-called concurrent power of legislation and gives the federation the right of legislation if there is a "need" for a federal law, however, the federation is in the position to take over more and more public functions. This development was strengthened through German unification. Currently, the Länder hold important functions only in sectors like education, universities and police, as well as in cultural and social affairs; they also have to support the communes through grants out of their budgets.

Two basic principles determine the functions of the federal level in the theory of public finance. On the one hand, the federation is in charge of providing national public goods; on the other hand, the federation is responsible for redistributional and stabilization activities. Consequently, the expenditures for social policy count for about 35 percent of the German federal budget (see Table 1). Other important competences of the federation are defense, highways and trains, as well as the support of the economy. Many public functions in Germany are fulfilled jointly by the federation and the Länder; this "cooperative federalism" makes it difficult to divide exactly their functions and expenditures.

Table 1: Expenditure Structure of the Federation and the Länder

Functions	in Million DM	in Percent
Federation(1994)		
Political leading and central administration	12,747	2.66%
Foreign affairs	15,453	3.23%
Defense	50,124	10.48%
Education, science, research, cultural affairs	19,816	4.14%
Social Security, social charge resulting from the war, reparation	168,180	35.15%
Health and sports	1,743	0.36%
Housing, urban development and communal services	6,637	1.39%
Nutrition, agriculture and forestry	5,657	1.18%
Electric power, water and regional policy	18,026	3.77%
Transport and communication	22,261	4.65%
Public enterprises, and maintenance of public real property and capital	39,646	8.29%
General financial policy (e.g. Grants, debt services, pensions)	114,452	23.92%
Total	478,400	100.00%
Länder (1991)		
Political leading and central administration	16,649	6.00%
Public Security	15,053	5.42%
Schools and kindergarten	47,531	17.13%
Universities	31,137	11.22%
Education related transfers	2,384	0.86%
Other educational institutions	1,526	0.55%
Science outside universities	3,336	1.20%
Social policy	25,877	9.32%
Health, sports and recreation	14,881	5.36%
Housing, regional policy, urban development	10,743	3.87%
Communal services	2,086	0.75%
Support of the Economy	13,002	4.69%
Transport and communication	10,058	3.62%
Public enterprises	5,945	2.14%
Maintenance of public real property and capital	3,260	0.12%
General financial policy(Grants, debt services, pensions)	57,965	20.89%
Other Expenditures		6.86%
Total	277,524	100.00%

Source: Federal Statistical Office (Ed.), Series 14, No. 3.1, p. 18-23 and Federal Ministry of Finance (Ed.), Financial Report 1994, Bonn 1993, p. 185.

2.2 The Structure of Public Revenues

In Germany the majority of public revenues are collected through taxes; for a detailed picture of the revenue structure see Table 2. The distribution of taxes to the levels of government therefore determines in an extraordinary way the fiscal capacity of the different levels. Besides taxes, which in Germany are defined as payments without a specific return service, contributions, fees and payroll-taxes are paid for a special public service, but count for a much smaller part of public revenues. To give a more detailed picture of public revenue sources, rents, leases, and concession payments have to be mentioned as well.

Table 2: Revenue Structure of the Federation and Länder

Sorts of revenues	in Million DM	in Percent
Federation (1994 planned)		
Taxes and dues similar to taxes	377,906	92.10%
Revenue out of economic activity	16,702	4.07%
Interest received	1,833	0.45%
Grants	3,464	0.84%
Other current receipts	6,675	1.63%
Revenue out of capital account	3,745	0.91%
Total	410,325	100.00%
Länder (1993 planned)		
Taxes and dues similar to taxes	246,302	75.87%
Revenue out of economic activity	6,153	1.90%
Interest received	922	0.28%
Grants	48,434	14.92%
Other current receipts	6,088	1.88%
Revenue out of capital account	15,476	4.77%
Other revenues	1,247	0.38%
Total	324,622	100.00%

Source: Federal Ministry of Finance (ed.), Financial Report 1994, Bonn 1993, p. 207.

The main technical problem is the assignment of taxes. The regulations are described in the following paragraphs.

2.3 Primary and Secondary Distribution of Taxes: An Overview

Regarding the assignment of taxes three different aspects can be distinguished:

- Which level is authorized to give the tax law (legislative power)?

- Which level is authorized to administer and collect the tax (administrative power)?

- Which level are the tax returns assigned to (assignment of revenue)?

Table 3: Primary and Secondary Distribution of Revenues

	Federation	Länder
Primary Distribution	**Federal taxes** – Spirits monopoly – Customs duties – Capital transaction taxes – Insurance tax – Solidarity surcharge – Levies required by the European Union – Excise taxes (with the exception of beer tax) on tobacco, coffee, tea, sugar, salt, sparkling wine, lamps and mineral oil **Share of common taxes** – Wages tax and assessed income tax (currently 42.5 %) – Non-assessed taxes on earnings and corporation tax (50 %) – Turnover tax, including import turnover tax (currently 63 %) **Share in trade tax apportionment(50 %)** **Remaining federal revenues (e.g. revenues out of economic activity)**	**Länder taxes** – Net worth tax – Inheritance tax – Real property transfer tax – Motor vehicle tax – Beer tax – Tax on betting and lotteries – Fire protection tax – Gaming casinos levy **Share of common taxes** – Wage tax and assessed income tax (currently 42.5 %) – Non-assessed taxes on earnings, and corporation tax (50 %) – Turnover tax, including import turnover tax (currently 37 %) **Share in the trade tax apportionment (50 %)** **Remaining Länder revenues (e.g. levies)**
Secondary Distribution	The federation receives nearly no revenues in a secondary way, but it is the payer of the aside mentioned grants. The common responsibilities of the Federation and Länder cause financial effects, which also have to be regarded.	**Distribution of the equalization destinated part of the turnover tax Länder share** **Fiscal equalization among Länder** **Grants** – Supplementary grants from primary federal revenue to financially weak Länder – Financial aids

From a fiscal point of view, the assignment of revenues is the dominant factor since the so-called primary tax distribution derives from it. However, the primary tax distribution does not correspond with the final revenues of a jurisdiction. The final revenues stem from the secondary distribution, which is the result of a redistributional process in the fiscal equalization system.

Table 3 illustrates the major elements of the primary and secondary distribution of taxes. The primary distribution on the one hand consists of so-called "separation-taxes", which are taxes solely assigned to one federal level. On the other hand there are "common taxes", which have been laid down in the Basic Law since 1969 and are shared between levels of government.

The secondary distribution firstly consists in a part (up to 25 percent) of the turnover tax Länder share, which is used for fiscal equalization between Länder budgets. After this a fiscal equalization system causing redistribution between financially strong and financially weak Länder becomes effective. Finally there are several kinds of grants, selective and general, which are given from the federation to financially weak Länder.

The legislative power to tax has to be regarded as subordinate to the assignment of tax revenues. Legislative power in taxation consists, for example, in the right to vary the rate of taxation or the tax-base. In Germany this right is assigned exclusively to the federation, a condition which is often criticized in public, political and scientific discussions. In contrast to Federalism in the US, the Länder in Germany hardly have the possibility to influence the structure and volume of their revenues; in this respect they depend completely on the federation.

To complete this overview, the administrative power in taxation has to be mentioned. This competence consists especially in the right to collect taxes from citizens, and belongs in Germany almost solely to the Länder (for the responsibility of tax offices see Figure 1).

Figure 1: Organization of the Finance Administration

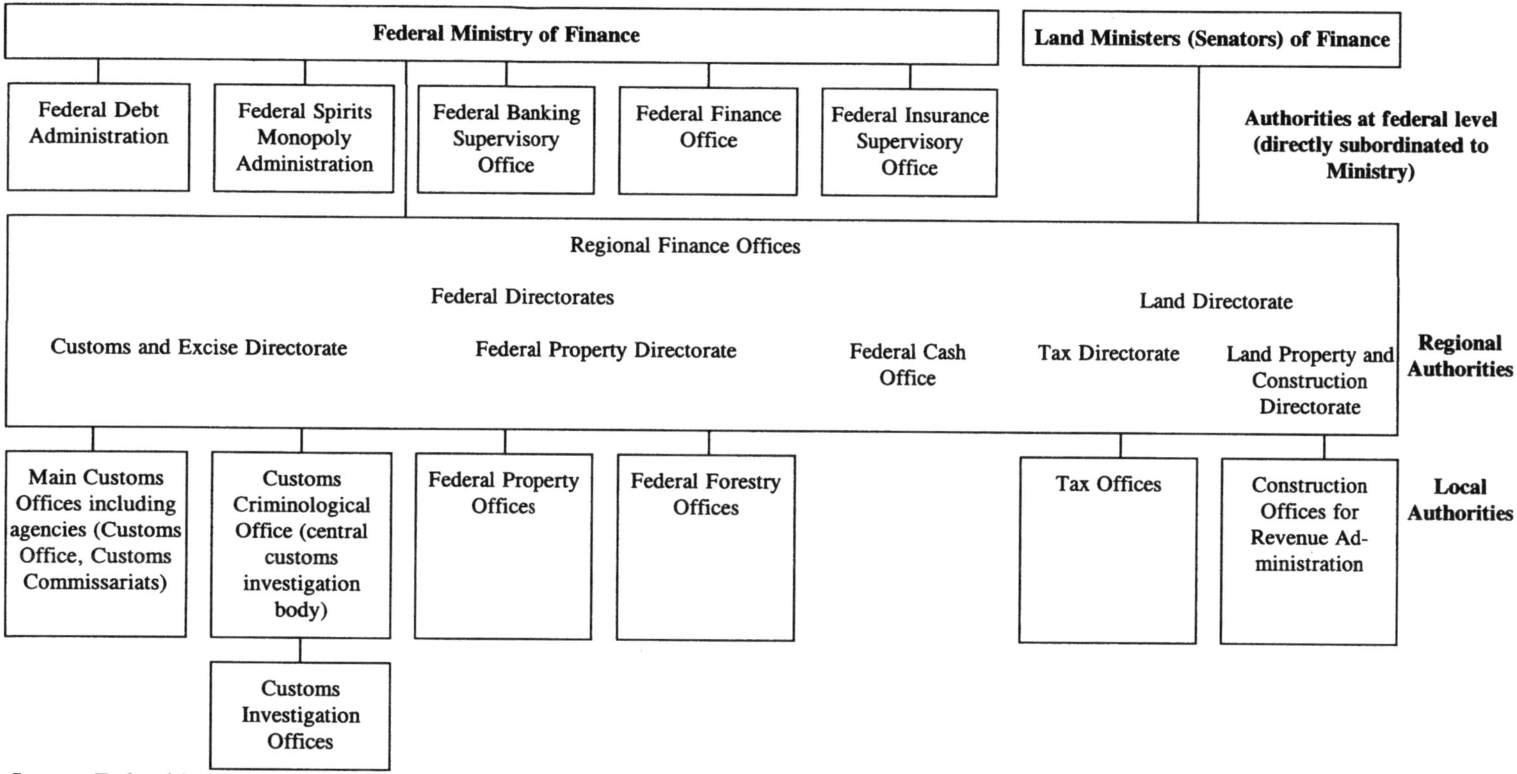

Source: Federal Ministry of Finance (ed.), An ABC of Taxes in the Federal Republic of Germany, Bonn 1993, p. 60/61.

These regulations, which were created during the inception-phase of the Federal Republic of Germany, were founded - among other reasons - due to fear that the Federation will get a too powerful position. The Länder should have the chance to refuse the transfer of tax proceeds, should a politically unstable situation require this. In the following paragraphs we will not consider the legislative and administrative power any further, but will only discuss the assignment and share of revenues in fiscal terms.

2.4 The Vertical Assignment of Tax-Revenues

As mentioned above, the returns of some taxes are assigned according to the "separation system". The so-called "separate-taxes" exclusively belong to one federal level; no other level of government participates directly in their proceeds. We foremost refer to the various federal taxes. Returns of the spirit monopoly belong to them, along with custom duties, capital transaction tax, insurance tax, and surcharges on income and corporation tax, which the federation can introduce autonomously. Even excise taxes, except for beer tax, are assigned to the federation; these include taxes on tobacco, coffee, tea, salt, sparkling, wine and the mineral oil tax, which is fiscally and ecologically of importance.

The equivalent to the federal taxes on the Länder side are the Land taxes. These are the net worth tax, inheritance tax, real property transfer tax, motor vehicle tax, beer tax, tax on betting and lotteries, fire protection tax, and gaming casinos levies; in Table 4 the communal taxes are also included. The main tax on this level is the trade tax, in which the Länder and the federation participate through an apportionment (Art. 106 (6) clauses 4 and 5 Basic Law). This trade-tax apportionment was implemented in 1970; at the time its volume counted for about 40 percent of total trade-tax revenues. Due to this apportionment, the trade tax cannot be named a separation tax in a strong sense. Several reductions of this apportionment since 1984 caused the Federation and Länder share to count for only about 15 percent of the trade tax proceeds. Another important communal tax is the real property tax. Besides these taxes, communes are able to obtain revenues through local excises and taxes on certain non-essential spending, e.g. from the dog tax and entertainment tax.

The distribution of taxes in the separation system corresponds with the normative criteria for the assignment of taxes to levels of government; these are discussed in the theory of public finance (Musgrave 1983). One of these criteria requires taxes with very different local tax proceeds to be centralized. Besides equity considerations, this is necessary because it would otherwise lead to unequal conditions between decentral jurisdictions. Another criterion is to assign taxes with immobile tax bases or taxes that are close to the equivalence principle to decentral levels. In this case decentral jurisdictions do not have any incentive to attract tax-bases with a subvention policy, which could cause global inefficiency. These criteria are mainly fulfilled in the German separation system. The taxes with a very unequal tax base, like the mineral oil tax (local returns differed in 1986 from 7 percent of the average local tax return in Schleswig-Holstein to 1664 percent in Hamburg), are thus assigned to the federation. Taxes with a relative immobile tax base, e.g. the net worth tax, are primarily assigned to the Länder. Table 4 illustrates that the separation taxes (Federal, Länder and Communal taxes) include only a small proportion of total tax revenues.

The main share of revenues is obtained from so-called "common taxes". These taxes were introduced in the financing reform of 1969 and are laid down in the Basic Law (Art 106). There is foremost a wage and assessed income tax, whose proceeds are assigned in equal shares of 42,5 percent to the Federation and Länder and a share of 15 percent to the communes. The non-assessed tax on earnings and the corporation income tax are equally split between Federation and Länder. Even the turnover tax is shared; the shares can be varied in intervals of several years by Federal Law, requiring the consent of the Federal Council (Bundesrat).

These shares should be determined according to the fiscal needs of the government levels. If the fiscal need of the levels increases disproportionally, the shares of the turnover tax should vary accordingly. The problem of this regulation lies in the measurement of fiscal needs. Since there are no valid indicators to measure the fiscal need, the development of public debt in the respective federal level was used as a substitutional indicator. In the context of German unification another problem occurred: To support the new Länder, the Federation increased its public debt considerably while the grants for the old Länder were reduced. If the old Länder had reacted with a reduction of their own spending, which would have been necessary to concentrate financial power in the new Länder, the Länder would have been in danger of decreasing their turnover tax share. Hence, the Länder had an incentive to increase their public debt instead of reducing their spending. To solve this problem, the Federation and Länder decided in the Federal Consolidation program to fix the shares at rates of 44 percent for the Länder and 37 for the Federation, without any time limit. The shares of the turnover tax therefore cannot be an objective of bargaining in the medium term, which is a solid basis for fiscal planning by the Federation and Länder.

Table 4: Distribution of Tax Revenues to Federal, Land and Local Government in 1992

Type of tax	Revenues in 1992 Absolute Number in Million DM	Revenues in 1992 in Percent of Total Tax Revenues
Federation		
1. Federal Taxes	105,093.3	14,36%
2. Federal share of Common Taxes		
a) wages tax/assessed income tax	122,762.4	16,78%
b) non-assessed taxes on earnings corporation tax	21,228.5	2,90%
c) turnover taxes	109,075.4	14,91%
d) trade tax apportionment	3,163.0	0,43%
Total Federal tax revenues	352,894.2	48,23%
Länder		
4. Länder taxes	32,962.6	4,50%
5. Länder share of		
a) wages tax/assessed income tax	122,762.4	16,78%
b) non-assessed taxes on earnings corporation tax	21,228.5	2,90%
c) turnover taxes	66,649.0	9,11%
d) trade tax apportionment	3,760.2	0,51%
Total Länder tax revenues (incl. supplementary grants)	247,362.7	33,81%
Communes		
6. Communal taxes	12,063.4	1,65%
7. Communes share of wages tax assessed income tax	43,327.9	5,92%
8. Trade tax less apportionment	37,924,5	5,18%
Total Communes tax revenues	93,315.8	12,75%
European Union		
EU own resources		
- Customs duties	7,741.8	1,06%
- VAT-based	21,987.1	3,00%
- GNP-based	4,473.7	0,61%
Total EU assigned German tax revenues	34,202.6	4,67%
TOTAL GERMAN TAX REVENUES	**731,730.1**	100

Source: Based on Federal Ministry of Finance (ed.), An ABC of Taxes in the Federal Republic of Germany, Bonn 1993, p. 58/59.

The common taxes were often criticized because they have reduced the fiscal independence of the Federation and the Länder and led to tremendous conflicts. This generated the idea to include the common taxes in the separation system, which is an unrealistic claim. It would indeed be possible to solely assign a common tax either to the Federation or the Länder, but the proceeds of the turnover tax cannot compensate for the loss of the portion of income tax; therefore, the income tax has to remain a common tax. The possibility of putting the turnover tax into the separation system, with compensation through a part of the federal share of the income tax, remains. The argument against this is that there is a different development in the returns of both taxes. The income tax has a higher responsiveness to the trade cycle and a higher reaction on inflation (cold progression). In sum, a regulation like this would only strengthen the existing problem of common taxes, which mainly consists in conflicts between levels of government about the share rates; this leads to the conclusion that there is no real alternative to the current system.

2.5 Horizontal Allotment of Local Tax Returns

Besides the problem of assigning taxes to the levels of government, the problem of allotting local tax returns between the Länder has to be solved. Regulations over the horizontal allotment influence the revenues of the respective Länder to a considerable degree. These regulations have therefore often been the subject of political controversy.

Regularly, tax proceeds are allotted to the Land which collected them. This regulation caused problems in the case of wage and corporation tax Länder share. As some of the Länder are "city-states" (Hamburg, Bremen and Berlin), there are many taxpayers who commute from the neighboring Land to a City State. Since the wage-tax is paid at the work place the City states would get the complete wage tax return from the commuters, although the Land where the commuters live has to provide a certain infrastructure, e.g. schools, cultural institutions, recreation facilities. Due to this, the distribution rules have been modified. The wage tax Länder share is assigned to that Land where the taxpayer has his or her residence, regardless of the Land the person works in. This regulation also has politico-economic advantages: The Land of residence is the Land where the taxpayer votes. This means that the taxpayer has the chance to sanction politicians for spending his or her tax payments.

A similar problem refers to the corporation tax Länder share. A combine´s corporation tax payments used to be collected in the Land where the headquarters of the combine are located. Although the economic activity of the combine often takes place in different Länder, only the Land where the headquarters are located received the tax returns. This problem is aggravated by resulting public expenditures in a Land, e.g. for transportation, infrastructure, industrial supervision, environmental protection. Due to these reasons, the corporation tax is currently allotted according to the place of economic activity. This regulation has politico-economic advantages too, because the Länder have incentives to support economic activities within their territory.

A special allotment problem occurs alongside the turnover tax Länder share. The German all-stage net turnover tax, which is a value-added tax incorporating an input-tax deduction, should put the burden on consumers; the tax liability is, however, attached to the entrepreneur, who realizes a taxable turnover. The entrepreneur should pass the tax burden to the consumers via price. Thus taxpayer and tax-carrier differ, while even the Land of collection must not be identical with the Land in which the burden occurs. The principal allotting the tax proceeds to the Land of collection therefore leads to undesired results in the case of the turnover tax. Theoretically, the turnover tax Länder share could be distributed according to the consumption expenditures in a Land; however, it is statistically difficult to measure the inhabitants consumption in a certain Land.

Table 5: The Regulations for the Allotment of Tax Returns to Localities

Kind of Tax	Allotment Principle	Regulated in:
Federal Taxes	No Allotment Required	-
Länder Taxes	Place of Collection	Art. 107 (1) Basic Law
Wage Tax	Taxpayer's Place of Residence	Allotment Law
Assessed Income Tax	Place of Collection	Art. 107 (1) Basic Law
Corporation Tax	Place of Economic Activity	Allotment Law
Turnover Tax	Number of Inhabitants	Art. 107 (1) Basic Law
Equalization Destinated Part of Turnover Tax	According to the Difference between Fiscal Capacity and Fiscal Need	Art. 107 (1) Basic Law

The political solution to the problem of allotting the Länder-shared turnover tax is to distribute it to at least 75 percent, according to the number of inhabitants of a Land, while reserving at most 25 percent of the Länder share for equalization purposes. The number of inhabitants could be viewed as an approximate measure for the consumption expenditures in a Land; differences in economic power indeed do not have any effect on the turnover tax returns, as is the case for income tax return. The turnover tax allotment already has significant equalization effects, especially the equalization-destinated 25 percent part; this is hence classified as part of the secondary distribution.

2.6 Fiscal Equalization Among Länder

2.6.1 Horizontal Turnover Tax Distribution

As previously mentioned, at least 75 percent of the turnover tax Länder share is distributed according to the number of inhabitants. This principle already includes an equalization element, because the local incidence of tax burden is not totally equal to the number of inhabitants. The inhabitants of the economically strong Länder pay relatively more turnover tax in relation to the inhabitants of economically weak Länder.

The equalization-destinated part of the turnover tax has an even higher equalization effect, which can amount to up to 25 percent of the turnover tax Länder share. Here, the major distribution criterion is the difference between the tax capacity of a Land and the average tax capacity. The tax capacity of a Land does not correspond with the absolute volume of the tax proceeds, since this would disadvantage the larger Länder. The absolute volume of the tax proceeds assigned to the Länder is divided by the number of inhabitants to ascertain the tax capacity; the average tax capacity is calculated as the sum of the tax proceeds of all Länder divided by the number of all inhabitants.

If 25 percent of the Länder share is not sufficient to bring all financially weak Länder up to 92 percent of the average tax capacity, their share of the equalization-destinated part of the turnover tax Länder share is curtailed. If a part of the equalization-destinated part of the turnover tax is left over after the financially weak Länder reached the threshold of 92 percent, it is distributed according to the number of inhabitants.

This regulation has often been regarded as an unnecessary and unsystematic element in the system of intergovernmental fiscal relations; it has been recommended to abandon this part of the system. It has often been proclaimed that the financial equalization system among Länder, which is discussed in part 2.6.2, would automatically bring all Länder to the above-discussed 92 percent threshold of the average tax capacity.

This argument does not take into account that this regulation has important effects on the distribution of the burden within the equalization system. As the equalization-destinated turnover tax part is taken from the turnover tax Länder share, which is normally distributed according to the number of inhabitants, the burden of the 92 percent filling up is carried by all Länder according to their number of inhabitants. In contrast to this, the burden of the financial equalization system among Länder is only carried by the financially strong Länder. In the context of German unification, where it was necessary to split a considerable burden, the turnover tax based equalization with its special incidence is an important element to share the burden in the politically desired way. This part of the financial equalization system can be described as a mostly "invisible" or "hidden" redistribution.

2.6.2 The Fiscal Equalization among Länder

In contrast to the turnover tax equalization, an equalization system called the *Länderfinanzausgleich* causes a redistribution from financially strong to financially weak Länder. On the one hand, this system should only correct the results of the primary distribution of the tax revenues if the turnover tax based equalization did not reduce the financial differences sufficiently. The fiscal equalization is based on several fundamental principles of the Basic Law. The federal state principle of Art. 20, I, Basic Law determines that a single Land has to be supported by other Länder and the Federation, if it is too weak to fulfill its constitutional tasks. On the other hand, the principle of federative diversity also derives from the federal state principle; this means that a total equalization between the Länder is not allowed. The heterogeneity of the Länder has to be preserved not only out of economic reasons.

The intensity of the fiscal equalization has to range between these two poles. The German unification revitalized the discussion on the proper intensity of fiscal equalization. Many economists are in favor of a low degree of equalization to give financially strong Länder the incentive to increase their economic activity; financially weak Länder should be encouraged to make own efforts to improve their economic situation. A high degree of equalization would reduce these incentives and lead towards immense transfer payments from the old to the new Länder. This transfer problem was the main reason behind the implementation of the German Unity Fund, which will be discussed in Chapter 3.2.2. After the Fund´s end in 1995, the new Länder will be included in the restructured fiscal equalization system featured, with a lower equalization intensity.

The central problem in a fiscal equalization system is to determine the basis for the assessment of equalization payments. In Germany this problem is solved by setting a standard, the so-called fiscal power. Thus, the payments a Land has to make or to receive result from the difference between the Land-specific fiscal power and the average fiscal power.

The fiscal power of a Land consists in its revenues, including the Länder share of common taxes, the share of trade tax apportionment, the Land taxes (with the exception of the betting tax) and some other levies. To these revenues half of the revenues from the communes of the respective Land are added; this is due to the dependence of the Land´s fiscal situation on the fiscal situation of its communes. The Land has the duty to support its communes with grants. If a Land has financially weak communes, quantitatively high grants are required, which have a negative effect on the Land's budget. For Länder with financially strong communes the reverse case is applied. To be able to compare larger and smaller Länder, all above-mentioned revenues are divided by the number of inhabitants of the respective Land.

An important question is whether special fiscal needs of a Land should be taken into account in the calculation of fiscal power. There are many special fiscal needs which apply only to certain Länder. The high costs of road construction in Länder with mountain areas, or the additional costs for building up an administration and an infrastructure in the new Länder, could be mentioned as examples. Another example are the costs to maintain harbors and airports in some Länder, or the high costs of leasing buildings for the administration in City States. These examples demonstrate that the number of special fiscal needs is nearly unlimited. If it were possible to submit special fiscal needs in the fiscal equalization system, the Länder would invent many special fiscal needs; this could lead to a permanent political debate on the allowance of these needs, without any prospects of a long term solution. Due to this, the inclusion of special fiscal needs is principally not allowed in the German fiscal equalization system.

One exception is the consideration of an assumed overproportional fiscal need in areas with higher population density. The progressive parallelism of fiscal need and population density was firstly discussed by the German economist Brecht. The situation of the City states (Hamburg, Bremen, Berlin) as capital cities without surrounding areas is taken into account by multiplying their number of inhabitants with the factor 1,35. Another case, where "Brechts Law" is considered, is the multiplication of the number of inhabitants of the communes according to their population density, to measure their fiscal power.

Besides these rules only the maintenance of harbors in coastal Länder is regarded as a deductible special fiscal need; this reduces the fiscal power of these Länder. This regulation was the subject of a long-lasting political debate, which was terminated by a decision of the constitutional court: It ruled that the regulation is valid for historical reasons. Economists criticized this decision as an unsystematic exception in the otherwise revenue-oriented fiscal equalization system. The discussion above also demonstrates that the current system was not created to integrate Länder with high extraordinary fiscal needs, like the new Länder.

Once the problem of measuring fiscal power has been solved, the next step is to determine the equalization tariff. This tariff is the functional relationship between the fiscal power and the payments and has to fulfill a set of requirements formulated by economists and constitutional jurists:

- The differences in fiscal power may not be totally equalized. This is necessary to keep incentives for financially strong Länder to increase their fiscal power, and to preserve the interest of financially weak Länder in improving their fiscal situation.
- The ranking of the Länder with regard to their fiscal power has to be identical before and after the equalization process. If one Land overtakes another Land through fiscal equalization, this Land would get a better treatment without any legitimization.
- The regulations in the fiscal equalization system must be in the position to cope with all fiscal situations. Even if the distribution of the fiscal power changes considerably, the system has to provide a solution. There should not be permanent conflicts resulting in high bargaining costs and uncertainty for fiscal planning. This demand could not be fulfilled within the current system, however, because it would have been overstrained by including the financially weak new Länder.
- The sum of the payments that financially strong Länder make and the sum of the payments that financially weak Länder receive must be identical. The achievement of this complicates the fiscal equalization system, since regulations have to be implemented to raise missing sums or to distribute surpluses.
- Another important criterion is that the system must be consistent and transparent. This demand is important because all Länder are endeavored to improve their position in the fiscal equalization system, e.g. with proceedings in the constitutional court. The intransparancy and inconsistency of the current system have caused cost-intensive conflicts and legal uncertainty.
- The final criterion is the guarantee of each Land achieving a minimum standard of fiscal power after fiscal equalization. This is necessary to assure that each Land is able to fulfill its tasks laid down in the constitution.

The final demand conflicts with the requirement that the increase of fiscal power before equalization must lead to a higher fiscal power after fiscal equalization. The realization of this demand for Länder whose fiscal power is lower than the minimum standard is very difficult, if not impossible.

After defining the requirements for a rational equalization tariff, we now turn to the current system.

Figure 2: Current Equalization Tariff

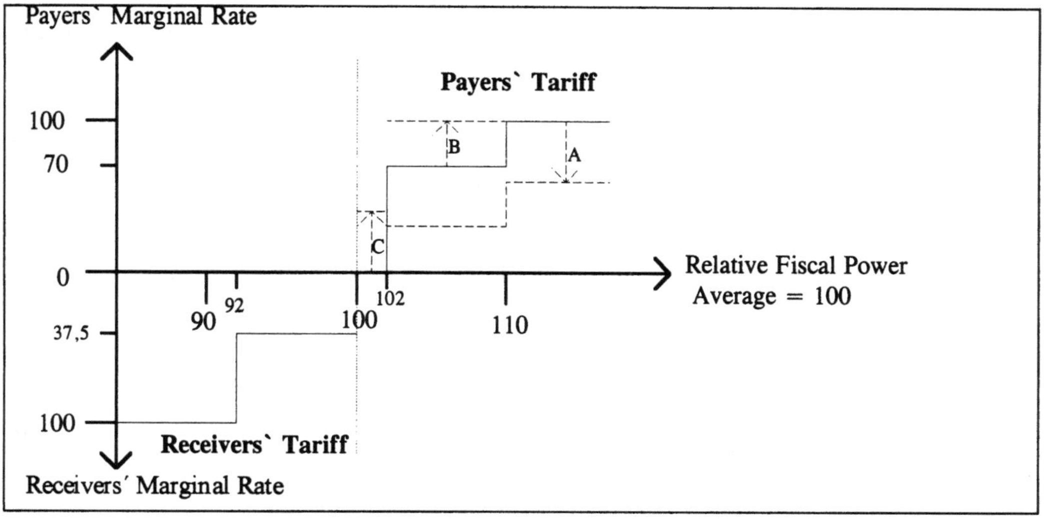

Figure 2 can be interpreted in analogy to a marginal tax rate. Länder that have more than 100 percent of the fiscal power are defined as financially strong Länder, while those under 100 percent are financially weak Länder. The area below the payers' tariff, up to the fiscal power value that a financially strong Land achieves, is equal to the payments it has to bring into the fiscal equalization system. The options B and C are used if the available payments are not sufficient; option A is used if the calculated payments are too high. The financially weak Länder receive payments in the amount of the area above the receivers' tariff from their fiscal power value (up to 100 percent).

This tariff indicates that efforts by a financially weak Land to increase its fiscal power do not have any effect on its fiscal power after equalization, until a value of 92 percent of the relative fiscal power is reached. This is contradictory to the important aim of preserving incentives for own efforts in the Länder. A similar case applies to financially strong Länder whose fiscal power is above 110 percent: If these Länder succeed in achieving more revenues, they will not receive any benefits from them.

In addition to the described procedure of calculating the equalization payments, another calculation is employed. It solely regards the Land revenues without revenues of the communes. This so-called "tax guarantee" attempts to guarantee that none of the financially strong Länder has under 100 percent of its original revenues after equalization, and none of the financially weak Länder less than 95 percent.

The "tax guarantee" is kept due to its political rationality - some of the Länder expect financial advantages. Economists often criticized the regulation: It does not only complicate the fiscal equalization system, but also violates the neutrality demand with regard to the fiscal power ranking before and after equalization. The main argument against the "tax guarantee" is that only fiscal power is a valid base for calculating the equalization payments. The introduction of a second base leads automatically to a violation of the above-mentioned requirements.

2.6.3 The Federal Supplementary Grants and Other Elements of the System of Intergovernmental Fiscal Relations

The Federal Supplementary Grants are aimed at strengthening the fiscal power of the financially weak Länder subsequent to the fiscal equalization among Länder. They are general grants which either raise the fiscal power of financially weak Länder or compensate for selected special fiscal needs.

So far the Federation has been very reluctant to consider special fiscal needs. Grants were only given for assumed overproportional costs of political leadership in small financially weak Länder. In future the special fiscal needs of the new Länder will be considered, giving these grants a more important role. The volume of the federal supplementary grants is currently fixed at 2 percent of the turnover tax proceeds in the old territory of Germany. Firstly, the grants for special fiscal needs are deducted; the remaining amount is then distributed to the financially weak Länder in relation to the remaining difference between the average fiscal power and their fiscal power after fiscal equalization. This could lead a financially weak Land, which received these grants, to overtake a Land without grants so that the ranking neutrality is not ensured; this has negative effects on the incentive structure. This problem is being solved in the new system (see Chapter 4.4).

As additional elements of the system of intergovernmental fiscal relations, the so-called financial aids must be considered. They are laid down in Art. 104a, 4, Basic Law and allow the Federation to give grants to the Länder to support economic aims of the entire nation. These grants can be given as selective or general grants of non-matching or matching type. This instrument also plays an important role in the unification process, as described in Chapter 4.4.

Finally, the so-called common responsibilities, which are laid down in article 91a and 91b Basic Law, have to be mentioned. These responsibilities mainly serve to internalize spill-over effects of certain public goods. The provision of public goods with a super-regional or national range, e.g. university education or coastal protection, are regulated in this way. The considerably high sums flowing from the Federation to the Länder for commonly financed projects are now mainly directed to the new Länder. This was one of the only possibilities to react with instruments of the current system of intergovernmental fiscal relations in German unification. As the amounts transferred in this way were not sufficient under any circumstances, many other interim regulations for the new Länder had to be found.

3. Interim Regulations for Unified Germany and their Necessity

3.1 The Political and Economic Framework after Unification: The Development 1990 - 1994

3.1.1 The Situation in East Germany

On October 3, 1990 the Unification Act, subscribed by representatives of the Federal Republic of Germany and of the former German Democratic Republic, came into force, ending the over 40 years lasting division of Germany. This act replaced the Socialist Economic System (Central Planning Economy) with the West German Economic System (Social Market Economy).

A few months after the introduction of the DM (Deutsche Mark) in the new Länder, several companies of the former GDR were forced to reduce their production or even close. The majority of firms in the former GDR was not able to compete in an open economy. Production and the GDP thus decreased considerably, whereas unemployment increased steadily, especially in the industrial sector. The reason for this development was the lacking competition for several decades, resulting in inefficient technological knowledge, experiences in management and market analysis, as well as adequately trained personnel. In addition, antiquated capital equipment, which was also immensely burdened by environmental pollution, deteriorated the situation. In the euphoria of unification these conditions were tremendously underestimated.

During the first year after unification, the differences in economic capacity between the old and new Länder became more obvious. In addition to the already-mentioned facts, the breakdown of trade relations between the new Länder and former socialist countries led to an even steeper decrease of production activities. The number of employed people decreased to 6.9 million persons in 1991, 1.4 million less than in the previous year and almost 3 million less than in 1989.

However, the economy of the new Länder did not suffer from a low domestic demand. In spite of the decreasing number of employees, disposable incomes increased in considerable scope because transfers were paid from public budgets. This additional demand was satisfied by higher imports into the new Länder, as most of their own products were not competitive. The spirit of enterprise in the new Länder was burdened by uncleared property rights, deriving from the expropriations in the territory of the former GDR. Complex regulations were necessary to handle this problem and to protect the constitutional right of property at the same time.

Beginning in mid 1991, the production recovered slowly. From a low level the production increased with rates of 9.7 percent in 1992 and 6.2 percent in 1993 (see Table 6).

Table 6: Production in the Industrial Sector, New Länder

Year		Percent Changes to Previous Year's Quarter
1991	1. Quarter	no data available
	2. Quarter	no data available
	3. Quarter	-38.0%
	4. Quarter	-25.7%
1992	1. Quarter	-4.7%
	2. Quarter	-2.5%
	3. Quarter	-3.7%
	4. Quarter	-0.1%
1993	1. Quarter	-1.1%
	2. Quarter	+9.3%
	3. Quarter	+15.9%
	4. Quarter	+11.6%
1994	1. Quarter	+21.7%
	2. Quarter	+25.3%

Source: German Bundesbank, Monthly Reports, October 1994 p. 7, May 1993, p. 71, March 1992, p. 61.*

The recovery was mainly caused by the building industry, while the industrial sector still suffered from the deep current recession in common Germany, which made it even more difficult for the new Länder to find new markets or to defend their market shares. The recovery of the industrial sector did not accelerate before the beginning of 1993.

The insufficient provision of public goods and services contributed to the problems of the East German economy to a high degree. The underdeveloped telecommunication, the bad quality of transportation networks, and the lack of open areas for industrial purposes impeded the engagement of foreign investors.

3.1.2 The Situation in West Germany

When unification took place in 1990, the West German economy was in an extraordinary boom situation. This boom was strengthened by unification since a high additional demand was generated by East German citizens, whose savings were converted into DM at a very benevolent exchange rate.

In the second half of 1991 the expansion of the West German economy slowed down. Due to the world-wide recession, the foreign demand slumped and the West German demand decreased. One of the main reasons for reduction in domestic demand was the rising burden of taxes, e.g. the so-called solidarity surcharge (7.5 percent of the income tax load) and the higher contributions to the social security system. Most of these additional revenues were used to finance fiscal or parafiscal transfers to the new Länder.

Nevertheless, most of the transfers for the new Länder were financed by public debt. See Table 7 for the considerable increase of public debt after unification. The increasing public debt was one of the main reasons for the rise in the interest rate, which can be viewed in Table 8. The high interest rate additionally lowered domestic demand for consumer and capital goods, especially for the interest rate responsive housing investments.

Table 7: Development of Public Debt[1], 1985-1994

Year	Total Debt in Million DM	Percent Changes to Previous Year	Total Debt in Percent of GDP
1985	760,192	-	42,5
1986	800,967	5.36%	42,6
1987	848,816	5.97%	43,8
1988	903,015	6.39%	44,4
1989	928,837	2.86%	43,2
1990	1,053,490	13.42%	43,5
1991[2]	1,173,864	11.43%	41,8
1992	1,345,224	14.60%	42,8
1993	1,505,000[3]	11.88%	46,2
1994	1,721,000[3]	14.35%	50,8

[1]Total public debt including all public instances
[2]From 1991 on data for Unified Germany
[3]Estimations from the "Deutsches Institut für Wirtschaftsforschung", Weekly Report 21/1994, p. 343.
Source: Federal Ministry of Finance, Financial Report 1994, Bonn 1993 p. 176-185 and OECD Economic Outlook, No.54, December 1993, p. 176.

Figure 3: Development of the Interest Rate, 1986-1992

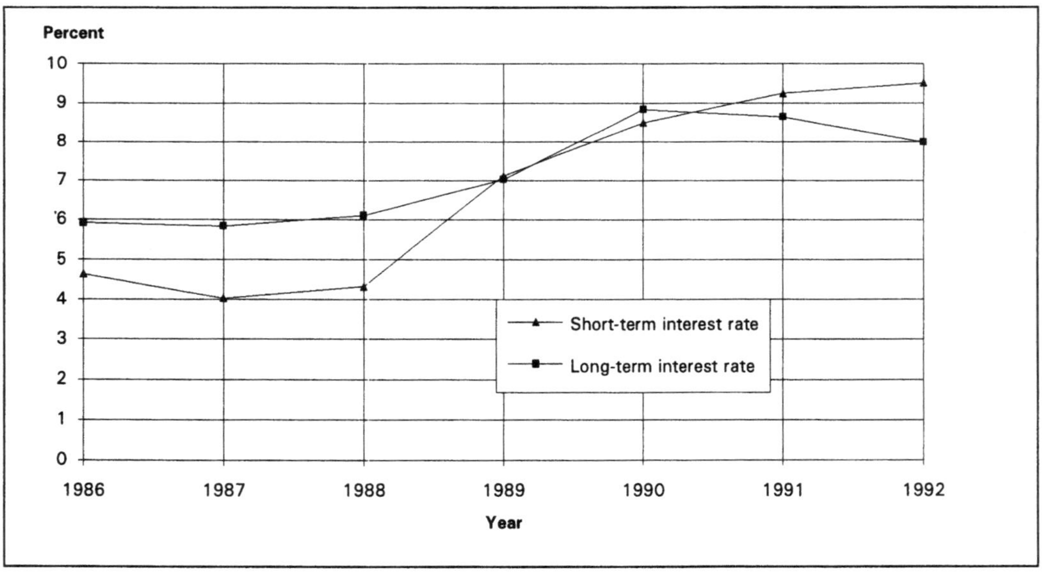

Source: Based on German Council of Economic Advisers, Annual Report 1993/94, Bonn 1993, p. 300.

Table 8: Inflation Rate, 1985-1992

Year	Price Index for Costs of Living[1]	Percent Changes to Previous Year	Price Index for Building	Percent Changes to Previous Year
1985	100,0		100,0	
1986	99,8	-0,2	101,4	1,4
1987	99,9	0,1	103,3	1,9
1988	101,0	1,1	105,5	2,1
1989	103,9	2,9	109,4	3,7
1990	106,7	2,7	116,4	6,4
1991	110,5	3,5	124,3	6,8
1992	114,9	4,0	131,3	5,6

[1]Based on a four person houshold

Source: German Council of Economic Advisers, Annual Report 1993/94, Bonn 1993, p. 405-407 and own calculations.

In spite of free production capacities and decreasing demand, the inflation rate remained high for a long period of time, as can been seen in Table 8. Some reasons included the shortage of housing space that raised residential rents, as well as the rise of administrated prices (fees for post, parking and co-payments for pharmaceuticals), as well as the increase of the turnover tax rate from 14 to 15 percent at the beginning of 1993. These increases temporarily lead to a restrictive monetary policy with negative effects on the trade cycle. In addition, the foreign demand weakness, especially on the capital goods market, had disadvantages for the export-oriented German economy.

The negative development of the trade cycle in West Germany led to a decline of public revenues, which strengthened the difficulties in financing German unification. Public revenues and therefore fiscal relations had many important functions in accomplishing German unification. Revenues of the Federation and the West Länder had to substitute the missing revenues of the East German Länder, to guarantee that they could fulfill their public functions. The fiscal need of the Federation was growing because additional public functions had to be financed in the new Länder, e.g. investments in environmental protection, in infrastructure and financial subsidies for newly founded enterprises and social transfers. Finally, the trade cycle caused losses in public revenues of all levels of government, which had to be managed.

These additional fiscal needs had to be financed under several restrictions:

- The total burden should be shared in an equitable way by the different levels of government.

- The financing must be long term oriented to create the possibility for fiscal planning in all jurisdictions.
- The problem of the rising public debt must be solved in the long run (consolidation).

These are the main objectives to be considered for restructuring the system of intergovernmental fiscal relations in newly-formed Germany.

3.1.3 The Necessity for Interim Regulations

Since the accession of the former German Democratic Republic to the Federal Republic of Germany, the regulations of the Basic Law, including those of intergovernmental fiscal relations, have been principally in force even for the new Länder. According to the tax assignment rules, the new Länder were immediately included; some exceptions were founded upon administrative difficulties or policy targets. The problem of insufficient data in the communes of the new Länder, for example, caused problems in allotting the communal share of wage tax and assessed income tax. The difficulties in book-keeping in conjunction with the policy target to enforce investments in the new Länder led to the renunciation of the collection of net worth tax and trade tax on business capital in the new Länder. The remaining taxes were collected with very low but increasing tax proceeds, as shown in Table 9, due to low economic activity and inefficient revenue administration.

Table 9: Tax Revenues of New Länder

Year		Absolute Numbers in Million DM	Percent Changes to Pervious Year's Quarter
1991	1. Quarter	4,020	-
	2. Quarter	4,658	-
	3. Quarter	5,256	-
	4. Quarter	5,205	-
1992	1. Quarter	5,827	+45.0%
	2. Quarter	5,468	+17.4%
	3. Quarter	5,380	+2.4%
	4. Quarter	7,133	+37.0%
1993	1. Quarter	6,167	+5.8%
	2. Quarter	6,563	+20.0%
	3. Quarter	6,955	+29.3%
	4. Quarter	7,862	+10.2%
1994	1.Quarter	7,847[1]	+27.2%
	2 Quarter	7,896[1]	+20.3%

[1]preliminary data

Source: German Bundesbank, Monthly Reports, October 1994, p. 71, May 1994, p. 71*, May 1993, p. 71*, March 1992, p. 61*.*

Until December 31, 1994 the new Länder are not included in the fiscal equalization system, the federal supplementary grants, and not completely in the regulations of the turnover tax distribution. In the case of an immediate inclusion, the automatically-working equalization mechanism would have caused an immense redistribution from the old to the new Länder. The old Länder would not have been able to carry this burden in the short run, because most of their expenditures are fixed.

Table 10: Prognosted Effects of the Inclusion of the New Länder in the Current Fiscal Equalization System in Million DM, 1995

Land	Fiscal Power without Inclusion of the New Länder in the Fiscal Equalization System, in Million DM	Difference in Case of Inclusion, in Million DM	Difference in Percent of Total Fiscal Power
Schleswig-Holstein	10,951	-0,717	-6.5%
Hamburg	9,478	-2,884	-30.4%
Niedersachsen	30,898	-2,173	-7.0%
Bremen	3,826	-0,399	-10.4%
Nordrhein-Westfalen	75,318	-6,700	-8.9%
Hessen	25,103	-2,284	-9.1%
Rheinland-Pfalz	15,684	-0,895	-5.7%
Baden-Württemberg	42,860	-3,900	-9.1%
Bayern	49,476	-4,081	-8.2%
Saarland	4,643	-0,498	-10.7%
Berlin-Ost-West	14,876	-0,133	-8.9%
Mecklenburg-Vorpommern	4,365	+3,495	+80.1%
Brandenburg	6,221	+4,260	+68.5%
Sachsen-Anhalt	6,628	+5,098	+76.9%
Thüringen	6,046	+4,598	+76.1%
Sachsen	11,066	+8,410	+76.0%
Total	317,439	0,0	0.0%

Source: German Council of Economic Advisers, Annual Report 1992/93, Bonn 1992, p. 214 and own calculations.

The volume of transfer payments that would have been caused in the following year by the inclusion of the new Länder in the fiscal equalization system was uncertain; the economic development and time range for setting up a functioning administration in the new Länder were difficult to forecast. Hence there would have been an incalculable risk for the budgets of the old Länder. A common fiscal equalization only makes sense if all Länder collect identical taxes, if the collection is pushed forward with the same intensity and if fiscal needs are comparable. These conditions were not met by the new Länder. Another problem is that equalization payments are general payments; hence there is the danger that these payments will be used for consumptive purposes and not to remove structural deficits in the new Länder. These are the main reasons for implementing interim regulations according to fiscal relations with the new Länder.

3.2 Interim Regulations for the New Länder until 1994

3.2.1 Separated Turnover Tax Distribution

The Unification Act determines the following regulations according to the turnover tax distribution: After the deduction of the share for unified Berlin, the turnover tax proceeds should be divided into an East and West share; this would result in the new Länder having only 55 percent of the turnover tax share per inhabitant of the Western Länder in 1991. In comparison to an equal share per inhabitant, this regulation would have incorporated a loss of revenues of some 4-5 billion DM in the new Länder. This regulation was publicly criticized as a discrimination without any legitimation and withdrawn.

The new Länder now participate in the turnover tax Länder share. The whole turnover tax Länder share is divided into an Eastern and Western share according to the number of inhabitants. 25 percent of the respective part is then destinated to help Länder with a low tax capacity, as in the procedure described in Chapter 2.6.1. In contrast to a turnover tax redistribution without separation of East and West Länder, this procedure saved the West Länder financial transfers of about 12 billion DM.

In 1993 the Länder share of the turnover tax was increased from 35 to 37 percent. On the one hand, it was to compensate for the discontinuity of federal grants for financially weak old Länder, on the other hand to strengthen the new Länder. The Federation, which also has high additional fiscal needs, could cope with the reduction of the federal turnover tax share since it benefited from the tax increases.

3.2.2 A Separated Fiscal Equalization System Among Länder

Due to the different tax structures in the old and new Länder, fiscal equalization among the new and old Länder (see Chapter 2.6.2) is performed separately (excluding Berlin). The redistributional effects of fiscal equalization among the new Länder (introduced in the Unification Act only upon the wish of former GDR officials) are very low, since their fiscal power is quite similar. In contrast, the fiscal equalization among the old Länder causes considerable payments between the financially strong Länder (e.g. Hessen) and financially weak Länder (Saarland and Bremen).

Table 11: Financial Effects of the Fiscal Equalization System, in Million DM, 1992 (Old Länder)

Land	Effected Payments, in Million DM	Received Payments in Million DM
Schleswig-Holstein	-	439.7
Hamburg	-	-
Niedersachsen	-	1,463.1
Bremen	-	530.0
Nordrhein-Westfalen	-	-
Hessen	1,992.8	-
Rheinland-Pfalz	-	704.1
Baden-Württemberg	1,555.2	-
Bayern	-	-
Saarland	-	411.1

Source: Federal Ministry of Finance, Financial Report 1994, Bonn 1993, p. 146-147.

The redistributive effects illustrated in Table 11 do not reflect the total redistribution between the old Länder. To evaluate the complete redistributional effects, other elements of the secondary distribution, e.g. the turnover tax redistribution, must also be considered.

3.2.3 The German Unity Fund

Since a fiscal equalization between the old and new Länder is not occurring, the Federation and old Länder must finance the German Unity Fund until the end of 1994. The Fund is destined to ensure the financial viability of the new Länder and their communes and substitutes the missing tax revenues of the new Länder. The payments are distributed according to the number of inhabitants in the new Länder and the Eastern part of Berlin; they are general payments, thus not endangering the fiscal autonomy of the new Länder.

It was primarily intended to transfer payments in a volume of 115 billion DM to the new Länder between 1990-1994. Retrospectively, the perceptions of economic development upon which these calculation were based were too positive. The volume of the German Unity Fund had to be raised several times to compensate for the miserable development of tax revenues, and to consider the very high additional fiscal need caused by the stronger than expected breakdown of the East German economy (see Figure 5).

Figure 4: Actual and Planned Payments from the German Unity Fund to the New Länder

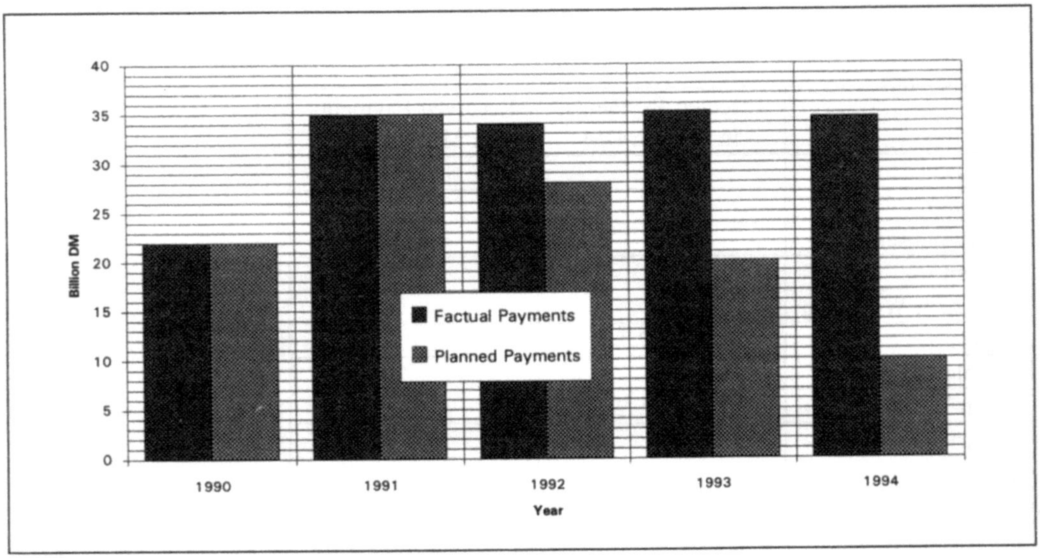

Source: German Council of Economic Advisers, Annual Report 1993/94, Bonn 1993, p. 152 and own calculations.

After the latest rise the total volume of the German Unity Fund is now 160,7 billion DM. A share of 66 billion DM of these payments is financed by transfers from the Federation and the old Länder. 49.6 billion DM of this amount are transferred from the Federal budget, and 16.1 billion DM derive from the budgets of the old Länder. 95 billion DM are financed out of public debt; the liquidation of this debt is equally shared by the Federation and the old Länder.

Due to the considerable transfers from the German Unity Fund, the new Länder will not receive any Supplementary Grants until December 31. 1994. These grants are solely destinated to the financially weak old Länder.

The German Unity Fund is a very problematic institution. It led to a tremendous increase of public debt with negative effects on economic activities. The sharing of the financial burden of the Fund was the subject of political conflicts among the Federation and old Länder, which always came under discussion when payments had to be raised.

Nevertheless, only some politicians and very few economists suggested the prolongation of the Fund past 1994. This demand was criticized by many economists, who instead recommended a final solution for including the new Länder in the system of fiscal relations. They underlined the importance of long term planning certainty as a presumption for consolidating the budgets of the German levels of government. The politicians followed this recommendation and created a solution called "Federative Consolidation Program", in the context of the "Solidarity Act Agreement", on March 13. 1993; this was an effort to include all public instances in building up the new Länder (see Figure 3).

4. Long-Term Solutions for Newly Formed Germany: The Federal Consolidation Program and Subsequent Measures

4.1 Overview

From 1995 on, a new system of intergovernmental fiscal relations including all Länder will be in force. In this system the new Länder will receive payments of approximately 56 billion DM p.a., which are to replace the German Unity Fund. The structure of the future system of intergovernmental fiscal relations will then be quite similar to the current system.

Besides the restructuring of the fiscal equalization system, a regulation according the unification-caused public debts had to be found. These debts resulted from the privatization of East German enterprises and the debts of the former GDR, especially the high debt in the publicly organized housing sector. Finally, a permanent solution for the heavily indebted Länder Saarland and Bremen had to be found; this is a special problem in West Germany.

Through the Federal Consolidation Program, the German Unity Fund was raised in 1993 and 1994 for a last time. This rise was financed partially by the increase of German interest rate deduction, a newly implemented method for more effectively collecting the income tax for capital earnings. After the old Länder agreed to increase the German Unity Fund, the payments of the Fund could be stabilized at approximately 35 billion DM p.a. for 1993 and 1994.

4.2 Changes in the Turnover Tax Distribution

The turnover tax will have a more important function in fiscal relations in the future than in the past. From 1995 on the turnover tax distribution will perform almost in the manner described in Chapter 2.6.1. 25 percent of the turnover tax Länder share will be distributed according to the lack of capacity of other taxes. All Länder should be filled up to 92 percent of average tax capacity out of this redistributed part of the turnover tax; the rest of the Länder share is distributed according to the number of inhabitants. The separation between old and new Länder will be abolished. This will induce high financial transfers from the old to the new Länder, because the new will acquire most of the filling-up payments. According to estimations for the tax proceeds in 1995, almost 20 billion DM will be transferred from the old to the new Länder by this regulation.

To compensate for the losses of the old Länder, the turnover tax Länder share will be raised from 37 percent to 44 percent; the Federation will lose about 17,5 billion DM. The remaining losses of the old Länder and their communes will be less than 1 billion DM, but they relieve the Federation by overtaking an additional amount of 2.1 billion DM p.a. for the financing of the German Unity Fund.

4.3 Changes in the Horizontal Fiscal Equalization System Among Länder

From January 1. 1995 Berlin and the new Länder will be included in the horizontal fiscal equalization system among Länder. As in Hamburg and Bremen, Berlin´s number of inhabitants will be multiplied by 135 percent to compensate for the fiscal burden caused by its special role as a City State.

The procedure for calculating the equalization payments will principally remain unchanged, except for a reformed equalization tariff as described in Figure 6.

The skimming of overaverage fiscal power is reduced; the maximal skimming rate is now 80 percent instead of the former 100 percent. The disincentives for the financially strong Länder to collect taxes were lowered by this regulation. The disregard of the fiscal power between 100 and 102 percent in calculating the equalization payments is removed, so that all Länder with fiscal power above average participate in the raise of the equalization payments; this relieves the Länder on the peak. According to the estimations of future tax proceeds, over 12 billion DM will be transferred annually to the new Länder through the horizontal fiscal equalization system.

Figure 5: Reformed Equalization Tariff

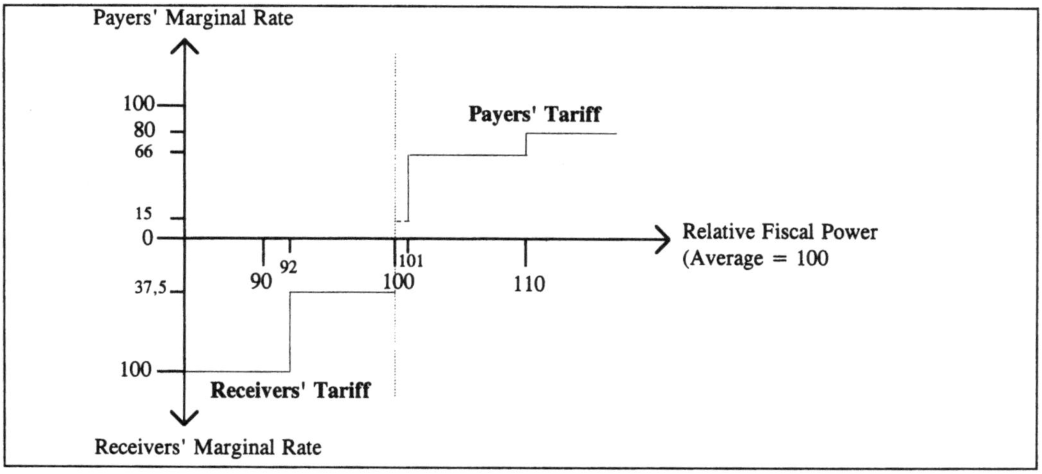

4.4 New Functions for the Federal Supplementary Grants and the Financial Aids

The Federal Supplementary Grants have several new functions in the newly formed system of fiscal relations, although the Basic Law gives them only a subsidiary function. From 1995 on the Federation will give "federal supplementary grants of the missing sum type" to the financially weak old and new Länder. Their volume will be calculated according to the difference between the average fiscal power and the fiscal power of a Land after fiscal equalization. The missing sum will be covered at 90 percent. According to estimations, the Federation will have to pay approximately 5-6 billion DM p.a. for these grants. The setting of the grants´ volume according to a fixed percent rate of the turnover tax proceeds (as practiced before) was given up. Now it is guaranteed that financially weak Länder cannot be pushed over the average fiscal power threshold. This is important, since a total equalization of the fiscal power was rejected with regard to the above-mentioned disincentives by economists; it lowered the incentives for the financially weak Länder to make own efforts to improve their situation.

In addition to this, the Federation pays newly invented federal supplementary grants to the new Länder to compensate for the burden caused by German separation. These grants also serve to compensate for the underproportional fiscal power of the East German communes, which must be supported by the East German Länder. Those grants have a volume of 14 billion DM and are limited until the year 2004. In 1999 the realization of the estimations on which the volume of these grants is based will be analyzed by the Federation and the Länder together. If the actual economic development in the new Länder then differs from the estimations, the volume of the grants will be adapted accordingly.

From 1995 on, small old and small new Länder will receive additional supplementary federal grants in a volume of app. 1.5 billion DM p.a. to compensate for their relatively high costs of political leadership. These often-criticized grants are designed to help financial institutions like the Land Parliament, the Land Government and other Land offices in Länder with a low number of inhabitants. Economists claim that a more efficient way would be to unify smaller Länder with other Länder to reach cost-efficient Länder scales.

As mentioned, the financially weak West German Länder will have tremendous losses in equalization payments when East German Länder are included in this system. Due to this, a new form of federal supplements was created to reduce the problem. These interim federal supplementary grants are limited until 2005 and lowered per annum by 10 percent; in 1995 the grants will have a volume of 1.4 billion DM. The financially strong old Länder support the financially weak old Länder additionally by overtaking parts of the Länder contribution for financing the German Unity Fund. These aids are degressively scaled as well.

The heavily indebted smaller Länder (Saarland and Bremen) will also receive from 1995 on special federal supplementary grants, which are matched towards the liquidation of their debt. The question is whether this is not only a symptomatic therapy, which might not solve the principle problem of unsolid management of public finances in these Länder.

The new Länder receive furthermore additional matching selective grants in form of financial aids, limited for 10 years and connected with co-payments of 10 percent. These aids have a volume of 6.6 billion DM per annum; they aim to build up the infrastructure in several fields.

4.5 Financing the New Regulations

The new regulations in the system of intergovernmental fiscal relations put a considerable burden of approximately 50 billion DM p.a. on the Federation. In contrast to the Federation, the total loss of the West German Länder counts only for about 1 billion DM. The West German communes participate in the burden through a rise in the trade tax apportionment, i.e. the part of the trade tax which the communes had to pay to the Federation and the Länder. Due to this regulation, it becomes necessary for the Federation to refund the additional burden. The main instrument of refunding is the reimplementation of the solidarity surcharge, an additional charge on the income tax load, from 1995 on. The additional revenues resulting from this regulation are estimated at about 28 billion DM in 1995 and 31.6 billion in 1996. The actual revenues will depend on the development of the trade cycle, which is the main uncertain element in the planning of the federal consolidation program. The second measure is the increase of the insurance tax, which will attain more that 4 billion DM per annum.

Table 12: Financial Effects of the Federal Consolidation Program in Billion DM, 1995

Measures	Total Volume	Federation	Old Länder	New Länder	Communes Old Länder	Communes New Länder
Raise of Turnover Tax Länder Share	18,4	-17,5	-0,7	14,4	-0,2	4,30
Inclusion of the New Länder in the Fiscal Equalization System	12,8		-10	10,0	-2,8	2,8
Additional Contributions of Old Länder to the German Unity Fund	2,1	2,1	-1,26		-0,84	
Supplementary Federal Grants of the Missing-Sum-Type	6,4	-6,4	1,8	3,2	-0,5	0,9
Supplementary Federal Grants for higher costs of political leadership	1,54	-1,54	0,52	0,68	0,15	0,19
Supplementary Federal Grants for separation caused burdens	14,0	-14,0		10,9		3,1
Interim Supplementary Federal Grants	1,4	-1,4	1,1		0,3	
Special Supplementary Federal Grants for Bremen and Saarland	3,4	-3,4	3,4			
Financial Aids for building up the New Länder	6,6	-6,6		3,3		3,3
Debt Service for Housing Cooperatives of former GDR	2,35	-1,175		-1,175		2,35
Financing Law of Communes	3,3		3,3		-3,3	

Source: German Council of Economic Advisers, Annual Report 1993/94, Bonn 1993, p. 153.

By cutting back expenditures, which is a part of the Federal Consolidation Program, the Federation is saving 1 billion DM. The negative development of the trade cycle required additional efforts. The Federal government therefore implemented the so-called "Saving,

Consolidating and Growth Program", which includes cuttings of federal public spending of nearly 6 billion DM in 1994 and nearly 10 billion DM in 1995 and the following years. Even the benefits of parafiscal institutions, especially of the Federal Labor Office, were cut back because their costs rose due to the negative development of the trade cycle. Finally, the increase of the mineral oil tax, which also took place out of ecological reasons, gives the Federation additional revenues of about 8 billion DM p.a. from 1994 on. Table 12 shows the financial consequences of the respective measures for the different levels of government.

5. Conclusion

Although the new regulations in the system of intergovernmental fiscal relations provide a solid foundation to solve the problems in the long run, the necessity to consolidate the budgets of the different levels of government still remains. The immense public debt, which occurred in connection with the German unification, has to be reduced. Therefore the future role of the trade cycle and the position of Germany in international trade will be a crucial issue.

The efforts to give more autonomy in law giving and revenue determination to the Länder, which were on the agenda before unification, had to be delayed in the medium term. The disparities between the old and the new Länder firstly have to be removed, so that more autonomy in collecting revenues and the lowering of the equalization intensity at the same time does not cause any disadvantages for the weak new Länder.

Although the fiscal equalization system met the challenge of German unification, it is already challenged again. Through European Integration the competences of the Federation are lowered while the political action potentials of the Länder will grow. The fiscal competition in Europe will be less between the national states than between the regions. The system of intergovernmental fiscal relations will have to cope with this challenge in the future.

References

BUNDESVERFASSUNGSGERICHT, Urteil vom 24.06.1986, in: Entscheidungen des Bundesverfassungsgerichts, edited by members of Bundesverfassungsgericht, No. 72, Tübingen, 1987.

FEDERAL MINISTRY OF FINANCE (ed.), An ABC on Taxes in the Federal Republic of Germany, Bonn 1993.

FEDERAL MINISTRY OF FINANCE (ed.), Financial Report 1994, Bonn 1993.

HENKE, KLAUS-DIRK, Finanzbeziehungen zwischen Bund und Ländern, Bestandsaufnahme und Entscheidungsbedarf, in: Wirtschaftswissenschaftliches Studium, Vol. 22. 1993, p. 67-74.

HENKE, KLAUS-DIRK, Schuppert, Gunnar Folke, Rechtliche und finanzwissenschaftliche Probleme der Neuordung der Finanzbeziehungen von Bund und Ländern im vereinten Deutschland, Baden-Baden, 1993.

MUSGRAVE, R. A., Who should Tax, Where and Why, in: McLure C., ed., Tax Assignment in Federal Countries, Canberra 1983, p. 2-19.

OATES, WALLACE E., Fiscal Federalism: An Overview, in: Public Finance with Several Levels of Goverment, Remy Prud´homme, ed., The Hague/Königstein, 1991, p. 1-18.

PEFFEKOVEN, ROLF, Deutsche Einheit und Finanzausgleich, in: Staatswissenschaften und Staatpraxis, Vol. 4, 1990, p. 485-511.

PEFFEKOVEN, ROLF, Finanzausgleich I: Wirtschaftstheoretische Grundlagen, in: Handbuch der Wirtschaftswissenschaft (HdWW), Stuttgart, 1980, p. 608-636.

PEFFEKOVEN, ROLF, Zur Neuordnung des Länderfinanzausgleichs, in: Finanzarchiv, N.F. Vol.. 45, 1987, No. 2, p.181-228.

SACHVERSTÄNDIGENRAT ZUR BEGUTACHTUNG DER GESAMTWIRTSCHAFTLICHEN ENTWICKLUNG, Jahresgutachten 1992/93, in: Bundestags-Drucksache 12/3774, Bonn, 1992.

SACHVERSTÄNDIGENRAT ZUR BEGUTACHTUNG DER GESAMTWIRTSCHAFTLICHEN ENTWICKLUNG, Jahresgutachten 1993/94, in: Bundestags-Drucksache 12/6170, Bonn, 1993.

WISSENSCHAFTLICHER BEIRAT BEIM BUNDESMINISTERIUM DER FINANZEN, Gutachten zum Länderfinanzausgleich in der Bundesrepublik Deutschland, in: Schriftenreihe des Bundesministeriums der Finanzen, No. 47, Bonn, 1992.

ZIMMERMANN, HORST, HENKE, KLAUS-DIRK, Finanzwissenschaft, Eine Einführung in die Lehre von der öffentlichen Finanzwirtschaft, 7th Edition, München, 1994, Chapter 5.

MACROECONOMIC ASPECTS OF GERMAN UNIFICATION

Hans-Werner Sinn

1. A New Germany

October 3, 1990, is German unification day. October 9, 1989, would have been Leipzig's Tianamin Square day had the GDR government had full control over its armed forces. Luckily there was no bloodshed and communist rule was swept away with incredible speed and unprecedented ease by the people's revolution.

Germany is not *re*united. The treaty that became effective on October 3rd, united West Germany with what was officially called "middle Germany", adding the six Laender Berlin, Mecklenburg West-Pommerania, Brandenburg, Saxony, Saxony Anhalt, and Thuringia to the Federal Republic of Germany. Silesia, East Pommerania, and East Prussia, the land of Nikolaus Kopernikus and Immanuel Kant, were not included. After the expulsion of 12 million Germans at the end of World War II, these territories were occupied and settled by Poles and Russians. The treaty is the first document in which Germany accepts the permanent separation of the eastern territories by stating that the unification of Germany is now "completed". A border treaty with Poland will soon (November 1990) confirm this interpretation.[1]

The unification is basically a "Hawaiian solution". Although substantial negotiations between the two remaining parts of Germany have taken place, the unification is not the kind of confederation between equal partners which article 146 of the West German constitution would have allowed. Instead, the unification followed article 23 which gave East Germany the right to unilaterally declare herself part of the Federal Republic of Germany.[2] As a consequence, practically all West German laws and institutions have been imposed on East Germany or will be imposed by the end of 1990. East Germany's role resembles that of Hawaii when it joined the United States of America. Hawaii did not significantly alter the legal system of the US.[3]

The expected economic consequences of the unification are regarded with mixed feelings. East Germans are afraid of the increasing unemployment; West Germans are afraid of inflation and excessive resource transfers to the East; and the world worries about Germany's economic might. Some observers, on the other hand, expect a united Germany to increase Europe's economic and political stability and help lead this part of the world to new prosperity.

Analyzing the present frictions and predicting the consequences of unification is a difficult, if not impossible, task, given the complexity of the problem. It may even be futile. The first German Economics Minister, Ludwig Erhard (1953), may have been right when he expressed his "mistrust, scepticism, and sorrow" concerning attempts to anticipate and predict the economic problems of unification. Nevertheless, this paper dares to comment on some of the issues involved.

Section 2 puts the unification problem in an international perspective and comments on its implications for the world economy. Section 3 discusses the monetary conversion problem with particular emphasis on a distinction between the frequently cited money overhang and the real asset overhang that characterizes communist countries. Section 4 describes the dangers of centralized privatization and Section 5 comments on the structural unemployment expected in the transition to a market economy.

2. Unification in International Perspective

The importance of unification for Germany's economic power is a matter of major concern among its neighbors and competitors in international markets. However, these fears are sometimes founded on misperceptions of simple economic facts.

It is true that West Germany has had the world's largest trade surplus ($ 72 b. ahead of Japan with $ 65 b. in 1989) and that the addition of East Germany will lead to an increase in industrial power. However, even if East German per capita output rises to the West German level, German GDP will only increase from currently 25% of EC output to 30%, and it will be just 29% of US GDP.[4]

The misperceptions frequently derive from overestimations of Germany's size.

Geographically, united Germany is only equivalent to an American state (cf. Figure 1). Its area is smaller than that of Texas, California, or Montana, and while its population (78 m.) is the largest in Western Europe, it is less than one third of that of the US and less than one fourth of that of western Europe. It even ranks well below Japan or the Russian Republic whose population sizes are 123 m. and 147 m. respectively.

Figure 1: The Germanies Compared to Another World

Perhaps the most common overestimation concerns the size of *East* Germany. It is a widespread feeling that the unification joined two Germanies of similar size, and that the German economy as a whole will soon be twice as strong as that of West Germany. The truth is very different. While geographically East Germany makes up 30% of the united Germany, its population is 21% and its (pre-unification) GDP only 15%.[5] Figure 2 illustrates the relative importance of the new Laender, both in terms of their population sizes and in terms of their productive powers. The whole territory of East Germany has only as many people as West Germany's biggest Land (17 m.), North-Rhine Westfalia, and, in 1989, it had a production capacity resembling that of Baden Wuerttemberg.

Figure 2: East and West Germany Compared

GDP [billion DM, before unification, 1:1 exchange rate]

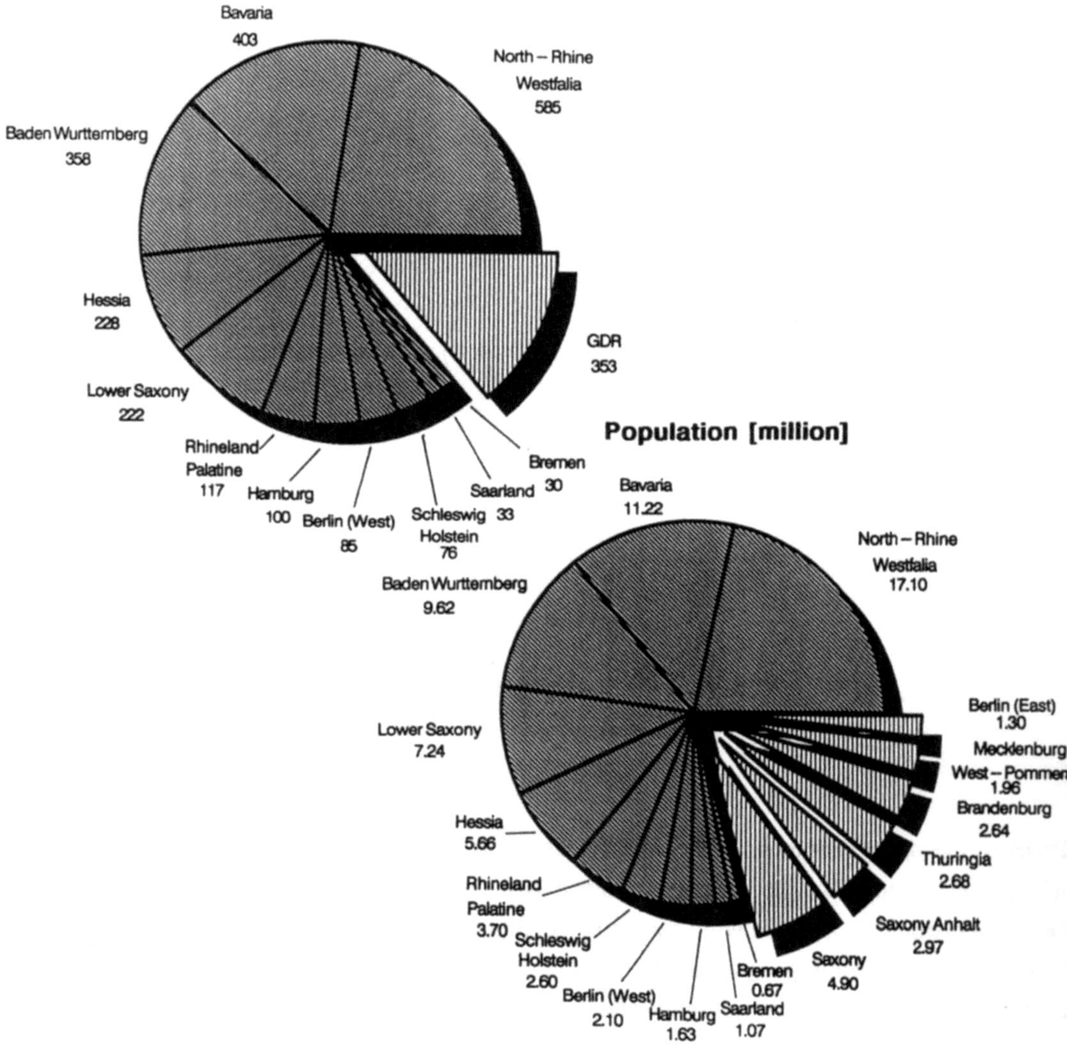

2.1 A Comparison With Other Eastern Countries

It is generally acknowledged that East Germany will have an easier transition to a prosperous market economy than other east European countries. West Germany's help makes an obvious difference.[6]

In Spring 1990, a German Unity Fund of DM 115 b. ($ 77 b.) was created by the West German Federal and Laender governments to cover East German budget deficits over this and the next four years. The plan is to use rates of DM 22 b. and DM 35 b. in 1990 and 1991.

However, as given in a joint report of the major West German research institutes, an additional DM 28 b. and DM 37 b. of annual public transfers are expected to flow from west to east in 1990 and 1991.[7] These transfers will primarily be necessary to maintain the East German social insurance system (45%) and to cover tax revenue losses (27%). East Germany has adopted a variant of West Germany's indexed pension system, and its pensions are fixed in proportion to the *eastern* average wage income. It also has, in principle, West Germany's tax system. For most taxes, including the income tax, there is, however, a transition period up to the end of 1990 during which not much revenue will be collected. By January 1st, 1991, all West German tax laws will apply in East Germany.

In addition to the financial aid coming from the West, East Germany's movement to a market economy will be greatly facilitated by the fact that it is the only eastern country that can offer the stable legal and institutional environment necessary to attract international capital flows. This is the advantage of the Hawaiian solution. Other countries like Poland or Czechoslovakia will go through a lengthy period of search during which unstable and changing political coalitions will experiment with different institutional settings, including different shares of the government sector, different organizations of private firms, different regulatory interventions, and different tax systems. Private investment will be deterred by this instability, and it may take a long time for these countries to catch up. East Germany has related problems with its privatization procedure (see section 4); however, they are of minor importance in comparison to the problems its eastern neighbors may face.

The third reason why East Germany is likely to succeed quickly is its heritage of craftsmanship and expertise in high quality industrial production. Before the war, some of Germany's most advanced industries, including famous aircraft, automobile, fine mechanical, optical, and chemical plants like Junkers, DKW, Horch, Zeiss, Schott, and Leuna-Werke were in East Germany. Thuringia and Saxony were at the forefront of the world's technological development. Of course, the knowledge itself has deteriorated, but the tradition of assiduous vocational education and the spirit of successful entrepreneurship are still alive. These provide excellent starting conditions which are paralleled to a large extent in Bohemia (in Czechoslovakia) and Slovenia (in Yugoslavia), but much less so in other eastern countries or provinces.

Observers from other parts of the world are often not aware of the heterogeneity of east European countries, but this heterogeneity is obvious to east Europeans and is clearly reflected in the data available on incomes and productivity levels for the period before the second world war. The left side of Table 1 compares the per capita income of Germany with that of other, primarily eastern, European countries. It shows that, in 1938, Czechoslovakia's per capita income was 52% and Poland's only 31% of Germany's, and the right side makes it clear that, at about the same time (1936), East Germany's per capita GDP ranked high compared to that of other regions in West Germany. In fact, on average, West Germany, as defined today (the British, American, and French zones including Saarland, but excluding Berlin), had a per capita output which was 7% below that of East Germany, as defined today.

Table 1: Europe before the War

Net national income per head of population (1938, US dollars)		*GDP per head of population (1936, Reichsmarks)*	
Bulgaria	68	British Zone	596
Romania	70-75	Soviet Zone	546
Yugoslavia	81	American Zone	427
Poland	104	French Zone	417
Hungary	112	Saarland	500
Czechoslovakia	176	Greater Berlin	697
France	236	Silesia, East Pommerania, East Prussia	229
Germany	337	German Reich	494
		West German territory (without Berlin)	510

Source: Kaser and Radice (1985, p. 532)

Source: Abelshauser (1983, p. 14)

These facts make it clear how large the gaps are which some eastern countries will have to overcome before they can catch up with western living standards. It is not only the gap caused by communist rule which will have to be bridged!

2.2 Implications for the West

The US policies of the eighties showed the extent to which international capital movements can disturb the world economy. While there are different opinions about whether the US budget deficit, the tight monetary policy, or the excessive investment incentives introduced in 1981 were the most important causes of the American greed for capital, there is broad agreement that the decade was characterized by an excessively large US capital demand. Estimates of the possible magnitudes put the long-run US capital import required to satisfy that demand at $ 1 trillion, and 90% of that figure has now been reached, although some of the causes of the US capital demand have weakened in the meantime.[8] The result of the extraordinary US demand for capital was a period of sharply rising interest rates (8% in real terms in the US, 1984), a high value of the dollar (DM 3.45 in 1985, more than 130% above its current value), and huge annual capital import flows (peaking at $150 b. in 1987).

It is rather obvious that similar effects can be expected from opening East Germany and eastern Europe to the international capital markets. The countries of the East are filled with lucrative investment opportunities, skilled labor, but a limited real capital endowment most of which can no longer be used. These countries' capital demand will raise world interest rate levels and absorb funds that otherwise would have been available for investment in western Europe, the USA, and other parts of the world. Whether the artificially overvalued currencies of the East will devalue or revalue is not fully clear. However, it is clear that the value of the Dollar in terms of Deutschmarks or other currencies of the EMS must temporarily decline to reduce Germany's current account surplus and the US current account deficit. A low value of the Dollar is necessary for as long as it takes to bring about the required new allocation of the world capital stock.

The world-wide shortage of capital will hurt the United States, which has relied so heavily on capital imports from Japan and Germany in recent years, and it will hurt wage earners throughout the western world whose factor supply becomes relatively more abundant. The lucky winners will be wealth owners who can enjoy a higher rate of return on their assets.

The simplest conceivable model which captures the steady state effects of the required adjustment is represented in the Kemp-MacDougall diagram of Figure 3. The figure depicts the world after the completed adjustment of the East, say in 10 years from now. The stock of wealth then owned by the West is AB and that owned by the East is BC. The curve falling from left to right is the West's marginal product of capital curve and the curve falling from right to left is the corresponding curve for the East, where the capital used by the West is measured from left to right and that used by the East from right to left. The world capital market equilibrium is characterized by point D, where DE is the interest rate and EB the amount of capital owned by the West and being used in the East.[9]

Figure 3 : Opening the East to the World Capital Market

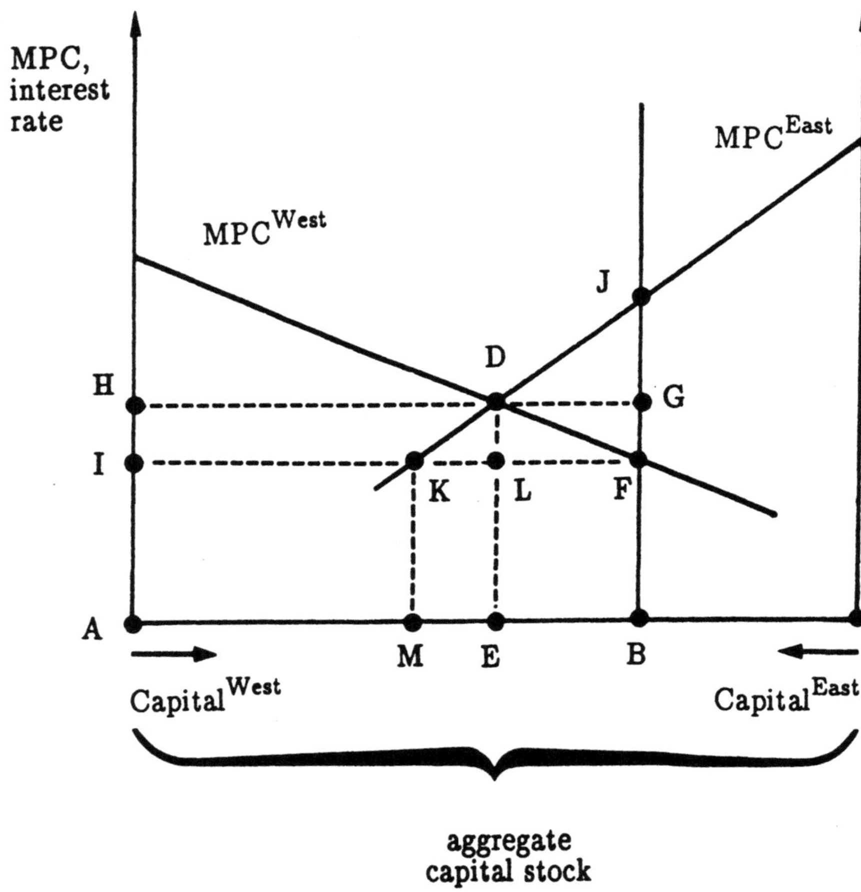

Without the attractive investment opportunities of the East, the West would use all its capital at home, and the interest rate would be FB. Opening the East for western capital therefore increases the capital income earned by westerners by the amount HGFI. This gain consists partly of a welfare gain in terms of an increased national product (DGF) and partly of a comparative reduction in western wage incomes which equals HDFI. While the "cake"

increases, wage earners receive a smaller part of it. It is clear who, in the West, gains and who loses from the elimination of the borders.

Apart from the actual class of capital owners in the East, i.e. the communist nomenklatura, people in the East gain from two effects. First they gain from getting access to western technologies. This effect is not shown in the figure. It could be represented by an upward shift of the MPC^{East} curve from a very low level towards the one depicted. Secondly, they gain from importing western capital. The imported capital (EB) increases their *domestic* product by the amount DJBE, but since the capital income earned by westerners is only DGBE, easterners experience a net welfare gain in terms of an increased *national* product which is represented by the area DJG.

The only losers from the fall of the borders are western workers. This may explain why the West German Social Democrats were so reluctant to follow Chancellor Kohl's pace in the reunification process. East German wages are currently only one third of those in the West.[10] Of course, western workers cannot gain from the increased competition for capital.[11]

Predicting the magnitudes of the relevant effects in the context of the world economy goes beyond the scope of this paper, and may hardly be possible at all. There are no reliable statistics for eastern economies and, at this stage, it is unclear how quickly the Soviet Union will disintegrate and when it will create the institutional environment necessary to attract foreign investment.[12] Clearly the demand can be huge, even relative to the total capital stock available in OECD countries.

Despite these uncertainties, it might be useful to apply the model to the isolated world of the two parts of Germany and make some exemplary calculations - just to develop a feeling for the orders of magnitude involved. Suppose the countries will use the same linearly homogeneous production function with capital and labor as factors, where capital is an aggregate capturing all private real assets including the land values. The stock of private capital in West Germany, the distance AB or IF in Figure 3, is currently about DM 7.90 trillion and West Germany's population is 62.3 million.[13] This means that the capital stock per capita is about DM 127.000 and that East Germany, with a population of 16.4 m., could usefully employ a stock of capital, including land, equalling DM 2.1 trillion at the pre-unification market rate of interest. In Figure 3, this stock is represented by the distance MC.

The size of the East German capital stock must be known before the amount of capital imports needed can be calculated. The official value of the eastern stock of real assets was DM 1.75 trillion in 1989, but this figure vastly overstates the value which the stock attains under market conditions. According to a new estimate of the East German Institute for Applied Economic Research (IAW), 67% of the official stock of assets must be written off under West German valuation rules; i.e., according to this estimate, the usable East German stock of real assets is only DM 576 b. This value could still be an overstatement if the popular view among West Germans that the East German economy is a "heap of junk" has any validity. However, no better estimate has been published so far, and for reasons that will be given in section 4.1.3 it would be wrong to base the discussion of this section on the expected *sales* revenues of the Treuhandanstalt. These will certainly be lower than the value of the East German stock of real assets in a situation of market equilibrium, where only marginal units of capital are traded.

Appendix II makes an attempt to evaluate the East German stock of land which can ultimately be used for private production. The current value of this stock, assuming eastern and western prices have become equalized in 10 years' time is DM 421 b., but for the purposes of this calculation it seems more consistent to value the East German stock of privately usable land at current West German land prices. Using this method the value is DM 524 b.

The total stock of capital, including land, which is available for private production in East Germany is therefore approximately DM 1.1 trillion (= DM 576 b. + DM 524 b.). Subtracting this from the DM 2.1 trillion stock of capital that could usefully be employed in East Germany with pre-unification interest rates, the East German excess demand for capital - the distance KF or MB in Figure 3 - becomes just DM 1 trillion.[14]

The excess demand for capital will necessarily increase the interest rate level and absorb part of the West German capital stock that would otherwise be available. With the assumed identical and linearly homogeneous production functions, the equilibrium capital import by East Germany, the distance LF in the figure, equals DM 1 trillion = $\Theta \cdot$ DM 770 b., where $\Theta = 0.77$ is the West German share in the joint work force.[15] Note that this is a static capital import based on 1989 figures and neglects the growth trend. The true dynamic capital import is likely to be higher than this and, unlike in the static model, it could be nourished by West German savings without its capital stock necessarily declining. The reason for concentrating on the static reallocation effects is that these give more cautious estimates of the absolute magnitudes involved and are unlikely to distort the relative magnitudes.

The relative increase in West Germany's capital income resulting from the increase in interest rates is, using the definitions of Figure 3,

$$GF / FB = (LF / IF)/\mu$$

wherein μ is the capital demand elasticity and LF/IF is the relative decline in the stock of capital employed in West Germany. It is a general result of production theory that

$$\mu = \sigma/\alpha$$

where σ is the substitution elasticity between capital and labor, and α is the partial production elasticity of labor or, under competitive conditions, simply the share of private sector wages in the private sector value added. In West Germany, $\alpha \approx 0.63$ and σ is known from various investigations in western countries to approximate 0.6.[16] Thus $\mu \approx 0.95$. Since LF/IF = DM 770 b. / DM 7.90 trillion ?? 0.097, the equilibrium *increase* in West German capital incomes resulting from the unification turns out to be

$$GF/FB \approx 9.2\%$$

The corresponding *decline* in labor incomes is

$$(GF/FB)\ (1 - \alpha)/\alpha \approx 5.4\%$$

minus the western part of the welfare gain in terms of an increased West German national income.

The West German welfare gain is, however, only a second-order effect. The figure makes it clear that the absolute annual welfare gain accruing to the West is half of the absolute increase in the rate of return to capital, GF = [GF/FB] FB, times the East's import volume LF. Equating FB with the pre-unification rate of return to capital, which the appendix I calculates as 7%, and using the results GF/FB $\approx$ 9.2% and LF $\approx$ DM 770 b. gives the absolute welfare gain as

(1/2) (GF/FB) FB LF $\approx$ DM 2.5 b. or as 2% of the DM 1,172 b. wage income. The overall decline in wages caused by the unification would therefore be 5.2%.

If the capital demand of other eastern countries is of similar significance for the rest of the western countries, these orders of magnitude would not necessarily change in a multi-country model, and whether they are large or small is partly a matter of judgement. It is, however, clear that the static West German welfare gain is negligible compared to the redistributive effects. The decline in annual wage incomes in absolute terms, on the other hand, is DM 61 b. (= 5.2% DM 1,172 b.). This happens to be slightly more than the average annual public funds which are estimated to flow from West Germany to East Germany in 1990 and 1991 (cf. section 2.1). This fact gives some indication of who in the West might ultimately foot the unification bill.

3. The Currency Conversion Problem

From July 2, 1990, the two Germanies were pre-united by sharing the Deutschmark as a common currency. Stocks of Eastmarks were changed into Deutschmarks at an average rate of 1.8:1 and all monetary contracts have been converted to a Deutschmark base.[17] Children below 15 years could exchange 2000 Eastmarks, adults below 60 years 4000 Eastmarks, and pensioners 6000 Eastmarks on a one-to-one basis. Most other amounts of money and financial claims, including company debt of about 260 b. Eastmarks, were exchanged or converted at a rate of 2:1. Price contracts, wage contracts, and pension claims were converted at a rate of 1:1 (where pensions were recalculated using the West German schedules amended with the eastern pension claims as lower bounds).

The currency conversion was aimed at achieving three major tasks. First, the wage conversion was to maintain or establish GDR competitiveness. Second, the money exchange was to inject just the right amount of liquidity. And third, the conversion of claims was to provide GDR citizens with a fair endowment for their new start in the united Germany. Satisfying all three goals was difficult, if not impossible, and it is understandable that there were heated debates among experts in West Germany on how, precisely, the conversion of the currencies should be organized. The actual outcome was a compromise between the government which had publicly committed itself to a 1:1 exchange and the Bundesbank which favored a much more restricted exchange.

In the international press, the compromise was considered as overly favorable for East Germans who were believed to enjoy significant windfall gains. The predominant opinion was that the currency conversion would boost commodity prices and erode the value of the Deutschmark.

So far, these fears have not materialized. Apart from a small reaction of the price level to the recent oil price increase, there has been no inflationary impact on the Deutschmark and, while there is a boom in West Germany, there is a severe depression in the East. It seems likely that large parts of the East German economy will collapse before the ultimate recovery. At the time of writing (November 1990) East Germany's production is only half what it was in 1989.

3.1 Purchasing Power Parity

The major reason for the misperception of the economic implications of the currency conversion was a general ignorance of the purchasing value of the Eastmark. It is true that the black market exchange rate in the beginning of the year 1990 was 7:1 or even 11:1, but this rate reflected little else than speculative expectations at the eve of the collapse of the East German state.

The purchasing power parity between the two currencies, based on average consumption baskets, was instead very close to 1:1, and in fact, there is increasing evidence that the Eastmark may even have had a somewhat higher purchasing value than the Deutschmark. Table 2 gives an overview of recent estimates of the exchange rate that would have maintained East Germans' purchasing power.

The comparisons between the currencies are difficult because relative prices in the East and the West differed significantly. The East German government spent about 50 b. Eastmarks each year to subsidize food, housing, and other elementary goods, and it collected 43 b. Eastmarks with particular excise taxes on luxury commodities. As a result, a TV set cost about 3 times as much as in the West and a loaf of bread only one sixth.[18]

Table 2 : The Exchange Rates Required to Maintain the Purchasing Power of East German Financial Wealth

Bundesbank[1]	100 Eastmark = 107 DM	pre-unification basket
DIW[2]	100 Eastmark = 120 DM	expected post-unification basket
DIW[3]	100 Eastmark = 128 DM	actual price change in East Berlin from January to July 1990, pre-unification basket
Joint office of statistics[4]	100 Eastmark = 98 DM	actual price change, October 1990 compared to average 1989, pre-unification basket
Ifo[5]	100 Eastmark = 98 DM	expected price change, pre-unification basket

[1]Unofficial estimate, as reported by K. Koehler, member of the directorate of Deutsche Bundesbank, in his lecture to the Department of Economics, University of Munich, May 5, 1990.

[2]DIW, Wochenbericht 21/90, 25 May 1990, p. 294.

[3]DIW, Wochenbericht 32/90, 9 August 1990, p. 446-450.

[4]Gemeinsames Statistisches Amt, Preisindex fuer die Lebenshaltung, November 1990. The equation was 100 Eastmarks = 94 DM in July 1990 which is equivalent to a 16% annual inflation rate in the East.

[5]Ifo Schnelldienst 43, 13/90, 7 May 1990, p. 24-26.

Given these large differences in relative prices, the choice of baskets is theoretically important for the comparison. However, as the first of the two DIW studies shows, it is not clear that a basket based on western prices would necessarily result in a lower value for the East German currency. The reason is that the negative income effect which the DIW estimated as resulting from the currency union can overcompensate substitution effects and increase the weight of basic products in the basket even though these are becoming more expensive.

It is important to note that the exchange rates given in the table represent expected or actual numerical price increases from the currency unification and cannot be identified with purchasing power parities in the usual sense. All estimates are based on the assumption that rents in the East are being kept frozen after the unification and that the Deutschmark has a higher value in East than in West Germany. A purchasing power parity comparison between the East and West German currencies would measure the pre-unification purchasing powers in the respective currency regions and would therefore have to take into account the fact that the rents in the West are much higher than in the East. Currently, West German households spend on average 20% of their incomes for rents, but East Germans used to spend only 3%. The rent per square meter in the East is only one fifteenth of what it is in the West. Adjusting the calculations for this effect would result in much higher values for the Eastmark than reported in the table.

At the moment, a true purchasing power comparison that takes the lower East German rents into account may be of limited relevance because the assumption that the rents are frozen is still correct. However, it is likely that the rents will soon be freed. When this happens, the theoretical exchange rate required to maintain the purchasing power of any pre-unification stock of East German financial wealth will jump up to the purchasing power parity. It is already clear at this stage that the utility costs included in the rent will strongly increase in the next few months and that this will boost the East German price level. The price increase is already visible. The official East German price index, which the table showed to have fallen from 100 in 1989 to 98 in October 1990, increased by nearly four percentage points in the first three months following the currency unification. If this trend persists, the official statistics will soon replicate the DIW's result that even a 1:1 exchange would have been unfavorable for East Germans.

An effect that works in the other direction is the significant quality differences between East and West German products. If the expected or calculated price increases that follow from the unification simply reflect quality improvements in the consumption baskets purchased by easterners then there is no need to offer exchange rates better than 1:1 in order to maintain the purchasing power of East German financial wealth. Unfortunately, there are no estimates that show the strength of this effect. The penetration of the East German market with luxury commodities is known to be high. However, these commodities cover only a small fraction of a typical household's budget, and it seems hard to believe that the bias resulting from the assumption of frozen housing rents will be overcompensated by the quality effect. Further statistical studies will hopefully clarify this issue.

Despite all the difficulties in interpreting the data it should be clear from this discussion that a 1:1 exchange would not have been as utopian as some commentators of the unification had believed and certainly it cannot be claimed that the actual average exchange of 1.8 Eastmarks for 1 Deutschmark created windfall gains for East Germany.

3.2 The Problem of Two-sided Competitiveness

A major concern in the debate preceding the currency unification was the appropriate conversion of wage contracts for ensuring the competitiveness of the East German industry. While it was (correctly) expected that many wage contracts would be rewritten soon after unification, there was a general agreement that the sluggishness of wage adjustments overall was sufficiently high to make the officially agreed wage conversion non-neutral during an extended transition phase.

The major problem was that competitive neutrality had two dimensions. On the one hand, East Germany was to become attractive for direct investment and East German firms were to be able to survive in the common market with West Germany. This called for low wages. On the other hand, East German workers were not to be stimulated to move to the West. This called for high wages.

The 1:1 conversion on which the governments agreed fixed the East's wage level at about one third of the western level. Previous studies of the DIW had indicated that the productivity of the East German industry was about 50% of that of West Germany, and the Bundesbank put this ratio at only 40%.[19] From both perspectives, a starting wage level of 33% seemed to be roughly compatible with the requirement of competitive neutrality in one of its two senses.

At this stage (November 1990) the wisdom of that decision seems somewhat dubious, though. The wave of bankruptcies and lay-offs sweeping currently through East Germany lends support to those who had recommended starting with lower wages in order to facilitate a widening of the wage spread which the transition to a market economy requires. On the other hand, starting with a wage of only 1/6 of the western level, as these commentators had suggested, would have created excessively large incentives for the population of the East to simply pack their luggage and move west. There was no real solution of the problem of two-sided competitiveness. Moreover, there is another explanation of the wave of bankruptcies that rivals with the view that wages in the East are too high. That explanation will be developed in section 3.8.

3.3 The Money Overhang and the Real Asset Overhang

All eastern economies seemed to be characterized by a substantial money overhang. They all had more liquidity than they needed for transactions purposes or at least more than a comparable western economy with the same income level was using. They could afford the money overhang, since an increase in the price level or a reduction in the interest rate, which would have resulted in a western economy, was prevented by state controls.

Similarly, and almost by the definition of a communist country, all countries of the East were characterized by a real asset overhang. The marketable private claims which people held in their hands were only a small fraction of the total real assets available. The governments were the owners of these assets, not the individuals. Thus, a stylized picture of the typical eastern country is one where the individual household is overly stuffed with money, but where money is about all it possesses.

The German Democratic Republic was no exception to this rule. In 1989, the stock of money balances in the M3 sense (i.e. including savings accounts) was 237 b. Eastmarks.[20] Relative to net money income, about the only reliable income aggregate offered by East German statistics, this was 142%.[21] By way of contrast, M3 relative to the personal disposable income in the West was only 89%. There was a money overhang of 53% of net money income or, in absolute terms, of 88 b. Eastmarks. Using the pattern of the West, 150 b., and not 237 b., Eastmarks would have been the appropriate stock of money balances for the German Democratic Republic.

Subtracting the money held by East German firms (61 b. Eastmarks) from the aggregate stock of money balances gives the stock of money possessed by East German households as 176 b. Eastmarks. If one adds 15 b. for insurance claims one obtains the total pre-unification stock of private marketable wealth of East German households. It equals 191 b. Eastmarks. This wealth is only 11% of the official value of the stock of net fixed assets which was 1.75 trillion Eastmarks in 1989("Grundmittelbestand", without land).[22] Of course, as argued above, a large fraction of this stock is useless under market conditions. However, even if only 33% of the net fixed assets are counted, as the IAW suggested, the private wealth would turn out to be just one third of the "true" value of the economy's stock of net fixed assets.

3.4 The Planned and the Actual Money Supply

The political debate in Germany largely neglected the real asset overhang and focussed nearly exclusively on the money overhang. This explains the policies actually chosen by the West German government and the Bundesbank. The exchange pattern described above was meant to provide just the required stock of M3 which was calculated above (150 b. DM). As shown in the appendix, the M3 endowment of East Germany would have been DM 151.4 b. if all inhabitants had exchanged exactly the maximum quantities allowed for their age.

Interestingly enough, however, the actual increase in the stock of money balances (M3) which has just been published by the Bundesbank is DM 180 b.[23] This shows that DM 30 b. of the DM 88 b. money overhang have not been abolished. The reason is a mistake in the Bundesbank's calculations resulting from the fact that there were some money stocks hidden in remote corners of the East German economy which unexpectedly qualified for exchange into Deutschmarks. These stocks were found in foreign trade organizations which had been previously counted as "banks" and whose monetary claims against normal banks had therefore not been included in the official measure of the East German money stock. The mistake is not negligible in absolute terms, but it clearly does not imply major inflationary risks. DM 30 b. is just 2.1% of the total stock of money balances (M3) in the two parts of Germany.[24]

3.5 Wealth Effects of the Currency Conversion

While the Bundesbank successfully managed the currency conversion in a way that eliminated two thirds of the money overhang, it was not successful in eliminating the real asset overhang. On the contrary, that overhang was increased rather than reduced by the policies chosen.

Some economists had argued that it would be best to choose a 1:1 exchange throughout and to solve the problem of the money overhang by not exchanging all money into money. They preferred the overhang to be first converted into "frozen" savings accounts which, in a second step, would then have to be converted into long term assets, preferably into the shares of the newly created East German joint stock companies.

The Bundesbank neglected such proposals. Sharing or fearing the opinion expressed in the international press, it argued that a 1:1 exchange for the total money stock would create "massive gains in purchasing power" and result in an "inflationary consumption wave".[25]

Given that the Bundesbank possessed at least some of the statistical information reported in Table 2, this was a surprising policy decision which was hard to understand at the time and is even harder to understand today. If the Bundesbank has tried to "err on the right side", it has done so with remarkable success.

The "success" is a substantial exchange loss for East German households. As mentioned above, before the unification East German households' financial wealth was 191 b. Eastmarks. Assuming a full exhaustion of the exchange limits, 66 b. of these could be exchanged at a rate of 1:1 against Deutschmarks. The remainder, 125 b. Eastmarks, was exchanged or converted at a rate of 2:1. Equating units of Eastmarks with units of Deutschmarks, as suggested by the purchasing power comparisons made above, this means that East German households experienced a loss of DM 62 b. or DM 3,765 per person. The loss is one third of their wealth.

It is true, of course, that the loss is not a net loss for East German households from the unification. They will certainly gain from the economic prosperity which the unification is very likely to bring about in only a few years. However, it is a *comparative* loss in wealth that could have been avoided with the "frozen accounts" strategy.

In addition to warning with regard to windfall gains, the Bundesbank objected to the 1:1 exchange because it feared that the East German company debt of 260 b. Eastmarks would not be sustainable under market conditions. It argued that forcing East German firms to pay the market rate of interest, rather than the symbolic interest rate with which their creditor, the East German State Bank, had been satisfied with previously, would drive a large proportion of them into bankruptcy.

This argument was probably correct. It was not necessary, however, to solve the bankruptcy problem the Bundesbank's way. It would have easily been possible to reduce the company debt without at the same time depriving households of part of their savings. Applying a 2:1 ratio to the company debt of 260 b. Eastmarks, but not to the stock of housing loans, which totalled 108 b. Eastmarks, would have left the East German banking system with claims of DM 238 b.[26] This would still have been enough to cover the private insurance claims(14.7 b.) and the bank deposits of companies (60.6 b.) and households(159.7 b.) which would have totalled DM 235 b. under a 1:1 exchange.

That this policy would have been feasible, becomes even clearer if one realizes that, from an economic point of view, there is no need to cover non-interest bearing demand deposits with interest bearing claims. The need to cover such items under ordinary book-keeping rules is a meaningless artifact resulting from the requirement that assets and liabilities be counted at their face values rather than the present values of the payment flows they induce. In present value terms, only the private sector's savings and time deposits are liabilities; the demand deposits, on which (in Germany) practically no interest is paid, are not. In West Germany, savings and time deposits are 73% of the private claims against the banking system. Applying this percentage to the DM 220 b. bank deposits of households and firms in the East shows that, with a 1:1 exchange, the interest bearing liabilities of the banking sector, including the insurance liabilities, could have been limited to DM 176 b. (= 73% DM 220.3 b. + DM 14.7 b.). This would have left a comfortable DM 62 b. surplus of interest bearing claims with which even the GDR government debt (DM 21 b.) or other liabilities could have been covered.

Accountants might not have been fully happy with this procedure. To satisfy them, and to cover formal accounting deficits, the banking system could have been given permanent, non-interest bearing and non-tradeable claims against the government sector. These claims are useless from an economic point of view, but they would have helped keep the books in order.

Admittedly, a unilateral cut in company debt would seem strange in a market economy where most of this debt is backed by claims of the household sector. However, East Germany was not a market economy. As shown, the company debt exceeded household sector claims by an amount sufficient to make the unilateral cut possible. An important function of the company debt in the communist state was to provide the government with a revenue source and, in fact, the companies had often been forced to borrow from the State Bank even though they did not want to. The interest on the company debt was a hidden form of profit tax. Replacing this tax with western corporate tax and cutting the debt in half was certainly an appropriate policy for the transition to a market economy. Reducing the already too small stock of savings was not a necessary complement.

3.6 The Bundesbank Unification Gain

The East German exchange loss is a fact that contradicts popular beliefs. Another such fact concerns the Bundesbank's "losses" from the currency conversion. Laymen in Germany often argue that the exchange of "good" western for "bad" eastern money implied Bundesbank losses equal to the volume exchanged. Every economist knows, of course, that such a view is nonsense. If a central bank extends its currency region by simply giving its money away, its only resource costs are the printing expenses, and if it can manage to lend rather than give the money away, it will even enjoy seignorage profits. As long as the money does not exceed the amount the new currency region needs for transaction purposes, the resource claims to which the owners of the money are entitled will never be realized.

The Bundesbank is supervising the East German State Bank and its system of local banks, but it did not make money gifts and it did not exchange a single Deutschmark for Eastmarks. As well, the compensation claims which the local banks received to avert bankruptcies arising from the uneven exchange pattern are directed towards the East German State Bank (now called "Credit Bank") and not the Bundesbank. The Bundesbank simply increased the monetary base in East Germany in exchange for promissory notes issued by the East German banking system which will have to be serviced at the current market conditions. Thus the Bundesbank enjoys the full seignorage of the newly issued base money. Using the West German M3 multiplier, which was 5.4 before the unification, this implies that the unification-induced increase in the monetary base is DM 180 b. / 5.4 = DM 33 b. This number expresses the (present value) Bundesbank gain from the unification.

3.7 Portfolio Reactions

The increased wealth overhang which resulted from the particular method by which the money overhang was eliminated has implications for the behavior of East German households in asset and goods markets. Two basic reactions can be expected.

The first reaction is a portfolio adjustment. Since East German households received only money and were not endowed with long-term assets, it can be expected that they will use some of their money to buy such assets. In West Germany, M3 is just 50% of the household sector's overall financial wealth.[27] East Germans started from a situation where M3 is nearly all their financial wealth. Clearly, the East German percentage of M3 in overall financial wealth will move some way towards the West German one.[28] It will not however become equal to the West German percentage since the overall financial wealth in the East is so small relative to other economic aggregates. If they adopted the western percentage East Germans would have too little liquidity relative to their transactions volume.

As was calculated in the previous section, the total financial wealth of East German citizens after the currency conversion is DM 129 b. (=DM 191 b.- DM 62 b. exchange loss). It consists of DM 7.5 b. insurance claims and DM 121.5 b. money in the M3 sense. If 50% of this wealth is kept in the form of M3, then DM 57 b., or nearly one third of the DM 180 b. increase in the stock of money balances caused by the currency conversion, will be changed into assets with longer maturities given the interest rate structure, and if only half of the adjustment towards the western percentage occurred, then the portfolio effect would still be about DM 28 b.

The attempt to change such large quantities of money into long-term interest bearing assets would increase the market values of these assets and induce a decline in long-term interest rates. The consequent stimulation of interest sensitive real investment would make inflation a potential danger. To prevent this obvious outcome, the Bundesbank will have to step in and make the preferred restructuring of East German wealth portfolios possible by exchanging money for interest bearing assets. In short, it will be forced to accommodate the restructuring process with a contractionary open market policy.

The Bundesbank has implicitly announced this policy by stating in its October 1990 report that it "expects" the portfolio effect to reduce the increase of M3 caused by the currency conversion from an initial 15% to 10% in the long run.[29] This corresponds to the full DM 57 b. portfolio shift calculated above. With the West German M3 multiplier of 5.4, the volume of contractionary open market operations would be about DM 10 b., and the Bundesbank unification gain would shrink from DM 33 b. to 23 b. Note that the latter figure must be considered a lower bound for the unification gain since, for the reason explained, the actual portfolio effect is likely to be smaller than one third of the East German M3.

3.8 Demand Reactions

The other reaction to the increased wealth overhang is a reduced level of consumption. Lifetime optimizers and Keynesian consumers alike will react to the elimination of one third of their wealth by cutting their consumption expenses. This will induce downward multiplier effects of the Keynesian kind and may steer the economy into a depression.

It is true that, theoretically, there are strong countervailing effects that mitigate the development. If East German households know that they will personally benefit from the transfers which West Germany pumps into eastern public budgets, there should be a positive wealth effect on consumption. Moreover, East German households may know or believe that they will not lose from the 2:1 exchange rate because the use of this exchange rate implies a devaluation of company debt and increases the revenue from privatization. In these cases, the depressive effects of the increased real asset overhang may not come through. However, such rationality arguments seem rather artificial in a rapidly changing, partly collapsing economy where no one is able to predict the future with reasonable accuracy. The mechanics of the Modigliani-Miller theorem or of Ricardian equivalence may simply not be applicable under such circumstances.

Unfortunately, the current situation in East Germany is characterized by a deep economic recession. The number of unemployed is rising rapidly from currently half a million to an estimated 1.5 million in 1991, more than 1.5 million people are working short-time, and, perhaps the most alarming figure, in August the retail sales volume in East Germany was 45% below the level reached under communist rule in the year before.

Part of this development is attributable to the fact that for some industries even a wage which is one third of that in the West is too high to be competitive. Another part is certainly attributable to the fact that East German consumers substitute western for eastern products. A third, however, simply results from the fact that the currency conversion impoverished East German households.

On the first day after the currency conversion (July 3rd) the pre-written stories on crowds of East German consumers plundering the banks and squandering their money appeared in the press. How wrong the stories were! The truth was that East Germans were overly cautious, consumed little, and withdrew much less cash from saving accounts than the Bundesbank and most other observers had expected.

4. The Privatization Problem

Apart from the problem of monetary transition, the privatization of industry is one of the main problems in transforming a communist system into a market economy.

Since the war, East Germany has been under communist rule. Between 1945 and 1949 it was occupied and ruled by the Soviet Union, and from 1949 onwards it was formally independent but in fact ruled by a communist puppet regime. During both periods, large parts of the East German stock of wealth were expropriated.

The Soviet occupation forces expropriated one third of the land of East Germany, ending the rule of the "Prussian Junkers" and great landowners, who had dominated Brandenburg, Mecklenburg, and West Pommerania. The land was redistributed to the half million small farmers who have been the landowners since then. The Soviets also nationalized large sectors of industry, including basic materials, banking, and insurance. It is estimated that this nationalization covered 40 percent of GDP or 7000 companies.[30]

The German Democratic Republic nationalized most of the remaining companies during its forty years of existence, exempting only very few small handicraft businesses. It also forced the farmers into production co-operatives (Landwirtschaftliche Produktionsgenossenschaften) where all profits were shared by the participants. However, there were no large scale expropriation programs for agricultural and residential properties. House owners and farmers were able to keep their formal property titles. Only the marketability and fungibility of their assets was severely restricted. Between 50% and 60 % of the East German land continued to be privately owned despite the communist rule.

Nevertheless, land was expropriated in many cases. Company lots and real estate left behind by hundreds of thousands of refugees were not taboo for the greedy state. The property was sometimes kept, sometimes sold to new private owners. No one knows exactly how many expropriations and nationalizations took place in East Germany. However, it is known that, in 1990, one million applications for the return or compensation of expropriated East German properties have been filed.

4.1 The 49 Rule and the Pre-Coasian State

The unification treaty sharply distinguished between the two expropriation waves. Everything expropriated before 1949 is treated as a result of history and does not qualify for compensation other than that already given to those who lost their properties in the East (Lastenausgleich). Everything expropriated since the foundation of the German Democratic Republic will, as a rule, be returned to the previous owners. The communist state is regarded as illegal, and its acts are nullified wherever possible. The wheel of history is turned back to 1949.

There are, of course, many exceptions from the rule. Whenever the previous property was converted by using it for social purposes, for complex residential constructions, or for business purposes, the previous owners can claim compensation, but not necessarily the return of the property. Moreover, new owners of expropriated land cannot be forced to return this land if they have built permanent structures on it. They or the government may only have to pay compensation to the previous owners. However, the unification treaty (article 41 and amendment III) leaves no doubt that the previous owners have the stronger rights. Unless further laws will significantly simplify the legal procedures, the previous owners will institute hundreds of thousands of law suits to clarify property rights.

The decision to reinstate old rights is a logical consequence of West Germany's claim to have been the only legal state in Germany. It reflects the way lawyers think about the course of history and, as a by-product, it offers them glamorous income possibilities over the next decade.

In economic terms, the decision may have been the biggest mistake in the otherwise efficient and well-designed unification policy of the West German government. Of course, economists know about the problems of time consistency in policy making and the importance of warranting property rights. However, consideration of these aspects does not lend any support at all to the policies chosen. The time consistency is not a real problem, since no one would have made the West German government responsible for its eastern counterpart's deeds and no one would have expected property rights in the West to be unsafe simply because the communists did not respect them in the East. And the establishment of well-defined property rights is exactly what has been prevented by the "49 rule". The decision to roll back the wheel of history has created unnecessary uncertainty and has pushed East Germany into a pre-Coasian state, where market forces cannot unfold their virtues.

It is the message of the Coase theorem that, for an efficient allocation of resources, it does not matter *how* property rights are established. A trade in endowments (for example rental or leasing contracts) will always allow scarce resources to flow to the place of their most efficient use. What is important is *that* property rights are established. If, and only if, the rules of the game are clarified and everyone knows exactly what he owns, can the market's invisible hand do its job.

Unclear property rights will be a major obstacle to investment in East Germany. The present owners will not invest and the previous owners will not do so either unless who ultimately owns the property is clarified. Nor will investors buy the contested properties and begin the new business as everyone expects them to do. The invisible hand is manacled.

4.2 The Legal Role of the Treuhandanstalt

The present owner of the companies in East Germany is the "Treuhandanstalt", a resolution trust of the German ministry of finance whose task is the privatization of the East German industry. The Treuhandanstalt is a bureaucracy that was established at the beginning of 1990 by the communist government in a desperate attempt to prevent the privatization of state owned property. It received its new role under the subsequent civil government of de Maiziere (Treuhand Law of June 1990) and came under the ministry's control with the unification treaty.

The Treuhandanstalt owns about 7900 East German companies most of which will have to be privatized. The exceptions are about 1900 public utility companies whose ownership will probably be transferred to local communities.[31] Some of the companies are East German "combines" (Kombinate), huge entities comprising complete industry branches which have no counterparts in the West. The combines will have to be split into many independent companies before privatization is possible. The 7900 companies represent no less than 40,000 separate factories!

Privatization is to be carried out in two steps. In the first step, the East German companies will be transformed into either joint stock companies or GmbH's, a particular German form of limited liability association characterizing most West German companies. To do this, association agreements and starting balance sheets had to be produced. The deadline for submitting these documents to the Treuhandanstalt was October 31, 1990, but half the firms were granted extensions and are expected to deliver the documents in November or December of 1990. The Treuhandanstalt will check and correct the balance sheets, and the final versions of the revised sheets are due by May 1991.

In the second step, the companies will then be sold on the international capital market. There are no restrictions on potential buyers other than those imposed by Germany's antitrust board.[32] In particular, there are no constraints on the nationality of the buyers. The Treuhandanstalt is, for example, already negotiating with buyers from the USA, Japan, Britain, and France, and a number of successful deals can be expected for the near future. At the time of writing (November 1990) 30 "pearls" have already been sold, and up to 200 companies might be sold by the end of the year.

4.3 Risks of the Privatization Process

It is too early at this stage to make ultimate judgements on the activities of the Treuhandanstalt. However, some risks in this institution's role as a catalyst at the start of the East German market economy are already visible.

4.3.1 Sluggish Privatization

The first risk is that the Treuhandanstalt may not be able to move fast enough to prevent the collapse of the East German economy. Selling a whole economy is not like selling apples. The British government needed a whole decade to privatize a few dozen companies. The Treuhandanstalt is expected to sell thousands of firms in the next few months. It will lag hopelessly behind these expectations.

4.3.2 Cross-Subsidization

The second risk is that the Treuhandanstalt will use its sales revenues to subsidize unprofitable firms by awarding them interest bearing compensation claims against itself. The right of cross-subsidization was given to the Treuhandanstalt by the unification treaty, and it can be justified with the fact that the East German companies' debt resulted often from political rather than economic decisions. Unfortunately, however, there is reason enough to fear that political pressure will force the Treuhandanstalt to save jobs in useless enterprises and thus prevent the necessary structural changes.

4.3.3 Competition and Market Concentration

The third risk is that East German companies will be bought by their West German competitors in order to increase or defend their market shares. It is an open secret that many recent purchases of East German firms have been motivated by such considerations. The unification opens up the chance of increasing the efficiency of the German economy by strengthening its competitive forces. If West German firms simply gobble their East German counterparts this chance will be missed.

4.3.4 The Erosion of Sales Prices

The fourth risk is that the Treuhandanstalt will not be able to sell its companies at satisfactory prices. The clearance sale of tens of thousands of factories will quickly drive the price of factories to zero and may ultimately force the Treuhandanstalt to give away its companies instead of selling them. While it is true, of course, that one of the reasons for low prices is simply the bad state of East German companies, there are at least three systematic effects pointing towards a strong undervaluation of East German companies under the sales policies chosen.

The Zero-One Problem

The first effect is a strange bias in the sales policy of the Treuhandanstalt towards selling companies as a whole rather than piecemeal. As far as the author knows, the Treuhandanstalt has not attempted to sell shares of East German companies in the stockmarkets where a large number of individual purchasers could each buy a small share of a company. The institution is instead looking for other companies to take over the East German ones and offers zero-one choices. Apart from the problematic competitive effects mentioned above, this procedure significantly narrows the set of potential purchasers and implies that there is a steep demand curve for eastern companies on which prices will fall sharply. It is said that even investment banks lost interest in purchasing East German stock when they realized that they would not be able to put together well-diversified portfolios of parts of companies but would have to buy companies as a whole.

A frequently cited argument in favor of the policy of selling whole companies to other companies is the facilitation of a transfer of technological knowledge. This argument cannot be fully neglected. It is not, however, in the author's opinion, ultimately compelling. After all, there are consulting firms which sell technological knowledge and it is possible to hire the skilled managers of competing firms who would bring the knowledge with them. The technology transfer requires management transfers, but management transfers are not limited to intrafirm relocation. Managers are not slaves; they have a market. A privatization of the East German economy, however this is done, will create strong incentives for buying the knowledge where available. There is no reason for mistrusting the market forces.

The Stock-Flow Mismatch

The second reason for an erosion of East German stock prices is simply that the Treuhandanstalt is trying to sell the existing stocks of East German assets rather than limiting sales to the increments of these stocks which are necessary to modernize the East German economy. Trying to sell a whole economy is a dubious activity from a macroeconomic perspective, for it may result in a serious mismatch between stocks and flows.

It is true that, in principle, the Treuhandanstalt can trade its stocks of East German assets for stocks owned by the West. This would happen if the Treuhandanstalt used its revenue to buy interest bearing assets in the West. It would thus supply the stocks of funds which its purchasers need to buy its assets. The policy would be feasible and avoid the stock-flow problem. Unfortunately, however, it does not harmonize well with the privatization idea. A bureaucracy owning the financial equivalent of a whole economy does not fit much better to a market system than one that owns this economy directly.

An alternative to the Treuhandanstalt's owning financial assets is transferring the sales revenues to the East German Laender governments or to the companies in need of financial aid. Actually, this is what is suggested by the unification treaty and what will most likely happen with any sales revenues the Treuhandanstalt will fetch. If these institutions rechannelled the funds to the capital market by lending them directly or indirectly to the western buyers, the policy would again be self-financing. However, clearly this will not happen. Needy governments and companies are borrowing constrained. They will use the transfers for everything but lending them back to the West.

The remaining alternative is therefore the exchange of East German assets for Western goods. As the Western purchasers cannot liquidate old assets by selling them to the East, they must use their savings to purchase the Eastern assets, thereby transferring claims on western investment and consumption goods to the East. This is the stock-flow problem. It is logically and practically impossible to sell the Eastern stock of assets at one point in time against the Western flow of savings. The sales necessarily have to be stretched over time if the Treuhandanstalt wants to get positive prices. A quick sale will necessarily drive the prices of East German assets to zero.

By way of contrast, there would be no fundamental problem if the resource transfer from the West to the East were limited to the necessary net investment. If the East sold claims on increments of capital and used the proceeds to buy these increments in the Western investment goods markets, flows would be matched by flows. The mismatch between stocks and flows would not occur.

Faked Balance Sheets

In addition to the zero-one problem and the stock-flow mismatch there is a third effect that may result in an undervaluation of East German asset prices. This effect originates from the system of compensation claims which was introduced in East Germany to avert unnecessary bankruptcies. Firms that can prove they are viable, but equity poor, receive interest bearing claims against the Treuhandanstalt to improve their equity base, and equity rich companies are punished by having to accept interest bearing liabilities from the Treuhandanstalt.[33] It is clear that East German managers, who are very experienced in fooling their authorities with faked balance sheets, will react to the compensation claims system by fabricating starting balance sheets for the Treuhandanstalt that make their companies appear worthless, though not hopeless. The Treuhand bureaucrats will then find it easy to crown their sales efforts with success by charging dirt-cheap prices.

4.4 Another Method of Privatization

As shown in section 3, a shortcoming of the monetary conversion was that the real asset overhang, which characterizes communist countries, was increased rather than reduced. No attempt was made to convert the Volksvermoegen, the "people's wealth", into marketable assets owned by East German households. The Treuhandanstalt is, in principle, an adequate vehicle for carrying out this task, and indeed the unification treaty (article 25) and the Treuhand Law (preamble) explicitly offer this option. However, it seems that the sales policies actually chosen will silently bypass the legal options.

The alternative to the institution's "clearance sales" of East German companies would be decentralized privatization where East German households became the legal owners of these companies and could then decide for themselves whether they wanted to sell them. The first step in this decentralized privatization process would be the foundation of corporations and the production of introductory balance sheets just as under the current rules. However, step two would not consist of the Treuhandanstalt's attempt to sell whole companies in the market place. Instead, it would consist of distributing shares to the East German population and, at the same time, introducing these shares in the world stock markets. The shares would quickly find their market values, and the East German households could then decide whether and, if so, when they wanted to sell them.

Apart from the fact that this privatization path would be a more liberal and market-oriented procedure than the sales via a bureaucracy, it would have a number of advantages that parallel the problems of the present privatization procedure as discussed above.

First, and most importantly, it could be much faster. In principle, the shares of the whole industry could be distributed in one step, very much as the distribution of Deutschmarks to East Germans was. It is true that, normally, the introduction of new shares in the stock market is also difficult and time consuming. However, given the unique historical situation, it would be appropriate to facilitate the process by making an amendment to the stock market law which introduces a special category of "Eastern Stock", tailored to the special conditions involved.

Second, there would be no cross-subsidization in addition to the initial allocation of compensation claims. No sales revenues could be used to extend the life of dying firms.

Third, distributing shares among households rather than selling East German companies to companies in the West would help establish more competition in goods markets and boost the efficiency of the German economy.

Fourth, the stock-flow mismatch could be largely avoided and it would thus be much easier for firms to raise the new equity required for real investment. As many East German households would decide to keep rather than sell their shares, the supply of a particular company's stock would in this case be smaller than with a centralized sale of the total stock by the Treuhandanstalt. And as the households would sell almost perfectly divisible shares rather than whole company units, more demand for a company's stock could be mobilized in international capital markets. For both of these reasons, share prices would be higher with a decentralized than with a centralized solution, and the possibilities for placing new shares and generating the equity capital needed for new investment would be much better. The success stories of newly founded joint stock companies in the United States are a good example of what could happen. It would be a big mistake not to make use of the wave of interest and enthusiasm for the German revolution that has recently swept right around the world. Wealth owners in Japan, the United States and elsewhere are just waiting for the opportunity to buy new shares issued by East German companies so they can participate in the profits these companies are expected to generate.

The Treuhandanstalt's policy is to sell existing companies and to use the proceeds for preventing other companies from going bankrupt and, hopefully in the future, for helping fund the government budget. Not a single Deutschmark out of these proceeds will be used for investment in the firms sold. In order to finance such investment the buyers will have to mobilize additional funds, but their capacity for doing that may already have been exhausted.

Fifth, the distribution of shares could compensate for the impoverishment of East German savers brought about by the currency conversion, and it could overcome the lack of consumption demand and the problematic consequences for aggregate demand that were described above.

Of course, it would be difficult to determine what the precise distribution of shares among the households should be. Some of the shares could be distributed in proportion to those parts of the savings accounts that had been devalued at a rate of 2:1. Others could be distributed on a per capita basis. Also it might be advisable to reduce the risks to be borne by the new and inexperienced shareholders by giving them shares in mutual funds rather than in the companies themselves. The details would have to be determined by political consensus very much like other redistributive measures of the state.

A more practical difficulty would be that the Treuhandanstalt has a number of expensive tasks in addition to the privatization. It has, for example, to satisfy the claims of previous owners whose properties cannot be returned and it will have to pay for environmental damage. For these purposes, a certain proportion of the shares could be reserved for the Treuhandanstalt which could then sell these in the international stock exchanges. Provided the proportion stays small, most of the virtues of the decentralized privatization process could be preserved.

5. Structural Unemployment

The paper's analysis concludes with a few remarks on the problem of structural unemployment. This problem arises from the fact that unification has suddenly endowed East Germany with new technological knowledge, new incentive systems, and new factor and commodity prices. The result of these changes will be a substantial reallocation of labor and capital among the economy's sectors.

Table 3 shows that the structure of the East German economy differed significantly from that of its West German counterpart. Some of these differences are characteristic of all communist countries and can be attributed to their ideological roots.

A good example is the underrepresentation of the trade and service sectors. In the communist ideology, such sectors were considered "unproductive" (though not useless) and were therefore not included in national output figures. The result was that planning authorities, which focussed on the measurable growth performance of the communist state, could improve their statistics by expanding the processing industries at the expense of the service sectors.

Another example of the dominant role of ideology is the relative strength of agriculture, energy, and mining. The reason for these capital intensive sectors being overrepresented relative to the West can be traced back to Marx's labor theory of value.[34] According to that theory, prices should reflect the labor content of commodities, but not the full capital costs. Capital costs in excess of depreciation were considered as the surplus which was wrongly expropriated from the workers in capitalism, but which had no role to play in a communist economy.[35] It is true that the communist countries soon learned painfully how expensive such an ideology was in terms of wasted resources and were themselves forced to introduce interest charges. East Germany made this step in the early sixties with the introduction of the "new system of planning and steering the economy" (NOeSPL), speaking bashfully of "production fund charges" (Produktionsfondsabgabe) rather than interest. However, these charges were compromises between western interest rates and the labor theory's requirement that there should be no such charges. As a result, the production costs of the capital intensive sectors continued to be underrepresented and the magnitudes of these sectors remained excessive.

Apart from the ideological reasons for structural differences, an east-west time lag in structural change is visible in the data. There was a time when clothing, textile, and food industries absorbed similar percentages of the labor force in West Germany as they do in East Germany today. New labor saving inventions and strong international competition made it both possible and necessary for West Germany to move to lower labor force percentages in these industries. East Germany would have done so too at some stage, but it was lagging behind.

There are certainly many other reasons for the structural differences between the two Germanies, but, whatever they are, most will no longer be relevant in the unified Germany. It is not implausible to suggest that East Germany's industry structure will approximate and even match that of West Germany with the passage of time.

Table 3: Structural Differences between East and West Germany

Sectoral labor market structure	East Germany[1]		West Germany[2]		Lay-offs[3]
Agriculture, forestry, fishing	9.9		4.2		5.7
Energy and mining	3.2		1.4		
Energy and water supply		1.3		0.8	0.5
Mining[4]		1.9		0.6	1.3
Processing industries	33.8		29.7		
Chemicals		1.6		2.0	-
Petroleum refining		0.6		0.1	0.5
Rubber products, plastics		1.0		1.4	-
Stone, clay		1.0		0.7	0.3
Porcelain, glass		0.7		0.5	0.2
Metal production and working		2.0		2.4	-
Steel, aluminium		1.2		0.6	0.6
Mechanical engineering		5.9		3.9	2.0
Vehicle construction and repair		2.2		4.1	-
Electrical engineering		4.3		3.7	0.6
Office machines and computers		0.6		0.3	0.3
Precision tools, optical equipment		0.6		0.9	-
Iron and sheet metal goods		1.2		1.1	0.1
Timber industry, paper industry, printing		2.2		2.9	-
Musical instruments, toys		0.7		0.2	0.5
Clothing, leather		2.1		1.3	0.8
Textiles		2.3		0.8	1.5
Food		3.6		2.8	0.8
Construction industry	6.1		6.6		
Trade	7.8		14.5		
Wholesale, distributors		2.8		5.1	-
Retail		5.0		9.4	-
Transport	6.8		5.6		
Railways[5]		2.6		1.0	1.6
Shipping, ports		0.4		0.2	0.2
Other transport		2.4		2.5	-
Communications		1.4		1.9	-
Services, government non-profit organisations	32.4		38.0		
Credit, insurance[6]		0.7		4.4	-
Hotels and catering		1.9		3.7	-
Health and veterinary services[7]		4.1		5.1	-
Consultancy		1.4		4.8	-
Other services		3.1		4.9	-
Education, science		6.8		4.9	1.9
Social services		1.7		1.1	0.6
Culture, media, sport		1.4		1.1	0.3
Public administration[8]		5.1		6.6	-
Other government services[9] (X-sector)		4.2		0	4.2
Churches, associations, parties[10]		2.0		1.4	0.6
Total	100.0		100.0		25.1

Sources:

[1] DIW Wochenbericht No. 17/90, 5 April 1990, p. 243. (The DIW estimates are based on figures published by the Zentralverwaltung für Statistik der DDR, Bericht über die Berufstätigen in der DDR per 30.9.1989); apprentices not included.
[2] Statistisches Bundesamt, Arbeitsstättenzählung vom 25.Mai 1987, Fachserie 2, Heft 4; figures for agriculture: Statistisches Bundesamt, Bevölkerung und Erwerbstätigkeit Fachserie 1, Reihe 4.1.1., 1989; microsurvey of 1987.
[3] Positive differences between East and West German percentages.
[4] Including uranium mining.
[5] Including railways saving bank.
[6] Including social insurance.
[7] Including university clinics.
[8] Including police and ministry for security, but no soldiers.
[9] Other government areas, not included in official statistics (so called X-sector).
[10] Including the so called mass organisations of the GDR.

During the transition process, structural unemployment will be unavoidable. A crude measure of the unemployment is calculated in the last column of Table 3. This column contains the positive differences between the East and West German participation percentages for the different sectors. These indicate the lay-offs that will be necessary in East Germany. The sum of all necessary lay-offs is one quarter of the East German work force or about 2.3 million people.[36]

Of course, the number of lay-offs is equal to the number of "vacancies" that can be calculated by adding the negative differences in the East and West German percentages. Note, however, that the match between these two numbers is a long-run phenomenon, and not something that can occur instantaneously. As the categories formed in the table represent industry branches, the lay-offs mean that the people will have to change their professions - and not just their jobs - if they want to find new employment. Given that the German economy relies so much on extensive vocational training and sharp distinctions between the professions this is a very serious problem.[37] Germany is not America where people have learned to be flexible and are used to switching from one occupation to another in the course of their lives.

It should also be noted that the number of lay-offs cannot be equated to measured unemployment figures. It merely indicates one major source of this unemployment. Inefficiencies will lead to bankruptcies and unemployment even if a sector is the same size as in West Germany, and the sector-internal employment structures may differ substantially from those in the West, causing lay-offs not captured in the table. Moreover, the problem of insufficient demand resulting from the unfavorable monetary conversion will arise in all sectors. Without a doubt, East Germany will have to pass through an extended period of severe unemployment that will affect every fourth employment contract.

6. Conclusion

A year ago, when the people of East Germany escalated their "Monday's demonstrations" into a true revolution they may not have known the course history would take as a result. But they did know that what they were doing was risky. While they escaped the bloodshed that could have followed, they cannot escape going through a period of austerity and restraint. The structural unemployment problem which the unification causes will task East Germans' patience.

Some of the anticipated problems of unification have been mastered with surprising ease. The monetary conversion went, except for the 20-30 b. Deutschmarks overlooked, exactly as the Bundesbank had hoped it would. It did not create inflationary pressures, and there is no reason to fear that the value of the Deutschmark will be eroded.

Nor is there any reason for West Germans to fear that they will have to pay for the currency conversion. The contrary is true. The Bundesbank gained from the conversion, and East German households lost about one third of their wealth. Unfortunately, this exchange loss may have contributed to the current depression in East Germany by causing negative Keynesian multiplier effects.

This is not to say that there are no costs to the West. Transfers in the order of magnitude of the West German trade surplus will be necessary to cover the East German budget deficits in the next few years, and the increased scarcity of capital and abundance of labor will have consequences for the West German income distribution. It is very likely that workers in the West will have to foot the lion's share of the unification bill, but this is an unavoidable consequence of history.

Perhaps the most serious mistake in West Germany's mainly successful unification policy was the decision to return the property expropriated by the East German state to the previous owners. This decision will occupy the courts for years to come and may create a serious bottleneck for investment.

The success of the transition to a market economy will crucially depend on the efficiency of the Treuhandanstalt in privatizing the East German economy. Privatizing the economy by organizing a clearance sale for 6000 companies and combines will quickly send the market price for East German companies down nearly to zero and is dangerously time consuming. One alternative would be privatization by distributing company shares to East German households and by leaving it up to them whether and, if so, when to sell those shares. That way the market price of shares would stay high and it would be much easier for East German companies to sell the shares they need to issue for the purpose of new investment.

A positive side effect of this decentralized privatization procedure would be the elimination of the real asset overhang, which characterizes the communist economy and which was enlarged by the currency conversion. The "people's wealth" (Volksvermoegen) would at last go to the people.

Whatever the policies chosen, it is clear that East Germany has a much better chance of catching up with western living standards than other eastern countries. It enjoys the help of its countrymen in the West, can offer a stable institutional environment for direct investment, and can build on its excellent pre-war tradition of craftsmanship and "high tech" production.

Hopefully the unification of Germany will be advantageous for all eastern Europeans. Poland, Czechoslovakia, Hungary, and other countries, perhaps in the end even the countries of the crumbling Soviet Union, will gain from the economic progress and stability of the united Germany. Germany has accepted the permanent separation of her former eastern territories, and there are no unsolved border problems remaining in Mitteleuropa. The period of peace and prosperity that lies ahead will benefit all. Trade is not a zero-sum game, and national success stories are not mutually exclusive.

Endnotes

* *I wish to thank Rudiger Dornbusch for useful comments; Knut Borchardt, Otmar Issing, and Lutz Hoffmann for providing valuable data sources; and my secretaries and research assistants for technical support. The support of Ronnie Schoeb, who helped collect the data, and of Juli Irving-Lessmann and my wife Gerlinde Sinn, who suggested various improvements, should be particularly acknowledged. The paper is part of the NBER's research program. It was written while I was Visiting Professor at the Department of Economics and the Center for Economic Policy Research of Stanford University and Visiting Fellow at Woodrow Wilson School, Princeton University; it benefitted from seminars given at these institutions and at the US Congressional Budget Office in Washington. Remaining errors are my sole responsibility.*

1. Brandt's Ostvertraege did not give up the formal claim on the eastern territories, but ruled out the use of military force to get them back and acknowledged the Polish right to live in "safe borders". The corresponding passages of the unification treaty induced some parliament members to appeal against it in the Supreme Court, arguing that separate votes would be necessary on the different issues covered by the treaty. The appeal was rejected, and the treaty was accepted by the East and West German parliaments with the necessary majorities of two-thirds of the votes.

2. This article will use the term East Germany to denote the territory of the former German Democratic Republic.

3. Like many comparisons, this one may not be fully adequate. Hawaii had no revolution and it had adjusted its institutions gradually to those of the US, before it became a state.

4. See OECD, Main Economic Indicators, October 1990, p. 24.

5. Assuming a 1:1 exchange. See section 3.1 for the justification of this assumption.

6. West Germany is also a large supporter of east European countries. Direct subsidies to Poland, for example, amount to some $78 m. in 1990 plus a cut in credit liabilities of $506 m. agreed on in November 1989. At the same time US subsidies mostly for the environment and for food supplies amount to $115 m. in 1990.

7. Cf. Arbeitsgemeinschaft deutscherwirtschaftswissenschaftlicher Forschungsinstitute (1990), Die Lage der Westwirtschaft und der deutschen Wirtschaft im Herbst 1990. The DIW (Wochenbericht 39/90, 27 September 1990, p. 553) even estimated that the transfers in addition to the unification fund transfer would total DM 44 b. ($ 29 b.) in 1991.

8. See Sinn (1984).

9. The analysis abstracts from labor migrations because, under the assumptions specified below, the wage rates in the two regions are the same in equilibrium.

10. See appendix.

11. The conclusion hinges in part on the static nature of the model. Among West German economists there is the wide-spread belief - unfortunately not one that has been founded on explicit model specifications - that the opening of the East will create so much "dynamism" that, in the long run, everyone will be better off than otherwise would have been the case. Western savings could be higher than otherwise and technological progress faster. To the

extent that such effects come true, western workers may face a more optimistic lot than that predicted by the simple neoclassical model. The author wishes he could share these views.

12. This is despite the plan to move to a true market economy in only 500 days which the Russian Republic recently adopted against the central government's advice.

13. See appendix I, section 6, and appendix II. The (1989) West German stock of private net fixed assets is DM 5.85 trillion and the stock of private land is DM 2.05 trillion.

14. This is more than the DM 574 b. which Siebert (1990) estimated. The reason for the divergence is primarily that Siebert assumed that 50% of the East German capital is obsolete while the IAW figures used here are based on the estimate that 67% is obsolete.

15. Cf. appendix I.

16. Arrow, Chenery, Minhas, and Solow (1961) estimated a value of 0.57 and Berndt and Wood (1981) estimated one of 0.63. For the value of σ cf. appendix I.

17. Cf. Monatsberichte der Deutschen Bundesbank, 42, No. 7, July 1990. For the exact quantities see appendix I.

18. Cf. Ifo Schnelldienst 43, 13/90, 7 May 1990, p. 24.

19. See DIW Wochenbericht No. 14/90, 5 April 1990, and Monatsberichte der Deutschen Bundesbank 42, No. 7, July 1990, p. 7.

20. Households owned only cash and savings accounts which carried interest but could be used like demand deposits.

21. Communist statistics did not show GDP or GNP figures according to the OECD definitions since these included the "unproductive" work of the service and government sectors. The net money income is roughly equivalent to the personal disposable income according to the OECD definitions.

22. East Germany did allow private land ownership but it severely restricted the marketability of land titles.

23. Monatsberichte der Deutschen Bundesbank 42, No. 10, October 1990.

24. The Bundesbank said that it had expected a M3 increase of DM 160 b. and admitted a mistake of DM 20 b. (ibid. p.7). Based on this figure, the unexpected M3 increase is 1.4%.

25. Monatsberichte der Deutschen Bundesbank, 42, No. 7, July 1990, p. 16.

26. The East German State Bank agreed that it would be necessary to cut the company debt in half, but argued that housing loans should be at a rate of 1:1.

27. See appendix I.

28. Another portfolio reaction is an adjustment in the liquidity structure of M3. Firms convert some of their demand deposits into time deposits and households convert savings accounts into cash and demand deposits. Anticipating these reactions and the resulting change in reserve requirements, the Bundesbank waited one month after the currency conversion until it subjected the East German banking system to minimum reserve requirements.

29. Monatsberichte der Deutschen Bundesbank 42, No. 10, October 1990, p. 7.

30. Cf. Schulte and Doeinghaus (1990).

31. See Frankfurter Allgemeine Zeitung, 30 August, 1990.

32. That board recently forbade Lufthansa from buying the East German airline Interflug. This made British Airways the most promising bidder. If British Airways does not ultimately want to buy Interflug and if no other purchaser can be found, Lufthansa may again have a chance.

33. The precise rule is that a company has to accept a liability if its debt falls short of its real estate property value, i.e. if its equity capital exceeds its value of real assets net of real estate. A compensation claim is given to a company if it has no equity, but seems profitable enough to be rehabilitated. See Dietl and Rommert (1990).

34. Thereby disproving Marx's view that "the being determines the mind" (Das Sein bestimmt das Bewusstsein.) and confirming Hegel's view of history. The irony of communism is that it claimed to follow Marx, but violated his precepts by dictating an ideology that was in sharp contradiction to the real productive conditions (reale Produktionsverhaeltnisse). The abolition of communism is exactly what Marx's abstract theory of revolution predicts (although not of course what Marx believed would happen). Because a state's ideology conflicts with its "material base" (materielle Basis), there is a revolution that adjusts the ideological superstructure (ideologischer Ueberbau: state, institutions, and ideology) to the material base.

35. Interestingly enough, the rate of surplus was larger in East than in West Germany. It follows from the figures of the appendix that the share of wages in GDP was 0.4 in East Germany, but 0.53 in West Germany. When depreciation had the same magnitude relative to GDP in both states, the above statement is implied.

36. Adding the "x sector" of employees not counted inofficial statistics (4.2%) to the official work force results in a total employment of (9.3 m.). The number mentioned in the text is one quarter of this enlarged measure of the workforce.

37. For most occupations, Germany has an education system with a period of theoretical and practical training rarely under 3 years. There is a hierarchy of qualifications which signal the exact educational status of a worker. For example, a painter is awarded the title "associate painter" after successful training in the occupation for 3 years, and a more elevated title that is awarded to some of the senior painters is "master painter". The vocational education system is the strength of the German economy in terms of producing high quality output, but is its weakness when it comes to speed of adjustment.

Appendix I

Unless stated otherwise, the data are taken from Statistisches Bundesamt, DDR 1990, Zahlen und Fakten, Wiesbaden 1990; Statistisches Bundesamt, Statistisches Jahrbuch 1990 fuer die Bundesrepublik Deutschland, Wiesbaden 1990; Monatsberichte der deutschen Bundesbank 42, No. 5, May 1990; Statistisches Jahrbuch 1990 der Deutschen Demokratischen Republik 34, Berlin 1990; and Jahresbericht 1989 der Staatsbank der DDR.

1) Labor Force	East	West
Population	16.4 m.	62.3 m.
	(ratio East/West = 26%)	
Work force	8.9 m.	29.7 m.
Employed	8.9 m.	27.7 m.
Participation rate	54%	48%
Female particip. rate	50%	37%
Unemployment rate	0%	7.1%

2) Output and Incomes	East (Mark)	West (DM)
Produced National Income (without services)	260.4 b.	----
- per worker	38,759	----
Gross value added without the service sector	----	1449 b.
- per worker	----	67,400
Gross domestic product	**353.4 b.**[1]	**2,237 b.**
	(ratio East/West =**15.8%**)	
- per employed worker	39,700	80,750
	(ratio East/West = **49.2%**)	
- per worker	39,700	75,300
	(ratio East/West = **52.7%**)	
- per capita of population	21,500	36,300
	(ratio East/West = **59.2%**)	
Private value added (net of indirect taxes)	----	1505.1 b.

Gross wage income (including employers' social insurance contribution)	141.2 b.	1,171.5 b.
Gross private sector wage income	----	948.8 b.
Share of private wages in private value added (partial production elasticity of labor under competitive conditions)	----	63.0%
Rate of return to capital (private sector value added - private sector wages) / (private net fixed assets + private land value); see section 6)	----	7.0%
Average monthly gross wage earnings (including employer's contribution to social insurance)		
- Whole economy	1322	3966
	(ratio East/West = **31%**)	
- Manufacturing	1324	3657
- Construction	1310	2958
- Agriculture and forestry	1242	2597
- Commerce	1168	2893
- Transport and communication	1436	3311
Net money income (= Y_{East}; similar to personal disposable income)	**167.5 b.**	
Personal disposable income (= Y_{West})		**1403.8 b**
	(ratio East/West = **12 %**)	
Net money income, personal disposable income per capita and		
- per year	10,200	22,500
- per month	850	1,900
	(ratio East/West = **45%**)	

3) Government Revenue and Expenditure

	East (Mark)	West (DM)
Tax revenue	269.7 b. (1988)[2]	535.5 b.
- VAT	----	131.5 b.
- Personal Income tax	10.0 b. (1988)	278.6 b.
- Corporate tax	----	34.2 b.
- Excise taxes	**43.1 b.** (1988)[3]	53.6 b.
- Others	----	97.6 b.
- Social insurance contributions	18.8 b. (1988)	413.5 b.
Subsidies (to firms, other than price subsidies)	106.8 b. (1988)	75.6 b.
Transfers (to households)	36.3 b. (1988)	61.8 b.
Price subsidies for elementary goods	**49.8 b.**[3] (1988) (1971: 8.5 b.)	
of which:		
- Food and beverages	31.9 b.	
- Manufactured goods	11.9 b.	
- Transport services	5.0 b.	
Pensions	17.2 b.(1988)	173.9 b.(1988)
Average monthly government pensions	427	1018
Taxes/GDP	----	23.9%
Social insurance contributions/GDP	5.3%	18.5%
Government deficit	-0.2 b.	26.3 b.
Government deficit/GDP	---- (1990: 2.7%[4] - 3.7%[5]) (1991: 3.2%[4] - 4.5% to 5%[5]) (USA 1989: 2.6%)	1.2%
Government contribution to NDP (value added)	----	222.7 b.
Government expenditures/GDP	76.3%	31.2%
Government consumption/GDP	----	18.5%

4) Monetary Aggregates	East (Mark)	West (DM)
Cash circulation with households and non-banking firms		
- total	17.0 b.	146.9 b.
- per capita	1036	2350
Demand deposits (East: savings deposits)	159.7 b.	303.7 b.
Demand deposits of firms with central bank	60.6 b.[6]	0
Savings deposits[7]	159.7 b.	715.2 b.
M1	237.3 b.	450.6 b.
M2	237.3 b.	776.4 b.
M3	237.3 b.	1255.5 b.
Household financial assets[8]		
- total	191.4 b.	(1988) 2515 b.
- per capita	11,670	40,400

Ratios to net money income (Y_{East}) and personal disposable income (Y_{West}), respectively

	East	West
Cash	10.1%	10.5%
Demand Deposits (East: savings deposits and demand deposits of firms)	131.5%	21.2%
M1	141.7%	32.1%
M2	141.7%	55.3%
M3	141.7%	89.4%
Household financial assets	114.3%	(1988) 187.2%

Money overhang with 1:1 exchange and applying western ratios (DM)

Lower bound (M3 overhang)

1989: 237.3 b. - 89.4% 167.5 b. = **87.5 b.**

Intermediate estimate (M2 overhang)

1989: 237.3 b. - 55.3% 167.5 b. = **144.7 b.**

Upper bound (M1 overhang)

1989: 237.3 b. - 32.1% 167.5 b. = **183.5 b.**

Explanation: money overhang = $M_{East} - k_{West}\, Y_{East}$, where

M_{East} = cash owned by households and non-banking firms + household savings deposits + demand deposits of non-banking firms with central bank

k_{West} = Cambridge k of West Germany (based on personal disposable income)

Y_{East} = net money income of private households in East Germany (similar to disposable income according to OECD definitions)

Due to the fact that savings deposits could be withdrawn at any time in East Germany, these deposits are fungible like checking accounts in West Germany. On the other hand, there are hardly any long term assets available (with the exception of insurance savings plans of 14.7 b.). The magnitude of the money overhang depends on the definition of money supply used (M1, M2, or M3). The Bundesbank focussed exclusively on the M3 overhang.

Given the price level in East Germany and using the above estimates the following DM money supply should have been provided:

M1 (cash + demand deposits)	= 167.5 b. 32.1%	= 53.8 b.
M2 - M1 (time deposits at less than 4 years notice)	= 167.5 b. (55.3% - 32.1%)	= 38.9 b.
M3 - M2 (savings deposits)	= 167.5 b. (89.4% - 55.3%)	= 57.1 b.
		149.8 b.

Assuming the conversion pattern described in the treaty on the monetary union, stocks of East German currency were exchanged according to the following rules by July 1st, 1990. All amounts were exchanged to DM-M3 equivalents and they could be withdrawn as cash on demand; no quantities were "frozen" as many consultants had suggested.

<u>Exchange 1:1</u>

Persons up to 14 years of age	2000
Persons from 15 through 59 years	4000
Persons above 59 years	6000

Given the East German population structure this implied a DM-M1 increase totaling 65.5 b.

<u>Exchange 1:2</u>

In principle, the excess of M3 over DM 65,500, that is 237.3 b. - 65.5 b. = 171.8 b., was eligible for this rate. The DM-M1 increase was 85.9 b.

<u>Exchange 1:3</u>

However, a small part of the excess of M3 over DM 66,000 was owned by non-GDR residents. To the extent this consisted of East German bank accounts created in 1990, the 1:3 exchange rate applied. It is unknown (to the author) which exact amounts fell under this category.

Sum: DM-M3 increase according to treaty **151.4 b.**

M3 Money overhang with exchange according to treaty and applying western ratios

151.4 b. - 32.1% 167.5 b. = **97.6 b.**

5) Prices	East	West
Inflation: cost of living index (1970 = 100)	99.5	197.7

<u>Purchasing power parity:</u> See Table 2 of the text.

6) Assets and Liabilities	East (Mark)	West (DM)
Private gross fixed assets[9]	----	10,032.7 b.
Net fixed assets (total)[10]	1,745.0 b. 575.8 b.[11]	6,512.6 b.
- in the manufacturing secto	1250.0 b. 462.5 b.[11]	----
Private net fixed assets	----	5,850.5 b.
Private land value	----	2,049.8 b.[12]
Private and privatizeable land value (East Germany)	420.9 b. -524.5 b.[13]	----
Capital-output ratio[14]		
- overall	----	3.3
- in the manufacturing sector	4.8	----
Net foreign debt	21.2 b.	-426.8 b.
Company debt (East: gross of accounts with central bank)	260.4 b.	1169.6 b.
Housing loans	108.5 b.	729.4 b.
Government debt	----	923.5 b.

7) Saving and Investment	East (Mark)	West (DM)
Gross investment	77.1 b.	435.6 b.
Depreciation	33.4 b.	276.7 b.
Net investment	43.7 b.	199.6 b.
Aggregate saving	----	267.9 b.
Savings propensity (out of personal disposable income and net money income respectively)	6.3%	13.6%

8) Foreign Trade	East (Mark)	West (DM)
Exports less imports	+3.0 b.	+134.7 b.
Current account[15]	----	+104.2 b.
Capital account	----	-128.2 b.

9) Expenditures as Percentages of Disposable Income[16]

	East	West
Food and beverages	41.5%	23.2%
Manufactured goods	45.3%	40.0%
Services (including housing)	13.2%	36.8%
of which:		
- Rent	2.7%	20.1%
- Utilities (electricity, gas, heating)	1.9%	5.7%

10) Endowment with Consumer Durables[17]

	East	West
Private car	54%	96%
TV-set	96%	99%
- of which: color TV	57%	95%
Telephone	17%	99%
Refrigerator (without freezer)	99%	81%
Freezer (with and without refrigerator)	43%	75%
Washing machine	99%	97%
Housing		
- Number of apartments and housing units	7 m.	26.6 m.[18]
- Number of people sharing a unit	2.3	2.3
- Living space per capita	27.6 m^2	35.5 m^2 [18]
Proportion of living space built after 1948	35%	70%[18]
Proportion of units equipped with bath/shower	82%	96%[18]

Endnotes (Appendix I)

1. An alternative estimate by DIW (Wochenbericht 57, No. 17/90, 26 April 1990, p. 223) is 346.1 b. Eastmarks.
2. Total government revenues.
3. With the unification (October 3, 1990) most price subsidies and excise taxes have been removed and, except for housing, all prices have been freed.
4. Arbeitsgemeinschaft deutscher wirtschaftswissenschaftlicher Forschungsinstitute, Die Lage der Weltwirtschaft und der deutschen Wirtschaft im Herbst 1990, in DIW Wochenbericht 57, No. 43 44/90, 25 October 1990.
5. Estimated by Deutsche Bundesbank (cf. FAZ, No. 260, 7 November 1990, p. 17).
6. Jahresbericht 1989 der Staatsbank der DDR.
7. Savings deposits in East Germany were equivalent to sight deposits: arbitrary amounts could be withdrawn at any time.
8. Financial assets include cash, savings deposits, and 15 b. personal insurance savings in the case of East Germany. Include bonds in the case of West Germany.
9. At replacement cost.
10. Without land.
11. Estimate of the Institute of Applied Economic Research (IAW), Die ostdeutsche Wirtschaft 1990/1991, 22 October 1990.
12. Own estimate: see Appendix II.
13. Own estimate: see Appendix II.
14. West Germany: net fixed assets divided by net domestic product at market prices; East Germany: net fixed investment ("Grundmittelbestand") divided by produced national income.
15. Statistisches Bundesamt, Volkswirtschaftliche Gesamtrechnungen Fachserie 18.
16. 1998 East: all households. West: 4-person-employee households with gross income between DM 2,900 and DM 4,400.
17. 1989 East: Percentage of households owning the respective specified consumer durable; West: 4-person-employee households with a gross income between DM 3000 and DM 4500 (Statistisches Bundesamt; Statistisches Jahrbuch fuer die Bundesrepublik 1990, Wiesbaden 1990)
18. 1987: Statistisches Bundesamt, Wirtschaft und Statistik No. 8, August 1989, p. 494.

Appendix II

Land Values in West and East Germany (1989)

In cooperation with Ronnie Schoeb

West German Land Values

The size and structure of private West German land as given in the first column of Table A1 is reported in the West German statistical yearbook 1990 and in the monthly statistical report published by the West German Ministry of Finance. The prices of the various land categories given in the second column are based on the West German statistical yearbook 1990 and on information provided to the authors by the Federal Forest Office, Stockdorf.

Table A1: Private Land Values in the West
Current Values (1989)

Land category	Size [m. ha]	Price per ha [DM]	Value [b. DM]
Agricultural land (without forests)	13,488.1	30,924	417.1
Forests	2832.6	12,500	35.4
Urban Land	1685.4	947,700	1597.3
Total,	18,006.1	----	2049.8
average	----	113,839	----

Sources: Statistisches Bundesamt, Statistisches Jahrbuch 1990 fuer die Bundesrepublik Deutschland, Wiesbaden 1990, Tab. 8.13, 8.18, 23.10; Bundesministerium der Finanzen, Statistischer Monatsbericht 6/1990, p. 401; information provided to the authors by Bundesforstamt Stockdorf. Own calculations.

The urban land prices are average reported sales prices in 1989. These prices underestimate the land values because most sales occur in suburban areas where land prices are lower than in urban centers. While public traffic areas like roads, railroads, airports etc. are not included in the figures, it was not possible to separate out urban areas covered with public buildings. These areas probably explain only a small fraction of the total land value reported in the table.

East German Land Values

The difficulty in calculating the East German counterpart of Table A1 is that there are no market prices for land and that it is unclear how much of the land can be privatized. This section reports two sets of calculations based on the alternative assumptions that i) western land prices apply immediately and that ii) they apply after an adjustment period, ending with the year 2000, during which no rent will be generated by East German land.

i) The structural composition of the total East German stock of land is reported in the West German statistical yearbook 1990 but, naturally, there are no estimates of the areas that would be available in a privatized economy. The figures reported in the first column of Table A2 have been constructed from the available information assuming that all (non-forest) agricultural areas will ultimately be privatized, that the same fraction of forested areas will be privatized as in West Germany (38%), and that the ratio of eastern urban areas to their western counterparts equals the ratio of the respective housing spaces available today (20%). Multiplying the areas reported in the first column with the current (1989) West German land prices gives the land prices reported in the third column. Based on current West German land prices, the total value of private and privatizeable land in East Germany is **DM 524.5 b.** This figure must be considered as an upper bound since it implies an immediate equalization of eastern and western land rents at the time of unification.

Table A2: Private and Privatizeable Land Values in the East

	Immediate adjustment			Adjustment at the year 2000	
Land category	Size [m. ha]	Price per ha [DM]	Value [b. DM]	Price per ha [DM]	Value [b. DM]
Agricultural land without forests	6171.0	30,924	190.8	24,817	153.1
Forests	1133.5	12,500	14.2	10,031	11.4
Urban Land	337.1	947,700	319.5	760,547	256.4
Total,	7641.6	----	524.5	----	420.9
average	----	68,637	----	55,080	----

Sources: Statistisches Bundesamt, Statistisches Jahrbuch 1990 fuer die Bundesrepublik Deutschland, Wiesbaden 1990, Anhang 1, Tab. 5.1. Own calculations.

ii) The other extreme is the assumption that East German land will be unable to generate any rents until the year 2000 and will thereafter yield the same rents as western land. This produces the results reported in the last two columns of Table A2.

In a perfect capital market, the market rate of interest equals the expected growth rate of the land price plus the land's rental rate. Inflating West Germany's land prices and discounting the result with the market rate of interest therefore is equivalent to discounting the current (1989) West German land prices with the rental rate over the adjustment period. The West German average agricultural rental rate in the period from 1975 to 1987 equalled 1.1%[1]. When all land prices grow at the same rate, this rental rate can be taken to apply to all land categories. To be on the safe side, a rate of 2% was used to calculate the implicit East German land prices. The prices are reported in the last but one column of Table A2 and the corresponding land values in the different categories are shown in the last column. A conservative estimate of today's value of the East German stock of land that will ultimately be in private hands is therefore **DM 420.9 b.**

Endnotes (Appendix II)

1. Source: Statistisches Bundesamt, Statistisches Jahrbuch 1990 für die Bundesrepublik Deutschland, Wiesbaden 1990, Tab. 8.8, 8.13.

Statistical Sources

Bundesministerium der Finanzen, Statistischer Monatsbericht 6/1990.

Deutsches Institut fuer Wirtschaftsforschung (DIW) Wochenberichte 57, No. 14/90, 5 April 1990; No. 17/90, 26 April 1990; No. 21/90, 25 May 1990; No. 26/90, 28 June 1990; No. 32/90, 9 August, 1990; No. 37/90, 13 September 1990; No. 39/90, 27 September 1990; No. 43,44/90, 25 October 1990.

Frankfurter Allgemeine Zeitung (FAZ), No. 260, 7 November 1990.

Gemeinsames Statistisches Amt, Preisindex fuer die Lebenshaltung, November 1990.

Institut für Wirtschaftsforschung (Ifo), Schnelldienst 43, No. 13/90, 7 May 1990.

Institut für angewandte Wirtschaftsforschung (IAW), Die ostdeutsche Wirtschaft 1990/1991. Trends und Perspektiven, 22 October 1990.

Jahresbericht 1989 der Staatsbank der DDR.

Monatsberichte der Deutschen Bundesbank 42, No. 5, May 1990; No. 7, July 1990; No. 10, October 1990.

OECD Main Economic Indicators, October 1990, Paris.

Statistisches Amt der DDR, Statistisches Jahrbuch '90 der Deutschen Demokratischen Republik, Berlin 1990.

Statistisches Bundesamt, Wirtschaft und Statistik No. 8, August 1989, No. 9, September 1990.

Statistisches Bundesamt, DDR 1990, Zahlen und Fakten, Stuttgart 1990.

Statistisches Bundesamt, Statistisches Jahrbuch 1989 fuer die Bundesrepublik Deutschland, Wiesbaden 1990.

Statistisches Bundesamt, Statistisches Jahrbuch 1990 fuer die Bundesrepublik Deutschland, Wiesbaden 1990.

Statistisches Bundesamt, Bevoelkerung und Erwerbstaetigkeit, Fachserie 1; Reihe p. 49, 4.1.1.1989.

Statistisches Bundesamt, Arbeitsstaettenzaehlung vom 25. Mai 1987, Fachserie 2; Unternehmen und Arbeitsstaetten, Heft 4.

Statistisches Bundesamt, Volkswirtschaftliche Gesamtrechnungen, Fachserie 18.

Staatliche Zentralverwaltung fuer Statistik, Statistisches Jahrbuch 1989 der Deutschen Demokratischen Republik, Berlin 1989.

United States Department of Commerce, 1990, Survey of Current Business 70, No. 7.

Laws and Treaties

Vertrag ueber die Schaffung einer Waehrungs', Wirtschafts- und Sozialunion zwischen der Bundesrepublik Deutschland und der Deutschen Demokratischen Republik. Bundesgesetzblatt 1990, Teil II, No. 20, 29 June 1990, 537-567. (Effective: 2 July 1990).

Vertrag zwischen der Bundesrepublik Deutschland und der Deutschen Demokratischen Republik ueber die Herstellung der Einheit Deutschlands - Einigungsvertrag - In: Presse - und Informationsamt der Bundesregierung, Bulletin No. 104, 6 September 1990, 877 - 1120. (Effective: 3 October 1990).

Gesetz zur Privatisierung und Reorganisation des volkseigene Vermoegens (Treuhandgesetz) vom 17. June 1990. In: Gesetzesblatt der Deutschen Demokratischen Republik, Teil I, No. 33, 22 June 1990, 300 -303. (Effective: 1 July 1990).

References

ABELSHAUSER, W. (1983) Wirtschaftsgeschichte der Bundesrepublik Deutschland (1945-1980), Frankfurt.

ARBEITSGEMEINSCHAFT DEUTSCHER WIRTSCHAFTSWISSENSCHAFTLICHER FORSCHUNGSINSTITUTE (1990) Die Lage der Weltwirtschaft und der deutschen Wirtschaft im Herbst 1990 in: DIW Wochenbericht 57, No. 43-44/90, 25 October 1990, pp. 605-635.

ARROW, K.J., M.B. CHENERY, B.S. MINHAS, and R. SOLOW (1961) Capital-Labor Substitution and Economic Efficiency, Review of Economics and Statistics 43, pp. 225-250.

BERNDT, E.R. and D.O. WOOD (1981) The Speculation and Measurement of Technical Change in U.S. Manufacturing, MIT, Energy Laboratory Working Paper No. Mitel 81-046 WP.

DIETL, R. and S. RAMMERT (1990) DM-Eroeffnungsbilanzen in der DDR, Boersenzeitung, Frankfurt am Main, 10 August 1990.

ERHARD, L. (1953) Wirtschaftliche Probleme der Wiedervereinigung, Bulletin des Presse- und Informationsamtes der Bundesregierung, 174, 12 September 1953, pp. 1453-1454.

KASER, M.C. and E.A. RADICE, eds. (1985) The Economic History of Eastern Europe 1919-1975, vol. I, Economic Structure and Performance between the Two Wars, Oxford.

SCHULTE-DOEINGHAUS, U. and R. STIMPEL (1990) Auf wachligem Grund, Wirtschaftswoche 30, 7/20/90, pp. 32-43.

SIEBERT, H. (1990) The Economic Integration of Germany, Kiel Discussion Papers, No. 160, Institut fuer Weltwirtschaft.

SINN, H.-W. (1984) Die Bedeutung des Accelerated Cost Recovery Systems fuer den internationalen Kapitalverkehr, Kyklos 37, pp. 542-576.

COMMENTS ON: MACROECONOMIC ASPECTS OF GERMAN UNIFICATION

Rudiger Dornbusch

Hans-Werner Sinn's interesting paper cuts into the major issues of the absorption of East Germany into a common economic venture. It appropriately addresses the question of monetary reform, capital requirements, labor market issues and the modality of privatization.[1] It thus adds to the first flow of speculation of what lies ahead. Should we think of East Germany as the land of Zeiss and Junkers, with potential for high value added work and high wages, or as an area devastated by the productivity-eroding influence of 50 years of mindless, hard communism? There is plenty of history to say that the region once was in the forefront (like Rome, Athens and Bogota), but there is also the *Trabant* to remind us that something went badly wrong. Sinn rightly leaves no doubt, any numbers we might make must be highly speculative because for the time being so little is known about the facts and even less about their economic interpretation.

1. Do It Fast

My first point is to agree vigorously with Sinn on the issue of privatization. That question has been mishandled and the mismanagement is extremely costly. Wilhelm Nolling has rightly argued that it is more important to get it done fast, than to do it well. And the same applies to much of the reform process. There is always room for perfection afterwards.

A major tension arises between the concern to maintain existing employment patterns and the immediate standards of living on one hand and the recognition that drastic changes are required and time is short on the other. An approach that is overly cautious and protective along the lines of a *dirigiste* welfare state risks handling the adjustment poorly. Germany of 1948 offers a precedent for using rapid, radical reform as the best bridge to the market. The drastic cut with the past in the form of monetary reform and radical deregulation was the key step. With general disruption and a flood of more than 8 million refugees, unemployment increased to nearly a million and a half by early 1950, but with strong growth unemployment fell year by year. (See Figure) Average GDP growth in 1950-59 amounted to 7.9 percent. In the United Kingdom, by contrast, unemployment was always below 2 percent but growth came to only 1.9 percent per year. Practicing the welfare state had its costs.

The administrative capacity for *successful* gradual reform simply does not exist. After all, communism even with the advantage of repression could not handle the task of allocating resources. Nothing has changed with new and highly committed, talented personnel joining the ranks. They too will be unable to mastermind an economy-wide soft landing. The lesson of the postwar period is that those countries who pushed reform most aggressively soon showed the best results, even if the transition period was very hard. The market is already there. The only choice is whether to work *with* the market or to lose out in a fight *against* the market.

In the grey area between a control-economy that no longer functions and a market economy that is not fully accepted, economic collapse is inevitable. Collapse occurs because the cooperation required by a high division of labor does not arise spontaneously. It requires either the coercion of a repressive regime or else the incentives of a market economy. That was apparent in the collapse of production in postwar Germany and it is apparent today in East Germany once again.

FIGURE 1

How to get from here to there? Surely, the answer must be that the transition needs to be accomplished extremely fast because the ice is melting, the distance is far and the task is overwhelming. The pace will be determined by the market which is already operating on the back stage. Countries that move fast will draw resources from abroad and stand a better chance to retain scarce human capital and political reserves; countries that drag their feet risk falling into deep poverty where even the unsatisfactory living standards of the past decade can no longer be mustered because the organization of the economy has vanished.

In some areas the pace has been fast, even ruthless. But in the area of privatization and property rights more generally a mess has been made quite unnecessarily. Too much time and political ground was given to the topic of monetary conversion, too little to rapid, effective institutionalization of private property.

2. Monetary Reform

Perhaps the most successful feature of the economic integration was the decisive monetary reform. Much discussion continues as to the appropriateness of the conversion rate and on the question of who gained or lost. But there is surely no doubt that the immediate substitution of a hard money, and the abolition of any scope whatsoever for independent monetary and fiscal policy, were highly beneficial. A comparison with any other Eastern European country makes that point immediately and, if anything, suggests that these countries would benefit from moving quickly on to a DM standard.

Sinn rightly argues that the handling of company debts may have been unfortunate -- why not just write them off across the board? He also draws attention to the modality of monetary reform: the Bundesbank supplied DM in exchange for interest bearing promissory notes of the East German banking system. But he is not persuasive in two arguments: that the Bundesbank strategy of differentiated conversion, rather than 1:1 with freezing, implied a wealth loss for East Germany and that the Bundesbank made profits on the operation.

East Germany had a lot of paper, the Bundesbank converted it into the hardest currency in the world, as a gift. True, the gift could have been even larger if the rate had been uniformly 1:1, and even more if East Germans got some money in the mail every morning. The appropriate question concerns resource transfers. East Germans have as assets the real capital stock; their paper was worthless. Whether they gained as holders of paper assets is uninteresting; the only serious question is whether the real value of their assets (human and physical) today are worth more than they were before. Surely the answer to that question is positive. I would argue that monetary reform played an important role in that quick transition.

As to the profitability of the monetary conversion, Sinn stretches a good point. Surely, the world capital market would not lend to the East German banking system at the German T-bill rate. If East Germany got hold of DM at so low a rate there is clearly a subsidy involved. I have no doubt that the Soviet Union also would like to borrow DM at the favorable rate, and all of Latin America.

3. The Collapse

The most interesting economic feature of the ongoing merger is, of course, not the monetary reform. That was so successful that it leaves nothing much to be said. The deeply interesting issue is the massive collapse of economic activity, some 50 percent decline in industrial production by early 1991. That collapse needs thorough analysis.[2]

One clue to what is going on comes from Table 1 which reports a massive increase in *retail* import penetration. The same phenomenon, though on much more moderate scale, can be observed in Mexico and Chile at the time these countries eliminated their pervasive import barriers.

Table 1: Import Penetration at the Retail Level
(Percent of Goods of West German Origin)

Margarine	35
Eating Oil	41
Dishwasher Detergent	53
Tea	66
Cookies	76
Household Detergent	90
Canned Soup	94
Coffee	96
Chocolate	96

Source: *Die Zeit*, Sept. 28, 1990

There are at least three plausible explanations. The first has to do with a taste for diversity. In East Germany there were few brands of any product, West Germany has many. Accordingly, as the ability to access the West German range appears, demand for the one or two East

German brands declines. A simple Spence-Stiglitz model, for example, would predict this outcome.

A second hypothesis suggests that West German goods have the "magic touch", they smell the same, they taste the same, but somehow nobody wants to believe they are quite the same. And if they are consumed long enough, they may even become a new habit. This argument makes East German goods look like "lemons" which simply cannot be sold, even at a price that is far below that of West German goods.

The third hypothesis, less appropriate in East Germany where shortages had not been a dramatic problem, is the superior ability of East German suppliers to actually put goods on the truck and on the shelf, including even with trade credit.

In reality each factor will play a role. We will have opportunity to see more of these effects at work as more and more economies are opened up. Of course, the East German experience may caution countries against opening if that means the instant demise of domestic production.

Of course, the decline in industrial production need not result exclusively from the shift in demand. We must also recognize that East German firms are not organized to survive in a market setting. With their emphasis on scale and autarchy, they are the antithesis of the "flexible production, customizing" design of modern production and their functioning requires a plan and cannot deal with prices and adjustment. They are a bit like NY stretch limousines brought into the Paris Latin Quarter. The sooner they are destroyed, viable firms can start to be built.

When we look for productivity growth, it must come of course from the unmantling of these aberrant production structures. Here may be another case where the Schumpeterian growth model applies. And precisely because we cannot predict, just as little as the Communists could, where resources should best be employed, the process must be left to a maximum degree free and unimpeded. There needs to be a social safety net, but surely there can be no sense in trying to plan the transition.

Where East Germany ultimately winds up is a wide open question. Looking at the wage surely does not get us very far. East Germany will have some development poles or agglomerations, and it will have depressed areas.[3] Distances are sufficiently small so that all goods can be shipped in from West-Germany. The only way East Germany will have a high standard of living comes from the rapid development (presumably by joint venture) of high value added, quality products. That justifies paying high wages and then supports a local service sector.

Table 2: Hourly Compensation in Manufacturing
(1989 Wage, Index U.S.=100)

W.Germany	123	Taiwan	25
Italy	92	Hong Kong	19
Japan	88	Singapore	22
France	89	Mexico	16
United Kingdom	73	Brazil	12
Spain	64	Korea	25
E.Germany*	40		

*Estimate by the author

Note: US compensation in 1989 was $14.30 per hour

Source: US Dept. of Labor

If the dynamics go wrong, and they surely will in many places, the regions will simply lose their highly skilled labor, they will fail to attract capital inflows and will ultimately become poverty traps. East Germans should travel to Barcelona where the understanding of these dynamics is very advanced and where integration has been very consciously translated into prosperity.

4. Prospects and Spillovers

How will the economic integration spill over to the rest of the world? The IMF has offered a scenario reproduced in Table 3.

The direction of effects cannot be in doubt: a strong expansion of demand in East Germany financed by the West; collapse of activity in the East at the outset; and a boom in the West. A combined deterioration in the current account can be expected. The spill over effects to the rest of Europe is negative: the current account deterioration notwithstanding, the boom forces high interest rates and that means slow growth.

Table 3: The IMF Unification Scenario
(Deviations from Baseline)

	1990	1991	1992-94	1995-7
FRG				
Real GNP	0.5	1.3	0.6	0.4
Real Demand	0.1	0.1	-0.1	-0.2
FRG + GDR				
Real GDP	0.5	2.0	3.6	5.8
Current Account[a]	-0.9	-1.8	-1.8	-1.4
Budget[a]	-1.3	-1.8	-1.2	-0.8
Other ERM Countries				
Real GDP	-0.1	-0.2	-0.4	-0.3
Current Account[a]	0.1	0.2	0.1	0.2
Other Ind. Countries				
Real GDP	0.1	0.2		
Current Account[a]	-	0.1		

[a]Percent of GNP
Source: IMF *World Economic Outlook*, October 1990, p.47.

The forecasts bring out a puzzling issue: how did West Germany manage to capture so much of the demand; why can France or Italy, or Korea not get a higher share of the action? The answer, one suspects, is that Germany is a little bit like Japan, managing to contain competition by an invisible hand.

Endnotes

1 See the references for further work.
2 It is my impression that more fortunes will be made in comparative economics in the few years of collapse now underway, than in the many decades of past practice.
3 More than neoclassical trade theory, the modern discussion on regional agglomerations, notably *Krugman and Venables (1990)* is relevant here.

References

BOFINGER, P. (1990) The German Monetary Unification: Converting Marks to D-Marks. Federal Reserve Bank of St. Louis Review, August.

CONGRESSIONAL BUDGET OFFICE (1990) How the Economic Transformation in Europe Will Affect the United States. Washington DC, December.

DE GRAUWE, P. (1990) The Economic Integration of West and East Germany. Two Tales Based on Trade Theory: Discussion Paper No. 72, CES, Katholieke Universitaet Leuven.

INTERNATIONAL MONETARY FUND (1990) World Economic Outlook, Washington DC, October.

KRUGMAN, P. and VENABLES, A. (1990) Integration and the Competitiveness of Peripheral Industry. CEPR Discussion Paper No. 363, January.

LEWIS, A. and J. GAGNON (1990) The Global Economic Implications of German Unification. International Finance Discussion Papers No. 379, Board of Governors of the Federal Reserve.

WOLF, H. (1990) From Plan To Market: Germany 1948 and 1990. Mimeo, Massachusetts Institute of Technology.

TRANSFORMING A SOCIALIST ECONOMY: CURRENCY UNIFICATION, BANKING REFORM AND CAPITAL MARKETS

Karl-Hans Hartwig

1. Socialist Economies and Systemic Transformation

Transforming an economic system means a radical change of its basic institutional principles: its property rights structure and its information and coordination structure. Traditionally the socialist economy is a centrally planned economy of the Soviet type. The structure of property rights (property rights order) is characterized by the overwhelming dominance of state ownership of the means of production. The essential characteristic of the coordination structure (planning order) is the detailed allocation by a centralized hierarchy of goods and services among producing and distributing organizations. This entails that the allocating bureaucracy issues binding plan targets to each organization for outputs and inputs. To secure plan fulfillment, the economic units are motivated by a system of premiums and bonus payments and monitored by central administrations.

Transformation of a socialist centrally planned economy involves the replacement of central planning and bureaucratic coordination by enterprise independence and market coordination, and a change in the property rights structure towards private and cooperative property. Although decentralization has been a central element of the reform concepts of the sixties in most of the socialist economies, the reforms failed (*Brus and Laski, 1989*). With the exception of Yugoslavia and Hungary, fundamental changes in the planning mechanism never occurred, and the dominance of state ownership of the means of production turned out to be a taboo. In the current decade the situation is changing dramatically. Now, after an economic slowdown of socialism, radical reforms and even a transformation into a market economy are under realization or are at least proposed in nearly all socialist countries.

Because economic systems are dominated by their planning and coordination structure as well as by the structure of property rights, all the other institutional arrangements of the economy are subordinated to and coordinated with both of these constitutional elements (*Hensel, 1977; Cassel, 1988*). Their radical change, therefore, demands complementary changes in the other institutional parts of the economic system (*Eucken, 1954*). A "supplementary order" of great importance in the transition from a centrally planned and controlled economy to a market economy is the monetary and financial system. The restructuring of money, credit and banking is a precondition for the efficient conduct of monetary policy and a well-functioning resource allocation by the market mechanism. To overcome its characteristic weaknesses and to match the new requirements emerging from current economic reforms the "monetary order" (the rules of the game in money and finance) and thus, of course, monetary policy, the banking structure and the allocation of credit and of capital resources have to differ considerably from its traditional socialist setting. This is obvious if one compares the functioning of money, credit and banking in the centrally planned economy in comparison with a reformed system.

2. Money and Banking in a Traditional Socialist Setting

The main features of the traditional socialist money and banking system are its subordination to the central planning mechanism and the intention to separate two types of money and two types of monetary flows (*Garvy, 1977; Hartwig, 1987*). The banking system acts as an arm of the central authorities. It is fully embedded in the central plan and has to secure the monetary alimentation of the planned activities and to control plan fulfillment.

2.1 Banking System

Because money enters the process only when the actual planning has already been made its importance is minor. Organized as a state-owned single mono-bank with branches and subordinated special banks, the state bank plays the usual role of a central bank and of a commercial bank. Besides being a bank of issue, it keeps the current accounts and deposits of enterprises and private households; it exclusively controls the supply of long-term and short-term credit to the consumption sector, manages the gold as well as the foreign exchange reserves, and carries out foreign payments. All parts of the state bank system have to check that the monetary funds are disbursed only for specific purposes.

Because money is totally supplied by the state bank system via credit operations, cash and all deposits in banks are liabilities of the state bank and represent high powered money or monetary base. Money supply itself is subject to central planning. Like physical planning, monetary stocks and flows are planned and coordinated by balancing methods. The result of the balancing procedure is the credit plan of the state bank which balances long-term and short-term credits on the assets side and money in the hands of the state sector and of the private sector on the liabilities side. The credit plan is used as the "money issuing directive" (*Ehlert, Hunstock and Tannert, 1984*).

2.2 Active and Passive Money

In the socialist economy money plays different roles (*Dembinski, 1988*). In the household sector money is a medium of choice. Anyone who possesses money is entitled to specify the period of time and the class of transactions in which he will spend it. Even if households are limited in their use of money, by shortage and by a small range of assets available to them, and if the buyers may not influence the volume and assortment of goods, the freedom of choice granted by money in principle exists. Therefore money in the household sector is active which means that money has influence on economic decisions. In the state productive sector money is essentially "passive" (*Brus, 1963*). Changes in prices and quantities do not respond to changes in the stock of enterprise money for two reasons: on the one hand, the range of choice open to enterprises is strictly limited, resources are allocated centrally and all receipts are channelled in fixed proportions into a number of earmarked funds; on the other hand, many ways exist for state enterprises to obtain money. Once a task is planned, the bank is bound to supply enough finance, even if the final transactions are more extensive and the final costs are higher than those originally estimated. Although producers cannot go into bankruptcy, they do face a "soft budget constraint" (*Kornai, 1986a*).

2.3 Two Distinct Monetary Problems

These institutional arrangements result in separate spheres of monetary circulation. This results from the rule that in the productive sphere transactions have to be conducted with deposit money, while those between households and enterprises and within the household sector are conducted with cash. For the monetary authorities, therefore, two distinct monetary problems exist. In the inter-enterprise sphere the state bank system has to perform the allocation of resources through the allocation of financial means. In the consumption sphere, where households are free to use their money, the problem is to avoid global monetary disequilibrium, which depends on the quantity of money in circulation. The easiest way to tackle the allocation problem is to generously provide firms with liquidity. In this way plan fulfillment is not hindered by financial constraints, and hindrances to the economic performance are negligible because of the institutional inactivity of enterprise money. To bring the monetary circulation in the consumption sphere into equilibrium, the state bank has to adjust the quantity of household money. While the money supply in the inter-enterprise sphere is endogenous, money supply in the consumption sphere is a control variable.

3. Money, Credit and Banking in a Reformed System

Even in the traditional environment of a centrally planned economy the socialist monetary, banking and credit system did not work effectively. Because of imperfections and inconsistencies in the central planning and coordination mechanism and in the incentive and motivation structure central authorities have not been successful in the allocation of financial resources nor in the control of money supply in the consumption sphere. Monetary central planning and a centralization of the monetary, banking and credit system, often compared with a "monetary straitjacket" (*Garvy, 1977*), could not prevent an automatism which extends credit to enterprises on request and leads, via scheduled and non scheduled wage payments, to an excess supply of money in the household sector (*Hartwig, 1987*).

The structure of the economic system is totally incapable of solving the monetary problems of the current economic reforms. As reforms increase enterprise independence, self management, and self financing the range of transactions into which money allows an enterprise to enter will expand, and the monetary problems will change. Firstly, the problem of allocation of financial resources in the inter-enterprise sphere is no longer a task of the state bank system. Secondly, economic equilibrium in this sphere loses its immunity to an excess supply of money. Excess liquidity being sterilized in the traditional system now becomes highly dangerous for the overall economic performance. The same lax monetary policy which traditionally was the surest way to handle the problem of allocation of financial means in the socialized sector, leads directly to shortages, bottlenecks, and price increases. Moreover, because reforms remove almost all devices that traditionally kept the two spheres of monetary circulation independent of one another, excess liquidity in the socialized sector now easily spills over to the consumption sphere (*Dembinski, 1988*). Inflationary pressure emerges which, in case of inflationary processes, distorts price relationships and calls into question their function as indicators of the relative scarcity of resources.

The de facto unification of the monetary circulation and of the role of money entails two different, and to some extent conflicting, dimensions of the monetary problems: the control of the overall quantity of money, which is a purely macro-economic problem, and the efficient allocation of financial resources within a large number of widely independent different economic units. No single institution, not even a state bank, is able to handle both problems simultaneously. For that very reason economic leadership in the centrally planned economies in the past tried to separate the monetary circulation into two spheres.

There is only one way (1) to control the overall quantity of money and (2) to allocate the financial resources given a specific quantity of money supplied: the creation of a two-tier banking system with a central bank at the top and a set of autonomous and competing commercial banks, supplemented by efficient money and capital markets. Contrary to the centrally planned economy with its unified centralized banking structure and its two spheres of monetary circulation, in the reformed socialist economy a unified monetary circulation has to be based upon a separated banking structure (*Hartwig, 1990*).

4. Monetary Problems in the Process of Transition

To require a new monetary, credit and banking system and smoothly working money and capital markets is one thing; to put it into practice is quite a different matter. This can be demonstrated by the experiences of Hungary and Yugoslavia. As the most advanced countries on the road of reforms, having started with the introduction of the market mechanism as early as the fifties and sixties, the reform of the monetary system has yet to be completed (*Gedeon, 1987; Erdoes, 1989*).

4.1 German Economic Unification

As has been noted recently, the transition from a capitalist to a socialist economic system has been described and analyzed in legions of books and essays. But no studies are available that might be used as a guide along the path from a centrally planned economy to a free market order. Whereas the other socialist economies have to create the institutional setting for a market system "from scratch", East Germany simply took over the institutional arrangements of West Germany. This means a very abrupt transition from a centrally planned economy to a market economy order. In some areas the introduction of new institutions will take some more time, but this is not so in the area of money, credit and banking. On July 1, 1990 the East German currency was replaced by the West German D-Mark as legal tender, medium of exchange, unit of account and store of value - an operation without a precedent in modern economic history. In line with the currency unification the Bundesbank's responsibilities were extended to cover the territory of the GDR.

The instant-approach of an early currency unification is anything but a textbook example. It operates as a crash program producing economic frictions and high transactions costs. Most economic experts therefore would have preferred a step-by-step approach with two currencies existing for a certain period of time using the exchange rate as a shock absorber for the East German economy, thus maintaining price competitiveness for East German companies for a time. In the light of pure economics first of all the institutional arrangements of a market order have to be created before implementing an intra-German currency union as a "culminating act". This would also have eased the transitional difficulties involved in adjusting wages and the social system and would have postponed the problem of the conversion of debts and liabilities of state enterprises. The current slowdown of the East German economy, therefore, still seems to be the logical consequence of the early currency union.

Even though this conclusion is correct from an economist's point of view, it lacks completeness. First of all, current unemployment, bankruptcies and the decline in industrial output are not only and not essentially the result of currency unification, but the burdens of four decades of state socialism. East Germany's industrial capital stock and public infrastructure is outmoded, the environment is heavily polluted, its service sector underdeveloped, and its manpower, management and economic behavior still influenced by attitudes developed under the previous command economy. The rapid transition to a market economy only brings to light all the distortions and inefficiencies in the socialist economy concealed in the past with some success. Poor competitiveness in terms of prices and quality standards, unemployment and inflation have been observed in the socialist countries, but the manifestation of these problems is changing and generally becoming more apparent.

Secondly, there are politico-economical reasons for using the instant-approach. The political reason was, however, that two currencies would not have stopped emigration from East to West Germany. It became more and more uncertain, whether East Germans would have been willing to continue to accept their own currency. The opening of the Berlin Wall left those looking for a better economic future with a chance to leave the GDR, thus burdening both states with incalculable risks and costs without any corresponding benefits in sight. Moreover, in the face of the elections forthcoming on March 18th, it was a strategical move to offer the West German D-Mark as a symbol of prosperity and stability. From the view of systemic transformation another aspect is much more important: the rapid monetary unification puts the whole economic system under a strong reform pressure. It acts as a vehicle of fundamental economic and political reforms. Experts who know about the difficulties and delays of socialist economic reforms and about the numerous ideological and personal reform-barriers will esteem the importance of such a pressure.

At the beginning the reform process in the GDR likewise pointed in the wrong direction - gradual reforms within the existing system. The Modrow-government was neither willing nor ready to transform the socialist economy into a market economy. In particular representatives had in mind the creation of a system based on a combination of market elements on the one hand and a central plan on the other. Likewise, the main task of the newly founded government trust agency was not privatization, as most western politicians and economists thought, but the restructuring and preservation of state ownership in case of a German unification (*Luft, 1990*). The result of this kind of reforms would have been the typical stop-and-go cycle of socialist reforms and counter-reforms originating from the fact that the first phase of more or less mild reforms never succeeded in achieving efficiency to a satisfactory degree (*Brus and Laski, 1989*).

With hindsight, in spite of the reservations of pure economics, the early currency union has been the fastest way to economic and political unification. Technically, the operation was performed without major problems. Economically, its success cannot be judged after such a short time, but there is hardly any doubt now that German monetary, economic and social unification offers the prospect of a rapid process of economic and social improvement in the former GDR.

While the problems connected with the transition from a centrally planned economy to a market economy are similar in all socialist countries, the question may be asked as to what extent the reform process in East Germany can serve as a model for systems transformation. In fact, with the exception of Korea, it cannot:

- German currency unification means the abolition not only of the East German currency, but a complete loss of sovereignty in monetary and, at least, in economic policy matters.
- Currency unification means an abrupt transition to a market economy with all consequences for prices, incomes, competitiveness, etc.
- Currency unification needs a strong economic partner, who, in the early stages of transition, is able to cushion the economic and social frictions of the restructuring process.

West Germany cannot offer a currency unification to Poland, Bulgaria and the whole rest of the socialist countries.

4.2 Some Lessons from East German Reform

Although the German monetary, economic and social unification cannot serve as a model for the other socialist countries which are at the beginning or in the midst of a multi-tier and lengthy process of transformation, it emphatically demonstrates the importance of radical monetary and financial reforms. This is of interest in so far as money, financial institutions and capital markets have been ignored or underestimated in most of the economic reform processes in the past. Hungary, for example, started with the introduction of a market economy order in 1968 but introduced a two-tier banking structure with a network of commercial banks 20 years later (*Erdoes, 1989*). Yugoslavia's decentralized socialist market economy created systematic laws in 1988 (*Cicin-Sain, 1990*). In the other socialist countries the restructuring of the monetary and financial system is in the phase of preparation or in the stage of discussion.

The reasons for the lack of monetary and financial reforms are manifold: inferiority of money in the socialist economy; lack of knowledge about the functioning of a market economy; the fear that independent organizations (enterprises, central bank, commercial banks) undermine the traditional power structure; the social implications expected from a tight monetary policy and from a banking system granting credits only by commercial criteria; ideological reservations. Especially commercial banks and capital markets are controversial on ideological grounds.

A further experience from the economic reform in East Germany is the fact that despite the necessity of a network of effective financial institutions and a tight monetary policy the GDR neither had the experience nor the instruments nor the human capabilities to implement such a radical reform. The rapid creation of a well-functioning monetary and banking system has been possible only under the discretion of the Bundesbank and with massive support of West German commercial banks. The Bundesbank established a network of regional branches in East Germany and is applying its regular monetary policy instruments in this area, too. An effective banking structure is being created by West German banks. Savings banks and cooperative banks in particular are deploying skilled and trained personnel to East German "partnership-banks" as consultants or in management positions on a good will basis. Employees of former GDR-banks were not able to carry out even simple banking operations necessary in a market system. They never learned banking business - all they had to do was execute central instructions. Poland is another example. There, the IMF is coordinating support of Western central banks in the fields of banking supervision, instruments of monetary policy, money market and short term securities, payments systems, foreign exchange market operations etc. The World Bank is mounting a parallel effort in the area of commercial banks (*Schrettl, 1990*).

4.3 Elements of a Monetary and Financial Reform

The general impression which is given by the reform process in East Germany as well as by all the other economic reforms in the socialist economics is that on the one hand only radical and rapid institutional changes in the direction of a market economy with private property offer the prospect of a process of economic and social improvement (*Sachs, 1990*); on the other hand, the process of transition needs time and foreign assistance especially in the field of institutional restructuring. This will be the case the more the population has become used to central planning and the more people have been strictly isolated from competition, behavior patterns oriented to market requirements, private property rights, and cost consciousness.

One of the vital prerequisites for the success of the reforms is monetary stability, above all for two reasons: First of all, prices are only capable of coordinating individual economic plans, and thus of steering production and distribution via the market, if they indicate the relative scarcity of resources as precisely as possible. This is achieved best on the basis of flexible individual prices, but a stable overall price level. Inflationary processes distort the price relations and lead to a misallocation of resources and impede the smooth operation of the market. Secondly, in socialist countries inflationary processes will weaken material and moral incentives to work and undermine the faith in economic reforms. After decades of price stability people are not willing to tolerate price increases for a sustained period. The reaction of the Soviet public when confronted with the relatively small-scale problem of cooperative price increases demonstrates the political explosiveness of open inflation in the socialist countries. Reform reluctance is growing, and reform opponents will find a good excuse for recentralization. Inflation for them provides legitimation for suppressing market forces and reviving tight bureaucratic control and central interventions (*Kornai, 1986b*).

Although monetary stability is a necessary precondition for reform success, inflation seems to be inevitable during the transition period in most of the socialist countries. The reasons are rooted deep in the socialist economic system. Decades of central planning and state property have left the economies ill prepared for undergoing the economic shock treatment which the rapid transition to a market economic system will entail. To diminish the social frictions emerging from reforms, to avoid riot and reform reluctance and, last but not least, to secure political power in the daybreak of democratic structures, governments will provide grants, subsidies, and employment programs financed by state bank credits. Furthermore, in connection with this, there may be a supply side aspect of inflation during the transition period. Because the structural reshaping of economies and the development of supply side forces proceeds only slowly, allowing prices to be set freely in the lack of competition and in the absence of active entrepreneurs initiates a process in which not only price relations are adjusted but the price level may increase as well (*Caselli and Pastorello, 1990*). At least, all socialist countries are more or less confronted with a monetary overhang at the beginning of the reform process as a legacy of the past (*Hartwig and Thieme, 1987*). In the traditional institutional setting, with prices tightly controlled and fixed for longer periods by central authorities, inflation has essentially a suppressed character. Under market conditions repressed inflation is transmitted into price inflation. Obviously, this only means a modification of its shape and not of its volume. But because visible price inflation is perceived more directly than repressed inflation and the functioning of a market economy is as yet not well understood, reform dissatisfaction will spread easily.

To avoid inflationary pressures in the early stage of transition and to create the basis for a future monetary stability the present monetary overhang has to be reduced as far as possible. There are three options at one's disposal: a currency reform introducing new "heavy money", inflationary adjustment by a once-and-for-all shock therapy or by a selective gradualism, and the sale of state property (housing stocks, firms, land) to private individuals. The choice of the most effective strategy is not easy. The initial situation differs from country to country and time to time. Estimations of the dimensions of excess money are hindered by the lack of statistical data (*Khandruev, 1990*).

Beside the problem of finding the adequate rate of conversion, enormous social conflicts are expected from a currency reform. Since average money balances are very small in most of the socialist countries, a currency reform would certainly damage medium and low earners. Moreover, under contemporary conditions it would be impossible to maintain secrecy about the preparations of a currency reform. As a consequence, propensity to keep current money balances will decline to zero and enormous allocationary shocks will spread out all over the economy.

A process of inflationary adjustment economically has the advantage that the selection of the correct rate of conversion is left to the market (*Kloten, 1990*). But the shock therapy, characterized by a radical price liberalization, entails the risk of a further inflationary acceleration. For most people a once-and-for-all price level adjustment, in the absence of past experiences, cannot be discerned from permanent inflationary pressures. A wage price spiral may be set in motion if monetary policy is accommodating. If not, unemployment will increase (*Welfens, 1990*). Gradualism via price increases, selected by the government, leads to a new form of misallocation of resources.

Compared with the other two principal methods of eliminating the monetary overhang, the sale of state property offers a very attractive solution. Indeed, it is not free of obstacles. To evaluate state-owned firms and to sell them in the absence of markets and clear evaluation procedures is difficult. Likewise, distributional problems will emerge because many balances are unequally distributed. Even criminal energy is released by privatization. The Soviet Mafia, for instance, is using the expanding network of private cooperatives and cooperative-banks in order to launder high amounts of black money hoarded in the past. Lastly, privatization does take some time. The sale of state property, nevertheless, has the great advantage of killing two birds with one stone: it allows the withdrawal of excess money and, at the same time, encourages privatization - an unavoidable step in the formation of efficient capital markets.

5. Perspectives

Because there is a lack of experience in the institutional settings of a market economy order and a lack of capital resources, the capital formation process, as well as the allocation process, is proceeding only slowly. Foreign support in forms of consultation, in forms of capital made available at the terms and conditions granted internationally and mainly in the form of foreign direct investment could fill the gap and have a major impact. Fears about "excessive foreign influence" and a "sell out" should be dismissed. In the case of the former GDR these fears have proven unfounded so far. The problem is not a sell out; on the contrary, the problem is that capital moves in too slowly.

One of the main difficulties in the creation of horizontal capital flows in all socialist countries will be the high level of uncertainty. The normal way to reduce the risk as seen from the side of capital-providing units is to come up with ample collateral. Collateral increases the net wealth of the capital seeking institutions, and it has to be the higher, the higher the uncertainty (*Schrettl, 1990*). A simple method to spread potential collateral is privatization, above all, of land because the value of physical capital is rather limited in all socialist economies. However, especially the privatization of land is one of the reform measures which is blocked up very often. The current discussion in the Soviet Union is a good example. Some reform plans tried to get around privatization of land. In some cases, although privatization is part of the reform plans, realization is hindered by reform opponents. Because privatization of land, on the one hand, is the cornerstone of transformation, but, on the other side, is one of the most controversial points on ideological grounds, enormous hindrances have to be overcome before reforms will succeed.

References

BRUS, WLODMIERZ (1963) Pieniadz w gospodarce socjalistycznej, Ekonomista, 5, 9-23.
BRUS, WLODMIERZ and LASKI, KAZIMIERZ (1989) From Marx to the Market: Socialism in Search of an Economic System, Oxford: Metropolis.
CASTELLI, GIAN P. and PASTORELLO, GABRIELE (1990) Poland 1990: From Plan to Market through Crash?, Forschungsberichte No. 166, The Vienna Institute for Comparative Economic Studies, Vienna.
CICIN-SAIN, ANTE (1990) The Role of Commercial and Central Banking: Yugoslavia, in: BOGOMOLOV, OLEG, ed., Market Forces in Planned Economies, London: Macmillan, 159-173.
DEMBINSKI, PAWEL H. (1988) Quantity Versus Allocation of Money: Monetary Problems of Centrally Planned Economies Reconsidered, Kyklos, 41, 281-300.
EHLERT, WILLI, HUNSTOCK, DIETHELM and TANNERT, KARLHEINZ (1984) Geld und Kredit in der DDR, Berlin: Die Wirtschaft.
ERDOES, T. (1989) Monetary Regulation and its Perplexities in Hungary, Acta Oeconomica, 40, 1-16.
EUCKEN, WALTER (1954) Grundlagen der Nationalökonomie, Stuttgart: Fischer.
GARVY, GEORGE (1977) Money, Financial Flows, and Credit in the Soviet Union, Cambridge Mass: Ballinger.
GEDEON, SHIRLEY, J. (1987) Monetary Disequilibrium and Bank Reform Proposals in Yugoslavia - Paternalism and the Economy, Soviet Studies, Vol. 39, 281-291.
HARTWIG, KARL-HANS (1987) Monetäre Steuerungsprobleme in sozialistischen Planwirtschaften, Stuttgart: Fischer.
HARTWIG, KARL-HANS and THIEME, H. JOERG (1987) Determinanten des Geld- und Kreditangebots in sozialistischen Planwirtschaften, in: THIEME, H. JOERG, 2nd, Geldtheorie, zud. ed., Muenchen: Nomos, 217-240.
HARTWIG, KARL-HANS (1990) The Role of Commercial and National Banking in a Reformed Socialist Economy: Comment, in: BOGOMOLOW, OLEG, ed., Market Forces in Planned Economies, London: Macmillan, 191-196.
HENSEL, K. PAUL (1977) Systemvergleich als Aufgabe, Stuttgart: Fischer.
KHANDRUEV, ALEXANDER (1990) Monetary Aspects of the Stabilization, Nomisma, 1, 43-51.
KLOTEN, NORBERT (1990) Beseitigung des Geldueberhangs und Inflationsbekämpfung, Deutsche Bundesbank, Auszuege aus Presseartikeln, 79, 11-12.
KORNAI, JANOS (1986a) The Soft Budget Constraint, Kyklos, 39, 3-30.
KORNAI, JANOS (1986b) The Hungarian Reform Process: Visions, Hopes and Reality, Journal of Economic Literature, Vol. 24.
LUFT, HANS (1980) Probleme des gesellschaftlichen Eigentums in der DDR, Wirtschaftswissenschaft, Vol. 38, 1027-1035.
SACHS, JEFFRY (1990) What has to be done?, The Economist, January 13, 1990.
SCHRETTL, WOLFRAM (1990) Transition in Depression: Soviet Monetary Issues, Osteuropa-Institut München, Working Papers No. 140, München.
WELFENS, PAUL J.J. (1990) Economic Reforms in Eastern Europe: Problems, Options and Opportunities, Paper prepared for testimony before United States Senate, Small Business Committee, Washington D.C.

COMMENTS ON: TRANSFORMING A SOCIALIST ECONOMY: CURRENCY UNIFICATION, BANKING REFORM AND CAPITAL MARKETS

Juergen Klose

At the very beginning I want to express my agreement with most statements of the paper, but I also have the requirement to offer some ideas from the standpoint of an economist of the former GDR.

This comment is focussing on only one question: What are the macroeconomic advantages and disadvantages of the "super shock therapy" for the transition of the economy of the former GDR into a social market economy?

Since the idea of a German Monetary Union (GMU) as an important part of a comprehensive German Economic and Monetary Union (GEMU) has occurred and its implementation became a necessity many discussions among economists, financiers, bankers, and entrepreneurs about the two fundamental possibilities and their variants of such a process have taken place. A GMU is to be understood as the establishment of a unified monetary system in the whole of Germany by introduction of the DM in the territory of the former GDR and extension of the monetary authority of the Bundesbank as well as introduction of a market oriented banking system and unrestricted money and capital markets in East Germany. Thus the Deutsche Bundesbank will assume monetary sovereignty in the uniform currency area of Germany.

The first possibility of a GMU was the step-by-step approach (transitional program) where the introduction of the DM in the territory of the former GDR would have taken place after a transitional period of transforming a former centrally planned economy into a social market economy. In the meantime the monetary sovereignty would remain with the central banks of the two states and a fixed exchange rate between the two currencies would have been determined. This was the way to a GMU also favored by the Deutsche Bundesbank in the first steps of the preparation activities, and this was in full conformity with the opinions of most German economists because shocks arising from transition could be diminished with a reasonable exchange rate between the two currencies. But the second possibility of a GMU (the instant approach or the shock therapy) was selected by the government of the FRG with the variant of a "super shock therapy" by the immediate introduction of the DM in the territory of the former GDR and the extension of the monetary sovereignty of the Deutsche Bundesbank to that part of Germany.

This also was agreed upon in the State Treaty between the two German governments because of three main political reasons:

a) to reduce the flow of emigrants from East to West Germany significantly,
b) to satisfy the expectations of most citizens of the former GDR who anticipated quick economic improvement and to utilize this in the forthcoming elections to the provincial parliaments of the five new Bundeslaender in October 1990 and to the Bundestag of the united Germany in December 1990 in favor of the CDU,
c) to realize the unique opportunity of the German unification within a historically short period of time as a prerequisite of which the GEMU had to be established.

The GMU is a unique case in the transition of a centrally planned into a social market economy and has some special characteristics:

- It is part of the unification of two states while the former socialist state is disappearing,
- total liquidation of the former socialist economic system with all its structures and institutions and taking over the economic model and legal system of the stronger state with a social market economy,
- establishment of a uniform currency area by introduction of another convertible currency and total liquidation of the former nonconvertible currency of the state with a centrally planned economy,
- very short period of transition.

In this respect the GMU cannot serve as a model for transforming the economies in the Central and East European countries. But for the future there are two cases where this model might be imaginable: first the two Korean states and second the special case of help for Cuba eventually by USA. In both cases the experience of the GMU could be utilized in the transition of these two states to a market economy because there is no chance that they could establish a successful socialist economic system.

The way in which monetary and financial questions within the economic transition are settled has a decisive impact on all other elements of the transformation, e.g. the GMU is determining the course of the German Economic and Social Union. The "super shock therapy" has a couple of benefits but also disadvantages for the political, economic and social situation in the new Germany.

Disadvantages are:

a) The radical change of the whole life in the former GDR involves a heavy burden for the new Germany which brings the country to the limits of its economic strength and creates the danger of temporary economic weakness which could have many negative internal and external consequences,

b) the immediate raising of huge funds to finance the high costs of this variant of a GMU causes enormous budget deficits. They are now at 140 billion DM and are expected to rise to 200 billion DM in 1991. This creates additional financial burdens to the budget as interest is rising and the heavy demand for loans makes the interest rates increase. The share of interest payments in the federal expenditures is expected to rise from 9.3% in 1990 to 17% in 1994. So a high part of budget deficits and interest payments has to be paid by the coming generation.

c) the introduction of the DM from July 1, 1990 in the former GDR creates an enormous extension of money supply while the production in this part of the new Germany is declining. That means that money supply is not acting according to the evolution of production. As GNP of the former GDR is estimated at 10-15% of the Federal Republic's GNP the figure of money supply M_3 may rise by 125-180 billion DM in the territory of the former GDR. But now M_3 here has reached 250 billion DM. That means that 70-125 billion DM plus the budget deficits of the five new Bundeslaender must be closed down by conversion of a certain share of savings into property titles in the course of reprivatization. Otherwise the danger of inflation could occur. Price increases in the five new Bundeslaender caused by heavy demand already exist in some sectors especially cars, certain consumer goods, services, etc. But this inflation as a consequence of high money supply is not incorporated in the official inflation rate of the new FRG because of lack of the corresponding data base,

d) a further macroeconomic impact and disadvantage of the "super shock therapy" within the GMU resulting from the financial burdens is a possible diminishing role of Germany in the framework of international help for Central and East European as well as developing countries. In this field also the policy of the former GDR assistance to developing countries cannot be continued,

e) the growing concentration of West German investors in the Eastern part of Germany could lead to a weaker role of Germany as a main exporter of capital and that could disappoint some aspirations in Central and East European as well as developing countries,

f) in the two parts of Germany a different economic situation as a consequence of the "super shock therapy" has occurred. The slogan "West is booming, East is consuming" is only the reflection of an insufficient result of this variant of the GMU as a consequence of too little time for restructuring enterprises in the five new Bundeslaender. Unfortunately the Eastern part of Germany is considered only as a goods and services market but not yet as a region for investments. So it is no miracle that the production capacities in the west of Germany are utilized by more than 90%. This is the realization of a dream of every entrepreneur. The still booming economy in the Western part of the new Germany is mostly based on the economic weakness of the five new Bundeslaender in the East. Also in the future there is a strong impact of this kind,

g) the introduction of a strong hard currency in an economically weak country as the former GDR increases its low international competitiveness and that is why the already dear exports because of high cost of production become still more expensive as a consequence of the applied exchange rate. Thus in the former GDR a heavy revaluation took place resulting in the increase of export prices. On the other hand imports are becoming cheaper. The result is that imports are growing and exports stagnating. With that East Germany is contributing to a certain decrease of the surplus in the trade balance of the united Germany. This and the extended delivery from West to East Germany may lead to a diminishing role of Germany as a main exporter of goods and services,

h) the most disappointing result of the "super shock therapy" is the extremely high rate of unemployment of 27% in November 1990. This rate is expected to increase even more because all enterprises are looking to improve their efficiency and especially by dismissing labor force. The intended comprehensive system of creating new jobs by new investments, retraining of unemployed East Germans and social measures is not yet working. The high costs for financing the unemployment should better be pumped into the creation on a favorable investment climate with low taxes, higher investment allowance, settlement of property issues, governmental financing the old environmental damages (Altlasten) of the enterprises, rapid improvement of the infrastructure, making available business space for new enterprises and the fast strengthening of the new provincial governments,

i) the success of reducing the flow of inhabitants from the five new Bundeslaender to the West after the introduction of the DM in the former GDR has disappeared because the worsening economic situation in this part of Germany has become more complicated and wages as well as salaries in the western part of Germany are still three times higher. Also the number of East Germans who are moving every day to work in the Western parts of Germany and Berlin has steadily increased in the last months. All this is causing additional difficulties in both parts of

Germany. In Western Germany housing problems are growing and the high offer of labor force is diminishing the possibilities to increase wages and salaries in a booming economy. In the former GDR highly qualified workers and scientists are leaving their homes and causing a lack in the labor market during the course of reconstruction of the economy. Thus far, this target of the "super shock therapy" for the former GDR has not been fulfilled.

Naturally, the "super shock therapy" variant of the GMU also has a lot of benefits that could compensate the above mentioned disadvantages:

Advantages:

a) The chance of a quick restructuring of the former GDR on the basis of a market economy and with that the establishment of a new Germany with a strong and healthy economy in the framework of a unifying Europe could be implemented. After the period when the whole of Germany is concentrating its economic power on the reconstruction of the five new Bundeslaender the new German state could take over higher responsibility for political and economic world affairs. It is likely that Germany will reach a stronger position in the EC, in Europe, and in the whole world,

b) the rate of emigrants leaving the five new Bundeslaender slightly decreased on an average because more East Germans see a chance to improve their living standard in that part of Germany,

c) the "super shock therapy" creates very high pressure on all enterprises to reconstruct a modern business on a corporate level of the market economy looking for partners in co-operation and extending their position in internal and international markets,

d) a quick retraining of labor force is required by the complicated economic situation as approximately half of the working population of East Germany has to learn a new profession or to reach higher sophistication by advanced study. This could lead to better meeting the requirements of the future labor market in Eastern Germany,

e) the new provincial governments are obliged to quickly organize their activities and take over their extended competences in restructuring the new Bundeslaender especially in improving infrastructure and investment climate,

f) the GMU with its "super shock therapy" contributed to a fast and comprehensive integration of the former GDR into the EC because with the economic and monetary unification of

Germany on July 1, 1990, three months before the official national unification of the two German states, the former GDR became a de-facto member of the EC as part of the uniform economic and currency area of Germany. The EC is regarding this new part of its territory in a transitional period as a region with a declining economy and a strong agricultural structure and has guaranteed net flow of financial help (taken temporarily by the government of the FRG) as well as many exceptions of EC regulations especially in the sectors of environment, agriculture and trade with third countries.

In summary, the "super shock therapy" variant of the GMU shows close connections between political aims and economic decisions and is likely to shorten the transitional period of the East German economy to a social market economy and lead to the faster establishment of a politically and economically strong united Germany at the cost of high financial and social burdens for the population, even for the coming generation. Thus, this "super shock therapy" was only the "second best" solution.

II. National Challenges

LABOR MARKETS AND SOCIAL SECURITY SYSTEMS FACING UNIFICATION: SYSTEMIC CHALLENGES IN GERMANY

Doris Cornelsen

1. Introduction

The changes in East Germany have occurred with breathtaking speed. Beginning with the 9th of November, there was only a very short time period to discuss the possible avenues of further development. Already in the early 1990s the people of Eastern Germany had been unambiguous in expressing their wish for unification with the Federal Republic of Germany. Meanwhile the foundations had been laid and unification had taken place.

Like all the other countries of Eastern Europe, the former GDR lacked the elementary basis required for a market economy to take hold. Certain structures must be in place for markets and market economies to function correctly. These include the whole legal and institutional framework to establish markets and competition. In the case of the GDR, unification with the Federal Republic of Germany has provided it with a secure foundation. It was decided to adopt the whole legal and administrative framework of Western Germany. In the first State Treaty (*Vertrag über die Schaffung einer Währungs-, Wirtschafts- und Sozialunion zwischen der Bundesrepublik Deutschland und der Deutschen Demokratischen Republik vom 18. Mai 1990*) the principles of the adoption had been laid down. The second State Treaty (*Vertrag zwischen der Bundesrepublik und der Deutschen Demokratischen Republik über die Herstellung der Einheit Deutschlands - Einigungsvertrag - vom 31. August 1990*) settled the details.

There was some discussion about this move, however. The legal and social framework in the Federal Republic of Germany had for many years developed in line with specific economic and social structures. Conditions in the former GDR are quite different in many respects. Also there are features in the framework of the FRG which are not quite satisfactory either. A resolution of these issues in connection with unification would have been favorable. However, under the circumstances a fast solution was better than a perfect one. Thus Eastern Germany was able to avoid the long and hard debate of how to change the system - a major obstacle to systemic changes in all the countries of Eastern Europe.

Unification is obviously a challenge for both sides of Germany. In East Germany, the population is faced with new economic and social conditions; the enterprises are suddenly confronted with competition in the global economy. To adopt new rules means changes in all the former habits. In West Germany, to cope with the financial burden of unification is a big task too.

2. Labor Markets

In the field of the labor markets, conditions in the two parts of Germany are very different. In the West, there is sustained economic growth, and the number of jobs has increased in the last year while unemployment has gone down. This development took place in spite of a difficult global economy and is partly due to the big demand push from the East. In the East, abrupt confrontation with international competition showed all the weaknesses of the planned economy. Some areas are no longer competitive and had to close down or at least to reduce the work force. Other areas have to be developed almost from scratch; new skills and qualifications are necessary.

2.1 Facts and Figures

In the field of labor markets, there are four aspects to consider:
- the migration to the West
- the commuters to the West
- the unemployment
- part-time workers (or underemployment).

As far as migration is concerned, there are two sets of statistics as of July 1st, both of them with different omissions. The Statistical Office in the West had registered all the immigrants but did not register people going back again: thus the real figure might be lower. The Statistical Office in the East registered all emigrants from the GDR who gave notice of their departure: thus the real figure might be higher. With economic union on the 1st of July, the approach to statistics in the West has changed completely. Migration from East to West is now treated like internal migration in Germany, the final results of which are usually published very late. The only statistical record since July is that of East Germany.

Anyway, migration to the West was especially high in 1989. According to Eastern statistics, 244 000 people left the country (Western statistics: 344 000). In the first half of 1990, another 175 000 went to the West (Western statistics: 238 000). It is estimated that around 70% were of working age. So in 1989 and in the first half of 1990 2.5% of the population or 3.1% of the labor force (Western statistics: 3.5; 4.2%) left the country. Eastern statistics show a total of 89 000 migrants in July/September, which is an increase compared with the preceding months.

A new feature is the number of commuters, living in the East and going to work in the West, especially in Berlin. This number is estimated to be around 100 000 in this year. Migration and commuting concern both parts of Germany. In the West, the new inhabitants compete with the old ones for jobs. Commuting is a special concern of the West German Trade Unions because they fear dumping in the field of wages. However, up to now it has been possible to integrate migrants and commuters without big problems. In the East, migration and commuting lighten the burden of unemployment. It is, however, a sort of brain drain because the percentage of young and qualified people in this group is high.

Unemployment had been unknown in the past of the GDR. Full employment was only maintained, however, through the inefficient use of labor. The changing framework had already resulted in growing unemployment (see *Table 1*). In November, there were about 590 000 unemployed in the country. The average unemployment rate amounted to 6.6%; in structurally weak regions, the rate was much higher.

Table 1: Unemployed and Part-Time Workers
(September 30, 1990)

	Unemployed		*Part-Time Workers*	
State	Persons	Unemployment Ratio (%)	Persons	Part-Time Workers Ratio (%)
Mecklenburg/ Vorpommern	68 928	6.2	174 134	15.7
Brandenburg	70 826	5.1	334 592	24.0
Sachsen-Anhalt	75 999	4.7	360 567	22.2
Sachsen	111 299	4.2	533 589	20.3
Thueringen	74 189	5.4	298 000	21.8
Berlin (Ost)	43 584	6.1	69 794	9.8
Total	444 825	5.0	1 771 576*	20.0*

* Revised total: 1 728 700; revised ratio: 19.4%.

A special feature is the number of part-time workers. This does not mean part-time work of one's own free will, but part-time work because of economic problems. According to West German law, social support is made available when enterprises face temporary difficulties. They are allowed to introduce part-time work for their employees, and unemployment insurance makes up the difference up to about two-thirds of the former net wages (63% for singles and 68% for married people). Thus in many cases open unemployment can be avoided. In Eastern Germany, the number of those part-time jobs has increased rapidly in the last months. In the final figure for October (1.77 Mill. people), the ratio is different in the various branches (see *Table 2 and 3*). The reduction in working time is different, too:

part time workers % of workers	working time % of normal time
25	less than 25
43	25 to 50
20	50 to 75
12	more than 75

So, in total, 25% of the working force was affected either by unemployment or by shorter hours.

2.2 Perspectives

The labor market in Eastern Germany is facing a severe test. Necessary structural change will cause another mass of unemployed or part-time workers; it is difficult to predict when the economy will be in balance again. Assessments of the future development have to take into account several points:

- The structure of the GDR economy had been based on the political idea of autarky. This had been combined with insufficient integration into international trade relationships. Whatever possible was produced at home. Thus many old, inefficient and noncompetitive industries were artificially maintained. Structural changes did not occur to the necessary extent. Compared with Western industrialized countries, the percentage of the labor force in agriculture and industry was high; the percentage of the labor force in trade and services was low. Structural change therefore will be combined with shrinking employment especially in agriculture and industry.

Table 2: Unemployment and Part-Time Work in the GDR in 1990

	Unemployed				Part-Time Workers		
	Number	Male (%)	Female (%)	Unemployment rate (%)	Number	Number of firms	Part-Time work rate
January	7 400	86.5	13.5	0.1			
February	11 000	64.5	35.5	0.1			
March	38 300	58.2	41.8	0.4			
April	64 900	58.1	41.9	0.7			
May	94 800	57.1	42.9	1.1			
June	142 100	51.3	48.7	1.6			
July	272 000	48.3	51.7	3.1	656 277	6 029	7.4
August	361 300	46.8	53.2	4.1	1 499 872	17 088	16.9
September	444 800	45.0	55.0	5.0	1 728 700	20 308	19.4
October	537 800			6.0	1 767 000		19.9
November							
December							

Source: Zentrale Arbeitsverwaltung der DDR

Table 3: Part-Time Work in the GDR in September 1990

	Part-Time Workers		
	Number	Part-Time Work Rate (%)	increase from previous month (%)
GDR Total*	1 771 576	20.0	23.1
of which:			
Energy	110 258	48.1	4.4
Chemicals	120 610	36.4	28.4
Metallurgy	101 098	74.1	-32.5
Engineering and metal construction	252 059	29.4	31.2
Electrotechnics	149 301	32.4	8.9
Light industry	33 673	7.3	-28.6
Textiles	96 761	45.0	-12.1
Construction	57 233	10.2	-7.2
Agriculture and forestry	260 916	28.3	-1.0

* revised total number 1 728 700; total ratio: 19.4%; and total increase: 20.1%.

Source: Zentrale Arbeitsverwaltung der DDR

- In many branches of the GDR economy the labor force had not been efficiently used. There was a remarkable amount of hidden unemployment, which will become open unemployment sooner or later. Hidden unemployment in the economy is estimated to be about 15% of the labor force.

- On the other hand the service sector is expected to expand. Small and medium sized enterprises in all sectors, which have had no place in the economy of the past, are already beginning to be established. From January to September 1990 about 200 000 new businesses were reported.

- The volume of the labor force in East Germany had already been reduced by retiring the old age pensioners, who had formerly been employed in many branches (total of formerly employed pensioners: 270 000), and by the discharge of the foreign workers, mainly from Vietnam, who had worked in the GDR on the basis of limited contracts with their home countries (total of formerly employed foreigners: 100 000). Early retirement, migration and commuting too will reduce the number of unemployed.

As a result the German Economic Research Institutes in their test publication (autumn 1990) had come to the following estimation: the number of unemployed in 1991 in Eastern Germany will reach an average of 1.4 million people; the unemployment rate will be as high as 17.5%. In addition to this, 1.75 million part-time workers are estimated. This estimate is on the optimistic side of the possible assessments. It is supposed that in mid-1991 a certain recovery of the economy will take place.

2.3 The Legal Framework

As mentioned before, the legal framework in the GDR prevented open unemployment in the past. The enterprises themselves had to care for their employees. If there were jobs to be abolished, the enterprises had to offer new jobs, either in the same company or in another one. Thus there was no risk of being unemployed and unemployment insurance had been dropped in 1978. In the first half of 1990, the government of Modrow issued some special laws in this field: to offer payments out of the public purse (around 70% of the former net wages) to the unemployed, to introduce the possibility of early retirement and to offer retraining for new qualifications.

On the basis of the first state treaty, the legal system of the Federal Republic of Germany is now in force in East Germany, too (1 July 1990). The central labor administration (Bundesanstalt fuer Arbeit) is responsible for the united Germany in the field of labor market and unemployment insurance. In East and West the employed and the employer have to pay a certain percentage of gross wages into this insurance; unemployment payments are based on the former net wage (63% for singles and 68% for married people). The legal status of part-time work in Eastern Germany is less restrictive than its counterpart in the West. Part-time work in the East is supported even if the prospects of the enterprise are not very good. Part-time workers' payments are 63 or 68% of their former net wages. In some special wage contracts the enterprises have to pay another 22%, so the income in the case of part-time work amounts to 85 - 90% of full time net wage. Besides this, public support with respect to promoting qualification and new skills is offered.

The Modrow-Government had already introduced the possibility of early retirement for older unemployed people. At that time, it had been possible to retire five years before the regular age limit (60 for women and 65 for men). According to the second State Treaty, beginning on the 1st of January 1991, everybody in East Germany can retire at the age of 57. The payment will be the same as in the case of unemployment: 63% or 68% respectively of the former net income.

2.4 The Promotion of Skills, Training

One main point in the whole bunch of measures to improve the situation on the labor market is the promotion of skills. In general, most observers agree that the average level of training in East Germany is quite good. The system of education was oriented to everybody obtaining vocational training. The percentage of unskilled people in the labor force is very low. The traditional German dual system of vocational training both in school and in the workplace had brought about a quite reasonable level of skills. But some areas, especially modern accounting, financing and marketing, were absolutely neglected during the time of the planned economy. In the production area, many old and outdated production procedures were followed, and modern skills had not been taught to the necessary extent. Now there is a great need for training, not only of unemployed, but in the work force too.

Up to now this problem has not been solved. It is very difficult to determine the best direction of training because nobody really knows the necessary structure of skills in the future. Besides this, there are not enough institutions and teachers in Eastern Germany to initiate new education. Finally, the high level of payments, especially for part-time workers, creates little motivation for learning new skills. The number of people in training up to now is remarkable: around 75 000 - but much below the necessary level.

3. Social Security Systems: Health Insurance, Old-Age Pensions

3.1 The Systems of Social Security

Social security systems in Germany have a long history. In general, they include health insurance, old age pensions, and insurance in case of accidents, all regulated by law, compulsory for most employees and financed by the contribution of both employees and employers.

In the GDR, the old roots of the systems of social insurance had been, in principle, maintained. But in the 40 years of socialism special features had evolved. Compared with the manifold systems in Western Germany, the system in the GDR was a very simple one. There was, in principle, one big institution for the different branches of social security, which collected the contributions and distributed the benefits. In fact, the only distinction was that concerning wage earners versus self-employed and members of cooperatives; accordingly, there were two different administrative units. Compulsory insurance was almost universal. An individual's contribution to social insurance was made in accordance with earnings, liable to deduction up to a limit of 600 Marks monthly. Ten percent of this had to be paid by the employee, another 12.5% by the employer. In addition to this, social insurance funds were fed to an increasing degree by contributions to the Voluntary Supplementary Pension Insurance, which was, in fact, a compulsory insurance, too, for which workers and employees earning more than 600 Marks monthly were eligible.

Social insurance benefits were financed through social insurance contributions and out of the state budget. But contributions were not adjusted to increasing expenditures. So social insurance was not self-financing and its institutions were increasingly dependent on grants from the state budget. According to the most recent figures, the state budget had to pay about 50% of the expenditures in this field.

In general, benefits in the GDR were reasonable where the efficiency of the society was concerned (e.g. health care); they were low, sometimes even at a minimum, in cases of people outside of the working population (old age payments). The basis on which pensions were calculated was similar to the practice prevailing in the Federal Republic, i.e. based upon years of paying contributions and income. But there was no periodic "dynamic adjustment" to incomes in the GDR. The levels of pensions were much lower than in the West, and there was very little difference between the lowest and the highest monthly payment. Most of the retired people got the average amount of payments. Provided normal working life and average income, the old-age payment in the GDR amounted to about 55% of the former net income; the ratio in West Germany is about 70%.

Now it has been decided to take over social security systems existing in Western Germany, with some special regulations with respect to timing. The Western system is somewhat different in organization, contributions and benefits. There is no single institution responsible for all the branches. In particular, health insurance is broken down into many different units according to profession and branch.

Thus the single administrative unit of the former GDR will be divided into several different units. Beginning on the 1st of January 1991, there will be a special health insurance with many independent branches. At the same time, old age insurance will be split into the institution for blue-collar and white collar workers in line with the West German organization.

Adjustment in the level of the social insurance contribution took place on the 1st of July 1990. At this time the percentage of the contribution had been increased remarkably:

- health insurance: 12.8%
- old age funds: 18.8%
- unemployment insurance: 4.3%

The total - 35.9% - will be paid for by the employer and the employee in equal shares.

3.2 Health Insurance

Major services and benefits for the insured and their families in the event of sickness were similar in both parts of Germany. They are comprised of medical treatment, medicines, treatment in hospitals and sickness benefits. There were some differences, though: in Eastern Germany sickness benefits had been paid by the social security system, beginning with the first day of sickness. In the West, the first 6 weeks of sickness are covered by the employer, the social insurance system kicking in only after 6 weeks. In Eastern Germany, there had been full coverage of medicines by social security; in the West the insured people have to pay part of the costs. Health insurance benefits will be adapted to the Western Germany system on the 1st of January 1991. Besides this, the whole structure of health care is expected to change in the future.

In the past, the Eastern German health sector was organized by the state, in ambulances and clinics. There had been very few private doctors. For a long time this model worked quite well. The number of medical people per 1000 of the population was almost as high as in Western Germany. But in the last years economic problems had caused severe neglect of the health care system. The ambulances and clinics were badly equipped and the average income in the health sector unsatisfactory. Thus large numbers of doctors had left the country by 1989. Now a structure is developing similar to that of Western Germany, with private doctors and hospitals. The second state treaty has stated that, in the beginning of the social union, the price of medicine and medical treatment shall remain well below the western level. But this will only last for a short time, until the level of prices and the cost of the health care are equal in both parts of Germany.

3.3 Old-age Insurance

The existing old-age system of East Germany will exist up to the end of 1991. But a law has already been passed to implement some basic features of the West German benefits, as of the 1st of July 1990. The main idea is to bring about the same ratio of pensions compared with net income as to be found in Western Germany. People working all their lives and earning an average income will get old-age payments of about 70% of their former net income. The second idea is to peg the old-age payment more closely to the working income, thus installing a more differentiated distribution in accordance with distribution of income. A calculation model was developed to adjust all the existing pensions to the new guiding principles. All the existing old-age payments had to be recalculated, in all about 3 million pensions. It was very surprising that the former GDR administration was able to manage this task in a very short time (see *Table 4*). Altogether there was an increase of the payments of about 30%, beginning mid-year 1990. It had already been decided to increase the level of pensions by 15% on the 1st of January 1991, which will further improve the situation of retired people.

Because many of the older people in East Germany get very low pensions even under the new regulations, a special solution has been found. Their monthly payment will be a baseline 495 DM, irrespective of the calculated amount. The difference is financed by the state budget, not by social security system funds. According to the law, this sort of "minimum payment" will last until mid-1995.

Table 4: Amount of Rents

Type of Benefits	12/31/89 Marks		7/1/90 DM	
	Men	Women	Men	Women
Old age payments	526	418	663	502
Old age payments including voluntary supplementary pension insurance (FZR)	632	454	798	548
Disablement payments	499	462	616	586
Disablement payments including FZR	643	529	793	672
Orphans' pensions	169		207	
Widows' pensions	264	327	-	-
Disablement old age payments	501	409	639	516
Disablement old age payments including FZR	615	452	784	572

According to polls, 56% of retired people interviewed stated they would get higher pensions under the new regulations; 41% of the interviewed will get the same amount as before; 5% will get the minimum payment.

4. Financing of the Social Security Systems

In Western Germany, social security system benefits are financed in general by contributions. Contributions are determined by expenditures; thus in the last decades the percentage of income to be paid to the social security systems had been gradually increased. Grants of the state budget are paid for the old-age payments and for the unemployment insurance. But this principle is not applied everywhere. The health insurance plan works without those grants.

The state grant for the old-age payment amounts to about 18% of the expenditures. This grant is fixed by law in an absolute amount, regardless of the financial situation of the old-age insurance plan. The state grant for unemployment insurance is a compensation in case of deficits in this branch of the social security system, and surpluses of former years have to be taken into account. So the state grant is dependent on the level of unemployment and is subject to changes from year to year.

With social union of the two parts of Germany, the same revenue structure will be applied in both parts: contributions by the insured and grants from public funds (fixed amount in the old-age insurance, deficit compensation in the unemployment insurance). Calculations have shown that in the East the social security systems concerning health and old-age payments can function under these regulations. The people in Eastern Germany have to pay the same percentage of their income as the people in the West. Because of lower gross income, the revenue of the social security systems will certainly be lower than in the West. But since the benefits are combined with the income level, the expenditures in the East will be lower, too. Thus it was hoped these systems will work the same way they do in Western Germany. Unemployment insurance will work anyway because of the deficit compensation.

But in the beginning of the social union there was a deficit in the coffers of the Eastern social security systems. As it turned out, this was mostly due to confusion in administration. In the past, the employers used to pay their contributions two months late. So, after social union the necessary revenues were not there. Besides this, it was decided to collect contributions through tax revenue offices.

But in fact, there was no well developed tax revenue administration in Eastern Germany. So the deficits in the security systems increased very rapidly. Benefits, then, could only be paid because money was available from several sources - starting financial support by the Federal Republic of Germany, contributions by the State budget of East Germany, and credits.

Obviously the short term confusion will not last forever. But some doubts remain about the financial structure of the social security systems in Eastern Germany.

As far as old age pensions are concerned, calculations were based on the structures of 1990. But it has already been decided to increase the pensions by 15% in January 1991 and there might be another increase by 10% in July 1991. Thus there are some doubts about the financial situation in 1991 and the years to follow. The situation in health insurance is difficult to survey because the whole structure of the health care certainly will change. The level of expenditure in this part of the social security system could increase faster than the level of contributions.

The critical burden on the social security system will be the high level of unemployment. The payments in this branch will be much higher than the contributions. Assuming 1.4 million unemployed and 1.75 million part-time workers, the deficit in the balance will be about 25 billion DM in 1991. Altogether, there is an expected deficit in the social security systems of 7 billion DM in 1990 and of 34 billion DM in 1991 (see *Table 5*).

In the framework of a united Germany, the benefits of the social system must be guaranteed, irrespective of the revenues. Therefore, contributions from West to East are inevitable.

Table 5: Revenue and Expenditure of the Social Security Systems
Second Half 1990 and Year 1991
(Billion DM)

	Old Age Insurance		Health Insurance		Unemployed Insurance	
	2/90	1991	2/90	1991	2/90	1991
Revenue	11.95	29.67	10.65	22.68	2.4	4.5
Contributions						
Employer	5.4	9.8	3.6	6.7	1.2	2.25
Employee	5.1	9.3	3.6	6.7	1.2	2.25
Self-employed	0.55	1.1	0.7	1.0	-	-
Contributions for						
Part-Time workers	0.55	1.4	0.5	1.9	-	-
Unemployed	0.35	2.1	0.7	2.9	-	-
Early retired	-	0.17	-	0.23	-	-
Health insurance for pensioners	-	-	1.55	3.25	-	-
State grant	-	5.4	-	-	-	-
Expenditure	13.8	33.2	9.5	22.0	7.45	29.65
Money transfers	12.2	29.4	2.0	4.0	4.85	19.95
Public consumption	-	-	7.5	18.0	0.5	1.0
Social insurance contributions	1.6	3.8	-	-	2.10	8.7
Revenue - Expenditure	-1.85	-3.53	+1.0	+0.28	-5.05	-25.15
Starting subsidy	+2.85	-	-	-	+5.6	+3.0
Financial balance	+1.0	-3.53	+1.0	+0.68	+0.55	-22.15

Source: DIW

5. Conclusions

In general, one main idea has guided events since the beginning of currency, economic and social union: people in Eastern Germany should not be worse off as compared with their former status. The outcome was different:

- Employed people obviously could improve their former status. In the first half of 1990 the average income did increase by 10%; the wage negotiations in summer 1990 came out with another increase of more than 20%. So in the end of 1990 the average income will be about 30% higher than 1989. Gross income on average will be 42% of the West German level, compared with 34% in 1989. Even with increased contributions to the social security systems, net income will be higher than before. This is true of course only on average. Especially the lowest income groups will have some problems.

- Retired people under the new regulations receive higher payments. In this case, too, the people with minimum pensions are on the bad side of the coin.

- The most difficult problem is unemployment. Unemployment did increase and will increase further. Part-time workers in some cases do get 85 - 90% of their former net income, in other cases only 63 - 68%. The latter is the ratio for the unemployed, too. Thus their real position is worse than before. Besides this, to be unemployed in many cases means social disaster.

There is still another problem in the evolution of Eastern Germany. Most people expected western living standards to accompany economic union. Now they are faced with many economic problems and uncertainty concerning their future jobs. So in spite of western assistance to improve the social net, uncertainty is growing. Thus the psychological uncertainty of the East German people will continue to be a difficult problem for the foreseeable future.

This problem cannot be solved within the framework of the social security system. It can only be resolved in the context of the larger economy, mainly by the investment of public funds to improve the conditions for economic activity - especially in infrastructure in a broad sense.

COMMENTS: THE NEW GERMANY - A DIVIDED SOCIETY

Gerhard Bäcker

1. Political Unification - Social Division

Since the national pathos has disappeared from everyday life, we are beginning to realize the societal and social realities: in the new single German state there are two societies with a highly uneven level of development and a highly uneven pace of development. This is most evident in the grave economic and social difference between the old and new states. East of the Elbe the whole economy finds itself in a desolate, even catastrophic condition; the economic situation is worsening rapidly, unemployment is reaching unusually high levels, and there is no light yet at the end of the tunnel. Despite the major increases in nominal wages which were attained in recent months, income levels are still about half of that in the West German states. Social policy is clearly cushioning the worst social effects of the fundamental economic upheaval, but it is in no way levelling out the trench between east and west.

With this deep social and economic rift, no one can speak of social and economic unity or of unity of living conditions or opportunities within Germany. Compared to the well-to-do West German citizens, the East German citizens are in many aspects structurally disadvantaged and have less satisfying jobs. The east Germans are second class citizens today and are likely to remain that way for the forseeable future. The new Germany is a polarized society. In addition to the former and continuing social structure differences between the two Germanies which include class division, level of education, and gender, the two now disassociate themselves regionally as well to an unfamiliar extent. In all the disparity in living conditions is rising in the officially unified Germany to an extreme degree.

The economic and social division is not the only factor preventing the societies and citizens of East and West from growing closer together. The division of Germany into two entirely different states with diverging social and economic structures brought with it differing lifestyles, value systems, and mentalities. What is of greater concern is that the unification process has actually enlargened the rift between West and East rather than having diminished it. Production and employment in the new states find themselves in a nosedive, with no end in sight. In complete contrast to the lofty predictions of an immediate economic upswing, it is not the East but the West which has profitted from the unification process. In any case the economically more powerful side is the winner of the unification process and will become even richer, whereas in the East, economic and social decline is accelerating without visible reconstruction taking place amidst the dismantling.

Such a contrast between rich and poor in a united state has been unknown in German history and in the four decades of the Federal Republic. Despite the regional structural and industrial crises in mining, the iron, steel, and textile industries, as well as in shipbuilding, the old

Federal Republic was and is a regionally relatively homogenous society. This changed drastically on the day of unification and it will take years before these regional disparities can be significantly reduced. Whether or not the standard of living in East and West will approach the same level in the near future, as specified in the Basic Law is uncertain; whether and within what time framework this occurs is among others dependent upon the economic, labor market, and social policies chosen.

The issue of regional dualism of rich and poor in one state is too broad and general for one to grasp the social reality in Germany and its medium-term development. An direct equalization of poverty and wealth in East and West would namely hide the fact that there are more and more differences within the two societies. In the old Federal Republic prosperity reached an all time high with things going very well for very many people; at the same time, however, there are more and more people who have been excluded from the rising prosperity and forced to the edge of this society. Never before were there so many people in the old Federal Republic who could be described as "poor" as at the beginning of the 1990s. Moreover, the disfavorable aspects of economic prosperity and efficiency are hardly given thought anymore. In the mean time they appear almost undisputed if not viewed as unavoidable and accepted norms of a market economy.

This separation between winners and losers will show itself very soon and very clearly in the former GDR as well, though to a much lesser degree. In contrast to the relatively egalitarian social structures predominant there (of course, with major priviledges of state and party leaders) what lies ahead for GDR citizens is an unheard of polarization of incomes, living conditions, and risks - perhaps even more radical than in the West. On the one hand, a larger portion of the population in the new states will be better off as a result of the transformation from socialism to a market economy and will find integrate with the West. This "new prosperity" especially for the middle class and the blue-collar workers in the highly modern, productivity-oriented manufacturing and service sectors, however, will stand in contrast to the "new poverty" of those excluded from this. Unemployment, precarious working conditions, insufficient income, the threat of losing one's apartment - these concerns will become more and more a part of daily life, perhaps even for the majority.

On this side, but predominantly on the other side, the number of people is growing who at least temporarily or even for extended periods of time are getting less than their fair share of prosperity in society with incomes at or under the poverty line and who are increasingly forced to rely upon social services for securing their material needs. In contrast to the promises of an economic miracle and prosperity for all, the new Germany will be a country with a very large and growing number of poor people. This change in the social structure in the form of a loss of societal homogeneity has far-reaching consequences not only for the East but for all of Germany.

2. Social and Sociopolitical Consequences of Regional Polarization

(1) The radical economic change upsets not only the economy of East Germany. The historically unique experiment of an transitionless transformation from "Realsozialismus" (real socialism) to "Realkapitalismus" (real capitalism) the people's entire social environment. The society as a whole is exposed to an equally abrupt and full adjustment pressure and modernization process and is experiencing an upheaval in its internal social structure. The usual working and living conditions are changing within a short period of time for the entire population. The old social security system (strongly coupled to industry and a secure job) and the traditional way of life is disappearing, qualifications are being invalidated, life-long plans are being cancelled, but at the same time new chances and suppressed freedoms are emerging. The people are now free from a repressive-paternalistic state, which surpressed and legally incapacitated, but which also cared for and supplied one's social needs. Now the state no longer takes automatic responsibility for everyone and everything. In a liberal market economic structure living conditions are distributed primarily via the market and only to some extent redistributed through social policies. The East German citizens thus have to take the burdens upon themselves without having learned until now how to deal with these new demands and contradictions.

(2) The uneven pace of development of the eastern and western society bears unknown regional and social conflict potential. The interests and political issues - and the socio-political issues - in the west are to a large extent completely different than those in the east. What matters for the largest portion of the population in the new states is plainly and simply to reach and secure the material basis for a positive outlook on life whereas in the west in recent years, "post-material" values have gained in significance more and more.

(3) The more extreme the regional disparity turns out to be and the longer it persists, the longer the migration from east to west - which was given as the central reason for the overhastily introduced monetary and economic union - will last and increase again. According to estimates approximately 250,000 people will resettle in the West in 1991 alone. In addition to this there is a growing number of people commuting to work (up to an estimated 400,000 people in the year 1991), and in many cases this is the first sign of a permanent move from east to west. This exodus leads to a continued desertification of the east German states; the young, talented, and mobile work forces are attracted the most, and they are precisely those who are needed most for the economic reconstruction. But many unemployed and those who have lost their status in the East will also try to find their way in the West, thereby increasing the number of the poor in the West.

(4) So long as production, productivity and employment levels in the two parts of Germany fail to approach the same level, significant financial payments will have to flow from west to east in order to avoid mass poverty, to support economic restructuring, and to make possible

an upswing in investment and production. The German Bundesbank estimates the amount due to be DM 140 billion for 1991; this corresponds to about two-thirds of the east German gross domestic product. And depending on the economic development in the new states, the sums in the coming years may reach similar dimensions. A large part of these transfers will have to be spent on social services because the tax incomes in the "Beitrittsgebiet" (annexed territory) will not come close to covering the expenditures. Because of the urgent requirements to achieve social unity and to finance it, the "gains" of the West Germans resulting from unification - and in personell, the "gains" are distributed differently - are again lost. Due to the tax increases required for unification the gross national product will hardly grow in the coming years. This is likely to result in a number of conflicts and disputes. If the division is to be overcome by means of the parts, the threat of social conflicts over distribution may be overshadowed and perhaps even dominated by regional conflicts over distribution. The question of how just is the distribution of the unification burdens may become a decisive socio-political issue in West Germany.

(5) In view of the enormous financial burdens resulting from the unification process and the serious social problems in the East, the issues of societal outcasts, undernourishment, and poverty are being given less emphasis in the West. The danger exists that every person or group of people who so far have been at below-average standards of living, will be pushed closer to the edge and/or completely cast aside due to the unification process. And the situtation is in no way better for the structurally unemployed, the recipients of welfare, those needing special care, and the homeless. The fact that in the eastern Laender many people have to live under somewhat more severe conditions in no way resolves a single social problem in the West. It is thus of concern that the financial burdens of unification become an additional factor for putting off the urgently needed socio-political reform measures to do away with undernourishment and poverty. And on the other side in the eastern Länder, the socially weak and outcast are being pinched on the one hand by a structural financial state of emergency and on the other hand by the numerous economic and socio-political demands and tasks.

East Germany - On the Path to a "Halved Society"

In the new Laender the standard of living remains low. The most important measure for this is the level of income/wages. No doubt, since 1990 employee income has risen sharply. Average gross wages and incomes increased last year by nearly 20%; the average gross wage per full time employee - that is excluding the large amount of part time employment - rose by about 25%. One must keep in mind, however, that the absolute amounts compared to West Germany remain very low - annual averages put the gross wage per full time employee at a total of DM 1317 monthly. Even for the coming year, the expected further increase of about 25% would raise the average to about DM 1650 per month. As a result of collective bargaining agreements on a step-by-step assimulation of wage levels between East and West, these increases will continue in such a way that the income level of the employed will fundamentally improve very quickly, but will not approach the West German level. Aiming for western levels in the industry-by-industry negotiations also implies that wages and incomes will fluctuate according to the regulations on the wage and income structure adopted from the old FRG system and according to the productive and competitive strength of industry. Large differences in income will result depending on the branch of industry and one's qualifications - a development which will place a burden on women in particular. This extreme spread of wages which is disguised by clauses based on averages will go hand-in-hand with low income levels nonexistent in the former GDR and with part time work and precarious and completely unprotected working conditions.

Even more important and consequential for the description of working conditions than indicating the inner differentiation of levels of income is the fact that the levels and their development say very little at all. It is namely foreseeable that during the economic and social transformation crisis up to two-thirds of the population will have to live on welfare and company-based social service programs. Lasting unemployment, erosion of the normal working conditions, increasing fragility of public funds for women - these socio-economic shifts already characteristic in western Germany will emerge much more drastically and much more clearly in the former GDR not just temporarily but for an extended period of time. At the same time, however, the official wage-oriented social security system has been adopted by the new Länder with all its design principles, gaps, and special classifications (but its advantages, as well).

It is thus foreseeable that the number of recipients of social services in the East will be (in relative terms) significantly higher than in the West. First of all, the problems there are accumulating due to the economic and social decline; secondly, the income levels and thus the compensation levels are only about half that of western countries. The closer the wages, pensions, unemployment compensation, and other social services are to the subsistence level, and the more the people who in the future remain without the protection of insurance or whose benefits are terminated, and the less one can rely on familiar support, the greater will be the number of social service recipients in the new Laender. The actual measure of undernourishment and poverty in East Germany naturally depends decisively on the definition of the poverty line. In comparision to the situation before 1990, that is the conditions in the former GDR, a general increase in income levels and standard of living is noticeable. But at least since the official state unification, the citizens of East Germany have taken the income levels of West Germany as their measuring stick. In one country, there can be but one socio-cultural subsistence level by which poverty is measured.

High Unemployment - Low Support Services

The process of separation and the impoverishment in the former GDR will show itself foremost in the erratically growing number of unemployed, especially in the number of structurally unemployed. The employment decline which is primarily a result of the economic decline goes well beyond registered underemployment to include migrant workers, migration, and the forcing aside of women. Assessments of this dramatic situation by the new federal states indicate that by the end of the year only as much as half of the former 9 million employed persons will receive their full income. In all, the quantity of those people in the new Laender who are excluded from the employment system and who are living at minimal subsistence levels of between DM 600 - 800 per month will take on a dimension which has never been seen before in the German federal social system: about 2 million unemployed this year; an equally high number of part time workers; about 500,000 recipients of retirement benefits; as well as welfare recipients averaging about 350,000 annually. This comes to a foreseeable potential of about 4 million people at this time alone, who for the most part have to live off of the services of the Federal Ministry of Labor. With an average net remuneration of presently ca. DM 1250 monthly the corresponding services amount to the following:

* DM 790 - 850 for unemployment compensation (depending on the number of children).
* DM 700 - 725 for unemployment assistance
* DM 810 - 910 for welfare benefits, and
* DM 810 for retirement benefits.

Unemployment in the East is also much different than a short-term, frictional transition phenomenon. Even a significant increase in industrial production will raise the total employment figures only slowly taking into account the parallel-running productivity increase. A level of employment like the one existing before the monetary and economic union is not is sight, and it is no longer promised by the politicians. From this perspective, the double selection and structuralization effect common in West Germany when becoming unemployed and employed again will reproduce itself in the East. The percentage of those who do not fulfill the legal insurance requirements (waiting period) for receiving compensation will rise, as well as the number of those whose unemployment or social assistance is terminated. In specific terms, the East German society threatens to become in itself a "Halved Society."

Outlook

If the state social charter is taken seriously, then it holds true that the societal divisions in the united Germany have to be dealt with right away by means of an appropriate reform-oriented social policy. It would be short-sighted to assume that a lasting dual structure of the economy, the labor market, and society in general would not show side-effects upon the social composition in Germany as a whole. The difficult socio-economic restructuring process in East Germany and the growing together of the two parts of Germany will only be possible on the basis of a guaranteed social security system. Acquiescence, hopelessness, dim prospects for the future, and poverty are the worst conceivable prerequisites for the development of a civil and democratic society; they serve more as a breeding ground for the spreading of radical right wing thought and behavior patterns. With this in mind, the introduction of a need-based social minimum security standard which complements the wage-oriented social security benefits is urgently required.[1]

---

1 See as references BÄCKER, G. and STEFFEN, J. (1990) Sozialunion: Was soll wie vereinigt werden?, in: WSI-Mitteilungen, 5, 1990. BÄCKER, G. (1991) Sozialpolitik im vereinigten Deutschland, in: Aus Politik und Zeitgeschichte 3-4, 1991.

ENVIRONMENTAL PROTECTION: PROBLEMS AND PROSPECTS IN EAST AND WEST GERMANY

Günter Streibel

1. Introduction

From a historical point of view, the unification of two politically, economically, socially and also ecologically different or even contrary systems as represented by the former Federal Republic of Germany and the former German Democratic Republic within an extremely short period of time is a unique process without any historical precedent.

After 40 years of separation, both German states united on October 3, 1990. On the other hand, this creates a favorable framework for the rapid economic upswing in this new Germany; on the other hand, this implies a process which will be rich in conflicts and require several years for the compensation of the existing grave differences. The present development is characterized by rapid economic growth and a drop in unemployment figures in the territory of the former Federal Republic of Germany which is in contrast to the economic decline and increasing unemployment experienced in the Eastern regions of the new Germany.

This difficult process becomes even more complicated due to the fact that the failed model of socialism in the territory of the former GDR left behind an ailing economy in a desperate environment with people visibly suffering from moral identification losses.

As regards the state of the environment, in spite of significant differences both German territories are characterized by features which are typical for industrial growth-oriented economic systems: broadly similarly growing consumption of natural resources implying the more or less visible destruction of nature inside one's own country and a share in the development of global environmental problems, i.e. the depletion of the ozone layer, the greenhouse effect, the dying of the forests, the extinction of species, erosion and desertification.

Since 1982, in the territory of the former FRG environmental protection has been a major aspect in the policy of the Government. Increasing investments, the development and application of relevant legal regulations, economically efficient instruments and the like helped in significantly reducing existing environmental impacts through controlled waste disposal putting more emphasis on the precautionary principle and supporting manifold international initiatives which are highly appreciated on the global scale as well.

In the field of air pollution control an internationally leading position could be reached. So, annual SO_2 emissions could be reduced from 2.85 million tons in 1982 down to 1.05 million tons in 1989.

Due to the rapidly expanding traffic NO_x emissions, however, which increased from 1.95 million tons in 1966 to 2.95 million tons in 1986, CO emissions were reduced from 12.4 million tons in 1966 down to 8.9 million tons in 1986 and dust emissions from 1.75 million tons in 1966 down to 0.56 million tons in 1986.

The protection of bodies of water also developed in a positive way. The households of 92% of the population are connected to the sewer system and 86% of municipal wastewater is treated biologically in central wastewater treatment plants.

However, the extensive use of herbicides more and more exceeds limiting values applicable for ground and drinking water. In particular, this refers to active substances such as atrazine, dichloropropane and simazine.

In some places, fixed limits in the drinking water supply are exceeded by more than 40 active substances. In more than 10% of the investigated wells, the contents of active substances of herbicides went beyond the admissible limits. For 10-20% of all waterworks special regulations apply since the drinking water supplied by them contains between 10-100 times more than the admissible amount of pesticides *(Arbeitsgruppe Alternative Wirtschaftspolitik 1990)*.

The quality of surface waters could be improved considerably, in particular, thanks to the significant reduction of the contents of oxygen-consuming substances and heavy metals.

The example of the Rhine river illustrates that reduction of pollution has gone fairly well:

Table 1: Pollution of the Rhine River

	1971 mg/l	1986 mg/l
five days biochemical oxygen demand	10	0.75
ammonia nitrogen	2.5	0.4
mercury concentration	2.3	0.2
cadmium concentration	3.3	0.3
halogen compounds	100	50
oxygen content	4.3	9

Furthermore, the level of heavy metals could be reduced which resulted in an overall increase in the diversity of microorganisms and species of fish.

However, the Elbe river is already heavily polluted when coming from Czechoslovakia and becomes even more polluted when passing the territory of the former GDR. High concentrations of ammonia, heavy metals, organochlorine compounds and mercury have an enormous impact on the North Sea.

Since 1984, the discharge of heavy metals into the North Sea via the Elbe, Weser and Ems rivers has been increasing, and in 1987 amounted to:

Table 2: Pollution of the Rivers Flowing into the North Sea

	t/a
cadmium	15.8
mercury	26.1
copper	461
zinc	3457
lead	354

Likewise, this holds true for the discharge of PCB, HCB, HCH, nitrogen and phosphorus:

	t/a
PCB	0.264
HCB	0.078
2-HCH	0.210
Beta-HCH	0.97
N	307,000
P	12,000

In spite of restrictions, 49,318 tons of wastes were still incinerated at sea in 1987.

"Risks for groundwater and the load on the North and the Baltic Sea are becoming more and more obvious."

In the field of waste management "big efforts are still required. The contents of harmful substances and the amount of wastes must be reduced significantly. The main problem, actually, is the insufficient infrastructure required for safe disposal. In fact, we have already today the state of emergency in this field."

Special problems concern the disposal of wastes containing harmful substances such as used oil, halogenated solvents, CFC-based refrigerants, used batteries as well as the huge amount of waste produced by the beverage, packaging material and building industries.

The quantity of domestic and domestic-like wastes remained almost at the same level (1980: 31.7 million tons; 1987: 31.0 million tons). The degree of re-utilization could be increased up to approximately 30%. The expanding beverage industry creates increasing problems: about one-tenth of the overall amount of packaging wastes are non-returnable cans and bottles amounting to 2 billion pieces in 1972 and about 8 billion pieces by 1984. The amount of wastes coming from producing sectors of industries and from hospitals increased from 158.3 million tons in 1977 to 205.7 million tons in 1987. The amount of wastes calling for special control and disposal increased from 7.1 million tons in 1983 to 10.6 million tons in 1985.

We have to face almost 50,000 "hot spots", i.e. probably contaminated sites.

The incineration of wastes represents a special potential danger. Regarding the contents of harmful substances, i.e. heavy metals and organochlorine compounds, unsorted waste is the dirtiest fuel and the incineration of waste an expanding means of waste disposal *(Neidhardt 1988)*.

Significant problems exist in the field of soil protection, since the soil is affected by the pollution of other environmental media. In particular, this refers to persistent harmful substances, contaminated sites, acid rain, substantial damage due to agricultural activities and radioactive substances.

Overload, misuse and competing requirements lead to effects on the soil substance and changes of the soil structure. The serious dangers associated with it have been recognized; however, a change in the trend could not be reached until recently.

One-fourth of the total territory of the former FRG and more than 85% of the area of arable land are being treated regularly with herbicides, thus affecting groundwater quality, microorganisms, plants, insects, birds and human beings as well.

In regions with intensive farming soils are affected by liquid manure and surface waters by sheet erosion. The cultivation of maize and sugar beets and the expansion of fields and grassland rotation result in soil erosion and loss, and drainage systems are clogged. About 12-15% of the area of arable land of the former FRG is "sealed".

One more specific problem is noise abatement. According to 1987 figures, traffic affects more than 50% of the former FRG population with 20% of them feeling most annoyed. 38% felt annoyed by aircraft noise. More than 12% of all inhabitants are exposed to noise levels amounting to 65 db(A) and more within their residential areas.

Harmful substances generated by human production and consumption habits enter the human organism via the food chain, drinking water and air.

A special risk to health are substances with a relatively long biological half-life which accumulate in the organism. In particular, this refers to heavy metals, polychlorobiphenyls (PCB), dioxins and furanes, and heavy halogenated CFCs (e.g. HCH/hexachlorocyclohexane, HCB/hexachlorobenzene, DDT, etc.)

Apart from the general investigation of cereal cropping, there is no continuous monitoring covering the whole area but only selective event-related investigation.

The example of maternal milk which contains a high share of residues from chlorinated hydrocarbons shows that in spite of massive restrictions imposed on the use of those substances the situation has not improved yet. Compared to the admissible maximum limits established for drinking milk, the limits are partially exceeded in maternal milk with regard to almost all components:

According to this, maternal milk has to be considered as a very poisonous kind of foodstuff! That is why the Commission of the Senate of the German Association for Research into Residues in Foodstuff recommended a maximum of four months for breast-feeding.

Table 3: Maternal Milk

FRG (1985) contents in mg/kg fat	Mean value	Maximum value	Maximum admissible value (for drinking milk)
HCB	0.431	1.803	0.2
Beta-HCH	0.138	1.829	0.075
total DDT	0.892	6.680	1.0
p,p-DDD	0.003	0.202	-
p,p-DDE	0.789	6.290	-
PCB	2.104	12.424	-
K 138	0.202	2.040	0.05
K 153	0.280	2.300	0.05

Although numerous activities have been undertaken by enterprises, public authorities, communities and citizens in the territory of the former FRG - many of them have been appreciated internationally as well - in order to stem the ecological crisis, the individual condition of the natural media is different, but in general, not at all satisfying.

Facing this fact and relevant risks, the Report on the State of the Environment indicates measures to be taken in each critical sector in the field of environmental legislation, the application of economic stimuli, technico-technological solutions, information and the like aiming at the further improvement of the situation in the years to come.

However, although they accept a significant reduction of the strain on the environment, critical voices emphasize the creeping environmental impact and pollution both in their own territory and on the global level. "This overall evaluation (of the Report) contradicts (in spite of significantly intensified activities in environmental policy) reality. Environmental policy is not 'over the hill'; it just slowed down degradation in most fields - but never turned it. Even in the few regions where a certain improvement of the situation could be reached, the level is ecologically incompatible and globally unacceptable in the long run" *(Kollatz-Ahnen 1990)*.

In summary one can say that "in spite of serious efforts and manifold laws the state of the environment is nothing less than satisfying" *(Glaeser 1990)*.[1]

In particular, one has to point out that the "state of the natural environment...is not widely investigated even in the Federal Republic of Germany" which refers especially to the impact imposed by chemicals *(Glaeser 1990)*.

All these critical remarks do refer as well - and to a much higher degree - to the environmental policy and situation in the territory of the former GDR.

In spite of the incomparably higher strain on the environment, one could not identify serious efforts of those who used to be responsible for environmental protection in the GDR. The priority of economy over ecology practiced in the centrally managed national economy of the GDR - despite good legal stipulations in this field and the unity of economy and ecology sworn to all over again - led to the fact that the "heirs" of the failed "really existing socialism" in the GDR inherited an obsolete, inefficient economy and an extremely desolate environment. On an international level, the former GDR held a leading position with regard to pollution. Compared to the most favorable case in the international spectrum - i.e., Japan - the per-capita pollution by CO_2 is almost three times as high, by SO_2 more than 30 times and by dust more than 100 times as high! *(Mez, Jaenicke, and Poeschk 1990)* (see *Table 8*).

In the following let me present some data relating to the load on the natural media in the territory of the former GDR:

Table 4: Air Pollution in the Former GDR (1988)

Pollutant (emission)	Quantity (kt)	Amount per capita (kg)	Load/km^2 (t)
SO_2	5209	313	48
NO_x*	408	0.025	3.8
NO_x	700	0.042	6.5
dust	2199	132	20.3
hydrocarbons	345	0.021	3.2

**without traffic*

36% of the population is exposed to inadmissibly SO_2-polluted areas; in the case of dust 30% of the population is affected.

Four-fifths of the total pollution caused by dust and SO_2 occur in the former districts of Halle, Leipzig, Cottbus and Dresden. In this region, more than 35% of the population of the former GDR live in an area which covers 27% of the former GDR territory, i.e. compared to the impact the population experiences in other districts, the per-capita pollution is more than 7.3 times and per km^2 more than 11 times as high with regard to dust or SO_2 emissions (1986). This enormous air pollution also results in serious forest damage (see *Table 9*).

In spite of a lot of expenditures on environmental protection measures amounting to 9.75 billion marks which have been spent since 1980, it was not possible to decisively reduce this environmental strain (see *Table 10*).

2. Water Management

More than two-thirds of the flowing waters are heavily or even very heavily polluted. Almost 33% of the overall amount of industrial wastewater to be treated is not purified; more than 48% of municipal wastewater is treated mechanically or not at all. 30% of the 18.5 million m^3 of feces produced annually are disposed in an uncontrolled way.

7.6 million inhabitants cannot be permanently supplied with drinking water of normal quality; 1.4 million inhabitants receive drinking water loaded with nitrate endangering their health; another 1.4 million inhabitants get drinking water which contains microbes thus also affecting their health; in approximately 1000 communities babies get extra water; 0.5 million inhabitants get partially considerably nitrate-polluted drinking water. Annually, approximately 50 million m^3 of liquid manure is produced, but only half of that amount can be stored.

Due to non-adequate methods of soil treatment in agriculture in the territory of the former GDR, ground and surface waters became highly polluted by liquid manure and fertilizers; soils, bodies of water and agricultural products were affected by herbicides; ecosystems were disturbed by extremely extensive agricultural management; soils were compressed and arable land was destroyed. 20-70% of the fields are compressed resulting in yield losses amounting to 5-30%. This again results in expenditures on the breaking-up of soils amounting to 20-25 million DM/a. In spite of the permanently increasing use of herbicides and fertilizers in agriculture, yields could not be increased to the same extent. (see *Table 11*).

3. Destruction of Areas

Annually, about 16,000 to 20,000 hectare of arable land were destroyed, e.g. due to lignite mining 567 km^2 were taken away from agricultural utilization between 1971 and 1988 and only 404 km^2 were returned.

4. Noise Abatement

Damages caused by noise amount to about 1 billion DM/a; partial pensions for those whose health was seriously affected by noise amount to 75-100 million DM/a.

From almost 1500 enterprises, about 2000 tons of heavy metals (nickel, zinc, chromium, copper) are emitted which is equal to a raw material equivalent of approximately DM 40 million. 420 exceptional permits - among them for the emission of about 180 harmful chemical substances and 130 non-toxic dusts - were granted.

Considerable investments were made mainly in the area of disposal in order to stem this environmental pollution. *Table 12* shows the international level in the field of investments in environmental protection.

Table 13 indicates the purposes of environment-related investments in the territory of the former GDR. From 1980-1988, air pollution control was given top priority. The breakdown according to industrial branches also helps identify the main sources of emission (see *Table 14*). (The high share of investments allocated to the Ministry of Water Management and Environmental Protection results from the fact that it used to be responsible for all measures in the field of water management).

Table 15 shows the "hypertrophy" of the former GDR capital (East Berlin) which was created consciously in the past - with respect to environmental protection as well: in spite of a very low share of Berlin in the total emission of SO^2, dust and hydrocarbons in the GDR, almost one-fifth of all investments in environmental protection was concentrated in Berlin between 1980 and 1988. Although the city of Berlin and the former district of Cottbus used to share the second position after thè former district of Leipzig with regard to SO^2 pollution (tons/km^2), the two districts mentioned received relatively much less investment for environmental protection measures than the former capital. Obviously, Berlin was intended to be not only an island with preferential supply of goods but also an ecological island in the heavily polluted territory of the GDR before the 1989 renewal.

The so-called problem of contaminated sites is a phenomenon implying largely unknown dimensions, danger potentials and expenditures towards their rehabilitation. According to data based on first investigations and preliminary registration which, however, are assumed to be absolutely fragmentary, the territory of the former GDR covers 1300 of those contaminated sites. According to international experience, the specific expenditures required for the sanitation of those "hot spots" range from 20 to 1400 DM/m^2 (encasement) or 50 to 1000 DM/ton (on-site treatment) - depending on the technology applied.

What were the causes for that precarious ecological situation?

1. Obsolete, morally and physically worn-out techniques and technologies and the respective out-of-date equipment implying the maximum use of available resources and a heavy burden on the natural media. This also involves an insufficient degree of renewal of products which require too much material and energy both for production and consumption compared to other products in the international market.

2. Long-lasting clinging to a highly nonrational energy and structural policy, high consumption of low-quality lignite (with an 80% share in energy generation) resulting in the devastation of large areas through extensive open-cast mining activities, extreme waste of energy, the large share of branches in heavy and chemical industries consuming too much energy and raw materials, long-lasting disregard of integrated environmental protection based on precaution, insufficient investments in environmental protection, and underdeveloped industry producing environmental protection goods.

3. Until now, the too low rate and mass of accumulation did not allow for the required essential ecological reconstruction of our financial and technical basis.

4. The unilaterally consumption-oriented thinking and behavior and the achievement of a relatively high material standard of living was obtained at the expense of health, of the financial and technical basis and national wealth - in particular, at the expense of natural resources. The spreading of excessive forms of consumption such as individual motorization, the spoiling of the landscape by indiscriminate spreading of summer houses, the incompatibly extensive utilization of areas by the army and other security services as well as by privileged individuals led to the waste of resources and such an impact on the environment.

5. The comparably low labor productivity and the too low profitability of exports resulted in the waste of social labor and, thus, also of energy and raw materials, which in connection with growing credit burdens forced the import of production and consumption wastes for disposal, thus aggravating the problem of contaminated sites.

6. The supercentralized, obscure, inflexible, and inefficient system of management, planning and economic accountancy led both socially and individually to the waste of resources and a strain on the natural media. The increasing incongruence of material and financial processes resulted in the infringement of the functional unity of the categories of values and the application of economic stimuli (fees, prices, sanctions and the like) as mere financial procedures without inducing the users of the resources to environmentally sound behavior in an efficient way. Thus, even reasonable legal stipulations were in vain in many cases.

A comprehensive body of environmental laws and investments in environmental protection measures amounting to 1 billion marks/a led to partial improvements or stemmed devastation; however, it was impossible to fundamentally change the desolate state of the environment in the territory of the former GDR. Also, fees levied on the utilization of natural media or sanctions imposed for exceeding limiting values failed to have the desired effect.

Table 5: Pollution Fees in the Former GDR 1988/1989 (millions of marks)

water use charges	400
land use charges	185.3
increased land use charges	1
fee for wastewater discharge	1200
wastewater charges	126
dust and exhaust gas emission charges	50.8
Total	1963.1

Although these data are incomplete and partially only estimated, the following "Ecological Overview" might be presented.

Table 6: Ecological Overview

	GDR	FRG
annual growth of national income or GNP, respectively (%)	3-4	1.8 - 3.4 (1985 - 1988)
annual environmental damage		
marks/DM, respectively	28-30 billion	103.6 billion
% of national income or GNP, respectively	11	6
annual returns from fees imposed on the use of natural media (marks)	ca. 1.9 billion	-
annual investments in environmental protection		
marks/DM, respectively	ca. 1 billion	ca. 36 billion
% of national income or GNP respectively	ca. 0.4	1.7 (1988)

This table illustrates that in the former two German states:

a) the value of environmental damages increased considerably more than the national income or GNP, respectively.

b) expenditures on environmental protection were essentially lower than the value of the environmental damages.
c) returns from fees imposed on the utilization of environmental media were considerably higher than relevant expenditures (GDR).

Since for other market - as well as planned economy systems - similar data are given, one has to conclude:
Neither market nor planned economy systems to date have proven to be able to combine economic growth and efficient environmental protection.

"The unconditional orientation towards growth of profit-controlled and centrally managed systems caused destructive exploitation of the natural fundamentals of life to an extent overstraining the ability of regeneration in many cases causing irreparable damages which result in massive effects on the quality of life, and partially, even threaten life." *(Arbeitsgruppe Alternative Wirtschaftspolitik 1990).*

With the rapid accession of the GDR to the FRG and the acceptance of the laws of the FRG by the former GDR there emerged the extremely difficult task of overcoming the big differences in the development of both - socioeconomically opposite - countries within an as short as possible period of time. This refers to the considerable difference in the levels of productivity, in the scientific and technical fields, in per-capita consumption and, of course, in the ecological situation.

It is quite clear that this can only be a process of step-by-step adaptation.

Provided that the environmental legislation of the FRG or even the relevant standards of the EC have to be applied to their full extent in the territory of the former GDR right now, then about 70% of all enterprises would have to be closed down immediately. That is why it is planned to apply these high standards when erecting new plants, to close down internationally non-competitive old and worn-out plants which consume a lot of energy and raw materials and pollute the environment, and to rehabilitate the remaining old plants until 1995 or 2000, respectively.

This, however, results in the massive conflict which has been known in the territory of the former FRG already since the early 1970s, i.e. the conflict between the preservation of workplaces and environmental protection.

So, many workers in the ecologically critical area around Bitterfeld are ready even today to accept environmental pollution for some years more, for here restructuring means the loss of approximately 30,000 workplaces. It must also be emphasized that due to the overhasty unification of the two German states the originally existing hope for possible ecological renewal in all Germany became pointless. This refers to the protection and conservation of natural landscapes, efficient management of secondary raw materials and the moderate use of individual motorization while improving public transport. However, these are only desires which have no chance to be fulfilled in the frenzy of enthusiastic shopping or which are to be further developed.

Since on the one hand the measuring screen and environmental control and monitoring systems are absolutely underdeveloped in the territory of the former GDR, and on the other hand, the available funds do not meet at all the requirements, one cannot exclude that the desired rapid economic growth shall be achieved at the expense of ecological demands.

This refers to the attempt to establish in the former GDR territory a system of low wages and the utilization of natural resources at low prices which might be illustrated by the now German domestic transport of wastes, the intended erection of 16 waste incinerating plants, touristic and possibly also industrial development including the expansion of traffic in hitherto almost natural landscapes, and the like.

The FRG Law on Stability and Growth of 1967 which now also applies to the territory of the former GDR ignores targets related to environmental policy, thus indirectly allocating the task to environmental policy of repairing afterwards the consequential damages generated by economic growth and economic policy. Now as before, reactive environmental policy implying the repair of damages is dominating - at the expense of preventive, integrated environmental protection *(Stratmann-Mertens 1990)*.[2]

Facing the ecological, economic and social challenges linked with the unification process it would be necessary to replace this "Law of Stability and Growth" with a new organic law for an ecological and social market economy. Introducing the target of "ecological sustainability" would change the famous "magic quadrangle" into a "magic pentagon".

The ecological restructuring of the former GDR should cover the following measures:

a) reduction of health hazards; sanitation of the ecologically critical areas (around the cities of Leipzig, Halle, Bitterfeld, Dresden and in the Lausitz region).

b) change of the economic structure; reduction of energy-intensive basic industries; phasing out of material-intensive and environmentally incompatible technologies and products; drastic reduction of primary and final energy consumption; reduction of lignite mining and lignite-based energy generation; replacement of lignite as an energy carrier by oil, gas, hard coal, and regenerative energy sources; modernization of inefficient power plants, fluidized bed combustion, unit-type heating stations, combined use of the thermal output of power plants and heating stations.

c) closing down, modification of use and completion of big polluting plants with filters and other required equipment (low-temperature carbonization plants, viscose fiber production, chlorine generation); this, however, includes two problems: loss of workplaces and increasing dependence on imports.

d) reorganization of agricultural production; break with the previously prevailing gigantomania (intensive animal farming, extensive crop cultivation); abandonment of the previous separation of plant and animal production; economical use of chemical fertilizers and herbicides; application of alternative methods of management.

However, one has to be prepared for the reaction of the enterprises competing in the EC market because more intensive management means the application of more chemical fertilizers and herbicides for the sake of cost reduction and increased productivity.

The adopting of the environmental legislation of the FRG involves the following problems:

1) stepwise overcoming of the significant environmental strain posed by dust, SO_2, wastewater; this positive development, however, should not obscure the fact that certain loads will increase, e.g. those caused by NO_x, CO_2, and CFCs due to the "full motorization" to be expected; furthermore, one should take seriously the evaluation of west German environmentalists with regard to the "creeping" progressive environmental poisoning of soils, rivers, seas and food.

2) The use of partially apparently or actually environmentally sound technologies and products from the FRG creates - in light of the "frenzy of consumption enthusiasm" of the GDR citizens - the illusion that this would allow for the absolutely safe achievement of Western outfitting standards. But - as the example of the catalytic converter-equipped motorcars shows, other substances which are injurious to human health are emitted, e.g. platinum. Furthermore, energy and material consumption as well as the stress on landscapes is strongly increasing - also the number of accidents which cost human life and destroy material values.

It has been found that in spite of the outfitting of more and more motorcars with catalytic converters, environmental pollution did not decrease because the number of motorcars is permanently growing.

3) growing consumption inevitably leads to growing amounts of waste. In particular, packaging material, newspapers, and advertising leaflets are flooding households thus increasing the quantity of waste by leaps and bounds. Through rigorous liquidation of the - internationally highly appreciated - secondary raw material recycling system of the former GDR the state of "waste emergency" is virtually being provoked. Thanks to systematic collection of industrial wastes turning them into secondary raw materials, about 40% of those wastes could be recycled, thus meeting approximately 13% of the material requirements of the national economy. A network comprising 1900 public collecting points, 5400 private collecting points, 7400 collectors working part-time, and 1400 individuals working in social collecting points allowed for the collection and recycling of about 44% of the total amount of domestic wastes, i.e. 300 kg/inhabitant/a (FRG: ca. 30%).

Since this efficient system will be eliminated before the FRG system of dual collection will be introduced, waste mountains will be growing simultaneously with the predictable level of production up to that of the former FRG (500 kg/inhabitant/a). However, it has not been taken into consideration here that the saving of about 100 million D-marks in this regard (i.e. subsidies for the secondary raw material recycling system) requires additional funds amounting to approximately 1 billion D-marks for the liquidation of these waste mountains. Furthermore, one has to add several billion D-marks which will be necessary for the organization of the dual system - and that will take some years.

4) as the details of the state of the environment are not known completely, almost every day new weak points are being discovered. This refers to pollution of bodies of water (groundwater, surface waters such as the Elbe and the Havel river), areas affected by air pollution, radiation-contaminated sites where uranium has been mined (mine dumps, sludge lagoons, groundwater). 20-30,000 eventually contaminated sites are assumed to exist in the former GDR territory.

5) according to recent studies (see *Mez, Jaenicke, and Poeschk 1990*) power supply to the former GDR territory could be guaranteed until the year 2000 without nuclear power and import of power even when reducing lignite combustion - if power consumption will be reduced by decreasing power consumption in the power stations themselves, by the exclusion of net losses and by heat insulation of buildings - provided that a community-based power industry can be established and alternative energy sources will be used to a larger extent. This

would also considerably reduce SO_2 and dust pollution. However, the takeover of the former energy-generating enterprises by three west German big business firms contradicts progressive international experience and sets tight limits to possible savings in energy generation and consumption as well as to decentralized solutions due to the monopolized offer of a restricted number of non-regenerative energy carriers.

6) The motorization wave in the territory of the former GDR led to the significant deterioration of air quality, to traffic jams and accidents. At present, 8 million motorcars are registered in the new five Federal Laender and 37.3 million motorcars in the 11 Federal Laender of the FRG, i.e. in East Germany there are 230 motorcars per 1000 inhabitants compared to 500 motorcars per 1000 inhabitants in West Germany. The high average age of the eastern cars (14 years) also means high noise annoyance and emission of pollutants. This situation is still aggravating due to the shifting of transport from railways back to roads. In the former GDR territory, the railway/road transport ratio was 75:20, but now it will change towards the present FRG ratio of 23:55. (However, it must be mentioned that in the GDR railway transport losses in 1987/88 were registered which were equal to the industrial growth within the same period of time!).

Traffic and area planning concepts, stipulations regulating higher prices for motorcars and lower prices for public transport in order to give a certain relief to the situation are not evident to date.

7) Increased capital flow will lead to further destruction of arable land resulting in expanding "sealing" of soils and the spoiling of landscapes by indiscriminate spreading of settlements of low density.

The comprehensive measures aiming at the stabilization and step-by-step improvement of the bad environmental situation resulting from the disregard of these problems over decades call for significant expenditures.

According to preliminary rough estimations, for the elimination of the worst environmental damages the following funds would be required during the next years: *(Weizsaecker 1989)*

Table 7: Funds Required to Alleviate Worst Damages (billion marks)

air pollution control	50 - 60
protection of the ozone layer/ combatting the greenhouse effect	25 - 30
water pollution control	80 - 100
soil protection	5 - 10
clean-up of contaminated sites	40 - 45
nature conservation and protection of landscapes	2 - 5
Total	202 -250

Note: The latest figures even refer to about 400 billion marks.

As everybody will understand, these enormous funds cannot be made available within a short period of time and not by the new Federal Lands alone. Facing these requirements, the funds amounting to 671 million D-marks allocated by the Federal Ministry of the Environment for the 35 environmental pilot projects in the new five Federal Laender are rather modest.[3] "The balance sheet to be drawn up for the environmental policy of the FRG is negative in so far as it stays far behind the necessities.[4] Neither in the use of funds - the Federal Government spends five times as much on nuclear research as on alternative energy sources, energy saving measures and alternative power technology development - nor in the field of environmental stipulations do really efficient areas of concentration become visible as regards environmental protection....In spite of contrary explanations and general theoretical concepts environmental policy still remains reactive and punctual; on the other hand, it is massively hindered by the interests and the lobbying of the associations concerned. In so far, the future prospects are bad as well." *(Arbeitsgruppe Alternative Wirtschaftspolitik 1990)*.

Since with the German-German unification positive attempts have been started in order to overcome the most serious environmental defects in the territory of the former GDR - although no substantial turn in the tendency of environmental policy exerted by traditional industrial systems is evident, especially with regard to the mitigation of global environmental problems - it has to be stated that it was not possible to achieve a model for lasting sustainable development of democratic societies by means of this historically unique process *(World Commission for Environment and Development 1988)*.

5. Outlook

Facing the conflict-laden situation of the world and the environment as described by various competent bodies (Report of the Club of Rome, Global 2000, the Brundtland Report, and others) with prognosticated "final periods" of 30-50 years, the periodization introduced by E.U.v. Weizsaecker is very interesting according to which the century of economy is over with the new one to be imaginable only as the century of ecology - of the environment *(Weizsaecker 1990)*.

According to a UN report indicating a daily world population growth of about 250,000 amounting to an annual growth of about 100 million people, in 2025 about 8.5 billion people will be living on Earth. However, already in the year 2000 34 countries will no longer be able to support their population.

This population growth is connected with an enormously increasing consumption of resources (energy, raw materials), increasing environmental pollution as well as an increase in social conflictual situations.

The "salvation" from this situation can only be the basic change of values and the strict turning away from euphoria and unquestioning belief with regard to economic growth, technical progress, innovation, development of material wealth and consumption.

A new "wealth model" is necessary *(Weizsaecker 1989)*.

The target cannot be *maximization* of wealth but *stabilization* of wealth (balancing at the same time indefensible international differentiation) at minimum consumption of the environmental media and minimum impact on the environment. Values such as health, social, ethical and other values must become the essential criteria of wealth.

The present and planned German environmental policy, however, does not meet at all these vital requirements which will be essential for survival.

Table 8: SO_2 and NOx Emissions of European Countries (1985) (kg/capita/a)

	GDR	CSSR	Hungary	Bulgaria	Poland	Yugo-slavia	UK	FRG	USSR (Eur. Part)
SO_2	301	203	133	127	116	78	63	40	57
NO_2	58	72	28	22	23	8	30	48	15

Source: 1988/89 Data on the Environment, Umweltbundesamt, E. Schmidt Verlag, Berlin (W) 1989

Table 9: Forest Damage (1989) (% of total forest stock)

Czechoslovakia	FRG	Poland	GDR
70.5%	52.4%	49.4%	54.3%

	Pine	Spruce	Beech	Oak
GDR	51.6	40.9	24.9	42.6

Source: "Schutz unserer Waelder", in "Was und Wie, Informationen, Argumente", No. 7, 1989.

Table 10: Development of Emissions (1988)
(1976 = 100)

SO2	Dust	NOx	CH
122	80	160*	299

* without motorcars, 239 (in 1980 = 100)

Source: Calculated according to the 1989 Report of the GDR Ministry of the Environment

Table 11: Agriculture: Herbicides/Fertilizers/Yield Ratio
1987 (1970 = 100)

Herbicides	Chemical weed control	Fertilizers				Yield
		N	P2O5	K2O	CaO	
161	167	170	77	90	144	123

Source: Calculated as above.

Table 12: Investments in Environmental Protection (international level)

Country	Share in GNP(%) 1988	1980	Expenditures Billions DM 1988	Per-capita Expenditures (DM) 1988	Share (%) in National Income 1990 (Plan)
Canada	1.11	1.46	8.8	344	
FRG	1.07	1.11	22.5	368	
USA	0.87	1.05	69.7	288	
UK	0.74	1.07	11.8	208	
Japan	0.69	1.72	33.0	275	
France	0.62	0.93	10.3	187	
Italy	0.46	0.58	6.7	118	
GDR	0.66	0.49	1.8	107	1.3
Bulgaria	National Income		(Billion Marks)	(Marks)	3
USSR	only investments				3

Source: Capital, July 1989; GDR figures in effective prices; 1989 Report of the GDR Ministry of the Environment

Table 13: GDR Investments in Environmental Protection

From 1980 to 1988, GDR investments included the following (figures in effective prices):

	Investments (in million marks)	Share (in %)
Total	9750	100
of which:		
- for wastewater treatment plants	4100	42
including		
- for housing programs	2171	22
- for industrial wastewater treatment	1929	20
- for liquidation of liquid manure/ storage of mineral fertilizers/ pasture formation/		
- protection from erosion	811	8
- for air pollution control	3376	35
including		
- for flue gas desulphurization	690	7
- for dust removal	2686	27
- for waste removal	1372	14
including		
- for removal of municipal wastes	175	2
- for removal of industrial wastes	1197	12
- for noise reduction	91	1

Source: 1989 Report of the GDR Ministry of the Environment

Table 14: Industrial Ministries Investment in Environmental Protection (million marks, effective prices)

Industrial Ministries	Million Marks	%
Coal and Energy	2046.5	21.0
Ore Mining, Metallurgy, and Potassium Production	944.5	9.7
Chemistry	2174.0	22.3
Electrotechniques/Electronics	200.0	0.2
Plant and Heavy Machine Building	162.0	1.7
Machine Tool and Processing, Machine Construction	94.3	0.9
Consumer Goods Industry	89.4	0.9
Construction of General and Agricultural Machines and Vehicles	117.7	1.2
Regional and Foodstuff Industry	74.7	0.8
Glass and Ceramics	344.4	3.5
Building	130.3	1.3
Agriculture, Forestry, and Foodstuffs Industry	810.9	8.3
Environmental Protection and Water Management	2172.5	22.3
Others	387.8	3.9
Total	9750.0	100

Table 15: Investments in Environmental Protection According to Conurbation Centers

	Population	Emission 1988 (kt)		Investments (1980-88)mill. M (effective prices)			
		SO2	Dust	CH	Total	Air	Water
Conurbation Centers	53.6	77.6	70.2	78.1	64.9	74.9	68.2
Conurbation Centers (without Berlin)	46.0	76.4	68.8	75.8	45.6	54.7	40.1
Berlin	7.6	1.2	1.4	2.3	19.3	20.2	28.1
Districts							
Berlin		67	30	3681		682	
Halle		986	471	62,896		678	
Cottbus		1373	475	4890		624	
Leipzig		936	236	0,257		187	

(calculated according to above)

Endnotes

1. See *GEISLER, T. (1990)* Rezension in: Wirtschaftswissenschaft Heft 9, p. 1340.

2. See also *JAENICKE, M. (1987)* Staatsversagen, Piper, Muenchen-Zuerich, 79.

3. See *Berliner Zeitung (1990)* October 11, p. 1.

4. According to OECD data, about 6-8% of the GNP should be spent annually on environmental protection (compare with *Table 12*).

References

ARBEITSGRUPPE ALTERNATIVE WIRTSCHAFTSPOLITIK (1990) Memorandum 1990: Im deutsch-deutschen Umbruch: Vorrang fuer sozialen und oekologischen Umbau, p. 5-8.

FEDERAL MINISTER FOR THE ENVIRONMENT, NATURE CONSERVATION AND REACTOR SAFETY (1990) The 1990 Environmental Report, May.

GLAESER, B.(1989) Umweltpolitik zwischen Reparatur und Vorbeugung, Westdeutscher Verlag GmbH, Opladen, 1989, 81.

KOLLATZ-AHNEN, M. (1990) Umweltbericht 1990, Kommentar in: IOeW-Ifo-Dienst, No. 3-4, 21.

MEZ, L., JAENICKE, M., and POESCHK, J. (1990) Zur Energiesituation in der DDR, Forschungsleitstelle fuer Umweltpolitik, FU Berlin, II.

NEIDHARDT, R. (1988) Muellverbrennung: Ein brennendes Problem fuer Mensch und Natur, Bund fuer Umwelt und Naturschutz Deutschland e.V.

PAULY, M. (1990) Grund zum Aufatmen, in: Horizont, No. 31, 45.

STRATMANN-MERTENS, E. (1990) Wachsen und Schrumpfen, in: Wirtschaftswoche, No. 31, July 27.

UMWELTBUNDESAMT (1989) Data on the Environment 1988/89, E. Schmidt Verlag.

WEIZSAECKER, E.U.v. (1989) Erdpolitik, Wissenschaftliche Buchgesellschaft, Darmstadt.

WORLD COMMISSION FOR ENVIRONMENT AND DEVELOPMENT (1988) Our Common Future, Staatsverlag der DDR, Berlin, 57.

COMMENTS ON: ENVIRONMENTAL PROTECTION: PROBLEMS AND PROSPECTS IN EAST AND WEST GERMANY

Peter Palinkas

1. Introduction

Already in the 1970s the former German Democratic Republic (GDR) had initiated a new approach to environmental policy; since 1974 environmental protection had been firmly based in Article 14 of the Constitution; and as early as 1971 a new ministry of environmental protection and water management had been established. But this by no means accurately reflected the state of the environment. Only the revolutionary changes that occurred in the GDR and in other Eastern European countries in November 1989 revealed the full scope of environmental mismanagement.

The status of the environment in the former GDR and in other Eastern European countries was in Western Europe long considered to be of secondary importance. But this has changed totally after the Chernobyl disaster in 1986 and following the revolutionary changes in Eastern Europe since November 1989. In particular, the Chernobyl accident brought home to us the fact that pollution is international and ignores differences in ideology.

In his speech on July 6, 1989 to the Council of Europe in Strasbourg (*Kraus, 1989*), the Soviet Head of State, Mr. Gorbachev, referred to the international character of environmental pollution in Europe; he thought it quite possible that environmental protection might be one of the first areas to be tackled through cooperation in the "European home".

Environmental policy and protection is not only a very promising field of further East-West cooperation, but also a tremendous burden on the process of German unification. The environmental legacy could well hinder the process of economic recovery in the former GDR and could make it even more difficult to build a united Germany with conditions more or less equal in the economic and social field.

In the case of the former GDR environmental problems are to a high degree caused by the combination of coal (lignite) dependence, few pollution controls, and energy inefficiency; all this has resulted in levels of sulphur dioxide (SO_2) in the atmosphere that are among the highest in the world. This paper, therefore, tries to describe briefly the main linkages between energy and air pollution in the former GDR and to give a short outlook concerning energy and environmental policy in the process of German unification.

Due to lack of space only air pollution, the most threatening environmental problem in the former GDR, is considered here.

2. Main Energy and Environmental Indicators

Statistical information concerning Eastern European countries (countries of the Council for Mutual Economic Assistance, CMEA, i.e. the USSR, the former GDR, Hungary, Poland, the CSFR, Bulgaria, and Romania) is, in general, insufficient and of poor quality (*EC Commission, 1990a*). In addition, it is now publicly admitted that statistics were frequently manipulated in the past to satisfy political objectives and planning targets. In other words, all quantitative data concerning this region must be treated with great caution. Especially in the former GDR various data and statistics concerning energy and the environment were insufficient, not published or even treated as a state secret.

But keeping in mind that all available statistics concerning energy and the environment in Eastern Europe are insufficient, it seems nevertheless justified to describe the former GDR as a highly polluted country. As far as air pollution is concerned, the GDR very often "leads" the international league table. An international comparison based on main energy and environmental indicators reveals (*Palinkas, 1988 and 1990*):

- After the USA (20.7 million tons per year; in 1985) and the USSR (11.1 million tons) the GDR (5.0 million tons) already placed third in the world as far as the total amount of SO_2-emissions are concerned. But the GDR was by far the world leader concerning SO_2-emissions per capita (301 kg per year and capita) and is followed by the CSFR (203 kg) and Poland (116 kg) *(see Table 1 and Figures 1 and 2)*.

- The GDR only reached an average position as far as emissions of nitrogen oxides (NOx) are concerned (vehicle ownership, one major factor concerning NOx-emissions, was of minor importance in the GDR) *(see again Table 1 and Figures 1 and 2)*.

- The GDR leads the international league table again concerning emissions of carbon dioxide (CO_2) per capita. The GDR came in first with 21.2 tons CO_2 per year (in 1988) and capita, followed by the USA (19.7 tons) and Canada (17.0). The USA was only in a "lead" position as far as the total amount of CO_2-emissions is concerned *(see Table 2 and Figure 3)*[1].

- The energy sector (energy production, transformation and consumption) is the main contributor to the above mentioned air pollution (mainly CO_2-, SO_2- and NOx-emissions). Thus, these very high levels of per-capita emissions in the GDR can mainly be explained by the amount and structure of energy consumption. The per-capita energy consumption in the GDR (7891 kg SKE per year and capita; in 1987) was very high - compared with figures in the former Federal Republic of Germany (FRG) (5624 kg) and other western industrialized countries *(Figure 4; note: SKE=equivalents of hard coal units)*.

- The consumption of energy per capita is one common indicator describing a country's energy efficiency. Another common indicator measuring energy efficiency is energy intensity. This indicator is often regarded as the most appropriate one for an international comparison of energy efficiency, as in this case the total amount of energy used per unit of output (GNP, measured in real terms) is indicated. Despite some weak points (problems concerning deflation and exchange rates to allow international comparison) energy intensity reveals clearly a country's strength and ability in the field of rational use of energy. This indicator shows that the input of primary energy in the former GDR was more than twice as high as the respective input in Western Europe (FRG, EC-12) to produce one unit of output (GNP; measured in US dollars, 1987-prices); the primary energy intensity was 0.71 for the GDR in 1987 (i.e. 0.71 kgoe per unit of GNP, measured in US 1987 dollars); the respective intensity was 0.32 for the FRG and 0.35 for the European Community (EC-12) *(see Table 3 and Figure 5)*.

- Another common indicator is electricity intensity (indicating the amount of electricity used to produce one unit of output). This indicator shows again the waste of energy or electricity in the Eastern bloc. This intensity was 0.54 for the GDR in 1987 (i.e. 0.54 kwh per unit of GNP, measured in ECU, 1987-prices); this intensity was in the same range for other countries in the Eastern bloc, whereas this ratio was considerably lower in Western Europe (0.32 in the FRG, 0.38 in EC-12).

Not only the waste of energy but also the structure of energy consumption in the GDR contributed to the high level of air pollution. A comparison of the structure of energy consumption in the former GDR and in the FRG reveals:

Table 1: Emissions: SO_2 and NOx (1985)

	SO2 (kt/a)	NOx (kt/a)	SO2 (kg/a * capita)	NOx (kg/a * capita)
Japan	1079	1416	9	12
USA	20700	20000	87	84
France	1846	1693	33	31
UK	3540	1690	63	30
FRG	2440	2930	40	48
GDR	5000	955	301	58
Poland	4300	840	116	23
CSFR	3150	1120	203	72
USSR	11100	2930	57	15

Source: Umweltbundesamt (UBA)

t = 1 ton = 1000 kg
kt = 1000 tons
kt/a = kt per year (annum)
kg/a* capita = kg per year and capita

Figure 1: Total SO2- and NOx-Emissions per year (1985) in kt

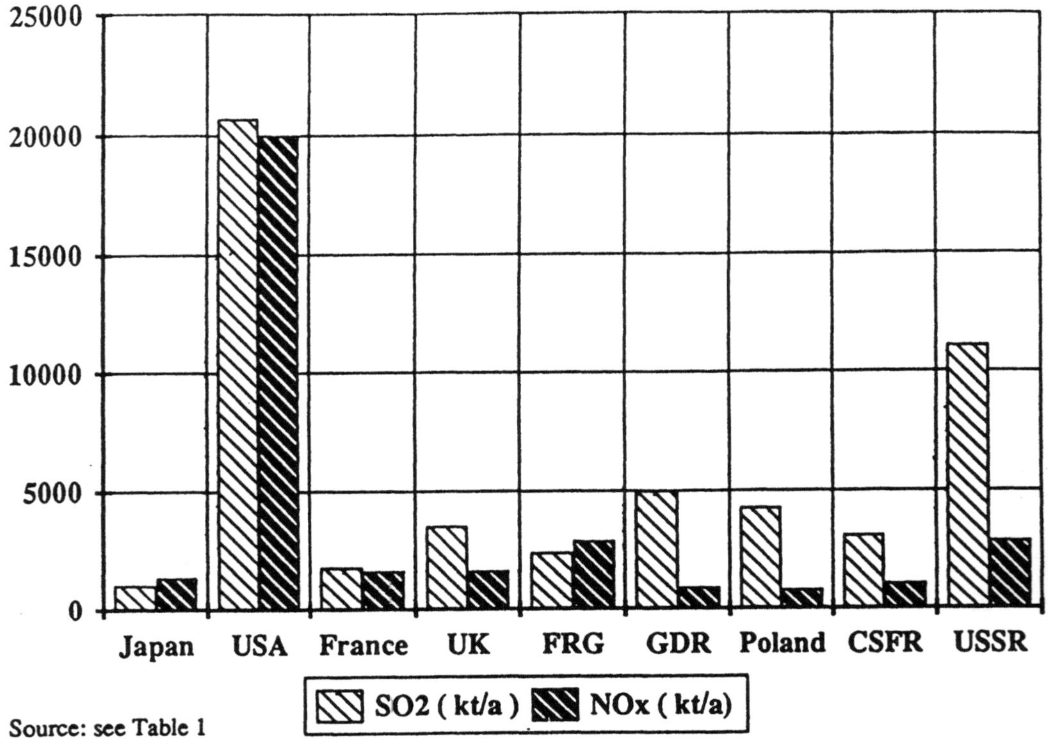

Source: see Table 1

Figure 2: SO2- and NOx-Emission: kg per year and capita (1985)

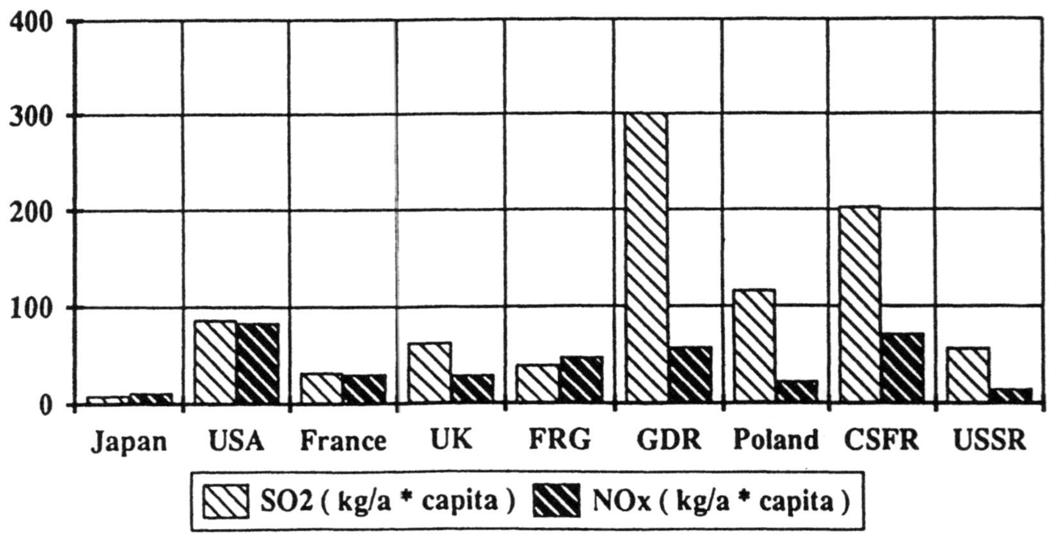

Source: see Table 1

Table 2: CO_2 Emissions (1986)

	Total emissions (Mio. t / a)	% of total world emissions	Emissions per capita (t / a * capita)
Japan	913,77	4,56	7,5
USA	4765,68	23,76	19,73
France	383,68	1,91	6,94
UK	676,39	3,37	11,92
FRG	715	3,6	11,7
GDR	352,46	1,76	21,2
Poland	478,15	2,38	12,7
CSFR	244,27	1,22	15,73

Source: Bundestag, Germany, Enquete-Commission (BT-EC)

Figure 3: CO2-Emissions:tons per year and per capita

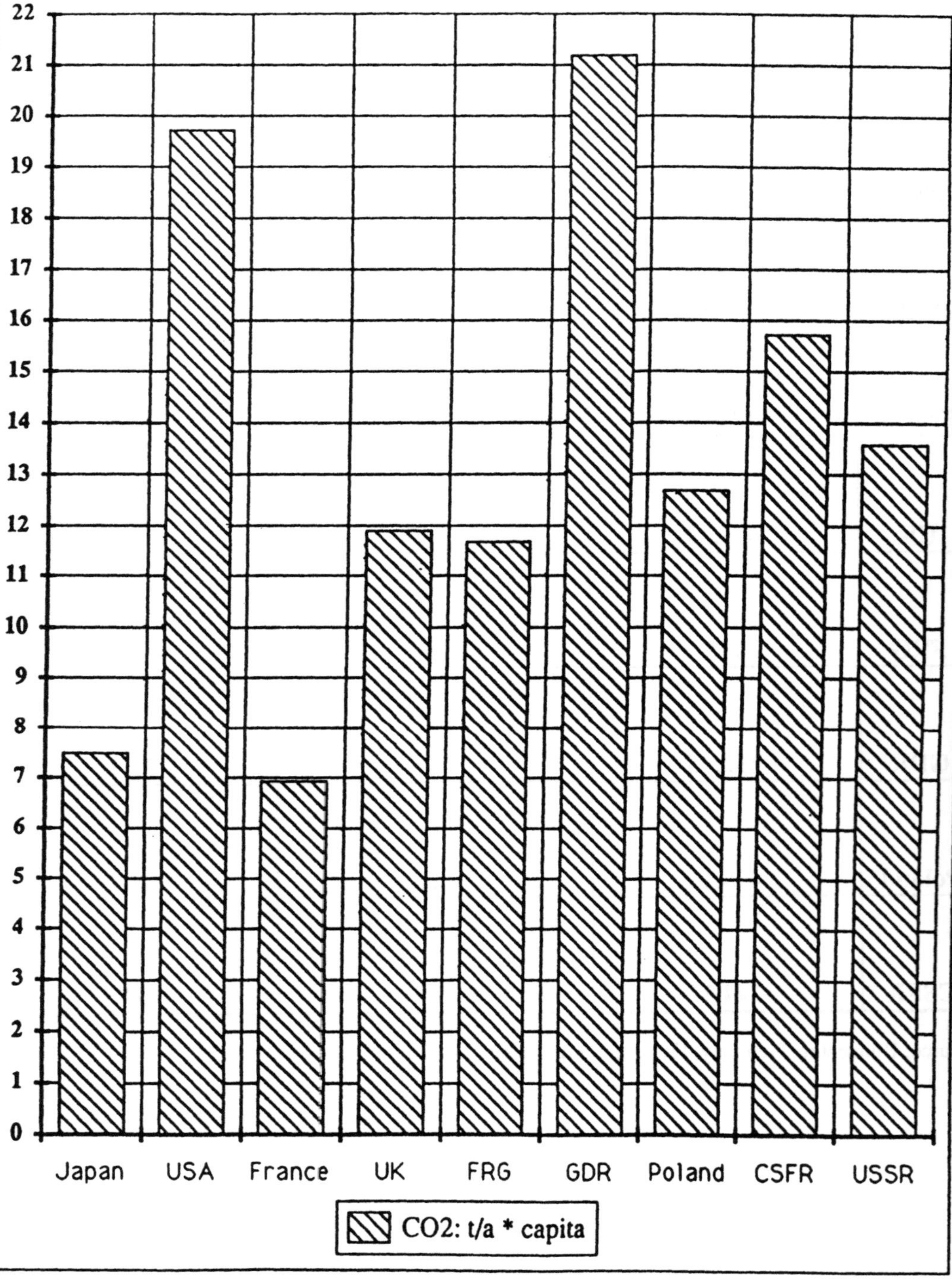

Source: see Table 2

Figure 4: Energy consumption per capita, 1987: kg SKE per capita

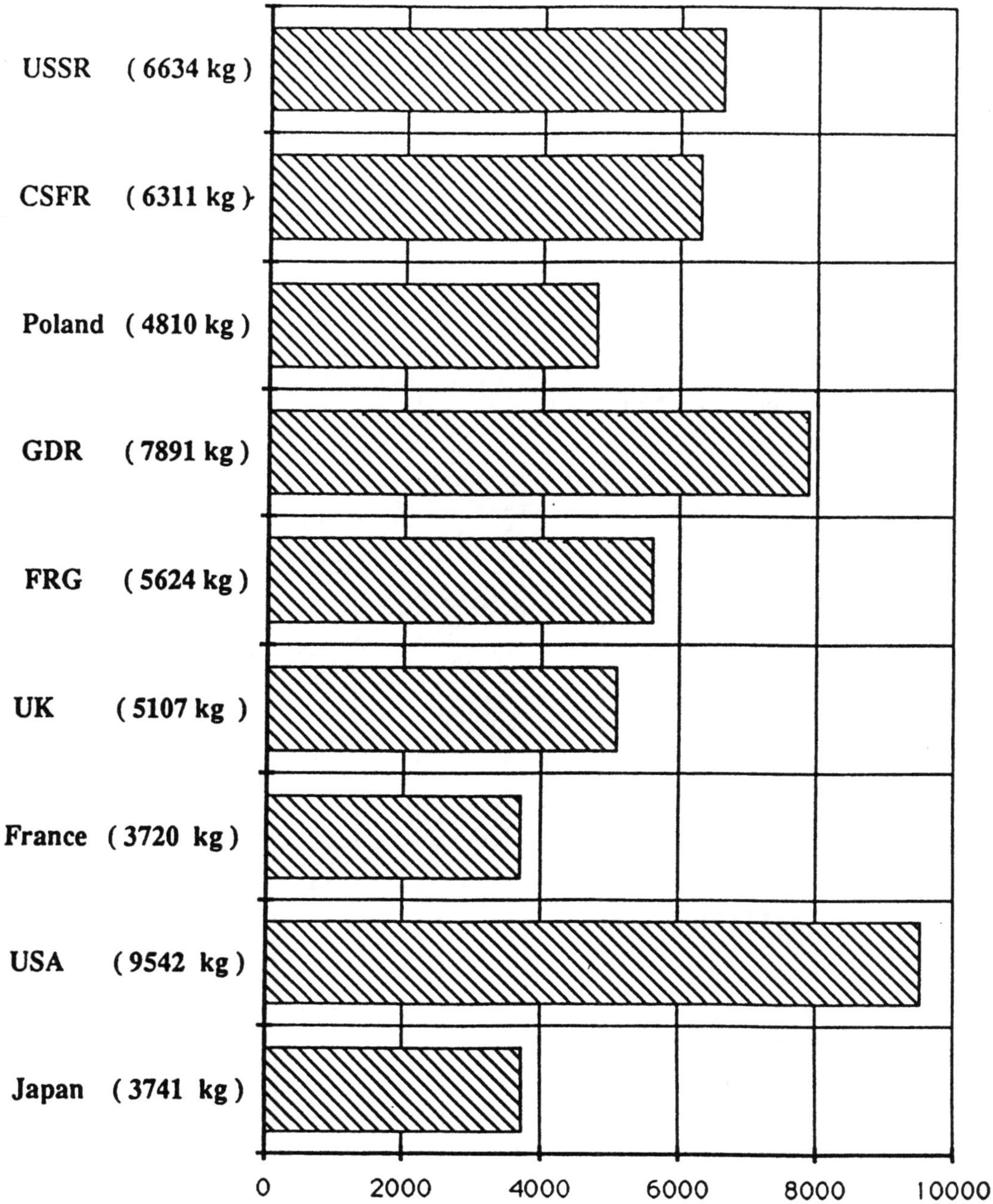

Source: Vereinigung Industrielle Kraftwirtschaft (VIK)

SKE = Steinkohleeinheiten (units of hard coal)

Table 3: Energy Intensity (1987)

	Primary Energy intens. (kgoe / US 87$)	Electricity intens. (kwh / ECU 87
EC 12	0,35	0,38
FRG	0,32	0,32
GDR	0,71	0,54
Poland	0,72	0,5
CSFR	0,73	0,57
EEUR7	0,66	0,55
USSR	0,85	0,67

Figure 5: Energy Intensity (1987)

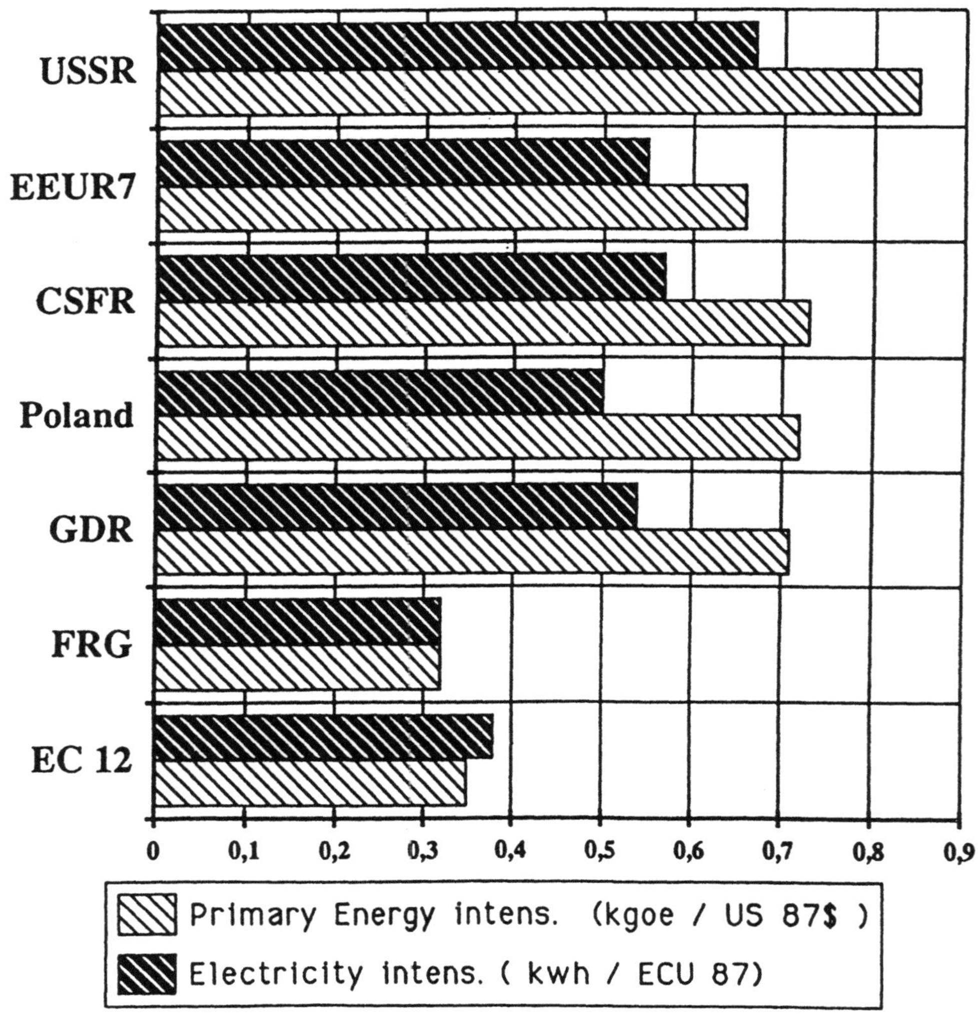

Source: EC-Commission and own calculations ; kgoe = kg oil equivalent; kwh =kilowatt-hours

Table 4: Energy Consumption: GDR and FRG (1987)

	GDR	FRG	GDR + FRG
Total: Mio t SKE	124,2	389,8	514
of which (in %) :			
Coal	3,8	19,2	15,5
Lignite	68,9	8,1	22,8
Oil	13,7	41,9	35,1
Gas	10	16,3	14,8
Electricity	3,6	13,9	11,4
Others		0,5	0,4

Source: BT-EC

Figure 6: Energy Consumption in the GDR and FRG (1988): Energy Sources (%)

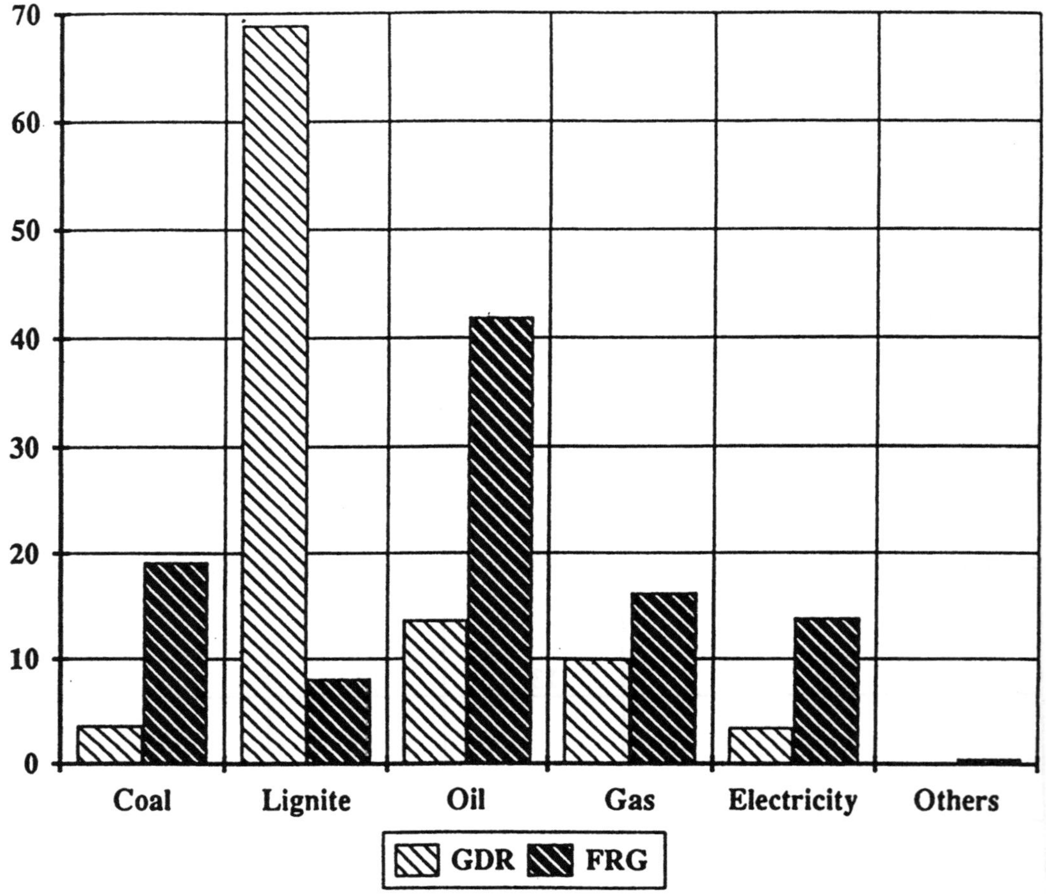

Source: BT-EC

Table 5: Stucture of Electricity Production: GDR and FRG (1988)
Percentage Share of Energy Sources

	GDR %	FRG %
Solid fuel		
- lignite	84.8	18.6
- coal	0.2	30.3
Oil	0.5	2.6
Hydro	1.5	4.8
Nuclear	9.9	33.6
Others	2.9	10.1

Source: BT-EC

- A very large proportion of total energy consumption in the former GDR is accounted for by lignite (68.9% in 1988), whereas in the FRG, by contrast, the main source of energy is still oil (41.9%) despite a declared policy of "Away from oil" *(see Table 4 and Figure 6)*.

- In the case of electricity production in the GDR an even higher proportion is accounted for by lignite (84.8% in 1988), whereas in the FRG only half of total production was based on solid fuels (with 30.3% from hard coal and 18.6% from lignite) *(see Table 5)*.

Thus, the high proportion of lignite with its inherent disadvantages from an environmental point of view (compared with other energy sources) is - among others - one of the reasons of the desperate environmental situation on the territory of the former GDR. Due to this high proportion of lignite (together with insufficient cleaning technologies like scrubbers etc.) the energy sector (production, transformation and consumption) was in the past the main contributor to total emissions in the GDR. In 1988 the energy sector in the GDR was responsible for *(see Figure 7 and Figure 8)*:

- 96.6% of total SO_2-emissions in the GDR;
- 87.0% of total dust emissions in the GDR;
- 41.9% of total NOx-emissions in the GDR.

The energy sector in a broader sense (including all processes concerning energy production, transformation and consumption) is exclusively responsible for all CO_2-emissions. In the case of the former GDR the "leading" role of lignite concerning CO_2-emissions is obvious again *(see Table 6)*:

- Lignite was responsible for 79.9% of total CO_2-emissions in the GDR in 1988.
- The role of all other energy sources concerning their contribution to total CO_2-emissions was of minor importance (percentage part of hard coal, oil and gas: 3.3%, 12.0% and 4.8%).

The above mentioned figures described to some extent the unique position of the GDR on a world scale as far as pollution and the threat to the environment is concerned. But even these average figures for the former GDR do not fully bring out the actual level of pollution in the individual regions. A regional break-down of emissions reveals that regional SO_2-, NOx- and dust-emissions are often four or five times higher than the respective average emission level for the whole former GDR. These most polluted regions (for example: Cottbus, Dresden, Chemnitz, Halle, Leipzig) are situated where (lignite), power plants and energy-related industries are located *(see Table 7)*.

Figure 7: Emissions in the GDR (1988): Contribution of the energy sector (%)

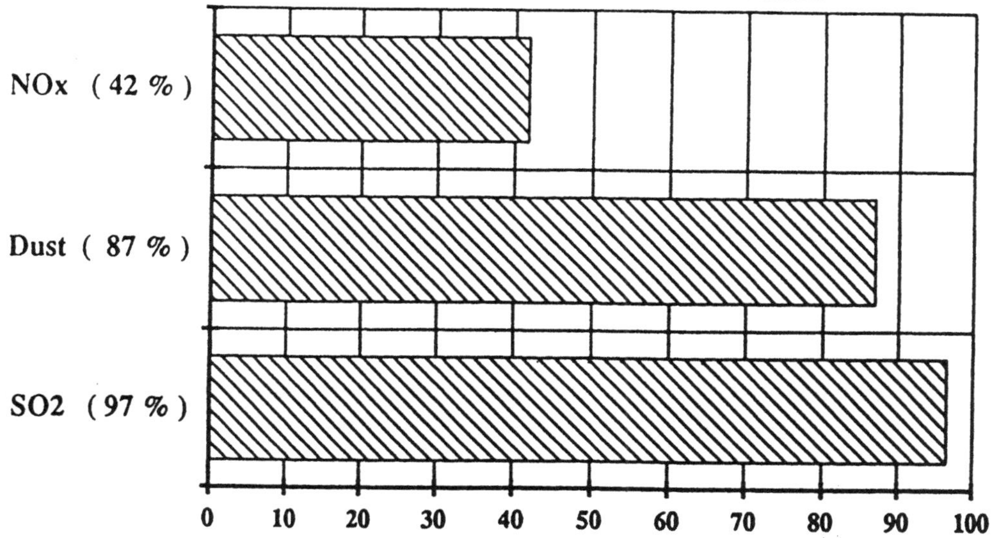

Source: BT-EC

Figure 8: Total Emissions in the GDR (1988; kt)

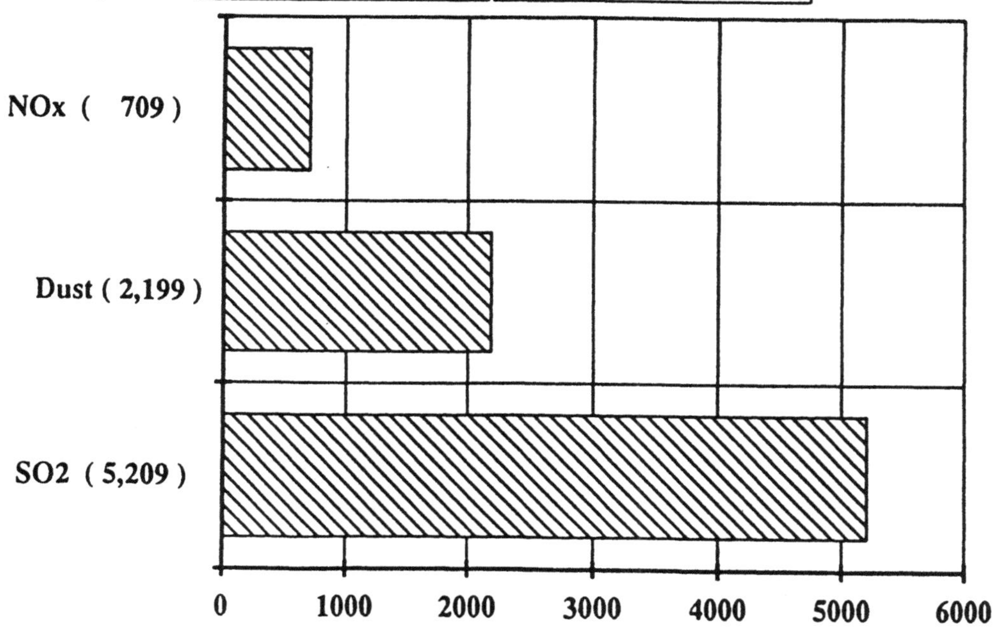

Source: BT-EC

Due to the enormous amount of SO_2-emissions in the former GDR, SO_2-pollution in some areas of the GDR reaches daily maximum values up to 4000 mg/m^3. The WHO has laid down a target maximum of 60 mg/m^3 on an annual average basis. In Weimar and in Erfurt these annual averages are in the order of 305 and 296 mg/m^3 (the maximum permissible threshold in the GDR was set at 150 mg/m^3). By comparison, the Ruhr area in the FRG has a figure of 60 and Frankfurt a figure of 59 mg/m^3 (annual average values) (*Schwinkowski, 1990*).

Pollution in the GDR has caused tremendous health problems, especially in highly-polluted regions (almost half the population of East Germany lives in areas in which the limits for SO_2-emissions are exceeded!). In the old industrial areas in the south of the former GDR, to take only one terrifying example, every second child suffers from respiratory ailments. In general, if emissions were cut by 50% in areas with excessive atmospheric pollution, the health situation could be improved substantially (*Würth, 1985*):

- mortality could fall by 4.5%;
- life expectancy could increase by 3 to 4 years;
- 25% of malignant tumors of the respiratory tract could be avoided in the long term;
- cases of cardiovascular disease could be reduced by 10 to 15%.

Another striking example for effects of air pollution is the situation of the forests. There is now general agreement that the direct and indirect effects of air pollution are the main cause of the widespread damage in Europe's forests and of the forests in Europe. It is accepted that SO_2, NOx and the acids and photo-oxidants they produce in the air (including ozone) have a damaging effect. The recent report (November 1990) on the health of forests in Germany showed that the extent of damage in the East (former GDR) is twice as high as in the West (former FRG).

3. Outlook: Options, Constraints, Future Trends

Before presenting a short outlook for the energy and environmental sector in the former GDR, it seems useful to summarize the main existing problems in this field:

Compared with the FRG and other EC-countries the GDR had a very low energy efficiency. The main reasons for the low energy efficiency are:

- an absence of energy cost-consciousness in centrally-planned economies;

Table 6: Sources of CO_2: Emissions in the GDR (1987)

	Mio. t	%
Lignite	281.8	79.9
Coal	11.8	3.3
Oil	42.3	12.0
Gas	16.7	4.8
Total CO2 - Emission	352.6	100.0

Sources: BT-EC

Table 7: Environmental Emissions in the GDR: A Regional Breakdown

Region	SO2			NOx			Dust		
	kt	t/km2	kg/cap	kt	t/km2	kg/cap	kt	t/km2	kg/cap
Berlin	67	166	53	9	22	7	30	74	243
Cottbus	1373	166	1551	138	17	156	475	57	537
Dresden	416	62	236	30	4	17	223	33	127
Erfurt	232	32	187	13	2	11	133	18	107
Frankfurt	121	17	170	18	3	25	101	14	142
Gera	178	44	240	10	3	13	56	14	76
Halle	986	112	555	67	8	38	471	54	265
Chemnitz	275	46	148	17	3	9	107	18	58
Leipzig	936	189	687	42	8	31	236	48	173
Magdeb.	190	17	152	12	1	10	141	12	113
Potsdam	116	9	103	33	3	30	64	5	57
Rostock	69	10	75	5	1	5	36	5	39
Schwerin	75	9	126	4	0	6	39	4	66
Suhl	112	29	204	6	1	10	44	11	80
Total	**5209**	**48**	**313**	**408**	**4**	**25**	**2199**	**20**	**132**

Source: BT-EC

t/km2 = tons per square km
kg/cap = kg per capita

- inappropriate price structure and subsidies in the energy sector (energy was often supplied at prices which are estimated as being only approximately one third of total production costs and which were scarcely an incentive to save energy);
- high energy conversion losses, particularly in heat and electricity generation, which are mainly due to the fact that most energy plants are technically obsolete (for example: 50% of all steam generators and 36% of all turbines in the GDR's power stations were more than 20 years old).
- the structure of energy consumption itself. In the case of lignite a high degree of energy is used to produce final energy. The internal energy balance is more favorable in the case of oil and gas. The energy sector in the former GDR with lignite as the main energy source thus had a structural bias towards energy inefficiency.
- lack of capital and technologies in order to reduce emissions.
- heavy dependence on energy imports (except lignite), in particular from CMEA countries.
- inherent risks and problems concerning security of nuclear plants.

It is virtually impossible at present to forecast future trends in energy production and consumption in the former GDR. Main determinants of energy consumption, such as the overall economic growth rate and the structure of industry, can only be the subject of speculation. Be that as it may, there is an urgent need to tackle the existing serious problems of energy and environmental policy. The key issue here is the diversification of the structure of supplies. But all problems concerning energy and environment can, at best, only be solved in the medium term. Close integration in the energy sector with the former FRG and the other Western European countries seems indispensable in this context. As the former GDR is now part of the European Community, energy and environmental policy need to be fully integrated at the EC level, too. These aspects may be summarized as follows:

- For the former GDR the issue of energy savings must have absolute priority. Since the expected economic upturn will necessarily be accompanied by an increase in energy demand, energy savings means, first and foremost, an improvement in energy efficiency.
- The absolute prerequisite for improving energy efficiency is the use of up-to-date technology and massive investments (the total amount of investments for the reconstruction of the energy sector is expected to reach nearly 200 billion DM). These two measures are also necessary as a way of tackling the other main problem of the energy sector in the former GDR: the excessive pollution of the environment.
- As far as the structure of energy production and consumption is concerned, it is expected that:

a) Lignite will continue to play an important part, albeit reduced (lignite production is expected to be cut to at most 160 and 170 million tons by 1995 for environmental reasons; today's production level is in the range of 300 million tons). Scientific and technical exchange of views and cooperation with producers in the former GDR (Rheinbraun) will - together with the respective investments - reduce the inherent environmental pollution.
b) Hard coal will play a more important role; imports from non-EC countries are expected to rise substantially in the medium-term, especially when nuclear reactors have to shut down (due to defective safety standards) in the longer term.
c) Gas will increase its part in energy consumption substantially within the next years. The existing grid in the GDR will soon be connected more closely with the Western European grid.
d) Electricity grids in the former GDR and FRG will be interconnected within the next few years.[2] After the takeover of the electricity sector in GDR in last August by three FRG-companies (RWE, PreussenElektra, Bayernwerke), often criticized as an infringement of competition rules and as an obstacle to an efficient and decentralized energy supply system, electricity supply in the former GDR can be provided within the near future by power plants in the West. This opens again the possibility of easing the environmental threat stemming from (lignite-based) electricity production in the former GDR.

According to the German Unification Treaty (Einigungsvertrag) and provisions concerning the application of Community law (*EC Commission, 1990b*) various exceptions and derogations allow transitional arrangements in such areas as safety and quality standards, environmental legislation and structural policy. But as far as secondary Community law[3] in the field of environmental protection is concerned, periods of grace extending to 1995/96 have been allowed for, taking into account the need for integrated medium-term measures. However, wherever a period of more than three years is allowed, there is an obligation to submit an improvement plan within one to two years. But the periods proposed are much shorter than those originally provided for in the directives. Thus, the periods of grace are very short in the case for the former GDR - much shorter than those periods granted, for example, to Spain and Portugal, when they joined the Community, and even much shorter than those originally provided for in the Community directives. Enormous efforts are needed to fulfil the strict FRG- or Community-standards (for example: directives on the reduction of air pollution) by the end of the short transition period. Severe problems are expected to arise when closure of firms and job losses will occur.

But the structural change in the former GDR can also be regarded as a unique chance to avoid mistakes and errors in the field of environmental protection, which are today common for most western industrialized countries. Environmental protection in these countries is based mainly on end-of-the-pipe-techniques and technologies. The task of restructuring nearly the whole economy, as is necessary in the case of the former GDR, allows most industrial sectors to be organized in a more efficient and sustainable way, which means closed industrial cycles (wherever possible) and orientation towards an "ecological economy" (including, for example, social costs in a revised private and national accounting system).

Finally, the restructuring of the economy in the GDR also gives a new perspective - not only with regard to the GDR - to the issue of protection of the environment in the "European House". Under present conditions the rate of return for all investments in the environmental sector in the former GDR and in other Eastern European countries is significantly higher than in western industrialized countries (e.g. if a given sum of money is invested in reducing harmful substances in the East, the reduction that can be achieved is many times higher than in the West!). Given this situation, is there a need for a change of direction - possibly only for a limited period of time - in the environmental policy currently being pursued? The example of the former GDR with its huge environmental burden indicates the urgent need to react and to develop an efficient strategy for all Eastern European countries with similar (or even more severe) problems. As a first step in the direction towards a kind of "green foreign policy" western countries could set up a new "Marshall plan" not only to provide the necessary funding but also, and more importantly, as a proof of the ability of the market-economy system to solve the serious transitional problems (from a planned to a market economy). A development strategy (with a strong environmental dimension) will have positive repercussions for the whole of Eastern Europe and will also help to reduce tensions in neighbor countries provoked by the process of German unification itself.

Endnotes

1. Ratios of CO_2-emissions per unit of energy input differ quite considerably for the various energy sources. This ratio is (on the average) 0.22 in the case of natural gas (0.22 kg CO_2/kwh), compared with 0.33 in the case of oil and 0.39 in the case of coal (and no direct CO_2-emissions in the case of nuclear power). Thus, national CO_2-emissions per capita differ from the respective national energy consumption per capita (due to differences in the respective national structure of energy consumption).

2. Due to differences concerning the stability of the frequency in the Western European electricity grid (including the former FRG) and the Eastern European grid (including the former FRG), electricity could only be supplied via appropriate direct current interconnection systems.

3. The unification of Germany entails the incorporation of the GDR ipso jure into the Community legal order. In other words, the entire Community law was automatically applied in the territory of the former GDR after the unification took place. This legal integration will not involve any amendment of the Treaties or other acts which constitute primary law. By contrast, the immediate, across-the-board application of secondary legislation is not feasible. As with any accession, various technical adjustments will first be needed on account of the specific features of the former GDR's socioeconomic and legal system (see *EC Commission, 1990b*).

References

DEUTSCHER BUNDESTAG (1990) Dritter Bericht der Enquête-Kommission zum Schutz der Erdatmosphäre, BT-Drucksache 11/8030, Bonn, October.
EC COMMISSION (1990a) Directorate General for Energy, Energy for a New Century, The European Perspective, Energy Outlook of the USSR and Eastern Europe, Working Document No 13, Brussels, May 3-4, 1990.
EC COMMISSION (1990b) The Community and German Unification, COM(90)400 final - Vol. I, Brussels, August 21.
FRENCH, HILARY F. (1990) Green Revolutions: Environmental Reconstruction in Eastern Europe and the Soviet Union, Worldwatch Paper 99, Washington, D.C., November.
KRAUS, HANS-HERMANN (1989) The State of the Environment in the Countries of Eastern Europe, European Parliament, Luxembourg (PE 137.119).
PALINKAS, PETER (1988) Outline of the Energy Situation in Eastern Europe (CMEA countries) European Parliament, Luxembourg (PE 126.129).
PALINKAS, PETER (1990) The Energy-supply Situation in the GDR - Evaluation and Perspectives, in: European Parliament, Research and Documentation Papers, Working Document No 1, The Impact of German Unification on the European Community, Luxembourg, pp. 87-97.
PETSCHOW, ULRICH, MEYERHOFF, JÜRGEN and THOMASBERGER, KLAUS (1990) (eds) Umweltreport DDR, Bilanz der Zerstörung, Kosten der Sanierung, Strategien für den ökologischen Umbau, Eine Studie des Instituts für ökologische Wirtschaftsforschung, Frankfurt a. M.: S. Fischer.
SCHWINKOWSKI, KARL (1990) About Pollution in the GDR, paper presented at the Congress "Public Health and Environmental Crisis in Central Europe", April 30 - May 2, 1990, Wilson Center, Washington, D.C.
WÜRTH, GERHARD (1985) Umweltschutz und Umweltzerstörung in der DDR, Europäische Hochschulschriften, Reihe XXXI, Politikwissenschaft, Vol. 70, Frankfurt a.M., Bern, New York: Lang.

STRUCTURAL ADJUSTMENT AND PRIVATIZATION OF THE EAST GERMAN ECONOMY*

Claus Schnabel

In every great monarchy of Europe the sale of the crown lands would produce a very large sum of money, which, if applied to the payment of the public debts, would deliver from mortgage a much greater revenue than any which those lands have ever afforded to the crown.... The crown might immediately enjoy the revenue which this great price would redeem from mortgage. In the course of a few years it would probably enjoy another revenue. When the crown lands had become private property, they would, in the course of a few years, become well-improved and well-cultivated.

Adam Smith (1776, book V, ch. II)

1. Introduction

Since October 3, 1990, West and East Germany are united, after having been politically separated for more than four decades by the iron curtain. In some respects - particularly from an economic point of view - another date might be even more important - since July 1, 1990, the Federal Republic of Germany (FRG) and the German Democratic Republic (GDR) are closely connected by an economic, monetary and social union. Although the State Treaty establishing the intra-German union represented but an intermediate step towards complete political unification, it heralded the end of the socialist "command economy" and its transition into the kind of "social market economy" established in West Germany more than forty years ago.

On July 1, the (East German) Mark was replaced by the Deutsche Mark as legal tender, unit of account, medium of exchange and store of value. Although many economists and politicians would have preferred a slower transition, the exodus of thousands of people per day to West Germany made it clear that there was no political alternative to an early monetary and economic union. The introduction of a currency union at an early stage of the reform process served to clarify the direction in which changes would have to be made and committed the FRG to support the transformation with more than financial help. The State Treaty and its supplementary documents bound the GDR to apply all key economic laws of the FRG, establish a market system with free price formation, restore a free enterprise system, reorganize and (re-)privatize state-owned companies, create a two-tier banking system, introduce private property rights in accordance with western legal requirements, and liberalize foreign trade and capital movements.

There is no historical precedent for the transformation of a socialist command economy with a non-convertible currency to a market economy with a fully convertible currency. A comparison with the experience of the 1948 economic and monetary reform in West Germany makes clear that the introduction of market economy principles represents a much greater challenge for the GDR economy and requires greater structural and behavioral adjustments than was the case after the end of World War II in the FRG. On the one hand, East Germany benefits from the advantages of a hard currency, the free access to the financial and real resources of western countries, the rapid transfer of human and technological know-how from advanced countries, and last but not least from West German fiscal support. On the other hand, four decades of socialist government have left East Germany's economy ill prepared for undergoing the shock treatment which unification entails.

Although long described as the leading economic power of the CMEA, the GDR economy is more a shambles than a powerhouse. The capital stock in industry is largely obsolete because outdated technologies are used, and output is often not competitive. Public infrastructure is outmoded and the environment is heavily polluted. The service sector is underdeveloped and the production and employment structure is strongly skewed towards the public sector: in 1989 only 5 percent of the labor force worked in private firms and only 2 percent were self-employed (*Table 1*). Workers and managers, consumers and investors are still very much influenced by attitudes developed under the previous command economy.

By pursuing a strategy of autarky and isolation from the West, East Germany shut itself off from the international division of labor.

GDR industry tried to produce the entire product set of the world economy - one shoddy version of each. In the metal industry, for example, about half of the range of products in the world assortment were produced, compared to only 17 percent in the same West German branch. Since each branch had been organized as a state monopoly with clearly segmented markets and since these monopolies were not checked by international competition, GDR industry was totally inefficient. When the Berlin wall came down, labor productivity in GDR industry was probably only about one-third of that in the FRG (*Siebert, 1990; Raith, 1990*).

Table 1: Basic Data on the German Democratic Republic, 1989

	unit	GDR 1989	in %
area	km^2	108,333	- -
GDP	bill. Mark	353.3	- -
population	1 000	16,433.8	- -
labour force	1 000	8,885.8	100.0
- by sex			
- - male	1 000	4,570.7	51.4
- - female	1 000	4,315.1	48.6
- by status			
- - self-employed	1 000	184.6	2.1
- - wage earners	1 000	7,541.5	84.9
- - members of cooperatives	1 000	821.2	3.2
- - apprentices	1 000	338.5	3.8
- by enterprises			
- - sozialized enterprises	1 000	7,100.2	79.9
- - cooperatives	1 000	1,312.9	14.8
- - private enterprises	1 000	472.7	5.3

Source: Statistisches Bundesamt (1990), Statistisches Amt der DDR (1990); own calculations

Productivity can be expected to rise fast because the introduction of the market economy removes restrictions and constraints which in the past have adversely affected output per employee. Underutilization of manpower and overmanning must change. Disruptions of production processes due to bottlenecks are reduced drastically. Firms no longer need large inventories in order to minimize the risk of nondelivery of essential inputs. Taking advantage of the division of labor among firms puts an end to the uneconomically low degree of specialization and the high degree of inhouse-production of intermediate goods and equipment. This can only happen, though, if the structure of the East Germany economy changes drastically: small and medium-sized private firms must be established, the service sector must grow, and the large state monopolies must be broken up and privatized. Structural adjustment, deregulation and privatization of the economy are of vital importance for the economic and social evolution of East Germany.

2. Structural Adjustment: Necessity and Perspectives

The sector structure of the GDR economy has been prevented by its isolation from developing in the standard way of advanced capitalist countries: agriculture dwindling to a small fraction of the work force, industry coming down to around one-third of it, and services employing an increasing number of people. *Table 2* shows that such an employment structure is typical for West Germany. In contrast, the East German sector structure is biased in favor of agriculture and manufacturing and against services.

Comparisons of this sort between countries with very different economic regimes, however, are difficult to make as price and production structures are totally different and as there are substantial differences in definitions and statistical classifications (*Halstrick-Schwenk, Loebbe and Wenke, 1990*). Particularly, the biased price relations in the GDR suggest the use of employment statistics rather than statistics on value added or production for meaningful comparisons of sector structures. Such a comparison, presented in *Table 2*, shows that the employment structure of the GDR in 1989 is quite similar to the sectoral distribution of West German employees in 1965! However, this does not necessarily mean that the GDR economy lags 24 years behind the FRG economy. Comparative studies have estimated the technological gap to be just 5 to 10 years (*Gerstenberger, 1990*). Nevertheless the comparison of employment structures can give an impression of the extreme structural adjustment necessary in East Germany.

Employment in agriculture and forestry will certainly decline. In 1989, the employment share of agriculture in the GDR was more than twice as high as in the FRG, whereas labor productivity was no more than 50 percent (*Balz, 1990*). This was due to the GDR strategy of national self-sufficiency and to overemployment which enabled farm workers to enjoy shorter working hours than in western countries. Around 95 percent of agricultural land belongs to cooperatives and only 5 percent is in private hands. Restructuring and privatizing the agricultural sector, reducing inefficient unit size and integrating East Germany into the Common Agricultural Policy of the European Community is an urgent task likely to produce a lot of political conflict.

Table 2: Sector Structures of the GDR and the FRG

sector	GDR gross value added 1989 in million Mark	GDR gross value added 1989 in %	GDR employment 1989 in 1 000s	GDR employment 1989 in %	FRG employment shares, in % 1965	FRG employment shares, in % 1989
agriculture & forestry	33,641	9.2	959.9	10.8	10.7	3.9
manufacturing	197,632	53.8	3883.0	43.7	40.0	33.1
construction	20,713	5.6	597.8	6.7	9.2	6.6
transport & communication	19,325	5.2	673.2	7.6	5.5	5.6
trade	25,843	7.0	908.1	10.2	12.4	13.0
others	70,460	19.2	1863.7	21.0	22.2	37.8
(of which: state*)	(27,645)	(7.5)	(?)	(?)	(9.8)	(15.4)
Total	367,614	100.0	8885.8	100.0	100.0	100.0

* Official data do not provide adequate information on what would be termed the state sector in western definitions. Particularly, the official employment figures do not include military and security personnel etc. in the order of up to 700,000. This means that total employment can be estimated at about 9.5 million in 1989.

Source: Statistisches Amt der DDR (1990), Statistisches Bundesamt (1990), National Accounts; own calculations

Massive structural adjustments will also take place in manufacturing. In 1989, 44 percent of total GDR employment was in manufacturing and the goods-producing crafts, while this share was only 33 percent in the FRG. Most branches of GDR industry are therefore expected to experience massive employment reductions, particularly in the consumption goods industries and the chemical industry (partly due to environmental reasons). Pollution- and energy-intensive branches will have to adjust. Ailing industries, which are no longer internationally competitive, such as shipbuilding and parts of the textile and steel industry, will also become a policy problem. Mechanical and electrical engineering may have a better chance of survival because of their relatively high technological standard, their skilled labor force, their potential for intra-industrial division of labor with the similarly specialized West German industry, and the increasing demand for their products when modernizing the East European economies. From the modernization of the East German economy and infrastructure, the construction sector is likely to benefit most; its employment share of 6.7 percent might even increase.[1]

The ideological emphasis on industry, which was based on the obsessive growth orientation of socialist economies and was characterized by an import substitution strategy attempting to produce the product set of the world economy, has severely hampered the development of the service sector. The underdeveloped service sector will therefore expand considerably. The expansion of employment in services will take place by privatization of state services (such as banking and insurance or parts of the health service), by the contracting-out of services from industrial conglomerates, by increasing trade and by creation of new services. Substantial growth potential exists in tourism and in legal advice and consulting (the GDR had just 600 lawyers, for instance, compared to 55,000 in the FRG).

The service sector as shown in *Table 2* has been restricted not only by the political focus on industry but also by the integration of services into production enterprises. Similar to the principle of national autarky described above there existed an autarkic production strategy in which firms eschewed specialization - at great cost to efficiency - in order to produce all the necessary components for the production process. Whereas West Germany adopted just-in-time production organization, in which large firms rely on small, highly specialized firms to provide inputs in a carefully timed manner, East Germany had only very few independent firms servicing large enterprises. Most of the work was done inhouse, and this included all sorts of services which were thought to be essential for the production process or for the workers. The result was that production enterprises employed large repair groups, construction workers, electricians, nurses, gardeners, farm workers etc., most of whom they have to lay off now.

As the organization of East German industry was designed to facilitate top-down planning, it was strongly skewed towards large state enterprises integrated both horizontally and vertically. All firms in a particular sector and their suppliers were grouped together in large conglomerates called Kombinate. In 1988 there existed 126 national Kombinate in industry, each consisting of 20 to 40 firms and employing more than 20,000 workers on average. There were also 95 regional industrial Kombinate with about 2,000 employees each, and further conglomerates existed in construction, transport and agriculture. The largest Kombinate were Carl Zeiss Jena, Cotton (Karl-Marx-Stadt) and Robotron (Dresden) with roughly 70,000 employees each. The share of industrial Kombinate in employment, production and export was in the range of 95 to 100 percent. Not surprisingly, their excessive size and the anticompetitive structure of industry proved to be impediments to innovation and productivity growth (for details, see *Cornelsen, 1990,* and the *Statistical Yearbook of the GDR 1989*).

The result of this centralization and integration is a virtual absence of small to medium-sized firms in East Germany - the kind of firm that is of vital importance for economic development in western countries. Similar deficiencies are found in other East European countries such as Hungary (*Kornai, 1986*) and Poland (*Lipton and Sachs, 1990*), but in the GDR concentration has been brought to an extreme. *Table 3* shows that in 1988 the average number of employees per enterprise in GDR industry was almost 900 (about ten times higher than in 1950), compared to just 190 in the FRG. Such differences exist in all sectors of industry.

As can be seen from *Table 4*, total employment and production shares of the 2,013 firms with fewer than 500 employees were as low as 12 percent in the GDR in 1988. This stands in sharp contrast to the importance of the Mittelstand in the FRG - the 2 million small to medium-sized firms that are the backbone of West Germany's economy. Such firms (with fewer than 500 employees and/or sales below DM 100 million) account for two-thirds of employment, roughly half of total sales, and almost 40 percent of total gross investment in the FRG (*Gruhler, 1990*).

Before the last wave of nationalizations in 1972, there existed more than 10,000 small to medium-sized firms in GDR industry with total employment and production shares of 25 percent. The decline of such firms was accompanied by a strong reduction in self-employment. In 1989 the number of self-employed persons was down to 184,600 (*Table 1*), compared to 258,500 in 1971 and even 2,304,000 in 1946. In other words, the share of self-employment in East Germany fell from 28.3 percent to 2.1 percent since the end of World War II.

Table 3: Industry Structures of the GDR and the FRG, 1988

sector	enterprises	GDR employees*	employees per firm	FRG employees per firm
chemical industry	236	335,000	1419	296
metal industry	43	138,000	3209	474
construction material	132	94,000	712	71
mechanical engineering / manufacture of vehicles	1157	970,000	838	217
electrical engineering / electronics	298	463,000	1554	333
light industry	733	492,000	671	95
textile industry	166	216,000	1301	169
food industry	577	277,000	480	125
total industry	3342	2,985,000	893	190

*excluding apprentices

Source: Statistisches Bundesamt (1990), Gerstenberger/Kischel (1989); own calculations.

Table 4: Enterprises, Employment and Production in GDR Industry by Size of Enterprise, 1988

size by number of employees	enterprises number	enterprises in %	employees* number	employees* in %	gross production in %
1 - 25	112	3,3	1555	0,0	0,1
26 - 50	175	5,1	6591	0,2	0,2
51 - 100	326	9,6	24,246	0,8	0,9
100 - 200	536	15,7	79,458	2,5	2,5
201 - 500	864	25,4	280,268	8,7	8,0
501 - 1000	556	16,3	395,007	12,2	10,8
1001 - 2500	527	15,5	837,193	25,9	24,4
2501 - 5000	214	6,3	731,751	22,6	20,7
5001 - 10 000	77	2,3	558,065	17,3	20,7
over 10 000	21	0,6	318,444	9,9	11,9
Total	3408	100,0	3,232,578	100,0	100,0

* excluding apprentices

Source: Statistisches Bundesamt (1990); own calculations.

In many sectors of the economy, particularly in industry, agriculture, transport and communication, there was almost no self-employment. Only in crafts did small private firms play a substantial role (see *Table 5*). However, as private firms were legally restricted to a maximum of 10 employees, their average size was only 3 employees per firm (compared to 61 employees in craft cooperatives). This explains why total employment in private enterprises was only 472,700 in 1989 (see *Table 1*).

Structural (re-)adjustment of the GDR economy by means of invigorating private firms and the Mittelstand is a prerequisite for economic development. The reversal of the nationalizations of the 1970s can be a first step to increase self-employment and the number of private firms. Often the former owners of nationalized firms are ready for a new start, although sometimes they are too old for business. Unfortunately, their young successors know costs, prices and balance sheets only as bureaucratic fictions.

This is a general problem in East Germany: 50 years of central planning since the beginning of World War II have been just long enough to kill off the understanding of how business works. The lack of experience in marketing, accounting, finance, price-setting etc. is an obstacle to more self-employment, establishment of new enterprises, and privatization.

Despite these teething troubles, increasing competition and pressure on productivity growth in the East German economy will favor division of labor and establishment of smaller firms as suppliers of products and services. Therefore in the long run the share of self-employment in East Germany can be expected to reach West German standards (11 percent). This would mean an increase in self-employment to almost one million in East Germany.

Particularly in those branches where initial capital requirements are relatively low, such as crafts, restaurants and other services, the number of small private enterprises will increase rapidly. In the first three quarters of 1990 there were already 200,000 registrations of new business.[2] It will take some years, however, until the East German economy reaches the sound mixture of small, medium-sized and large firms which is typical for West Germany and which is so vital for the growth, flexibility and stability of a market economy. The most important step in this direction besides establishing new firms is deregulation and privatization of existing enterprises.

Table 5: Enterprises and Employment in GDR Craft Sectors by Legal Form of Enterprise, 1988

	enterprises			employees*			employees per enterprises		
sector	cooper-atives	private firms	total	cooper-atives	private firms	total	cooper-atives	private firms	total
manufact.	1263	58,100	59,363	71,700	194,200	265,900	57	3	4
construc.	1058	14,295	15,353	51,800	45,200	97,000	49	3	6
services	398	9,839	10,237	42,000	26,200	68,200	106	3	7
Total	2719	82,234	84,953	165,500	265,600	431,000	61	3	5

* excluding apprentices

Source: Statistisches Bundesamt (1990); own calculations.

3. Deregulation and Privatization

Deregulation and privatization are government strategies of increasing the scope of the market in the production and allocation of goods and services by removing excessive government control, promoting competition, and assigning property rights from the state to private persons or corporations. Thus they are the opposite of government regulation and nationalization, which used to be the dominant government strategies in East Germany for 40 years.

After the founding of the GDR in 1949, expropriation took place in several waves. In agriculture, farm collectivization à la Stalin started in 1952, finally putting almost all arable land in the hands of the state or of farm cooperatives. This collectivization did not necessarily remove the owner's basic title to his land - it simply made it non-negotiable and worthless. Private citizens could also go on owning houses, but they were often "persuaded" to hand over their houses to the state by state-set rents which did not cover costs. Throughout the 1950s and 1960s the private sector of industry was reduced more and more, either by direct nationalization or by the state increasing its shareholdings in many industrial firms. This was achieved, for instance, by denying supplies to private companies or by forcing them to take out loans with the State Bank for repairs and investments that their controlled cash-flows would not pay for. In 1972, most remaining small private enterprises were nationalized and finally integrated into large conglomerates (Kombinate).

When attempting to reverse this process, it might be useful to have a look at western experience with deregulation and privatization. Such policies are currently in progress in many advanced countries such as the U.S., Japan and France as well as in numerous developing and newly industrialized countries, but nowhere are they carried out as extensively as in the U.K. under Mrs. Thatcher (see *Vickers and Yarrow, 1988; Schnabel, 1990*). In West Germany, the first privatization program was announced by Ludwig Erhard as early as 1957, and the number of federal state participations has been reduced substantially particularly by the Kohl government, which recently sold its remaining shares in large companies such as Volkswagen, Veba and Salzgitter AG (see *Knauss, 1990*). Both the experience of the U.K. and of West Germany are therefore of special interest for restructuring the East German economy. Of course, priorities may differ and East Germany may have additional problems, but the following principal aims of privatization and deregulation in western countries will still be relevant.

3.1 Promoting Competition

An important aspect of deregulation and privatization in western countries has been the promotion of competition by liberalizing markets, reducing government control and bureaucracy, removing barriers to entry, abolishing legal monopolies, and breaking up and selling state monopolies. Particularly the British experience shows that competition and deregulation are crucial prerequisites for the transfer of property rights into private hands. For, if market dominance persists, regardless of the change of ownership, then a monopoly position in the private sector could turn out to be worse or no better than the public sector monopoly it replaces. Whereas the privatization of firms in reasonably competitive industries (including Jaguar, Rolls-Royce, BP etc.) has generally been successful, the Thatcher government has strongly been criticized for failing to introduce sufficiently effective frameworks of competition and regulation before privatizing such utility industries as telecommunications and gas (*Vickers and Yarrow, 1988; Bishop and Kay, 1988*).

The East German situation has more parallels with western experience than with the situation in other countries of Eastern Europe. Since Poland, Hungary or the CSFR are largely isolated from international competition, they must urgently break up their monopoly companies in order to encourage competition and the functioning of the price system on their domestic markets. In contrast, the monopoly power of the GDR Kombinate disappeared as soon as the two Germanies merged their economies. The State Treaty and unification made sure that all key economic laws of the FRG apply in East Germany, that there is strong competition from western firms, that government control is reduced, and that barriers to entry for new firms are removed. The serious financial problems of many East German firms demonstrate how intense competition from western firms is. Of course, the existence of effective competition on East German markets does not relieve the government of dismantling state monopolies into smaller organizational units. In wholesale and retail, the GDR government had to learn this lesson the hard way, because its delay in breaking up the state monopoly in trade, retail outlets, etc. temporarily led to monopolistic price increases after the introduction of the D-Mark in July 1990.

Taking over the legal framework of the FRG has definitely helped East Germany in encouraging competition, but it has also created similar problems as in West Germany. Even in the "capitalist" FRG, economic activity is highly regulated in some fields such as the service and the crafts sector with the result that competition is artificially reduced and private initiatives are discouraged. Prominent examples are rigid store hours, excessive regulations on craftsmanship, the telecommunications monopoly of the Deutsche Bundespost and the highly regulated transport and energy sectors. Suggestions by economists that East Germany should seize its chance and leap-frog West Germany to a more privatized, less regulated telecommunications, transport and energy infrastructure have proved to be wishful thinking. East German politicians agreed to take over the existing and relatively successful model of the West German economy without any "theoretical improvements". As a result, the monopolistic structure of the West German energy sector has been extended to East Germany because only under this condition were West German energy suppliers willing to finance the huge investments which are necessary for reconstructing the energy sector in East Germany. It might be possible, however, that under the pressure of the task ahead, the German government will undertake initiatives to liberalize the public infrastructure sector by removing institutional barriers to private investment.

3.2 Improving Economic Performance

The principal objective of privatization is improving economic efficiency and productivity. Those activities which had previously been sheltered in the public sector are exposed to the pressure of the market, and the new challenge brings about a change of attitudes by both management and workers. By reducing government involvement in enterprise decision making privatization eliminates another frequent source of distortion. Privatization policies rest on the assumption that private firms exhibit superior economic performance than their state-owned counterparts with respect to costs, productivity and profitability. An increasing number of international studies (*e.g. Borcherding, Pommerehne and Schneider 1982; Picot and Kaulmann, 1989*) as well as the British experience (*Bishop and Kay, 1988; Vickers and Yarrow, 1988*) provide empirical confirmation of this superiority hypothesis.

All these aspects are relevant for East Germany (and for the other countries of Eastern Europe): there used to be massive government intervention; competition and incentives for working efficiently hardly existed; labor productivity was low. So privatization can be seen as a good way of overcoming these problems. But privatization means more for former communist countries, which used to be isolated from technological developments and innovations in the West: it is probably the best way for quickly filling their technological and managerial gaps. Western firms buying former state enterprises in East Germany will drastically modernize the capital stock, and they will bring technological know-how and managerial experience, which are in short supply in the East. Such a transfer of capital and knowledge can only work, however, if the firms to be privatized can be sold to foreign investors. Due to the State Treaty and unification, this is no problem in East Germany, but some other countries of Eastern Europe are more reluctant to let foreigners in.

3.3 Improving the Public Finances

In many countries, an important motive for privatization has been the government's need to raise revenue or reduce expenditure. Net proceeds from the sale of state-owned enterprises and dwellings in Britain almost reached £ 50 billion in the 1980s and significantly helped to eliminate the budget deficit. In West Germany, revenues from the 1984-1990 sales of federal assets amounted to DM 9.9 billion, but here financial aspects have played a minor role compared to efficiency considerations (*Knauss, 1990*). As already suggested in the introductory quote by *Adam Smith (1776)*, if the assets are more productive under private than public operation, privatization will raise more revenue than the expected income stream under public ownership. Thus privatization improves both economic efficiency and the public finances.

This aspect is of crucial importance to East Germany. Here income streams in most state enterprises are negative and the government cannot expect this to change soon. In order to reduce the huge losses which have to be covered by the public budget, fundamental reconstruction of state companies would be necessary. The measures to be taken include replacing or retraining management, modernizing machinery and equipment, importing technological know-how, etc. But government has neither the manpower nor the experience for such drastic changes. Therefore, in order to reduce the probability of bankruptcy and to improve prospects for profitability in the future, East Germany has to privatize its state enterprises as soon as possible, even if this means accepting relatively low bids or writing off companies' debts. The sale of state companies does not only reduce the amount of government subsidies; it is also likely to increase future tax revenues when these companies are working profitably under private ownership.

The financial motive for privatization has recently been stressed by the Deputy Governor of the Deutsche Bundesbank, Mr. Helmut Schlesinger. He suggested utilizing privatization revenues as an additional source of finance for reducing the huge budget deficit caused by unification. Since privatization in East Germany might not yield substantial amounts in the near future, Mr. Schlesinger has proposed intensifying privatization in West Germany. According to his estimates, revenues from sales of public assets in West Germany could amount to DM 370 billion.

3.4 Widening the Ownership of Economic Assets

By giving preferential treatment to small investors, employees and tenants, sales of public assets can be structured so as to promote wider ownership of economic assets. This has been an important objective of Mrs. Thatcher's privatization program in Britain, where the proportion of adult share owners has risen from 5 to 27 percent and where more than one million tenants have been able to buy their houses from the state (*Schnabel, 1990*). Widening share ownership also played an important role in the reductions of FRG participation in companies such as Volkswagen and Veba in the 1960s, whereas the privatizations in the 1980s did not make use of such preferential treatments (*Knauss, 1990*).

However, in both countries the new shareholders typically own few shares, and many subscribers to subsidized share issues quickly sold their holdings after flotation, unless there were strong incentives to retain shares, such as vouchers and share bonuses for loyalty. Furthermore, from an economic point of view, privatization is generally a poor instrument for widening share ownership in comparison with alternatives such as changing fiscal incentives for individual share ownership (see *Vickers and Yarrow, 1988, ch. 7.4*).

Despite these theoretical and practical problems, the question of giving preferential treatment to individuals, employees and tenants when privatizing state assets has played an important role in East Germany. Some politicians have demanded that all inhabitants of East Germany be given equal shares in state wealth and thus claims to privatization revenues. Even the State Treaty (Article 10.6) mentions the possibility that savers could be compensated for their nominal losses in the two-for-one conversion of East German Marks into D-Marks by conceding them claims to socialized wealth. This seems unlikely to happen, however, because according to the State Treaty revenues from privatization will primarily have to be used for covering the costs of reconstruction, of government subsidies, of debt relief, and for improving the public finances, so that not much will be left for distribution among the general public.

More promising ways of securing broad participation of the public in economic wealth and growth might be employee share ownership and privatization of state dwellings.[3] Giving employees preferential access to a modest fraction of the shares of their enterprises might motivate them and could increase acceptance of privatization and of the social market economy. It is unlikely, however, that East German workers will retain their shares longer than their western counterparts if there are no financial or legal incentives to do so.

In contrast to share ownership, house ownership could be an incentive for East Germans not to start moving again to West Germany. In 1989 only 42 percent of residential property in East Germany was in private hands. Privatization of state houses - perhaps with preferential treatment of those tenants who have invested in modernization of their dwellings - might improve the physical state of the buildings as well as the public finances and the motivation of people. Of crucial importance for the success of privatization will be its organizational implementation.

4. The Treuhandanstalt: Organization, Objectives and Problems?

In order to organize privatization and structural adjustment of the economy, the GDR government has established the Treuhandanstalt, a giant trustee agency responsible for almost 8,000 state firms. Since unification, the Treuhandanstalt is formally linked to the Federal Ministry of Finance in Bonn, but it enjoys wide-ranging autonomy in its decisions. In an attempt to import managerial experience and to send a signal to potential investors, Mr. Detlev Rohwedder, chairman of Hoesch, the West German steel and engineering group, has been appointed chairman of the agency's supervisory board. The Treuhandanstalt's headquarters are in East Berlin, but there exist 15 regional offices responsible for small to medium-sized local firms.

The Treuhandanstalt is subdivided into four departments reflecting the agency's main tasks, namely Reconstruction, Privatization, Labor Market/Social Policy, and Finance. According to the Treuhand Act, the agency is not only charged with privatization, but also with reconstruction and liquidation of state enterprises. "In anticipation of future privatization revenues" (§2), the Treuhandanstalt may give financial injections and back up loans from private banks which help companies overcome liquidity problems during reconstruction. In the Unification Treaty the credit limit of the Treuhandanstalt has been extended to DM 25 billion. Most observers seem to agree that the Treuhandanstalt is but a second-best solution, but there is less consensus about the kind of first-best solution.[4]

The basic concept of the Treuhandanstalt is breaking up the Kombinate and selling off the pieces, using proceeds from successful privatizations for facilitating the reconstruction and privatization of less attractive firms. But the difficult puzzle is how to privatize a vast array of firms in a manner that is swift, efficient, fair, politically acceptable, and likely to create an effective structure of corporate control. Whereas Mrs. Thatcher, the world's leading privatizer, has overseen the transfer of a few dozen state enterprises to the private sector in the past decade, East Germany has about 6,000 candidates for privatization. The ownership of roughly 2,000 public utility companies will be transferred to local authorities. In autumn 1990, only about 200 firms had been sold by the Treuhandanstalt, with revenues amounting to DM one billion. Progress is slow because there are many obstacles to rapid privatization, such as the sorry state and the indebtedness of GDR industry, valuation problems, liabilities for past pollution, unsolved problems of property ownership, and political interference.

As is clearly visible to any visitor, East German industry is in a poor state. Although the lack of western methods of accounting makes evaluation of enterprises very difficult, official and unofficial sources in East Germany indicate that less than one-third of state enterprises might be capable of competing in a free market, up to one-third might have to close down, and the rest need complete overhauling and financial support to stay in business. Conversations with western experts and East German businessmen suggest that these "guesstimates" might even be too optimistic. Only one-third of GDR machinery and equipment was not older than five years, while 21 percent were older than 20 years. Official depreciation was too low, so that the real value of physical assets might be as low as one-quarter to one-tenth of their book value (*Institut der Deutschen Wirtschaft, 1990; Pohl, 1990*).

A better impression of the real situation of East German industry can be obtained from the western-style balance sheets and profitability plans which the state firms were asked to hand in to the Treuhandanstalt by October 31, 1990 (although many firms have not been able to meet this deadline). These enable the agency to direct its loans to those companies which have a realistic prospect of survival. Before, the Treuhandanstalt had severe problems in finding out which claims for financial assistance were promising and which were not. In July tight spending limits set by Bonn meant the agency could grant only an across-the-board 41 percent of all amounts requested, thus at the same time damaging promising firms and keeping alive firms without any chance of long-term survival. The absence of realistic balance sheets made evaluation of firms and assessment of credit risks almost impossible, thus delaying privatization.

Even without balance sheets it was obvious that the economic situation of most communist state enterprises is much worse than of those companies which were privatized in the U.K. or West Germany, making privatization in East Germany (and other East European countries) much more difficult. For example, after taking a close look at East German chemical plants, most West German chemical firms have been reluctant to take them over, on any terms. Although East German chemical industry has had a reputation of being the best in Eastern Europe, the Treuhandanstalt may count itself lucky if western firms bother to take GDR chemical plants for free. The problem is not just the sorry state of industry, but also the fact that most industrial sites are deeply polluted. Since GDR industry used to be one of the worst polluters in Europe, the clean-up bill is expected to be enormous. It is quite understandable that western firms do not want to pay much for such companies and that they demand to be protected against the companies' liabilities for past pollution.

Another problematic inheritance from socialist planning is companies' huge debt to the State Bank. In order to secure state control, East German managers were not allowed to finance investments by making appropriate use of depreciation charges. All "profit" after paying variable costs had to be sent straight to the government, which decided about capital spending. Firms were forced to take out loans with the State Bank for needed investments or repairs, and even for paying company taxes. The result was that the Kombinate's collective debt amounted to M 212 billion on June 30, 1990, which were converted into DM 106 billion in the currency reform. Since state companies' debts were in fact hidden state debts, since many firms are not able to pay their debts when interest rates of a free capital market apply, and since the huge amount of debt clearly deters potential investors, many West German economists have suggested that the companies' debts be written off or taken over by the government or by the Treuhandanstalt. The hesitation of the government to do so has substantially delayed privatization (for details see *POHL, 1990*).

Privatization is also difficult to implement when there are unsolved questions of property ownership. The process of nationalization described above and the expropriation of residential property belonging to GDR citizens who fled to the West has left a mass of claims of former owners. Until these claims are sorted out, western firms are reluctant to invest in East Germany: they want to be certain that they can have title to what they are buying. The Unification Treaty has tried to solve this problem by making nationalizations and expropriations reversible in principle. In order to get back their property, former owners must quickly apply to the state and pay back what they then received. At the end of August 1990, 1,565 small firms had been returned to their original owners this way. If restitution is not possible, former owners will be compensated. Since in many cases final decisions are likely to be made in court, the process of privatization and reprivatization can be expected to take some time, and uncertainty will not end soon.

Last but not least there is the problem of bureaucratic rigidity and political interference. State bureaucracy in East Germany is not only huge and inflexible, but also composed of members of the former communist party, SED. These often are neither able nor willing to implement the sale of state assets, or they try to sell off prime assets to other SED members. Potential investors are also deterred by municipalities' reluctance or inability to provide land for business purposes, by legal job guarantees in companies to be sold, and by politicians' demands to preserve jobs by not liquidating inefficient parts of enterprises and branches. Although the Treuhandanstalt enjoys a high degree of autonomy, there is a definite risk that the political process will dominate and retard privatization and structural adjustment.

5. Privatization Strategies

The Treuhandanstalt as well as the German government must take the privatization problems mentioned above into account and try to overcome them as soon as possible, e.g. by clearly defining property rights and by protecting investors from liabilities originating in the past. It is essential to establish institutional arrangements which enable the trustee agency to operate efficiently. Important principles must be the political independence and the temporary nature of the Treuhandanstalt.

The prime task of the Treuhandanstalt should be dismantling state monopolies into smaller organizational units, extracting organizational sub-units such as repair crews, suppliers, services etc., and selling these enterprises. Priority should be given to rapid privatization, and not to nursing through and reconstructing inefficient firms. For successful reconstruction, the Treuhandanstalt would need a large staff of highly-qualified experts, who are in short supply in East and West Germany. Such a large staff would also be in danger of confirming Parkinson's Law and perpetuate the agency's existence.

Since the government or the Treuhandanstalt have neither the manpower and experience nor the time for reconstructing and modernizing state firms, they should sell them rapidly, even if this means accepting lower revenues in the short run. The increase in revenues from privatization after reconstruction would not cover the costs of reconstruction and the opportunity costs of liquidity injections, interest payments and tax revenues foregone. Privatization proceeds should be used for improving the public finances, for financing the modernization of public infrastructure etc., but not for polishing up state companies or softening the process of structural adjustment. Modernizing and reconstructing privatized firms should be left to private investors.

The British experience has shown how important positive psychological effects from successful early privatizations can be for the success and acceptance of the whole program. Therefore the transfer of ownership into private hands should start with reprivatization of nationalized firms and with privatization of enterprises and sub-units that are easy to sell. These include firms with special know-how, with valuable residential property, with competitive advantages, with promising strategies and with good prospects on a free market.

In order to prevent investors from skimming the cream off and leaving government with problematic firms, it has been suggested to tie up parcels which combine a very attractive firm and a company in need of reconstruction (*Lipp, 1990*). This, however, might delay privatization and create more problems than it solves. From an economic point of view, there is nothing wrong with firms picking the few dozen "pearls" of East German industry, provided there exist arrangements which secure realistic pricing of assets.

Mechanisms for selling state assets - or transferring them free of charge - to the private sector must be devised that are rapid, transparent, equitable and that prevent the inadvertent creation of new monopolistic structures. There are several ways of privatization:

- Transfers free of charge can be a means of getting rid of unattractive firms, but they can also be used to encourage management buy-outs (provided that East German managers and workers are able and willing to take the risks involved).

- Shares can be offered to the public, perhaps accompanied by giving employees or small investors preferential access to a modest fraction of the shares. The shares offered could be shares of single companies as well as shares of the Treuhandanstalt itself, in such a way transforming the agency into a private investment fund (a more detailed proposal of this kind can be found in *T. Mayer's comment, this volume*). However, the public offering of shares is time-consuming and it is hampered by problems of valuation and by underdeveloped capital markets in East Germany.

- In view of the severe financial and logistical difficulties involved in the sale of several thousand companies through public offerings, the Treuhandanstalt must largely rely on direct sales of shares and mergers with western firms. In these sales, elements of auctions should play an important role.

Auctions are an effective, fair and transparent means of selling state enterprises. They make use of market forces and can be expected to lead to much more accurate pricing and finally to higher revenues than fix-price offers for sale. When selling state enterprises, the Treuhandanstalt could invite bids for shares above a given minimum price, making use of two alternative mechanisms: either all the shares would be sold to the highest bidder, or shares would be allocated to those who entered the highest bids in a tender offer.

Institutional mechanisms should be established by which individual firms can dissociate themselves from the Treuhandanstalt, for example by management buy-outs or by pointing out a potential investor. The agency could be forced either to give its consent to the privatizations proposed or to present better alternatives (see also *Siebert, 1990; Lipp, 1990*). When state enterprises are sold directly to investors or when there are management buy-outs, the negotiated contracts should be made public and checked for correctness, and other potential investors should be given some time (say, one month) to make better bids. Such a procedure would have prevented the problems which arose when the Treuhandanstalt had to veto a deal between the East German Interhotel chain and the West German Steigenberger Hotels, which would have allowed Steigenberger to swallow Interhotel on extremely favorable conditions.

Privatization can and should be carried out by many means. The pace must be rapid but not reckless, competition must be ensured, and various other aspects discussed above must be taken into consideration. Firms with no prospect of long-term survival should be liquidated quickly, and structural adjustment must not be delayed. Although some enterprises might have to remain in the state sector for some time, this should not counteract the privatization efforts of the West German Federal Government, which has reduced the number of its participations in companies from 808 in 1982 to 132 in 1989 (*Knauss, 1990*).

6. Conclusions

The analysis above has shown the urgent need for structural adjustment and privatization of the East German economy. The similarity found when comparing sectoral employment structures of East Germany in 1989 and West Germany in 1965 indicates that East Germany will have to undergo a rapid structural change for which West Germany had 24 years time. Employment in agriculture and in industry will certainly decline while the underdeveloped service sector will expand considerably. The large and inefficient state monopolies must be dismantled into smaller organizational units and privatized. Self-employment and the establishment of private small to medium-sized firms, which are the backbone of West Germany's economy, must be encouraged in East Germany. It will take some years, however, until the East German economy reaches the sound mixture of small, medium-sized and large firms which is so vital for the growth, flexibility and stability of a market economy.

Important steps in this direction are deregulation and privatization, which have been used (more or less) successfully by western governments for promoting competition, improving economic performance and the public finances, and widening the ownership of economic assets. Western experience can be helpful to the Treuhandanstalt, the trustee agency responsible for almost 8,000 state firms, when devising privatization mechanisms that are rapid, equitable, transparent, politically acceptable, and that guard against the creation of new monopolistic structures. But there are additional aspects that must be taken into account, such as the huge number of firms to be privatized, the virtual absence of capital markets in East Germany, the sorry state of industry, and the importance of selling state enterprises to western investors for quickly filling the technological and managerial gaps in former communist economies. Furthermore, many obstacles to rapid privatization have to be removed, such as the indebtedness of GDR industry, liabilities for past pollution, unsolved problems of property ownership, and political interference.

It has been argued that the prime task of the Treuhandanstalt should be privatization rather than reconstruction of state enterprises. Since the agency has neither the manpower and experience nor the time for reconstruction, it should sell state assets rapidly, leaving reconstruction to private investors. Increases in revenues from privatization after reconstruction would not cover the costs and opportunity costs of reconstruction. Extensive reconstruction could also seriously delay the privatization process and perpetuate the existence of the Treuhandanstalt. In view of the many problems involved in the sale of several thousand companies through public offerings, the Treuhandanstalt must largely rely on direct sales of shares and mergers with western companies. In these sales, elements of auctions should play an important role because they can be expected to maximize transparency, pricing accuracy, and revenues.

A final question remains: Can the structural adjustment and the privatization of the East German economy be interpreted as a model for other former communist countries in Eastern Europe? On the one hand, the basic structure of centrally planned economies is quite similar, so each CMEA country can learn from the transformation experience of its neighbors. On the other hand, East Germany is a special case because it has been at one sweep fully exposed to the operation of an open market economy, while at the same time being supported by West Germany with financial resources and with technological, managerial and political know-how. The State Treaty and unification made sure that all key economic laws of West-Germany apply in East Germany, that there is intense competition from western firms, that government control is reduced, and that there are no barriers to entry for new firms. The existence of effective competition and the appeal of a hard currency to foreign investors promote structural adjustment and privatization in East Germany. As the situation in other East European countries is quite different, one should be reluctant to draw general conclusions from the East German experience.

7. Postscriptum: The Privatization Results

German unification has been more difficult and the economic transformation of Eastern Germany much more costly than most observers expected. In particular, expectations and results diverge substantially regarding the privatization of the Eastern German economy, albeit in two different ways. On the one hand, the Treuhandanstalt has privatized much more rapidly and extensively than similar government agencies in other post-communist countries in Central and Eastern Europe. On the other hand, privatization revenues were much lower and expenditures for reconstructing and keeping alive inefficient firms much higher than expected, which resulted in huge net losses. This postscriptum attempts to sketch briefly the main results of privatization achieved by the end of 1993 (for extensive descriptions and evaluations of the Treuhandanstalt and the privatization process, see *Carlin and Mayer, 1992, Lichtblau, 1993* or *Fischer et al., 1993*).

Privatization involves three different categories of property: land (including houses) where the former owners have a right to be restituted, nationalized firms to be given back to their former owners (reprivatization), and state-owned firms to be sold to private investors. As already suspected in 1990 (see Section 4), from an economic point of view, the decision to reinstate expropriated owners in their former position has proved to be a major flaw in the Unification Treaty. Turning back the wheel of history to 1949 has created unnecessary uncertainty, inhibited investment and delayed economic recovery by preventing the establishment of well-defined property rights.

By the end of 1993, privatization in Eastern Germany had proceeded as follows:

- *Restitution of the ownership of land*: About 2.15 million restitution applications have been submitted by expropriated land-owners, and in 190,000 cases (or 9%) the land had been returned to former owners by September 30, 1993. The problem is that each of these applications has to be decided on administratively (which is complicated by dubious title records), and each decision can be challenged in the administrative courts. Therefore it may well be that the clarification of all ownerships claims will take ten years (*Siebert, 1993*).

- *Reprivatization of firms*: There are about 15,000 applications for restitution, 9,038 of which had been decided by December 1993. 6,048 firms, parts of firms and assets had been returned to their former owners, 2,100 former owners will receive compensations, and 890 applications had not been successful.

- *Privatization of firms*: The Treuhandanstalt had sold 13,643 firms and parts of firms by December 1993. Due to the breaking up and restructuring of firms, this figure exceeds the original number of 8,000 firms owned by the agency at the start of the privatization process. 2,591 of these privatizations (i.e. 19%) were management buy-outs. The regional distribution presented in *Table 6* shows that the largest number of privatizations took place in the state of Saxony, whereas revenues were highest in East Berlin.

Table 6: Privatization of Firms (by December 31, 1993)

State	Privatized firms and parts of firms	Privatizations by management buy out	Privatization revenues (billions DM)	Investment "guarantees" (billions DM)	Employment "guarantees" (number of employees)
Brandenburg	2,161	394	6.820	32.417	291,631
Mecklenburg-West Pomerania	1,784	409	3.474	12.899	128,159
Saxony-Anhalt	2,116	392	5.093	22.356	187,136
Saxony	3,989	794	13.665	45.168	419,338
Thuringia	2,558	425	4.911	14.741	199,668
Berlin (East)	921	175	13.733	26.063	258,990
Others (e.g. GDR firms located outside eastern Germany)	114	2	0.425	32.964	1,953
Total	13,643	2,591	48.123	186.608	1,486,875

Source: Treuhandanstalt.

Total revenues from selling 13,643 enterprises as well as large areas of state land and agricultural estates amounted to DM 48.1 billion. According to the sales contracts, investments of DM 186.6 billion are to be expected, including an investment of DM 30 billion in the energy sector. Furthermore, private investors have "guaranteed" to secure almost 1,5 million jobs.

Foreign investors were involved in 818 privatizations (*Table 7*). At first sight, this number seems to be relatively low, but other indicators give a more accurate picture of the importance of foreign investment: revenues from these sales were DM 5.6 billion or 11.6% of total revenues, investment and employment "guarantees" by foreign investors are roughly 10% of total commitments. Swiss, British and Austrian investors each bought more than 100 firms, whereas French investors contributed most to privatization revenues.

Table 7: Privatization Sales to Foreign Investors (by December 31, 1993)

Origin of foreign investors	Privatized firms and parts of firms	Privatization revenues (millions DM)	Investment "guarantees" (millions DM)	Employment "guarantees" (number of employees)
Switzerland	129	746	1,162	18,893
Great Britain	125	887	2,177	16,888
Austria	101	317	1,004	16,135
Netherlands	93	384	1,181	9,930
France	86	1,433	5,431	25,434
United States	74	530	2,936	12,753
Italy	36	303	651	4,777
Denmark	25	331	545	3,158
Luxembourg	12	280	406	2,208
Canada	10	34	1,848	16,712
Others	127	343	2,734	19,106
Total	818	5,588	20,076	145,994

Source: Treuhandanstalt

For several reasons, privatization revenues have been much lower than widely expected: The most important one may be that, contrary to suggestions from many economists (see e.g. Section 4; *Siebert, 1990*; *Fels and Schnabel, 1991)*, elements of auctions have not played an important role in privatization sales. Claiming that the sale situation is complex and cannot be standardized, the Treuhandanstalt has used an informal bargaining approach involving multiple criteria: Prospective investors were asked to give assurances about the amount of investment planned and the number of jobs a firm would continue to offer, and these, as much as the sale price and the reputation of the buyer, influenced the Treuhandanstalt's decision. Major drawbacks of this informal bargaining appoach are that it is discretionary, allows strategic behavior of bidders, and does not result in revenue maximization. In many cases, the Treuhandanstalt has accepted lower bids connected with higher investment and employment guarantees in order to save as many jobs as possible. The agency also had to accept negative sale prices caused by firms' indebtedness, liabilities for past pollution, etc.

Liabilities for past pollution and for debts of GDR state-owned firms, substantial costs of reconstruction, privatization and liquidation, and political pressure to cover operating deficits of inefficient firms as long as possible resulted in huge expenditures of the Treuhandanstalt, which exceeded privatization revenues by far. Consequently, the agency's credit limit of DM 25 billion laid down in the Unification Treaty had to be extended considerably. When the Treuhandanstalt finishes its privatization activities by the end of 1994 (unfinished business, supervision of contracts, etc., will be continued by five smaller agencies), it will have accumulated a total debt of DM 275 billion, to be borne by the German taxpayer !

By December 1993, the Treuhandanstalt had liquidated 78 firms, and 3,118 firms were in the process of liquidation. 951 firms with 187,000 employees were left to be privatized by the agency. Out of these, 463 are companies with 20 employees or less, located mainly in the agricultural and service sector. In contrast, 19 firms, mainly in manufacturing, have more than 1,500 employees and account for a total employment of 96,170.

Since closing down these largely inefficient big firms would further reduce employment and increase regional problems, there have been political calls for an explicit structural policy in Eastern Germany. Particularly, the governments of the five East German states talk of preserving firms with "regional significance", and some of them (foremost Saxony) have taken steps to rescue such firms (for details, see *Lichtblau, 1993*). However, the vague concepts of preserving "industrial cores" and of industrial targeting have major drawbacks, and they may well prove to be counterproductive.

As other experiments in industrial policy have often shown, politicians are not competent to decide which firms are worth rescuing, which products will sell well, and which industries will flourish in the future. The inefficient firms would have to be subsidized heavily. Once governments have granted subsidies, they usually find it difficult to withdraw them. Therefore, keeping uncompetitive firms in business would be a very costly way of softening the adjustment process and would have strong negative implications for fiscal policy.

Moreover, the availability of subsidies might induce managers and investors to engage in rent-seeking instead of fulfilling their role of innovating and implementing new allocations of production factors. Subsidized old firms might also get in the way of new firms, e.g. by competing unfairly on the product markets or by blocking scarce location space that is needed for the creation of new firms (*Siebert, 1993*). All in all, by being orientated towards the old structures, such a conservationist policy risks perpetuating the inefficiency of the socialist planning system, inhibiting structural adjustment, and delaying the modernization and transformation of Eastern Germany.

Although preserving unsellable Eastern firms may be economically senseless, it looks as if keeping alive at least some of these firms is politically unavoidable in order to restrict unemployment in certain regions and preserve social peace. This means that - though being up for sale - many of the firms in the portfolio of the Treuhandanstalt can be expected to have a long future as public enterprises. Such a strategy, however, risks recreating a system of subsidies and state ownership in Eastern Germany, which has long drained the economy of Western Germany; it furthermore counteracts government policies of deregulation and privatization in Western Germany.

Endnotes

* ***I would like to thank Hans-Peter Fröhlich and Hans-Peter Klös for helpful comments on a preliminary draft of this paper. The usual disclaimer applies.***

1 For more detailed discussions of sectoral prospects see the paper by ***Lutz Hoffmann, this volume***, and ***Halstrick-Schwenk, Loebbe and Wenke, 1990***; see also ***Gerstenberger 1990***.

2 For details, see the paper by ***Henning Klodt, this volume***.

3 For an extended discussion of various alternatives, see ***Institut der Deutschen Wirtschaft, (1990)***.

4 Some of the ideas discussed are mentioned in section 3.4 and in Hans Werner Sinn's contribution in this volume.

References

BALZ, MATTHIAS (1990), Probleme einer Integration der DDR-Landwirtschaft in den EG-Agrarmarkt, Ifo-Schnelldienst 19/90, 9-18.

BISHOP, MATTHEW, and KAY, JOHN (1988), Does Privatization Work? Lessons from the UK, London Business School.

BORCHERDING, THOMAS E., POMMEREHNE, WERNER W., and SCHNEIDER, FRIEDRICH (1982), Comparing the Efficiency of Private and Public Production: The Evidence from Five Countries, in: Bös, Dieter,Musgrave, Richard A. and Wiseman, Jack, eds., Public Production, Zeitschrift für Nationaloekonomie, Supplementum 2, Wien/New York, 127-156.

CARLIN, WENDY, and MAYER, COLIN (1992), Restructuring Enterprises in Eastern Europe, Economic Policy, 15, 311-352.

CORNELSEN, DORIS (1990), Die Wirtschaft der DDR in der Honecker-Aera, DIW-Vierteljahresheft 1-90, 70-79.

FELS, GERHARD, and SCHNABEL, CLAUS (1991), The Economic Transformation of East Germany: Some Preliminary Lessons, Group of Thirty Occasional Papers No. 36, Washington, D.C.

FISCHER, WOLFRAM, HAX, HERBERT, and SCHNEIDER, HANS KARL (eds.) (1993), Treuhandanstalt: Das Unmögliche wagen, Berlin: Akademie Verlag.

GERSTENBERGER, WOLFGANG (1990), Das zukuenftige Produktionspotential der DDR - ein Versuch zur Reduzierung der Unsicherheiten, Ifo-Schnelldienst 7/90, 13-22.

GERSTENBERGER, WOLFGANG and KISCHEL, WOLFGANG (1989), Deutsch-deutsche Industriestruktur im Vergleich, Ifo-Schnelldienst 34/89, 3-4.

GRUHLER, WOLFRAM (1990), Schwerpunkt DDR: Unternehmensstruktur, IW-Trends 2/1990, II-1 - II-11.

HALSTRICK-SCHWENK, MARIANNE, LÖBBE, KLAUS, and WENKE, MARTIN (1990), Die sektoralen Wirtschaftsstrukturen der Bundesrepublik und der DDR, RWI-Mitteilungen, Vol. 41, 11-28.

INSTITUT DER DEUTSCHEN WIRTSCHAFT (1990), Möglichkeiten einer breiten Streuung des volkseigenen Vermoegens in der DDR in Zusammenhang mit seiner Privatisierung, Study for the Federal Ministry of Labor, Cologne June 1990.

KNAUSS, FRITZ (1990), Privatisierung in der Bundesrepublik Deutschland 1983-1990, Beitraege zur Wirtschafts- und Sozialpolitik des Instituts der deutschen Wirtschaft No. 183, Cologne.

KORNAI, JANOS (1986), The Hungarian Reform Process: Visions, Hopes, and Reality, Journal of Economic Literature, Vol. 24, 1687-1737.

LICHTBLAU, KARL (1993), Privatisierungs- und Sanierungsarbeit der Treuhandanstalt, Beiträge zur Wirtschafts- und Sozialpolitik des Instituts der deutschen Wirtschaft No. 209, Cologne: Deutscher Instituts-Verlag.

LIPP, ERNST-MORITZ (1990), Der Staat ist kein Sanierer, Frankfurter Allgemeine Zeitung, August 11, p. 11.

LIPTON, DAVID, and SACHS, JEFFREY (1990), Creating a Market Economy in Eastern Europe: The Case of Poland, Brookings Papers on Economic Activity, 1/1990, 75-147.

PICOT, ARNOLD, and KAULMANN, THOMAS (1989), Comparative Performance of Government-owned and Privately-owned Industrial Corporations - Empirical Evidence from Six Countries, Journal of Institutional and Theoretical Economics, 145, 298-316.

POHL, REINHARD (1990), Alt-Schulden der DDR-Betriebe: Streichung unumgaenglich, DIW-Wochenbericht 36/90, 503-509.

RAITH, MICHAEL (1990), Die Arbeitsproduktivität in der Industrie: die Deutsche Demokratische Republik im Vergleich mit der Bundesrepublik Deutschland, mimeo, Institut der deutschen Wirtschaft, Cologne, April.

SCHNABEL, CLAUS (1990), Privatisierung und Deregulierung in Grossbritannien, List Forum für Wirtschafts- und Finanzpolitik, 16, 148-166.

SIEBERT, HORST (1990), The Economic Integration of Germany - An Update, Institut für Weltwirtschaft, Kiel Discussion Papers No. 160a, September.

SIEBERT, HORST (1993), The Big Bang with the Big Brother: German Unification in its Third Year, Institut für Weltwirtschaft, Kiel Discussion Papers No. 211, May.

SMITH, ADAM (1776), The Wealth of Nations, Cannan edition, Chicago 1976: University of Chicago Press.

STATISTISCHES AMT DER DDR (1990), Statistisches Taschenbuch '90, East Berlin: Rudolf Haufe.

STATISTISCHES BUNDESAMT (1990), DDR 1990: Zahlen und Fakten, Stuttgart: Metzler-Poeschel.

VICKERS, JOHN and YARROW, GEORGE (1988), Privatization: An Economic Analysis, Cambridge/London: MIT Press.

COMMENTS ON: STRUCTURAL ADJUSTMENT AND PRIVATIZATION OF THE EAST GERMAN ECONOMY - GUIDELINES FOR A PRIVATIZATION STRATEGY

Garry J. Schinasi

The paper by Dr. Schnabel is well-written and well organized. It is a comprehensive presentation of three important aspects of reform in the former German Democratic Republic (GDR): (1) the need for restructuring and privatization; (2) the daunting task of the Treuhandanstalt, and (3) the various strategies that can be pursued to privatize the state owned enterprises in the GDR.

On the main points of the paper there can be little disagreement. The paper advocates relatively rapid privatization based on market principles and advocates far-reaching structural adjustment in the former-GDR. Dr. Schnabel even goes a step further and suggests there is a need to continue structural adjustment in the FRG. These are themes that will be echoed again and again throughout eastern Europe by policymakers from the west, and hopefully from the east.

There is of course very broad agreement about the need for structural adjustment. Though the subject of deregulation and privatization in the industrialized western world is interesting, for example in the U.K., this experience probably has only limited practical significance for the eastern region of Germany and the rest of eastern Europe, except in-so-far as it highlights the difficulties of deregulation and privatization, even in places where markets are well-established. Governments cannot manage profit-making very well, partly because they often lack the expertise but also because of conflicting government objectives: on the one hand to maintain employment and income through periods of recession and crises and on the other hand to create an efficient and productive business sector.

It was suggested in the author's discussion that there has been little practical experience with economic reforms that can be examined and utilized by German policymakers to provide guidance for the challenges ahead in reforming the former-GDR. This is an opinion I do not fully share, for two reasons. First, there are several countries that have attempted to move from nonmarket- to market-orientations over the past twenty years, in Europe and in Asia. The IMF and other multilateral institutions have been involved with many of these reform processes and have accumulated some knowledge about what elements of reform have been, and have not been, successful. Secondly, the economic successes of the major industrial countries, their continued ability to make productive use of scarce resources, and their apparent resilience in the presence of repeated economic shocks, all provide ample evidence that a market orientation is worth establishing and maintaining. Furthermore, such experiences provide source-material for understanding markets and how and why they work (or fail).

With this perspective in mind, there is much to say about the Treuhandanstalt, its organization, its objectives, its performance to date, and the general subject of privatization strategies. Rather than address the specific issues raised in the paper about the Treuhandanstalt and privatization schemes, most of which are aptly covered in the paper, it might be useful to provide a broader perspective, to place the challenge of the Treuhandanstalt in the relevant context, and to perhaps indicate where further thinking might be desirable. This broader perspective is one that brings together the essential themes that have been useful in countries that have adopted market-oriented reforms, themes that in effect have been known by economists in market-oriented countries for a long time. Some of these themes are particularly relevant for the decisions that Germany will face in the coming months, especially regarding the policy of the Treuhandanstalt.

There are four main themes: first, there is no "third way" between central-planning and a market-oriented system; second, to achieve economic efficiency, economic reforms must be comprehensive and if at all possible simultaneous; third, as far as privatization is concerned, it would be preferable if the time horizon were relatively short, as short as possible; and fourth, because the public sector cannot be the only source of capital - - the amount of capital required for reform is enormous -- the macroeconomic and microeconomic environments must be conducive to attracting private capital flows very quickly and for a sustained period of time.

1. The first theme is that as far as the allocation of resources and pricing is concerned, there is no "third way" somewhere between central-planning and market economies. Except in clear cases of market-failure, either one allows prices and resource-allocation to be more-or-less determined freely by the market, hopefully more rather than less, or one will likely suffer from the misallocation of resources the East has experienced over the last 40 years. This does not imply that the transition to a market-orientation needs to be inequitable or "heartless;" it just means that prices, rather then politics or a central plan, allocate resources. If redistribution of incomes is also an objective there are well established means for achieving this objective, through fiscal policy adjustments.

The lesson from experience is that privatization should proceed in a free and open environment. Transparency is a key element and policies should be guided by market principles. In addition, procedures should be accessible by all interested purchasing parties. As suggested earlier in the conference by Thomas Mayer, it would be particularly attractive in some countries to organize several funds that manage their portfolios of properties with one objective in mind: maximizing the market value of the portfolio. This necessarily means quickly closing enterprises that have no chance of survival and quickly selling those that do. Of course, many jobs are at risk temporarily but this is most likely a necessary part of the adjustment process towards a market-orientation. For the majority of enterprises -- those companies that may be saved with some managerial and financial help -- perhaps the solution is to find able partners for mergers, for transferring knowledge and technology.

2. A second theme is that structural reforms must be comprehensive. That is, all of the main elements of a market-oriented system have to be in place to achieve economic efficiency and to establish and sustain a desirable distribution of income. Prices, wages, asset-prices, income flows, trade flows, and capital flows are all completely intertwined. Both demand-side and supply-side policies can be grounded in the principles ofthe marketplace.

Hence, the reform process would be at risk if goods (and perhaps labor) markets operate on market principles while the values of companies were arbitrarily and artificially determined, by political or social imperatives. One cannot expect to have this mix to achieve an efficient allocation of material and human resources. Even in western European countries that are market-oriented, State ownership and control of enterprises has not been able to produce satisfactory results. This is why countries such as Canada and the United Kingdom have attempted to privatize their nationalized industries.

3. A third theme involves timing. There is less of a consensus in the economics profession about how rapid the adjustment process should be. There is currently a debate about whether countries bent on economic reform should apply shock therapy or a more gradual approach. My own judgement is that a relatively rapid adjustment is essential for two reasons. First, one cannot expect some of the fragile political coalitions that have been responsible for the recent dramatic political changes in eastern Europe to be sustained through a very long, protracted, and costly period of low-or-no-growth, and in some places prolonged recessions or depressions. Secondly, and this to some extent anticipates the fourth theme, longlasting and sustainable reform will require large injections of private western capital. For the former-GDR, only the second problem is relevant. Unless rapid progress is made on several policy

fronts, private foreign capital will not flow to eastern Germany on the scale required. Among other important policy initiatives, rapid adjustment requires careful macroeconomic management, extensive microeconomic restructuring, and elaborate social safety nets. If it is at all possible to accomplish this adjustment rapidly, it is likely to be accomplished within the social-market-framework of West Germany.

To echo what Rudiger Dornbusch said yesterday, it is perhaps more important that the Treuhandanstalt do its job quickly than it is to do its job well. Clearly, in an ideal world, it would be preferable to have it done quickly and well.

4. Another theme is that public capital can not do it alone. The eastern region of Germany requires a tremendous amount of private capital. But this capital will not flow east unless market participants expect a stable economic and financial environment; in the rest of eastern Europe, political stability is also an essential requirement. Macroeconomic policymakers in Germany are committed to providing a stable economic and financial environment. But even with this macroeconomic stability, if it is perceived that microeconomic efficiency is not a clear objective in the eastern region of Germany during the transitional period, then the necessary flow of private capital will be delayed. For example, if it is generally expected that formerly state-owned enterprises can be bought tomorrow for prices well below today's then western companies will wait until such companies suffer capital losses. Likewise, capital flows east will be delayed if potential buyers are uncertain about property rights, the status of legal institutions and precedents, and political outcomes.

In the first instance, the Treuhandanstalt is the business sector of the eastern region of Germany. To attract private capital the Treuhandanstalt should behave like an investment bank, bringing together buyer and seller, and leave employment and social policies to the appropriate agencies of government.

Some have suggested that privatization would have occurred more quickly without the creation of the Treuhandanstalt, or any other agency like it, or that at least its constitutional mandate should have been to maximize its own market-value. What is important as the privatization process moves forward is the establishment of a broadly-based capital market in which equity shares in east German private companies can be freely traded, ultimately, and in which managers are exposed to the demands of the marketplace. Such a broadly-based capital market would establish a vital interest on the part of a large segment of the German population to see that productivity and efficiency were quickly established as the objectives of enterprises and workers. Thus, it is important that market principles be employed to select companies for the auction-block or the junk-pile. The major risk in the operations of the Treuhandanstalt is that the proceeds from selling viable companies will be used to support companies that have no chance of survival.

Henning Klodt

GOVERNMENT SUPPORT FOR RESTRUCTURING THE EAST GERMAN ECONOMY

1. Introduction

Restructuring the economy of the five East German states surely needs a helping hand from the federal budget. Infrastructure in the former GDR is in poor shape, productive capacities are in a wretched condition, product-lines are not adapted to world-market demand, and the labor force is lacking experience with modern technologies.[1] Since these deficiencies are the legacy of more than five decades of central planning (first fascism, then communism) the most appropriate remedy is establishing a viable market economy. It is open to doubt, however, if mere market forces are able to solve the whole bunch of problems.

A clear-cut market solution would require a wage differential between East and West Germany that completely compensates for efficiency differences of any kind. Considering the expectations and hopes that were raised by German unification and considering the low barriers to westward migration it seems rather unlikely that East German workers would be ready to accept such a low level of wages. If real wages fail to adjust to productivity, the "Mezzogiorno syndrome" could be round the corner, i.e. the former GDR could be stuck with regional underdevelopment and structural unemployment for decades (*Burda, 1990*).

It is the central question of this paper which type of governmental intervention should be preferred in order to improve the economic performance of East Germany. For this purpose part 2 presents some empirical evidence on the position of the East German economy since currency unification with West Germany in July 1990 as compared to the preceding period.

The analysis mainly focuses on labor market problems, especially on the rise in unemployment. Part 3 investigates the impact of different forms of government support on labor demand in the framework of neoclassical production theory. In addition, it presents a survey of policy measures that have already been adopted by the German government. Part 4 summarizes and briefly comments on policy options.

2. The East German Economy in Transition

The conversion from a centrally planned economy to a market economy in the GDR came in four separate steps:

- The opening of the Berlin Wall on 9th October 1989 removed the barriers to migration between East and West Germany. Since the legal authorities of West Germany had always regarded East German people as German citizens, the whole West German labor market was open to them without any institutional barrier. Up to mid 1990 the West German government even provided special financial assistance for people coming from East Germany.

- Since the general East German election of 18th March 1990 the GDR was no longer governed by the Communist Party. The new coalition of Conservatives and Social Democrats quickly abandoned the search for a "third way" and was determined to adopt the political and economic system of West Germany.

- On 1st July 1990 an almost complete economic unification was achieved. The treaty between the East German and the West German Government not only included currency unification but also the endorsement of a substantial part of West German business laws to the East German territory.

- On 3rd October 1990 economic unification was complemented by political unification. The joining of East Germany to the jurisdiction of the West German Basic Law automatically extended the range of validity of all West German laws to the East German territory. Specific modifications were stipulated for a few cases only, for instance in the areas of environmental protection, antitrust policies and labor market regulations.

Of course, these steps are only prerequisites for establishing a market economy. The main unsolved issues are the clarification of property rights on real estate, the privatization of state-owned enterprises and the reduction and transformation of an oversized public administration (*Schnabel, 1990; Schmieding, 1990; Siebert/Schmieding, 1990*). At present, it seems most urgent to remove these impediments to the inflow of western capital and technology.

But even under these restraints, it could have been expected that releasing an economy from central planning would result in an immediate increase of output, productivity and wealth. Removing bureaucratic slack and ceasing price and quantity controls should improve economic efficiency from one day to the next even without any reconstruction of the capital stock or the introduction of new technologies.[2] In reality industrial production in the GDR region fell by half and unemployment (including short-time work) increased to more than one quarter of the total labor force (Fig. 1).[3]

Fig. 1: Unemployment, Short-Time Work and Industrial Production in the (Former) GDR 1990

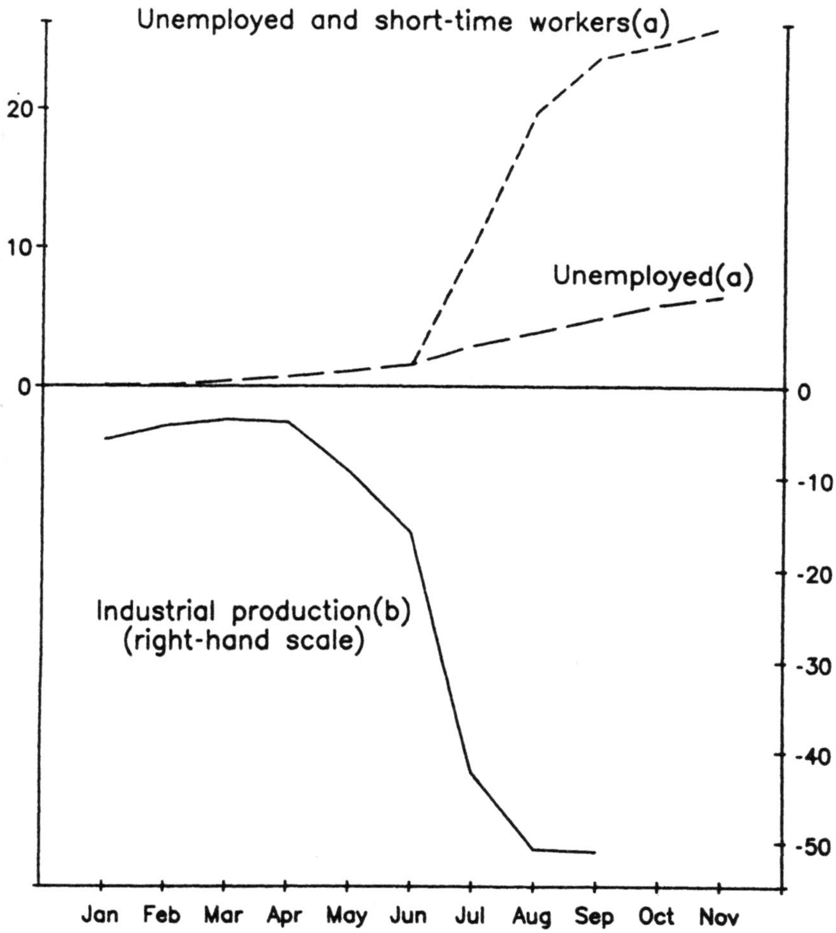

(a) Percentage of total labor force. (b) Change from 1989.

Source: *Statistisches Amt der DDR (1990).*

The whole size of labor market problems is even underestimated by these figures. About half a million people (6 percent of the labor force) accepted pre-retirement that is offered to workers who are older than 55 years and younger than the regular retirement age of 65 years (*Institut für Angewandte Wirtschaftsforschung, 1990*). An unknown number of workers from public institutions have been suspended from work while their salaries are granted for an additional period of six or nine months (depending on age). Moreover, several people, especially women, totally retreated from the active labor force. And, last but not least, about half a million workers from the former GDR are now working in the western part of Germany. Hence, the decrease in the number of jobs is much sharper than the increase in unemployment.

Sure enough, nobody had expected a soft landing of the East German economy. But for most observers the extent and the rapidness of decline came as a surprise. In part the dismissal of workers simply reflects a shift from covert to overt unemployment. Under the system of central planning there were only limited incentives for reducing labor input and it was almost impossible for enterprises to get rid of idle workers. In addition many working hours were lost due to shortage of inputs and other forms of inefficient planning. Recent estimates based on questionnaires are indicating that "disguised unemployment" in the GDR reached a level of about 15 percent in past years (*Vogler-Ludwig, 1990*). Discharging these people will probably continue to fuel open unemployment for a considerable time. It should be kept in mind that this type of adjustment by definition only affects labor input and cannot explain the reduction in output.

An increase in unemployment may also result from asymmetries in the adjustment speed of ailing and prospering industries. By and large, central planners in the GDR (and in other CMEA-countries as well) were favoring raw-material intensive and smokestack industries at the expense of light industries and services (*Stehn/Schmieding, 1990; Kostrzewa, 1988; Weiss, 1983*). Since July 1990, liberalization of prices and strengthened budget-constraints imposed a strong pressure for structural adjustment on traditional industries.[4] In part, these pressures showed up in shifting relative consumer prices after currency unification with West Germany (Table 1). It should be recognized, however, that shifts in producer prices were much more distinct, since subsidies and product-specific levies have also been removed.

The argument of asymmetric adjustment speed simply says that less time is required for closing down obsolete activities than for expanding promising new activities. The available data on industrial production are suggesting, however, that the decline of output is not an industry-specific phenomenon. Within the manufacturing sector there is not a single industry with an increase of production in August 1990 as compared to June 1990 or to the average of 1989 (Table 2).[5]

Table 1: Absolute and Relative Price Changes in the GDR from July 1989 to July 1990 (percent)

Expenditure category	Absolute price change	Relative(a) price change
Food, beverages, tobacco	15.4	22.1
Textiles, apparel, leather	- 42.5	- 39.2
Furniture, household appliances	- 25.5	- 21.2
Health and beauty	19.4	26.3
Transport and Communication	- 14.8	- 9.8
Education and Recreation	- 11.5	- 6.3
Other goods and services	- 1.0	4.8
Rents, energy	0.0	5.8
Total consumer prices	- 5.5	0.0

(a) Absolute price change in the respective expenditure category divided by change of total consumer prices.

Source: Deutsche Bundesbank (1990); own calculations.

Table 2: Index of Industrial Production in the GDR (1989 = 100)*

	Jan.	Feb.	Mar.	Apr.	May	June	July	Aug.	Sept.
Total	94.0	95.6	96.3	96.0	90.5	84.0	57.6	49.1	49.0
Industry	95.0	95.6	95.9	96.1	91.0	84.5	57.9	49.2	48.9
Energy	97.0	93.8	93.2	85.2	92.3	87.9	59.9	52.3	61.6
Chemicals	93.6	90.4	91.1	94.3	85.2	79.9	59.8	48.5	49.8
Basic metals	94.4	92.0	95.1	94.0	90.3	77.0	39.7	33.1	34.5
Construction	92.3	95.5	96.0	93.5	97.4	97.3	63.0	40.8	34.3
Water supply	106.8	99.8	104.7	102.9	105.8	110.1	89.6	100.8	100.3
Non-electrical machinery, Transport equip.	88.7	93.1	97.0	99.1	97.5	103.8	71.2	64.2	62.6
Electrical machinery	93.3	96.0	99.8	99.2	98.9	93.4	67.3	53.3	53.3
Light industry	95.8	96.2	97.7	92.3	87.1	75.2	48.9	44.6	46.2
Textiles, apparel	96.8	94.1	98.6	96.0	81.2	72.2	48.7	44.9	45.7
Food, beverages, tobacco	98.6	97.3	95.1	91.7	86.7	72.0	42.3	38.6	37.9

** Adjusted for working days.*

Source: Statistisches Amt der DDR (1990).

Hence, the East German industry is facing a global problem, not a sectorally concentrated one. This is not to say that no sector-specific output reductions are required, but at present they are obviously outweighed by economy-wide depression.

For the economy as a whole it is estimated in the joint forecast of the five leading institutes for economic research that real GDP will be 17 percent lower in 1990 than in 1989 (see *Deutsches Institut für Wirtschaftsforschung et al., 1990*, p. 46).[6] These figures are annual averages, i.e. the estimate for 1990 also includes the first two quarters when output was rather stable. No monthly or quarterly data on real GDP of the GDR region are available, but it can be expected that the decline in the third quarter was much sharper than in the whole year on average. Nevertheless, most observers agree that adjustment pressure is strongest in manufacturing industries.

It could be objected that the decline in output is simply a statistical phenomenon - at least in part. Up to June 1990, the GDR was still a centrally planned economy, even if the plans were observed only to a limited extent. As premiums and gratuities mainly depended on reported output, it paid to blow up production statistics by fictitious output that was never produced. This practice is commonly called "Pripiski", the Russian word for writing down in addition (*Winiecki, 1990*). Since July 1990, the incentives for Pripiski disappeared because the revenues of companies now depended on factual sales and not on reported production.

Notwithstanding these considerations, there is no doubt that East German enterprises suffer from insufficient competitiveness in open markets. Up to November 1989 East German consumers had no choice and even after the break-down of the Wall their choice was limited by the non-convertibility of the GDR currency. East German enterprises were still able, therefore, to sell low quality at high prices. As an immediate reaction to currency unification, however, retail trade in the GDR almost totally replaced GDR products by imports from West Germany or other western countries - literally overnight.

For most producers of consumer goods this strong demand reaction was an unexpected shock. They had been well aware of partial demand shifts, but not of an almost complete plunge of their sales. Declining demand rapidly diffused to producers of intermediate and investment goods. Moreover, their customers too faced enriched choices and often preferred to purchase western products.

Fig. 2: Evaluation of Inventories in Wholesale and Retail Trade of the GDR, July 1990 (percent of reviewed enterprises)

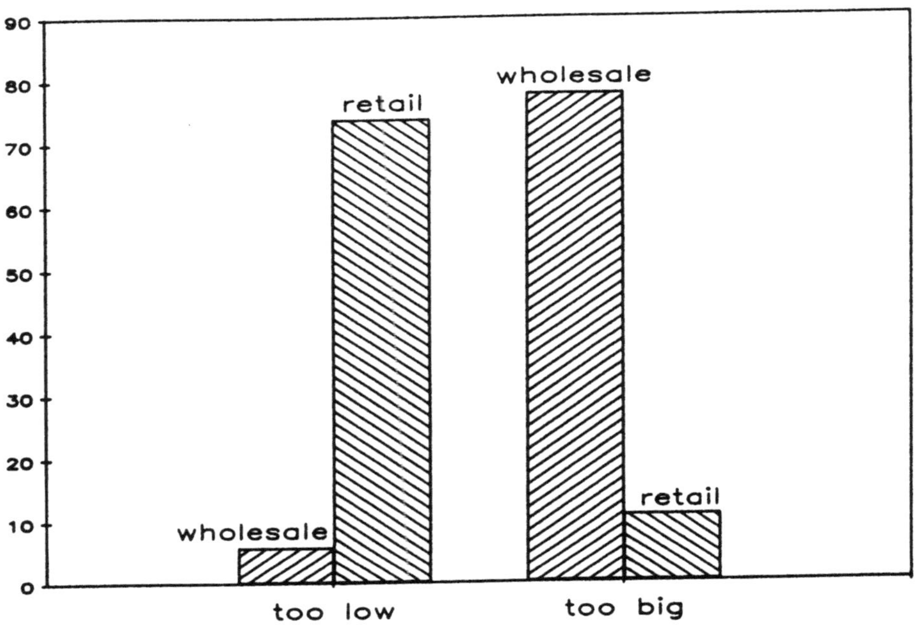

Source: *Ifo-Institut für Wirtschaftsforschung, Institut für angewandte Wirtschaftsforschung (1990).*

The situation after currency unification is reflected in the stock of inventories in wholesale and retail trade (Fig. 2): In July 1990 retail trade would have preferred higher inventories while wholesale trade inventories were judged as being too high. A shift of inventories between these two branches was impossible since retail trade was mainly demanding western products and wholesale trade was offering eastern products. It has been argued that the resulting difficulties for eastern producers have been aggravated by monopolistic behavior of western trade companies. There is some casual evidence that West German suppliers tried to tie GDR shops exclusively to their products. It must be recognized, however, that most GDR consumers highly welcomed the opportunity of spending their new money on those products that had not been available to them before.

East German producers reacted to declining demand in a quite market-oriented manner: In July 1990 producer prices were cut by 48.3 percent as compared to the average level in 1989.[7] Nominal factor prices, by contrast, even increased. Government levies for investment funds were substituted by interest rates, and nominal wages increased by about 35 percent on average.[8] Hence, East German companies are now facing a significantly deteriorated cost price ratio.

There are also some signs of hope, especially from the establishment of new enterprises in the service sector (Table 3). In the past, central planners had almost ignored this part of the economy and its share in total employment remained at a level of about 40 percent, whereas the corresponding share in western industrial countries was 60 percent or even higher. In the future, expanding service industries will probably absorb the majority of workers that are dismissed from manufacturing. In the short and medium run, however, the buoyancy of services seems much too weak for bearing the whole burden of labor market problems.

Some economists are primarily attributing rising unemployment to the conversion rate of 1:1 that was chosen for currency unification with West Germany. They would have preferred a substantially lower rate for the Mark of the GDR in order to keep real wages down (see, e.g., *Vaubel, 1990*). It can be doubted, however, that a less favorable conversion rate would have substantially improved the competitiveness of East German companies.

Table 3: Registered Openings and Closings of Enterprises in the GDR 1990

	January-June	July	August	September	January-September
Openings					
Total	100 482	35 849	30 790	29 768	197 286
thereof:					
Handicrafts	18 399	4 965	3 665	3 232	30 126
Trade and restaurants	46 364	18 865	17 414	15 879	98 332
Closings					
Total	3 456	2 307	2 924	3 641	12 328
thereof:					
Handicrafts	1 696	814	844	828	4 182
Trade and restaurants	1 231	964	1 241	1 800	5 236
Balance					
Total	97 026	33 390	27 769	26 127	184 958
thereof:					
Handicrafts	16 703	4 137	2 823	2 404	25 944
Trade and restaurants	45 133	17 920	16 200	14 079	93 096

Source: Statistisches Amt der DDR (1990).

From the theory of optimum currency areas it is well known that a real depreciation is impossible between currencies of countries with a high factor mobility. If the nominal value of one currency is reduced, the outflow of capital and labor will quickly drive up nominal factor prices. With perfect factor mobility the increase in nominal factor prices will just offset the decrease in nominal exchange rates, i.e. real exchange rates will remain stable.

In fact, the political motivation for a conversion rate of 1:1 was exactly the intention to stop or at least slow down migration from East to West Germany.[9] The events since 9th November 1989 had clearly demonstrated that the mobility of labor between the two Germanies was much higher than, say, between Germany and Spain or other low-wage regions of the EC. Admittedly, in the first days after the breakdown of the Wall many East Germans came to the West for political reasons, since the credibility of the new freedom to move was far from clear.[10] In the course of spring 1990, however, economic motives for migration increasingly dominated.

It must be noticed, therefore, that the two German governments did not have the choice of determining the price ratio between East and West Germany by fixing a more or less favorable conversion rate for currency unification. With no barriers to trade and migration, output and factor price ratios between East and West are determined by market forces, not by government treaties. Economic policies that are designed at restructuring the East German economy must accept as a fact that prices of East German products sharply declined and factor prices moved up. There is no way of reversing these events.

3. Criteria for Evaluating Different Types of Government Support

In the context of neoclassical production theory all price adjustments that occurred in East Germany can be interpreted as an increase in real factor prices. From the producers' viewpoint a deterioration of output prices is equivalent to an increase of factor prices. The basic features of the changed situation are illustrated by Fig. 3, showing a production function that relates different levels of capital intensity (k) to different levels of labor productivity (y). Before entering the details it should be carefully examined how to interpret the concept of a production function for the former GDR. In traditional growth models international factor mobility is in general ruled out; the production function describes the productive capacities of a country with given factor endowment and technology. Hence, factor intensity is exogenous and the factor price ratio is endogenous.

Fig. 3: Production Function, Factor Prices and Subsidies

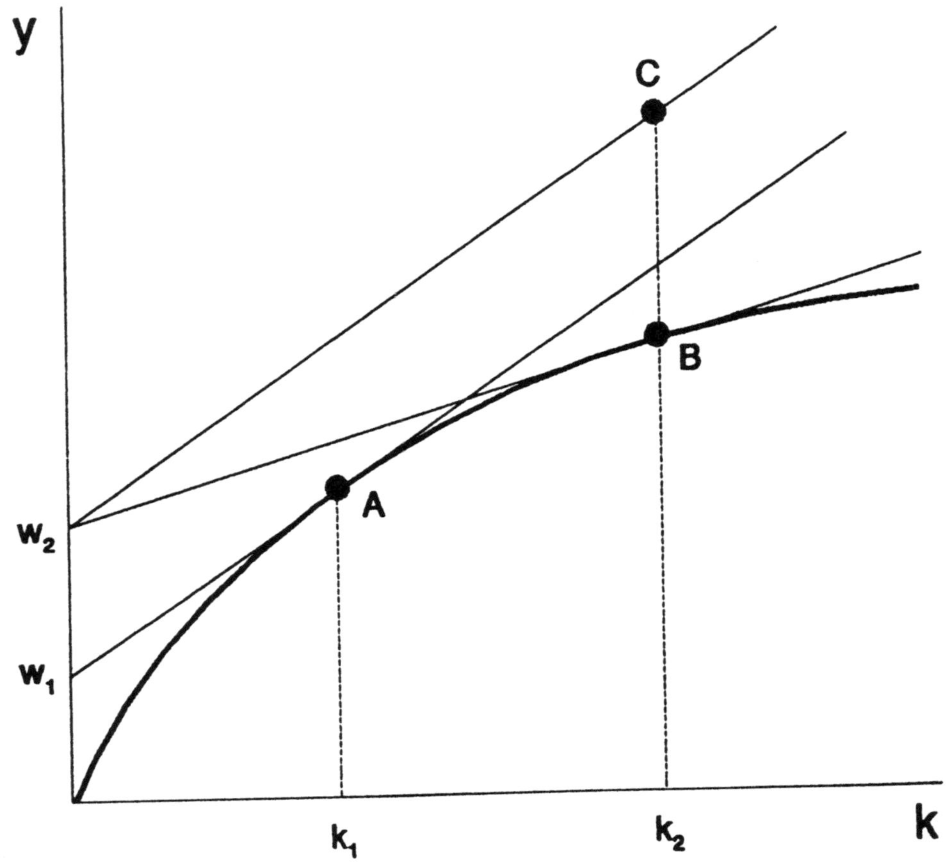

Such a model obviously does not apply to East Germany after the breakdown of the Wall. Factor prices rather than factor intensities are exogenously determined, notably by prices that prevail in West Germany. In this situation, the production function of Fig. 3 simply describes the state of technology that is available in the eastern part of the German economy.

Real interest rates (determined on world capital markets) are given by the shape of the straight lines running through points A and C, and w_1 is the level of real wages that would enable East German companies to compete on world markets. If wages were lower, competition among producers would drive them up; if wages were higher, fixed capital would be distracted from the region and unemployment (or emigration) would steadily rise. Economic stability can only be achieved at a wage level of w_1, and this level automatically leads to full employment.

Unfortunately, w_1 is not feasible, since it would not be accepted by the labor force. Real wages in West Germany are much higher and w_1 is often even lower than social security payments.[11] Instead, East German producers have to accept a real wage of w_2.

The most comfortable way out of this dilemma would be an increase of productivity that corresponds to the increase in real wages, i.e. an upward shift of the production function until it touches the straight line running through w_2 and C. In the long run, such an increase can be expected from the inflow of western capital and from technological cooperation between eastern and western companies. At present, however, technology transfer is strongly hampered by uncertainties on property rights on real estate, by slow and bureaucratic decisions on privatization by the Treuhand-Anstalt, by idle transport and telecommunication facilities, and - last but not least - by a qualification of the labor force that is not adapted to western technologies.[12] In the long run, these problems will probably disappear, but it must be recognized that the East German economy right now faces a significant transition period with severe labor market distortions.[13]

There is some need, therefore, for temporary government assistance. The appropriateness of specific types of government intervention can be evaluated by four criteria:

(a) The adopted measures should be effective, i.e. they should increase aggregate demand for labor.

(b) They should be temporary, i.e. labor demand should remain high when government support will be gradually reduced in the course of the transition period.

(c) They should be fast-working, i.e. they should increase labor demand at early stages of the transition period when unemployment problems are most severe.

(d) They should be efficient, i.e. they should yield the desired result at minimum costs.

There is a broad variety of possible forms of government intervention. If the economic situation of East Germany is correctly described by Fig. 3, however, they can be classified into three basic categories: A first type of measures aims at shifting the production function upwards by increasing overall economic efficiency, for instance by modernizing infrastructure or by public investment in the qualification of the labor force.

A second (and commonly used) type of measures reduces the user's costs of capital, in general by public grants or tax credits for private fixed capital formation. As these measures are basically equivalent to an interest rate subsidy, they can be illustrated in Fig. 2 by a downward twist of the line connecting w_2 and C to the line connecting w_2 and B. A third type of measures that reduces the producer's costs of labor input by subsidizing wages would bring this line down to the one running through w_1 and A.[14]

All of these measures comply with the above stated criterion (a), since they increase the profitability of economic activity and hence increase aggregate demand for labor. With respect to criterion (b), however, type-one measures are to be preferred against type-two and type-three measures, since improvements of infrastructure and qualification will raise economic efficiency and thus help to close the gap between real wages and productivity. After closing the gap no further subsidies will be needed. To some extent, subsidizing factor prices will also increase productivity by stimulating investment in new jobs. These investment activities will introduce modern capital-embodied technologies into the GDR region and hence shift the production function upwards. Hence, the amount of factor price subsidies that is necessary for sustaining full employment will gradually decline in the course of time. Nevertheless, the upward shift of the production function will be more rapid with type-one measures, since they are directly improving economic efficiency.

Unfortunately, type-one measures are inferior to the others concerning criterion (c), i.e. their positive impact on labor demand will not immediately show up. One can easily understand, therefore, why the two German governments decided to emphasize cost-reducing measures against efficiency increasing ones. At present, government support for reconstructing and modernizing infrastructure and for improving the qualification of the labor force are only a small fraction of total subsidies to the former GDR.

Within the area of cost-reducing subsidies there is an unequivocal order of preference between interest rate and wage subsidies with regard to criterion (d). In Fig. 3, the wage subsidy per head that is necessary to achieve full employment is equal to the distance w_1w_2. The corresponding interest rate subsidy per head is given by the distance BC. With any neoclassical production function BC is larger than w_1w_2.[15] It can be concluded, therefore, that a given increase in labor demand can be achieved by a less amount of wage subsidies than of interest rate subsidies.

The difference simply arises from the fact that wage subsidies are directly adjusting labor costs to labor productivity, whereas interest rate subsidies are indirectly closing the gap between wages and productivity by raising the capital-labor ratio. In other words: part of interest rate subsidies are utilized for increasing the capital intensity of existing jobs and not for creating new jobs. Of course, interest rate subsidies would result in higher levels of labor productivity and total output, but it must be recognized that wage subsidies will attain full-employment at lower costs.

An evaluation of actual economic policy for restructuring the economy of eastern Germany in light of these criteria is quite difficult because there is a manifold and rapidly increasing collection of different government programs. They are in general not documented in easily available publications and relevant information is scattered over numerous leaflets, booklets and newspaper articles. A selection of the most important cost-reducing programs is presented in Tables A2 and A3 in the appendix.

A brief glance at these tables clearly indicates that the majority of programs is concerned with fixed capital formation, whereas subsidization of labor costs is of minor importance. This impression is confirmed by a comparison of financial volumes; the programs listed in Table A3 are in general less expensive than those of Table A2. There exists, however, one important exception - payments for short-time work. This is the most expensive one among the government programs in support of the GDR region.

It should be noted, however, that these payments do not exactly fit into the above described categories of efficiency increasing or cost-reducing subsidies. Payments for short-time workers are not increasing labor demand but are simply preventing dismissal. The government intends to combine short-time payments with qualification measures, but the available evidence suggests that most short-time workers of eastern Germany are simply disguised unemployed.

4. Prospects for Economic Policy

The sharp recession in East Germany mainly arises from the widened gap between real wages and labor productivity. As the barriers to migration between East and West Germany have disappeared, a significant rise in the level of wages was inevitable. A corresponding rise in productivity is hampered by various factors, notably by unsolved questions about property rights on real estate, by sluggish decentralization and privatization of state-owned companies and by deficiencies in infrastructure and qualification. Closing the productivity gap will probably take several years.

The central issue in economic policy is to remove these impediments to the reconstruction of the East German economy in order to retrench the transition period. In face of rapidly increasing unemployment, however, it seems inevitable to direct at least part of government funds towards mitigating the transition problems. Government support for sustaining labor demand should be effective, temporary, fast-working and efficient. It is a fundamental problem for policy makers that efficiency-increasing measures are in general not fast-working and that cost-reducing measures tend to turn into ever-lasting subsidies. The German government responded to this trade-off by presenting a mixture of different programs. A critical evaluation of these programs should acknowledge that economic policy resisted the temptation of designing interventionistic subsidy programs for the support of specific industries. The government does not pretend to know the winners of tomorrow and almost all programs are open to any branch of the economy.

It can be criticized, however, that public funds are heavily concentrated on the promotion of fixed capital formation. In light of neoclassical production theory, reducing unemployment by subsidizing labor costs would be cheaper. It might be objected that the concept of the production function would be somewhat strained when drawing the policy conclusion that subsidies on capital input should totally be replaced by temporary subsidies on labor input. For instance, it could be argued that it may be more difficult for political reasons to get rid of wage subsidies when the transition period is over. Nevertheless, the analysis presented above should cast at least some doubts on the present approach of the German federal government that completely ignores the alternative of subsidizing wages.

Finally, the problems of improving the qualification of the labor force are not solved at all. It has been analyzed elsewhere that many workers from East Germany are lacking experience with modern technologies (*Klodt, 1990*). According to official announcements, the system of short-time benefits is intended to solve this problem by combining short-time work with qualification arrangements wherever possible. The central problem is, however, that those who want to get short-time payments are forced to stay in their old companies. And very often these old companies are unable to provide new qualifications. It should be considered, hence, to substitute short-time payments by personal grants that can also be used for qualification programs outside old companies.

Table A1: Unemployment and Short-Time Work in the (Former) GDR*

1990	Unemployed			Short-time-workers	Unem-ployed	Unemployed and short-time-workers
					as a percentage of total labor force	
	Total	Male	Female			
January	7 440	6 409	1 031	-	0.1	x
February	10 994	7 080	3 914	-	0.1	x
March	38 313	22 273	16 040	-	0.4	x
April	64 948	37 670	27 278	-	0.7	x
May	94 807	54 078	40 729	-	1.1	x
June	142 096	72 893	69 203	-	1.6	x
July	272 017	131 536	140 481	656 277	3.0	10.3
August	361 286	169 082	192 204	1 439 412	4.0	20.1
Septemb.	444 875	200 073	244 802	1 728 700	5.0	24.2
October	537 800	.	.	1 767 000	6.0	25.7

* Estimated total labor force: 8.97 million.

Source: Statistisches Amt der DDR (1990).

Table A2: Selected Measures for Promoting Fixed Capital Formation in the Five New States

Measure	Duration
Investment grant for equipment (until 6/30/91: 12 %; until 6/30/92: 8 %)	07/1/90 - 6/30/92
Special depreciation for equipment purchased in 1990 (50 %; 30 %; 20 %)	01/1/90 - 12/31/90
Two-year exemption from personal and corporate income tax up to 10 000 DM for enterprises established before 1/1/91	1/1/90 - 12/31/90
Additional grant for building society depositors (unmarried: 1 200 DM; couples: 2 400 DM)	1/1/91 - 12/31/93
Creation of appropriations for tangible assets transferred to companies in the (former) GDR and for initial losses of affiliates in the (former) GDR	1/1/90 - 12/31/91
Investment grant (up to 23 %) from the joint program "Improvement of regional industry structure" (total grants of 3 billion DM per year; jointly financed by the federal government and the five new states)	7/1/90 - 6/30/95
Investment grant (up to 90 %) for business-related municipal infrastructure	
Low-interest credits for municipal investment (credit volume: 10 billion DM, interest rate reduction: up to 3 % for 10 years)	1/1/90 - 12/31/93

Table A2 (continued)

Measure	Duration
ECCS-credits for investment in mining regions of the (former) GDR	unlimited
Disbursement credits for modernizing houses and flats (credit volume: 10 billion DM; maximum individual amount: 10 000 DM)	since 6/30/90
Promotion of equity capital of SMEs (low-interest credits up to 40 % of investment expenditures)	1/1/90 - 12/31/93
ERP-credits for establishment of new enterprises, modernization of enterprises a. investment in environmental protection (credit volume 1990: 7.5 billion DM; 1991: 6 billion DM; maximum individual amount: 10 million DM)	unlimited

Table A2 (continued)

M e a s u r e	D u r a t i o n
Investment-credits of the Deutsche Ausgleichsbank (max. individual amount: 1.5 million DM)	unlimited
Guarantees for liquid loans (80 % of credit volume, up to the liquidity requirements for 3 months)	unlimited
Payment guarantees for West German deliverers (80 % of deliveries guaranteed by the federal government)	7/1/90 - 12/31/90
ERP-credits for private investment in the (former) GDR (50 % share of the finance; maximum individual amount: 1 million DM)	unlimited
Program for promoting tourism (low-interest credits for establishing, expanding and modernizing hotels and restaurants)	unlimited
Low-interest credits of the KfW for modernizing houses and flats (credit volume: 10 billion DM; interest rate reduction: up to 3 %; duration: 25 years)	

Table A3: Selected Measures for Promoting the Employment of Labor in the Five New States

- Short-time payments also for non-temporary loss of working hours (limited until 6/30/91; can be extended until 12/31/95)

- Access to qualification programs also for workers who are not unemployed

- Grants and credits to enterprises for promoting commencement of work

- Bridge-over financing for founders of new enterprises (equivalent to unemployment benefits for up to six months)

- Job-creating measures of private and public institutions (financial contribution to wages and salaries between 50 % and 100 %; regular duration: 1 year; maximum duration: 3 years)

- Promotion of external institution for qualification and technology transfer (financial contribution to investment up to 90 %)

- Promotion of arrangements for information and qualification (financial contribution to arrangement costs)

- Promotion of consulting services for SMEs (80 % of consulting fees, maximum individual amount: 3 000 DM)

Endnotes

1. For a detailed analysis of the weakness of the East German economy see *Siebert (1990)*.
2. For a careful and illuminating evaluation of the determinants of low efficiency in centrally planned economies see *Winiecki (1988)*.
3. There is an intense discussion about the question whether short-time workers should be added to the unemployed for calculating the true rate of unemployment. It must be recognized that the conditions for receiving short-time benefits from the Federal Institution of Labor are substantially weaker for the GDR region than for the West German region. In fact, for many East German enterprises short-time work is just another form of dismissal and many short-time workers are working zero hours a day. More detailed statistics on unemployment and short-time work are presented in Table A1 in the appendix.
4. For a comparison of the sectoral structure of East and West Germany see *Halstrick-Schwenk/Löbbe/Wenke (1990)*.
5. The comparably good performance of water supply can mainly be attributed to the fact that this sector is still subsidized and not yet exposed to competition.
6. For 1991, a further decline of 10 percent is predicted.
7. See *Bundesministerium für Wirtschaft (1990)*.
8. *Sachverständigenrat (1990)*.
9. One of the most popular slogans on East German rallies in early 1990 ran as follows: If the D-Mark does not come to us, we shall come to the D-Mark.
10. The changing political situation in the GDR since 1989 is analyzed by *Hamilton (1990)*.
11. Since July 1990, East German citizens are entitled to receive the same amount of social aid as West Germans, with some adjustments only for the lower level of rents in East Germany. The social security system hence fixes de facto minimum wages for East Germany (and West Germany as well).
12. For an analysis of the qualification requirements in East Germany see *Klodt (1990)*.
13. The five leading institutes of West Germany are expecting that the extreme point of depression in East Germany will be reached in summer 1991 (see *Deutsches Institut für Wirtschaftsforschung et al., 1990)*.
14. It has been suggested that strict price controls on nontradables should be preferred to direct wage subsidies, since residence decisions of rational workers would depend on real and not on nominal wages (*Burda, 1990*). It might be agreed that low rents and low tariffs for public transport would give an incentive for staying in the GDR region, but freezing these prices at present low levels would severely discourage the modernization of the East German housing stock and transport facilities.
15. In this context, the term neoclassical refers to diminishing returns.

References

BUNDESMINISTERIUM FÜR WIRTSCHAFT, Die wirtschaftliche Lage in der Bundesrepublik Deutschland. Monatsbericht 9 '90, Bonn 1990.

BURDA, Michael C., Capital Flows and the Reconstruction of Eastern Europe: The Case of the GDR after the Staatsvertrag. Paper prepared for the Kiel Week Conference, 19-22 June 1990.

DEUTSCHE BUNDESBANK, Die Wirtschaftslage in der Bundesrepublik Deutschland und in der DDR im Sommer 1990. Monatsberichte, Vol. 42, 1990, No. 9, 5-45.

DEUTSCHES INSTITUT FÜR WIRTSCHAFTSFORSCHUNG et al., Die Lage der Weltwirtschaft und der deutschen Wirtschaft im Herbst 1990. Berlin, 18 October 1990 (mimeo).

HALSTRICK-SCHWENK, Marianne, Klaus LÖBBE, Martin WENKE, Die sektoralen Wirtschaftsstrukturen der Bundesrepublik und der DDR. RWI-Mitteilungen, Vol. 41, 1990, Heft 12, 11-28.

HAMILTON, Daniel, After the Revolution: The New Political Landscape in East Germany. American Institute for Contemporary German Studies/The Johns Hopkins University, German Issues No. 7, Washington, D.C. 1990.

IFO-INSTITUT FÜR WIRTSCHAFTSFORSCHUNG, INSTITUT FÜR ANGEWANDTE WIRTSCHAFTSFORSCHUNG, Erste Anzeichen eines Aufschwungs der ostdeutschen Wirtschaft in Sicht? Ergebnisse einer Unternehmensbefragung, Berlin, 1 October 1990.

INSTITUT FÜR ANGEWANDTE WIRTSCHAFTSFORSCHUNG, Arbeitslosigkeit auf dem Gebiet der DDR? Ergebnisse einer Befragung, Berlin, 1 October 1990.

KLODT, Henning, Arbeitsmarktpolitik in der DDR: Vorschläge für ein Qualifizierungsprogramm. Die Weltwirtschaft 1990, Heft 1, 78-90.

KOSTRZEWA, Wojciech, Verpaßt Osteuropa den Anschluß auf den Weltmärkten? Kiel Discussion Papers, No. 144, September 1988.

SACHVERSTÄNDIGENRAT ZUR BEGUTACHTUNG DER GESAMTWIRTSCHAFTLICHEN ENTWICKLUNG, Jahresgutachten 1990/91. Stuttgart, Mainz 1990.

SCHNABEL, Claus, Structural Adjustment and Privatization of the East German Economy, this volume.

SCHMIEDING, Holger, "Unschätzbare Vorteile". Wirtschaftswoche, 1990, No. 42, 12 October, 171-175.

SIEBERT, Horst, The Economic Integration of Germany - An Update. Kiel Discussion Papers, No. 160a, September 1990.

-------, Holger SCHMIEDING, Restructuring Industry in the GDR. Kiel Working Papers, No. 431, July 1990.

STATISTISCHES AMT DER DDR, Monatszahlen. September 1990, 2. Folge. Berlin 1990.

STEHN, Jürgen, Holger SCHMIEDING, Spezialisierungsmuster und Wettbewerbsfähigkeit: Eine Bestandsaufnahme des DDR-Außenhandels. Die Weltwirtschaft, 1990, Heft 1, pp. 60-77.

VAUBEL, Roland, German Monetary Reunification: The Economic Consequences of Returning to the Pre-War Parity. August 1990 (mimeo).

VOGLER-LUDWIG, Kurt, "Verdeckte Arbeitslosigkeit in der DDR". Ifo-Schnelldienst, 1990, No. 24, 3-24.

WEISS, Frank D., West Germany's Trade with the East. Hypotheses and Perspectives. Kieler Studien, No. 179, Tübingen 1983.

WINIECKI, Jan, Heilsamer Druck. Beim Übergang zur Marktwirtschaft sinkt die Produktion, ohne daß sich der Lebensstandard verschlechtert. Wirtschaftswoche, 1990, No. 44, 26 October, 104-106.

--------, The Distorted World of Soviet-Type Economies. Pittsburgh, 1988.

COMMENT ON: GOVERNMENT SUPPORT FOR RESTRUCTURING THE EAST GERMAN ECONOMY: CAPITAL OR LABOR SUBSIDIES

George M. von Furstenberg

1. The Central Policy Objective and Proposal

The paper by Klodt contains one central policy recommendation about how to subsidize the economic assimilation of East Germany while keeping workers from leaving the territory that, until recently, comprised the GDR. This recommendation deserves to be examined carefully. It is of interest not just for Germany. Rather, it may apply to analogous movements toward economic integration of high-productivity and low-productivity economies when mass movement from the latter to the former is not desired by policymakers. For instance, the economic integration of Mexico and the United States that will start to be formalized in the North American Free Trade Area may also raise the issue of choosing subsidies to discourage labor flight. Indeed, with confidence, that state planning and rigging can serve as an effective engine of development, waning all over the world, more low-productivity countries have become prepared to seek rapid development through economic integration with advanced industrial countries.

This integration may not proceed entirely on market terms, and temporary subsidies may be offered. In this connection Klodt argues that reducing unemployment and raising real consumption wages by subsidizing labor costs would be cheaper than doing so by promoting fixed capital formation in East Germany. He grants that increased investment in infrastructure capital, i.e., capital that raises the productivity of both business capital and labor, is indispensable for the long term. But for the German government to concentrate its subsidies on the formation of business capital in East Germany would be inefficient. In his view, wage supplements or the reduction of earnings-related taxes should be used there instead.

I will first take Klodt's qualitative argument and quantify its implications on its terms in Section 2. It turns out, however, that these terms of reference are not well chosen to represent the transition of the East German economy. Section 3, therefore, outlines an alternative analysis more supportive of temporary subsidies for business capital formation. Such capital subsidies accelerate the transition to a state-of-the-art economy which wage subsidies would slow down. By cutting down the length of time for which either type of subsidy must be paid, capital subsidies thus provide an additional benefit, not recognized by Klodt, that tips the balance of argumentation more in their favor. Even though this comment thus ultimately casts doubt on the cogency of Klodt's recommendation, he is to be congratulated for having raised a central question of policy in a clear way.

1.1 Agreed Constraints

To arrive at his point, Klodt assumes that the supply of labor willing to remain in East Germany becomes infinitely elastic at a real wage of $\underline{w}$. This elevated floor for worker remuneration is loosely related to the real consumption wage in West Germany to which East German workers have improved - though by no means certain, - access through the unrestricted migration option provided by unification. He further assumes that, with the opening up of the East German economy, capital has become perfectly mobile. Thus, ignoring any risk premium, it needs to earn a net real rate of return $\underline{r}$, where $\underline{r}$ is the real interest rate "determined by world capital markets," at all times. The corresponding gross real rental rate, $\underline{g}$, on the net stock of capital, K, would then be $\underline{r} + \underline{d}$ in the simplest case first without taxes and subsidies. In this expression $\underline{d}$ is the exponential depreciation rate applicable to the class of assets considered. The upshot is that $\underline{g}$ and $\underline{w}$ would be factor-price constraints imposed on the East German economy by the new-found mobility of its factors. That economy can not, however, satisfy these constraints except at intolerably high rates of unemployment and out-migration. Hence the purpose of the subsidies is to keep the level of employment in East Germany, L, from falling below the minimum target level that is politically acceptable, L*.

While accepting these constraints and objectives as the basis for discussion throughout, this comment is divided between internal elaboration (Section 2) and external critique (Section 3) of how best to achieve them. At first it therefore accepts both Klodt's purpose and his framing, seeking only to put his conclusion in quantitative perspective. It then moves on to question the framework in which the problem of subsidizing the East German economy is addressed and outlines a more appropriate model yielding different conclusions.

2. The Cost of Subsidies Compensating for Chronically Inferior Productivity

First, how can Klodt's qualitative conclusion be made more telling on his own terms? Politicians are used to having their favorite subsidy programs denounced as inefficient by economists. But because politicians recognize objectives and constraints beyond those normally entered into economic calculations, purely qualitative demonstrations of economic inefficiency have little chance to connect with the legislative process. What could be more helpful is specific information on what percentage of the total cost of a program could be saved by choosing more efficient means.

2.1 A Comprehensive Measure of the Relative Efficiency of Labor Subsidies

Since Klodt provides a graph but no metric, let me first derive a measure of the relative efficiency, E, of wage subsidies to guage how large their efficiency advantage, 1-E, may be under various conditions.

Three assumptions appear to be implicit in Figure 3 of his paper and in the interpretations that surround it:

(1) Capital earns an internationally-competitive rate of return, even in the short run, presumably because it can be installed and withdrawn in an instant, as if it were putty-putty.
(2) I spite of this implied flexibility and homogeneity, total factor productivity is substantially lower in East than in West Germany.
(3) New investment in business capital does not convey any higher level of total factor productivity since the production function is unbroken and unique. This indicates that a simple, inferior level of technology prevails in East Germany regardless of any change in the capital-intensity of production that now involves investment in "Western" technology.

With these assumptions we can readily quantify how the relative efficiency of wage subsidies compares with that of return-to-capital subsidies for meeting the employment target, L*, at the net real consumption wage $\underline{w}$. Referring to his Figure 3, the relative efficiency measure, E, is equal to the distance from point w_1 to w_2 divided by the distance from B to C, where B is a point on the linear homogeneous production, Y, or output per unit of labor input function, $Y/L^* = y = f(K/L^*) = f(k)$. The distance w_2w_1 is the difference between the intercepts of two lines which are tangents to the production curve. One passes through point B with slope $f'(k_2)$ and the other through point A with slope $f'(k_1)$. Hence:

$$w_2w_1 = y(k_2) - y(k_1) + f'(k_1)k_1 - f'(k_2)k_2 \qquad (1)$$

Using the quadratic approximation lemma[1] to obtain

$$y(k_2) - y(k_1) \approx 0.5\,[f'(k_1) + f'(k_2)]\,(k_2 - k_1), \qquad (2)$$

and substituting in equation (1) for the change in output (average labor productivity) produced by the increase in capital intensity from k_1 to k_2 yields:

$$w_2w_1 \approx 0.5[f'(k_1) - f'(k_2)]\,k_2 + 0.5\,[f'(k_1) - f'(k_2)]\,k_1 \qquad (3)$$

From Klodt's Figure 3, the distance CB is easily seen to be a function of the same slope difference:

$$CB = [f'(k_1) - f'(k_2)]\, k_2 \qquad (4)$$

Hence the relative efficiency of wage subsidies, with their cost expressed as a fraction of the cost of return-to-capital subsidies also achieving L*, $\underline{w}$, and g is:

$$(w_2 w_1 / CB) \approx E = 0.5 + 0.5\, (k_1 / k_2) \qquad (5)$$

This first result shows that the inefficiency of return-to-capital subsidies depends on the increase in capital intensity they produce. For instance, if k_2 is 10% higher than k_1, labor subsidies would be 4.5% more efficient. Of course if k_2 is double k_1, which is about what is shown in Figure 3, 100 (1-E)% is much higher, 25% - all on Klodt's terms.

2.2 The Marginal Rate of Substitution of Capital for Labor Subsidies

The measure offered in equation (5) is quite precise because the quadratic approximation used to derive it is close. Unfortunately it requires knowledge of the current replacement cost of the East German stock of business capital per unit of L* (k_1) and how far this capital intensity would have to be raised (to k_2) if East Germany were to meet the factor-price constraints and the employment objective by means of capital subsidies alone. Such information would not readily be forthcoming even if we could abstract from the fact that the old stock of net capital, in k_1, and the investment that now follows, are not at all homogeneous. Furthermore, no one has yet proposed relying on capital subsidies exclusively. For these reasons it may be more helpful to derive a price-based measure of the marginal rate of substitution of return-to-capital subsidies for wage ("employment") subsidies. The total budget outlay for the former is $S_k = s_k K$, and it is $S_e = s_e L$ for the latter. To estimate the extra marginal cost of capital subsidies, this measure will be seen to rely on the subsidy rate, s_k, in relation to the gross marginal product of capital deployed in East Germany, $g - s_k$, alone. It shows the rate at which return-to-capital subsidies can be traded-off for wage subsidies when the combined subsidies, $S = S_k + S_e$, are just sufficient to meet the specified constraints ($\underline{w}$ and g) and objective (L*).

Instead of the quadratic approximation lemma, we now use an explicit (CD) form of the production function to get specific results. Formally, the problem is to minimize:

$$S = \underline{w}L + gK - Q(L,K)$$

subject to:

$$L = L^*; \ Q(L,K) = L^{\alpha}K^{1-\alpha}$$

Hence the first-order condition for the Lagrangean (with σ representing the Langrange multiplier), is:

$$G = S - \sigma(L-L^*), \qquad (6)$$

$$\delta G/\delta L = \underline{w} - \alpha\,(Q/L) = \sigma;\ \sigma = s_e \qquad (7)$$

$$\delta G/\delta K = g - (1-\alpha)(Q/K) = 0;\ s_k = 0 \qquad (8)$$

$$\delta G/\delta \sigma = L - L^* = 0 \qquad (9)$$

While the optimum program clearly shows that return-to-capital subsidies should be zero on Klodt's terms, how much costlier is it if they are used partially to substitute for wage subsidies? To answer this, equations (7), (8) and (9) are replaced with the production-equilibrium (profit-maximization) conditions for given subsidy rates s_e and s_k:

$$\underline{w} - s_e - \alpha\,(Q/L) = 0 \qquad (7a)$$

$$g - s_k - (1-\alpha)(Q/K) = 0 \qquad (8a)$$

$$L - L^* = 0 \qquad (9a)$$

After substituting the Cobb-Douglas production function for Q, equations (7a) and (8a) are solved for s_e and K, respectively:

$$s_e = \underline{w} - \alpha\,(K/L^*)^{1-\alpha} \qquad (10)$$

$$K = L^*\,(1-\alpha)^{1/\alpha} / (g - s_k)^{1/\alpha} \qquad (11)$$

Now the amount of the labor subsidy, S_e, saved as a result of increasing the rate of the capital subsidy, s_k, is:

$$dS_e/ds_k = (ds_eL^*/dK)(dK/ds_k)$$

$$= -\alpha(1-\alpha)\,K^{-\alpha}L^{*\alpha}\,(dK/ds_k) \qquad (12)$$

$$= -\alpha(g - s_k)\,(dK/ds_k)$$

The cost of the increased return-to-capital subsidy which Klodt applies to the entire stock of capital, old and new, on the other hand, is:

$$dS_k/ds_k = K + s_k\, dK/ds_k,$$

where

$$dK/ds_k = (1/\alpha)\,(1-\alpha)^{1/\alpha}\,L^*\,(g - s_k)^{-(1+\alpha)/\alpha} \qquad (13)$$

Hence the marginal rate of substitution in the amounts of the two types of subsidies is:

$$dS_k/dS_e = [(K/(dK/ds_k)) + s_k] / (ds_e\, L^*/dK)$$

$$= -\{1 + [s_k / \alpha(g - s_k)]\} \qquad (14)$$

Clearly, how much more expensive return-to-capital subsidies are at the margin depends entirely on the subsidy rate, s_k, in this second result.

An example may be helpful. In Germany, labor's share in the net national product is about two-thirds, and the gross return to capital may be around 18%. Hence αg is about 12 percent, and a subsidy rate, s_k, of 2 percentage points would mean that the marginal rate of substitution of subsidies of the return on capital for wage subsidies is just under 1.2. At a g of 18% per annum, a subsidy of the annual return on capital equal to about 2% of capital would be conferred by a tax credit of 10% of investment. With $s_k = 0.02$, $g = 0.18$, and $\alpha = 0.67$, such a credit would represent, at the margin, a 19% more expensive way of achieving the employment objective than the wage subsidies it replaces. This result from equation (14) is about as concrete as we can get quantifying relative inefficiency on Klodt's terms.

In the next section I try to point out that staying at the low level of capital intensity indicated by point A and k_1 in the preceding author's figure is not the correct recommendation when increased capital investment allows the economy to move to a higher production frontier faster, a move that will allow it to dispense with future subsidies. No such movement has been provided for by Klodt or credited to future capital formation in the East German economy. We now turn to giving such credit and showing why it is deserved.

3. Alternative Terms of Reference

So far we have derived two measures showing precisely that, on Klodt's terms of reference, return-to-capital subsidies are always less efficient than wage subsidies, though not necessarily much less efficient for his purpose. If East Germany in transition could be characterized as a one-sector economy in equilibrium we would not need to probe further. In fact, however, it is now a two-sector, or dual, economy in disequilibrium. Instead of having a single aggregate level of total factor productivity, at least two such levels must be distinguished: one representing the old conditions and one the new possibilities that have opened up.

The job of economic policy is to help the East German economy move from one production function on to a uniformly higher one. Once that economy has approached world-market standards, there is no occasion for further subsidies. However, adjustment costs are surely substantial for business in the interim and they rise at an increasing rate with the rate of change, - in this case with the rate of net capital formation.

To boost the adjustment process against the natural braking effect of adjustment costs to some degree, temporary subsidies may be justified and, indeed, cost-efficient. The reason is that introduction of the new technology, and only this up-to-date technology, can ultimately raise real wages and the gross rate of return accrued on business capital toward West German levels by market means. By contrast, continuing to pay wage subsidies would prolong working with inferior technology and retard the process of technology catch up.

I conclude, therefore, that reasoning about optimal subsidies in a static one-sector economic region, that is somehow chronically disadvantaged, is not conclusive for a dynamic, dual economy in disequilibrium seeking to overcome that disadvantage. Rather, using appropriate modelling, such as that outlined below, shows that temporary subsidies of both capital and labor form part of the optimal program for the transformation of the East German economy. Klodt's categorical preference for wage subsidies thus does not stand up in a setting where new capital investment raises total factor productivity by helping to catapult the East German economy on to a higher production function rather than just moving it along its inherited low-possibility frontier.

3.1 An Outline of the Alternative Model

Attempting to give credit to capital subsidies for accelerating the conversion from a low- to a high-productivity economy involves first of all moving from a comparative-static to a multiperiod conception of economic transition and its costs in the form of subsidies. The second step is to replace the assumption of a single technology in use with that of two putty-clay technologies: the old "socialist" (s) and the new "world" (w) technology. New capital goods installed henceforth in East Germany will be up to the world standard. But because they are long-lived, the configuration chosen for them will reflect not only current but also expected future costs of capital and labor, $\underline{g}$ and $\underline{w}^*$, with tax features expected to be the same as elsewhere in Germany in the long run. However, temporary investment subsidies apply in the Eastern part to encourage a faster transition from low-productivity ($_s$) to high-productivity ($_w$) operations. Because these subsidies are known to be temporary and adjustment costs steep, temporary investment tax credits do not raise the capital intensity desired for the long run in East Germany appreciably above the levels prevailing in West Germany for comparable world-class operations.[2]

Now the production functions in the two sectors and the joint employment constraint in East Germany are:

$$Q_s = a_s (K_s, L_s); \; Q_w = a_w (K_w, L_w); \; a_s < a_w \quad (15)$$

$$L_s + L_w = L^*$$

Profit maximization in each of the two sectors, the first of which is not attracting any further investment, implies:

$$\underline{g} > dQ_s/dK_s \geq 0; \; dQ_w/dK_w = \underline{g} = (1-\alpha)(Q_w/K_w) \quad (16)$$

$$\underline{w} > dQ_s/dL_s = \underline{w} - s_e; \; dQ_w/dL_w = \underline{w}^* = \alpha(Q_w/L_w),$$

where $\underline{g}$ and $\underline{w}^* \geq \underline{w}$ denote the same rate of user costs of capital and the same real wage as elsewhere in Germany.

Purely to economize on notation and to keep the deductions as simple as possible, we assume that there would be no net investment in East Germany without investment tax credits at the present time and that these credits are new and apply to net rather than gross investment in the world-technology sector. Furthermore, total adjustment costs, which rise at an increasing rate with the amount of change in the net stock of capital per period, dK/dt (=I), are represented by $0.5a\dot{K}^2$. Hence adjustment costs at the margin of net investment are adK/dt. Now if the marginal user cost of capital is to remain g, the rate of net investment in "world" capital, I_w, will be driven to the point where the capitalized marginal adjustment costs, net of the present value of the tax savings from their depreciation, are just equal to the rate of the special investment tax credit granted in East Germany, v. The tax saving per unit of historical cost incurred is uz, where u is the corporation income tax rate and z the present value of depreciation allowances per unit of original cost. Under these assumptions and with a dot over a variable representing a change started by a policy intervention:

$$v - (1-uz)\, a\, I_w = 0 \qquad (17)$$

The fiscal cost of the investment tax credit is:

$$\dot{S}_k = dS_k = v\, I_w \qquad (18)$$

Since the inherited stock of "socialist" capital is obsolete in East Germany, it will be taken out of service as soon as the labor it worked with is transferred to the modern industrial sector using K_w. Were it not for the accelerated scrappage induced by investment subsidies for K_w, capital and labor still employed in the "socialist" sector using K_s would both decline at the depreciation rate $\underline{d}$. Hence, starting from a level of employment in the old sector equal to $L_s(0)$, the present value of labor subsidies connected with the inferior technology tied to K_s is:

$$S_e = s_e \int_0^{\infty} e^{-(r+d)t}\, L_s(0)\, dt \qquad (19)$$

$$= s_e\, L_s(0)/(\underline{r} + \underline{d})$$

Then the entire saving from transferring labor to the world-class sector with the inducement of the investment tax credit is:

$$dS_e = s_e\, d\dot{L}_s/dt \;/\; (\underline{r} + \underline{d})$$

$$= -s_e\, dL_s/dt \;/\; (\underline{r} + \underline{d})$$

$$= -s_e\, I_w\, L_w \;/\; (\underline{r} + \underline{d})\, K_w \qquad (20)$$

The last substitution is derived from factor-price ratios being fixed at the level prevailing elsewhere in Germany, as required in equations (16), so that capital and labor inputs grow at the same rate in the expanding sector. Using equation (17) to substitute for I_w and equations (18) and (20) for dS_k and dS_e, the change in the total cost of subsidies from substituting the investment tax credit for some part of the wage subsidies paid in the socialist sector is:

$$dS = v^2 / [(1-uz)a] - s_e v L_w / [(1-uz)a(\underline{r} + \underline{d}) K_w] \quad (21)$$

Clearly dS is negative for very small v because of the presence of v^2 in the positive term, so that introducing an investment tax credit or other types of subsidies for new investment initially reduces the total cost of subsidies. The level of v at which the budgetary savings from the subsidy substitution are maximized is obtained by setting the partial derivative of dS in equation (21) with respect to v equal to zero and solving for the optimum value of v:

$$v^* = s_e L_w / [2(\underline{r} + \underline{d}) K_w] \quad (22)$$

This result shows that the optimum value, v*, is equal to what wage subsidies would cost if they were applied to labor employed in the world-technology sector, divided by twice the annual gross return on capital in that sector. Thus, in the alternative model, granting both investment tax credits and wage subsidies is efficient in the aggregate: If s_e is positive, then so is v*.

On a disaggregated basis the availability of two types of subsidies would imply a choice. Producers who want to stick with the old technology until their capital becomes worthless to use could be entitled to wage subsidies to the end, or at least until L* can be met even while their output and employment sink faster. On the other hand, those who wish to make a rapid transition or start new businesses would choose investment subsidies, thereby forgoing wage subsidies for their employees. The net result of any such differentiation would be a budgetary saving on a present-value basis in meeting the factor-price constraints and the employment objective that Klodt had stipulated.

Endnotes

1 The quadratic approximation lemma is so named because it holds exactly for quadratic functions but only approximately for other nonlinear functions. For the CD production function the approximation is close. Take, for instance, $Y = K^{0.5} L^{0.5}$ and evaluate output, Y, and hence $y = Y/L^*$ at the points $(K_1, L^*) = (4,9)$ and $(K_2, L^*) = (9,9)$ to obtain $y(k_1) = 2/3$ and $y(k_2) = 1$, with $k_1 = 4/9$ and $k_2 = 1$. From $y = f(k) = k^{0.5}$ the slope values at the end of the range, $f'(k_1)$ and $f'(k_2)$, are found to be 3/4 and 1/2, respectively. Substituting these values into equation (2) yields $1/3 \approx (5/8)(5/9) = 25/72$. Hence the approximation misses by 1/72 in this example, which is an error of about 4% in relation to 1/3.

2 If investment tax credits were either introduced or raised permanently in one part of Germany but not in the other and both parts were treated as a unitary economy in which they had started on the same footing, distortions would develop: The gross rate of return on capital would gradually decline as capital intensity would be raised through faster growth of capital in the "favored" part. During this period, costs of adjustment connected with the faster growth of capacity would be incurred that would offset the advantage conferred by the special investment tax credits at the margin. Ultimately, however, the gross rate of return on capital would have to fall (or congestion costs would have to rise) so far in the favored part of Germany as to fully offset the advantage of the special investment tax credits granted there.

In reality, no such distortions will be allowed to materialize. Because labor from the shrinking "socialist" sector is in highly elastic supply and because investment tax credits are temporary and adjustment costs rise steeply with rate of net investment, capital deepening will be negligible compared with capital broadening in the foremost-technology sector. Fiscal and economic competition between the states (*Laender*) in the federal system will assure that federal tax incentives will not be maintained in the five Eastern states for such a long time that they could actually lead to systematically *higher* capital intensities in the world-market sector than elsewhere in Germany. Any such disequalizing outcome would obviously pervert the redistributive rationale of the subsidies, and there is no political reason to expect that it would be tolerated by the majority of German states.

III. International Perspectives

GERMAN ECONOMIC UNIFICATION AND EUROPEAN INTEGRATION: PROSPERITY WITHOUT STABILITY?

Paul J. J. Welfens

1. Introduction

The new Germany is Europe's leading economy, the biggest trading nation in the EU, and Europe's second most important source of foreign direct investment. Germany is thus a strongly internationalized country, even if, as a result of German unification, it is an economically divided country. Overcoming more than 40 years of different institutional, economic and political developments naturally is difficult; yet problems may be limited if the country's unification spreads gains equally across regions and professional groups, and if there are mechanisms leading to convergence. Within a country, capital exports from capital-rich to capital-poor regions, fiscal transfers, one-time corrections in the regional wealth endowment and, of course, interregional trade, should bring about a gradual narrowing of differentials in income and wealth. If market forces and political interference cannot bring about convergence, migration could; the German economic, monetary and social union of July 1, 1990 was indeed motivated by a fear of a massive westward migration of East Germans. 388,000 East Germans left the ex-GDR in 1990, another 395,000 and 250,000 in 1991 and 1992, respectively. Since in 1991, 80,000 moved eastward in Germany; the net outflow in 1991 fell to about half the level of the previous year, to 169,000 (FEDERAL STATISTICAL OFFICE, 1994a).

Of the 16.5 million people in the ex-GDR, only about 1 million left eastern Germany in the period 1989-93; since 1992 the number of West Germans moving to eastern Germany has increased. Yet the intra-German net balance for the ex-GDR will remain negative for many years to come. Outward migration will slow down if high economic growth in eastern Germany and relatively modest land and housing prices are maintained, and if Berlin can restore its position as an economic and political center in Germany. In western Germany some regions and cities already face declining importance as major companies relocate production facilities and headquarters, or shift major investment projects to eastern Germany, or even further east. Expected high productivity increases, anticipated high subsidies, relatively abundant land and proximity to cheap suppliers in Poland and the ex-CSFR support the view that eastern Germany can catch-up with western Germany in productivity and income levels in the coming decade. This indeed would be a remarkable process, since the GDR's per capita income was only about 1/3 (level of Greece) of that in western Germany in 1990. In 1950, per capita income levels in the ex-GDR were about 50 % of those in the Federal Republic of Germany (STOLPER, 1960, p. 272-273).

The ex-GDR still has a long way to go toward economic catching-up with western Germany. Eastern Germany's population is 25 % of that in western Germany, but gross domestic output in the former GDR was only 1/10 of that in western Germany in 1993. The ex-GDR's economy accounted for only two percent of overall German exports in 1993. Eastern Germany is also much less internationalized: the share of foreigners living in the Ex-GDR is about 1%, in western Germany almost 8 %.

Opinion polls show that a solid western German majority supports EU integration. The European Union supports the restructuring of the ex-GDR with increasing funds, thus becoming more visible in the political sphere. Eastern Germany's population however, is a weaker supporter of European integration than that in western Germany. Since the East German electorate accounts for about 20% of overall voters (while GDP accounts for about 9 % of overall GDP in 1994), Euroskeptical East Germans could decisively influence Germany's attitude towards future EU integration. Moreover, about 1/4 of the young German generation associates the EU with the terms " Europe bureaucracy " and Germany as the " paymaster " of the EU (DER SPIEGEL, 1994, No. 38, p.81).

In the following analysis we will focus more closely on the major ingredients of the East German catching-up process, pointing out that there are positive prospects for a third German economic miracle - if and only if the unemployment problem can be overcome (Section 2). In Section 3 the emphasis is on European integration, which is shown to raise productivity levels and income growth. Yet while prosperity might increase, the political stability could erode in the European Union; this would lead to economic stagnation and disintegration in the long term. We will also raise the question of whether the new affluent Germany could be less pro-EC in its policy stance than the old Federal Republic of Germany.

In a period of high budget deficits and rising political nationalism in Europe, resistance against rising net contributions of the EU budget is increasing in the whole European Union; this is seen foremost in the traditional highest net contributor, the Federal Republic of Germany. Voter turnout at the 1994 EU Parliament elections fell to historical lows, while even traditional supporters of integration - e.g. western Germany and the Netherlands - showed signs of political fatigue over EU integration. In a wider EU community, comprised of new EFTA member countries as of 1995, Germany might become more influential; this may be due to a successful German economic convergence process, and since internal political impulses encourage a greater role of the new Germany. This paper will analyze whether this is consistent with the decision-making processes in the EU.

2. German Economic Unification

German unification is the rare case of a divided country that was able to reunite. In Europe, only the Polish reunification in the early 20th century is a similar case; here, however, the division lines remained markedly visible throughout decades. While the industrial heartland of Germany was located in Saxony in the interwar period, the leading high-tech region of reunited Germany is in the West, in the triangle Frankfurt-Stuttgart-Munich. Nevertheless, except for the Saarland, West Germany's Länder all have major economic centers. The political division of Germany in the period 1945-90 stimulated not only political federalism, but also regional decentralization of economic power, which facilitates German economic unification. All the West German Länder actively endorsed the integration and transformation process in the five newly-restored Länder of East Germany throughout financial transfers, manpower training and administrative support.

German Unification in Retrospective

German unification imposed systemic transformation on the people in the ex-GDR, who obtained economic and political freedom after six decades of totalitarianism. While the switch to a market economy and parliamentary democracy is opening up a range of new opportunities for the younger generation, many among the older generation feel that their "very personal wealth" is heavily discounted having much of its value. Memories and good personal relations built over decades often seem worthless ex post, which can be interpreted as a kind of immaterial capital loss of the elderly, in some regions major supporters of the post-communist PDS party. Most people in the military and party bureaucracy have been discredited, thus losing relative economic privileges, not to mention a sharp drop in the social status. In contrast, many West Germans view eastern Germany and unification as creating new career opportunities in business, politics and academia. The old nomenclature as well as many skilled and highly-educated East Germans are in contrast suffering a relative loss of income, influence and status, which might be felt as more than outweighing the absolute gain in real disposable income experienced by most households; the individual utility index U_i of the representative individual is here assumed to depend positively both on absolute income y_i and the ratio y_i/Y (Y=average income). All East German employees and workers face the risk of open unemployment, which, until 1990, was unknown in the GDR and other CMEA countries.

Losers and winners in the unification process are unevenly spread both the former GDR and within the whole of Germany.

German economic unification began in 1990 in the form of a currency unification: East German wages and salaries were converted at a favorable 1:1 exchange rate, while rates applied to deposits were slightly less favorable. Given the effective external exchange rate of 1:4, which implicitly had been applied to trade with western Europe, the conversion rate was rather generous; given a favorable initial monetary wealth position of many groups in the ex-GDR, one might have expected wage moderation to be a guiding principle of unification. As is well-known, this was not the case, partly because the FRG's trade unions, eager to obtain a new clientele in the ex-GDR, were fighting hard to reach wage parity. They furthermore attempted to prevent East Germany from remaining a low-wage area with sustaining downward pressure on West German wages, partly because there was no real counterweight against the trade unions' demand; firms were still to be privatized, while employer organizations in eastern Germany (often dominated by West Germans hardly interested in transforming the ex-GDR into a broad platform for newcomers) accorded generous wage increases.

In the metal-working and electrical industries, wage rates were increased by 25% in 1990; basic pay rates were to rise in a four-stage approach from spring 1991 to spring 1994 to 100% of the level in respective West German partner areas. The 1994 deadline was later postponed to July 1, 1996. The boost in wage income in the ex-GDR was rationalized to help stem the expected westward migration wave. Even with high wage growth, intra-German migration continued; fear of unemployment, however, and high levels of regional unemployment in eastern Germany, often caused by the rapid rise in wages, became a major cause of westward migration.

Adjustment to West Germany's relative prices brought about a jump of the price level of about 1/3 in the period 1990-1994. Rents and energy costs quadrupled. The eastern German inflation rate fell to 3 % in the last quarter 1994; hence prices in eastern Germany and western Germany are increasing at rather similar rates. Subsidized housing - a trait of the GDR - no longer plays a decisive role in eastern Germany, although rents often are somewhat below market levels. In January 1995 consumer price inflation fell to 2.3 % in western Germany, the lowest figure since spring 1990. Unification effects on the FRG's price level have petered out within five years.

2.1 Rapid Progress in East German Economic Restructuring

In the ex-GDR, basic pay rates reached about 50% of West German levels in late 1990; by the end of 1993, basic rates had already reached 4/5 of the level in West Germany. Taking into account the lower fringe benefits in eastern Germany, the east-west pay ratio was 3/4 at the end of 1993 (DEUTSCHE BUNDESBANK, 1994, p. 39). A shorter East German standard working week (40 instead of 42 hours in 1990) and longer holiday entitlements (+ 3.5 days, which gives 27 days p.a.; western Germany 29 days) imply that pay rates increased by roughly 10 percentage points more than on a monthly basis since 1990/91. Actual earnings were raised slightly less than negotiated wage increases: 12% of East German employees in industrial enterprises, and 23% of those in craft enterprises, generally earned less than the agreed-upon rates. With labor productivity in 1950 only half as high as in western Germany, an east-west wage ratio of 70% in late 1993 was still excessive from a short-term perspective. Moreover, the price level of everyday goods was 6% below that in western Germany (FEDERAL STATISTICAL OFFICE, 1994b, p. 425). Facing such high wage pressure, the shocking exposure to international competition, and an associated fall in the industrial producer price of about 40% after unification, East German industry lost three million jobs out of an initial stock of 9.5 mill. between 1990 and 1994.

The price divergence fetched in markets by West German and by East German companies explains part of the intra-German differential in value-added per employee. Based on a sample of small firms in both parts of Germany, FRITSCH and MALLOCK (1994) found that the physical productivity in the ex-GDR increased from 36.2% of the West German level in 1987 to 66.8 % in 1992, while gross value-added per employee reached only 46.1%. Expected figures for 1995 are 90.9 % for physical productivity and 65.8 % for gross value-added per employee (Tab. 1). This indicates a problem in the reputation of East German products, possibly also to quality-control problems, and, of course, to insufficient vertical integration, which allows many West German firms to exert market power, i.e. to raise prices above pure competitive levels. Reputation and quality-control problems, as well as problems in the efficient reorganization of the flow of work within the company, could be mastered in small firms within several years; the overmanning in management and search for the cheapest and most reliable suppliers (in terms comparable to those of established western firms) might be more difficult issues. Efficient restructuring and catching-up in labor productivity and quality-control might be challenging in big firms, but their access advantage to capital markets should compensate for potential disadvantages in the reorganization of production, marketing and distribution. Therefore, there is a fair chance that the East German industry will come close to West German productivity levels by the year 2000, and to gross value-added per employee some years later (on an hourly basis, this will take longer because employees in the ex-GDR have longer working hours than their West German colleagues). This leads to the conclusion that the intra-German income and productivity gaps will have almost vanished by the turn of the century. Such a convergence result presents no reason, however, to believe that westward migration will cease. Relatively increasing rents and housing prices in eastern Germany, and only moderately increasing prices in western Germany, could stimulate unemployed people to move to western Germany; housing shortages have fallen in the mid-1990s, due to massive new housing starts.

Table 1: Physical Productivity and Gross Value-added per Employee in Small Firms in Eastern Germany

	East-West-Ratio (%)		
	1987	1992	1995*
physical productivity	36.2	66.8	90.9
gross value-added per employee		46.1	65.8

* estimate

Source: FRITSCH and MALLOK (1994), p. 16.

Unemployment and Structural Change

The overall loss of employment in eastern Germany was more than 1/3 (see Tab. 2); women were among the main losers of transformation, their unemployment rate of 21.9 % was more than twice the male unemployment rate in early 1992. The absolute number of jobs increased in the service sector and in construction. In the crafts and service sectors, continuous employment growth can be expected in the future. However, without a profitable industry there is little hope of maintaining a dynamic service sector. The restructuring of the East German business sector is hence so important, as is the restoration of profitability in industry; wage payments exceeded net social product at factor costs, so that the average profit rate was negative in the ex-GDR in 1993.

Table 2: Employment and Unemployment in Eastern Germany, 1989-93 (in 1000)

	1989	1991	1993	Change 1989-93
Persons employed				
in ex-GDR	9 747	7 279	6 242	-3 505
Agriculture & Forestry	976	454	242	-734
Producing Sector	4 386	2 960	2 146	-2 240
Manufacturing*	3 758	2 282	1 277	-2 481
Construction	628	678	869	+241
Service	2 130	2 173	2 236	+104
Public Sector	2 255	1 692	1 618	-637
Memorandum Items				
Participants in job-creation schemes/training		449	642	
Short-time workers		1 616	181	
Unemployed		913	1 149	
Unemployment Rate (%)	0	10.4	15.8	
		12.6 (m)**		
		21.9 (f)**		

* including energy; ** unemployment rate for male and female, January 1992 (microcensus)

Source: DEUTSCHE BUNDESBANK (1994), p. 42 and p. 84; FEDERAL STATISTICAL OFFICE (1994a), p.19.

Firms in eastern Germany all cope with the problem of higher unit labor costs than in western Germany, causing incentives to substitute labor by capital to remain high in the 1990s. Employer federations have been criticized for offering too-generous wage concessions in the first half of the 1990s; some firms have indeed left the employers' federation, while newly-created firms are often hesitant to become members of an employer federation whose collective bargaining results would be binding.

Underestimation of the Costs of Unification and Catching-up

An important surprise of German unification is that its costs were much underestimated by officials in the Bonn government. False analogies with the first 1949 West German economic miracle circulated in the government - these did not take into account that private entrepreneurs were waiting to raise production in West Germany under the political guidance of Ludwig Erhard, whereas in the ex-GDR private ownership of industrial assets had to foremost be organized. Moreover, while World War II created destruction and devastation mostly outside Germany, and thus leaving large part of the production potential functioning, a large part of eastern Germany's industrial capital stock was obsolete after unification.

Labor market problems were not generally underestimated prior to unification. Yet negotiations between the FRG and the GDR in 1989 were based on the misleading statistics of the Report on the Nation in the Divided Germany (Bericht zur Lage der Nation im geteilten Deutschland) of 1987, which very much overestimated the GDR's economic potential: the ratio of East German per capita income to West German per capita income was set at 50%, while in reality a value of less than 1/3 correctly described the situation (VON DER LIPPE, 1994). The report was unaware of the enormous distortions created by ever-increasing state subsidies, insufficient reinvestment in industrial capital and the infrastructure, and negative value-added in the form of nature's destruction as a basic production factor. Estimates of environmental destruction are twice as high as the absolute increase of net material product in the 1980s, so that an ecologically-augmented national accounting system could have shown the continuous fall of the GDR's true value-added (WELFENS, M., 1993, p. 65). Rising foreign debt, increasing environmental degradation, and the contradiction between generous welfare system and inefficient production system, as well as political suppression, all contributed to the collapse of the GDR.

The shrinking of the ex-GDR's industrial base in the period 1990-94, major investments in filters, as well as sewage water treatment and the general modernization of the GDR's capital stock, brought a rapid improvement in the ecological situation. Low aspiration levels in regard to environmental protection and poor information ensured that emission control and environmental policies played no major role in the GDR; moreover, the secret police controlled any potential opposition. Government invisibly, and sometimes visibly, committed criminal offenses (e.g. robbing parcels sent from western Europe). In the new open society with a market economy, there is a rise of "ordinary crime", which does not necessarily indicate that the GDR had less crime than post-GDR eastern Germany.

The limited history of environmental awareness, and the rapid ecological progress in the first years of unification, might explain why the Green Party faces major difficulties in politically surviving in eastern Germany. For the Green Party environmental issues in the context of unification caused an unexpected occurrence: When West Germans learned after unification the truth about the poor environmental quality in the socialist GDR after the unification, the ecological situation in western Germany looked brighter than ever. Green issues hence do not rank among the top priorities of the median voter. He is often more concerned with the developing problems of unemployment and increasing fiscal pressure - i.e. the rise of tax rates and social security contributions in the context of unification. Rising pension payments for the elderly, as well as unemployment benefits for people in East Germany, were financed by West German members, which in effect reinforced the trend of workers and employees bearing the financial burden of unification.

While early estimates by the Ministry of Finance estimated the costs of unification at about $ 100 bill. the final true costs of unification were at least 10 times as high: West Germany's net transfers to eastern Germany amounted to some $ 100-120 bill. annually in the first five years of unification, while the second half of the 1990s is unlikely to see much smaller transfers. The Bonn government's misperception of the costs of unification did not cause a political disaster only because eastern Germany - in terms of population and economic size - is so small relative to western Germany. Politicians and economists might rightly call German unification a unique situation, since major errors could not be avoided; yet the order of magnitude was out of acceptable proportions.

Political credibility problems emerged in 1990/91, when the federal government raised taxes to finance the burden of unification; this contrasted earlier promises that no tax increase would be necessary. Underestimating the costs of unification implied a disappointment for taxpayers and voters in western Germany, yet also for those people in eastern Germany who had believed that achieving income parity with western Germany would be quick and painless.

Massive transfers only to a small degree supported investments and economic restructuring. To the extent that disposable income in eastern Germany was increased, transfers had a favorable effect on the overall savings rate: Since East German household savings rates almost doubled (and that of West Germans only transitorily reduced) between 1989 and 1994, the upward pressure on real interest rates was not as accentuated as it could have been. The major reason for maintaining modest real interest rates was, however, the massive influx of foreign capital - the negative corollary was a negative current account balance, which switched from a high pre-unification surplus to a minus position after 1990.

Nominal and real interest rates in Germany increased only in the period 1990-92, decreasing thereafter. The transitory increase of German interest rates, necessary to attract foreign capital inflows, hit EU partner countries in a period of declining economic growth. The need to raise interest rates parallel to Germany's as long as fixed exchange rates (within the standard margin) held, made consistent EU policy cooperation difficult. The old European Monetary System fell victim after a series of speculative attacks in 1992/93 (WELFENS, 1995a). German unification switched the zero position in general government balances to a negative figure of about minus 3 percent; a consideration of THA deficits would raise the figure by another percentage point. The 1992/93 recession in the EU, in combination with rising interest rates due to the pressure of German unification, raised the public deficit in UK and France dramatically: from less than 2 percent of GDP to 6-7% in 1993 (OECD, 1994b). Compared to this development, Germany's deficit ratio remained low, although it increased by 3 percentage points after unification. With the restructuring and expansion of the East German capital stock, the demand for DM-denominated bonds - complementary assets to real capital under modern portfolio theory - should increase, creating new opportunities for lower long-term German interest rates. However, the decrease in nominal rates could be lower than the fall in the inflation rate, as measured by the producer price index; for the manufacturing industry, this would imply rising and high real interest rates. Due to intensified competition in the single market, producer price increases are likely to remain below the 1990's increase in the consumer price index. While Germany contributed to the rise of the G-7 deficit ratio from about -1 to -7% in 1993, hence creating some upward pressure on interest rates in the OECD area, the long-term impact of German unification on the EU could be favorable: an enlarged, prosperous and stable Germany will reinforce the attractiveness of the DM and of those EU currencies tied to it. An enlarged and prosperous Germany will reinforce the attractiveness of the DM as an international reserve currency, which should allow Germany to keep its real interest rates slightly below its EU partners. The EU as a whole might benefit from lower real interest rates, which in turn stimulate economic growth.

The GDP growth rate in western Germany jumped from 3% in 1989 to 5.7% and 4.5% in 1990 and 1991, respectively; it was followed by a drop to 1.6% in 1992, and a recession in 1993, when output fell by 1.9%. One may expect growth rates of 2-3 % for 1994 and 1995. After a strong collapse of GDP in eastern Germany in 1990/91, high growth rates of about 10 % and 6.5 % were realized in 1992 and 1993, respectively; 9-10% economic growth is expected in 1994-96.

In 1993, production in the ex-GDR for the first time increased faster than real domestic demand. In the second half of 1990, private consumption was 88 % of GDP in eastern Germany; in 1991 that share jumped to 100 %, while the figure for West Germany was 54 % (FEDERAL STATISTICAL OFFICE, 1994a, p. 10). Since government consumption and investment, relative to GDP, each reached about 45 % in 1991, it is clear that the ex-GDR's current account deficit vis-à-vis the rest of the world - including West Germany - reached 90 % of GDP. In 1993 investment per employee in eastern Germany was for the first time higher than in western Germany, so that one may expect an acceleration in the catching-up process with West German productivity levels, as well as a steep rise in GDP. Even during the recession year 1993, sales to western Germany - accounting for 20% of overall sales in manufacturing industry - increased. Firms' main market focus is still local and regional: 60% of sales were in eastern Germany, while only 20% were exported to the rest of the world (IFW/DIW, 1994). Privatization, the creation of new firms and massive retraining of the labor force were key ingredients for rapid structural change, which, in combination with modernization and lay-offs, which raise productivity via a backward move on the production function, raised productivity strongly.

Table 3: Sectoral Shares in Gross Value-Added in Eastern Germany, 1990.2 (second half) and 1993

	1990.2	1993.2	1993
	East Germany		West Germany
Agriculture & Fishery	7.3	3.3	1.1
Manufacturing	42.7	34.3	38.3
Distribution & Transportation	18.3	12.5	14.8
Services	11.2	26.2	36.7
Government*	20.6	23.6	14.4
Total	100.0	100.0	100.0

Shares may not add-up to 100 because of rounding; * including households

Source: Federal Statistical Office, Deutsche Bundesbank.

Structural adjustment indeed has been quick: the shares of agriculture in gross value-added fell from 7.3 in the second half of 1990 to 3.3% three years later (Tab. 3); the share of manufacturing fell by more almost 10 percentage points. The share of services increased by 15 points, which suggests overall that East German economic structures are converging to the pattern of western Germany. There is only one exception, namely the increasing share of government in output in eastern Germany - a development which largely reflects the fact that redundancies in the state sector remained relatively rare. By contrast, privatization in industry led to a rapid shrinkage of industrial output shares.

Privatization

Within five years, the Treuhandanstalt privatized the East German industry; this is, despite some individual pitfalls in privatization of firms, a remarkable achievement. The Treuhandanstalt was created in June 1990 by the last GDR government and parliament. The

Trusteeship Act gave the THA a task as summarized in the preamble to the act: "Through privatization to reduce the entrepreneurial activity of the state as rapidly and as extensively as possible; to make as many enterprises as possible competitive and by doing so to safeguard jobs and create new employment; to make real property available for business purposes." Article 25 (par. 1) of the German-German Unification Treaty stipulates that the Trusteeship Act of June 17, 1990 would continue to apply after unification, with the following proviso:

"The Trust Agency (THA) shall continue to be charged in accordance with the provisions of the Trusteeship Act, with restructuring and privatizing the former publicly owned enterprises to bring them into line with the requirements of a competitive economy. It shall become a direct institution of the Federation vested with legal capacity and subject to public law. Technical and legal supervision shall be the responsibility of the Federal Minister of Finance, who shall exercise technical supervision in agreement with the Federal Minister of Economics and the respective federal minister. Stakes held by the Trust Agency (THA) shall be indirect stakes of the Federation. Amendments to the Charter shall require the agreement of the Federal Government."

In 1990 the Treuhandanstalt (Berlin), which later gained 15 regional offices to take care of smaller privatization cases, started out with some 8,000 state firms; these were split up into almost 14,000 companies. Only 450 firms were still in the THA's books in mid-1994. Until mid-1994, there were 10,158 reprivatizations (restitutions). Foreign investors had acquired 839 firms or plants for DM 5.6 bill.; there were 2,700 management buy outs. About 3,500 firms with some 350,000 jobs were liquidated; about 1/3 of these jobs were safeguarded. A major achievement, in contrast to privatization procedures in other ex-CMEA countries, indeed is the splitting-up of big industrial firms to facilitate privatization along long-term profitable lines of business (LICHTBLAU, 1993; FISCHER/HAX/SCHNEIDER, 1993). There were 34,000 cases of property transfers (e.g. swimming hall, kindergarten) in favor of cities and towns until the end of 1994; some 60,000 cases in which local governments reclaimed property still had to be settled in mid-1994.

Within the small-scale privatization of restaurants, hotels, shops, pharmacies and cinemas there were 14,257 privatizations, 4,298 reprivatizations, 25,030 small privatizations and 38,000 cases of land-selling. The latter was organized under the auspices of the THA subsidiary TLG. Until mid-1994, the overall number of privatizations in the ex-GDR reached 81,600 (TREUHANDANSTALT, 1994). Privatization revenues reached DM 53 bill., which is about 1/4 of the GDP in eastern Germany. However, since many privatizations became feasible only at a negative price - the THA provided funds for restructuring or additional equity capital - the overall net revenue from privatization will be negative. Instead of the DM 160 bill. expected by the THA in 1990, the net revenue will be in the red, at about DM 200 bill. This negative revenue balance should, however, not be over-emphasized, since the government's main issue in privatizing should be the discounted future tax revenues from value-added in privatized firms, as well as the number of jobs able to be maintained.

The typical Treuhand privatization approach was to get a private investor with a credible and success-promising business plan; in most cases the THA required a firm commitment for medium-term investment and job guarantees. The THA had obtained investment commitments of DM 200 bill. and job guarantees for 1.5 mill. jobs by mid-1994. Contracts stipulated that violation of the terms of the deal would lead to penalty payments by the investor. In the ex-GDR, privatization contracts were almost always strictly enforced by the contract supervisory system of the THA (SCHMIDT, 1994), this contrasted some other countries in the ex-CMEA, where both the legal system and technical enforcement of contracts is weak. Between July 1990 and April 1992, some 77,300 jobs were privatized, of which 551,000 could be maintained (IAB, 1992); in this period the THA recorded 226,000 redundancies, so that 2/3 of political critical job losses was accounted for by the Treuhandanstalt, while 1/3 occurred in the course of privatization.

Between January 1, 1991 and spring 1994, the number of people employed in Treuhandanstalt firms was reduced via privatization and redundancies; switching into special employment creation schemes furthermore reduced employment from 2,922 mill. to 0,14 mill., a reduction of 95.3%. THA firms employed only 2.6 % of all employed in the ex-GDR in mid-1994. The THA balance looks somewhat less favorable if one does not view 1991 and its 3 mill. employees as the starting point, but rather 1990, when 4 million people, and thus almost half of the GDR employment, worked in firms of the Treuhandanstalt. Privatized firms developed more favorably than firms remaining on the portfolio of the Treuhandanstalt (GÜRTLER, 1992). This suggests that firms acting in a competitive environment under private ownership are typically quicker to restructure, more efficient in the choice of investment projects, and more responsive to market signals, than firms owned by government.

From a strategic point of view, the THA and federal government, respectively, can be criticized on several counts:

(1) Investment commitment and job guarantees, maintaining minimal R&D activities in eastern Germany, should have been leading privatization criteria, while pro-competition effects should also have been stressed. Eastern Germany, as a high-wage region, can foster profitable firms

and high per capita GDP in the long-term if a critical minimum of R&D activities is located within the ex-GDR. Since many young researchers are leaving THA firms in eastern Germany, special investment incentives will be required to attract major firms producing technology intensive goods. Government also failed to impose a general requirement stating that competition should be reinforced by privatization in the whole of Germany, in several important cases, privatization has weakened competition (e.g. in the energy sector and the oil refining industry). The government-owned (West German) Deutsche Telekom AG's crude strategy to quickly modernize, by massive capital investment, the outdated telecom system in eastern Germany meant an extension of state-owned West German monopoly firms; yet the EU has stipulated an end to the telecom monopoly in 1998. Under an innovative regime of network competition catching-up in telecoms density in eastern Germany could have been achieved at a lower price in terms of investment costs, ultimately reducing East German subscriber rates to levels below those in West Germany (and in the long-term stimulating competition in the all-German economy).

(2) Government provided almost no special incentives to create broader strata with equity or wealth in other forms of real industrial capital; the THA furthermore did not develop innovative privatization forms. Those MBOs and MBIs that were encouraged by THA workers had no special incentives to save for investing into investment funds or in the firm where they were employed. Both the federal and regional (Länder) governments provided incentives for the creation of new firms, but one may question whether this is an adequate approach to creating a broad strata of middle- and upper-income households with industrial wealth; this group typically politically supports the market economy (and sometimes democracy).

(3) Government and the THA failed to adequately disentangle social facilities (e.g. kindergartens, youth clubs) and firms intimately linked together under the GDR system. In cases of pending restitution claims, public access to both the firm and social facilities became impossible.

(4) Government and the THA underestimated the negative effects of xenophobia in eastern Germany, which discouraged foreign would-be investors in many cases; it raised the prize of privatization since foreign investors required higher subsidies and capital injections than otherwise might have been necessary.

(5) Government failed to impose a special capital gains tax, which would have allowed the tax payer to ultimately benefit from the network effects of privatization. With more and more

privatized firms - e.g. suppliers becoming more innovative and cost-efficient over time - the value of industrial assets and land will increase.

(6) It took the West German government more than two years after unification to cope effectively with its self-created investment impediment: namely the principle that restitution proceeds before compensation cum privatization. Special laws were adopted to make sure that in cases of unclear historical ownership of industrial premises and land, outside investors could acquire the firm without having to fear uncertainties in their property title.

(7) In the ex-GDR, the role of small and medium-sized firms is likely to remain limited in comparison to West Germany. The size distribution inherited from the socialist GDR was clearly biased toward big firms, while aggressive West German competitors - often the big firms - kept newcomers at bay in many East German industries. Big firms will play a greater role in the politics and economics of the new Germany; this tendency is reinforced by incentives in the single market to create bigger firms by national and international M&As.

A final critique can be raised with respect to the "business-as-usual policies" that characterized the first two post-unification years in western Germany. Privatization in West Germany should have accelerated in a period in which privatization of the East German economy was perceived as a major policy priority (HARTWIG, 1993).

2.2 Germany's Labor Market Disequilibria

The unification boom postponed the need for structural changes and cost-trimming in the West German industry. Facing a sharp recession in 1993 and structural problems in some international markets, German industry undertook a massive restructuring operation. West Germany dipped into recession as a consequence of weakening export demand, high unit labor cost increases in 1991-92, and the rise of real interest rates. Unit labor costs in the period 1989-92 increased by 11%, which equaled the total rate of increase over the preceding seven years; wage moderation only came in 1993, when effective fixed pay rates reached 1.5% (DEUTSCHE BUNDESBANK, 1994). The workforce in many firms - even in Germany's leading automotive producers - was reduced severely in the recession of 1993/94. Unemployment rates (as a percentage of total labor force) in western Germany fell in 1990 and 1991 to 6.4% and 5.7%, respectively, but increased to 5.9% in 1992, 7.3% in 1993, and about 8% in 1994. From 1.9 mill. in 1990, the number of unemployed jumped to 2.6 mill. in mid-1994. Since 1974, mass unemployment has been a problem in Germany and all EU member countries; the exceptions are Portugal, which is, likely to face a massive shake-out in agriculture in the 1990s because of internal market forces, and Greece, which never was a member of the exchange rate mechanism in the EMS. The oil price shock adjustment in labor markets remained incomplete in the Federal Republic of Germany and most EC countries. Since the second oil price shock, both the share of long-term unemployment (unemployed over one year) and level of unemployment have increased in the EU (Fig. 1), whereas there was no persistent increase in these indicators in the US, Japan and the EFTA countries.

After the oil price shocks of the 1970's almost all EU countries suffered a gradual increase of the unemployment rate, which rose from cycle to cycle. Insufficient wage dispersion is a major reason for this unfavorable development. In the 1980s the percentage wage increases of the least skilled workers were higher than average in major EC countries (OECD, 1994, p. 22); this induced firms to replace unskilled, relatively overpaid workers with modern machinery constructed and built by more skilled workers. While the trade unions argument is valid proof that unskilled workers often have to pay rents as high as skilled workers, it is an open question whether unskilled workers' disposable income should be raised by massive gross increases or by a modest gross wage increase in combination with reduced tax rates. In terms of safeguarding employment, the latter is clearly preferable, since labor costs for the firm are much lower than under the alternative strategy of sharply-rising gross wages, which stimulate the substitution of capital for labor.

There is also insufficient wage dispersion in Germany: the wage drift has narrowed in the second half of the 1980s, while German unification, with its increase in the number of workers, would have called for general wage moderation and increasing wage differentiation. Between 1985 and 1992, the actual wages and salaries per employee increased in West Germany by 3.9% p.a., which is less than fixed pay increases of 4.1% (DEUTSCHE BUNDESBANK, 1994, p. 36). Hence, wages lost part of the incentive function necessary for a spatial and sectoral reallocation of labor, which would have been particularly necessary in the context of German unification and the unfolding of single market dynamics.

In eastern Germany productivity growth matched wage growth in 1994. Overall labor costs per unit of output showed no increase - for the first time since unification. Under the pressure of rising unemployment rates and the credible threat of major companies to relocate production activities to southern or eastern Europe, wage demands and fixed pay rates moderated in Germany in 1993/94. Together with a modernization of the capital stock, this brought about declining unit labor costs, rising profits and improved capacity utilization rates in western Germany. However, the main impulse for overcoming the recession came from rising foreign demand, which raised German exports despite the fact that Germany suffered a real DM appreciation in 1992/93. Germany's exports are relatively robust with respect to real exchange rate changes (DÖPKE and FISCHER, 1994).

Germany suffers from declining FDI inflows, relative to other EU partner countries, declining employment in the high technology sector, and from insufficient innovation and capital formation. The high rate of unemployment is a key to the innovation problem: a high unemployment rate suggests that trade unions will often resist technological changes. While full employment would include an unemployment rate of 3-4%, the present all-German rate is about 10%, namely 8% in the country's West and 16% in the East (1994). While one may anticipate a reduction in unemployment to 10% in eastern Germany at the end of the 1990s, and a reduction of 1-2 percentage points in western Germany in the course of a cyclical upswing, the rate of economic growth will be insufficient to restore full employment. East German growth rates will remain high for at least a decade; yet this could destabilize Germany through a rise in westward migration from eastern Europe. The majority of immigrants is likely to move to western Germany, where the high share of foreigners, in many cities creates a natural bridgehead for immigration. However, as long as the unemployment rate in western Germany remains high, xenophobic reactions are likely to remain a major problem in the whole country (experience shows that even in the US in the 1930s, when immigration quotas were effectively cut, unemployment created resistance against immigration). For eastern Germany, which lacks multinational company investment and attracts only 4% of overall FDI flows into Germany, xenophobic reactions of a part of the population would reduce prospects for attracting more FDI, thus improving opportunities for economic catching-up. FDI inflows bring significant technology transfer and contribute to high economic growth. It is no coincidence that those German Länder with the highest GDP growth are also those with the highest FDI inflows: Baden-Württemberg and Bavaria (IWD, 1994); not surprisingly, Saxony is the leading location for foreign investment in eastern Germany.

High unemployment is a grave social, economic and political problem, to which people and parties in the FRG adapted to in the 1970s and 1980s. The unemployment overhang of the 1970s has never been eliminated, the German government not taking the unemployment problem seriously. The same could be said about trade unions, for which net real wage maximization strategies might imply excessive wage rates, and, more importantly, insufficient wage dispersion between skilled and unskilled workers. Not surprisingly, employer federations are not really interested in full employment either; unemployment is welcomed for raising the working efforts of the employed. Since the single market has intensified competition in markets, companies might silently welcome the disciplinary effect of high unemployment rates.

While a part of unemployment would be eliminated if the unemployment insurance system were redesigned in an incentive-compatible way (WELFENS, 1994), namely that regions with above-average (below-average) unemployment rates pay contribution rates above-average (below-average), the growth of job opportunities might still be insufficient for full employment if obstacles to economic growth are not removed.

Figure 1: Labor Market Disequilibria

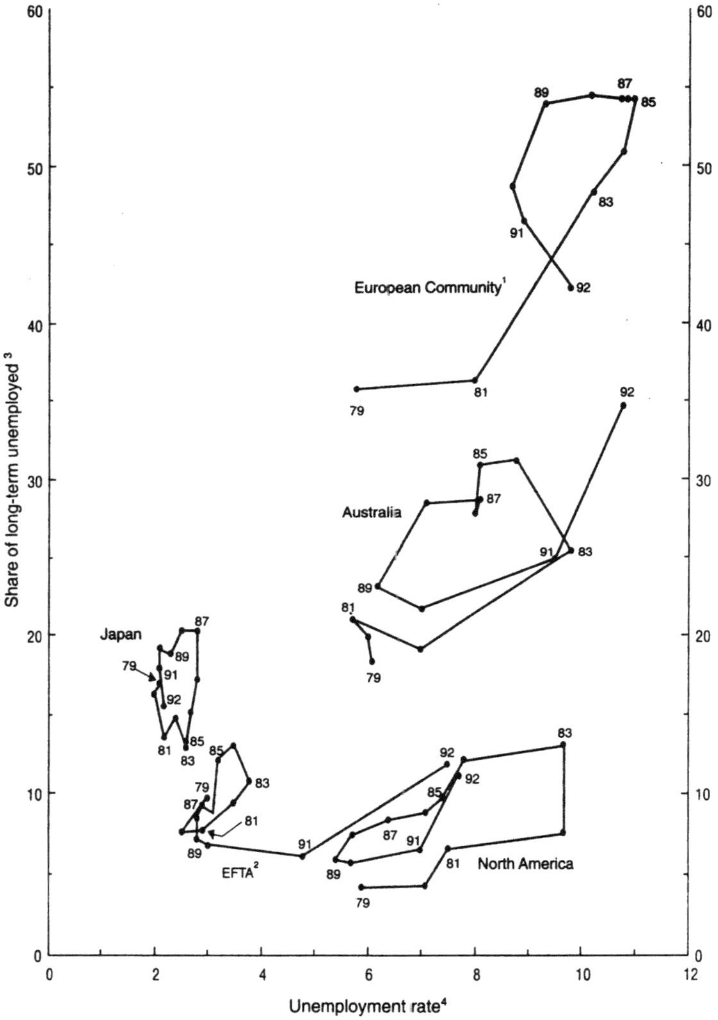

1. Excluding Luxembourg and Portugal for all years and Greece for 1979.
2. Finland, Norway and Sweden only.
3. Unemployed for one year and over as a per cent of all unemployed.
4. Standardised unemployment rates.

Source: OECD (1994).

2.3 Supply-Side Changes in Germany and Prospects for a New German Economic Miracle

There are many barriers to economic growth in Germany. The shock of German unification, which brings so many hard changes to people in eastern Germany, also raises new questions in western Germany: Old answers are no longer automatically valid in a period in which high government budget deficits require an economization of resources. Major bottlenecks in infrastructure are visible in the whole of Germany. Asian NICs have raised new challenges for Germany, as has the economic opening-up of eastern Europe. There are many reasons not to proceed with business-as-usual policies. The dramatic events of German unification, leading to major changes in public attitudes, removed many barriers in the political arena that traditionally blocked reforms in western Germany. Finally, intensified political competition on the "junior policy level", namely on that of the FRG's Länder (16 instead of 11 prior to 1990), implies greater locational competition, and thus greater pressure for the competition of policy regimes in Germany.

Facing enormous economic adjustment problems, some East German Länder might pioneer institutional innovations, adopting new regulations which under normal circumstances, never would have had a chance to be realized in the FRG. The private financing of infrastructure projects is one example; the consideration of replacing Federal Labor Offices in Saxony by new and more flexible local offices for employment creation in 1994, another. In western Germany itself, some supply-side oriented reforms have been adopted in a big party alliance; this would have been more difficult to achieve, had not exceptional unification problems time and again called for cooperation among leading political parties. Under new legislation, both the Deutsche Telekom, the third-biggest telecom company in the world, and the Deutsche Bahn AG were turned into joint-stock companies, both to be privatized. Since the telecom sector is, together with the electronics industry, the most technologically-dynamic industry in OECD countries, one may expect new impulses for investment, employment, growth and trade from its liberalization. The Deutsche Bahn AG and energy supplier VEBA (actually a conglomerate) will launch their own terrestrial network; network competition can be expected in the late 1990s. Other energy producers are following suit, and one may expect the ongoing EU liberalization of the telecoms business to stimulate the expansion of all information-intensive industries; this will create a boom in the multimedia business, opening-up new EU-wide investment opportunities. Germany, as the main producer of capital equipment, is expected to benefit most from this.

The massive reforms in the ex-GDR's university system (HAMACHER and GUTMANN, 1994), and the creation of new universities in eastern Germany, majorly contribute to rejuvenating and improving human capital formation in the whole of Germany. If leading national and multinational companies can be attracted to the ex-GDR in the medium-term the combination of a modernized university system, new infrastructure system, and intensive competition among privatized firms, might well generate growth impulses for the whole of Germany. If the ex-GDR achieves parity with West Germany, its share in the overall GDP would be 25%; assuming 5% growth in the ex-GDR implies a contribution of 1.25% to the all-German growth rate. Thereby, the all-German growth rate might exceed that of its EU partners by about 1 percentage point.

If low unemployment rates reduce the pace of liberalization and innovation in many fields, prospects for higher growth in Germany and the whole EU will be much better than in the mid-1990s. In western Germany, the 1980s brought a revival of entrepreneurship: The share of entrepreneurs and self-employed increased for the first time in decades (already before unification), while new growth opportunities in eastern Germany could open up new fields for newcomers in the long-run.

If modest EU growth can be maintained and the catching-up potential of smaller ex-CMEA countries fully mobilized, Germany could benefit from both internal rejuvenation and external growth impulses. While ecological problems require pro-ecological growth strategies to be implemented, it is obvious that the prospects for higher growth in Germany have improved. With Japanese competitors struggling under weakened domestic demand and a rising Yen, German firms enjoy the advantage of reduced external competitive pressure from East Asia. The new Germany could become the economic powerhouse of western Europe if it combined internal liberalization and a restoration of full employment with growth impulses from eastern Europe, to which German FDI outflows could actively contribute. This optimistic scenario, which could lead to a (modest) third economic miracle, is an option requiring the EU to remain a stable political entity. A caveat concerns the appreciation of the DM which continued in early 1995. Supply-side changes will positively influence eastern Germany's export performance. The Bundesban (1995, p. 59) notes: "Real gross fixed capital formation which has been surging ahead since as early as 1991 increased once again in 1994 by 15.5 %. Last year a major part of the capital goods was probably produced in the new Länder themselves, contributing to the increase in output there. The acceleration in economic growth is mainly attributable to the trend in manufacturing, the sector with the greatest need for adjustment after the collapse of communism. Not only the branches of the manufacturing sector which were already expanding their output the year before accelerated the pace of their production in

1994; other industries, too, reached the area of growth - the chemicals and the textile industries, for instance. The successes of east German industry are not based solely, as was still the case in 1993, on rising domestic sales; the enterprises are succeeding more and more in gaining a foothold in the export markets. In the first eleven months of last year manufacturing turnover as a whole was 19 % higher and domestic sales were 20.5 % higher than in the corresponding period of the previous year. At the same time, export business rose by 9.5 %, although export turnover reached only 11.5 % of overall turnover (compared with 28.5 % in western Germany)."

3. European Integration

EU integration has decisively been driven by the German-French twin engine in the 1950s and 1960s. During the 1970s, all of the EC faced major and sometimes divergent, economic problems: they had to absorb two oil price shocks, as well as the advent of newly-industrializing countries. After a period of Eurosklerosis in the first half of the 1980s, the single market program adopted in 1987 brought renewed economic growth and optimism into the Community. However, with the collapse of the common adversary, the USSR, and the adoption of the Maastricht Treaty, which envisages foreign policy cooperation and a monetary union, Eurofatigue is spreading throughout the Community of twelve.

A brief look at the declining voter turnout (Tab. 4) at EC parliamentary elections suggests that EU issues are considered less interesting and important, despite the new competences given to the European Parliament under the Maastricht Treaty.

Except for Denmark, France, Spain and Luxembourg, voter turnout fell in the 1994 election; ignoring Greece and Luxembourg because of compulsory voting, all small countries, except for Denmark and Belgium, reported less than 50%. The UK had a very low turnout figure, too. This points, together with the opinion polls of the EU Commission, to declining political support in major EU countries. Smaller countries might receive the impression that their economic influence in a wider EU (with a bigger Germany) is declining.

Table 4: Voter Turnout in EC Parliamentary Elections (ranked according to 1994 turnout)

	1989	1994	Change 1994/89 (percentage point)
Belgium	90.7	90.6	-0.1
Luxemburg*	87.4	88.5	1.1
Italy*	81.0	74.8	-6.2
Greece*	79.7	71.2	-8.5
Germany	62.3	60.4	-1.9
Spain	54.6	59.1	4.5
Denmark	46.2	52.9	6.7
France	48.7	52.7	4.0
Ireland	68.3	44.0	-24.3
Netherlands	47.2	35.6	-11.6
Portugal	51.2	35.5	-15.7
UK	36.2	36.4	0.2

* compulsory voting

Source: Federal Statistical Office, EC Bulletin.

While support for supranational policy in western Europe is eroding, regionalism is reviving in almost all EU countries. Taking into account the combination of xenophobia and the revival of nationalism in many EU member states, the centrifugal forces within the Community are gaining in influence. Paradoxically, the economic success of integration in the EU could create problems of policy consistency; while integrated markets and multinational business call for common economic policy, rising per capita incomes raise the demand for individual autonomy and decentralization. It is difficult to reconcile decentralization or regionalism with the rising influence of supranational policy-making in the EU. One may doubt whether the new Committee of Regions in Brussels will be a major step towards bridging the requirements of cooperation and decentralization.

Centrifugal forces will be an even greater problem if integration and German unification weaken the German-French twin-spark integration motor. German unification is clearly to Germany's economic advantage. France, as Germany's most important trading partner, will gain on the trade side, but the rivalry between German and French companies in third markets could tilt in favor of Germany. This, along with French perceptions that Germany's relatively greater economic role is undermining power parity, could destabilize the EU. No pair of countries can credibly replace German-French cooperation.

3.1 The Dynamics of the Single Market

The creation of a single EU market has on the one hand reinforced competition in goods markets; on the other hand, locational competition, and hence the quest for foreign direct investment, have intensified. The elimination of intra-EU trade barriers and resulting move from a customs union (achieved in 1968) to a single market have created economic benefits in terms of higher employment and transitorily higher economic growth. The EC COMMISSION (1993, p. 10) argues that the single market is a tangible reality:

* *70 million customs documents revoked;*
* *A 3% saving on the costs of international transport;*
* *Three times more company mergers and acquisitions in the Community over the period in question;*
* *Twice the number of European companies involved in mergers and acquisitions in the rest of the world;*
* *A doubling of trade in those Community sectors previously regarded as sheltered from competition;*
* *Investment increased by one third between 1986 and 1990;*
* *Nine million jobs created between 1986 and 1990;*
* *One half of a percentage point extra growth each year.*

While the EC single market has yielded visible benefits in the period 1986-92, the official start of the integrated market in 1993 was rather disappointing: 1993/94 was the first all-EC recession since 1974/75. The single market is creating new growth opportunities only in the long-term; even with higher growth, there is little hope that the EU will be able to reduce the unemployment rate. The IFO (1994) Institute, together with its EU partner institutes, expect growth rates to reach only about 2% in the EU in the period 1992-98. This would be a rather modest performance if one takes into account that the growth of the EU population could reach 1/2 percentage point; per capita income would hence increase only by about 1.5%, much less than expected in the US.

According to the EU Commission, the single market has yielded economic benefits. Yet additional benefits may only be expected through a massive EU infrastructure program: Network services in telecom, railways and energy are considered to be the key to overcoming unemployment and achieving economic growth. While there is little doubt that a modernization of infrastructure can raise economic growth, one may doubt whether it will reduce unemployment significantly over a long term. Infrastructure programs do not eliminate the malfunctioning of EU labor markets; they are therefore likely to lead to higher real wage growth, but not to greater wage dispersion nor the removal of barriers to entry in the labor market. Hence the EU twin problem of high unemployment rates and long unemployment duration will hardly be changed by the EU program.

Facing rising intra-EU competition, German industry has intensified its search for cheaper production locations within the EU and third countries. With increased capital mobility and a wider area of investment location for leading companies, German firms can improve their position in the EU market; this holds especially due to the special advantage of an increased domestic market (after unification).

3.2 Problems with EU Enlargement

Germany and France launched an initiative at the EC Commission level to create a task force to study problems of an EU enlargement. The EU enlargement by (at a maximum: four more) EFTA countries in 1995 will raise the EU's GDP and influence in the global economy (Tab. 5). However, the set of EU institutions needs urgent reform, since a Community of 15 or 20 member countries cannot function like the initial EC-6 group.

Table 5: Prospective Enlargements of the EU
(figures refer to 1992)

	GNP ($ bill.)	Population
EU 12	6 814.3	347.1
EU 16	7 495.0	373.0
EU 20*	7 639.7	437.3

EU20=EU 16 plus Visegrad Countries (Poland, Hungary, Ex-CSFR)

Source: ERECO (1994), Europe in 1998, forthcoming.

The Bhanzaf index (defining power as a country's ability to change a losing coalition into a winning one by joining the existing coalition) calculations for various EU groupings indicate that with both the EFTA enlargement of the 1990s and future Visegrad-countries-enlargement, the big countries lose political influence. These countries could thus find the EU harder to accept, leadership becoming more difficult to implement.

Germany and France (where some leading politicians suggested that the two countries are the core of a smaller "EU hard core", one moving ahead of the pack in the future) could solve the contradiction between the aspiration to control decision-making and declining weight in Community decision-making, by either renationalizing certain policy fields or excluding some other EU countries from "core decision-making". The latter will be achieved by simply creating a two-speed Community, with an attached outer-ring of countries in the European Economic Area.

Table 6: Bhanzaf Index for EU Countries/Candidates

	1958-1973	1973-1981	1981-1985	since 1986	EU (16)	EU (20)
FR	0,238	0,167	0,158	0,129	0,1088	0,0865
GE	0,238	0,167	0,158	0,129	0,1088	0,0865
IT	0,238	0,167	0,158	0,129	0,1088	0,0865
BG	0,143	0,092	0,082	0,067	0,0567	0,0464
NL	0,143	0,092	0,082	0,067	0,0567	0,0464
LX	0,000	0,016	0,041	0,018	0,0226	0,0186
UK		0,167	0,158	0,129	0,1088	0,0865
DK		0,066	0,041	0,046	0,0348	0,0282
IR		0,066	0,041	0,046	0,0348	0,0282
GR			0,082	0,067	0,0567	0,0464
PR				0,067	0,0567	0,0464
SP				0,109	0,0896	0,0718
AU					0,0433	0,0364
SW					0,0433	0,0364
FL					0,0348	0,0282
NO					0,0348	0,0282
PL						0,0718
HU						0,0464
CR						0,0464
SR						0,0282
Total	1	1	1	1	1	1

Source: Hosli (1993), p. 640.

The transformations in eastern Europe developed quickly, causing enormous adjustment problems in the ex-CMEA (WELFENS, 1992). Transitions have created new export markets for the EU, as well as new production locations that provide a cheap basis for labor-intensive production (even of goods which require relatively skilled labor inputs). Similar to the US in Latin America, and Japan in East Asia, the EU faces the option of having a low-wage economic neighborhood of considerable potential growth. It is not surprising that EU foreign direct investment increasingly flows to ex-CMEA countries. In the period 1990-92, Hungary and the ex-CSFR were the most prominent investment targets (Tab. 7).

Table 7: Twelve Most Active 3rd Countries in Number of M&As Concerning EC Enterprise, 1990-92

3rd Country as Bidder		3rd Country as Target	
US	417	US	345
Switzerland	200	Switzerland	82
Sweden	135	Hungary	59
Japan	104	Sweden	49
Finland	61	Norway	35
Austria	55	Canada	35
Australia	32	CSFR	30
Canada	31	Austria	27
Dual Nationality	22	Poland	23
Hong Kong	22	Finland	21
Norway	21	Australia	21
South Africa	12	Japan	16

Source: EC COMMISSION (1994), European Economy, No. 57, Brussels, p. 29.

The prospective EU enlargements by the four EFTA countries Austria, Sweden, Norway and Finland will increase the economic weight of the EU, shifting the economic gravity center towards eastern Europe. 18% of Finland's exports in 1990 were with the former Council of Mutual Economic Assistance; yet due to the collapse of the CMEA and the transformation crisis in eastern Europe, this share declined to about 12 % in 1993. Austria held almost the same share: 18% of its foreign direct investments flowed to eastern Europe in 1993. Behind the US, Germany, France, the UK and Italy, Austria held the highest stock of FDI in eastern Europe (incl. the former USSR); in terms of the number of deals, Austria ranked third behind the US and Germany. Hungary and the Czech Republic are receiving the majority of Germany's East European investments. German foreign investors launched foreign direct investments of DM 0.8 bill. in 1992 in Hungary, which equaled German FDI flows into Spain (total German FDI outflows: DM 29.9 bill. in 1992; 18 bill. in 1993).

Germany accounted for 50% of EU trade with eastern Europe (exports DM 43 bill.; imports DM 36 bill.), followed by Italy with a share of 16%, France with 9% and the Netherlands and the UK with each 7%; these were trailed by Belgium, Luxembourg and Denmark (combined 2%), and the four countries Spain, Greece, Portugal and Ireland (combined 4%). Trade is developing in a manner consistent with economic theory (see Tab. 8): RCAs of the Visegrad countries have improved both for labor-intensive industries and skill-intensive mobile Schumpeter industries (defined by medium or high technology content, but with options to separate R&D from the production location) in the period 1990-92.

Table 8: Competitive Position of Eastern Europe in Trade with Germany

		Poland	Ex-CSFR	Hungary	Bulgaria	Romania
Mobile Schumpeter Industries	1980	-120.1	-100.6	-81.6	-66.7	-152.3
	1990	-67.1	-77.1	-59.9	-92.3	-144.9
	1991	-65.2	-64.3	-50.6	-88.4	-150.3
	1992	-88.3	-63.1	-43.6	-72.7	-154.3
Immobile Schumpeter Industries	1980	-161.1	-163.8	-130.3	-157.3	-207.7
	1990	-166.9	-147.6	-105.8	-176.3	-86.2
	1991	-162.3	-86.7	-92.5	-142.6	-140.0
	1992	-164.1	-83.7	-88.6	-157.4	-177.9
Resource Intensive Industries	1980	133.1	165.0	85.1	19.8	83.8
	1990	158.7	190.3	142.4	90.0	48.7
	1991	146.3	103.9	71.0	182.0	59.9
	1992	178.9	119.5	77.7	186.2	88.1
Capital Intensive Industries	1980	28.4	72.1	32.2	101.0	4.7
	1990	-26.6	94.5	30.5	118.0	-140.5
	1991	-26.8	57.2	45.3	17.8	-98.2
	1992	-40.5	51.2	25.7	7.0	-99.9
Labor Intensive Industries	1980	63.0	63.7	111.7	97.4	96.6
	1990	87.6	84.3	75.1	109.0	206.2
	1991	89.7	86.0	69.5	107.6	166.8
	1992	82.8	70.2	69.2	117.7	148.8

Source: KLODT, H. (1993), Perspektiven des Ost-West-Handels: Die komparativen Vorteile der mittel- und osteuropäischen Reformländer, in: Die Weltwirtschaft, Heft 4, p. 424-440.

3.3 Instability in the Political and Economic Sphere?

When Japan's long-term LDP government fell in 1992, the Asian economic giant suffered a period of slow growth, falling share prices and inconsistent economic policies. Regardless of the October 16 all-German election results, Germany is not likely to face political instability in the short-run; this holds even if the post-communist PDS musters enough seats to be represented in Parliament (the minimum is three seats, which make the 5% threshold of votes redundant.

There are three possible dividing lines which could cause social and political tensions in the long-term in Germany:

(i) The division between western and eastern Germany: In a natural process in which the old generation of eastern Germany (the main loser of German unification) is dying, potential conflicts between winners and losers of German economic unification will become increasingly irrelevant in the long run.

(ii) The division between the younger and older generation: the "greying" of Germany and the whole EU, which will have a share of 19-20% people aged above 65 in 2010. This is 5 percentage points higher than the current 14.5%. Problems in financing pension schemes will lead to conflicts: raising taxes will become increasingly difficult in societies in which tax burdens are already perceived as high or excessive, and in which the tax burden increasingly falls on labor. The latter occurs since very mobile capital enjoys, often as a consequence of the creation of the single market, many options to avoid or reduce taxation. If the retirement age is raised (it was already raised in Germany in 1994, revising former reductions), it might reinforce the problem of unemployment, which very often concerns those aged 50 and above.

(iii) The division between the employed and unemployed, or those suffering frequent unemployment spells. Unemployment in Europe is likely to remain a stubborn problem, particularly in Germany.

Revival of Economic Nationalism in Germany

In post-unification Germany, nationalism is gaining influence. This holds not only for the extreme right of the political spectrum, but also more generally. The leader of the conservative CDU fraction in Parliament declared in 1994 that nationalism is necessary (again) because it generates solidarity; this is welcomed during German unification, which requires affluent West Germans to finance 4-5% transfers of West Germany's GDP to eastern Germany over many years. Nationalism might also be considered as a prerequisite to raising tax rates: for the sake of the nation, each individual should sacrifice an increased share of his/her gross income. HARRY JOHNSON argued that economic nationalism raises peoples' utility level in developing countries, since it reinforces their sense of identity and makes them feel better-off through a psychological satisfaction (quasi-income) and nationalism. In Europe in general, and in Germany (with seven million foreigners living among 80 mill. inhabitants) in particular, economic nationalism could become a political problem. The right wing might be affected because industrial interests among heavily-internationalized German multinational companies are not in favor of economic nationalism nor the associated risk of politically-motivated protectionism. The more internationalist and interventionist political left also faces problems, since economic nationalism seems to suggest a higher degree of policy autonomy. Part of the "green left" is sometimes openly hostile toward international trade, which is identified to be a major cause of ecological problems worldwide. A revival of German economic nationalism in the long-term cannot be excluded, but it might take time for such a new political paradigm to gain momentum on the right or the left. Economic nationalism is difficult to reconcile with the idea of an integrated European Union.

Instability in Germany could result from the fact that the marginally most influential West German party, the liberal FDP, faces the risk of political extinction after unification. The party fares worst in eastern Germany which is not surprising since there is no comparable West German clientele; here, civil servants, craftsmen and entrepreneurs are major voter groups. Civil servants in eastern Germany traditionally supported the SED and the post-communist PDS, respectively. The number of craftsmen and entrepreneurs will remain under-represented in the former GDR: the legacy of former "big state" firms in eastern Germany, and the often overwhelming challenge by large West German companies, will prevent the emergence of a "Mittelstand" (medium-size-firms) of major importance.

Since the left-wing PDS is strongly regionally represented in the ex-GDR, the political left will be represented by two parties in the German Parliament. This new phenomenon, along with FDP's threatened political survival, could make the formation of governments in Germany much more difficult than in the old Federal Republic of Germany. Moreover, all West European party systems face the following problem: the former political glue of anti-communism and fear that the USSR has lost its significance, causing pure self-interest to become the dominating impulse in party life. This could make the formation of stable political coalition governments much more difficult than in the European past.

A wider European Union is already in the making, since Hungary and Poland are in favor of EU membership in the near future (WELFENS, 1995b). Whether a Community of 15 or 19 countries can be governed as effectively as the original Community of six (or the Community of 12 countries) is doubtful. In a larger EU club, the smaller countries could feel fully dominated by big countries, who manipulate of the Brussels EU bureaucracy. The formerly equal econmic heavyweights Germany, France, Italy and the UK, have to now look for a new balance with an enlarged Germany.

References

DEUTSCHE BUNDESBANK (1994), Monthly Report, August 1994, Frankfurt/M.

DEUTSCHE BUNDESBANK (1995), Monthly Report, February 1995, Frankfurt/M.

DÖPKE, J. and FISCHER, M. (1994), Was bestimmt die westdeutschen Exporte?, Die Weltwirtschaft, 1994/1.

EC COMMISSION (1993), Growth, Competitiveness, Employment, White Paper, Brussels.

EC COMMISSION (1994), European Economy, No. 57, Brussels.

FEDERAL STATISTICAL OFFICE (1994a), Zur wirtschaftlichen und sozialen Lage in den neuen Bundesländern, Stuttgart: Metzler-Poeschl.

FEDERAL STATISTICAL OFFICE (1994b), Zwischenörtlicher Vergleich des Verbraucherpreisniveaus in 50 Städten, Wirtschaft und Statistik, No. 6.

FISCHER, W.; HAX, H. and SCHNEIDER, H. K., eds. (1993), Treuhandanstalt. Das Unmögliche wagen, Berlin: Akademie-Verlag.

FRITSCH, M. and MALLOK, J. (1994), Productivity in Small East and West German Industrial Plants - A Matched Pair Analysis, paper presented at the 3rd Conference of the European Association for Comparative Economic Studies, "The Transformation of Economics Systems", Budapest, Sept. 8-10, 1994.

GÜRTLER, J. (1992), Neue Bundesländer: Privatisierte Unternehmen nach wie vor deutlich erfolgreicher, in: IFO-Schnelldienst, 34/92, München, 15-19.

HAMACHER, S. und GUTMANN, G. (1994), Humanvermögensentwertung durch die Vereinigung - Das Beispiel der Hochschulen, in: GUTMANN, G. and WAGNER, U., Ed., Ökonomische Erfolge und Mißerfolge der deutschen Vereinigung - Eine Zwischenbilanz, 227-252, Stuttgart: Fischer.

HARTWIG, K.-H. (1993), Privatisierung in Westdeutschland: Vertane Chancen bei der deutschen Privatisierung, in: THIEME, H.J., Ed., Privatisierungsstrategie im Systemvergleich, Berlin: Duncker & Humblot, 41-64.

HOSLI, M. O. (1993), Admission of European Free Trade Association states to the European Community: effects on voting power in the European Community Council of Ministers, in: International Organization, Vol. 47, No. 4, 629-643.

IAB (Institut für Arbeitsmarkt- und Berufsforschung, 1993), Kurznachrichten Nr. 15, 16, 17, Nürnberg.

IFO (1994), Europa bis 1998: Eine Zeit der Neuorientierung, Ifo Schnelldienst, Vol. 47, July 22, 18-20.

IFW/DIW (1994), Gesamtwirtschaftliche und unternehmerische Anpassungsfortschritte in Ostdeutschland, 10. Bericht, Kieler Diskussionsbeiträge, No. 230, Kiel.

IWD (1994), IWD Mitteilungen, Vol. 20, No. 27, Cologne: Institut der deutschen Wirtschaft.

KLEIN, M. and WELFENS, P.J.J., eds. (1992), Multinationals in the New Europe and Global Trade, Heidelberg and New York: Springer.

KLODT, H. (1993), Perspektiven des Ost-West-Handels: Die komparativen Vorteile der mittel- und osteuropäischen Reformländer, in: Die Weltwirtschaft, Heft 4, 424-440.

LICHTBLAU, K. (1993), Privatisierungs- und Sanierungsarabeit der Treuhandanstalt, Köln: Deutscher Instituts-Verlag.

OECD (1994a), The OECD Jobs Study, Paris.

OECD (1994b), OECD Economic Outlook, No. 55, Paris.

SCHMIDT, K.-D. (1994), Treuhandanstalt and Investment Acquisitions: How to Ensure that Contracts are Kept?, Kiel Working Paper No. 632, Institute für Weltwirtschaft.

STOLPER, W. (1960), The Structure of the East German Economy, Cambridge, Mass.: Harvard UP.

TREUHANDANSTALT (1994), Monatsbericht, Berlin.

VON DER LIPPE (1994), Materialen zum Bericht der Lage der Nation im geteilten Deutschland 1987 als statistische Grundlage für die Staatsverträge mit der ehemaligen DDR, in: GUTMANN, G. and WAGNER, U., eds., Ökonomische Erfolge und Mißerfolge der deutschen Vereinigung - Eine Zwischenbilanz, Stuttgart: Fischer, 3-36.

WELFENS, M. (1993), Umweltprobleme und Umweltpolitik in Mittel- und Osteuropa. Ökonomie, Ökologie und Systemwandel, Heidelberg: Springer-Physica.

WELFENS, P.J.J. (1992), Market-oriented Systemic Transformations in Eastern Europe, Heidelberg and New York: Springer.

WELFENS, P.J.J. (1994), Growth and Full Employment in the European Union, Volkswirtschaftliche Diskussionsbeiträge der Westfälischen Wilhelms-Universität Münster, No. 201, Münster.

WELFENS, P.J.J. (1995a), European Monetary Integration, 3. ed., Heidelberg and New York: Springer (forthcoming).

WELFENS, P.J.J. (1995b), The Single Market and the Eastern Enlargement of the EU, Heidelberg and New York: Springer (forthcoming).

EXTERNAL ASPECTS OF GERMAN UNIFICATION: THE POLISH VIEW

Andrzej Budziński

1. Introduction

German unification is of utmost importance for Poland for at least two reasons:

(a) It concerns one of Poland's largest trade partners. United Germany's share in Polish exports and imports amounts to some 20%. Germany is also Poland's main creditor, supplier of technology and partner in exchange of capital, labor and tourists;

(b) The unification of Germany is taking place at a time of other historical changes in Europe. New democracies are emerging in Eastern Europe - the part of the old continent which for over 40 years was ruled by communist regimes building political and economic walls dividing Europe.

Tearing down the Berlin wall gives way not only to German unification but also to pan-European integration. It is even more challenging that the speeding up of integration processes in Western Europe - marked by establishment of the Single European Market - contrasts with the collapsing CMEA tràde system.

Poland's official position on German unification is based upon the following assumptions:

(1) It will have no direct or indirect negative impact on the economy of Poland - the united Germany's immediate neighbor. It specifically means that the pre-unification volume of trade between Poland and the former GDR will not decrease as a result of deteriorating market access for Polish goods and services;

(2) The United Germany will inherit and uphold rights and obligations under previous agreements concluded between Poland and the GDR. The contractual obligations between firms will be met regardless of bankruptcies, liquidations, ownership transformation, restructuring, etc. of state-owned enterprises following the introduction of market conditions in the territory of East Germany;

(3) The Oder-Neisse border will not divide our two countries. Rather, Poland and Germany will be brought closer together as firms and individuals from both countries are more able to interact.

2. Short-Term Consequences for Poland of German Unification

Against this background let me now look briefly at recent developments in trade between Poland and the former GDR. In 1989 the trade between Poland and the GDR was based upon the government-to-government trade protocol. Exports from Poland amounted to 1360 Million transferable roubles and our imports reached 1310 Million TR. The share of the GDR in Poland's foreign trade was 4%. It was the fourth largest trading partner of Poland, preceded by the Soviet Union, the Federal Republic of Germany and Czechoslovakia.

From the statistical appendix it may be seen that two-thirds of Polish exports and imports consisted of machinery and equipment. In the remaining trade some 20% was accounted for by fuels, raw materials and semi-finished goods. A major item in Polish exports was services, which under the CMEA trade nomenclature were classified in the same category as exports of machinery and equipment. In 1989 these exports amounted to 380 Million TR.

The structure of trade between Poland and the GDR described above could be regarded as highly stable since it did not change significantly over the last 5 years. The 1990 trade agreement between Poland and the GDR provides for a trade volume equal to only 15% of the previous years trade. The main items included in the agreement are raw materials and some products of the electro-engineering industry. It was resolved that contracts for the remaining trade were to be negotiated freely between enterprises with no direct guidance from either government.

In the first half of 1990, during the period prior to establishment of economic, monetary and social union between the two German states, Poland exported to the GDR goods and services of 560 Million TR and her imports valued 510 Million TR. The trade balance was in favor of Poland and amounted to 50 Million TR. Taking into account the requirements of the union, it was resolved to continue in 1990 trade of goods in transferable roubles, whereas services have been traded in convertible currencies since July 1, 1990. The firms exchanging services were requested to renegotiate their contracts accordingly.

Since July 1, 1990 the trade position vis-a-vis East Germany has been steadily deteriorating. According to the data through the end of September, Polish exports amounted to 650 Million TR, but imports increased by 720 Million TR and valued 1230 Million TR. During the first three months of the economic, monetary and social union the balance of trade has deteriorated by 630 Million roubles.

There are various reasons for these negative trade developments:

(a) A rate of exchange of 2.34 DM per 1 TR has been introduced by the GDR and is still maintained, which makes exports in roubles extremely attractive for East German exporters, and imports very expensive. The over-valued rouble vis-a-vis the DM has caused deep distortions in the trade flows between Poland and the former GDR;

(b) East-German firms have withdrawn from many import contracts, partly due to the overvalued rate of exchange of the rouble.

(c) Shifting demand in the GDR to Western products, and the bankruptcies of many East German businesses newly exposed to market conditions were other reasons for dropping import contracts by German firms. Their value for the end of September 1990 totalled 300 Million roubles.

These are immediate effects of the changes brought about by German unification. They are however likely to persist in 1991. Polish exports to the former GDR fall into two broad categories: the products exported only to the GDR and other CMEA countries, and those also exported to Western countries. Basically, if products have only been exported to the CMEA countries, they, as a rule, are not competitive on the world market in convertible currency. This concerns mainly investment goods which played a dominant role in Polish exports to the former GDR. In 1989 these goods amounted to some 500 Million TR. If these exports are exposed to international competition, they will fall in 1991 to less than one-third of their 1989 level. Exports may continue for a limited number of final products, certain spare parts, components and elements. However, this will only occur if the importing German firms do not go bankrupt in the meantime. The dollar value of machinery and equipment (excluding services) which will be exported next year will probably not exceed 100 Million.

Polish goods exported to East Germany and Western countries such as coal, sulphur and chemicals are competitive on the world markets at current prices. Despite the prevailing preference of GDR consumers for goods of Western, and mainly FRG origin, such Polish exports may be maintained. Traditional exports to East Germany of coal, coke and sulphur denominated in convertible currency will amount to 60 Million dollars in 1991.

There is every indication that in this short-term perspective Polish exports of services are also endangered. In 1989 33,000 Polish workers were employed in the former GDR providing services on a contractual basis. These exports have unfortunately been shrinking since the establishment of the economic, monetary and social union. East German firms did not confirm many contracts concluded earlier in roubles. Their value for the second half of 1990 amounts only to 35% of that for the first six months of the year or the second half of 1989. The number of Polish workers employed in East Germany dropped to 16 thousand at the end of September 1990.

As a result of bankruptcies of many enterprises in the former GDR, changes in investment programs under new market conditions, and financial difficulties of investors, the market for services will remain depressed in 1991. Additionally, rising unemployment in East Germany will act to discourage contracts with foreign firms.

The above analysis indicates that with the exception of raw materials, all other Polish exports in 1991 will suffer under changing trade conditions between Poland and the former GDR. Supplies of machinery and equipment as well as services, which traditionally comprised a dominant share of Polish exports, will most probably fall to one-third their previous level.

The value of contracts for investment goods already concluded for 1991 indicates even more dramatic trade developments. As of the middle of September, Polish firms concluded with East German firms such contracts worth 11.5 Million DM on the export side, and 65 Million DM as far as imports are concerned. Traditionally, by September some 70-80% of the next year's deliveries of investment goods were already contracted.

3. Long-Term Impact of German Unification on the Polish Economy

The long-term impact of German unification on the Polish economy may be somewhat more optimistic, but before it is discussed, let me point out some measures which could reduce the negative consequences of short- term trade developments:

(a) The unification of Germany entails the incorporation of the GDR into the Community legal order. It means that all EC laws will automatically apply in the territory of the former GDR. However, the transitional scheme is envisaged to allow the GDR's legislation to be gradually adopted to the Community system, especially in such areas as technical norms, safety and quality standards as well as environmental legislation. As a general rule the application of Community rules in the former GDR will need to be phased in by the end of 1992.

The application of transitional measures will permit the marketing of products in the territory of the former GDR which do not meet conditions laid down by Community law. Polish exports will take advantage of the transitional arrangements. They should apply to all goods traded with the former GDR under the annual protocol in 1989. This solution will help to uphold exports of Polish products which at present do not adhere to EC norms and standards.

(b) The transitional system, which is designed to absorb disruption of trade with East European countries, provides for tariff-free treatment of Polish goods exported to the former GDR. These goods will enjoy all the advantages of the internal market; however, the tariff concessions will only be granted if these goods are consumed in the territory of the former GDR and do not reach other parts of the Community.

The impact of the application of the transitional measures to tariffs is limited in the case of Poland, which already benefits from the full extension of the Generalized System of Preferences in the framework of the G-24 PHARE program for a temporary period of five years from January 1990. Further, the transitional regulations do not apply to agricultural products.

(c) EC regulations provide for quantitative restrictions on certain imports on a regional basis in the Community. German unification implies the extension to the former GDR territory of those restrictions applied by the FRG against the CMEA countries. They concern textile and steel products.

The conditions for Polish exports will be improved if the number of import licenses for these products could be increased this year. For 1991 the quotas should be raised to levels which take into account Polish traditional exports of textiles and steel products to the former GDR. These increases should be added to the existing share of the Federal Republic.

Elimination of all quantitative restrictions towards imports from Poland must be the ultimate objective. Trade relations should be extended on a market basis, and Poland as well as other reforming East European countries should be helped to improve their competitiveness on the world market.

(d) Taking into account the requirements of the "Staatsvertrag" Poland also requests an increase in the number of labor permits for Polish workers in the united Germany. These should at least reflect the number of workers employed in the Federal Republic (11 thousand workers) and those employed in the GDR in 1989. Altogether in 1991 labor permits should be issued to 46 thousand Polish workers.

As was already pointed out services were the most important part of Polish exports to the former GDR. Besides balance of payments consequences, the collapse of those exports will result in a net increase in unemployment in Poland equivalent to the number of workers released from contracts in Germany.

German unification will have a positive effect on economic growth in the Federal Republic. This is mainly a result of a shift of GDR internal demand towards imports from the FRG. Community countries will also feel the effects of greater import demand from the GDR economy, given the high rate of capacity utilization in the FRG. Additionally EC countries will benefit from growing activity in the Federal Republic brought about by the unification of Germany. West Germany accounts for some 25% of GDP for the EC-12, compared to a share of just below 20% for the next largest economy, France. The united Germany's share rises to 30%.

Taking into account that the EEC countries - and among them Germany - are Poland's main trade partners, their accelerated growth will attract more imports from Poland. This is one of the reasons why Poland may consider with some optimism the medium- and long-term impact of German unification on her economy.

In 1989 the EC-12 accounted for 32% of Polish exports, of which 18.8% was shared by the united Germany. The importance of the EC and especially of Germany for the Polish economy is going to grow, following the collapse of the CMEA trade system and the subsequent need for Poland to find new outlets for her exports and sources of supply. The privatization and restructuring of the Polish economy is certain to result in increased demand for capital goods from western countries.

4. Policies Towards Poland's Integration into the United Europe

Extension of the EC territory to East Germany means that Poland will have a joint border with the Community. As was indicated earlier, this border cannot become another wall separating Poland from an integrating Western Europe.

In June 1990 Poland applied for an association agreement with the Community. According to the Polish request, the association status should evolve into full EC membership by the end of this century. As you know Poland has chosen the path of economic and political freedom. The program of Polish reforms aims at achieving full democracy, recognition of human rights, and political pluralism. These are all universal European values. At the same time Poland has entirely changed her economic system by abolishing central planning and by introducing market economy institutions.

The Polish economy has become open to the world market through liberalization of domestic prices, convertibility of the Polish currency for current transactions, demonopolization of foreign trade, elimination of all import restrictions, etc. Recently, the privatization program has been initiated.

Polish efforts to transform her economy into a market economy and to integrate into the European economic system are assisted by the industrialized countries. The Group of 24 is acting in unison to support economic stabilization and restructuring of the Polish economy. This includes better access to western markets, the promotion of investment and financial assistance or joint operations in agreed priority areas, e.g. in the protection of the environment.

The present assistance program cannot, however, replace the envisaged integration of the Polish economy with the EC-12 through coordination of trade and other policies and the adaptation of the Polish economic system to that of the Community. United Germany, our largest trade partner in the EEC and the major economic power in the Community, should actively support Polish efforts in this respect.

As part of our policies aimed at exposing the Polish economy to world markets, we have also opened the economy to foreign investment. Germany is the largest foreign investor in Poland holding 40% of the invested foreign capital. They are represented by over 800 joint ventures and fully-owned foreign firms licensed to be established in Poland through the end of September 1990. The majority of investments are of small and medium size with capital below 100 thousand dollars.

Poland is seeking ways to make conditions for foreign investment favorable and attractive to larger investors. The privatization law has allowed for acquiring shares by foreign investors in privatized enterprises. Also new regulations concerning direct investments, which are now being prepared, will introduce a liberalized system of profit transfers and further promote the establishment of joint ventures and foreign firms in Poland. Many major Western corporations have already started their businesses in Poland, and among them are German firms such as Siemens.

It must be pointed out that in the immediate future the firms from the Federal Republic - due to German unification - will concentrate on investments in the territory of the former GDR, and as a result they may not develop substantial investments in Poland. This negative consequence of German unification will be reversed after some time, when East Germany becomes saturated with new capital.

One of the attractions of Poland for Western businesses is our relatively large domestic market. The second important factor is the availability of high quality but low cost labor. The distribution network which Poland has in Eastern Europe and also in the USSR is certainly another asset. Polish companies have been doing business throughout the region for 40 years now and have in place networks that could be very useful to Western businessmen. Firms from Poland and Germany should use these opportunities and develop joint businesses in the Soviet market and in other markets of the region. Another important factor is proximity to the European Community market including the market of the united Germany. This proximity to vast markets creates further opportunities in Poland for the development of transit services.

Prospects

Facing the legacy of the socialist command economy and inherited external constraints - including a high foreign currency debt - the Polish economy will undergo a dramatic transformation in the 1990s. Hard currency exports of Poland have sharply increased in 1990 such that a current account surplus is recorded. Despite the positive development of the trade balance debt reduction programs are necessary if the Polish economic reforms are to be successful, and Germany (even more so, the U.S.) will play an important role in a debt reduction program whose significance is emphasized not only by the Polish government but by Western experts as well (*Budzinski, 1991; World Bank, 1990*). The rapid export growth of 1990 is partly due to shrinking ruble markets and a falling domestic demand in Poland; however, it also testifies to the improving supply-side response. As the Polish privatization program which is comprised of many difficult organizational, distributional and political aspects (*see Lipton and Sachs, 1990*) is accelerated in the early 1990s one may expect not only internal efficiency gains but also an improved external competitiveness. Privatization will entail problems in the labor market as firms will try to reduce costs, but one may also hope for trade creation effects that help to stimulate economic growth and provide new opportunities for investment and employment. Open markets in Western Europe and elsewhere will be important for Poland's attempt to restore growth and stability within a complex reform program that actively seeks a full integration into the international economy in the long term.

Table 1: Structure of Polish Foreign Trade with Germany in 1989

Branches	*West Germany** *Export* Bil. Zloty (%)	*Import* Bil. Zloty (%)	*East Germany* *Export* Bil. Zloty (%)	*Import* Bil. Zloty (%)	*United Germany* *Export* Bil. Zloty (%)	*Import* Bil. Zloty (%)
Fuels & Energy	285.4 (9.9)	8.6 (0.4)	41.6 (5.1)	51.2 (7.7)	327.0 (8.8)	59.8 (2.0)
Metallurgical Industry	628.6 (21.8)	248.4 (10.4)	17.8 (2.2)	25.3 (3.8)	646.4 (17.5)	273.7 (9.0)
Electro-Engineering	477.0 (16.5)	1060.9 (44.4)	516.9 (63.4)	410.6 (62.0)	993.9 (26.8)	1471.5 (48.2)
Chemical Industry	271.1 (9.4)	524.5 (21.9)	46.2 (5.7)	87.6 (13.2)	317.3 (8.6)	612.1 (20.1)
Mineral Industry	52.4 (1.8)	15.0 (0.6)	4.9 (0.6)	18.5 (2.8)	57.3 (1.5)	33.5 (1.1)
Wood & Paper Industry	174.4 (6.0)	24.3 (1.0)	2.6 (0.3)	15.3 (2.3)	177.0 (4.8)	39.6 (1.3)
Light Industry	175.0 (6.0)	106.7 (4.5)	27.1 (3.3)	20.7 (3.1)	202.1 (5.4)	127.4 (4.1)
Food Industry	470.8 (16.3)	199.7 (8.4)	13.4 (1.6)	4.4 (0.7)	484.2 (13.2)	204.1 (6.7)
Other Industries	15.9 (0.6)	45.1 (1.9)	4.6 (0.6)	11.9 (1.8)	20.5 (0.6)	57.0 (1.8)
Construction	139.4 (4.8)	0.5 (0)	135.9 (16.7)	0.8 (0.1)	275.3 (7.4)	1.3 (0.1)
Agricultural Products	183.1 (6.3)	153.0 (6.3)	1.8 (0.2)	13.0 (2.0)	184.9 (5.0)	166.0 (5.4)
Other Goods	13.9 (0.6)	4.8 (0.2)	2.6 (0.3)	3.4 (0.5)	16.5 (0.4)	8.2 (0.2)
Total Trade	2887.0 (100)	2391.5 (100)	815.4 (100)	662.7 (100)	3702.4 (100)	3054.2 (100)

* Including West Berlin
Source: Foreign Trade Statistical Yearbook 1990

Table 2: Structure of Polish Foreign Trade with Selected Countries in 1989

			EXPORTS TO: / IMPORTS FROM:				
Branches	*World* Mil. Zloty	*World* %	*CMEA** %	*EEC* %	*FRG*** %	*GDR* %	*United Germany* %
Fuels & Energy	1 873 686 1 907 357	100.0 100.0	25.4 74.4	36.4 3.1	15.2 0.4	2.2 2.7	17.4 3.1
Metallurgical Industry	2 035 384 1 360 998	100.0 100.0	11.9 28.7	55.6 45.7	30.9 18.2	0.9 1.8	31.8 20.0
Electro-Engineering	7 475 108 5 593 269	100.0 100.0	56.3 37.9	14.8 34.4	6.4 19.0	6.9 7.3	13.3 26.3
Chemical Industry	2 050 184 2 343 236	100.0 100.0	33.9 15.0	29.5 51.5	13.2 22.4	2.3 3.7	15.5 26.1
Mineral Industry	252 324 198 118	100.0 100.0	11.4 38.2	37.1 32.5	20.8 7.5	1.9 9.3	22.7 16.8
Wood & Paper Industry	570 865 296 739	100.0 100.0	6.2 33.8	60.4 18.5	30.5 8.2	0.5 5.1	31.0 13.3
Light Industry	1 072 873 1 171 396	100.0 100.0	19.6 16.0	39.2 22.6	16.3 9.1	2.5 1.8	18.8 10.9
Food Industry	1 868 635 1 466 270	100.0 100.0	9.2 8.7	57.8 36.6	25.2 13.6	0.7 0.3	25.9 13.9
Other Industries	109 968 267 242	100.0 100.0	37.1 20.8	38.1 38.6	14.5 16.9	4.1 4.4	18.6 21.3
Construc-tion	1 151 665 4 216	100.0 100.0	53.4 80.9	13.1 17.8	12.1 11.9	11.8 19.0	23.9 30.9
Agricultural Products	862 937 762 609	100.0 100.0	16.0 6.2	65.9 49.3	21.2 19.4	0.2 1.7	21.4 21.1
Other Goods	152 545 44 600	100.0 100.0	28.1 78.0	12.3 9.2	9.1 10.7	1.7 7.6	10.8 18.3
Total Trade	19 476 174 15 416 050	100.0 100.0	35.1 31.9	32.0 33.9	14.8 15.5	4.2 4.3	18.8 19.8

* CMEA: Council for Mutual Economic Assistance
** Including West Berlin

Source: Foreign Trade Statistical Yearbook 1990

References

BUDZINSKI, ANDRZEJ (1991), Economic Relations of Poland with the CMEA Member Countries, in: UN Commission for Europe, Reforms in Foreign Economic Relations of Eastern Europe and the Soviet Union, New York, 146-153.

THE WORLD BANK (1990), Poland. Economic Management for a New Era, Washington, D.C.

LIPTON, DAVID and SACHS, JEFFREY (1990), Privatization in Eastern Europe: The Case of Poland, Brookings Papers on Economic Activity, Washington, D.C., 293-342.

COMMENTS ON: EXTERNAL ASPECTS OF GERMAN UNIFICATION: THE POLISH VIEW*

John P. Hardt

Dr. Budzinski's paper on External Aspects of German Unification: The Polish View provides a useful critique on Germany focusing on the net advantages of change in production relations and resolution of the problems of a divided Europe. However, the broader problems from the viewpoint of Poland and other Central and East European countries may be the lack of, or slowness to move toward integration within Central and East Europe, all-Europe and into the global economy. The case should be made for a European Regional Market as a key to success of European economies in transition. Let me highlight the issues involved.

The Soviet Union and East European countries in transition aim to open their economies and integrate into the European and global market systems. This process of economic transformation in Eastern Europe thus far has not been supported by coordinated regional development within the former Bloc trading area. Moreover, developments in intraregional trade promise to continue to be very disruptive to the domestic economies of the region. This absence of regional cooperation runs counter to one of the major accomplishments of the Marshall Plan period - successful regional market integration. Feasible remedies would be complex and currently do not command much support.

Western countries and international agencies are doing little to foster the development of an open, all-European market for transforming economies. In part due to preoccupation with their own integration in EC-1992 and its domestic priorities for protectionism; in part due to concern, shared with Eastern countries that to integrate in the East might perpetuate the old system of Soviet-led modified autarchy. To meet the goal of open, competitive economies the Soviet Union and Eastern Europe might first integrate through their new *Organization for International Economic Cooperation* within their region, then with Western Europe and with the global market economy. All actors support regional integration in principle, but not in practice. Western Europe could do much more in providing a liberal environment within which the transforming economies could integrate. Western governments and institutions could, by encouraging regional development and opening Western economies, contribute to the success of East European economies in transition. However, their efforts toward a market economy and the effectiveness of Western aid is restricted by inadequate regional markets in the East and access to Western markets. A coordinated effort would provide a better basis for stimulating integration into the Western markets, encouraging foreign direct investment into the transforming countries, and integration into the global market.

1. Regional Integration for the East?

Regional cooperation toward a common market in Eastern Europe may be as important in this transition decade as steps by individual countries toward integration into the European Community and the global economy. Each country in the region currently appears dedicated to a policy of maximizing relations with the West and minimizing relations with each other. Integration of developing market economies in the East is held back by shunning cooperative ties with members of the former Eastern economic organization, the Council for Mutual Economic Assistance (CMEA). Forging new regional cooperation to ease and further the overall process of market integration and interdependence might mitigate severe transition shocks resulting from too rapid open market transition within both the west and the east. This reasoning suggests that Western nations consider encouraging rational regional development based on the objective of developing an all European market model for orderly transition. Indeed, the international organizations such as OECD, IMF, and World Bank, and Western nations would appear to be necessary participants if East European regional cooperation is to be effectively pursued.

The Soviet Union and East European countries are moving toward cooperation, even integration, with Western Europe, the global market and international organizations. European Community (EC) trade and cooperation agreements with the USSR and Eastern Europe are considered steps toward membership in EFTA and later the EC. Soviet observer membership in GATT, moving toward some form of IMF/World Bank membership, are concrete examples of increased participation in international organizations. Increased openness of Eastern markets to foreign goods as well as to investment to increase competition in the domestic markets is occurring. A proposed restructuring of regional organization using the Conference on Security and Cooperation in Europe (CSCE) "international norms" as guidelines, as suggested by the Kadar Committee (Bela Kadar) at the January 1990 CMEA meeting also has possibilities.[1] While many have supported the inclination to "kill the CMEA and dance on its grave," this sentiment - while understandable - has severe short term costs if no effective regional commercial relations arise in its place. A new regional market and cooperative organization merits serious, immediate consideration. The newly formed Organization for International Economic Cooperation may provide such an institutional opportunity.[2]

Regional cooperation early on in the Marshall Plan, encouraged by the only major economy viable at that time, the United States, is now thought by many to have been a key contribution to the resulting "economic miracles." There was no doubt in the 1950s that Western Europe should move expeditiously toward currency convertibility; modern, competitive and open economies; and toward early resolution of regional approaches to common problems in infrastructure and other region-wide issues. The transitions were organized to minimize disruption and instability while resolutely pursuing an organized regional program. This regional discipline was reinforced by the emerging cold war. Would a new Western approach that accelerates the integration of competitive East European economies in transition be feasible and beneficial? This would, in effect, be obligating the West to provide a liberal environment concurrent with the requirement that the Eastern countries move toward liberal market economies. Although a liberal environment is widely supported in Europe and the United States, it is not generally addressed in an Eastern regional market context. This is partly due to resistance to any regional effort seen as support for the old CMEA system.[3] What may be needed is a counterpart of the Treaty of Rome and the development of the European Common Market. A surrogate may be a process of accession to existing regional market organizations such as European Free Trade Association (EFTA). In the interim, some greater attention by the Bretton Woods institutions, the OECD, the European Bank for Reconstruction and Development (EBRD), and related organizations, may be in order.

Consideration of the transition to a liberal East European regional market should include the following issues:

(1) *Currency convertibility* is an appropriate and necessary goal, but the precipitous shift to world prices for Soviet energy to East Europe on January 1, 1991, has caused a severe shock. The costs to Poland, Czechoslovakia, and Hungary are several billion dollars per country from the price change alone. Soviet receipts will increase by a comparable amount.[4] In terms of "hard goods" saleable from Eastern Europe in the Western market the price impact would also be severe. With the debt service of the West requiring more than Poland, Hungary, Yugoslavia, and Bulgaria could readily afford and the continued requirement of repayment of Soviet debt, these countries will be seriously handicapped in transformation; they could not carry both the price rise and hard currency debt service burdens at the same time and proceed with transformation. Regional cooperation may facilitate a more measured transition to convertibility as previous integration processes have involved sequenced rather than sudden or shock conversions to convertible currency pricing. Peter Kenan makes a strong case in arguing that an Eastern "Payments Union" is not an appropriate remedy at this time but some new mechanism is nonetheless indicated.

(2) *Industrial transformation* requires careful forecasts of the interregional and international aspects of structural change and access to modern technology and external investment.[5] For example, in the steel industry of the region, movement away from open-hearth to oxygen and/or electric furnaces and introduction of continuous casting capability is appropriate, but scheduling is important as well as access to the latest Western technology and external financing. What may happen as some countries apply the "shock treatment" is a precipitous closing of a large percentage of metallurgical enterprises with its attendant disruption in production and unemployment within countries and regionally. The highly centralized output in Poland is very dependent on the Soviet market; the centralized Soviet output in the Urals is dependent on all-Union consumption. The closing of Nova Huta in Poland and Magnitagorsk in the USSR would be very disruptive without some organized transition. Knowledgeable restructuring of industrial enterprises before they are disposed of through privatization, and with consultation by private banks, international organizations such as the World Bank, and other Western consultants could ease the transition.

(3) *Agricultural transformation* depends not only on a number of domestic factors including privatization and farm-to-market system improvements but on external market access. A regional policy in East European agriculture might be helpful in gaining access to West European markets as well as promoting some rational degree of specialization. Full domestic success in East European agricultural modernization would bring limited benefits when faced with the restrictive European Common Agricultural Program (CAP), and East European integration probably would be opposed if agricultural policy remained unchanged in the Common Market.[6]

(4) *Infrastructure modernization* in communications, transportation, and transmission of energy require a regional approach to be effective. A unified Germany alone seems to be addressing this problem; the Shatalin plan in the USSR called for virtually freezing at current levels all new investment, including infrastructure. Regional transition plans would include considerable investment in infrastructure to promote efficiency.

(5) The trinity of *Health-Environment-Energy* pose serious common problems throughout Eastern Europe and the Soviet Union. Little is being done on the coordination of a regional approach on any of these issues.[7] Debt-to-nature swaps under the new Bush initiative might be helpful. A *European Energy Community* was proposed to the European Community by Dutch Prime Minister R.F.M. Lubbers in Dublin, on June 23, 1990, perhaps to emulate the beneficial experience of the European Coal and Steel Community after the Second World War. The purpose would be to tie closer together the market-oriented European states to regionally develop sources of oil and gas, encourage conservation, avoid environmental pollution on the

basis that "the production, transportation and use of energy must be organized in a different, more integrated and better way." The Soviet Union with its vast resources of oil and gas and the East European countries with serious shortfalls in supplies of clean, safe energy to replace polluting coal and unsafe nuclear power represent needs that are likely to be deficient in capital and technology without Western assistance. Payment for some of this necessary investment could come from an international "concession" system that permits substantial control by the Western partners of technical and management decisions in return for substantial investments and possible subsidies.

> A European concession system, particularly for natural gas, could be developed on the basis of the charter, which would exist alongside the national concession system in the country producing the gas, which should govern the receipts of profits or royalties. Such a European concession system could provide political safeguards for the transportation of products and sales across national borders, thereby ensuring access to both reserves and markets. The Community could also investigate the possibility of acquiring ownership of transport systems where this proves necessary.[8]

This would appear to imply added stability of supply and energy costs for West European consumers and more profit for West European utilities in return for earlier market integration and Eastern development as well as environmental gains.

(6) *An open Scientific Research and Development Facility for Integration of Transforming Economies* could initiate mechanisms to facilitate technology transfer through the OECD, World Bank technology and institutional appraisal facilities, and bilateral institutions.[9]

2. Creating a Liberal Economic Environment for European and Global Integration of Transforming Economies

Market Access could be facilitated, particularly in European agriculture. Were all the transforming economies to have the Western market access that the former GDR has, they could be much more competitive. Transforming countries would then have an opportunity to compete on the basis of price, quality, and transport costs. Western countries and multilateral organizations might not only take the view that any restrictions on the goods, services, and financial markets are poor policy because of the West's commitment to encouraging the transition, but might also take the position that the West should actually stimulate competitive integration. Were that the policy, full market access might be in order using the unification of Germany as a model. Such an open market development would likely be opposed, at least, by the West European subsidized and protected agricultural sector. Renewal of the Uruguay Round GATT proposal on reduction of agricultural trade restrictions would be helpful to the economies in transition.

Export Controls could be reduced to promote modernization and competition. CoCom is still a formidable constraint on modernization of the economies in transition. Economies in transition require the latest technology and management techniques to be competitive. While some modification of CoCom makes access to Western computers, telecommunications, and other critical technology possible - often on a case by case basis - restricted supply of advanced products and techniques limits competitiveness. Development of a "new paradigm" for export administration may remove only "core military technology" from normalized trade, while freeing most, if not all, technology keyed to civilian industrial competitiveness. The risk for the West is that some commercial technology markets could be lost in the East and that much improved inexpensive weapons would become major manufacturing exports of the USSR and some others. The threat of sustained disintegration in the USSR is also worrisome. At the same time, if the Soviet Union - potentially the world's largest, new importer of plant and equipment to modernize civilian enterprise - could pay for imports with increased energy income, all machinery manufacturing countries in the region might benefit.

Debt Burden and Access to Capital Markets. Foreign debt inherited from the old regimes is difficult to service for the economies in transition, especially Poland, Hungary, Bulgaria, and Yugoslavia. Initiation of a major restructuring of the Polish official debt by the United States in the Paris Club and adoption of the Brady Plan for private debt would help deal with this problem. However, new access to capital markets and a flow of foreign direct investment would still be needed. The Bush Administration's initiative on Polish debt reduction may invite new efforts to make debt servicing manageable.[10]

National Export Credit Shortages restrict competitiveness of transforming countries in the global market place; establishment of Eastern export credit agencies would address this problem. While Western export credit agencies provide about six billion dollars a year in financing exports to Eastern Europe and the Soviet Union, the transforming countries have no comparable financing facilities to be competitive on the basis of price, quality, and delivery. Daniel Bond and Anthony Solomon suggest that the West could help "by providing about $4 billion in export credit reassurance... To cover claims, the reinsurance facility would need to be supported by reserves equal to about one-tenth of outstanding guarantees. Given a five-year average repayment term, reserves of $2 billion would eventually be required." These facilities could be marketed through the OECD and conditioned on introduction of market-oriented economic reforms.[11]

Endnotes

* Helpful comments by Rozanne Ridgeway, President of the Atlantic Council are gratefully acknowledged.

1. Information Bulletin, CMEA meeting in Sofia, January 9-10, 1990.

2. In its final session, February 27-28, 1991, the nine-nation CMEA, when disbanded, will be replaced by an association based "on a market basis" called the Organization for International Economic Cooperation. Washington Post, January 6, 1991.

3. Curt Tarnoff, "The Marshall Plan: Design, Accomplishments and Relevance to the Present". CRS Report 91-3F, January 2, 1991, pp. 35.

4. L. Husain and L. Diwah, "External Debt and Expected Capitol Flow to Eastern Europe"; World Bank paper at Conference on The Transformation to a Market Economy in Central and Eastern Europe, OECD Paris, November 28-30, 1990. Estimates of Jozef Van Brabant of the United Nations.

5. David Cantor, "Steel Industries of Eastern Europe: Can They Compete With the West?" CRS Report #90-402E, August 24, 1990.

6. John P. Hardt and Jean F. Boone, "Strategies for Facilitating East European and Soviet Transformation", The Atlantic Council, October 1990.

7. Murray Feshbach, "Economics of Health and Environment in the USSR: Implications for Civilian and Military Sectors", Basic Books, 1990.

8. "A European Energy Community," presented by Rudd Lubbers to the Dublin EC Summit in June 1990. A British inspired charter was the core of the European Communities energy aid program for the Soviet Union. Financial Times, August 1990, p. 20.

9. S.3212 to establish the Industrial Development for Eastern Europe Foundation introduced by Senator Joe Lieberman in the U.S. Senate in 1990 may be reintroduced in 1991.

10. See letter from President Bush to the Polish Prime Minister, November 1990. The G-7 meeting in January 1991 recommended substantial reduction in official Polish debt.

11. Daniel Bond and Anthony Solomon, "Leveling the Playing Field for Central Europe for Exports", presented at the Institute for East-West Security Studies, December 1990.

ECONOMIC REFORM IN THE USSR AND PROSPECTS FOR TRADE AND ECONOMIC RELATIONS WITH UNIFIED GERMANY

Ruslan S. Grinberg

1. Introduction

The USSR and the two Germanies have had important trade links for many decades. In the early 1990s the USSR faces difficult internal reforms, and internal and external adjustments are required. Improving trade and investment relations with Western Europe could play an important role in the future, and the role of a unified Germany will be influential. Growing international trade could support the internal reforms aimed at raising economic growth and restoring economic stability.

In my paper I will focus on two principal issues. First of all, I will try to assess the "Basic Guidelines of Stabilization of the National Economy and Transition to Market Economy" recently adopted by the USSR Supreme Soviet. Then I'll present some ideas on the possible participation of the West in general and unified Germany in particular in the process of our economic recovery and transition towards the market.

2. Difficult Reform Situation

Without any risk of exaggeration it can be stated that the present socioeconomic situation in the country is extremely difficult, and what is especially displeasing, is that it continues to worsen swiftly. According to the data by the USSR State Committee for Statistics (which, in contrast to previous years, is likely to stop beautifying reality), the national income for January-September (current year) decreased by 2.5 percent. The situation in the investment sphere is aggravating. In fact, the putting into operation of the most important production facilities, housing and social-and-cultural projects failed. In the agriculture sector the output of many kinds of agricultural products declined compared to January-September of last year. Accordingly, the satisfaction of the population regarding industrial consumer goods and foodstuffs sharply worsened. As a result of the accelerated growth of money incomes of the population as compared to the production of goods, the state shops are largely empty. The only indicator which shows a real gain this year is trade turnover in strong beverages, with vodka at the top of the list.

The country (as in Poland in the 1980s) faces the combination of a suppressed and open inflation on so-called free and kolkhoz (collective-farm) markets. Despite the drop in production, the amount of money emitted in circulation in the first nine months of this year is twice that of the respective period of last year. For this reason, under the conditions of fixed retail prices, money swiftly loses the property of a versatile means of payment. The trend towards naturalization of the commercial exchange became widespread. Rationing of foodstuffs has been introduced substantially everywhere. During recent times the difficulties with foodstuffs has become especially acute in Moscow, Leningrad and other industrial centers which is due mainly to the destruction of economic links and the violation of contractual and executive discipline. As a result of a sharp amassing of economic difficulties and social phenomena crime is growing in the society. The life of people becomes more and more difficult, and their interest in labor goes down. Labor discipline is falling in all branches of the national economy. The growing losses of working time (1.6 times higher than in 1989) are also strongly influenced by strikes and inter-ethnic conflicts. As a result, direct losses of output alone amounted to one billion roubles. It should be noted that this figure does not take into account the even more considerable losses of related industries due to resulting troubles in deliveries of raw materials and components. Moreover these losses are accumulating due to the growing trends of separatism of the Republics (quest for sovereign fields of policy) and individual regions which is splitting the unified economic mechanism of the country. The prestige of the central government has fallen to nearly the zero mark.

In short, the Soviet economy is now in a very dangerous stage; the traditional administrative system of management is almost broken, while new motivation mechanisms for labor efficiency have not been created yet. The scale of the crisis is quite clearly recognized by everybody now, both on the top and bottom. As a result of a 5-year discussion of traditionally Russian questions - "Who is to blame?" and "What is to be done?" - the society (or in any case its overwhelming majority) is inclined to perceive the only reasonable answers: The command-administrative territorial economy based on the dictate of the "eternally" ruling party is guilty; As regards what is to be done, the answer is to go speedily along the road to the market economy. The vivid ideological discussion whether the transition to the market contradicts socialist principles is likely to lose its importance. The question of "How does one do it?" is being placed at the forefront of public debates, i.e. what steps must be taken for a maximum painless transition to a self-regulated market economy.

This means that today the main subject of the discussion is one of pragmatic issues, while the reforms themselves (after 5 years of ritual incantations) become the matter of a practical policy. In this sense, what is the importance and probability of realization of the "Basic

Guidelines of the Stabilization of the National Economy and the Transition to a Market Economy?"

You might know that these "Basic Guidelines" were prepared on the basis of two programs. The first was elaborated by the group of Mikhail Gorbachev and Boris Yeltsin at the beginning of this September. This program (known as "500 days") was almost unanimously approved by the Russian parliament and officially began on November 1 of this year. The second program was prepared by the Nikolai Ryzhkov Union Government. Both these programs were debated at the September Session of the Supreme Soviet of the USSR which did not adopt either of them. Under these conditions the President of the USSR took personal responsibility for the preparation of a new program document. The result of this was the above-mentioned draft of the "Basic Guidelines" which was also nearly unanimously adopted by the Union parliament on October 19, 1990. This time the radical reform promises to be really radical. The authors of the adopted guidelines have envisaged a whole system of both stabilization and systemic transformations of an almost unquestionably market-oriented nature. I see certain inconsistencies and half-measure characteristics in this program only in regard to the delayed pace of price control; I also doubt the reasonableness of a large-scale centralized price increase. These are nuances, although not insignificant ones. In general, the choice which has historical importance for the country's destiny has apparently been made. However, a sacramental and poignant question arises: "For what country"? In this regard, while reading the "Basic Guidelines" one involuntarily recalls an old maxim: theory differs from practice first of all in that in theory everything is possible. I'm sure that the basic guidelines could be realized only in the case that disintegration of the Soviet Union is avoided. For me it is also clear that in order to preserve the single economic space it is necessary to ensure integrity of the country in the form of a new Union of sovereign republics. Every sovereign republic, of course, should have the possibility to elaborate and implement comprehensive measures in the transition towards a market economy taking into account the specificity of the socioeconomic situation, national and historical particularities. By the way, the "Basic Guidelines" suggests this very approach. They are rather flexible and are not of an imperative nature.

Nevertheless, the formation of an All-Union market seems unrealizable to me if all republics (of course, on a voluntary basis) fail to delegate a number of most important duties to the Union authorities. From merely an economic perspective, I have in mind, first of all, the provision of unified money (the rouble must be the single means of payment on the territory of all republics incorporated in the Union), the realization of a common customs law, as well as the formation of a central budget financed by Union (federal) taxes.

The problem, however, is that such a new Union has not occurred yet, but there is still a unitarian-imperial state which is being rapidly broken under the influence of a "triumphal quest for sovereignties" all over the country. For me it is obvious that the majority of nations inhabiting the USSR are, so to say, doomed to unification by the whole course of historical development. However, viewing the situation realistically, one should recognize that the ratio between centrifugal and centripetal forces today is quite clearly not in favor of the Union. Furthermore, the socioeconomic situation in the USSR is such that it only enhances the former and weakens the latter. Moreover, one can see that tendencies of pure separatism are also gaining momentum. In addition to the Baltic countries I'd mention in this context growing separatist moods in Georgia, Moldavia and the Ukraine.

I think that today it is not so urgent to boost the signing of a new agreement on the Union of sovereign republics. I'm also afraid that the stronger the pressure by the Center on the republics to sign this agreement, the greater the counteraction on the part of the republics it will face.

I agree with those analysts who think that the Union Treaty is extremely necessary in principle. But it should be signed only when fundamental socioeconomic stability is restored to a lesser or greater extent. At the present moment it would be reasonable to limit oneself to the adoption of a memorandum of declarations on joint measures for preservation of already existing inter-republican relations within the framework of a single economic space. It is very important to reach consent with respect to common monetary, money and customs policies in order to avoid disintegration of the country.

In this regard, I set great hopes in the realization of Gorbachev's idea of the formation of a so-called Inter-republican Economic Committee intended to coordinate measures taken by the republics concerned.

All this seems to me to be quite realizable on condition of a close political collaboration between President Gorbachev and Chairman of the Russian Supreme Soviet, Boris Yeltsin. It is to be hoped that the next period of uncertainty in relations between them is close to its expiration. In any case, the destiny of the reform in general and of the "Basic Guidelines" in particular depends to a great extent on their readiness to find reasonable compromises.

Now let me tell you about the possible role of, so to say, the external factor in the context of the "Basic Guidelines". From the fact that the West is objectively interested in a stable and democratic Soviet society the question inevitably arises: in what manner could it contribute in particular to the stabilization measures and, at the same time, to the systemic transformations in this country? Since we are discussing the German problem here, the issue of the specific character of German participation in the Soviet perestroika processes is a natural one.

First of all, let me make several general remarks. It is quite clear that this severe economic crisis which the country is now facing can hardly be overcome without large-scale assistance from the West. Mass-scale deliveries of foodstuffs, pharmaceuticals and a number of primary consumer goods are needed. In view of the expected very cold winter, the extraordinary, urgent character of such deliveries is of major concern. Nevertheless, while rendering such assistance the West, in my opinion, should see to it that even these deliveries would stimulate, not block, the systemic transformations. In this regard, I recollect the words of the present U.S. Vice-President who allegedly said that "perestroika in the USSR seems to me to be irreversible, but everything can still change". It is important to take into consideration the fact that the present central government is more conservative than the President, to say nothing about the managerial authorities of Russia. It cannot be excluded that the government might place emphasis only on stabilization, and the process of marketization of the economy would thus be decelerated. Everybody should clearly understand that both the one-way assistance and commercial credits are reasonable at this time only in the case that the main focus in both domestic and external economic activities becomes the enterprise. This means that decentralization of the external economic activity with delegation of commercial transactions to the level of enterprises must be carried out simultaneously with the stabilization measures rather than after their realization.

3. Economic Relations with Germany and Western Europe

In general improving economic relations with Western market economies will be important for a successful reform program, but capital and trade flows with Western countries can create problems, too. There is a certain paradox here which could complicate the economic participation of the West in our transition to a market economy.

The point is that Western businesses have become accustomed to dealing exclusively with the government, more specifically with industrial ministries. The latter, as a rule, have regarded the granted loans as free financial means and have not always used them efficiently. The results are very disappointing: even today under conditions of a total deficit we have stockpiles - nearly $10 billion worth - of non-installed imported equipment. Nevertheless, Western partners were always certain that the granted money would be returned in time, since every deal was backed exclusively by the government. A principally different situation appears when newly-formed Soviet entrepreneurs become their business partners. Unlike the branch ministries, they understand that "money must make money"; but the risk of business contacts with such entrepreneurs is considerably higher for the Western side, since such contacts are deprived of any real governmental support. In this regard, in particular, the problem of credit guarantees becomes more acute. It seems to me that for resolving this problem it would be reasonable to consider the idea of creating a joint share-holding company for insurance of import credits. This company could operate on the same principles as the "Hermes" society, and I see the German link in that "Hermes" could be the nucleus of such a joint company. It could have a special importance for supporting small and medium size Soviet business.

3.1 Economic Relations with Germany

Soviet-German trade has played an important role for decades. Trade flows with the GDR were about twice the size of total trade with West Germany. The GDR accounted for about 10 percent of Soviet trade in the late 1980s, whereas the Federal Republic of Germany accounted for about 5 percent. (*see Tables 1-4*). German unity creates problems for the Soviet Union in the short run, namely reduced prospects for trade with Eastern Germany, but at the same time one may expect a long term increase of overall Soviet-German trade.

Table 1: Foreign Exchange Between USSR and West Germany (Billions of Foreign Exchange Rubles*)

	1985	1986	1987	1988	1989
Exports	3991.5	2720.1	2327.3	2397.2	2478.3
Imports	3103.1	2857.8	2629.8	3231.3	4076.4
Total Trade	7034.6	5577.9	4957.1	5628.5	6554.7

Sources: Statistical Yearbook: Vnyeshnyaya torgovlya SSSR v 1985, p. 10; ibid. v 1987, p. 10; Vnyeshniye ekonomicheskiye svyazi SSSR, 1989, p. 11.

Table 2: Foreign Exchange Between USSR and East Germany (Billions of Transferable Rubles*)

	1985	1986	1987	1988	1989	1990**
Exports	7669.9	7884.2	7635.9	7193.2	6662.5	4920
Imports	7591.7	7128.1	7093.2	7024.4	7175.4	6290
Total Trade	15,261.6	15,012.3	14,729.1	14,217.6	13,837.9	11,210

* foreign exchange ruble (Russian: invalutniy ruble) and transferable ruble (Russian: pierievodnoy ruble) are notional accounting units whose exchange rates to US dollars is estimated at approximately 0.65 - 0.55 in corresponding years.

** estimated par contracts at the beginning of 1990.

Sources: Statistical Yearbook: Vnyeshnyaya torgovlya SSSR v 1985, p. 9; ibid. v 1987, p. 9; Vnyeshniye ekonomicheskiye svyazi SSSR, 1989, p. 10.

Table 3: West German Share in USSR Total Trade (Percentages)

1985	1986	1987	1988	1989	1990*
5.0	4.3	3.8	4.3	4.7	5.8

* estimated

Source: Statistical Yearbook: Vnyeshnyaya torgovlya SSSR v 1985, pp. 9,10; ibid. v 1987, pp. 9,10; ibid. v 1989, pp. 10,11.

Table 4: East German Share in USSR Total Trade (Percentages)

1985	1986	1987	1988	1989
10.7	11.5	11.4	10.8	9.8

Source: *Statistical Yearbook: Vnyeshnyaya torgovlya SSSR v 1985, p. 9; ibid. v 1987, p. 9.*

A comparison of the structure of bilateral trade with the GDR and West Germany leads one to expect that Soviet exports of chemicals and food products could increase in the long term, while the export of machinery and equipment (reaching about 15 percent of Soviet exports to the GDR (see Table 5) will reduce to a relatively low share - the latter reached 2.5 percent of the USSR's exports to West Germany in 1989 (see Table 6). Moreover, trade with West Germany which expanded in the first half of the 1980s (Table 7) could further grow in the 1990s. If the volume of trade could be increased significantly, the structural change in exports and imports of the USSR should not inflict serious long term adjustment problems in the USSR.

Table 5: Structure of Bilateral Trade Between USSR and East Germany by Commodity Groups (in Percentages)

USSR Exports	1985	1987	1988	1989
Total Exports	100	100	100	100
Machinery and Equipment	11.8	13.5	16.4	17.6
Fuels and Mineral Raw Materials	69.7	67.2	63.4	63.8
Chemicals	2.0	2.0	2.0	1.2
Agricultural Raw Materials	6.2	5.5	5.6	5.8
Raw Materials for Food Products	0	--	--	--
Food Products	0.1	0.1	0.1	1.1
Consumer Goods	0.6	0.7	0.7	0.9
USSR Imports	**1985**	**1987**	**1988**	**1989**
Total Imports	100	100	100	100
Machinery and Equipment	68.2	65.9	64.4	62.2
Fuels and Mineral Raw Materials	5.7	5.9	5.6	3.9
Chemicals	4.7	5.2	5.3	2.5
Agricultural Raw Materials	1.2	1.2	1.3	0.9
Raw Materials for Food Products	0.5	--	--	--
Food Products	1.5	0.8	1.0	--
Consumer Goods	14.9	16.1	17.1	17.6

Source: Statistical Yearbook: Vnyeshnyaya torgovlya SSSR, 1985, pp. 125-182; ibid. v 1987, pp. 127-135; Vnyeshniye ekonomicheskiye svyazi SSSR v 1989, pp. 139-147.

Table 6: Structure of Bilateral Trade Between USSR and West Germany by Commodity Groups (in Percentages)

USSR Exports	1985	1986	1987	1988	1989
Total Exports	100	100	100	100	100
Machinery and Equipment	0.8	1.6	2.0	1.9	2.5
Fuels and Mineral Raw Materials	89.0	84.2	81.1	78.2	75.7
Chemicals	3.5	2.5	3.3	3.0	3.8
Agricultural Raw Materials	1.6	3.7	5.0	4.7	4.8
Raw Materials for Food Products	--	--	--	--	--
Food Products	0.5	0.7	0.7	0.8	0.7
Consumer Goods	0.4	0.9	1.1	1.2	1.1

USSR Imports	1985	1986	1987	1988	1989
Total	100	100	100	100	100
Machinery and Equipment	40.7	40.4	32.9	40.2	47.9
Fuels and Mineral Raw Materials	28.8	27.9	29.6	27.9	17.8
Chemicals	8.2	7.4	10.2	9.3	8.9
Agricultural Raw Materials	2.5	3.7	4.0	3.6	3.6
Raw Materials for Food Products	--	--	1.9	2.6	1.4
Food Products	--	1.0	1.1	1.9	0.7
Consumer Goods	3.1	2.8	3.0	2.4	5.4

Source: Statistical Yearbook: Vnyeshnyaya torgovlya SSSR, 1985, pp. 167-171; ibid. v 1987, pp. 171-176; Vnyeshniye ekonomicheskiye svyazi SSSR v 1989, pp. 182-187.

Table 7: Annual Percentage Changes in Bilateral Trade Between USSR-East Germany and USSR-West Germany

	USSR-East Germany	USSR-West Germany
1981-1985	10.6	4.2
1986-1989	-2.4	-1.95
Change from Previous Year (previous year 100)		
1986	98.4	78.6
1987	98.1	88.9
1988	96.5	113.5
1989	97.3	116.5

Source: Statistical Yearbook: Vnyeshnyaya torgovlya SSSR, 1980, pp. 9,10; ibid. 1985, pp. 9,10; ibid. 1987, pp. 9,10; Vnyeshniye ekonomicheskiye svyazi SSSR v 1989, pp. 10,11.

With regard to trade expansion with Western Europe, one may expect a key role for Soviet-German trade (not ruling out significantly rising trade and investment links with other countries). The leading economic role of Germany in Europe and the key position of the German mark in the European monetary system could be used, in my opinion, in two other relatively autonomous but still interrelated spheres.

First of all, it should be noted that from the beginning of next year the so-called currency independence of enterprises is to be substantially enlarged in the USSR. In fact, a domestic currency market is to be created with free buying and selling of currencies at a market exchange rate. This will necessitate the formation of a certain centralized stabilization fund of a freely convertible currency to prevent the exchange rate of the rouble from swiftly dropping.

Secondly, it seems to me that the problem of the introduction of currencies in the USSR and other countries of Central and Eastern Europe could be solved best through the formation of a multilateral system of regulation of payments with the European Payments Union. This Union functioned from 1950 to 1958 and within its framework convertibility of West European currencies was attained step by step. And if a multilateral currency clearing could function exclusively on the basis of the U.S. dollar in the past, today the central balancing role of mutual accounting of payment requirements of East-European countries and the USSR might be taken by the German mark.

Short-term Aspects

As regards the prospects of trade and economic relations between the USSR and Germany in the short run, I'd like to limit myself to the following remarks.

As it is known, during recent years the FRG occupied first place in our trade turnover with the West, while the GDR was always the leading partner in Eastern Europe. Their share in Soviet foreign trade is 6 and 10 percent respectively. It seems to me that within the coming years the share of the former GDR in our trade will somewhat reduce, while the share of West Germany will noticeably increase. I also think that one can expect a weakening of the traditional link between enterprises of East Germany to deliveries of Soviet raw materials. Besides, some enterprises of the former East Germany are being closed due to their inefficiency, while others are starting to orient themselves to the markets of West Germany and the EEC.

Nevertheless, as far as I know, many West-German economists who directly implement measures for shifting the economy of East Germany to market relations are convinced of the necessity to preserve and even expand economic relations with the USSR for at least two reasons. First of all, this is desirable in order to retard a rapid growth of unemployment. (It should be taken into consideration that more than 1.5 mil. former GDR residents are directly or indirectly involved in the activities associated with trade with the USSR). Secondly, the experience of cooperation with Soviet enterprises gained in East Germany might be used for a further active penetration of industrial products from a unified Germany into the Soviet market. I should note here that over many years of economic cooperation (though not always efficient) with Eastern Germany, a unique potential has been formed - about 300,000 specialists know the Russian language to a lesser or greater extent and are familiar with specific features of work with the USSR.

Medium-term Prospects

That is why I, like numerous Western experts, think that the economic space of the former GDR can become a kind of bridge in East-West trade and economic relations.

I'd also like to note that the experience of privatization of East-German enterprises has great importance for our country. It is in this very sphere that I see the greatest difficulties for our economic reform even in the case of a sound consensus between all political forces and national republics.

In general, though with the risk of simplification, the following scheme of mutual economic interests between the USSR and a unified Germany can be imagined: West Germany has technologies to offer and gets free access to the Soviet market; the Soviet Union has its market to offer and gets access to the technologies; East Germany has existing channels of cooperation and uses them as a stabilizing factor. The understanding of these interests could facilitate the transition to properly coordinated practical measures.

3.2 Perspectives

The complex reform situation in the USSR has been analyzed by Soviet (*Abalkin, 1986, Aganbegyan, 1988; external reforms: e.g. Lavrov and Teodorovitch; Schagalow*) as well as by Western analysts who have focussed on real and monetary aspects of systemic reforms while suggesting divergent - sometimes gradual, in some fields radical - adjustment strategies (*e.g. Hewett, 1989; Bryson, 1990; Welfens, 1990*). It is obvious that progress in the external sphere is connected to reforms in the internal economic and political sphere, and indeed the USSR faces the most complicated reform tasks of all (former) CMEA countries.

Sustaining internal reforms in the USSR will be important for a successful economic transition period in the USSR. However, given the scope of the problems encountered, broad support on the side of Germany and other EC countries could be helpful. Pragmatic adjustments in the EC could be required, and a reduction of import barriers in Western Europe is particularly important. Moreover, a relaxation of the Cocom rules should promote the growth and diversity of Western exports to the USSR. Radical short-term improvements are not to be expected. However, a series of gradual improvements could bring sustaining economic reforms in the USSR. The international organizations have prepared a rather gloomy report on the economy of the USSR (*IMF et al 1990*). The proposed radical reforms in the USSR are not easy to realize. Indeed, if the major OECD countries adopt only traditional gradual support for increasing West-East economic relations, long-term success of economic reforms may not be feasible in the USSR. The complicated economic intra-German adjustment process after unification will illustrate for Germany, and for other countries as well, how complicated the transition to a market economy can be even under favorable side-constraints.

References

ABALKIN, LEONID (1986) The Strategy of Economic Development in the USSR, Moscow: Progress Publishers.
AGANBEGYAN, A (1988) Economic Challenge to Perestroika, Bloomington, Indiana: Indiana University Press.
BRYSON, PHILLIP J. (1990) Soviet Economic and Social Reform (Perestroika and Glasnost): Claim and Reality, in: Cassel, D., ed., Wirtschaftssysteme im Umbruch, Muenchen: Vahlen, 122-152.
HEWETT, ED A. (1988) Reforming the Soviet Economy: Equality Versus Efficiency, Washington, D.C.: The Brookings Institution.
IMF et al. (1990) The Economy of the USSR, Washington, D.C.
LAVROV, S. and T. TEODOROVITCH (1988) Problemy perestrojki vnesnich ekonomiceskich sviasej, Voprosy Ekonomiki, 2/1988, 45-54.
SCHAGALOW, G. (1988) Novyi mechanism vneschneekonomitscheskich svjasej i meschdunarodnogo sotrudnitschestva, Voprosy Ekonomiki, 5/1988, 138-148.
WELFENS, MARIA J. (1990) Internationalisierung der UdSSR? Bedeutung der sowjetische Reformpolitik für die Stellung der UdSSR im RGW und im Ost-West-Handel, in: Cassel, D., ed., Wirtschaftssysteme im Umbruch, Muenchen: Vahlen, 196-221.

COMMENTS ON: ECONOMIC REFORMS IN THE USSR AND PROSPECTS FOR TRADE AND ECONOMIC RELATIONS WITH UNIFIED GERMANY

Angela Stent

German unification has created major new economic challenges for the Federal Republic not only in terms of the absorption of the former GDR but also because of the assumption by Bonn of the GDR's external trading obligations. Germany has inherited a number of commercial agreements between the former GDR and the Soviet Union that it is obliged to honor. Moreover, given the unstable political and economic situation within the Soviet Union, Germany has been called upon to assume a disproportionate share of the financial support for the weak Soviet economy. How far can and will Germany go in supporting the Soviet economy? What are the prospects for continued German economic involvement in the USSR once the 380,000 Soviet troops have withdrawn from the former GDR? Does the past provide any answers to these questions?

Germany and Russia have a long history of profitable complementary economic relations, involving the exchange of Russian raw materials for German manufactures. This trade was always more important for the Russian economy than for the German. At the height of their commercial ties, in 1913, 47% of Russian imports came from Germany and 29% of Russian exports went to Germany. The Cold War period of trade restrictions and low levels of bilateral commerce was an aberration in historical terms. Yet, as Germany confronts current Soviet demands for much greater economic involvement, it has to weigh both the costs of unification domestically and the wisdom of investing in a declining economy during a period of great political uncertainty, where there are major questions about the current leadership's commitment to economic reform.

Since the fall of the Berlin Wall, there have been a number of positive developments in Soviet-German economic relations. Since West Germany was the USSR's most important capitalist trading partner and East Germany its most important communist trading partner, united Germany, as Dr. Grinberg shows, is now the USSR's number one trading partner. The Federal Republic, as part of the negotiations that preceded unification, agreed in principle to assume all the economic obligations of the GDR to the USSR, under the current five-year plan.

However, the process of privatizing the East German economy and the difficulties of this transition period have complicated the fulfillment of many of these obligations. Nevertheless,

West Germany is absorbing East Germany and has inherited economic specialists who are familiar with the Soviet market and are oriented toward commercial relations with the USSR and Eastern Europe. After all, prior to unification, about 70% of GDR exports went to the CMEA region. It is unlikely that there would be a complete reorientation of this trade once the process of unification has been completed.

Germany has also "paid" the USSR for unification in a variety of ways. After all, the external aspects of Germany's unification could not have been completed without Soviet consent and, not surprisingly, Gorbachev expected something concrete in return for renouncing one of the fundamental pillars of postwar Soviet foreign policy - the need to keep Germany divided and woo West Germany away from NATO. At the end of 1989, the FRG had extended 13 billion DM of credit to the USSR, 2.6 billion of which were state-subsidized. Since then, an additional 13 billion DM credit has been given in payment for unification, 7.8 billion of which is for the construction of new housing for Soviet soldiers returning from the GDR. By delaying the ratification of the "Two Plus Four" agreement guaranteeing Soviet assent to unification, Moscow was able to secure further economic concessions from the FRG. Moreover, Bonn has also given substantial food aid to the Soviet Union to help stave off a potentially disastrous economic situation and ensure that floods of refugees do not leave the Soviet Union.

Germany has, therefore, granted substantial credits to the Soviet Union before and after unification. However, German business has been more reluctant to become deeply involved in investing in the Soviet economy for the same reason that most Western firms shy away from the Soviet market - the uncertainty about the future direction of the Soviet economy and the Soviet political system.

There are, however, a number of constraints on Germany's future economic involvement in the USSR.

a) There are competing claims on Germany's resources, as this book amply demonstrates. Bonn's first priority is to integrate the former GDR economy into the Western system, and this is proving to be a Herculean task. The successful completion of economic unification requires tremendous energy and resources, and leaves little to spare for other claimants. Moreover, the Gulf War has also taken resources from Germany, at a time when it was not in an optimal position to provide such resources.

b) It is not only the Soviet Union which seeks German economic involvement. All of the newly-emerging democracies of Central Europe look to Germany as their major source of assistance, despite their fears about the political consequences of German economic domination of the region. Polish, Czech and Hungarian officials are asking for assistance, as well as representatives of Croats, Slovenes and Slovaks, who are dealing with the various Laender.

c) Since the rejection by Gorbachev of the Shatalin Plan for a rapid transition to a market economy, and the growing uncertainty about whether the Soviet Union will indeed embark on a program of meaningful economic reform, potential German investors have become quite wary about the wisdom of investing in the USSR.

d) The major deterrent to German investment is the unresolved question of the relationship between the Union and the Republics, and who owns the natural resources of the Soviet Union. With Yeltsin claiming that the Russian Republic, and not the Soviet Union, owns the oil, gas and other natural resources in Russia, it is very difficult for a potential investor to be sure that he has negotiated with the right partner. Until the political issue of the future sovereignty of the union republics is decided, it will be difficult for the Soviet Union to attract large-scale investment. The Ost-Ausschuss der deutschen Wirtschaft, the major German East-West trade lobbying group, is actively involved in promoting more investment in the Soviet Union, but acknowledges that its members are deterred by the disorganization in the country and the difficulty of dealing with central and republic authorities, both of whom claim that they are the ultimate repositories of power and authority.

e) Germans also believe, as do other Western economic partners, that they cannot solve the economic problems of the Soviet Union. Dr. Grinberg urges that the West stimulate the transformation of the Soviet economy, but there is a growing feeling in the West that the USSR must first put its own economic house in order - or at least agree on how it might go about doing this - until it becomes a more attractive investment prospect. The key to the resolution of the Soviet economic crisis lies at home, not abroad.

For the next few years, the Federal Republic will remain committed to helping out the Soviet Union financially as much as its other responsibilities allow it. As long as there are Soviet troops on German soil, there will be an incentive to maintain the economic involvement. However, once the troops have withdrawn, and if the Soviet Union does not embark on a far-reaching program of reforms, the German government and German industry may well reassess how far they should go toward reviving the traditional Russo-German commercial relationship.

GERMAN UNIFICATION AS AN INCENTIVE FOR INSTITUTIONAL AND ORGANIZATIONAL CHANGES WITHIN THE EC: A FRENCH VIEW

Claude Menard[1]

1. Introduction

German Unification, coupled to the processes going on in Eastern Europe, is definitely a major event in Europe, if not the most important one since World War II. This is so because it opens new paths to freedom in Eastern Europe and because it increases, both politically and economically, the weight of Germany. But, as decisively, it is also a major change since it will probably shift the center of gravity of the European Economic Community in the long run and induce significant changes within its organization.

The 1980s were a period of expansion of the EC to the South of Europe. The entrance of Greece, Portugal, and Spain into the Community created a completely new situation. Of particular importance was the entrance of Spain since its economic dynamism, as well as the dynamism of Italy and the restructuring of the French economy with an increasing economic weight of its southern area, created a new pole of development in Europe, reequilibrating the EC to the south. At the same time, the German economy, though the most powerful in Europe, was confronted with a severe threat: its demographic decline.

Therefore, several observers thought that in the long run, the economic core of Europe could shift to the South, to the Mediterranean area. It is now obvious that German unification, as well as the changes going on in Eastern Europe, will seriously challenge this evolution.

It is the purpose of this paper to explore some of the consequences of this new situation which was created by historical events that nobody would have predicted two years ago. After a short summary of the rapid changes that happened over the last year as perceived from the point of view of their economic consequences on the EC (Section 2), I shall analyze some institutional changes that have already happened or that may be necessitated by German unification (Section 3). Finally I will shortly point out some significant organizational effects that may be expected from the economic processes already going on (Section 4). Though the analysis developed here is focused on economic aspects, it is intertwined with political factors: one must recall that in regard to recent events, political factors were very often, and still are in several aspects, the engine to which economic factors had to adjust.

2. New Perceptions and Old Apprehensions

It is very instructive to retrospectively read some major newspapers published in Europe, but elsewhere than Germany, so as to remember what was said by leading decision-makers of the EC as well as by several analysts, on German unification and its consequences.[2]

2.1 An Accelerated Process

When the flow of German migrants from East Germany as well as from several other East European countries became important in the summer of 1989, emphasis was placed on the failure of the planning system in "command economies", but also on the fact that reforms would be a long process, particularly as far as inter-German cooperation was concerned. This would be the case, so it was argued[3], because of differences among their political regimes but also because of major differences in cultures and traditions rooted in the history of the German States which, up to the end of the nineteenth century, were rivals in terms of power and which had very different structures, economically as well as politically.

Therefore, so ran the argument at least, if ever there were to be a convergence between East and West Germany, it would be in the long run. "Reunification is hardly around the corner" read the headlines of the *International Herald Tribune (09/22/89)*. And, as late as in January of this year, Lord Weidenfeld argued (*Times, 01/19/90*) that the European partners of West Germany should "Face the inevitable and help forge a unified state" by the mid 90's! The important point is that Europeans were slow to realize what was going on, not only because they thought that neither NATO nor the USSR would allow a unification process, but also because they overemphasized the importance of the economic and cultural gaps and correlatively underemphasized the power of the social pressure within East Germany.

The sudden acceleration of history, from October 1989 to May 1990, e.g. from the amplification of demonstrations in East Germany and the opening of the Berlin Wall to the announcement of the Treaty on Economic and Monetary Union between East and West Germany, obviously changed the analysis.

2.2 Two Attitudes

Over the whole period, and up to now, though there will surely be disagreements on this, there were two basic attitudes in Europe as far as German unification is concerned. These two attitudes were perfectly summarized at the Dublin Summit of the European Community in January 1990. At that time, there was significant tension between two groups: those who were opposed to any special treatment that would distinguish East Germany from other East European countries and that would help its European integration (Hurd, from the U.K., van den Broek from Holland, and Eyckens from Belgium made explicit statements on that point); and others (mostly Delors, acting as president of the European Commission and Mitterand, from France, though this is more controversial as we will see) who insisted on according East Germany special treatment, particularly as far as economic help was concerned. At that time, the first attitude prevailed, so that in January 1990 the European Commission was still talking of "intensifying cooperation with East Germany" through a commercial agreement that would be signed for ten years (Report by Andriessen, Vice President of the European Commission), while Delors, developing arguments of his own, was already talking about rapid German unification as the best way to have East Germany "fully integrated within the Community".

Obviously, these two opposite attitudes were spread all over the European Community, often times with elements from both views present. But looking carefully at the different positions adopted by some of the major leaders of the EC-12 as well as at the positions developed by the most influential newspapers, there were clearly two polarized views.

Opposition to unification has been particularly strong in the U.K. and, though to a lesser degree, in the Netherlands and in Belgium. This is clearly evident when looking at several headlines and articles published in the U.K. in the fall of 1989. "The Spectre of German Unification" (*Guardian, 09/20/89*), and "Beware of Reich Resurgent" (*Times 10/31/89*) were some major headlines. And, while the *Financial Times (12/11/89)* talked of "Apprehension" and of a "Pandora Box", the *Guardian (11/13/89)* published a very negative analysis by George Kennan ("German Reunification Remains an Unrealistic Option"), and the *Times* reprinted the long, and rather violent, paper that Gunther Grass initially published in the *New York Times (01/07/90)* ("Don't Reunify Germany"). The basic thesis developed in these papers and several other ones was that German reunification would threaten the equilibrium of the European Community in creating a too powerful German area and would destabilize its economy in integrating too rapidly an underdeveloped country (East Germany).

The attitude was radically different in France and, though to a lesser degree, in Spain and Italy. French leaders, and on this they were massively followed by French citizens as revealed by an opinion poll quoted in the *Financial Times (10/27/89)*, rapidly recognized, as early as September 1989, German unification as a priority on the agenda of Europe and as inevitable. Therefore, the earlier, the better, if certain conditions were met: the restoration of democracy in East Germany, and, most of all, a significant reinforcement of the European Community so as to firmly anchor a unified Germany in the EC. It seems that in Germany, the visit of Mitterand to Moscow at the end of 1989 was interpreted as a strong sign of opposition to unification, or, even worse, as open support for Gorbachev if he would slow down the process. Though there may be some exceptions, the predominant interpretation in France was totally different: Mitterand was seen as an early supporter of German unification, and his trip to Moscow, while he was acting as the President of the European Council, was seen as a search for guarantees that the Soviets would not interfere militarily in East Germany. That Mitterand was much more open to German unification than several other European leaders can easily be documented. Talking about the situation in Germany on October 27, 1989, Mitterand explicitly developed the point: "Our Answer is Europe". He also agreed with his friend Delors, the President of the Brussels Commission, who had declared in an interview with *Le Monde* as early as October 7, 1989 that "German unity will be realized by and within the European Community". At that time, they both were labelled "Eurovolunteers" by the *Express*, the most widely distributed French weekly magazine. *Le Monde*, the most influential newspaper in France, also published a long paper by a well-known French Ambassador (H. Froment-Meurice) entitled "Assume German Unity" ("Assumer l'Unite Allemande") almost at the same time as the *Guardian* was publishing the already quoted anti-unification paper by George Kennan. And Delors once again insisted that East Germany be considered as "a potential member of the EC" (quoted by the *Times, 01/09/90*) at the Dublin Summit, though he was clearly in a minority position at that time. The basic thesis that all pro-unity proponents developed was that a unified Germany was unavoidable, and that the best attitude was to accelerate the process and to seize that opportunity to reinforce the EC in deepening it.

2.3 Five Problems

History has already decided in that unification is almost accomplished now. It is clear, though, that the problems underlying these opposite attitudes are still there. What were and are these problems? I will list five of them and will come back to the analysis of some of them and other aspects in the last two parts of my paper.

1) There is the question of the new political power, some would say superpower, created by a unified Germany. As emphasized in a special section published by the *Economist (06/30/90)*, the question is: How will the new Germany be different from the one that plunged Europe into three wars, from 1870 to 1940? And will this new "Mitteleuropa" weaken its link with Western Europe so as to turn its resources toward Eastern Europe (a related question being the German temptation of "neutralism").

2) A second uncertainty is about the consequences of the new economic order that will develop in the EC. West Germany already had the most powerful economy. The unified Germany will

clearly be much more powerful. As emphasized by Flora Lewis (*New York Times, 10/08/90*), will there be "A European Germany or a German Europe"?

3) A related question is about the effects that German unification will have on the structures of the major economic areas within the EC. More precisely, will there be a shift of the center of gravity from South to North, as asked by the Spanish magazine *Economica* in a special issue of January 1990? In other terms, will the creation of such a strong pole in Northern Europe, and a pole that is much more open to Eastern Europe than to Southern Europe, divert financial resources so that it would seriously weaken the new and fragile dynamism of the South?

4) What will be the consequences for the institutions of the EC? Will the unified Germany ask for a new distribution of power (number of seats in the European Parliament, number of bureaucrats in Brussels, etc.)? Can it go so far as to remodel the institutions of the Community, based, for example, on its economic power to impose, more or less, its conception of what the coming European Central Bank should be?

5) And what will be the consequences of unification for the EC budget? Clearly, West Germany will have to make a major effort to integrate East Germany: this means that its subsidies will go to Germany rather than to other backward areas of the European Community[4].

We will now go a step further in looking more closely at some aspects of these questions.

3. Institutional Changes

Obviously, the unification process already involved, and will continue to involve, several institutional changes. This is now very clear for East Germany, but there will also be consequences for West Germany as well as for the EC, though it is not easy to predict yet what these changes will be. Therefore I shall raise questions here rather than give answers. One can try to establish some order in these questions by distinguishing institutional changes, and specifically changes in institutions that have to do with the economy, in Germany and within the EC before succinctly discussing some potential effects on the relations between the EC and the rest of the world.

3.1 Within Germany

As far as Germany is concerned, it is very difficult to isolate changes that affect the rules of the economic game from their political environment. First of all, one must recall how fast things have changed. One year ago (October 7, 1989), a suggestion made by Delors, namely that a Confederation between East and West Germany could represent a smooth transition toward a better integration of East Germany since such a special association would allow the future partner to structurally adjust to the EC, was considered as premature. What Delors had in mind, at that time, was an association like the one which benefitted Spain and Portugal in the early eighties and helped them to adjust within ten years. Six months later this proposition was already obsolete, though several members of the European Commission, backed by the U.K., still supported the idea that East Germany should be kept out of the EC for several years; later, however, they accepted the idea of a special agreement. The announcement of a Treaty on Economic and Monetary Union by Chancellor Kohl in April and then that there would be general elections simultaneously in East and West Germany before the end of the year so as to accomplish total unification dramatically changed the situation. It meant full political integration based on the West German Constitution with the possibility of some minor changes.

But if this has dissipated a lot of uncertainties about the political structure of a unified Germany, what about economic institutions? Here again, it is clear that most transformations are for East Germany, though there may be some consequences for West Germany. As far as East Germany is concerned, these major changes concern: 1) principles of ownership; and 2) labor relations.

As to the first point, the Treaty signed in May already made it clear that the Union would restore the principles of private property and a functioning property market. Putting these principles into practice, however, is not an easy task. First, one must recall that if there are some common principles shared by all market economies, there are also fundamental differences in the institutional patterns through which these principles are monitored. Second, one cannot forget that East Germany was under a command economy without experience in the functioning of a free market for almost fifty years so that assimilating the rules of the game of a market economy may not be that easy for individuals as well as for organizations. Third, there is the lack of institutions related to the functioning of markets (laws, courts, etc.) so that implanting West German structures into East Germany may not be that easy.

These difficulties can be exemplified by looking at the privatization program. The questions raised are now well known: What will happen to collectivized farms, to nationalized small industries, to town-house owners, and to the properties of those who fled to the West? Should all of the 8000 companies already in the government trusteeship (the famous Treuhandanstalt) be privatized? And according to what procedure? How can the EC and the European partners be involved in that process? One possible scenario for privatizing, apparently the one that is predominant today, is that the problem should be split into three components: East German counterparts of companies that are already in the public sector in West Germany should be kept within the public sector so that sectors like postal services, railroads, etc. would be integrated into already existing West German companies. As for the cooperatives as well as the firms owned by local governments that are not part of the public service sector, they would be sold to the employees or to local savers and entrepreneurs - a solution that sounds realistic if one takes into consideration the availability of savings in the East German economy. But what about the third component, the famous "Kombinate"? Should they be split into smaller companies before being sold, and how? And what should be the procedure for evaluating their assets? Should shares be sold on a free market (that does not yet fully exist in East Germany), or should they be distributed to the population?

Clearly the solutions adopted have already transformed and will continue to revolutionize East German institutions. But they may also modify significantly some institutional aspects in West Germany: for example, it is likely that under the new circumstances, the unified German government will have to manage one of the largest public sectors in the EC. Will it do so according to the previous rules, or will it adopt new rules?

The same question can be raised about labor relations. East Germans lived in a command economy for fifty years. This means that almost all of the labor force has been educated in a system that did not work, but one that established work standards that gave them some advantages. What will happen to their rights (e.g. the number of weeks allowed for pregnant women to be on leave, the social security system, etc.)? And will West German unions be able to maintain their power of negotiation by rapidly integrating this low-paid labor force that does not believe in unions anymore? And what will the reactions of entrepreneurs be in West Germany? Will the process alter labor relations? What rules will be adopted so as to harmonize these relations between the two areas? Again this means some substantial changes in economic institutions within Germany.

3.2 Within the EC

Now, will this also induce significant changes in the institutions of the European Community? So far the German government has adopted a low profile saying that it would not ask for more seats nor for more representatives on the different commissions, committees, groups, etc. of the EC. But, more realistically, and particularly if European institutions intend to be representative of the populations concerned, there will be necessary changes in the longer run. This is already a matter of discussion within the Community. The basic debate, these days, is between those who would like to broaden the Community, and those who would like to have a tighter community.

The broadening approach, so to speak, would like to build an enlarged common market - but only a common market - open not only to East Germany, but also, in the coming years, to other East European countries. There should be no new institutions, no new structures, but the possibility should be open to other countries to join the unified market of 1992. This is clearly the position of the Thatcher government (but there is now some uncertainty on that in relation to recent changes in the government of the U.K.) as well as, though to a much lesser degree, some major German decision-makers (like Karl Otto Poehl) and some Italian leaders. Mrs. Thatcher seemed to hope that German unification and the opening of the Common Market to eastern European countries would slow down French and Italian pressures for stronger links (pressures for a so-called "social policy", pressures for a tight Monetary Union, pressures for political institutions that would prevail over national Parliaments) and would also weaken the Paris-Bonn collusion in European affairs.

On the other hand, the deepening approach, as developed by Mitterand in France, by Delors as President of the European Commission in Brussels, as well as by the German President von Weizsaecker is that it is urgent for Germany as well as some other partners to become more strongly committed to the EC by reinforcing the existing structures and by creating new links, both at the economic level (through a tightened Monetary Union that would be completed by the creation of a common Central Bank and a common currency) and at the political level. In an interview with *Le Monde (10/05/90)*, President von Weizsaecker suggested that what is needed now is much more than an internally integrated market, and that major steps should be accomplished toward creating the United States of Europe. Though he did not use that expression, President Mitterand talked about the necessity of building a European Confederation that would complete the EC by means of an adequate political superstructure; this view was supported, at least partially, by a former Minister of Foreign Affairs in a conservative government, J.F. Deniau, who argued that in order to have a balanced European Community, it is necessary to have a united political power where German foreign affairs could be dealt with (*Le Figaro, 03/07/90*). Acting again as a free lance, President Delors of the European Commission, was very explicit on this issue (*Liberation, 09/26/90; Le Monde 10/12/90*). It is necessary, according to Delors, to recognize that the reinforcement of the already powerful Germany will accentuate German economic "expansionism". But, he argues, this could be very positive for the EC if economic as well as political integration, including military aspects, would be reinforced with the development of more democratic institutions that would reduce in the medium run the technocratic power of the European Commission.

One can be sure that this debate will continue and will develop within the Community. But some major steps in the direction defended by Delors were already taken at the European Summit held in Rome in 1990 with the decision to go further along the way of a total Monetary Union in the EC, even if it is necessary to overcome the U.K.'s veto. It is probable that, though there was clearly German opposition to certain aspects of the project, for example by the Bundesbank, EC monetary integration has been supported by the German Government as concrete proof that unification is not threatening, nor slowing down, European construction. It reinforces considerably the French position as well as that of the European Commission, while it isolated Mrs. Thatcher (and weakened her internally, as illustrated by the resignation of Sir Howe followed by her own resignation).

3.3 The EC and the Rest of the World

The last point that I would like to mention is about the possible consequences of these changes within the Community for the relations between the EC and the rest of the world. As asked by the *International Herald Tribune (12/27/1989)* as early as December 1989, will German integration and the consecutive reinforcement of European institutions generate a "Eurocentrism"? Though it is too early to give a precise answer to this question, it is clear that the tightening of the EC, as already observed, will modify the economic relations between Europe on one hand, and three groups of countries on the other.

Regarding economic relations with the U.S. and Japan, it is obvious that the strategy of a more united community is oriented toward building an economically more competitive area, of which Germany would be the center, and building a politically more consistent Europe that would progressively learn to speak as a single actor in international affairs[5]. Regarding Eastern Europe and the USSR, an integrated Europe could facilitate the role of Germany as "the natural link" (Genscher, interview with *Le Monde, 09/18/1990*) with this area since it would eliminate the suspicion that Germany is motivated by its exclusive interest, or, even worse, the suspicion that Germany is trying to create a new "Mitteleuropa" under its dominance and directed away from the EC. There is some debate, though, about the institutional pattern through which these links should be established. Should the relations with Eastern Europe and the USSR be developed on a bilateral basis (in such a case Germany would be the great benefactor: one must recall that West Germany has continuously been the major western partner of the USSR for the past 20 years), or should all EC partners be involved? One need not be a visionary to predict that this issue will be a source of tensions within the Community in the coming years. And, last but not least, there is the question of the relations between the EC and its Mediterranean partners that are either within the Community (Spain, Portugal, Greece) or that have special economic relations with it (Turkey, North Africa). Since the EC is clearly refocusing its attention toward Eastern Europe and since German unification should accelerate this process, it is not clear whether these relations will be considered as important in the future as they were over the past years.

To summarize, I think that German unification has already induced and will continue to induce some major institutional changes, the result of which will be a tightening of the EC and a strong development of economic relations between the EC on the one hand and Eastern Europe and the USSR on the other. These institutional changes will have some significant effects on the internal organization of European economies.

4. Organizational Effects

Institutions are designed so as to define the rules of the game, while organizations have to operate and to adjust within these rules. Therefore it is not surprising that the important institutional transformations related to German unification should have some powerful effects on economic organizations, both in Germany and in the EC. It is difficult, though, at such an early stage, to exactly anticipate what these effects will be. In this section I would like to explore some of them. After having pointed out several organizational changes that will be needed by the structural adjustment of the East German economy, I will highlight some potential consequences, at an aggregate level, for the unified German state as well as for its EC partners, and I will then proceed to indicate some induced effects at the micro level.

4.1 Structural Adjustments

Structural adjustments that will be needed for fully integrating the East German economy into the EC are quite similar to those necessary for unifying the two components of the German economy. We will summarize these adjustments under four categories.

First, there is the technological gap. Most observers do agree that East Germany failed in meeting the computer revolution, though it spent a lot of money to fill this gap over the last ten years. But these investments were misallocated, and the logic of autarky behind them pushed the economy into a dead end. Most of the computer industry built under the centrally planned economy is not competitive so that related firms will either be absorbed by western firms or, more likely, will be shut down. Moreover, these heavy investments diverted resources away from other sectors so that machines are obsolete in several key sectors: the postal system, public transportation, telephone, communication systems, etc. As for the "just in time production" techniques, the gap is evaluated at 20 years - e.g. in most sectors the East German economy utilizes techniques of production that are equivalent to those used in the early seventies in West Germany or in France. This means that East German firms that are going to survive will need heavy investment in new technologies, and, therefore, a radical reorganization of jobs.

Second, this will be accentuated by the productivity gap. Data on this productivity gap is very difficult to get, and estimations concerning the productivity of East German workers as compared to their western counterparts vary from 30% to 60% (40% according to the Deutsche Bank, and 52% if one looks solely at the industrial sector according to the D.I.W.). There is again agreement among most experts that this gap can be filled quite rapidly, particularly because of the highly qualified labor force that is available. But this is possible only if there are massive investments - evaluated at more than one billion DM for the coming five years (*Lipp 1990*) - in the manufacturing sector coming from Germany as well as from its European partners. Considering the uncertainties related to the efficiency of these investments in the short run, it is not clear that the private sector will provide enough resources: one major consequence would then be increasing public interference with private investments. One other major consequence of the productivity gap will be the necessity to implement a new organization of labor in East German firms, and once again, this is a source of some uncertainty, though one can expect several incentives for workers to accept these changes.

This incentive problem is related to a third structural adjustment that will be needed: economic behavior will have to change. The introduction of market prices should provide better incentives in the medium and long run, but in the short run it will mean substantial increases of prices for some basic goods (food, clothing), services (rents, public transportation) and social goods (day care, medication). Changes must also be implemented very rapidly, as emphasized by the Deutsche Bundesbank in its official statement of April 3, 1990, in labor contracts, retirement plans, rents, etc. But this is a new source of uncertainty for private investors since it is not clear exactly what the new rules will be and since there is no historical experience of such a sudden transition from one economic regime to another; thus, it is not clear at all how economic actors will react in the short run.

Fourth, there are also some structural adjustments that will be needed because of the European Economic Policy. Let me just mention three aspects here. It is well known that EC farmers are heavily subsidized on a per product basis. East German agriculture was even more heavily subsidized on a totally different basis (related to the state-cooperative system - see *The Economist, 6/30/90*). The European Commission already indicated that Community prices should be valid for all German products by 1992. How will East German agriculture adjust to this? The environmental question is also a crucial one since the European Commission would like its tough standards to be applied by 1996. But since East German industry is so massively polluting, this may involve the shutting down of a very significant number of firms (*Bafoil 1990*). Finally there is the competition policy that the EC has firmly implemented in the eighties: cracking down on state aids and monopolies is of direct concern for most East German firms so that the application of the EC rules will mean some very fundamental reorganization, particularly in the industrial sector.

4.2 A More Activist Government

What can be the organizational consequences of these structural adjustments? Several indications have already been given. At the state level, these adjustments will induce a more active role for the government and also more interference with market mechanisms, while the trend among European partners is in the opposite direction (even in the traditionally state-interventionist France). It is obvious that West Germans will have to pay for these structural adjustments.

It has been estimated by the Dresdner Bank (*Lipp 1990; see also D.I.W. 1990*) that the efforts needed in terms of public investment will induce an increased deficit (the deficit represented 1.5% of GNP in 1989; it would represent at least 2.5% over the three years 1990-1992), though one that is still reasonable. But the public deficit is only part of the picture since the government will also interfere with the markets and subsidize the East German economy through specific programs like the modernization of the telephone system (the Bundespost is planning to spend 55 Billion DM on this program of which 30 would be borrowed in the financial markets - see *Financial Times 06/21/90*) or like subsidies to private investments for the coming two years (up to 12% of equipment bought for modernizing East German firms). Also, the government will have to interfere with markets (it already does so) in order to avoid massive population flows from east to west: keeping rents at a low level so as to compensate for the gap in wages particularly among qualified workers or guaranteeing transfer revenues (retirement plans, etc.) so as to maintain and even improve standards of living and to avoid the abandonment of East Germany are some aspects of the problem. All these measures mean that German citizens will have to pay. Taxes may have to be raised, or, at least, the decline in rates of taxation that was observed over the last years would have to be stopped. More importantly, the financial needs of the government are likely to have a crowding out effect so as to slow down the intended investments by the private sector. This may induce a favorable situation for the European partners of Germany, particularly for countries with high rates of savings (as in France). But it also means that a unified Germany will have to focus on its internal problems, so that one must expect a slow down in German contributions to European policies (funds for disadvantaged areas, etc.). This may induce some shift of power among some major public organizations of the European Community.

4.3 Effects on Industrial Organization

Finally, there will be innumerable organizational effects at the microeconomic level. Within Germany, unification means that new management and new labor relations will have to be introduced in East Germany. Since low productivity there is largely related to the poor organization of production and to the lack of incentives, it means that to survive firms will have to drastically change their internal organization as well as their labor relations. A new corporate culture will have to be created: taking into consideration the specific historical experience of East Germany, it will probably be different from the corporate culture of their western counterparts. The financial system will also have to be totally restructured. Major changes in the banking system have already been introduced. The "Staatsbank" has been dismantled as of April 1, 1990, one third of the staff having been transferred to the central bank while the others were grouped into a newly created bank, the Kreditbank, closely related to the Deutsche Bank. This looks very much like an absorption by West German banks that will induce a more concentrated banking system in the new unified Germany. How will this affect relations between German banks and banks from other EC members? And what will be the effects - if any - on the structure of the financial markets in Europe?

More generally, since this is not a problem restricted solely to the financial markets, what will be the consequences of a restructured German industry (including banks and services) on market structures in Europe? Through its integration into the West German economy, East Germany will be a part of the division of labor within the EC. Economic unification will reinforce advantages that were already favorable to West Germany: machine tools, crafts, chemicals industry, electrical engineering, and data systems are sectors already competitive and are as well developed in East Germany as in West Germany. Privatization of these firms may signify an increased German domination of these strategic sectors within the EC. In the long run this is a major challenge to EC partners like France.

In other terms the internal reorganization of the German economy may induce some significant restructuring in several major firms within the EC.

5. Conclusions

Three fundamental questions, fundamental at least for a European, were raised in this paper in relation to German unification.

1) Does German unification mean the emergence of a new economic superpower that will disequilibrate the European Economic Community? As for the first aspect of the question,

Germans have generally adopted a very low profile arguing that the new demographic advantages would be cancelled in the medium run by the distorted pyramid of ages in West Germany, while economic unification would lower the GNP per capita for a long period of time and will reequilibrate the balance of payments by drastically reducing German surpluses (see a good summary of these arguments in the *Frankfurter Allgemeine Zeitung 02/15/90*). But I would suggest that the dominant feeling in the EC is definitely that a new economic giant is borne. Some have tried to evaluate its impact and have labelled it "the emergence of a fifth dragon" (*Harasty and Le Dem, 1990*). Will it disequilibrate the European Community, though? This is a very difficult question to answer. Basically, there are two opposing arguments. On the one hand German unification is definitely changing the center of gravity of the EC, shifting it from South to North, to the relative disadvantage of southern areas that were just taking off; but on the other hand the new dynamism of a unified German economy, with its expected rate of growth, will be an engine that will stimulate - and be beneficial to - its major partners, particularly France and Italy.

2) What institutional changes will unification induce in the long run? Basically, I have argued in this paper that it should have two major effects for the coming years: first, it will induce an increasing role of the German state, quite a different evolution from that of the other EC partners; and, second, it will focus German attention and resources on internal problems so that Germany should be less active within EC institutions at a time when these institutions will probably be restructured in depth (Economic and Monetary Union and so forth).

3) Last, but not least, what organizational effects can be expected from unification? Here an even more subtle analysis is needed since organizational changes are mostly at the micro level. There are three aspects, though, that I have emphasized. First, it seems clear that the needed structural adjustments will induce more interference of the public sector with markets. This may have consequences in the long run since it may stabilize the weight of the public sector at a significantly higher level than it was before unification. It is also highly probable that complementarities between some industrial sectors in East and West Germany will generate, through the unification process, groups that will be larger, more concentrated, and more powerful than before unification. This is already observable in the banking sector. One consequence is probably the restructuring of some key sectors of activity within the EC. To be clear, it means more concentration.

In the long run, it also means that competition should be accentuated among large groups within the EC but also on international markets. Indeed, one major organizational effect of German unification is likely to be the formation of bigger industrial groups with a dynamic strategy in Eastern Europe and the USSR. These groups will be competing more aggressively on international markets, too.

The crucial question in Europe for the coming years is: will these changes be mostly to the advantage of a new Mitteleuropa? Or will it mainly benefit the existing EC?

Endnotes

1 I would like to thank my research assistant, Delila Allam, for her help.

2 In preparing this paper, the following newspapers and magazines were reviewed from 1 June 1989 to 1 October 1990: *Financial Times, Guardian, International Herald Tribune, The Economist, Times, L'Express, Le Figaro, Liberation, Le Monde, La Tribune d'Allemagne, La Tribune de l'Expansion.*

3 See "Le debat sur l'identite Allemande" Problemes politiques et sociaux. Paris: Documentation Francaise, 1988. See also: Gunther Grass, *New York Times 01/07/90* and *Times 01/08/90*; and several German contributions to a special issue of *Le Figaro, 10/01/90.*

4 Report to the European Parliament, introduced by A. Donnely (Labor Party, U.K.) 07/14/90.

5 This point of view is explicitly developed by the official spokesman of the French Socialist Party (which controls the government) in *Le Monde 03/07/90.*

References

ALLEMAGNE D'AUJOURD'HUI (1990) January - March.
BAFOIL, F. (1990) L'introduction du Deutsche Mark en R.D.A.: la dimension sociale, Economie Prospective Internationale, No. 43, July 1990, 49-62.
DEUTSCHE BUNDESBANK (1990) The Monetary Union with the German Democratic Republic. Monthly Report of the Bundesbank, July 1990.
DEUTSCHES INSTITUT FUER WIRTSCHAFTSFORSCHUNG (D.I.W.) (1990) Wochenbericht Nr. 26.
ECONOMIE PROSPECTIVE INTERNATIONALE (1990) Special Issue: Une Economie Allemande, Nr. 43, July 1990.
EUROPEAN COMMISSION (1990) The Community and German Unification, Vol. 1, COM 90-400, Brussels, August 21.
GUERARD, F. (ed.) (1988) Le Debat sur l'Identite Allemande, Problemes Politiques et Sociaux, Paris, Documentation Francaise, February 19, 64.
GUERARD, F. (ed.) (1990) L'Unification de l'Allemagne, Problemes Politiques et Sociaux, Paris, Documentation Francaise, August 3, 65.
HARASTY, H. and Le DEM, J. (1990) Les Consequences Macroeconomiques de la Reunification Allemande, Economie Prospective Internationale, Special Issue, Nr. 43, July, 91-120.
IN PRESS (1990) Inter Nationes Bonn, Weekly.
LIPP, ERNST-MORITZ (1990) Des capitaux pour l'Allemagne Orientale, Economie Prospective Internationale, Nr. 43, July 1990, 13-28.
I.F.R.I. (1989) Rapport Ramses, Paris, Economica.
REVUE DE PRESSE: EUROPE DE L'EST (1990) Caisse des Depots et Consignations: Delegation aux Affairers Europeennes et Internationales, Paris, January 30.
REVUE DES QUESTIONS ALLEMANDES (1990) Special Issue, Paris, Nr. 3, March 1990.
WELFENS, PAUL J.J. (1990a) Politique de Stabilisation en R.F.A.: Maitriser l'ajustement a la C.E.E., in: MERLIO, G. and PELLETIER, N. (eds) (1990) Les Allemands et l'Argent, Bordeaux, Presses Universitairees de Bordeaux, 73-103.
WELFENS, PAUL J.J. (1990b) EC Integration and Economic Reforms in CMEA Countries: Germany as a Bridge Between East and West, this volume.

GLOBAL ECONOMIC RIVALRY: NEW PERSPECTIVES ON GERMANY (THE EC), JAPAN AND THE UNITED STATES

Michael Aho

1. Introduction

Overview

Throughout the postwar period, the United States was accustomed to being master of its own economic fate. As the world's predominant economic power, America had the ability to mobilize other industrialized economies in time of crisis and to act unilaterally if necessary to protect its interests. But Washington and New York, once the world's preeminent political and financial capitals, must now share the spotlight with Tokyo, Bonn, Frankfurt and London. In this new multipolar economic world, the United States is still the first among equals. But it no longer has the economic leverage to dictate the course of events. Leadership has of necessity become a collaborative effort. European and Japanese economic and political concerns now place real limits on U.S. action. The U.S. economy and American economic decision-making must now be adapted to an emerging global economy that no longer revolves around the United States.

Furthermore, the waning of the Cold War has changed the environment for U.S. policymaking. German unification has been hailed as a victory for Western principles and practices but the enormous problems and costs of rebuilding lie ahead. These problems will preoccupy the European Community at a time when the U.S. is looking for more cooperation on economic issues. In the past, U.S. foreign economic objectives were often subordinated to security concerns in a desire not to alienate allies. But without the constraint of the Cold War, America will not be as reluctant to aggressively pursue its economic goals on trade or macroeconomic issues. At the same time, it will have less leverage because Europe and Japan are less reliant on U.S. military protection. As a result, a more assertive America will confront a more assertive world, a prescription for confrontation. This paper surveys the potential for conflict on trade and macroeconomic issues and makes suggestions for reducing global economic rivalry.

With the waning of the Cold War between the military superpowers the possibility arises of a new capitalist cold war over economic and trade issues. Japan is posing compelling competitive threats to America's leading-edge industries often in ways branded as "unfair" by American firms. But unfairness is in the eye of the beholder and no international rules cover many practices or forms of business organization that can yield competitive prowess. Frictions are sure to foment.

The European Community has awoken from over a decade-long sleep to become a bold and dynamic force. Its 1992 effort to create a community without borders together with German unification and the new-found freedoms in Eastern Europe have captured the attention of businesspeople and policymakers alike. Now European monetary union, once a pipe dream, could become a reality before the turn of the century.

For its part, the United States is preoccupied with its perpetual fiscal problems and how to behave now that it is no longer the only elephant on the world's economic stage. America finds itself in the unaccustomed role of having to interact with two other elephants -- Japan and the European Community -- the latter, increasingly led by Germany.

Although other sources of rivalry will undoubtedly surface -- burdensharing being the most obvious example -- the main rivalries will occur in the trade and macroeconomic areas. Indeed, the waning of the cold-war makes it less likely that economic issues will be subordinated to security issues. The United States will not be as reluctant to aggressively pursue economic goals but at the same time America will have less leverage because Europe and Japan will be less reliant upon American security protection. As a result, tensions over trade and macroeconomic policy could easily erupt into bitter disputes.

This paper will examine emerging trends in trade and monetary policy to identify the new sources of rivalry in the world economy. Rather than focus solely upon the big three countries -- Germany, Japan and the United States, the paper focuses more upon the European Community, Japan and the United States because I believe more decisions over time will be made by the Community with Germany as its largest component playing the key role. The first section will survey trade issues, in particular the first big test of cooperation in the post Cold War world -- the Uruguay Round of multilateral trade talks. The second section will examine macroeconomic coordination and the emerging global capital shortage -- largely exacerbated by European developments. The final section will briefly propose reforms to minimize frictions and rivalries in the future.

2. Trade Talks or Trade Tangles?

The early 1990s will mark a critical juncture for the international trading system. The world's trading system is in disarray, and multilateralism hangs in the balance. Meanwhile, the two largest entities -- the European Community and the United States -- are at loggerheads over agricultural issues and are taking steps that threaten the multilateral order that has served the world economy so well for the past forty years.

The United States, having embarked upon a new, multifaceted policy in the mid-1980s, is still groping to find its way by employing a mixture of unilateral, bilateral, and multilateral approaches for resolving its trade problems.[1] Future U.S. trade policy will depend upon four unknown factors. How will the 1988 trade bill be implemented? Will additional bilateral free trade agreements (following those with Israel and Canada) be negotiated? How much will be accomplished in the Uruguay Round of multilateral trade talks under the auspices of the General Agreement on Tariffs and Trade (GATT)? Those talks have already exceeded their deadline of December 1990 because of an impasse over agriculture.

The eventual outcome of the multilateral talks depends upon the biggest unknown of all -- and the one that may be the deciding factor in determining future U.S. trade policy: the European Community's behavior on trade issues. The EC's 1992 unification effort, along with the breathtaking events unfolding in Eastern Europe as well as in Germany, is preoccupying Community policymakers. According to the Italian Trade Minister, the European Community is 'distracted' from the Uruguay Round of multilateral trade talks.[2]

American trade relations with the European Community (EC), not Japan, will dominate the headlines in the 1990s. For years, the EC has gotten off lightly as U.S. frustrations were vented principally at Japan. But as its 1992 unification effort moves forward, the Community is incrementally changing its rules of the game governing trade and domestic regulations. The U.S. trade policy process cannot ignore incremental changes in laws and regulations abroad that discriminate against U.S. interests. Moreover, the Community has proven to be a frustrating footdragger in the Uruguay Round of multilateral talks. Ideally, the Community could eliminate barriers among its twelve members while simultaneously liberalizing market access for foreign firms. Yet it is more likely to continue to protect against foreign interests while it liberalizes internally. On agriculture, the Community stubbornly resists reforming the Common Agricultural Policy, claiming it is the glue that holds the Community together. Helmut Kohl's call to Jacques Delors, urging him to go slow on agricultural reform in advance of the December 2 all-German elections, was a strong indication that multilateral progress on agriculture would not be forthcoming at the Brussels Ministerial meeting of GATT. And indeed it was not. As a result, several developing countries followed by the United States walked out saying that negotiations were not possible until the EC came up with a better offer on agriculture. If the Community continues to block progress in the GATT talks, the pressures for the existing multilateral trading system to fragment into regional trading blocs could become overwhelming.

Indeed, the emergence of some form of regional blocs is probably inevitable in the 1990s; but how benign -- as opposed to belligerent -- they will be will depend upon the outcome of the Uruguay Round. If those talks fail to achieve major progress on trade issues of importance to influential U.S. domestic constituents, as seems likely, the United States will be faced with difficult decisions all of its own. Lacking a viable multilateral option, America may choose aggressive unilateralism and/or additional bilateral agreements that could hasten the fragmentation of the global trading system, thus, causing hardship for all. Before weighing alternative U.S. responses, European developments, both actual and potential, must be surveyed.

2.1 European Unification and European Preoccupations[3]

After an initial flurry of concern about fortress Europe, politicians, trade policy officials, and businesspeople in the United States are still too focussed on Japan. Their myopia could leave them unprepared for the policy challenges and business opportunities that will be greater in Europe than in Japan and the Far East in the 1990s.

Europe is in flux. The European Community (EC) has embarked upon an ambitious program to achieve what was not accomplished 30 years ago; that is, a unified, dynamic common market. But the unshackling of restraints in Eastern Europe and the unification of Germany occurring simultaneously with the 1992 integration effort have raised fundamental questions about the future shape of Europe and it is distracting Community policymakers. The premises of the NATO alliance have been shattered -- the perception of a common threat has diminished and the United States is less dominant today. A new generation of leaders is coming into power that was not even born when NATO was founded 40 years ago. How far to reduce conventional forces is a source of widespread disagreement, and the future role of nuclear weapons is now in question.

These geopolitical issues will obviously predominate in the political debates in Washington but trade problems and the prospects for profits should also motivate policymakers and business interests to turn their attention more toward the Atlantic and away from the Pacific.

The United States certainly has a host of trade problems with Japan, but the Japanese distribution system and old-boy network are long-standing issues. The European Community is changing the commercial rules of the game with potentially profound implications for the world trading system. The possible entry of new members into the Community would increase the size of that bloc to the detriment of outside interests. Meanwhile, the Community is proving to be a stumbling block in the multilateral trade talks.

Besides the multilateral talks, immediate trade problems are being created by the 1992 unification effort itself. That effort has undoubtedly picked up momentum. The process may not be completed by December 31, 1992, in part because of the economic ramifications of German unification, but the shape of Europe will be altered.

What might 1992 unification effort mean? The economic effects could be substantial if all or most of the program is completed: European national income could increase by 9-30 percent over the medium term[4]; up to 5 million more jobs could be created; consumer prices would be lower and a wider variety of products would be available; 12 different sets of regulations and standards would be harmonized; economies of scale could be achieved on a European-wide basis enhancing competitiveness; and national cartels could be broken up providing for greater flexibility.

But the Community also is apprehensive and has fears that United States and Japanese firms may be in a better position to take advantage of 1992 than EC firms; that labor standards will be eroded to the lowest level permitted among member states; that regional imbalances will be accentuated; that the economic dislocations will be significant; and that a two-tiered (or two-speed) Community will result, with the original six members moving further, faster than the United Kingdom and the southern tier countries.

How much will be accomplished? The road to unification is littered with a wide variety of obstacles. The most significant is surely fiscal harmonization. And of course there is always the possibility of national objections to giving Brussels additional authority. Past efforts have foundered on national resistance to the sacrifice of autonomy. National parliaments could be expected to react negatively to widespread dislocations or to the potential demise of a national champion (e.g., Fiat, Peugeot). In addition, the member states will likely disagree over other issues including inconsistent immigration policies due to colonial preferences, widely differing labor standards and the possibility of the poorer countries claiming they are unequal partners. Finally, of course, unification of Germany has created new concerns and revived the debate over whether Community membership should be broadened or if Community commitments should first be deepened. The odds against achieving economic -- and ultimately political -- union are formidable. The process will be difficult, but the potential for change in Europe should not be underestimated. A slumbering giant is waking up, and the outside world had better pay attention.

The battles over the external consequences of the 1992 unification effort have not been fought yet. They will be fought out issue by issue, directive by directive, with alliances shifting from one issue to the next. The outside world should not let the Community lose sight of the implications for the multilateral trading system.

Instead, it should be on the look-out to see:

- Will Community directives call for a narrow application of reciprocity and establish European preferences to discriminate against outsiders?

- Will the directives provide long phase-in times and safeguards for lagging sectors or for the poorer European countries? If the European economies should undergo substantial restructuring and adjustment problems, (perhaps exacerbated by a recession) the pressure for continued protection against outside competition could become irresistible. Without multilateral scrutiny and agreements, "transitional" protection could become permanent.

- Who will negotiate regulatory standards for the Community, and on what basis can outsiders get mutual recognition of standards? Adoption of a Community-wide standard would reduce transactions costs for many firms now trying to cope with a dozen different national standards but it could also turn into another form of non-tariff barrier. Analytically, the establishment of a common standard would appear to be equivalent to the classic trade creation and trade diversion effects associated with the formation of a customs union. But whenever you change a regulation or a price, someone is surely going to complain and in this case there is no mechanism for compensation as exists when customs unions are formed or expanded.

- Will local content provisions be established and how will rules of origin be drafted? If the EC tightens up rules of origin, how long will it take for local content legislation to move through the U.S. Congress?

- How will bilateral quotas on cars and textiles at the national level be converted into EC-wide quotas?

- How will competition policy be revised and antidumping laws be used? Within the EC, what will constitute sufficient market power to block proposed mergers and acquisitions and on what basis will they be barred? How are foreign interests treated under any emerging competition policy? In the absence of a far-reaching antidumping agreement in the Uruguay Round, outside interests can expect wider use of antidumping actions to minimize foreign competition.

- Will negotiations over the European Economic Space lead to discrimination against outside interests? Will new members be admitted to the Community? The EC is negotiating with the members of the European Free Trade Area (EFTA), in part, to defer requests for membership from the EFTA countries. But, in practice, it has led to the adoption of parallel legislation by the EFTA countries to ensure continued preferential access to the EC. As this continues, the potential for trade diversion increases and could be realized if, for all intents and purposes, the EFTA countries achieve their goals of preferred access.

- Will the directives be produced in a transparent way or behind closed doors with maximum uncertainty? Uncertainty would have the same effect on outside firms as an increase in trade barriers, leading to forced investment in the Community on the part of those firms with sufficient resources. But much of the forced investment is likely to occur in industries like automobiles and semiconductors with existing worldwide excess capacity. Such investment diversion will only exacerbate the problem of excess capacity. And what about the smaller firms without the ability to invest in the EC? Those firms will certainly descend upon Washington looking for legislative solutions or unilateral action against the EC. Although they may be small, the complainers often get their way in Washington as Micron Inc. proved in precipitating the semiconductor agreement with Japan.

Needless to say, outside interests have much to monitor and to be concerned about. The external consequences of all these issues will not be known for some time, but the outside world can not wait until 1992 to see what the results will be because by then the Community's position will be set in concrete, with no room to maneuver.

Now is the time for other governments and firms to put pressure on the Community to open up its deliberations over its internal restructuring to comments and criticism and to make certain that outsiders are not discriminated against. If the EC is not constrained, the world risks willy nilly evolving into an economic order characterized by economic blocs. How benign these blocs could be would depend upon the strength of multilateral discipline. Greater multilateral discipline is on the table in the Uruguay Round, but if the round is not successfully concluded, the Community may not be constrained and what little multilateral discipline now exists in the world trading system may not be preserved. Absent multilateral pressure, the only country that can contain or constrain the EC is the United States. How should the United States respond?

2.2 U.S. Policy Responses

In order to keep Europe open, or indeed, to open it further, some would prefer to use the 1988 trade bill as a crowbar and to brandish retaliation but security and alliance concerns may take precedence. Extensive discussions with the allies are needed on a whole range of security issues including the future of NATO following the reunification of Germany, the reduction of conventional forces, and the Western response to reform in Eastern Europe. All of the unsettled alliance and defense issues, however, create a dilemma for U.S. trade policy officials because they may not be able to push too hard on the Community. Historically, U.S. commercial policy responses have been constrained by broader security issues and by the desire not to alienate allies.

Indeed, in May 1989, the Community was not named as an unfair trader under Section 301, in part, because President Bush was to attend a sensitive NATO meeting the following week. Apparently, the desire not to alienate allies lives on and for the time being the Bush administration is putting all of its eggs in the multilateral basket as far as the EC is concerned.

As a result, the Bush administration's credibility on trade is on the line. If the multilateral talks fail to produce significant agreements that satisfy domestic constituents and Congress, the demands for new unilateral initiatives could become overwhelming. After all, the Bush administration has demonstrated that section 301 can produce results. Those demands for unilateral action will certainly multiply if the EC is not constrained in its adoption of implementing directives, and, as a result, the directives discriminate against foreigners.

Compared to a multilateral solution with well-defined rules and sanctions, unilateral action under Section 301 is clearly inferior because it tends to politicize trade issues. It carries with it the risk of retaliation and counterretaliation. The alternative, however, may not be a multilateral solution but a bilateral or regional solution that would hasten the fragmentation of the trading system.

Several proposals for other bilateral trade agreements have come on the heels of the negotiation of the bilateral agreement with Canada, the United States' largest trading partner.[5] But bilateral free trade agreements are justified only in special cases. Israel, for political reasons, and Canada, for reasons of proximity and interdependence, are special cases. The European Community, in the development of its internal market, is also a special case on the latter score. Mexico is also a special case and the U.S. administration has announced its intention to begin negotiations in 1991. But after Mexico other countries would surely protest if the United States tried to negotiate additional bilateral agreements. Additional bilaterals would change the behavior of other countries. Can the United States say no to the other Latin American countries that will clamor for similar agreements? Furthermore, if other countries were to follow the U.S. lead by trying to negotiate through bilateral agreements offering mutually incompatible privileges, predictability would be destroyed for all countries. Such discriminatory bilateral agreements cannot combine to form a globally consistent and stable trading system.[6]

The arguments against a series of bilaterals are both political and economic. In terms of international politics, the essence of bilaterals is that you play favorites: and that creates foreign policy problems with those that are discriminated against. Inevitably, some countries will be left out. How will they be chosen and who will decide? In the United States, Congress will have to play a role. Thus, domestic political problems are created as well. Do members of Congress want to get involved in such micromanagement of trade and foreign policy initiatives? I doubt it.

The economic argument is that if the trading system should fragment as a result of a misguided bilateral strategy the United States would be unable to generate trade surpluses of up to $50 billion to service its trillion dollar foreign debt in the 1990s. Without an open multilateral trading system, that will be next to impossible to achieve.

Some legislators have proposed negotiating a bilateral accord with Japan because of the European Community's 1992 unification effort. The assumption is that the EC will discriminate against outside interests as it liberalizes internally. The EC may indeed try to do this, but isolating the Community would create more problems than it resolves. As a reaction, Community policymakers might turn toward Eastern Europe and the Soviet Union for markets and support.

Furthermore, a bilateral trade agreement with Japan would tie the hands of American trade negotiators. The launching of the Uruguay Round demonstrated the importance of coalition formation as a means for making progress.7 But coalitions shift from issue to issue. On market access to Japan, the United States might agree someday to join with the EC to gang up on Japan in a multilateral forum. But the United States and Japan may have to join together to ensure that the EC does not use its 1992 unification effort as a means to discriminate against outside interests. It is better to retain the flexibility to form different coalitions and to use unilateral retaliatory measures to prod the process, than to limit options by joining a bilateral with another major pillar of the trading system. And if other bilaterals are contemplated, it is not at all obvious which is the most appropriate partner, Japan or the EC. Each has been proposed by a different member of Congress[8].

Granted, new options are needed in this highly pluralistic world to bring more pressure on free riders and footdraggers. The preferred approach, however, should be a conditional most-favored-nation approach as was done with the Tokyo round codes (e.g., subsidies, government procurement) in which only those signatories to the code get the benefits from abiding by the additional discipline. Since the recalcitrant countries will vary from issue to issue, this approach allows for greater flexibility.[9] Such agreements, however, can be negotiated most easily in a multilateral forum. Multilateral negotiations are the best policy instrument available to influence the Community in the implementation of its 1992 directives because they are least likely to lead to confrontation and would help to minimize misunderstandings because more countries than the United States would be involved.

Many of the key issues in the 1992 effort and the Uruguay Round of multilateral trade negotiations are the same -- services, telecommunications, government procurement, and voluntary restraints. Can this coincidence be used advantageously by bringing international pressure to bear on EC internal decisions? Or, will the Uruguay Round be held hostage to the EC's restructuring -- crowded out because of limited time and resources, pushed into the background with internal EC directives taken first? With the internal rules of the game changing, creating uncertainty and new competition for EC firms, many EC firms would probably prefer to hold off liberalizing vis-a-vis the rest of the world. This is not to argue that the EC will raise new barriers but it may not be eager to make new commitments and to lower barriers. After all, signing on to substantial agreements in the multilateral talks would limit their flexibility in reaching internal agreements.

Seven rounds of multilateral trade negotiations have been conducted since the GATT was founded, and through them the member countries of GATT have been able to liberalize trade and integrate more fully with one another. The eighth round, the Uruguay Round of multilateral negotiations, began in September 1986. Progress in the negotiations is necessary to begin to restore confidence in the fairness and efficacy of the trading system. But these talks are the most ambitious undertaken since the GATT was founded. They are different and more difficult and could prove more disappointing than any that preceded them.[10]

To restore the credibility of multilateral negotiations as a way of solving problems, concrete results will be needed on subsidies, agriculture, services, investment, and intellectual property, or on some portion of the above. In order to obtain agreements in these areas, the United States will probably have to permit greater market access for textiles, steel, footwear, and apparel from developing countries, and it may be asked to revise its trade remedy laws -- for example, by curbing Section 301 actions. If a sufficiently large package of trade-liberalizing measures and new rules cutting across most of these issues cannot be developed, and if the ultimate package does not enjoy widespread support in the private sector, the administration will have a hard time winning congressional ratification.

If the Uruguay Round negotiations are resumed but further progress is limited, then some high priority U.S. objectives will not be accomplished, and influential domestic constituents are going to be disappointed. If agriculture -- the "Beirut" of trade negotiations -- continues to be the stumbling block because of EC intransigence, then the next U.S. farm bill will certainly include provisions for unilateral efforts to boost farm exports. If little progress is seen in services or intellectual property, key components of the coalition in favor of freer trade will be annoyed and may push for more limited bilateral and regional agreements or for aggressive unilateral action.[11]

2.3 Some Policy Recommendations

If the Brussels Ministerial meeting to "conclude" the Uruguay Round was the first example of economic coordination in the post-Cold War world, then a failing grade is in order. But this could be just an interim mid-term grade. An extension of the talks for two more years could prove to be beneficial. After all, why stop the multilateral process just when valuable momentum has been developed? Why take the risk of not having a viable multilateral option for resolving pressing trade disputes? Completion of the talks would also have left the EC free to complete its internal integration effort without the intense scrutiny of an ongoing multilateral negotiation. The key steps toward a successful conclusion will be a substantial offer from the EC on agriculture and an extension of expedited negotiating authority by the U.S. Congress.

In the United States the Constitution specifically empowers Congress to "regulate foreign commerce." The president's ability to negotiate credibly with other countries comes from the delegation of this negotiating authority by the Congress. Once a package is negotiated, it must be submitted to Congress for ratification. Under the "fast track" provisions of the 1988 trade bill, Congress agrees to consider any agreement reached within ninety days and no amendments are in order. These provisions required the negotiated package to be submitted to Congress by March 1, 1991, hence the emphasis on completing the round in December 1990 or shortly thereafter. Since the Brussels meeting broke up in disarray, conclusion of an agreement was not possible by March 1 so the Bush Administration asked for an extension of "fast track". As long as neither house of Congress votes a resolution of disapproval before May 31, 1991, the delegation of authority would continue until May 31, 1993.

This could be a blessing in disguise. These additional two years would provide sufficient time to negotiate substantial agreements, would provide a venue for continued multilateral scrutiny of the European Community's internal restructuring and would restrain aggressive unilateral and bilateral tendencies on the part of the United States. The two years could also be used to address the substantive proposals by Canada and Italy to establish a full-fledged world trade organization with stated authority comparable to the IMF and World Bank. The talks could also be used to clarify GATT provisions (Article XXIV) covering customs unions and free trade areas to minimize the distortions inherent in the emerging regional blocs.

However, if multilateral negotiations continue for another two years and some countries still continue to frustrate efforts to achieve a substantial multilateral accord on key issues, such as services and intellectual property, the major industrial countries should not agree to the minimum acceptable to the footdraggers. Instead the major industrial countries should opt for stronger agreements among a more limited number of countries. Such agreements -- achieved on a conditional most-favored-nation basis -- should be open-ended, including provisions for others to accede to the agreement if they are willing to accept its disciplines.

Even if the talks are successfully concluded and the round is ended, there will be increased pressure to sit down, possibly under the auspices of the Organization for Economic Cooperation and Development (OECD), to deal with the myriad government policies that now affect trade but are not governed by GATT rules. For example, just as national governments have had to devise antitrust regulations in response to the growth of national corporate power in the past, so the international system must devise antitrust regulations in response to the growth of global corporate economic power today. Similarly, there is a need to harmonize national standards, government procurement policies and public subsidies for research and development, which can distort trade. In particular, rules are needed for government-led research consortia such as Sematech, the U.S. computer chip manufacturing research facility, which champion high tech domestic industries.

The goal of such negotiations would not be to have mirror image legislation in each country but to bring laws and regulations closer together. As Sylvia Ostry, Canada's former chief multilateral trade negotiator, recently asked, "How much divergence in policy systems can an ever-more interdependent international economy sustain?"[12] Convergence in these policies within the OECD would reduce international friction, but if the OECD became the focus for further efforts to liberalize trade, that would surely revive North-South disagreements.[13] To avoid such an outcome, GATT should be turned into a forum for ongoing negotiations. After all, one of the major goals of the Uruguay Round was to integrate the developing countries more fully into the trading system.

3. Macroeconomic Coordination and the Coming Global Capital Shortage[14]

In May 1990 when President Bush called a weekend meeting of congressional leaders to propose a budget summit, he conveyed a sense of urgency about the budget not seen during his administration. Something had changed and his lips appeared to quiver. By late June, he abandoned his campaign pledge of no new taxes and said that tax revenue increases were needed to reduce the budget deficit. Projections of future U.S. budget deficits were almost $100 billion over previous estimates and his advisors convinced him that more trouble might lie over the horizon---not just because of a possible recession but because of unfolding events in Europe and Japan.

The advisors' reasoning was simple. German unification would dramatically expand internal demand in the united Germany and reduce the funds available for investment abroad. Plans to create a barrier-free internal market in Western Europe by 1992 are expected to more than double European business' demand for capital over the next decade. The investment-starved economies of Eastern Europe are likely to begin soaking up funds like a dry sponge in the near future. And, the Japanese were no longer investing money on net in the United States.

As with any scarce commodity, rising demand for money will drive up its cost. And, thanks to the relaxation of controls on international capital flows over the last decade that have created one global financial market, such action can reverberate around the world, driving up interest rates everywhere.

The capital shortage of the 1990s would be a shock to the world economy comparable to the oil embargoes of the 1970s and the Third World debt crisis of the 1980s. The only difference is, this time a principal casualty could be the United States because it has become too dependent upon foreign capital.

The unification of Western Europe and the introduction of capitalism into Eastern Europe have long been American goals and widely viewed as a net plus economically. But American public officials, who came of age in the Cold War when an economically vibrant Europe was needed to fend off communism, and investment bankers, who stand to benefit from European dynamism, have often given short shrift to the potential downside for the United States of macroeconomic developments in Europe. Similarly, U.S. trade officials that have for years pressured Japan to expand internal demand did not give sufficient consideration to the consequences of a drop-off in Japanese capital flows to the United States.

To keep the foreign capital coming, the United States will have to bid up interest rates to attract capital from overseas. And, in a world of higher interest rates, the United States, with the slowest economic growth and the highest inflation rate of the major industrial powers (except for the United Kingdom), will find its economic woes aggravated by having to pay more to balance its books.

As governments inexorably ratchet up interest rates in the future there will be growing pressure from the international business community that must operate in this uncertain environment for industrial nations to coordinate monetary and fiscal policies better to keep things from getting out of hand. When that happens, the United States will not necessarily dominate the process as it has in the past. The planned creation of a European Central Bank, with the power to negotiate for a single European economic and monetary union (EMU) fundamentally changes the power relationship between the United States and Europe on monetary issues. No longer will the United States be able to employ divide-and-conquer tactics to get its way with Europe. In the future, the United States will have less influence and will have to offer policy concessions of its own to get reciprocal concessions from other governments.

Apart from the budget summit, the Administration has been a passive observer of European and Japanese economic developments. How long that can continue remains to be seen. West Germany's increase of its interest rate in the spring of 1990 and then again in the fall of 1990, underscores the volatility of the current situation. The spring hike was quickly mimicked in Tokyo, helping precipitate the May collapse of the Tokyo stock market, as Japanese investors adjusted their portfolios from low return equities to higher yielding bonds. The continued decline of the Tokyo stock market in the summer and fall of 1990 exposed the weakness of Japanese banks and cut their lending to the rest of the world.

The United States barely dodged these ricocheting financial bullets. But luck may not hold. It won't be long before events in Europe and Japan leave their imprint on U.S. economic policies. Ultimately, international macroeconomic developments will place almost irresistible pressure on the United States to increase savings (reduce government dissavings) by raising taxes and/or cutting public spending. The October budget agreement, cutting the deficit by

$492 billion ($250?) over five years, is a start but that agreement rests upon optimistic assumptions.

Such initiatives are long overdue and should be welcomed. But the fact that they may be forced on the United States by events beyond American control is unlikely to sit well with most Americans. This psychological shock may be the most difficult and abiding consequence of European and Japanese retrenchment. It is yet another indication of America's declining dominance and a sign that American economic policies will have to begin to be reshaped accordingly.

3.1 Economic Shock Wave

The unification of Germany is generating the first economic shock wave to emanate from Europe. The costs of absorption are staggering. Each successive estimate is higher than the previous estimate. Although the East German economy was the strongest among the former Soviet bloc nations, it trails far behind its Western cousin. Productivity, once thought to be half Western levels, may be less than a third that in the West. As uncompetitive plants are forced to close, the German unemployment rate could soar into double digits for a 2-3 year transitional period.

To stem the exodus of East Germans, which is already causing friction in the West, Bonn must quickly turn around East Germany's problems. Initial estimates put the annual price tag for rebuilding the East at about $60 billion, roughly 100 billion D-Marks at the current exchange rate, but as more careful analysis of the state of the East German economy has been taken into account, the price tag has escalated. "To raise income levels of the 9 million [East German] workers to the point at which immigration might be choked off might involve spending around DM 150 billion per year on income support," noted a recent study by Barclays Bank.[15] "To put this in perspective, total federal expenditure this year is scheduled at DM 300 billion." Barclays' economists think that unemployment benefits might cost an additional DM 25 billion and new pensions obligations DM 50 billion annually. These three expenditures alone would more than double the initial estimates, with public infrastructure costs for new telephone lines, electrified railroads and pollution cleanup still to be added on.

The benefits of unification can finance some of these outlays. Anticipated faster growth, probably at least a full percentage point higher than the current 3.7 per cent figure, will generate more revenue. Subsidies to West Berlin and border areas can be cut, as can the defense budget.

But most of the cost can only be met through deficit financing. The 1989 West German federal deficit was at a fifteen year low of DM 19 billion. In 1990 it is expected to rise to at least DM 33.5 billion. As a portion of the German gross national product (GNP), it would only be about 1.5 per cent this year, which is still a far cry from the more than 6 per cent level experienced during the 1975 recession. But with the projected spending increases because of East Germany it could easily double or triple in the next few years, unless taxes are raised.

As a recent analysis by Shearson Lehman Hutton notes, "if the deficit just pushed back up to, say, 4 per cent, historical experience suggests that would put nearly 50 basis points on bond yields."[16]

3.2 Shifting Investment Patterns

Such interest rate moves are the stuff of headlines. But their impact could be dwarfed by the effect developments in Europe, East and West, are likely to have on global savings and investment patterns and the subsequent redirection of capital flows around the world.

The economies of Eastern Europe have foreign investors salivating. Double digit economic growth in East Germany is possible in the next few years. And the prospects for the rest of the region are only slightly less optimistic because of its skilled work force, large domestic market and proximity to the European Community. Anticipating a higher real rate of return money in the east than in the west, firms are already flocking in. The Japanese plan to build auto plants in Hungary and Poland. Some 140 West German companies are committed to 1,100 joint ventures in East Germany alone.

But before these industries can cash in on the expected bonanza, the piper must be paid. Barclays Bank estimates that to raise the East German capital investment per worker to West German levels, for example, will require approximately DM 1,000 billion ($5.8 billion).[17] And East German firms are probably the best prepared in the Soviet bloc to compete on a world level.

The impact on world financial markets of this diversion of capital depends on the rate of investment. Projecting capital needs is one thing, projecting business investment expansion is another. That depends upon the voluntary decisions of tens of thousands of individual enterprises. Moreover, if anticipated Eastern European growth rates materialize, these economies will rapidly begin to generate substantial funds for reinvestment, easing the demand for western capital.

But Eastern Europe is only one source of the increased demand for capital. Over the next decades, Western Europe's demand for investment is likely to have the more significant influence on world capital markets and on the future of the U.S. economy. DRI/McGraw-Hill estimates that fixed investment by business in Europe will grow an average of 8.3 per cent per year from 1990 through 1995. By the end of that period, companies' annual capital demand will be more than triple what it was in 1985.[18]

This investment will come from U.S. businesses expanding their European operations and American firms trying to gain a foothold in Europe to take advantage of the soon-to-be-unified market. U.S. direct investment in the European Community has already been growing by 15 per cent per year over the last four years. It will come from Asian investors: Japanese investment in the Community grew substantially last year. And, most important, it will come from European companies keeping their money at home. This increased demand for capital will make it much harder for the United States to attract the capital it needs to finance its trade and budget deficits. Indeed, in the first six months of 1990, foreign investment in the United States in all forms combined was down by 70 per cent while U.S. investment abroad rose by 17 per cent.

This is of concern to the United States because, contrary to popular misconceptions, the U.S. Treasury is more dependent on borrowing European capital to balance its books than on Japanese capital. Over the last two years $153 billion in net EC capital flowed into the United States as direct investment in plant and equipment, for the purchase of government notes, corporate bonds and stocks and as bank deposits. By comparison, Japan supplied the United States with only $104 billion in capital net over the same period.[19]

This dependency makes the United States particularly vulnerable to the drop-off in exports of German capital expected in the early 1990s. For years West Germany has run a mounting current account surplus. Unable to absorb all this capital at home, some went to the United States, but most of it went to Western Europe, where, in turn, it freed up French and British capital for investment in the United States.

But this flood of German capital may soon slow to a trickle and could reverse direction. Because of unification, more investment will be made at home in Germany and the German propensity to consume may rise because of higher spending levels by East Germans. In addition, higher interest rates and the promise of EC '92 will drive up the D-mark, leading to a decline in the German current account surplus. Last year's surplus of DM 99 billion could be eliminated within a few years.

Japan's current account surplus is also shrinking rapidly. It has tumbled from a peak of $87 billion in 1987 to $57 billion in 1989. In the first half of 1990, Japan's current account surplus was only $20.5 billion, for an annual rate of $41 billion. During the first half of 1990, Japanese institutions were net sellers of $8.9 billion of U.S. securities compared with net purchases of $17.4 billion in such securities in the second half of 1989. Furthermore, Japanese investors have switched toward direct investment rather than portfolio investment. Direct investment now comprises 70 per cent of Japanese investment, up from 14 per cent in 1987. The United States is finding it harder to attract Japanese capital given the developments in Europe and the collapse of the Tokyo stock market, together with the weakening of major banks in Japan.

The Germans and Japanese turning off their capital spigot does not mean the United States will be unable to balance its books. There is no scarcity of capital in the world, if the price is right. But it probably does mean higher interest rates for quite some time in order to attract that capital.

3.3 Emerging Monetary Union

The planned creation of a European economic and monetary union (EMU) also poses a challenge to traditional post-war U.S. leadership in global economic affairs. Most members of the Community already synchronize exchange rates among themselves. Starting July 1, 1990, EC members began formally coordinating macroeconomic policy and central bank decision making, under a plan devised by a special committee headed by EC president Jacques Delors. Even the United Kingdom agreed to enter the European Exchange Rate Mechanism in October 1990. Over the next few years economic coordination will intensify, currency fluctuations will narrow and groundwork will be laid for a European system of central banks. At some yet to be determined date in the future (1997?), the ECU (or a new currency with a different name) will become the single European currency and a European central bank, comparable in structure and powers to the American Federal Reserve System, will take over control of European monetary policy and exchange rate intervention.

The drive toward monetary union stems from actions taken in the narrower 1992 effort to create a unified European Community by eliminating internal barriers . With the abolition of capital controls agreed upon in June 1988 and phased in over 4 to 7 years, economic policymakers in the EC are faced with an inconsistent triple -- free movement of capital, fixed exchange rates and independent monetary policy. With free capital movements and fixed exchange rates in the European Monetary System, it is virtually impossible for national monetary authorities to conduct an independent monetary policy except in the very short run. They must constantly be aware of what other monetary authorities -- especially in the larger countries -- are doing. As a result, in 1988, the European Council called for an examination of the issues under Delors' chairmanship.

The Delors Report, published in 1989,[20] called for three stages in the movement toward economic and monetary union. The first stage which began in July 1990 calls for movement toward greater convergence of economic performance through the strengthening of policy coordination.

In the second stage, the basic organs and structure of EMU would be set up following approval of a new treaty to be negotiated at an intergovernmental conference beginning in December 1990. The new institutional framework would monitor and analyze macroeconomic developments and promote a process of common decisionmaking. National economic authorities would still retain their own policy instruments for regulating economic activity. If the institutional framework can be agreed upon, the intent is to begin the second stage in January 1994. The third stage would see the move to "irrevocably" locked exchange rates and the assumption of monetary policy competence by the new Community institutions.

The momentum towards EMU accelerated in mid-March 1990 with the agreement among European central bank authorities to adopt a "Eurofed", that is, a European central bank. The agreement envisions moving to a single European currency sometime in the second half of the decade. Under the proposal drafted by the Commission and national bank authorities, the twelve central bank heads of the EC member countries will serve as a council that would decide monetary policies for the Community as a whole. A smaller group of appointed directors will implement the council's decisions. To ensure that they are independent of the day-to-day pressures of national politics, the directors will be appointed for long terms, perhaps 8 to 14 years.

The "Eurofed" will establish a central banking system for the European Community with a structure somewhere between the Federal Reserve System and the Bundesbank. The new monetary authorities will enjoy autonomy but not as much as the Bundesbank. Just as the chairman of the Fed must appear before Congress, some accountability will be built in by requiring periodic testimony before the European Parliament and meetings with EC and national officials.

But as much as the agreement is a step forward, the politicians in member states still need to be heard from. Different countries have different preferences over the course of macroeconomic policy and different decisionmaking processes. Giving up the ability to conduct their own monetary policy is likely to be viewed by them as the ultimate sacrifice of sovereignty. There is also a question of the Bundesbank's willingness to push ahead on European monetary union at the same time it is struggling to move forward on German monetary union with all of its attendant difficulties, both politically and economically. The acrimony over the exchange rate chosen to convert the two currencies is just the beginning. The real effects on living standards and competitiveness will linger for years. Only when these problems have been sorted out will the Eurofed have the credibility it needs.

Oddly enough, the drive toward European monetary union may have been accelerated by the unification of Germany. Certainly German unification is putting strains on the European Monetary System, but the prospect of a united Germany has caused France and Italy to exert pressure to speed up EMU in order to anchor Germany within the European Community. Politics is driving the EMU process just as politics drove German monetary unification. And with the increased investment spending in East Germany and the higher propensity to consume by residents of East Germany, total German absorption will rise, thereby reducing if not eliminating its current account surplus. Without the persistent imbalances of recent years, macroeconomic convergence in the EC could be accomplished sooner than before. Nonetheless, the Bundesbank will play a critical role in determining how fast EMU moves forward.

Another important development in March was the downplaying of the need to have "binding restraints on budgetary policy" as called for in the Delors Report. Rather than central restraints on budgetary policy, the agreement left the discipline to the marketplace. Although politicians running for reelection will often be tempted to increase government expenditures and/or reduce taxes to maximize their chances for reelection, they will be held accountable by financial markets. The central bank authorities pledged not to print money to cover any budgetary shortfall and promised no guarantee of a bailout for countries that get into financial difficulties. Like the states of Massachusetts and New York, countries with inadequate fiscal discipline might suddenly find their credit rating lowered and the costs of borrowing raised. Nonetheless, some oversight and scrutiny of national fiscal policies will be necessary because the market does not always operate smoothly or incrementally but instead can signal a change in confidence suddenly and dramatically. Since national governments will retain substantial power to tax and spend compared to Brussels, this will be a source of constant concern. How well the process will work, will not be known until one or two countries are subjected to the harshness of financial market discipline.

The speeded-up timetable to converge economic performance and to strengthen central bank coordination means Washington will have to deal with EMU's consequences sooner rather than later. Because of Germany's economic preeminence in Europe and the leadership role the D-mark and the Bundesbank already play and because the proposed Eurofed structure mimics that of the Bundesbank, it is likely that the Eurofed will be led by Germans and dominated by German economic philosophy.

Both the Delors committee and the EC Commission agree that the Eurofed will be "explicitly committed to price stability," an anti-inflationary bias now shared by governments of all major industrial nations, but most identified with the Bundesbank. Current exchange rate coordination has already led to a marked convergence of inflation rates among most European economies. (France now has a lower inflation rate than Germany!) EMU will only amplify this process.

To date, European inflation fighting has had little influence on American economic policy. But the United States faces the prospect of a global economy in which both a united Europe and Japan are more successful than Washington at controlling inflation. In the past, Washington could ignore such international pressure because foreign trade accounts for only a small portion of the U.S. economy. But in the future, with the growing importance of international capital movements and the expansion of world trade, it may not be so easy to remain aloof.

It is still too soon to be certain of the consequences of creation of a Eurofed. It is not clear that a Eurofed will insure a rock solid fight against inflation at any cost. There will still be arguments, just as there are in the U.S. FED open market committee, on how to strike the balance. Clearly, the balance will not be struck always on the side of price stability. Indeed, one of the reasons cited by France and Italy to push forward faster on EMU is to give them more of a say on monetary policy.

The Eurofed's creation will mean that a lot of the world's money supply will be coming under a single, new manager. Until now the United States has led the effort to define the accounting and fiduciary rules for the new global financial system. But, in a Eurofed the central banking and regulatory functions will go together. If Europe is working together on future international financial negotiations, they will have a much greater influence in terms of regulating the international banking system. Who knows, the reform of banking regulations on a Community-wide basis might finally stimulate Congress to pass a bill reforming U.S. financial regulation including Glass-Steagall.

Finally, the EMU is likely to transform the international economic coordination process industrial nations have fitfully been pursuing over the last decade and a half. The emergence of an industrial world Big Three---Europe, Japan and the United States---places a higher premium on coordination. At the technical level, creation of the Eurofed, with one currency and one bureaucracy, will presumably make that coordination easier---transaction costs will be reduced. But, in fact, coordination could at times become all the more difficult. Greater symmetry could generate more instability if it creates more of an incentive to manipulate exchange rates for domestic reasons.

If the European central bank has a clearly stated mandate in its charter of price stability above all else, it could hinder its ability to ease monetary policy when conditions might require that for international coordination. Moreover, so much depends on the personal chemistry of the decision makers. U.S. officials have long found Bundesbank personnel much more difficult to get along with than the leaders of the Bank of Japan. An emboldened Bundesbank leadership, newly confident in its leadership of the Eurofed may be even less likely to cooperate with Washington.

And, if the Eurofed is truly independent of the political process, like the Bundesbank and the FED, then it may be even harder for governments to insure that the international economic agreements they reach are put into practice. Because Brussels lacks substantial power to tax and spend, fiscal outcomes in the member states will condition the EMU monetary policy. But central monetary policy under EMU will put greater pressure nationally on fiscal policy to achieve domestic objectives. A situation like in the United States in the early 1980s---tight monetary policy and loose fiscal policy---is entirely possible with its adverse effects on interest and exchange rates. This means that international coordination of fiscal policy becomes more important but also more difficult. The head of EMU's central bank might be able to agree with his counterparts in the United States and Japan, but who (among the twelve) will serve as the EC's finance minister to negotiate on fiscal policy? The United States and Japan could find negotiating macroeconomic policy with the EC as difficult as negotiating trade policy where the Community position is almost immutable after it has negotiated internally.

Despite the progress on European monetary union in 1990, several potential problems still loom. The Delors Report assures that the European central bank will be "embedded in the democratic process." But how? What is the nature of the democratic compromise? Are periodic appearances before the European Parliament or consultations with EC and national economic officials, enough to satisfy demands for accountability? How do the different central bankers agree upon the rate of growth of the Community's money supply? What structure and instruments of monetary policy will be adopted? Who are eligible market participants and what is the nature of the regulatory framework? If national currencies are retained, how can "irrevocably" locked exchange rates be assured? How do the central bank authorities arrive at a common position for international coordination of macroeconomic policy? If exchange rate intervention is needed, who intervenes and on what basis? The details remain to be worked out.

The fiscal arrangements in the European Community could prove to be a problem in moving forward on EMU. The lack of sufficient power by Brussels to tax and spend could cause difficulties in gaining the assent of the poorer countries for EMU. By sacrificing the ability to change their exchange rate, countries are giving up a policy instrument that could be used to address declining economic activity and unemployment. The poorer countries are now lobbying for significant compensation -- in the form of structural adjustment funds -- for going along. As integration proceeds, industrial restructuring will inevitably cause layoffs and plant shutdowns. Lagging regions will complain to national parliaments. Poorer countries will complain to the EC. The relative lack of labor mobility contributes to regional imbalances. Unlike the United States, the European Community's labor force is not very mobile. Europeans tend to be well-rooted. People don't often move north and south in Belgium much less move from Belgium to Portugal. Furthermore, the EC member countries do not have the same cushion available to U.S. states during economic decline because of the lack of a strong federal role. When economic demand declines by $1 in Texas, Texas income only declines by $.60 because of smaller federal taxes and higher unemployment insurance expenditures. What will it take to buy off the poorer countries?

The answers to these questions are of grave importance. If the Eurofed is not accountable to political authority, tensions could arise in Europe that would trigger instability in world financial markets and higher interest rates. A Eurofed judged too subservient to politicians would lack credibility in the marketplace. Similarly, the Eurofed's mode of operations will be graded by the financial markets. If its procedures are cumbersome and deemed ineffective, the actions of this big elephant on the world's economic stage will cause big problems for the rest of the world.

The next big step will be the intergovernmental conference which began in December 1990. What is unknown is whether the intergovernmental conference will go for a "small treaty" merely to implement the institutional structure of EMU or a big treaty to try to tackle the "democratic deficit" of the Community, including enhanced powers for the Parliament to provide greater checks and balances over the unelected European Commission. A push for a bigger treaty could bog down progress over EMU.

Even if the European Commission and some national authorities should wish to go further, faster on monetary union, it is highly probable that not all countries will go along. Under Prime Minister Margaret Thatcher, the United Kingdom was the odd island out although the new PM, John Major, seems to be more flexible. The Southern countries -- Greece, Portugal, and possibly Spain -- might have a difficult time accepting the central discipline of monetary union and might prefer to retain the option of adjusting the exchange rate. If so, a two-tier or two-speed Community may result.

But whatever transpires, the question of EMU is no longer if, but how and when.

3.4 Ebbing Dollar Influence

As the new European currency comes into its own it will challenge the dollar's role as the world's key currency. The dollar has long been the medium of exchange all over the world. But more and more trade and assets are yen and D-mark denominated. And in a symbolic gesture, at least some of the assets of the new European bank will be denominated in ECU, the first truly multilateral institution to make this move. The use of other currencies to denominate transactions could accelerate if the dollar were to display continuing weakness. The evolution of a European currency block is now imaginable and with it U.S. leverage as the key currency country may also ebb.

EMU means the United States will have less influence through the market. In the past, the United States could rely on currency market forces to induce allies to change their economic policies in ways that the United States danted. For example, in the Reagan Administration then Treasury Secretary James A. Baker III talked down the value of the dollar to force Germany and Japan to begin expansionary domestic economic policies. This influence will not be available to the United States after monetary union in Europe. The arm-twisting effects of dollar depreciation will be diffused over a broader economy and will therefore be less effective. Thus, EMU fundamentally changes the power relationship between the United States and Europe on monetary issues. Indeed, this may have been one of the primary driving forces behind EMU. A united Europe through EMU would have greater negotiating leverage and would increase European confidence perhaps as a self-fulfilling prophesy.[21] The EC could then trade off macroeconomic changes for other objectives on trade or security issues.

The full ramifications for the United States of these macroeconomic developments in Europe have only begun to come into focus. But the need for eventual action already seems clear. It would be short-sighted if the United States did not realize that the growing global demand for investment will increase competition for savings. Now is the time for the United States to reduce its reliance on external savings. That means cutting the federal budget deficit even further.

But cutting the U.S. deficit is not the only necessary consequence of developments in Europe. The United States should also contemplate taking some initiatives internationally about how the world economy should be organized, in the wake of German unification, Western European unification and Eastern European liberation. Greater symmetry among the major countries means that the need for and benefits from closer economic coordination have swelled. The only question is will the coordination be led by the United States. Target zones for exchange rates may still be out of the question but the adoption of objective indicators to guide macroeconomic coordination could be the next step together with new procedures to ensure following and monitoring of Economic Summit agreements.[22] Only such an initiative now can protect the United States while it still has some clout, before Europe feels its weight and the U.S. economic role has declined even further.

4. Conclusion and Policy Recommendations

The policy recommendations are straightforward. They are: (1) Take and implement whatever modest result is available from the Uruguay Round but continue negotiations to establish a full-fledged world trade organization. (2) Take steps to increase global savings and reduce dissavings, that is the U.S. budget deficit. (3) Reinvigorate the process of macroeconomic coordination by establishing objective indicators and institutional follow-up for Economic Summit agreements. (4) Ensure more face-to-face contact among high-level officials including heads of state concerned with economic policy. If these steps are taken, the rivalry will be reduced and more emphasis can be placed on pursuing common interests.

Endnotes

1 See C. MICHAEL AHO (1990), Critical Issues: U.S. Trade Policy at a Critical Juncture, New York: Council on Foreign Relations, No. 3, for an examination of unilateral, bilateral and multilateral trade initiatives by the United States. Significant portions of this paper are derived from the aforementioned.

2 Financial Times, March 24, 1990, p. 3. The Italian Trade Minister, Renato Ruggiero, was speaking at a conference sponsored by the Confederation of British Industry and the Royal Institute of International Affairs in London. He went on to accuse the European Commission and fellow ministers of neglect and a lack of leadership on the multilateral talks.

3 Much of this is drawn from a testimony "On Europe 1992" before the House Foreign Affairs Committee, February 23, 1989. For an excellent overview of U.S. interests in the 1992 integration effort as well as sectoral analyses, see GARY C. HUFBAUER, ed. (1990), Europe 1992: An American Perspective, Washington, DC: The Brookings Institution.

4 The wide range for estimates for growth in national income depends upon the assumptions made for investment spending. For a review of the estimates, see RICHARD BALDWIN (Fall 1989), The Growth Effects of 1992, Economic Policy.

5 See RUDIGER DORNBUSCH (September 12, 1989), Is there a Case for Aggressive Bilateralism and How Best to Practice It?, Brookings Trade Conference, for an advocacy of bilateral trade agreements but without an explicit recognition of many of the drawbacks noted below. For a proposal for a U.S.-Japan bilateral, see SENATOR MAX BAUCUS (1989), A New Trade Strategy: The Case for Bilateral Agreements, Cornell International Law Journal, 1.

6 For an extended analysis see C. MICHAEL AHO (1989), More Bilateral Pacts Would Be a Blunder: What the New President Should Do, Cornell International Law Journal, 1, and JEFFREY J. SCHOTT (1989), More Free Trade Areas?, Washington, D.C.: Institute for International Economics.

7 See C. MICHAEL AHO (Winter 1987), The Uruguay Round: Will It Revitalize the Trading System?, The Fletcher Forum, Vol. II, No. 1.

8 In addition to Senator Baucus' proposal for a bilateral with Japan, Representative Richard Gephardt had proposed a bilateral with the European Community. Address by REPRESENTATIVE RICHARD GEPHARDT (October 12, 1988), United State Trade Policy for the 1990s, George Washington University Law Society. For a discussion of tactical problems of a bilateral with Japan, see AHO (1989), More Bilateral Pacts Would be a Blunder.

9 See C. MICHAEL AHO and SYLVIA OSTRY (1990), Regional Trading Blocs: Pragmatic or Problematic Policy?, in: William E. Brock and Robert D. Hormats, eds., The Global Economy: America's Role in the Decade Ahead, New York: W.W. Norton & Co.

10 See C. MICHEAL AHO and JONATHAN ARONSON (1987), Trade Talks: America Better Listen!, New York: Council on Foreign Relations, for a more complete treatment.

11 The President's chief advisory committee, the Advisory Committee for Trade Policy and Negotiations, chaired by James Robinson III, the chief executive officer of American Express, has already voiced its dissatisfaction and impatience by calling for a "results-oriented" trade policy vis-a-vis Japan in its report to U.S. Trade Representative Carla Hills on February 10, 1989.

[12] See SYLVIA OSTRY (1990), Governments and Corporations in a Shrinking World: Trade and Innovation Policies in the United States, Europe & Japan, New York: Council on Foreign Relations Press, p. 89.

[13] See GARY C. HUFBAUER (Winter 1990), Beyond GATT, Foreign Policy, for a proposal for an OECD free trade area.

[14] Much of this section is derived from my testimony before the Joint Economic Committee, June 21, 1990 and from a draft chapter from a forthcoming book on the European Challenge by myself and Bruce Stokes. See also AHO and STOKES (1990/91) The Year the World Economy Turned, Foreign Affairs, Vol. 70, No. 1.

[15] German Unification: Issues and Answers (Spring 1990), Barclays Bank PLC, Economic Department.

[16] International Economic Monitor (Spring 1990), Shearson Lehman Hutton.

[17] Barclays Bank, op cit.

[18] DRI/McGraw-Hill, personal interview with economist David Blond.

[19] U.S. Treasury Bulletin (1990). For an analysis of U.S. dependence on foreign capital, see C. MICHAEL AHO and MARC LEVINSON (1988), After Reagan: Confronting the Changed World Economy, New York: Council on Foreign Relations.

[20] J. DELORS (1989), Report on Economic and Monetary Union in the European Community, European Community.

[21] GEORGE ALOGOSKOUFIS and RICHARD PORTES (June 1990), International Costs and Benefits of EMU, Centre for Economic Policy Research, Discussion Paper Series, No. 424, London.

[22] For a discussion of objective indicators and target zones, see JOHN WILLIAMSON and MARCUS MILLER (1987), Targets and Indicators: A Blueprint for the Intended Coordination of Economic Policy, Washington D.C.: Institute for International Economics.

COMMENTS ON: GLOBAL ECONOMIC RIVALRY: NEW PERSPECTIVES ON GERMANY (THE EC), JAPAN, AND THE UNITED STATES

Gary R. Saxonhouse

Michael Aho provides a compelling projection of the international setting within which European development will proceed in the 1990's. He foresees a regionally pre-occupied Europe changing the rules of the international economic system to such an extent that American trade relations with it, and not with Japan, will dominate the headlines in the 1990's. While trade relations with Europe deteriorate, America will find it increasingly difficult to meet its savings deficit with European finance. In the capital-shortage 1990's, Western European savings will increasingly be used to finance the rebuilding of Eastern Europe.

However intriguing Aho's analysis may be, I am not fully persuaded that the 1990's will be quite as different from the 1980's as he imagines. For example, consider the question of relative tension in U.S.-Japanese economic relations and U.S.-European economic relations. If the height of foreign barriers against U.S. goods and services is the prime determinant of U.S. trade policy, and if Europe is really becoming substantially more protectionist, it might be possible to agree with Aho's projection. It is by no means clear, however, that either of these premises is correct.

It is doubtful that it is simply the degree of Japanese discrimination against American products that has made U.S. trade policy vis-a-vis Japan so aggressive in the 1980's. The actual degree of this discrimination remains a matter of hot debate. After all, Japan has very low tariffs and few quotas against industrial products, and today Japanese imports from the U.S. as a share of Japanese GNP are larger than U.S. imports from Japan as a share of U.S. GNP.

What Japan does continue to maintain, however, is a substantial surplus in its bilateral current account with the United States. While declining by over 35% in the past three years, Japan still has a $35 billion surplus in its current transactions with the United States. The substantial Japanese surplus with the United States makes it particularly vulnerable to pressure from the United States. In any confrontation there are more Japanese hostages than American hostages. Japan needs the U.S. market more than the U.S. needs the Japanese market.

This continuing leverage over Japan shapes the thrust of U.S. trade policy. There is a return to resources committed to U.S.-Japanese trade relations which seems unlikely to decline in the coming decade. With Japan uniquely poorly endowed with natural resources, it is likely to continue to run surpluses with the other advanced industrialized economies that are its trading partners. Continuing Japanese structural transformation will yield yet new industries in the United States which will feel the pressure of trans-Pacific competition. And for almost any foreseeable liberalization of barriers at the Japanese border and for almost any foreseeable harmonization of Japanese domestic institutions, there will still remain distinctive features of the Japanese economy that aggrieved American industries will find highly objectionable.

While a new international economic regime emanating from the European Community may trigger grave concern in the United States, none of the contemplated changes in the European Community *modus operandi* are even remotely capable of generating the kinds of structural imbalances in United States - European trade that have characterized U.S.-Japanese trade. In the absence of such imbalances, there is little profit in headline-generating, high profile campaign against European protection. Countermeasures may abound but they are likely to be highly discrete by comparison with the lectures to which the Japanese are regularly subjected.

It is important not to confuse the 1990's with the 1930's. The drive towards economic unification of Europe by 1992 will certainly provide more of a regional focus for the international economic system than had hitherto been the case. This is not the same, however, as the international system breaking into economic blocs. The pre-conditions for economic blocs in the 1930's were high tariffs and sharply declining world trade. The 1990's will not resemble the 1930's on either count. In this liberal environment, if the European Community members further lower barriers among themselves, it is hard to see that a large amount of trade diversion will result. As Aho notes, many of the key issues of the Europe 1992 effort and the Uruguay Round are the same. Perhaps progress in the Uruguay Round has been held hostage to EC restructuring. It is also possible, however, that ultimately more progress is being made on issues such as services, telecommunications, and government procurement because the compromises made by the Europeans in hammering out the internal EC 1992 directives will ultimately create the basis for far-reaching global agreements.

In commenting on Aho's analysis, I have discussed the future course of U.S.-European economic relations and U.S.-Japanese economic relations entirely in terms of trade policy. Does the shape of the future course of U.S. foreign economic relations change when the capital shortage of the 1990's is considered? Will Japan's and the EC's creditor statutes with respect to the U.S. give them new influence on U.S. economic policy making? This is doubtful. By comparison with markets for goods and services, financial markets are near perfect. The sources of Japanese and European finance are many and diverse. It is hard to imagine these large groups acting effectively in concert to influence U.S. policy. The scope of international financial markets is such that resources withheld from U.S. markets and diverted elsewhere are likely to be arbitraged back to the United States before very long. Restraining participation in a U.S. Treasury Bill auction is a very ineffective tactic by comparison with restraining imports of Japanese automobiles. The high costs of arbitrage in most manufactured goods markets prevent this.

More generally, at this point I should also venture a bit of cautious skepticism about the likelihood of a global shortage of capital in the 1990's. Aho's projection rests on the assumption that the U.S. budget agreement of last Fall will have little bite, that Japan will cease to be a major capital exporter and that Eastern Europe will realize its potential demand for capital and become a major capital importer. Each of these assumptions is debatable and the probability that they are correct is not very high at all. Small wonder, then, that financial markets give little indication that a global capital shortage is widely anticipated.

EC INTEGRATION AND ECONOMIC REFORMS IN CMEA COUNTRIES: A UNITED GERMANY AS A BRIDGE BETWEEN EAST AND WEST?

Paul J.J. Welfens

1. Introduction

The German unification that took place economically on July 1, 1990 and politically a few months later on October 3 creates a new Germany in the center of Europe. Integrating the former GDR with its 16.4 million inhabitants into the Federal Republic of Germany means not only a 26.7 % increase in its population, but also the movement of the EC border by some 200 miles eastwards - the (former) CMEA thereby losing a member country and the Federal Republic of Germany becoming the immediate neighbor of Poland. Germany faces the challenge of organizing the systemic transition to a market economy in the territory of the former GDR with its labor force of 8.5 million, about a quarter of them working in one of 8000 state enterprises grouped under the last Communist government in a state holding company, the "Treuhandanstalt".

The collapse of the GDR which was supposed to be the economically most advanced country of the socialist CMEA group revealed not only the problems of a socialist system; it now raises the unique problem of a systemic transformation - similar to the transition faced by the whole Council of Mutual Economic Assistance which disbanded in January 1991. After Ludwig Erhard led the West German economy in 1948/49 from a state-administered economy (with private property) on the way to prosperity and growth in a free enterprise system the question arises whether East Germany can now also hope for an economic miracle: possibly by using West German financial support, mobilizing entrepreneurial spirits and making best use of the now free access to EC markets and the inherited trade links to the former central planning economies (CPEs).

With nearly 2/3 of the exports of the GDR going to CMEA countries, East Germany had considerable trade links to Eastern Europe and the USSR upon which a united Germany could draw. With a much higher national income and a 4 percent share of CMEA exports in 1990 the FRG shows somewhat weaker trade links in absolute terms. Credit financing of most CMEA countries by German banks and government (DM 50 bill. of net claims) provide together with foreign direct investment projects - so far mostly joint ventures - various financial links to East European countries and the USSR with which new treaties for cooperation have been signed or are under negotiation. Finally, there is an invisible East-West link consisting of common environmental problems and the role of transborder pollution. Since

Eastern Europe and the USSR face tremendous environmental challenges in a period of increasing environmental public awareness, the FRG could become a welcome partner in environmental policy and in the attempt to reduce the high energy intensity of GNP in the CMEA.

All CMEA countries have embarked upon radical market-oriented reforms which include opening the economy to the West, achieving currency convertibility, preparing privatization of industry, organizing capital markets and joining or considering membership in the IMF, the GATT and other international organizations. Except for Rumania and Czechoslovakia all CMEA countries face high foreign indebtedness - most of which was accumulated under Communist governments. The foreign debt and the debt service, respectively, make high export proceeds necessary which are also required to achieve modernization of industry by rising imports of goods, services and capital.

The politico-economic collapse of the GDR after the fall of the Berlin Wall in November 1989 raises new challenges and offers new opportunities in central Europe. This is important because the Federal Republic of Germany plays a vital role in the EC in the present transition phase to a single market (*Cecchini, 1988*) and in developing the Economic and Monetary Union (EMU). With the EC 1992 project well under way and market-oriented reform steps taken in all the countries of the CMEA, a united Germany - arising from merging a strong West German and a formerly socialist, weak East German economy - means that a country of some 80 million inhabitants has been established with a huge unsatisfied consumer and investment demand in its Eastern part. The medium-term impacts mainly concern systemic transformation problems, prospects of high real interest rates worldwide and the satisfaction of a structural demand overhang. As Germany is a big open economy on the one hand, and, on the other hand, can generate considerable demonstration effects, there are various international effects to be expected. The long term impact of unification concerns the role of an enlarged Federal Republic of Germany which is the EC's leading economy in terms of income, trade and - together with the U.K. and the Netherlands - outward foreign direct investment (FDI). Moreover, Germany is a G-7 nation and an important member in international organizations whose role is increasing with the rising number of members from the CMEA group.

For the OECD countries the Federal Republic of Germany has been a valuable partner with five major traits: (1) it has been a stable and prosperous ally for Western countries and has played a leading role in the G-7 meetings; (2) postwar (West)Germany has been a defender of free trade and is the EC's biggest trading power; (3) it is a major source and host country of FDI as well as a technologically leading country; (4) Germany was an early advocate of detente as well as economic reforms in the CMEA countries. (5) together with France, the

Federal Republic of Germany has been the driving force of integration in the EC which represents a new way for nations and their respective business communities, institutions and people to cooperate and compete. This is a rare kind of international federalism and economic integration at the same time.

Regarding German unification much is at stake for the international community, where the economic and geopolitical position of Germany implies a particular interest of both the EC countries and the reforming CPEs. The U.S. and Japan, both strongly represented with trade flows and foreign direct investment in the EC and in Germany in particular, will contribute to the developments in the new Germany that emerged from a politico-economic rush to unification. In the context of German unity Europe faces higher real interest rates associated with rising and high German public deficits, but this growth-impairing effect of German unity could be offset by export growth in the EC and Eastern Europe which will benefit from rising German imports as a result of pent-up demand in GDR households and required modernization of the East German capital stock.

After a description of the German unification process and its major problems for which structural adjustments and investment are required on an enormous scale, we address the potential German bridging functions and analyze the effects of rising deficits and changing private household's savings in an international context (section 2). We then address the question to which extent German unification stimulates economic growth and politico-economic cooperation in the EC on the one hand, and, on the other hand how German unity will affect the EC's trade policy stance - particularly vis-à-vis Eastern Europe (section 3). If a united Germany is not in itself an ideal bridge between Western and Eastern Europe, German unification induced changes in the EC might indirectly reinforce Germany's bridging function, where German attitudes towards EC widening - i.e. enlarging the EC - are of critical importance for the CPEs; the latter might also benefit from the East German systemic transformation experiences and the transformation itself (section 4). Finally, we briefly raise some global economic policy issues that are related to German unification (section 5).

2. German Unification from a European Perspective

Having at first envisaged a gradual process of German-German unification the government of the Federal Republic of Germany - faced with a flood of immigrants from the GDR - offered in February 1990 monetary unification on the basis of the DM as the exclusive legal tender for both Germanies. In summer 1990 the USSR accepted Germany's integration into NATO and the withdrawal of Soviet troops from East Germany by 1994. What had begun as an effort for

German-German economic union had unfolded into a full political unification within less than a year after the fall of the Berlin Wall.

2.1 The Path to Unification

Setting aside his gradual merger approach envisaged in a 10-point plan proposed in November 1989, the Federal Chancellor offered German-German monetary union in February 1990 in the expectation of thereby stopping the westward migration of East Germans. The mass emigration had not only created disruptions of production in the GDR, but had added together with an influx of ethnic Germans from Eastern Europe to pressure on the FRG's generous welfare system and the housing market. 350,000 ethnic Germans from Eastern Europe plus another 350,000 immigrants (1989) caused severe problems in West Germany.

The initial policy approach of the FRG was simple: With the DM as a stable convertible currency at hand, the East German population would in principle gain access to all Western goods, so that the incentive for westward migration would reduce. The currency unification of July 1, established by the first German-German State Treaty on Monetary, Economic and Social Union (*Deutsche Bundesbank, 1990a*), accelerated the drive for a fast political merger and was seen by some observers as a precedent for a fast EC monetary integration process.

With more and more people in the GDR using the opportunity to travel to the capitalist West-Berlin (located in the midst of the GDR) and to the FRG after the fall of the Berlin Wall, the slogan of the demonstrations in East-Berlin, Leipzig, Dresden and elsewhere changed from "We are the people" to "We are one people". While the first slogan represented the desire for internal reforms and the dissatisfaction with a socialist government that claimed to have established the first socialist German republic, the second slogan represented the wish to end the existence of the socialist East Germany as a country and to integrate its territory into the market-based pluralistic system of West Germany. Indeed, the first free elections in the GDR in March 1990 brought a clear majority for the "bourgeois parties" which formed a grand coalition and resorted to a rapid political German-German merger as a means to avoid a total collapse of the East German economy. As the Communist party and power system plunged into open crisis and dissolved in early 1990, the state-run economy no longer followed an accepted state plan that would coordinate production activities nor could the labor force be expected any longer to work for slogans, party favors or monetary income paid in a non-convertible currency.

The introduction of the DM at an average conversion ratio of 1.8 M : 1 DM improved the working morale, but it accelerated liquidity problems in industry which had to pay high market interest rates for the first time while facing the relative price shock of an integration into the social market economy of the FRG. East German consumers increasingly turned to West German goods and services, so that East German firms suddenly fully felt the competitive pressure of West Germany's and the other EC countries' enterprises which offered a richer variety of qualitatively superior products.

Firms in East Germany that had been used to soft budget constraints, easy market conditions in the form of monopolistic positions plus structural excess demand (as a consequence of low state-administered prices) and cheap credits all of a sudden faced a new environment: an economy with non-rationing, functional competition and market interest rates on loans of three times the former 3 percent. The latter implied in view of a 2:1 conversion rate for firms' liabilities that the financing burden had increased much, while the sales prospects had sharply weakened. If one additionally takes into account that price subsidies reaching 18.5 percent of public expenditures and national income, respectively, in 1989 are to be rapidly phased out,[2] it is clear that German unification implied a coincidence of massive supply and demand shocks for East Germany where production has to adjust to relative world market prices and global competition. In the quest for international capital East Germany is at a disadvantage vis-a-vis other EC regions where wage pressure is much more moderate and labor productivity growth considerable (e.g. Spain, Portugal). Attracting capital to East Germany therefore requires special tax incentives and massive public investment which imply sustaining high public deficits in Germany.[3]

The GDR's switch from CMEA membership to EC membership brought not only unrestricted access to West European markets, but it also fully exposed the industry to EC competition, already sharpened by the EC 1992 project; moreover, the supply-side pressure was even increased from EFTA with which the EC has a free trade agreement for industrial goods. Finally, the introduction of the DM posed major problems for the GDR's traditional main trading partners in the CMEA. The countries in Eastern Europe and the USSR which accounted each for about 1/3 of East German exports reduced their orders rapidly.[4] Facing falling internal and external demand, rising factor costs and production facilities that were outdated in comparison with Western firms, impending bankruptcy of firms and unemployment became serious problems. After the fall of the wall the GDR experienced negative supply and demand shocks at the same time.

High investment flows are required for adjustment but were not recorded until late 1990. Only after October 3 when the new legal framework was established in the former GDR - in essence, that of West Germany - and after the first all-German election of December 2 did prospects for profitable investments improve. However, property rights uncertainties and effective contractual constraints or legal obligations connected with ownership impaired the prospects to privatize East German industry. Membership in the EC implies another supply shock for industry because the high technical and ecological standards to be met by East Germany by end-1995 further accelerate the obsolescence of know-how and capital. Facing short adjustment periods there is therefore the risk that the area that was formerly the GDR would become the Mezzogiorno of a united Germany - a continuous economic rift which could divide the country and lead to social unrest and political instability.

2.2 The Economic West-East Divide in the Unified Germany

The 16.4 million people of East Germany, which is less densely populated than West Germany, have a monthly income which is only about 1/3 of that in West Germany. The East German gross national product thus represented about 10 percent of that in West Germany in 1990 (*see Tab. 1*). Private households in the GDR had minimal access to modern communication and less than 10 percent of private households enjoyed the amenity of a telephone. There is less dwelling space available in the GDR and qualitatively it is inferior to West German housing - one striking and explainable paradox of the socialist GDR. In East Germany monetary wealth per capita amounted to about 19 percent of West Germany's levels, with the discrepancy being much greater if non-monetary assets (consumer durables and real estate) are included.

The structure of East German industry in 1988 was close to that of West Germany in the mid-1960s. While a clear majority of the West German labor force is active in the services industry today, the East German economic structure is still dominated by agriculture and manufacturing industry: 11 percent of the labor force were employed in agriculture and 47 percent in the socialist industry sector in which small and medium sized enterprises (with less than 500 employees) do not play a significant role. This is much in contrast to West Germany which owes much to small and medium sized enterprises: in terms of adjustment flexibility, employment growth and innovativeness.

The path to a social market economy will transitorily raise unemployment rates significantly in East Germany. The East German manufacturing sector is not only oversized in comparison to the West German market economy, but it is also much less productive.

Part of this inefficiency is due to the capital stock which is much older than in West Germany where only about 5 percent of the capital stock is more than 20 years old compared to 21 percent in East Germany. Not only by age but also by quality standards the East German capital stock is largely outdated. This holds even more so by the assortment of goods produced

Table 1: Key Indicators for West and East Germany in 1989
currency units M for the GDR, DM for West Germany

Population, income, standard of living indicators and wealth	West Germany	GDR (relative to W.Germany)	
GNP	2260 bill. DM	230-300 M (about 10 %)	
population	61.7 mill.	16.4 mill.	(26.6 %)*
population density (per km^2)	248	152	(61.3 %)
average monthly income in industry (Jan. 1990)	3809 DM	1184 M	(31.1 %)
telephones per 100 households (1988)	98	9	(9.2 %)
dwelling space per capita (in m^2)	35.5	27.0	(76.1 %)
monetary wealth p.c.	40747 DM	11022 M	(27.0 %)
		7654 DM**	(18.8 %)
Employment and capital	*figures in percent*		
employment structure			
agriculture	3.9	10.8	
industry	39.6	47.1	
services	56.5	39.6	
employment in firms with > 500 employees	20.8	78.5	
unemployment rate***	6.4	3.1	
age structure of the capital stock			
0-10 years	69.9	49.5	
over 20 years	5.3	21.1	
Savings and trade			
private household's savings ratio	13.9	7.0	
exports to EC-12('90#)	54.5	5.9(.6% of W.Ger.)	
share of trade with Eur. CMEA countries (ex/im)	3.8/3.8	69.5/68.7	
exports to the USSR	1.7	36.9	
export-GNP ratio	34.4	19-25****	

figures are for Jan.-July 1990; * is equivalent to 21 % of the all-German population; ** checking and savings balances of GDR residents, held in M(ark) in the state banking system were converted at an average rate of 1.44:1 into DM on July 1, 1990; *** figures are for July 1990; short-term employment in East Germany reached 656,000 in July which implies an effective unemployment rate of 10 %. On the conversion factors see Deutsche Bundesbank (1990a), Monatsberichte der Deutschen Bundesbank, July 1990. The conversion factor applied to income payments and pensions was 1:1. Assets and liabilities of industry were converted at a rate of 1:2. **** Author's estimate (multiple exchange rates imply uncertainties).

Sources: Council of Economic Experts, Zur Unterstützung der Wirtschaftsreform in der DDR: Voraussetzungen und Möglichkeiten, Sondergutachten vom 20. Januar 1990, Wiesbaden; Statistisches Bundesamt, Statistisches Jahrbuch der Bundesrepublik Deutschland, Wiesbaden 1989; DDR 1990, Zahlen und Fakten, Wiesbaden 1990; Staatliche Zentralverwaltung für Statistik, Statistisches Jahrbuch der DDR 1989, Berlin 1989. Institut für angewandte Wirtschaftsforschung Berlin, Ursachen der Wirtschaftskrise in der DDR, Berlin 1990. Trade figures for Jan.-July 1990 were directly obtained from the Deutsche Bundesbank (DB); DB: Reihe 3, Zahlungsbilanzstatistik. Own calculations.

which became immediately obvious when the German monetary unification exposed GDR products to the full competition from West Germany and other market economies - GDR goods could be sold only at high price discounts, and production in the respective East German industries fell overproportionately.[5]

With a capital-income ratio of about 4.5 in West Germany (FRG capital stock 1989: DM 10,725 bill., evaluated at replacement costs) and other OECD countries, the long term challenge for East Germany is to first replace the old capital stock and then rapidly increase it parallel to the growth of income. The order of magnitude for required investment in East Germany is around DM 600 bill. in the 1990s if one assumes that 50 percent of the present capital stock is outdated (*Siebert, 1990, p. 15*).

The savings rate of private households in the GDR was only half as high as that in the Federal Republic of Germany which implies in view of an intra-German income differential of 1:3 an enormous absolute divergence in the average savings, with the average West German citizen saving more than 5 times that of his East German counterpart. East German income levels are assumed to approach West German levels within 15 years or so, so that savings will gradually increase. Moreover, with the integration into West Germany, East German citizens will no longer emphasize that they are the best in the CMEA group, but will instead desire to reach higher West German levels in income and wealth. This reorientation can be modelled in a savings function $S = S(Y, W^{**}/W)$, where Y represents real income and W^{**} the desired higher West German per-capita-wealth, W actual wealth; also, after unification a greater asset menu is available than before. The exogenous regime switch from the former target wealth under socialism (W^{*}) to W^{**} - a "preference shock" - implies a stock-adjustment process which will be brought about by a rapidly rising savings rate in East Germany, once fear of unemployment becomes less widespread. This is to be expected in the mid-1990s after some successful macroeconomic adjustment.

Finally, the degree of openness, measured by the ratio of exports to GNP, was relatively low in the GDR (taking due account of the fact that smaller OECD countries show export-GNP ratios of about 50 percent) and trade patterns differed markedly between West Germany and East Germany, where about 2/3 of GDR trade was with CMEA countries, while the share of West Germany's trade with Eastern Europe and the USSR was about 4 percent. West Germany's exports to the EC amounted to 54.5 percent of total goods exports in the 1990, while the East German exports were only 5.9 percent of its total exports; the East German exports reached 0.6 percent of the West German figures, while on a per-capita basis the East German figures would have to be 21 percent (under the simplistic assumption that West Germany's trade pattern would be matched by East Germany). Intra-industry trade was hardly existent in the CMEA which had adopted a strategy of monopolistic international specialization, often based upon bilateral trade treaties and multiple exchange rates which implied price distortions within CMEA trade; moreover, the opportunity costs of goods exported to Western countries at world market prices diverged from that in CMEA trade.

West Germany recorded 2/3 of its trade surplus in the second half of the 1980s vis-a-vis the EC countries, but German unification will lead to a gradual reduction of the current account surplus which hovered between 4-5 percent of GNP in the late 1980s. Tremendous modernization needs of private and public capital in East Germany and the rising consumer demand in the area of the former GDR will accelerate imports and reduce exports. The DM 600 bill. or so needed for investment in East Germany - much relative to West Germany's (internal) investment of DM 480 bill. in 1989 - requires a change in Germany's intertemporal pattern of expenditures. The investment requirements in East Germany are manageable if phased over a decade or so. What is more problematic is that high German public deficits, namely around 4-5 percentage points of GNP, will lead together with the EC 1992-induced investment boom in Europe to sustaining high real interest rates that affect the whole stock of Germany's public debt of DM 1000 bill. with its annual roll-over financing needs. Higher interest rates will, of course, affect other EC countries and Eastern Europe.

Fortunately, the EC 1992 project of creating a single West European market generates considerable growth momentum for the (West) German economy which is Europe's main producer and exporter of capital goods. Economic growth of real gross national product reached 4 percent in West Germany in 1989 and is expected to be within the 3-4 percent range in 1990/91, slowing down thereafter in West Germany (*IMF, 1990*). Despite high growth rates in some industries East Germany will face a difficult transition period of falling production and, in some areas and industries, incomes.

.3 Major Aspects of Germany's Bridging Function

Many observers suggest that a united Germany could rapidly become an important bridge between Western Europe with its dynamic core, the EC, and Eastern Europe and the USSR. The integration of East Germany into the EC might be viewed as providing a new bridge for East-West trade. The EC Commission notes (*EC Commission, 1990, p. 15*):

The macroeconomic impact of German monetary, economic and social union on the rest of Europe will be significant and positive. The changing balance between demand and supply within the Union will affect trade flows and savings in partner countries. ...In the longer run, it can be expected that the beneficial effects anticipated from the single market will be reinforced. Moreover, to the extent that the other East European economies progress towards a market economy, the advantages of a progressive division of labour within Europe may increase further. Given the relatively high integration of the GDR economy into the East

European economies, the GDR can act as a bridge between the Community and Eastern Europe.

However, one may raise various counter-arguments to this view - at least from a medium-term perspective that takes into account the dynamic adjustment processes. Arguments in favor of a German bridging function might point to East German systemic transformation as a model for Eastern Europe and could stress that an East-bound enlargement of the EC poses limited problems as the GDR case seems to show. With the integration of East Germany the new Germany and the EC embrace established trade links between the former GDR and the East European economies. Finally there is the fact that East German politicians and business leaders have built up valuable networks of personal contacts to firms and institutions in the CMEA. However, since the East European countries and the USSR are heading towards a market-based system the value of links established in the former socialist world economy is rapidly eroding. Nevertheless, Germany could become a bridge in the long term, but its pillars would be different from those suggested by the EC Commission.

More important in the long term is Germany's role as the EC's leading exporter of capital goods and know-how which are at a premium in Eastern Europe and the USSR. This aspect is important since the CoCom rules have been relaxed in 1990 and because military disarmament is making progress in Europe (*Welfens, 1988*). For decades system-endemic impediments for Schumpeterian dynamics and inefficient technology trade have characterized the socialist command economies (*Poznanski, 1987; Balcerowicz/Welfens, 1988; Cassel, 1990*). Facing reforming CPEs that are eager to implement market-based systems and want to modernize their capital stock, Germany's industry - Europe's technologically leading country - has favorable prospects provided a successful debt-cum-growth strategy can be implemented in Eastern Europe. Fear of German dominance is widespread in Eastern Europe which is opening up to FDI only gradually and still relies mostly on joint ventures with low amounts of paid-up capital (*Inotai, 1990*).

However, there are prospects that diversified investments from most EC countries and the ongoing Europeanization of the EC industry - with a wave of cross-border mergers since 1985 - will raise the political acceptance level for international investment in Eastern Europe and the USSR; oligopolistic rivalry could bring about a rather diversified investment pattern in the CMEA countries. The multinationalization of production and the internationalization of industrial property rights which has become a common phenomenon in OECD countries (*Welfens, 1990a*) has yet to be introduced in Eastern Europe; since technology trade among OECD countries is mostly intra-company trade on the one hand, and, on the other hand, consists of cross-licensing, the internationalization of industry in the CMEA countries is the only reliable way to get wide access to proprietary and non-proprietary know-how and technologies. It is true, however, that after decades of emphasizing nationalism and socialism while not being exposed to multinational business, mass tourism and free trade the psychological threshold against foreign direct investment is still high in Eastern Europe and the USSR.

The question arises to which extent and under which conditions a united Germany could indeed become a stable bridge between the rich West European economies and the reforming East European countries. With per capita incomes and prices for output goods as well as assets in East Germany expected to rise to the high West German levels in the medium term, considerable incentives for higher imports from Poland, the USSR and other CMEA countries - with their still low prices and per capita wealth - can be anticipated in principle. Moreover, German multinationals in other EC countries will contribute to new East-West trade links as will the whole EC which could benefit from a prosperous German economy and stability-oriented successful economic policy in Germany. Even if German unity itself does not make Germany an ideal East-West bridge, the German role in the EC and the G-24 group could amount to such an (indirect) function.

3. EC Problems

As regards a united Germany's role in the EC both real and monetary aspects are relevant. At first Germany's functions in major EC institutions and in the formation of EC economic policy - in particular trade policy - are the focus here. In a period in which political consensus in Germany is at a premium the avoidance of intra-EC conflicts and prospects for sustaining West European growth could be particularly important.

German unification represents not only a silent eastward enlargement of the EC, but it also raises new problems because shifts in German political preferences, unification-induced high public budget deficits and conflicts over adjustment patterns as well as an erosion of German parties' basic political consensus could create instability in Germany and impair intra-EC political cooperation. Germany and France have been the driving forces of EC integration since 1957. However, with German unification the old French fear of German dominance in Europe is rising once again. Germany's share in the EC gross national product could rise from 25 percent in 1989 - trailed by France, the U.K. and Italy with 20, 17.5 and 17 - to nearly 30 percent in the long run. Indeed, to add East Germany to West Germany means that a country with the population of slightly more than that of the Netherlands is joining the EC. While political considerations might emphasize aspects of an intra-EC disequilibrium of power, economic considerations suggest that German unification will affect the various EC member countries in different ways.

3.1 European Opportunities for Trade and Investment

In a situation in which East Germans want to catch up to the level and patterns of consumption of the West Germans and in which a huge demand for public and for private investment in East Germany will occur, those countries are well positioned whose trade and investment links with West Germany are strong (see Tab. 2); West German imports strongly increased in the second half of 1990, and those from the EC countries increased with 14.3 percent by almost 4 points more than overall imports. If Germany's and the other EC countries' share of imports from Eastern Europe would increase in the future, German unification would indirectly contribute to trade creation and economic growth in the whole of Europe. Germany's imports from the former CPEs increased strongly after unification, namely by 17.9 percent; however, exports reduced by 9 percent and probably will show only moderate growth as the East European countries are likely to reorient their imports in favor of Asian NICs and other price competitive suppliers which could help to minimize the problems associated with the switch to CMEA hard currency trade.

Table 2: Trade and Investment Links with West Germany 1989/90**

change in West German trade July-Oct. 1990 exp.***	imp.***		% of total exports to West Germany	Eastern Europe	share in FDI stock in FRG	share in the German FDI
		West Germany		5.0		
-0.1	+14.3	EC-12			35.1	39.3
0.1	+11.7	Netherlands	27	1.8	12.1	5.6
-2.9	+25.8	Denmark	18	2.0	1.0	0.6
+4.8	+17.4	Belgium/Lux.	18	1.2	2.1	8.4
+2.0	+13.7	France	17	2.0	6.3	7.9
+8.9	+13.7	Portugal	17	3.3	-	0.4
		Greece	17	6.5	-	0.4
+1.7	+15.5	Italy	16	7.1	2.1	4.8
-6.7	+7.7	U.K.	12	1.8	10.3	5.8
+6.9	+31.0	Spain	12	2.8	0.3	5.0
		Ireland	11	1.3.	-	0.5
		Switzerland	*21*	*4.1*	*14.7*	*4.8*
		Austria	*31*	*11.9*	*1.4*	*3.7*
		Sweden	*12*	*3.5*	*2.2*	*0.6*
+0.9	-7.2	USA	5	1.5	32.6	27.0
+6.7	+7.6	Japan	6	1.0	7.3	2.2
-9.0	+17.9	Eastern Eur.+USSR	15-20*	55-70*	0.6	0.2
-0.2	+10.6	ALL COUNTRIES	N.A.	N.A.	100.0	100.0

* range of uncertainty is related to non-convertibility problems in total trade figures; ** shares for FDI (foreign direct investment; stock values) are for 1988; *** change against July-Oct. 1989. Sources: Statistische Beihefte zu den Monatsberichten der Deutschen Bundesbank, Reihe 3, April 1990, OECD, Paris; Deutsche Bundesbank, own calculations.

Those countries which are currently major exporters to West Germany are the ones which stand to directly benefit most from German unification. France, the Netherlands, Denmark,

Belgium, Portugal, Greece and Italy expect positive growth effects in the EC, as do Austria and Switzerland. If Eastern European growth benefits from German unification in the medium term, countries with a relatively high CMEA share of trade will benefit as well, where Italy, Greece and Austria - along with Germany - are countries that would be expected to gain most.

Since East Germany will adopt the FRG's politico-economic system design knowledge about West German markets, business practices and institutions is most valuable, so that German and foreign firms producing in West Germany are most likely to benefit from the switch to the Social Market Economy in East Germany.

Restructuring and development of East Germany will also involve the 10,000 foreign firms which represented inward foreign direct investment of DM 109 bill. in the Federal Republic of Germany at end-1988. If one assumes that they will maintain their per capita capital stock in Germany they would have to provide within a once-and-for all adjustment move (over several years) DM 29 bill. and would create some 420 000 jobs directly, bringing the total number of employment in foreign controlled firms to 1.9 mill. The U.S., Switzerland, the Netherlands, the U.K., Japan, and France would be major investors if the country shares for Germany in 1988 would persist: 32.6, 14.7, 12.1, 10.3, 7.3 and 6.3 percent were the respective shares for these six countries which account for more than 2/3 of Germany's inward FDI. West Germany's 16,500 firms abroad which represented a stock of outward FDI of DM 184 bill. and directly accounted for some 2 mill. people employed abroad in 1988 can be expected to reduce the growth of outward FDI, while transitorily increasing investment in Germany. The U.S. - with a share of 27.0 percent -, Belgium-Luxembourg, France, the Netherlands, Spain and Italy - accounting for shares between 8 and 5 percent of German FDI - would be affected in particular.

East Germany should not be expected to become a permanently disadvantaged German Mezzogiorno. With massive public investment, the full mobility of production factors in Germany, and the prosperous West Berlin, located in the midst of East Germany as an economic growth pole, no long-term economic division of Germany is to be expected. Only in the case that Eastern Europe would become trapped in a permanent crisis of high external debt, stagnation and political unrest, would one expect that the Eastern periphery of Germany will permanently be much worse off than the West with its favorable proximity to the most dynamic EC regions.

3.2 German Unification and Economic and Monetary Union in the EC

The EC has entered the first stage of Economic and Monetary Union on July 1, 1990, bringing about the total removal of capital controls in all major EC countries and EC-wide coordinated monetary policy under the auspices of the reorganized European Committee of Central Bank Governors. Its first elected chairman is the head of the Deutsche Bundesbank which has dominated the European Monetary System of fixed exchange rates so far. The Bundesbank and monetary policy in the EMS play a crucial role at present. Low inflation rates - between 0 and 3 percent in the period 1983-1990 - and a strong economy allowed the Bundesbank to exert monetary leadership in the EC. Germany's monetary policy contributed to a strong downward inflation rate convergence in Western Europe in the second half of the 1980s. Under the leadership of the Deutsche Bundesbank and based upon increasing German-French cooperation as well as a general convergence of policy views in the continental EC countries, the EMS with its low frequency of nominal and real exchange rates has developed successfully and supported the expansion of intra-EC trade (*Welfens, 1991a*).

In October 1990 the U.K. joined the Exchange Rate Mechanism (ERM) and thereby became a full-fledged member of the EMS; that is, the central bank has to defend a fixed parity of the pound in the future. As this is the more difficult the further one is from the lowest inflation rate in the EC, the considerable divergence between British and German inflation rates cannot persist in the long term which causes downward pressure on inflation expectations, and, with a certain lag, on nominal wage increases in the U.K. For the British economy the once-and-for-all adjustment burden is the heavier, the stricter Germany sticks to its goal of price stability. After German unification it is an open question whether or not inflation rate convergence will be achieved at higher average EC inflation rates. This would be the case if the Bundesbank embarked in the medium term upon a less strict anti-inflation policy as a consequence of internal plus external shocks and a shift in political preferences in the context of the integration of East German voters which might strongly favor full employment over price stability.

Apart from short-term monetary control problems caused by the enlargement of the DM currency area, a relaxation of German monetary policy is unlikely for specific reasons. Facing the coincidence of systemic shock adjustment in East Germany, the Iraq-induced oil price shock and a high capacity utilization in West Germany, inflationary pressures will build up faster than normally. At this point one should, however, keep in mind that money demand in East Germany - after the conversion to the DM and political unification - probably rose faster than suggested by short term output variation and medium term increases in the production potential; this is so because system transformation is perceived as a surge in permanent income which enters the money demand function with a positive sign. If the Bundesbank continues to follow a monetary target that is guided by the expansion of the (all-)German production potential, monetary policy is unlikely to accommodate rising inflationary expectations and thus to tolerate higher inflation rates in the long term.

More important is the problem of exchange rate adjustment in the EC after the U.K. joined the ERM with a wide +/- 6 percent exchange rate band which is also valid for Spain. The EMS has two major international currencies: the DM which might increasingly become subject to speculative capital (in-)flows focusing on Germany's particular exposure to Eastern Europe and the USSR, and the British pound which is a major international vehicle currency. The British pound is a currency that is subject to the high volatility of international capital flows going through London. If one takes into account that policy approaches of Germany and France were often difficult to reconcile with the EMS, one can imagine even more difficult triangular scenarios in the future, especially, if external shocks (such as the Iraq shock) suggest different national responses of monetary policy. The small +/- 2.25 percent standard exchange rate margin in the EMS could turn out to be too narrow in the 1990s such that a transition to parity interlocking and the switch to a convertible ECU issued by an EC central bank could become difficult. The Bundesbank's monetary leadership could erode under the impact of increasing regional volatility of intra-EC capital flows and rising conflicts between the Bundesbank and the German Ministry of Finance. Therefore the attempt to set up an EC central bank with a convertible EC currency could be viewed as a step to maintain exchange rate stability and effectiveness of monetary policy control in Western Europe, where Germany's monetary leadership creates fear in many countries of being dominated by German economic policy and thus becoming indirectly exposed to the repercussion of intra-German adjustment problems to which monetary and fiscal policy have to react.

In the medium term German unification means a greater weight of the DM in the European Currency Unit (ECU). The DM's present weight of 30.1 percent in the ECU, which is a "basket" of EC member currencies, is likely to be increased in 1994 when the next revision of weights is to take place. 1994 is also the date when stage II of EMU is to be enacted - at least according to the view of the continental EC members as expressed during the EC summit of Rome in October 1990. The rapid formation of the German monetary union (GMU) may have set a precedent for EC monetary integration.

Foreign policy considerations, namely the emphasis given to a united Germany being devoted to EC integration and firmly embedded in a European policy framework, seem to have influenced the German position, and thus have worked in favor of a fast track proposal for progress in EMU. To the extent that German unity reinforces the Bundesbank's position in the medium term the chance of organizing a future EC central bank along the lines of the

Bundesbank model increases: namely one with a clear commitment to price stability and a position which is relatively independent of government. Neither GMU nor German political unification seems to have seriously impaired the position of the Bundesbank and its ability to set a model for organizing EC monetary policy in the 1990s.

Since non-EC members, such as Austria, Norway, Yugoslavia and other countries are implicitly pegging their exchange rates to the DM and the ECU, respectively, the development of EC monetary union has an impact upon monetary and fiscal policies in both the EFTA countries and - possibly in the 1990s - the ex-CMEA countries with their gradually increasing trade with Western Europe as well. The Deutsche Bundesbank has not only become an institutional model for organizing central banks in several European countries, but it generally influences the course of economic policy by its successful leadership in the EC as well.

3.3 German Unity and the EC's Trade Policy Stance

As a major trading power, Germany plays a key role in the multilateral GATT rounds and in EC trade policy. The liberal quartet FRG, Denmark, the Netherlands and the U.K. are no longer shaping the EC's trade policy in the 1990s. French-Italian industrial policy approaches are spreading in the EC because of the generally increasing competitive pressure in global high-tech industries and because cross-border mergers in Europe not only create "Euronationals" but also powerful EC lobbying groups pressing for R&D grants and subsidies (*Welfens, 1991b*). In addition, heavy German subsidies to East Germany's ailing industries set a bad precedent in Germany and in the whole EC. Considering 40 years of Communist-led economic distortions in East Germany, many subsidies are indeed an investment in the transition to a market economy; however, market-creating subsidies and subsidies obtained in the context of rent-seeking are often difficult to separate.

As is evident in Tab. 3 the EC dominated the CMEA countries hard currency trade in 1989 which creates a strong short-term interest on the part of the former CPEs in central Europe and the USSR to maintain and increase these trade flows. Given the miniscule trade flows - in absolute terms - with Japan and the U.S., these two countries offer the greatest long term potential for a significant growth of trade. However, because the U.S. and Japan are starting from a weak trade level there is little political support to promote trade with the former CMEA countries. At the same time the present asymmetries of trade flows is conducive to conflict of interests between the EC, the U.S. and Japan. Whether opening up Eastern Europe and the USSR will lead to global trade creation effects will in the medium term depend largely on the EC. Expanding existing trade links with Western Europe provides the best basis to exploit static and dynamic economies of scale and to acquire experience and expertise in a competitive market environment such that this know-how as well as the improving cost competitiveness can later be used to enter other markets in the global market system.[6]

Table 3: Imports and Exports from the USSR and Central Europe in 1989 (bill. US $)

	Imports from							
	World	USSR	Bulgaria	CSSR	GDR	Hungary	Poland	Romania
Western Europe	1,361	21.3	.7	3.7	2.6	3.9	5.4	3.0
EC	1,165	16.5	.6	2.8	1.8	2.9	4.3	2.8
US	493	.8	.07	0.1	0.2	0.4	0.4	0.09
Japan	211	3.0	.05	0.1	0.1	0.1	0.1	0.2
	Exports to							
	World	USSR	Bulgaria	CSSR	GDR	Hungary	Poland	Romania
Western Europe	1,317	19.0	2.0	3.4	2.8	4.4	5.3	0.8
EC	1,130	13.6	1.6	2.6	1.8	3.3	4.3	0.8
US	364	4.3	0.2	0.05	0.09	0.1	0.4	0.2
Japan	275	3.1	0.2	0.06	0.02	0.1	0.2	0.05

Note: Trade between the FRG and the GDR is not included.
Source: GATT (1990), International Trade 1989-90, Geneva, Appendix Tab. 1.

3.3.1 EC Protectionism

German unification and the tremendous adjustment problems in East Germany's non-competitive agriculture and industry build up pressure in the political system not to accept additional adjustment pressure from multilateral negotiations. The final stage of the Uruguay GATT round already reflected this when Germany watered down a proposal of the EC Commission - responding to U.S. pressure - to reduce EC agricultural subsidies by 30 percent within a decade. Unless a longer time horizon for staggered trade concessions is adopted Germany will face difficulties in maintaining its traditional free trade stance.

Agricultural trade is a key to economic development and structural adjustment in Eastern Europe (and Latin America). With around 20 percent of the labor force employed in agriculture Poland, Hungary, Rumania and the Soviet Union face major and increasingly important problems in agricultural exports. The EC in general, and Germany in particular, has developed a system of gliding import tariffs and large export subsidies which make agricultural exports from Eastern Europe and the USSR very difficult. The major would-be agricultural exporters in Eastern Europe are also the countries with the highest foreign debt problems for which German government loans extended to Poland, Hungary and the USSR and the heavy lending activities by German banks in the 1980s play significant roles.

The transformation towards a market economy can hardly succeed in the reforming socialist countries if a modernized agricultural sector is not progressively allowed to export its product to the nearest high-income markets: those in Western Europe. The 4 to 9 percent of the labor force employed in agriculture in major EC agricultural exporting countries have powerful lobbies in their respective capitals as well as in Brussels. Germany provides only a few weak pillars for a bridge to Eastern Europe when it comes to the question of trade liberalization.

Necessary for adjustment and growth in central Europe would be a long term policy approach which takes into account transitory problems in Germany but presses for binding liberalization commitment in the long term. The CMEA group disbanded because of internal politico-economic conflicts and the growing obsolescence of existing CMEA organizations. However, the new common challenge to get open access to West European markets and to jointly organize systemic transformation to various brands of market-based systems could constitute a new basis for a radically modified CMEA. A gradual movement towards an East European free trade area which actively seeks free trade agreements with the EFTA and the EC could be a new approach to creating a European Economic Space.

3.3.2 Restoring Historical Trading Patterns in Central Europe?

Germany's trade orientation is likely to increasingly focus on Eastern Europe and the Soviet Union as the former CPEs advance to a market economy system. This would mean to some extent restoring the world market economy that existed prior to World War I. Germany's trade orientation in 1913 gives certain clues to a higher East European trade potential, and Tab. 4 shows Russia - then comprising part of Poland - as a market economy ranking with the U.S., the U.K., Austria-Hungary and France as a primary trading partner, whereas in 1989 its trade was of minor importance to Germany.[7] With the switch to hard-currency trade in the former CMEA countries the intra-regional trade in Eastern Europe is likely to decline in the medium term, while East-West trade should expand in Europe. However, CMEA trade with the Asian NICs and Japan is also likely to rise which in a triangular trade perspective could support European trade growth in the long term.

Table 4: German Trade Orientations in 1913 and 1989*
(shares for merchandise trade with selected countries)

	Country Share in German Imports		Country Share in German Exports	
	1913	1989	*1913*	1989
USA	*15.9*	7.6	*7.1*	7.3
Russia**	*13.2*	1.7	*8.7*	1.8
(Poland)		0.7		0.7
Great Britain	*8.1*	6.8	*14.2*	9.3
Austria-		(A)4.1		(A)5.5
Hungary**	*7.7*	(H)0.5	*10.9*	(H)0.6
(CSFR)		0.5		0.4
France	*5.4*	11.9	*7.8*	13.2
Italy	*3.0*	8.9	*3.9*	9.3
China****	*0.7*	1.1	*1.2*	0.7
(Taiwan)		1.1		0.6
Rumania	*0.7*	0.3	*1.4*	0.1
Serbia*****	*0.1*	1.3	*0.5*	1.1
Japan	*0.4*	6.3	*1.2*	2.4
Bulgaria	*<0.1*	0.1	*0.3*	0.2

* figures for 1989 are for West Germany.
** figures for 1989 refer to the Soviet Union.
*** figures for 1989 are comprised of the country shares of Austria, Hungary and the CSSR.
**** figures for 1989 refer to the People's Republic of China.
***** figures for 1989 are for Yugoslavia.

Sources: Statistisches Handbuch fuer das Deutsche Reich, Vol. II., Statistisches Bundesamt and Deutsche Bundesbank, own calculations.

For various reasons the pre-World War I situation is, however, unlikely to be restored in the long-term, mainly because of the rise of Japan and the Asian NICs on the one hand, and, on the other hand, because trade in services and differentiated products play such a greater role in the present economy than in the period 1870-1913 when primary products shaped world trading patterns. However, it is clear that Germany's trade policy stance is of prime importance for the development of trade between the EC and Eastern Europe (plus the USSR).

4. Germany and the CMEA Countries in a Divided Europe

German restructuring attempts in the context of German unity will require tremendous private and public investment that will strain national and international credit markets. The expectation of high real interest rates worldwide will impair capital formation and restructuring in heavily indebted East European countries and the USSR (and in Latin American economies). Prospects of overcoming the economic division of Europe in the 1990s are limited not only by high real interest rates which make the industrial restructuring of the East European economies difficult;

moreover, the reemergence of nationalism in Eastern Europe and the USSR, while intra-CMEA trade links are weakening suggests a rather fragmented CMEA group facing an increasingly integrated and compact Western Europe.

The coincidence of a partly German unification-induced real interest rate shock plus an oil price shock that stems from both the Iraq-Kuwait crisis and the Soviet Union's switch to hard currency trading confronts the East European reforming economies with tremendous problems. This holds all the more because with a gradual switch to world market prices the CMEA trade pattern will change from a complementary intra-bloc trade to a more diversified intra-industry trade with a greater weight of industrial market economies (mainly Western Europe). These economies accounted for only between 6-33 percent of total exports in 1988 - with higher values of Poland and Hungary being an exception which partly reflects country-specific debt problems. These two countries traditionally also show a strong orientation in Western trade towards the FRG which accounts for about 13 percent of all exports of these two countries and for an import share which is slightly lower in the Polish case and reaches 18 percent in the case of Hungary (see Tab. 5). These percentage shares are comparable to the German position in trade with some of its major EC partners while the level of per capita trade is much higher.

A unified Germany can be expected to account for about 15-20 percent of East European trade. Compared to historical trading patterns the present figures for Poland and Hungary are low. In 1930 Germany accounted on the import side for a percentage share of 27.0 and 21.2 percent, respectively. Similar shares were recorded by Czechoslovakia (25.4 %), Bulgaria (23.2 %) and Rumania (25.1).[8] In these three countries and the USSR the GDR accounted for almost double the share of West Germany on the import and export side which is in marked contrast to Poland's and Hungary's much stronger West German and West European trade orientation. In any case a united Germany will be the most important Western trading partner of Eastern Europe and the USSR. Given the comparatively low export-GNP ratios of the East European economies (with Hungary reaching the highest ratio, namely about 1/3 in 1989 which is low if compared to e.g. Holland's 2/3 ratio), one may expect a considerable growth of East-West trade in the 1990s. The real export growth rate g_X is in its own right a source of economic growth (*Balassa, 1978; Riedel, 1990*).[9] The historical experience and theoretical considerations based on the gravity equation model of international trade suggest that trade between Germany and Eastern Europe will expand in the long run provided that recurrent debt problems and internal politico-economic problems in the former CPEs do not undermine trade expansion.

[T]able 5: Trade Pattern of the CMEA Countries in 1988 (imports/exports in percent)

	Eastern Europe**	USSR	GDR***	FRG***	All Indust. Market Econ.	Developing Countries	Other*
USSR	54.1/48.9	-	8.1/ 7.9	4.6/ 3.8	25.1/21.9	8.2/14.2	12.6/15.0
CSSR	32.3/29.9	40.3/43.1	8.7/ 6.6	5.8/ 5.1	18.6/16.3	3.5/ 4.7	5.3/ 6.0
Romania	24.6/16.8	24.0/24.0	9.3/ 6.0	3.2/ 5.2	13.5/33.7	18.8/19.0	19.1/ 6.5
Bulgaria	20.1/18.1	53.7/62.8	5.0/ 4.1	3.2/ 3.0	15.5/ 6.4	7.8/ 9.1	2.9/ 3.6
Poland	17.2/16.2	23.4/24.5	4.9/ 4.4	12.9/13.5	45.7/43.3	7.1/10.2	6.6/ 5.8
Hungary	18.7/17.0	25.0/27.6	6.5/ 5.9	18.3/11.6	43.3/39.5	7.7/ 9.9	5.3/ 6.0
(GDR)	25.3/26.1	53.7/34.8	- -	12.2/11.1	15.5/29.9	7.8/ 3.6	2.9/ 5.6

including China; ** CMEA-6; *** figures are for 1989; for the USSR, the CSSR and Bulgaria the GDR-share [i]n Ruble Trade was 16.1 % on the import side (15.8 % on the export side), 12.6 (10.8) and 7.7 (6.4), [re]spectively. If overall trade is evaluated in dollar prices PLANECON estimates for the country's Ruble Trade [sh]are is 50 % (50 %), 69 % (61 %) and 65 % (64%) for the USSR, the CSSR and Bulgaria, respectively.

[S]ources: SCHRENK, MARTIN (1990), The CMEA System of Trade and Payments: Today and Tomorrow, SPR [D]iscussion Paper No. 5, January 1990; figures represent UN estimates and official national statistics of the [C]MEA countries; IMF (1990), Directions of Trade Statistics, Yearbook 1990; PLANECON, own calculations.

[T]he ratio of interest payments to exports to the market economies reached critical values - [e]ndangering trade expansion - in Bulgaria, Hungary and Poland with 24.2, 24.6 and 41.7 [p]ercent, respectively, in 1989 (*UN Economic Commission for Europe, 1990, p. 206*); [i]ncluding invisibles in export figures somewhat improves the picture for Hungary and Poland. [F]igures for the USSR, the CSFR and Rumania were below 5 percent, but as the case of the [S]oviet Union showed in 1990, organizational disruptions in ad-hoc reforms can seriously [i]mpair the creditworthiness of CMEA countries and raise effective financing costs: switching [fr]om a state monopoly for trade to firm-based decentralized competences for trade while not [a]dopting price reforms, dismembering and privatizing state-run firms and making policy [ch]anges can make things worse than in the old socialist system.

[O]ne may note that the USSR is particularly important on the import side for Bulgaria, the [C]SFR and the GDR which means that those countries would also be affected the most by [po]litico-economic disruptions in the Soviet Union. As regards exports Bulgaria and the CSFR [ar]e very dependent on the USSR. The developing countries and China play a considerable role [fo]r most CMEA countries which implies that they are vulnerable to the repercussions that [m]ight result from interest rate shocks affecting the Third World.

[G]ermany's current account surplus - hovering in the late 1980s around 5 percent relative to [G]NP - will reduce as a consequence of economic restructuring in East Germany and the real [a]ppreciation of the DM. This development benefits in the form of higher exports the EC [co]untries and most CMEA countries, especially Poland and Hungary. However, achieving a [ra]pid modernization of Eastern Europe and thus high economic growth as well as political [st]ability of the new democracies faces the problem that high sovereign debt (involving the

Paris Club) in most CMEA countries poses a major threshold for the import of Western technology and capital. At the same time there are further impediments reducing the East-West income gap: namely, difficulties in disentangling formerly state-run firms, improving the capability to adopt foreign know-how by long-term human capital investment and widely accepting foreign direct investment. People and politicians often have too short a time horizon in the critical transition phase to a market economy to realize a prudent supply-side oriented policy. Hence, prospects to increase trade - in its role as an engine of growth - are most vital for the CMEA countries.

With rising per-capita income in what was formerly the GDR, CMEA countries in particular should gain from higher exports of goods and services. To fully exploit the potential benefits massive infrastructure investment would be necessary in the CMEA countries, where East-West transportation links are underdeveloped and hence transportation time and costs are often prohibitive for full access to European markets. Multinational public investment projects co-financed by international organizations seem to be useful in this field, where fast and comprehensive decisions are needed.

Since East Germany's relatively low prices for formerly subsidized staple goods will adjust to the higher West German level, Poland, Hungary and the CSFR - where prices are still relatively low - can expect an increasing demand from East Germany, but impulses for price increases as well. Indeed, by way of these price impulses additional momentum for economic restructuring along world market prices will emerge in the East European countries.

4.1 Support for Eastern Europe: EC-Widening?

German unification could make EC widening (in the sense of integrating Hungary, the CSFR and other countries) more difficult, namely as a side effect of German-Polish problems arising from unification. The EC 1992 program which will realize a single EC market creates a particular problem for Germany and its neighbors. The single market program requires free intra-EC flows of goods and services, capital and labor. Even if the East German economy catches up only gradually to West Germany, one can expect an increasing economic East-West division of Europe and growing incentives for East-West factor movements. The economic frontier will run along the German-Polish border: (West) German per capita incomes stood at \$ 19,000 in 1990, while Polish incomes reached some \$ 2000.[10] Only gradually, in the course of improved German-Polish relations that could develop from German support for the Polish desire to reduce part of the external debt and from strong growth of trade and investment relations between Germany and Eastern Europe, could the intra-European economic divide be overcome.

There will be short-term and long-term effects of German unification on the former CPEs in Eastern Europe. The modernization of industry in East Germany will transitorily lead to high unemployment rates and an intensified quest for jobs and incomes within Germany that could impair the growth of East-West trade; but at the same time the Polish market-based reforms (among others in Eastern Europe) such as privatization and currency convertibility will create new opportunities for investment, trade and employment growth in central Europe. Considerable trade creation effects are to be expected.

However, to the extent that FDI and trade in goods and services move parallel, there is - even with sustaining economic growth in the former CMEA - an obvious threshold for higher trade with Poland, Hungary and the other former CPEs. While becoming an EC member would remove all barriers to trade it would also open up the East European economies to foreign investment. Obviously, the EC 1992 principle of a free flow of capital and labor poses a specific German-Polish problem with considerable international side-effects for all countries that seek full membership in the EC in the 1990s. To the extent that Poland is not ready to accept a free inflow of German capital (fear of dominance) - unavoidable in case of a Polish EC membership - , Germany is not ready to accept a mass immigration of Polish workers which would certainly be triggered by the combination of geographic proximity, existing large Polish expatriate communities in Germany and high income differentials. Adding 16.4 million East Germans, many of whom have strong Prussian, often anti-Polish and anti-Russian sentiments, to the 61.5 mill. West Germans does not in itself create a climate which is receptive to foreigners and "guest workers" coming into the country.

While Germany is likely to support "EC deepening" it is almost certain to block any comprehensive EC widening, that is a further enlargement of the EC. In contrast to the British government which favors a gradual integration of East European economies into the EC, the German government is reluctant to actively support EC widening. Since Poland and the other East European countries - themselves facing migrations pressures from the USSR - will have to be treated equally, the German-Polish problems could prevent EC widening for decades.

Apart from economic considerations there might be functional problems that arise when the number of member countries exceed a certain threshold. It is, however, doubtful that these impediments to an EC enlargement are relevant in the long term provided economic adjustment programs work in the right direction and institutional innovations can help to overcome practical problems. As the case of the EMS shows - representing a treaty among EC central banks which is not part of the EC Rome Treaties - different fields of international cooperation can be organized at first separately in specific regional scopes and then be joined later.

From this perspective one might envisage European cooperation in fields of common persistent interests: in the protection of the environment; in the definition of technological standards; in transportation and telecommunication; and in monetary policy. There is another area in which the whole of continental Europe lags behind the U.S., namely in the nurturing of new Schumpeterian talents and firms by providing venture capital. This is most needed in the reforming CMEA countries, but useful for the EC and EFTA countries as well so that this type of active competition and growth policy could represent a field of common interest. A common umbrella organization such as a European Venture Agency ("EVA") could be a useful starting point. One possibility would be to set it up as a sub-agency of the European Bank for Reconstruction and Development.

As regards the more complex field of trade liberalization in Eastern European economies and the USSR, one could envisage stronger ties with the EFTA (*Kostrzewa/Schmieding, 1989*) and increasing reliance upon free trade agreements. A different option would be the formation of a Baltic Free Trade Area (*Welfens, 1990b*). Such a BAFTA might comprise some republics of the USSR as well and could reestablish historical links between the Scandinavian countries, the central European economies and Russia. Overlapping liberalization schemes in the form of free trade arrangements between the various regional integration schemes could be useful.

West Germany's trade with the USSR and the other CMEA countries is still miniscule, i.e. smaller than the trade volume with Switzerland and Austria. The prospects for higher trade in Europe depend to a large extent on successful economic reforms in Warsaw, Budapest, Prague and Moscow. CMEA trade with Japan and the U.S. would more than triple as well if per capita figures of trade volume common among OECD countries could be reached. In a period in which Germany might be tempted to embark upon protectionism and thereby trigger global trade diversion effects and a spiral of trade contraction, it is important that the strongest advocate of liberal trade assumes a more long-term, but also a firmer position in multilateral trade negotiations. Fortunately, it is true: The U.S. interest in liberalizing agricultural trade - emphasized at the Houston G-7 meeting in 1990 - is much fueled by domestic interests and concern about indebted Latin American exporters; however, external benefits of trade liberalization would very much accrue to Eastern Europe and the USSR. The U.S. strategy to press for agricultural trade liberalization was initially aimed at obtaining developing countries' concessions in the field of trade in services and protection of property rights; however, now these issues should be envisaged in a broader perspective which includes the CMEA countries.

Since at the beginning of the Uruguay GATT round the radical market-oriented reforms in the CMEA countries could not be anticipated, the final stage of the Uruguay round should take into account the need of organizing trade creation by more long-term staggered concessions in all trade-relevant areas. A broader EC commitment to free trade within the GATT framework that at present covers only 1/3 of global trade can only be expected if the potentially strong exposure of EC countries to higher exports from CMEA countries is adequately considered.

For the reforming CMEA countries there is a risk that their attempts to adopt market-based economic systems end up in a "permanent provisional state" combined with social unrest, economic stagnation and political instability. Latin American problems in the 1970s and 1980s clearly point to the globally negative effects of such a failure to realize prosperity and stability along a sustainable adjustment trajectory.

4.2 Germany's Systemic Transformation as a Model for Eastern Europe?

German unification is a historical case of systemic transformation which mainly consists of opening up the economy, the switch to currency convertibility, the restoration of private property rights and competition in industry, the replacement of state-administered low prices - coupled with price subsidies - as a means of social policy by a Western-style incomes policy and the adoption of a unitary tax system that is based on income and value-added taxes. Finally there will be a retrenchment of the state as an economic actor which is no longer de facto responsible for investment, employment and pricing decision in industry. The systemic transformation certainly entails a sharp reduction of production and employment in the short term, but resistance against this will be limited as long as expected future income and employment opportunities as well as the immediately more diversified supply of (Western) consumer goods compensate for short-term uncertainties and real income losses that can result both from lower nominal incomes and a rise in the effective price level. Taking into account the socialist shadow economy with its comparatively high prices (P*) and the relatively low price level in the official economy (P) with its permanent shortage characteristics,[11] one can define the effective price level P' in a socialist economy as:

$$P' = (P^*)^{\beta}(P + b\, a_{ij})^{(1-\beta)}$$

With b denoting the marginal disutility of compromising on the most preferred variety of goods and with a_{ij} denoting the average divergence in "variety space" that is suffered by the representative consumer who buys a good i that diverges with its characteristics from the most preferred variety j, the real income loss faced by the switch to a market economy is smaller than shown by the increase in the official price index P reflecting a rise to market-clearing levels in major markets.[12] Moreover, prices in the socialist shadow economy will fall to the much lower level of a capitalist economy, while the income share (ß) of income spent in the unofficial shadow economy will also reduce.[13]

Elements of success and failure in German unification could become valuable experiences upon which the reforming CMEA countries could draw. This perception might be valid despite some qualifications which mainly relate to the access to massive "external transfers" - in the form of the U.S. Marshall Program this type of support also helped to start West Germany's postwar economic miracle.[14] German unification is unique in the sense that no other CMEA country was exposed to such a radical and high-speed systemic transformation;[15] but this is also so in the sense than no other (former) CMEA country will enjoy the benefits East Germany attained after unification: full access to the markets of the EC with its 340 million inhabitants; free labor mobility within Germany and the EC; a position where about DM 100 bill. annually - some $ 4000 per capita p.a. - will be available as intra-government transfers from the federal government (+ the "old states") in the 1990s; broad opportunities to attract highly qualified labor and experienced Western management; and finally special incentives for private investors as well as incentives for foreign investors who enjoy tax credits of the host country which are mostly effective because of appropriate bilateral income tax treaties.

Investment Incentives

In contrast to the German case the CMEA countries which offer generous tax credits for foreign direct investment face the problem that tax regulations of major source countries - above all the U.S. - imply that tax credits of the resident country cannot effectively be used to make more investment profitable: Lower taxes paid by foreign subsidiaries increase the tax burden of the parent company which can only be avoided by so-called tax-sparing regulations in international income tax treaties. Moreover, the $ 35 bill. West-German investment (partly from subsidiaries of foreign multinationals) in the former GDR in 1990 represents more than double the amount of foreign direct investment inflows for all remaining CMEA countries combined. Since between 1/3 and 1/2 of all Western trade is multinationals' trade, namely intra-company trade or trade between subsidiaries of different multinationals, systemic transformation in East Germany supports trade creation much beyond the scale the former CMEA countries can expect with their restricted ability to attract FDI.[16]

Tax Payers' Deep Pockets vs. Internal Adjustment Priority

In general, the conclusion to be drawn for the reforming CPEs is that appropriately tailored internal adjustment in each country as well as outward-oriented reform steps - arranged in an adequate sequence - are most important. Attaining static and dynamic efficiency as well as implementing sustainable macroeconomic policies must be a strategic priority. Other important elements include rapidly implementing reforms that establish a stable, but flexible institutional framework that supports the guiding and coordinating forces of a market economy and adopting credible and sustainable economic policies. This could help to minimize uncertainty and to attract FDI. "External" transfers are not available as in Germany.

Sequencing Aspects

A system transformation makes comprehensive institutional adjustment steps necessary which have to be arranged in a certain sequence and with a certain speed. German unification that took place with sometimes breathtaking speed suggests one lesson: comprehensive and fast transformation steps might be necessary in a first stage in order to make system transformation credible or to build up momentum against entrenched defenders of the old system. Rent-seeking coalitions were effective under the socialist regimes in the CMEA countries (*Winiecki, 1990*) and their tight networks could very much impair a gradual transition phase at the beginning of a systemic transformation processes. Certainly, individual CMEA countries have specific traits, but common problems include the old networks phenomenon, a monetary overhang (except for the CSFR), monopolistic industry structures and hyper-bureaucracy, distorted trade patterns and as well as group specific access to state property (*Lipton and Sachs, 1990; UN Commission for Europe, 1990b; Welfens, 1990b*).

The sequencing problem concerns, on the one hand, the question to which extent internal and external reform steps have to be parallel; on the other hand, there is the problem of the link between a reform of the monetary regime and an adjustment of the real system - the supply-side of the economy.

Establishing a Two-tier Monetary Regime

German monetary union is an exception in the sense that only the GDR could hope for strong psychological effects of a conversion to the DM and accept politically the sharing of the Bundesbank's reputation that required the full transfer of monetary policy control to this institution; moreover, only the all-German context ensured that the West German federal government would provide subsidies and start-up financing for the associated switch to world market prices. Other CMEA countries would have to adopt a more gradual approach for hardening their monetary regime in the sense of achieving a convertible and stable currency. Reputation of monetary policy institutions can be achieved only gradually or by adopting policy rules that effectively mean giving up monetary policy autonomy. In this respect an enlargement of the EMS in some distant future could be of interest to East European economies. Provided that comprehensive systemic reforms and convertibility have been achieved by the late 1990s, it could be attractive for them to join the EMS and subject domestic monetary policy to the leadership of a European central bank - provided it would work in line with the present Bundesbank model.

In Germany and in the CMEA countries a reallocation of production factors is necessary in a way that corresponds to comparative advantages, that is one which brings relative labor productivity in line with international relative wage differentials. In contrast to the German case where monetary union and full labor mobility exclude a role of exchange rate policy in improving the competitiveness of the economy, the CMEA countries could in principle make use of prudent exchange rate policies during the opening and modernization process of their respective economies.

Reorganization of Industry

German unification implied for East Germany fast potential access to sophisticated management skills and industrial know-how of German firms and multinational companies represented in West Germany. This potential can be mobilized by privatization of the formerly socialist industry or by attracting greenfield investments and the creation of a modern service industry. Fear of foreign dominance in industry might not be less widespread in East Germany than in other CMEA countries, but it is clear in the East German case that privatization means in most cases that West German ownership is established (foreign ownership represents a stronger psychological problem in CMEA countries).

This kind of Western industrial dominance stems not only from the availability of experienced managers and firms with ownership specific advantages, but is also a result of the East-West divergences in per capita wealth. Relatively poor citizens have a low marginal propensity to pay which implies that any auction model allocating property rights of formerly state-owned firms are biased in favor of wealthy private and corporate citizens of the West and the Pacific Basin.

In this respect there is a parallel in the East German and the East European case, the only modification being that relative to West German per capita wealth the East European position would be much worse than in the case of the GDR for which GMU brought a de facto appreciation of the currency and of nominal wealth, respectively.

External Aspects

In contrast to East Germany it holds that embarking upon a market-oriented system transformation typically entails a strong currency depreciation (favorable only to citizens holding foreign exchange as part of their portfolio). Privatization schemes that transfer part of national wealth to all domestic citizens in a first round might be advisable not only in East Germany but in Eastern Europe as well; Poland adopted such a privatization plan.

EC countries which often still restrict the M&A menu for domestic and foreign residents are likely to understand part of the problems described. This might cause a bias for intra-European solutions and arrangements in the field of foreign direct investment policies, leaving aside the U.S. which has neither government owned industries that are used to dealing with state-run or state-owned companies in Europe nor the European tradition of government-business cooperation on a regular basis.

Finally, common CMEA attempts and strategies vis-a-vis international organizations and regional integration schemes are required in order to mobilize two-way trade and investment opportunities in a world economy in which individual and group interests of Western countries, of Japan and some NICs are powerfully organized. In contrast to East Germany which enjoyed institutional windfall benefits in international organizations after political unification, the new or would-be members from CMEA countries have to build up their own positions.

5. Global Perspectives and Conclusions

German unification as well as the Gorbachev reforms are changing Germany's perception of Eastern Europe and the Soviet Union. Germany is building up special economic relations with the Soviet Union for many reasons, and this is likely to lead to a conflict of interest between the U.S. and its major ally on the European continent. Germany has an active interest in the success of reforms in the Soviet Union and in its political stability. The huge Soviet market to which about 40 percent of East Germany's exports were directed will continue to be an important market in the future. This is true not only because the size and proximity of the USSR have always had an attraction for Germany's trade activities, but also because the Bonn government has an active interest in maintaining at least part of existing (East)German-Soviet trade links in order to reduce the structural adjustment pressure and to contain the unemployment figures in East Germany.

From a Soviet point of view the German economy is the only major one with which reliable long term relations can be developed. The risk of political preference shifts in the U.K. and France, most likely in the context of changing security policies and global power rivalry, encourages Gorbachev or any other Soviet leader to first seek improved relations with a unified Germany. German industry offers nearly all the know-how and products a Soviet Union trying to modernize its economy needs. And finally, one may note that resource-poor

Germany provides a huge market for the export of Soviet natural resources whose share in German commodity imports might rise even further as the political East-West antagonism declines while Arab oil sources become increasingly problematic. Germany's EC partners will certainly benefit from increasing German-Soviet trade. What might be more important, U.S. and European investment in Poland and the other smaller East European countries will reach considerable amounts only if the Soviet Union can be stabilized. With a "fuzzy big bear's smell" no investor can sleep well.

In this view German unification could ultimately help lead Russia back to Europe and into the world market economy. Hence a united Germany which will financially support the Soviet reforms and will pay $ 8 bill. to the USSR for stationing troops and later bringing them back to the USSR could assume a specific role in the international burden sharing among the big G-7 nations. Indirectly this would support the success of reforms in Eastern Europe. Even the resources of a united Germany would be totally insufficient to fully mobilize the economic potential of a market-oriented Soviet Union. Japanese firms could become the other preferred Soviet economic partner if only the dispute over the Kurile Islands could be resolved and if the USSR could reform its trade system (*Welfens, M., 1990*).

Nobody knows whether the political system of the Soviet Union can achieve sufficiently credible reforms in the 1990s, and there is indeed the risk that the Gorbachev reforms will fail and the entire Soviet Union and, consequently, the whole of Eastern Europe will become deeply destabilized. If Germany were to face major financial problems and sustaining unemployment, central Europe could face new unrest. The Old World has become more complex after unification. However, the cyclical but steady economic progress of the EC sets a model for political diversity, different economic standards and competition of institutions. West Germany is just one economic miracle in Western Europe. One may hope that Eastern Europe and the USSR can develop their own federalist outward-oriented politico-economic system designs, where the NEMEs (New European Market Economies) meet increasing West European support for reorganizing the Old World.

A united Germany could become a viable East-West bridge - built partly from the debris of the Berlin Wall - only in the long term, namely after the EC and the CMEA have adjusted internally to the challenges of 1992-cum-EMU and to a market economy, respectively. A two-way multi-lane bridge built upon solid politico-economic pillars is needed as are vital connections to the heartland of the EC and the CMEA, respectively. To assume important bridging functions Germany would have to contribute to increased two-way trade in Europe; to help radically improve the transportation infrastructure in Europe; to encourage financial restructuring of outstanding debt in the CMEA countries; to support a stability-oriented EC central bank which provides a stable monetary policy framework for sustaining economic growth in the EC on the one hand, and, on the other hand, to encourage free trade agreements in the whole of Europe; to encourage trade in technology and in environmentally relevant know-how; to promote open minds in East Germany that would help to accept considerable labor migration from Eastern Europe in the late 1990s when a united Germany might already face shortages in the labor market; finally, to promote a new strengthened role for the main international organizations in which the U.S. might face more interventionist policy approaches by the Japanese or - increasingly important - by the Europeans. Such interventionist policies are likely in the medium term unless the advocates of a liberal global trade and financing regime envisage long-term reforms of traditional policy patterns. One can only hope that integrating Eastern Europe and the USSR into the world market economy and overcoming the economic and political divide of Europe does not lead to a weakening transatlantic cooperation.

The fact that the united Germany kept a low profile in the US-led military efforts to enforce the UN resolutions concerning Iraq's withdrawal from Kuwait has reduced prospects that Germany could ever replace the U.K. as the United States' favorite EC country for transatlantic policy cooperation. For historical, geopolitical and internal reasons Germany faces limited degrees of freedom when it comes to international leadership and responsibility. German unification is reinforcing the side-constraints of Germany's international role for quite some time.

References

BALCEROWICZ, LESZEK and WELFENS, PAUL J.J., eds. (1988), Innovationsdynamik im Systemvergleich, Heidelberg: Physica.

BALASSA, BELA (1978), Exports and Economic Growth: Further Evidence, Journal of Development Economics, 181-189.

BUCHHEIM, CHRISTOPH (1990), Die Währungsreform in Westdeutschland im Jahre 1948. Einige ökonomische Aspekte, in: Fischer, Wolfram, ed., Währungsreform und soziale Marktwirtschaft, Berlin: Duncker, 393-402.

CASSEL, DIETER, ed. (1990), Wirtschaftssysteme im Umbruch, München: Vahlen.

CECCHINI, PAOLO (1988), The European Challenge 1992, Aldershot: Gower.

COUNCIL OF ECONOMIC EXPERTS (Sachverständigenrat zur Begutachtung der gesamtwirtschaftlichen Entwicklung, 1990b) Jahresgutachten 1990/91, Bonn.

COUNCIL OF ECONOMIC EXPERTS (Sachverständigenrat zur Begutachtung der gesamtwirtschaftlichen Entwicklung, 1990a), Zur Unterstützung der Wirtschaftsreform in der DDR: Voraussetzungen und Möglichkeiten, Sondergutachten vom 20. Januar 1990, Wiesbaden.

DEUTSCHE BUNDESBANK (1990), The Monetary Union with the German Democratic Republic, Monthly Report of the Deutsche Bundesbank, July 1990, 13-28.

DRABEK, ZDENEK (1985), Foreign Trade Performance and Policy, in: Kaser, M.C. and E.A. Radice, eds., Economic Structure and Performance between the Two Wars, Vol. 1 of the Economic History of Eastern Europe 1919-75, Oxford: Oxford University Press.

EC COMMISSION (1990), The Community and German Unification, Vol. 1 (COM (90) 400, Brussels, August 21, 1990.

IMF (1990), World Economic Outlook, October 1990, Washington D.C.

INOTAI, ANDRAS (1990), Foreign Direct Investments in Reforming CMEA Countries: Facts, Lessons and Perspectives, forthcoming in Klein, Michael and Welfens, Paul J.J., eds., Multinationals in the New Europe and Global Trade, New York: Springer.

INSTITUT FÜR ANGEWANDTE WIRTSCHAFTSFORSCHUNG BERLIN (1990), Ursachen der Wirtschaftskrise in der DDR, Berlin.

KLUMPP, RAINER (1990), Die Waehrungsreform von 1948. Ihre Bedeutung aus wachstumstheoretischer und ordnungspolitischer Sicht, in: Fischer, Wolfram, ed., Währungsreform and Soziale Marktwirtschaft, Berlin: Duncker, 403-422.

KOSTRZEWA, WOIJCIECH and SCHMIEDING, HOLGER (1989), The EFTA Option for Eastern Europe: Towards an Economic Reunification of the Divided Continent, Institut für Weltwirtschaft, Kiel Working Papers, 297, October 1989.

LIPTON, DAVID and SACHS, JEFFREY (1990), Creating a Market Economy in Eastern Europe: The Case of Poland, Brookings Papers on Economic Activity, Vol. 1990, 75-124.

MENDERSON HORST (1949), Prices, Money and the Distribution of Goods in Postwar Germany, American Economic Review, Vol. 39 (1949), 652-660.

MURRELL, PETER (1990), The Nature of Socialist Economies, Princeton: Princeton University Press.

POZNANSKI, KAZIMIERZ (1987), Technology, Competition and the Soviet Bloc in the World Market, Berkeley: Institute of International Studies.

RIEDEL, J. (1990), The State of Debate on Trade and Industrialization in Developing Countries, in Pearson, Charles and Riedel, James, eds., The Direction of Trade Policy, London: Basil Blackwell, 130-149.

SCHRENK, MARTIN (1990), The CMEA System of Trade and Payments: Today and Tomorrow, SPR Discussion Paper No. 5, January 1990.

SIEBERT, HORST (1990), The Economic Integration of Germany, Kiel Discussion Paper, Institut für Weltwirtschaft, Kiel.

UN COMMISSION FOR EUROPE (1990a), Economic Survey of Europe in 1989-90, New York.

UN COMMISSION FOR EUROPE (1990b), Economic Reforms in the European Centrally Planned Economies, New York.

VAN BERGEIJK, PETER A.G. and OLDERSMA, HARRY (1990), Détente, Market-oriented Reform and German Unification: Potential Consequences for the World Trade System, Kyklos, Vol. 43, 599-610.

WELFENS, MARIA J. (1990), Internationalisierung der UdSSR? Bedeutung der sowjetischen Reformpolitik für die Stellung des RGW und im Ost-West-Handel, in: Dieter Cassel, ed., Wirtschaftssysteme im Umbruch, München: Vahlen, 196-222.

WELFENS, PAUL J.J. (1988), The Economics of Military and Peacekeeping: An Emerging Field, Jahrbuch für Sozialwissenschaft, Vol. 40, 358-385.

WELFENS, PAUL J.J. (1990a), Internationalisierung von Wirtschaft und Wirtschaftspolitik/Internationalization of the Economy and Economic Policies, Heidelberg: Springer.

WELFENS, PAUL J.J. (1990b), Economic Reforms in Eastern Europe: Problems, Options and Opportunities, paper prepared for testimony before U.S. Senate, Small Business Committee, March 23, 1990, updated version published in: Intereconomics, 1991..

WELFENS, PAUL J.J. (1990c), Privatizations, M&As and Intra-Firm Cooperation in the EC: Improved Prospects for Innovation?, in: PERLMAN, MARK, ed., Entrepreneurship, Technological Innovation, and Economic Growth: Papers in the Schumpeterian Tradition, University of Michigan Press, forthcoming.

WELFENS, PAUL J.J., ed. (1991a), European Monetary Integration. From German Dominance to an EC Central Bank?, New York-Heidelberg: Springer.

WELFENS, PAUL J.J. (1991b), International Implications of German Monetary Unification , in: DETTKE, D., ed., The European Monetary System and International Financial Markets, Bonn/Washington, 58-62.

WELFENS, PAUL J.J. (1992), The Market-Oriented Systemic Transformation of Socialist Economies, forthcoming.

WINIECKI, JAN (1990), Why Economic Reforms Fail in the Soviet System - A Property Rights-Based Approach, Economic Inquiry, Vol. 28, 195-221.

APPENDIX

Tab. A1: Key Economic Data for Eastern Germany and Western Germany 1990/91

	EASTERN GERMANY					*WESTERN G.*
	New orders and output					
	Industry		Construction		Business Registrations:	Output (1985=100)
	New Orders	Output	New Orders	Output	number in 1000	
	% change from previous period (prev. year)					
1990 III	-	-44.5(-48.1)	-	-	95.4	120.4
IV	-11.9	-4.5(-50.9)	3.2	0.9	84.5	120.9
1991 I	-	- -	-	-	73.4	123.1
	Labor Market Developments					
	Employed number in 1000	% from previous year	Vacancies number	Short-time Workers in 1000	Unemployment Rate in %	Unemployment Rate in %
1990 III	8,759	-10.8	27.0	1,295.0	3.5	6.4
1990 IV	8,193	-16.0	24.0	1,735.9	6.3	6.1
1991 I	-	-	21.8	1,925.8	8.6	5.6
	Prices					
	Producer Prices of of Industrial Products (Dome. Sales) 1989=100	% from previous per.	Cost of Living Index Total 1989=100	% from previous period	Clothing, Footwear 1989=100	Cost of Living 1985=100
1990 III	63.4	-	95.3	-	60.6	107.3
1990 IV	62.5	-1.4	98.5	3.3	68.2	108.4
1991 I	63.3*	1.9*	107.0	8.6	69.6	108.7**

* January (no estimate for I. quarter available); ** in April 1991 the year-on-year change was 2.8 percent.
Source: Deutsche Bundesbank (1991), Monatsberichte der Deutschen Bundesbank, May 1991.

Tab. A2: Exports to European CMEA Partners as a Percentage of Total Exports*

	Soviet Union	Other eastern Europe	of which						Yugoslavia**
			Bulgaria	CSFR	GDR	Hungary	Poland	Romania	
non-convertible trade valued at national rouble/dollar cross rate									
Rub/$ rate	0.63	-	0.65	1.51	1.74	2.09	2.96	0.96	-
Soviet Union	-	32	66	31	24	25	21	23	22
GDR	10	5	6	7	-	5	4	5	2
Other east. E.	36	15	12	17	18	10	10	10	11
non-convertible trade valued at 2 roubles to the dollar									
Soviet Union	-	28	49	27	22	26	25	14	-
GDR	5	4	4	6	-	5	4	3	-
Other east. E.	17	13	9	14	17	11	12	6	-

* Data refer to 1989. ** Yugoslavia's non-convertible trade with the Soviet Union is not denominated in transferable roubles.
Sources: CMEA. UN Economic Commission for Europe and national data/BIS, Annual Report, Basel 1991.

1 I am grateful for comments by Martin Schrenk, The World Bank, and research assistance provided by Tim Yarling.

2 As a percentage of government expenditures the share of price subsidies rose from 10.5 in 1980 to 18.5 percent in 1988, while the official price index (1970=100) stood at 99.4 and 99.5, respectively. See *Statistisches Bundesamt (1990)*. Saving deposits rose at the same time from M 99.7 bill. to 151.6 which suggests the existence of some monetary overhang - possibly being absorbed by rising prices in the shadow economy.

3 In 1990/91 this impairs economic growth in the whole EC, where Spain and Italy cope with stagnant growth because of their currency overvaluation in the EMS, while the Italian industry faces strong adjustment needs in the context of EC 1992. This could entail slow growth for the whole EC unless a united Germany grows fast. Weak German growth is to be expected if restructuring Eastern Germany is politically poorly managed.

4 The West German government will subsidize exports to the (former) CMEA countries until mid-1991. However, imports from Eastern European countries suffered immediately after July 1 since monetary unification brought for consumers full access to Western - and East Asian - goods and services with their higher quality and greater product variety. West Germany's trade balance surplus in German-German trade, representing some DM 15 bill. of trade in 1989, rose from DM 0.3 bill. in 1990.I to more than 3 bill. in the two following quarters. Imports from the CMEA countries fell from 15.4 bill. Mark in 1990.I to 7.8 bill. DM in 1990.II.

5 From an index value of 106.9 (1985=100) in the first quarter of 1990 production in industry fell to 56.7 (-46.8 percent) in the third quarter in East Germany; in light industry, in the textile industry and in the foods industry, where product quality and variety are important, the reduction was relatively highest: -54.3, -53.9 and - 59.1 percent, respectively. If the GDR had maintained its own currency but had made it fully convertible the GDR would have suffered a strong depreciation of its currency vis-à-vis most market economies, especially vis-à-vis the Federal Republic of Germany. Computations of changes in industrial production are based on *Sachverstaendigenrat zur Begutachtung der gesamtwirtschaftlichen Entwicklung (1990)*, Tab. IV.

6 The former CPEs' switch to convertible currency trade and the collapse of the CMEA suggest that traditional bilaterilism will be given up, and this alone should raise the overall volume of trade in the medium term while creating bilateral trade imbalances at the same time.

7 With respect to the changing regional breakdown of German trade Italy and France were the main winners of the emergence of CPEs in Eastern Europe and Russia.

8 Historical figures for 1930 are taken from *Drabek, Zdenek (1985)*. One approach to assess unification-induced effects on the future German trade orientation is the use of the gravity equation, where empirical results and simulations for the 1980s also suggest a potential growth of trade between a united Germany and Eastern Europe. See *Van Bergeijk, Peter A.G and Oldersma, Harry (1990)*.

9 The investment-output ratio, the growth rate of the labor force, the skill level and R&D-GNP ratios are major sources of economic growth in a theoretical perspective; monetary, or more generally, economic policy stability as proxied by the variance of the inflation rate also affect economic growth.

10 The income gap between the U.S. and Latin America is similar to that between Germany and its CPE neighbors and that between the EC and the former CPEs in Eastern Europe which suggest similar migration pressures.

11 Low state-administered prices induce a structural excess demand that is typical for the official economy in CPEs.

12 This aspect - mostly neglected in the analysis of the monetary overhang and so-called repressed inflation in CPEs, respectively - is important for purchasing power calculations and the assessment of welfare losses and gains in the transition from a socialist shortage economy to a market economy with its broad variety of products that are obtainable at comparatively low transactions costs. See *Welfens* (1991b).

13 See on the ratio of P*/P in the socialist and the capitalist shadow economy *Welfens, Paul J.J. and Welfens, Maria J.* (1991).

14 See for some aspects *Buchheim, Christoph (1990)*; *Klump, Rainer (1990)* and *Menderson Horst (1949)*.

15 Moreover, although opening up to the world economy certainly means for all former CPEs that aspiration levels with respect to long-term living standards and per capita income are rising, the former GDR provides an extreme example of sharply rising aspiration levels and expectations (with considerable "overshooting" that reflected a short-term lack of realism) which restrict sustainable options for economic policy. Opinion polls in East Germany immediately after monetary unification in July 1990 showed that a majority of the population expected to reach the much higher West German living standards within three years.

16 Murrell has emphasized that lack of multinational activities in socialist countries has been a reason for stagnating growth of output and trade in the CMEA countries. See *Murrell* (1990).

COMMENT ON: EC INTEGRATION AND ECONOMIC REFORMS IN CMEA COUNTRIES: A UNITED GERMANY AS A BRIDGE BETWEEN EAST AND WEST?

Martin Schrenk

1. Introduction

Welfens' paper stakes out the vast range of topics covered by the theme of this conference, and he introduces the evolving major strands of economic and political analysis. The paper raises five major questions:

(1) Can the EC serve as a model for CMEA reform?
(2) Can system reform in East Germany serve as a model for CMEA countries?
(3) How does German unification affect the EC?
(4) Can a unified Germany serve as a bridge between the EC and CMEA?
(5) What are the global repercussions of German unification?

I want to comment briefly on each of these questions which are likely to dominate the agenda for these two days. In most instances my comments paraphrase thoughts expressed or implied in Welfens' paper.

2. EC as a Model for CMEA Transformation

During the first half of 1990, one could imagine a legitimate role for a suitably reformed CMEA, an East European counterpart of the EC as it were. By now, however, it has become evident that a reformed CMEA would at best be a clearing house for experiences and thoughts without any operational mandate, an institution akin to the OECD.

I am not arguing that there would be no role for a reformed operational CMEA; I merely fail to see a constituency for it. The USSR, being in a structural creditor position vis-à-vis the East European Five, seems to have lost all interest. And the Five, while hoping for some bilateral transitional arrangements to soften the blow from the unravelling of the CMEA, seem not to be interested either in any new permanent framework, which includes the USSR as the biggest single member. Even the proposal for the creation of an East European Payments Union, which could make eminent sense as a possible bridge between the EC and a reformed CMEA, seems to remain an orphan.

Nevertheless, the term CMEA remains useful to designate a well-defined group of countries, and I understand that this is the meaning Welfens attaches to it. It seems preferable to the fashionable but fussy new terminology of "East Central" or "Central Europe", reflecting a vacuous political agenda rather than serving as an unambiguous, neutral shorthand.

3. East German Systemic Reform as a Model for CMEA Country Reform

I agree with Welfens that the system reform in East Germany should be a highly relevant model, not in the sense of a blueprint to be emulated, but as an experiment in vitrio to be evaluated for lessons of success or failure. To derive applicable lessons, however, one has to isolate features in regard to which East Germany is a special case in terms of manifest failure or advantages.

Welfens identifies a number of serious failures. For instance:

(1) Massive defects in the productive and physical infrastructure. The quoted figure of $400 bill. as the resource requirement for productive investment alone points to the awesome size of the task. As East Germany was widely considered the success story among the CMEA countries, the requirements of the rest of the CMEA are almost beyond imagination and certainly dwarf any number one can at this point imagine for the size of Western credits or direct investment.

(2) Pervasive obsolescence of output mix and critical technical and managerial skills. Again, as East Germany is commonly assumed to have been the best performer within the CMEA, the position of other members must be truly desperate.

(3) Absence of an "entrepreneurial culture" in the Schumpeterian sense.

(4) After a beginning has been made to harden the budget constraints of firms through monetary reform, crippling liquidity problems will surface.

Welfens identifies a number of advantages which none of the other CMEA countries shares. For instance:

(1) Huge amounts of "external" grant resources are available. Welfens mentions annual government transfers in the order of $60 bill. in the 1990s. This would translate into about $3,800 per capita per year, equivalent to almost three quarters of GNP per capita of the GDR in 1988/89, and exceeding that of several CMEA countries and dwarfing what any of them could ever hope for under most optimistic assumptions about the generosity of Western countries in the form of credits.

(2) Unrestricted access to the West German pools of investment resources and of technical and managerial skills critical to "jump start" economic growth.

(3) Instant monetary stability; instant monetary, fiscal and price reform; import of a tested legal system; a well-developed and financially sound safety net system for unemployed workers as well as for firms in temporary liquidity squeeze in the wake of the "shock".

(4) The secure financial "anchor" of a fixed exchange rate, which does not require reserves and measures for defense, and absence of any external constraint. However, this particular advantage may well turn out to be the Achilles heel of the notion of a rapid take-off in East Germany if the precarious initial balance of productivity and wage differentials in comparison with West Germany cannot be maintained, with potentially devastating effects on competitiveness in East Germany.

Yet, in spite of these advantages, Welfens, like most other analysts, does not seem to be quite certain about the success of the operation. His paper reflects such doubts by invoking the Mezzogiorno scenario - a metaphor for an economic structure consisting of isolated enclave activities in a sea of subsistence services and agriculture, and of structural unemployment, highly subsidized and without the prospect of a self-sustaining take-off. But the relevance of the possibility of such outcome is discounted without much discussion. But are the conditions under which this worst case scenario could materialize, and are not the courses of action available to avoid it, analytical questions of the highest order?

There is no more prima facie reason to take for granted that the vacuum in East Germany would pull in financial and human resources from West Germany than to assume the opposite: that the gravity of West Germany will absorb the scarce voluntary savings and talent from East Germany. Both movements will undoubtedly happen simultaneously, but it is impossible to predict that the balance will be in favor of East Germany. Nor can one assume that a large administrative transfer of financial resources from West to East would be a sufficient condition regardless of specific policies. One can also point to at least one mechanism, which would almost invariably lead into the Mezzogiorno scenario: wage levels racing ahead of productivity levels.

Needless to say, such an outcome, in fact any outcome other than a fairly rapid "economic miracle" in East Germany would be a political disaster and a serious blow to reform in Eastern Europe. For if system reform fails to deliver rapid self-sustained growth in East Germany with its unique starting position and "external" conditions, where else could it succeed? Such a failure would also be a serious blow to the vitality of the EC, for a Germany entangled in intractable economic and social problems in its eastern part is likely to turn from proponent of advancing EC integration, and of integration of the EC into the world economy, into an adversary.

It would seem then that the chances for the first best scenario - a swift economic, social, and political integration of East Germany into the Federal Republic in response to generous official resource transfers and the powers of the market forces - although better than even, are far from being certain. If one accepts that proposition, then the line of investigation would have to focus on the potential causes of failure and the scope for support programs and contingency actions. The first order issue would be the analysis of the dynamics of the integration process, and most importantly the conditions of and the time horizon for the "turning point" from downswing to recovery.

4. German Unification and the EC

It is difficult to imagine a positive link between German unification and the further development of the EC. If the effort to achieve a credible momentum of economic integration fails, then the perception of irreconcilable conflicts between the interests of Germany and those of the rest of the EC would arise, reducing the political support for further EC integration. At the least a failure of economic take-off in East Germany is likely to strengthen protectionism. As it can under the rules of the EC not be directed against other members, it would strengthen protectionism of the EC against the rest of the world, and perhaps most prominently against Eastern Europe.

If economic and political integration of East Germany succeeds, it is likely to attract a large voluntary flow of investment resources from West Germany. While financial resources in general do not seem to be a serious constraint, the supply of entrepreneurial initiative to engage in movement of resources to ventures in an uncertain environment is limited, and the capacity to explore a wide range of options is limited because of the transaction costs involved in exploring them in sufficient detail. West German firms that are ready to enter new ventures would tend to look at a booming East Germany first for a great number of obvious reasons, and Leipzig is likely to crowd out, say, Lisbon or Warsaw.

5. Unified Germany as a Bridge Between the EC-CMEA

For a unified Germany to serve as a bridge between the EC and the CMEA two conditions would have to be met. First, that East German economic and social integration be concluded swiftly, so that the political fall-out associated with the Mezzogiorno scenario for East Germany does not occur. And second, that the CMEA countries including the USSR succeed in avoiding the "Latin America" scenario of permanent political and social crisis, so that the German-Polish border will not become the border between the Europe of prosperity and the

Europe of misery, a "Welfare Wall" in Antall's words. The specter of migration pressures to the EC would be just one of the political and social implications. In short, a unified Germany is, merely by its existence, not likely to serve as a bridge between the EC and the CMEA; its function as a bridge is rather the by-product of success of reforms in both East Germany and the CMEA.

6. Global Repercussions of German Unification

Almost regardless of success or failure of the East German experiment, some "crowding out" of the rest of the world from German financial resources and the "investment horizon" of West German investors is bound to happen. The same is implied in the medium term projections of a drastic decline of the West German current account surplus from its recent peak in excess of $80 bill. on an annual basis in the wake of unification. Some projections suggest that the balance may in fact turn negative. As a casual look at the economic and financial indicators in the back of *The Economist* suggests, such a reversal would cause ripple effects in trade and capital flows felt throughout the world economy, particularly as it would be accompanied by a sizable decline of Japan's current account surplus, now universally expected for the next few years, and by rising capital requirements of the CMEA countries. Clearly the borrowing binge of some countries cannot continue, although the ultimate victims would be the Third World which would face higher interest rates and a reduced level of external financing.

The paper suggests in its last section that Germany "is building up a special relationship with the Soviet Union, and this is likely to lead to conflict of interest with the US." Conversely, it suggests that from the Soviet point of view "the German economy is the only major one with which reliable long-term relations can be developed." And the paper closes by expressing the "hope that integrating Eastern Europe and the USSR into the world market economy and overcoming the economic and political divide of Europe does not lead to a weakening of transatlantic cooperation." The recent events and the unfolding new challenges in Europe will unquestionably absorb resources and political energies of the EC in general and of Germany in particular, at least for a lengthy transition period. And in the longer run they will more likely than not strengthen the momentum toward evolution of a multipolar economic and political global order without a clear-cut leadership position of any individual country or group of countries. As either development constitutes a departure from familiar roles and rules, some political conflicts seem inevitable. But I find it difficult to see such conflicts rising to the level of a new "German Question".

Map of Western and Eastern Germany
(courtesy of Westermann Verlag and Bundespresse- und Informationsamt)

Germany Map of Länder

The Federal Republic of Germany is a grouping of 16 independent Länder.
The powers of the Länder directly affect the daily life of the individual. The Länder have their own constitutions and their own laws pertaining to such matters as education, communal organizations, and police. The Länder also have extensive administrative authority.
The Länder administer and enforce most of the Federal laws along with Länder laws. They function as "agents of the Federation" (Article 85 of the Basic Law) in such matters as autobahn and Federal highway construction.
The Federation's own areas of administrative responsibility include the Foreign Service, national railways, the Postal Service, the Border Police and the Armed Forces.
The Länder derive revenue from taxes on property, automobiles, inheritances, land, beer, gambling and lotteries. They also receive a percentage of income tax, corporate tax, and value added tax, which is a kind of sales tax.

Legend

■	More than 1,000,000 inhabitants
⊙	More than 100,000 inhabitants
•	50,000 – 100,000 inhabitants
○	Less than 50,000 inhabitants
	National frontier
	Land boundary
Berlin	Capital of the Federal Republic of Germany
Mainz	Capital of Land

Schleswig-Holstein	
Capital:	Kiel
Area:	15,730 sq km
Population:	2.6 million

Bremen	
Capital:	Bremen
Area:	404 sq km
Population:	0.67 million

Lower Saxony	
Capital:	Hanover
Area:	47,349 sq km
Population:	7.3 million

North Rhine-Westphalia	
Capital:	Düsseldorf
Area:	34,068 sq km
Population:	17.1 million

Hesse	
Capital:	Wiesbaden
Area:	21,114 sq km
Population:	5.7 million

Rhineland-Palatinate	
Capital:	Mainz
Area:	19,849 sq km
Population:	3.7 million

Saarland	
Capital:	Saarbrücken
Area:	2,570 sq km
Population:	1.1 million

Baden-Württemberg	
Capital:	Stuttgart
Area:	35,751 sq km
Population:	9.6 million

Mecklenburg-Western Pomerania	
Capital:	Schwerin
Area:	23,835 sq km
Population:	2.0 million

Hamburg	
Capital:	Hamburg
Area:	755 sq km
Population:	1.6 million

Brandenburg	
Capital:	Potsdam
Area:	29,060 sq km
Population:	2.6 million

Berlin	
Capital:	Berlin
Area:	883 sq km
Population:	3.4 million

Saxony-Anhalt	
Capital:	Magdeburg
Area:	20,444 sq km
Population:	3.0 million

Saxony	
Capital:	Dresden
Area:	18,338 sq km
Population:	4.9 million

Thuringia	
Capital:	Erfurt
Area:	16,251 sq km
Population:	2.7 million

Bavaria	
Capital:	Munich
Area:	70,554 sq km
Population:	11.2 million

Appendix: Selected Data for Western Germany and Eastern Germany

(all data are from Deutsche Bundesbank, Monthly Report, July 1991)

General economic conditions – western Germany

1. Origin, distribution and expenditure of national product

Item	1986	1987	1988 p	1989 p	1990 p	1987	1988 p	1989 p	1990 p	1987	1988 p	1989 p	1990
	DM billion					Change from previous year in %				Percentage of total			
	at current prices												
I. Origin of national product													
Gross value added													
Agriculture, forestry and fisheries	34.0	30.2	33.7	38.0	39.1	— 11.1	+ 11.5	+ 12.6	+ 3.0	1.5	1.6	1.7	
Producing sector	786.5	795.0	826.5	882.1	953.7	+ 1.1	+ 4.0	+ 6.7	+ 8.1	39.7	39.2	39.3	3
Energy supply, 1 mining	65.9	68.7	67.8	69.6	71.0	+ 4.2	— 1.2	+ 2.6	+ 2.1	3.4	3.2	3.1	
Manufacturing	620.4	624.7	652.4	697.8	752.6	+ 0.7	+ 4.4	+ 7.0	+ 7.9	31.2	30.9	31.1	3
Construction	100.1	101.7	106.2	114.7	130.1	+ 1.5	+ 4.5	+ 8.0	+ 13.4	5.1	5.0	5.1	
Distribution, transportation 2	269.6	279.5	294.5	309.9	331.3	+ 3.7	+ 5.3	+ 5.2	+ 6.9	14.0	14.0	13.8	1
Services 3	520.5	548.6	592.3	625.2	683.8	+ 5.4	+ 8.0	+ 5.6	+ 9.4	27.4	28.1	27.8	2
All enterprises	1,610.5	1,653.4	1,746.9	1,855.1	2,007.8	+ 2.7	+ 5.7	+ 6.2	+ 8.2	82.5	82.9	82.6	8
do. adjusted 4	1,526.9	1,571.1	1,661.9	1,765.9	1,912.8	+ 2.9	+ 5.8	+ 6.3	+ 8.3	78.4	78.8	78.7	7
Government	217.1	225.8	231.9	238.8	253.2	+ 4.0	+ 2.7	+ 3.0	+ 6.0	11.3	11.0	10.6	1
Households 5	46.4	49.3	51.5	53.8	58.2	+ 6.2	+ 4.5	+ 4.4	+ 8.2	2.5	2.4	2.4	
All sectors	1,790.4	1,846.2	1,945.2	2,058.5	2,224.2	+ 3.1	+ 5.4	+ 5.8	+ 8.0	92.2	92.3	91.7	9
Gross domestic product 6	1,925.3	1,990.5	2,094.9	2,219.4	2,403.4	+ 3.4	+ 5.2	+ 5.9	+ 8.3	99.4	99.4	98.9	9
Net factor incomes from abroad	+ 10.8	+ 12.5	+ 13.1	+ 25.8	+ 22.1	.	.	.	.	0.6	0.6	1.1	
Gross national product at market prices	1,936.1	2,003.0	2,108.0	2,245.2	2,425.5	+ 3.5	+ 5.2	+ 6.5	+ 8.0	100	100	100	10
II. Distribution of national product													
Wage and salary income 7	1,079.5	1,124.7	1,169.2	1,221.5	1,312.6	+ 4.2	+ 4.0	+ 4.5	+ 7.5	56.2	55.5	54.4	5
Entrepreneurial and property income	418.1	425.3	466.4	512.8	557.1	+ 1.7	+ 9.7	+ 9.9	+ 8.7	21.2	22.1	22.8	2
National income	1,497.6	1,550.0	1,635.5	1,734.2	1,869.7	+ 3.5	+ 5.5	+ 6.0	+ 7.8	77.4	77.6	77.2	7
III. Expenditure of national product													
Private consumption	1,066.4	1,108.0	1,154.5	1,207.3	1,291.3	+ 3.9	+ 4.2	+ 4.6	+ 7.0	55.3	54.8	53.8	5
Government consumption	382.6	397.3	412.4	418.9	447.3	+ 3.9	+ 3.8	+ 1.6	+ 6.8	19.8	19.6	18.7	1
Machinery and equipment	160.9	169.4	182.5	204.9	234.5	+ 5.3	+ 7.7	+ 12.3	+ 14.5	8.5	8.7	9.1	
Construction	212.6	216.4	227.4	247.2	276.1	+ 1.8	+ 5.1	+ 8.7	+ 11.7	10.8	10.8	11.0	1
Increase in stocks	+ 2.9	— 0.6	+ 9.0	+ 23.5	+ 25.5	.	.	.	.	— 0.0	0.4	1.0	
Domestic expenditure	1,825.4	1,890.5	1,985.8	2,101.8	2,274.8	+ 3.6	+ 5.0	+ 5.8	+ 8.2	94.4	94.2	93.6	9
Foreign balance 8	+ 110.7	+ 112.5	+ 122.2	+ 143.4	+ 150.8	.	.	.	.	5.6	5.8	6.4	
Exports	637.0	637.5	687.5	785.5	868.3	+ 0.1	+ 7.8	+ 14.3	+ 10.5	31.8	32.6	35.0	3
Imports	526.3	525.0	565.3	642.1	717.5	— 0.2	+ 7.7	+ 13.6	+ 11.8	26.2	26.8	28.6	2
Gross national product at market prices	1,936.1	2,003.0	2,108.0	2,245.2	2,425.5	+ 3.5	+ 5.2	+ 6.5	+ 8.0	100	100	100	10
	at 1985 prices												
Private consumption	1,072.0	1,106.9	1,137.4	1,154.3	1,204.2	+ 3.3	+ 2.8	+ 1.5	+ 4.3	58.2	57.7	56.4	5
Government consumption	375.0	380.9	389.1	382.7	393.9	+ 1.5	+ 2.2	— 1.6	+ 2.9	20.0	19.7	18.7	1
Machinery and equipment	159.5	167.3	178.3	195.7	220.9	+ 4.9	+ 6.6	+ 9.8	+ 12.9	8.8	9.0	9.6	1
Construction	209.0	209.0	215.4	226.4	238.1	— 0.0	+ 3.1	+ 5.1	+ 5.2	11.0	10.9	11.1	1
Increase in stocks	+ 2.7	+ 1.0	+ 11.4	+ 24.7	+ 27.4	.	.	.	.	0.1	0.6	1.2	
Domestic expenditure	1,818.2	1,865.0	1,931.5	1,983.7	2,084.5	+ 2.6	+ 3.6	+ 2.7	+ 5.1	98.0	98.0	96.9	9
Foreign balance 8	+ 56.2	+ 37.4	+ 40.3	+ 63.1	+ 54.2	.	.	.	.	2.0	2.0	3.1	
Exports	645.2	651.3	689.3	766.0	840.2	+ 0.9	+ 5.8	+ 11.1	+ 9.7	34.2	35.0	37.4	3
Imports	589.1	614.0	649.0	702.9	786.0	+ 4.2	+ 5.7	+ 8.3	+ 11.8	32.3	32.9	34.3	3
Gross national product at market prices	1,874.4	1,902.3	1,971.8	2,046.8	2,138.7	+ 1.5	+ 3.7	+ 3.8	+ 4.5	100	100	100	10

Source: Federal Statistical Office. — 1 Including water supply. — 2 Including telecommunications. — 3 Banks, insurance enterprises, letting of dwellings and other services. — 4 Enterprises' gross value added less imputed remuneration for bank services. — 5 Including private non-profit organisations. — 6 Gross value added by all economic sectors plus turnover tax receipts and turnover tax withheld because of statutory special regulations and import levies (import duties, excise taxes on imports, price adjustment levies and monetary compensatory amounts on imports of a cultural products). — 7 Including employers' contributions to social security funds other social security expenditure by employers (inter alia on company old-age pens schemes). — 8 Including transactions in goods and services with the former GDR p Provisional.

Discrepancies in the totals are due to rounding.

ıdex of net output in the producing sector *

ıd for working-day variations

	Producing sector, total		of which: Basic and producer goods sector		Capital goods sector: Total		of which: Mechan-ical engi-neering	Road vehicle manu-facture	Electri-cal engi-neering	Consumer goods sector: Total		of which Textile industry	Construction	
	1985 = 100	Change from previous year in %	1985 = 100	Change from previous year in %	1985 = 100	Change from previous year in %				1985 = 100	Change from previous year in %		1985 = 100	Change from previous year in %
·erage	102.7	+ 0.3	100.0	+ 0.4	104.7	+ 0.2	102.6	107.9	105.6	103.4	+ 1.2	100.4	105.8	— 0.5
,,	106.5	+ 3.7	106.3	+ 6.3	108.1	+ 3.2	105.0	108.2	111.1	106.5	+ 3.0	98.0	110.3	+ 4.3
,,	111.8	+ 5.0	108.6	+ 2.2	116.4	+ 7.7	115.9	116.3	120.7	111.1	+ 4.3	99.2	117.6	+ 6.6
,,	117.7	+ 5.3	110.9	+ 2.1	123.0	+ 5.7	123.3	122.1	127.6	118.1	+ 6.3	100.9	124.1	+ 5.5
ın.	109.7	+ 5.5	108.4	+ 2.7	111.1	+ 8.3	98.7	123.8	114.8	112.4	+ 5.2	104.5	91.3	+ 0.8
·b.	110.2	+ 5.2	106.2	+ 2.8	116.9	+ 7.5	111.6	124.6	122.6	112.5	+ 4.7	102.8	94.7	+ 5.5
arch	123.5	+ 6.8	117.0	+ 3.8	131.0	+ 8.0	129.5	134.5	135.8	125.7	+ 6.5	111.9	125.8	+12.7
·ril	113.8	+ 0.4	110.3	+ 0.4	118.6	— 0.5	117.1	121.7	122.8	113.4	+ 0.9	100.3	128.0	+ 5.7
ay	116.3	+10.1	111.8	+ 4.4	122.1	+12.7	122.4	123.7	124.9	114.5	+11.7	101.3	135.6	+12.8
ne	116.6	+ 2.3	110.6	— 0.8	124.8	+ 3.0	132.0	122.9	125.1	113.9	+ 1.1	100.6	131.4	+ 1.2
·ly	113.1	+ 5.8	110.7	+ 2.4	116.0	+ 6.0	119.4	108.2	124.7	108.9	+ 7.1	88.5	137.0	+ 8.6
·g.	108.8	+ 5.8	108.3	+ 1.4	106.2	+ 6.2	106.3	95.2	111.4	109.2	+ 7.4	77.3	128.5	+ 2.9
·p.	123.5	+ 5.4	113.1	+ 2.1	129.9	+ 5.0	128.1	128.2	136.9	127.8	+ 6.1	109.2	141.3	+ 5.0
:t.	132.5	+ 6.3	119.5	+ 2.3	136.7	+ 5.6	130.0	142.1	144.4	137.5	+ 8.4	117.0	152.9	+ 6.6
·v.	126.8	+ 5.3	114.5	+ 3.2	131.8	+ 3.9	129.5	130.9	137.5	129.6	+ 8.8	106.7	130.5	+ 2.8
·c.	117.0	+ 4.0	99.9	+ 0.1	130.7	+ 4.0	155.1	109.2	130.1	111.9	+ 7.9	90.3	92.7	+ 0.8
ın.	116.3	+ 6.0	112.2	+ 3.5	117.1	+ 5.4	103.1	128.2	122.8	122.2	+ 8.7	106.8	95.7	+ 4.8
·b.	114.5	+ 3.9	106.2	+ 0.0	122.4	+ 4.7	112.0	128.2	129.2	122.5	+ 8.9	106.7	67.5	—28.7
arch	127.0	+ 2.8	117.0	+ 0.0	133.3	+ 1.8	126.5	135.9	142.3	131.8	+ 4.9	111.9	130.0	+ 3.3
·ril p	122.0	+ 7.2	115.1	+ 4.4	127.6	+ 7.6	118.1	133.6	132.4	122.6	+ 8.1	103.3	136.1	+ 6.3

Federal Statistical Office. — * Results for kinds of activity units. —
ıonal.

3 Prices

Period	Index of producer prices of industrial products in domestic sales 1					Index of producer prices of farm products 1			Indices of prices in foreign trade		Indices of unit values in foreign trade			Index world market prices of raw materials 3, 4
	Total		of which Products of			Total		of which Vegetable products	Exports	Imports	Exports	Imports	Terms of trade 2	
	1985 = 100	Change from previous year in %	the basic and producer goods sector	the capital goods sector	the consumer goods sector	1985 = 100	Change from previous year in %		1985 = 100		1980 = 100			1985 = 100
1981 average	88.3	+ 7.8	90.4	88.0	89.4	103.3	+ 6.1	107.5	88.7	91.2	106.3	113.8	93.4	[illegible]
1982 ,,	93.5	+ 5.9	93.8	93.0	92.9	107.0	+ 3.6	106.3	92.5	93.3	110.9	114.5	96.9	[illegible]
1983 ,,	94.9	+ 1.5	93.4	95.5	94.5	105.4	— 1.5	108.0	94.1	93.0	112.4	114.1	98.5	[illegible]
1984 ,,	97.6	+ 2.8	97.2	97.6	97.5	104.1	— 1.2	107.3	97.4	98.6	116.3	120.8	96.3	[illegible]
1985 ,,	100	+ 2.5	100	100	100	100	— 3.9	100	100	100	120.8	123.9	97.5	[illegible]
1986 ,,	97.5	— 2.5	89.1	102.1	101.0	94.3	— 5.7	98.3	98.2	84.3	116.8	104.1	112.2	
1987 ,,	95.1	— 2.5	86.3	103.8	101.9	91.7	— 2.8	98.9	97.3	79.8	o 113.8	97.8	116.4	
1988 ,,	96.3	+ 1.3	87.9	105.5	103.8	91.8	+ 0.1	96.0	99.3	80.8	114.8	98.7	116.3	
1989 ,,	99.3	+ 3.1	93.4	107.8	106.5	99.8	+ 8.7	97.4	102.1	84.4	120.0	106.0	113.2	[illegible]
1990 ,,	101.0	+ 1.7	93.1	110.7	109.1	94.7	— 5.1	97.4	102.2	82.5	118.5	103.3	114.7	[illegible]
1990 May	100.8	+ 1.5	91.7	110.5	108.8	98.7	+ 0.4	103.4	102.1	81.1	118.7	101.1	117.4	
June	100.8	+ 1.6	91.3	110.7	108.9	98.9	— 1.9	102.4	102.2	80.6	119.4	100.7	118.6	
July	100.7	+ 1.4	91.4	110.9	109.2	98.1	— 3.5	101.0	102.3	80.6	120.5	102.4	117.7	
Aug.	101.3	+ 1.9	93.4	111.1	109.4	94.3	— 9.2	98.3	102.3	81.9	117.9	101.4	116.3	[illegible]
Sep.	101.7	+ 2.1	94.9	111.3	109.6	93.3	— 11.4	99.6	102.5	83.9	118.3	104.5	113.2	[illegible]
Oct.	102.1	+ 2.0	96.8	111.5	110.0	90.7	— 11.8	95.3	102.5	85.0	117.7	106.2	110.8	[illegible]
Nov.	101.8	+ 1.8	95.4	111.6	110.1	91.2	— 10.0	97.0	102.4	84.1	117.0	104.2	112.3	[illegible]
Dec.	101.5	+ 1.5	94.1	111.6	110.2	91.9	— 8.7	100.0	102.3	83.4	119.2	104.1	114.5	[illegible]
1991 Jan.	102.4	+ 2.3	95.6	112.2	110.9	91.5	— 5.3	101.4	102.7	83.2	116.5	103.3	112.8	
Feb.	102.3	+ 2.2	94.5	112.5	111.2	p 94.3	p — 2.8	104.5	102.8	82.2	117.1	103.5	113.1	
March	102.0	+ 1.8	92.5	112.9	111.3	p 94.9	p — 2.9	106.3	103.2	82.4	117.0	103.2	113.4	
April	102.9	+ 2.2	92.4	113.7	111.5	p 94.5	p — 3.8	108.4	103.7	83.3	...	...	...	
May	...	...	...	...	...	...	...	...	...	...	...	...	...	

Period	Overall price index for residential buildings 5		Price index for road construction 5		Cost of living index for all households						Cost of living excluding			
					Total						food		sources of energ[y] 6	
	1985 = 100	Change from previous year in %	1985 = 100	Change from previous year in %	1985 = 100	Change from previous year in %	Food	Other consumer goods	Services and repairs	Rents, including garage rents	1985 = 100	Change from previous year in %	1985 = 100	Change from previous year in %
1981 average	91.8	+ 5.8	100.0	+ 2.7	88.0	+ 6.3	92.0	88.7	87.1	83.9	87.3	+ 6.5	87.7	+
1982 ,,	94.8	+ 3.3	97.7	— 2.3	92.6	+ 5.2	96.5	93.3	91.9	88.5	92.0	+ 5.4	92.3	+
1983 ,,	96.7	+ 2.0	96.9	— 0.8	95.7	+ 3.3	98.0	95.7	95.6	93.5	95.3	+ 3.6	95.8	+
1984 ,,	99.3	+ 2.7	98.2	+ 1.3	98.0	+ 2.4	99.8	97.8	97.9	97.0	97.6	+ 2.4	98.1	+
1985 ,,	100	+ 0.7	100	+ 1.8	100	+ 2.0	100	100	100	100	100	+ 2.5	100	+
1986 ,,	101.4	+ 1.4	102.1	+ 2.1	99.9	— 0.1	99.6	97.7	102.3	101.8	99.9	— 0.1	101.6	+
1987 ,,	103.3	+ 1.9	103.2	+ 1.1	100.1	+ 0.2	99.1	96.6	104.3	103.4	100.3	+ 0.4	102.7	+
1988 ,,	105.5	+ 2.1	104.3	+ 1.1	101.4	+ 1.3	99.1	96.9	107.2	105.6	101.7	+ 1.4	104.4	+
1989 ,,	109.2	+ 3.5	106.6	+ 2.2	104.2	+ 2.8	101.3	99.9	109.9	108.7	104.6	+ 2.9	106.8	+
1990 ,,	116.0	+ 6.2	113.2	+ 6.2	107.0	+ 2.7	104.9	102.1	112.6	112.5	107.3	+ 2.6	109.5	+
1990 May	115.8	+ 6.3	113.1	+ 6.4	106.7	+ 2.3	106.2	101.2	112.6	112.0	106.8	+ 2.0	109.5	+
June	.	.	.	.	106.8	+ 2.3	106.0	101.1	112.9	112.3	106.9	+ 2.1	109.7	+
July	.	.	.	.	106.8	+ 2.4	105.3	101.0	113.1	112.7	107.0	+ 2.2	109.7	+
Aug.	117.2	+ 6.7	114.2	+ 6.7	107.1	+ 2.8	104.8	102.2	112.5	113.1	107.5	+ 2.7	109.5	+
Sep.	.	.	.	.	107.5	+ 3.0	104.2	103.1	112.6	113.4	108.0	+ 3.0	109.6	+
Oct.	.	.	.	.	108.2	+ 3.3	104.4	104.3	112.8	113.6	108.7	+ 3.3	109.9	+
Nov.	118.0	+ 6.7	115.5	+ 7.1	108.0	+ 3.0	104.4	103.8	113.0	113.9	108.6	+ 3.1	110.0	+
Dec.	.	.	.	.	108.1	+ 2.8	104.9	103.5	113.2	114.2	108.6	+ 2.8	110.4	+
1991 Jan.	.	.	.	.	108.8	+ 2.8	106.0	104.2	114.0	114.6	109.2	+ 2.9	110.9	+
Feb.	121.0	+ 7.2	117.3	+ 6.6	109.1	+ 2.7	106.7	104.3	114.2	115.1	109.5	+ 2.9	111.3	+
March	.	.	.	.	109.0	+ 2.5	107.1	103.5	114.5	115.7	109.3	+ 2.5	111.6	+
April	.	.	.	.	109.5	+ 2.8	108.0	104.0	115.0	116.2	109.7	+ 2.8	112.1	+
May	...	...	...	...	109.9	+ 3.0	108.7	104.3	115.3	116.8	110.1	+ 3.1	112.4	+

Source: Federal Statistical Office; for index of world market prices: Hamburgisches Welt-Wirtschafts-Archiv. — 1 Excluding value-added tax. — 2 Index of export unit values as % of the index of import unit values. — 3 Food and industrial raw materials; on a dollar basis. — 4 Rebased from original base 1975 = 100. — 5 Including value-added tax. — 6 Mineral oil products, electricity, gas and coal as well as contribu[tions] towards the cost of central heating, warm water and district heating (calculated b[y] Bundesbank). — p Provisional. — o Series levels not fully comparable (some [...] changed in 1988; the 1980 unit values are therefore partly estimated).

Selected economic data for eastern Germany

riod	Labour market												Memorandum item	
	Wage and salary earners 1				Short-time workers 2		Unemployed 3				Placements		New businesses registered	
	Industry	Construction	Transportation, postal and telecommunications services	Distribution	Number	Change from previous month	Number	Change from previous month	Unemployment rate in % 3, 4	Vacancies 3	in the relevant month	cumulative since start of 1990	in the relevant month	cumulative since start of 1990 5
	Thousands									Thousands				
90 May	6 2,961	6 371	6 580	6 722	.	.	95	+ 30	1.1	54	7	60	17	.
June	.	.	.	.	.	.	142	+ 47	1.6	41	6	66	54	101
July 7	2,777	361	553	671	656	.	272	+ 130	3.1	28	5	72	34	.
Aug.	2,710	367	558	661	1,500	+ 844	361	+ 89	4.1	20	10	81	31	.
Sep.	2,584	350	552	634	1,729	+ 229	445	+ 84	5.0	24	12	93	30	196
Oct.	2,452	343	525	582	1,704	— 25	537	+ 92	6.1	25	17	111	29	.
Nov.	2,388	337	512	554	1,710	+ 6	589	+ 52	6.7	24	18	128	28	.
Dec.	...	...	...	...	1,794	+ 84	642	+ 53	7.3	23	18	146	28	281
91 Jan.	...	...	...	...	1,841	+ 47	757	+ 115	8.6	23	26	172	8 26	.
Feb.	...	...	...	...	1,947	+ 106	787	+ 30	8.9	21	26	198	25	.
March	...	...	...	...	1,990	+ 43	808	+ 21	9.2	21	30	228	24	357
April	...	...	...	...	r 2,019	+ 29	837	+ 29	9.5	23	43	271	29	386
May	...	...	...	...	1,963	— 56	842	+ 5	9.5	25	47	318	...	...

	Producing sector													
	Manufacturing						Construction							
	Net output 9		New orders		Turnover		Output 10		New orders 10		Domestic turnover 10		Orders on hand 10	
	3rd qtr 1990 = 100	Change from previous month in %	2nd half of 1990 = 100	Change from previous month in %	2nd half of 1990 = 100	Change from previous month in %	DM billion	Change from previous month in %	2nd half of 1990 = 100	Change from previous month in %	DM billion	Change from previous month in %	2nd half of 1990 = 100	Change from previous quarter in %
90 Feb.	.	.	.	.	.	.	.	.	.	.	.	.	.	.
March	.	.	.	.	.	.	.	.	.	.	.	.	.	.
April	.	.	.	.	.	.	.	.	.	.	.	.	.	.
May	.	.	.	.	.	.	.	.	.	.	.	.	.	.
June	.	.	.	.	.	.	.	.	.	.	.	.	.	.
July 7	108.5	.	135.7	.	108.6	.	1.9	.	76.5	.	1.5	.	.	.
Aug.	100.7	— 7.2	105.1	— 22.5	106.2	— 2.2	2.0	+ 9.9	93.3	+ 22.0	2.3	+ 48.7	.	.
Sep.	90.8	— 9.8	85.5	— 18.6	94.7	— 10.8	2.0	— 1.8	125.4	+ 34.4	2.6	+ 13.0	118.0	.
Oct.	90.6	— 0.2	85.7	+ 0.2	92.2	— 2.6	2.1	+ 2.3	100.9	— 19.5	2.6	— 0.5	.	.
Nov.	98.3	+ 8.5	89.3	+ 4.2	96.1	+ 4.2	2.0	— 2.0	100.6	— 0.3	2.6	+ 2.0	.	.
Dec.	80.5	— 18.1	98.7	+ 10.5	102.1	+ 6.2	1.9	— 5.5	103.4	+ 2.8	3.8	+ 45.7	82.0	— 30.5
91 Jan.	64.7	— 17.6	...	...	...	...	...	...	...	...	...	...	.	.
Feb.	61.8	— 4.5	...	...	...	...	...	...	...	...	...	...	.	.

	Retail trade, prices 11													
	Retail turnover 12				Index of producer prices of industrial products (domestic sales)		Cost of living index 14							
		of which					Total							
		Enterprises mainly dealing in												
	Retail trade, total	food, drink and tobacco	household furniture and appliances 13	vehicles, vehicle parts, tyres, etc.	1989 = 100	Change from previous month in %	1989 = 100	Change from average of 1989 in %	Food, drink, tobacco	Clothing, footwear	Furniture, white goods and other household appliances	Goods for health care and hygiene	Goods for transport and telecommunications	Goods for education, entertainment, leisure
	3rd qtr 1990 = 100								1989 = 100					
90 May	.	.	.	.	.	.	98.3	— 1.7	100.9	89.0	96.0	92.3	100.2	106.4
June	.	.	.	.	.	.	87.9	— 12.1	97.4	51.7	84.8	88.5	93.4	88.3
July 7	.	.	.	.	64.2	.	94.5	— 5.5	115.4	57.5	74.5	119.4	85.2	88.5
Aug.	.	.	.	.	63.1	— 1.7	94.9	— 5.1	111.9	59.9	74.9	121.4	89.2	90.9
Sep.	.	.	.	.	62.8	— 0.5	96.6	— 3.4	111.4	64.4	76.3	122.6	89.8	95.2
Oct.	105.9	99.4	130.8	110.2	62.9	+ 0.2	98.2	— 1.8	112.2	66.9	76.6	123.4	92.5	99.6
Nov.	106.6	101.2	145.4	102.2	62.5	— 0.6	98.1	— 1.9	112.4	68.1	76.6	123.7	90.3	99.2
Dec.	120.4	114.8	128.7	101.6	62.1	— 0.6	99.1	— 0.9	113.8	69.5	77.5	126.6	89.1	100.2
91 Jan.	90.5	93.4	95.4	95.0	63.3	+ 1.9	106.4	+ 6.4	114.9	69.3	78.8	127.5	96.2	102.6
Feb.	...	...	...	...	63.4	+ 0.2	106.8	+ 6.8	115.4	69.6	79.1	128.1	95.0	104.8
March	...	...	...	...	63.2	— 0.3	107.7	+ 7.7	116.8	69.8	79.3	129.2	96.6	105.4
April	...	...	...	...	63.2	± 0	108.5	+ 8.5	117.5	70.1	79.6	130.5	98.4	106.0

ırce: Federal Statistical Office, Joint Statistical Office of the Lånder Brandenburg, ;cklenburg-Western Pomerania, Saxony, Saxony-Anhalt and Thuringia or former ɛtistical Office of the GDR, Federal Labour Office. — 1 Wage and salary earners, uding trainees; monthly averages. — 2 Mid-month figures; short-time working also ɹdes retraining and further training. — 3 End-of-month figures. — 4 Unemployed percentage of the total labour force; up to May 1990 calculated by the Bundes-k. — 5 The cumulated figures contain revisions not included in the individual monthly figures. — 6 Quarterly average. — 7 Inception of the monetary, economic and social union. — 8 From January 1991 excluding Berlin (east). Of a total of 281,096 new business registrations for 1990, 23,690 were accounted for by Berlin (east). — 9 Index for kinds of activity units; per calendar month. — 10 Construction enterprises with 20 or more employees. — 11 From July 1990, prices in Deutsche Mark; previously, prices in GDR Mark. — 12 At current prices. — 13 Excluding electrical equipment and apparatus. — 14 All households. — r Revised.

List of Authors and Conference Participants

Claudia Ade
Universität Hannover

Dr. Michael Aho
Council on Foreign Relations

Dr. Gerhard Bäcker
Wirtschafts- und Sozialwissenschaftliches Institut des DGB

Dr. Stefan Baron
Die Wirtschaftswoche (session chair)

Dr. Andrzej Budzinski
Polish Ministry of Foreign Economic Relations

Dr. Doris Cornelsen
Deutsches Institut für Wirtschaftsforschung

Prof. Dr. Rudiger Dornbusch
Massachusetts Institute of Technology

Prof. Dr. George M. von Furstenberg
Indiana University

Dr. Lothar Griesbach
Representative of German Industry and Trade (session chair)

Dr. Ruslan Grinberg
Institute of International Economic and Political Studies - Moscow

Dr. John Hardt
Congressional Research Service

Prof. Dr. Karl-Hans Hartwig
Universität Münster und Universität Bochum

Prof. Dr. Ullrich Heilemann
Rheinisch-Westfälisches Institut für Wirtschaftsforschung

Prof. Dr. Klaus-Dirk Henke
Universität Hannover

Dr. C. Randall Henning
Institute for International Economics (session chair)

Prof. Dr. Lutz Hoffmann
President, Deutsches Institut für Wirtschaftsforschung

Dr. Jackson Janes
Director, American Institute for Contemporary German Studies at the Johns Hopkins University

Dr. Henning Klodt
Kiel Institute for World Economics

Prof. Dr. Jürgen Klose
Hochschule für Ökonomie Berlin und American Institute for Contemporary German Studies at the John Hopkins University

Dr. Steven Kramer
American Institute for Contemporary German Studies at the John Hopkins University

Dr. Robert Lawrence
The Brookings Institution (session chair)

Dr. Robert Livingston
Director, American Institute for Contemporary German Studies at the Johns Hopkins University

Klaus Löbbe
Rheinisch-Westfälisches Institut für Wirtschaftsforschung

Peter Lutz
Universität Hannover

Dr. Thomas Mayer
Salmon Brothers, London

Prof. Dr. Claude Menard
Université de Paris, Sorbonne

Dr. Peter Palinkas
The European Parliament

Dr. Detlev Rohwedder
President, Treuhandanstalt

Prof. Dr. Gary Saxonhouse
University of Michigan

Dr. Claus Schnabel
Institut der deutschen Wirtschaft

Dr. Garry Schinasi
International Monetary Fund

Dr. Martin Schrenk
The World Bank

Prof. Dr. Hans-Werner Sinn
Universität München

Prof. Dr. Angela Stent
Georgetown University

Prof. Dr. Günter Streibel
Humboldt-Universität Berlin

Dr. Manfred Wegner
ifo Institut für Wirtschaftsforschung

Prof. Dr. Paul J. J. Welfens
Universität Potsdam

Prof. Dr. Nick Ziegler
Massachusetts Institute of Technology

List of Tables and Figures

Chapter A

Table 1: Gross Outputs of Manufacturing Industry (including Mining) in Eastern Germany by Kinds of Products 28
Table 2: Composition of Mechanical Engineering in Eastern Germany - 1992 29
Table 3: Composition of Electrotechnical Industry in Eastern Germany - 1992 29
Table 4: The Chemical Industry in Eastern Germany - 1992 30
Table 5: Turnover and Wage Costs in the Manufacturing and Mining Industry in Eastern Germany - 1991 and 1992 30
Table 6: Sectoral Employment in Eastern Germany - 1989 and 1992 31
Table 7: Labor Cost in the Manufacturing Sector in Eastern Germany - 1993 32

Figure 1: Employed in Eastern Germany by Aggregated Sectors 33
Figure 2: Employed in Eastern and Western Germany by Aggregated Sectors 34

Chapter B

Table 1: Employment Potential in the GDR by Sector 47
Table 2: GDR Exports to Eastern European Countries 55
Table 3: GDR Imports from Eastern European Countries 55
Table 4: Key-Economic Indicators of East Germany in current prices 61
Table 5: Investment in East Germany by Industry - in billion DM 65
Table 6: Production in Manufacturing in East Germany - Structure 1990 - 1993 67

Figure 1: Daily Industrial Production of the Economy. Annual Average 1985 = 100 42
Figure 2: Unemployed 43
Figure 3: Immigration and Outmigration Across the Borders of the Former GDR 44
Figure 4: Supply and Demand in East Germany (Million DM, in constant 1991 prices) 63
Figure 5: External Balance (Billion DM, in constant 1991 prices) 63
Figure 6: Ratio of Consumption to GNP (1) and Ratio of Investment to GNP (2) in East and West Germany 64
Figure 7: Share of Manufacturing (1), Services (2) and Construction (3) in GDP in East and West Germany 66
Figure 8: Marginal Productivity of Capital (MPK), Ratio of Gross Investment to GDP (IQ), Rate of Growth (GDP % p. a.) in East Germany 72

Chapter C

Table 1: Real Gross Value-Added In East Germany, 1991 - 1994 (Annual percentage change, at prices of 1991) 80
Table 2: Gross Value-Added and Employment in the New and Old *Länder*, 1989 - 1993 (Shares in percentage of total economy) 81
Table 3: Net Production in the Goods Producing Industries, 1991 - 1994 (Indices, second half year 1990 = 100, corrected by working days 82
Table 4: Real Gross Capital Formation, 1992 - 1995 (Annual percentage changes, at 1991 prices) 86
Table 5: Investment per Employee in Manufacturing - in DM 87
Table 6: Gross Capital Formation by Sectors, 1991 - 1994 (At current prices and shares in percentage) 87
Table 7: Macroeconomic Labor Productivity in East Germany, 1992 - 1995 (Annual percentage changes) 88

Table 8: Regional Divergence and Growth Performance in East Germany 90
Table 9: Productivity and Wage Levels in the New *Länder* (Total New *Länder* = 100) 91

Figure 1: Real Growth in the New Länder, 1992 - 1995 (Annual percentage changes, at prices of 1991) 79
Figure 2: East German Industrial Production in Important Branches, 1990 - 1994 (Index of net production; second half year 1990 = 100) 83
Figure 3: „Trade Deficits" in Eastern Germany, 1990 - 1995 (In billion DM and in percentage of total domestic demand) 92

Chapter D

Table 1: Expenditure Structure of the Federation and the Länder 101
Table 2: Revenue Structure of the Federation and Länder 102
Table 3: Primary and Secondary Distribution of Revenues 103
Table 4: Distribution of Tax Revenues to Federal, Land and Local Government in 1992 108
Table 5: The Regulations for the Allotment of Tax Returns to Localities 110
Table 6: Production in the Industrial Sector, New Länder 118
Table 7: Development of Public Debt, 1985 - 1994 120
Table 8: Inflation Rate, 1985 - 1992 121
Table 9: Tax Revenues of New Länder 122
Table 10: Prognosted Effects of the Inclusion of the New Länder in the Current Fiscal Equalization System in Million DM, 1995 123
Table 11: Financial Effects of the Fiscal Equalization System, in Million DM, 1992 (Old Länder) 125
Table 12: Financial Effects of the Federal Consolidation Program in Billion DM, 1995 131

Figure 1: Organization of the Finance Administration 105
Figure 2: Current Equalization Tariff 115
Figure 3: Development of the Interest Rate, 1986 - 1992 120
Figure 4: Actual and Planned Payments from the German Unity Fund to the New Länder 126
Figure 5: Reformed Equalization Tariff 129

Chapter E

Table 1: Europe before the War 140
Table 2: The Exchange Rates Required to Maintain the Purchasing Power of East German Financial Wealth 148
Table 3: Structural Differences between East and West Germany 168
Table A1: Private Land Values in the West 184
Table A2: Private and Privatizeable Land Values in the East 186

Figure 1: The Germanies Compared to Another World 137
Figure 2: East and West Germany Compared 138
Figure 3: Opening the East to the World Capital Market 142

Chapter F

Table 1: Import Penetration at the Retail Level 193
Table 2: Hourly Compensation in Manufacturing 195
Table 3: The IMF Unification Scenario 196

Figure 1: German Unemployment Rate 191

Chapter I

Table 1: Unemployed and Part-Time Workers 221
Table 2: Unemployment and Part-Time Work in the GDR in 1990 223
Table 3: Part-Time Work in the GDR in September 1990 223
Table 4: Amount of Rents 229
Table 5: Revenue and Expenditure of the Social Security Systems 231

Chapter K

Table 1: Pollution of the Rhine River 241
Table 2: Pollution of the Rivers Flowing into the North Sea 241
Table 3: Maternal Milk 244
Table 4: Air Pollution in the Former GDR (1988) 245
Table 5: Pollution Fees in the Former GDR (1988/1989) (millions of marks) 249
Table 6: Ecological Overview 249
Table 7: Funds Required to Alleviate Worst Damages (billion marks) 255
Table 8: SO_2 and No_X Emissions of European Countries (1985)(kg/capita/a) 257
Table 9: Forest Damage (1989) (% of total forest stock) 257
Table 10: Development of Emissions (1988) 257
Table 11: Agriculture: Herbicides/Fertilizers/Yield Ratio 258
Table 12: Investments in Environmental Protection (international level) 258
Table 13: GDR Investments in Environmental Protection 259
Table 14: Industrial Ministries Investment in Environmental Protection 260
Table 15: Investments in Environmental Protection According to Conurbation Centers 261

Chapter L

Table 1: Emissions: SO_2 and NO_X (1985) 267
Table 2: CO_2 Emissions (1986) 269
Table 3: Energy Intensity (1987) 272
Table 4: Energy Consumption: GDR and FRG (1987) 273
Table 5: Structure of Electricity Production: GDR and FRG (1988), Percentage Share of Energy Sources 275
Table 6: Source of CO_2: Emissions in the GDR (1987) 279
Table 7: Environmental Emissions in the GDR: A Regional Breakdown 280

Figure 1: Total SO_2- and NO_X-Emissions per Year (1985) in kt 268
Figure 2: SO_2- and NO_X-Emission: kg per Year and Capita (1985) 268
Figure 3: CO_2 Emissions: Tons per Year and Capita 270
Figure 4: Energy Consumption per Capita, 1987: Kg SKE per Capita 271
Figure 5: Energy Intensity (1987) 272
Figure 6: Energy Consumption in the GDR and FRG (1988). Energy Sources (%) 274
Figure 7: Emissions in the GDR (1988): Contribution of the Energy Sector (%) 277
Figure 8: Total Emissions in the GDR (1988, kt) 277

Chapter M

Table 1: Basic Data on the German Democratic Republic, 1989 289
Table 2: Sector Structures of the GDR and the FRG 291
Table 3: Industry Structures of the GDR and the FRG, 1988 293
Table 4: Enterprises, Employment and Production in GDR Industry by Size of Enterprise, 1988 294
Table 5: Enterprises and Employment in GDR Craft Sectors by Legal Form of Enterprise, 1988 295
Table 6: Privatization of Firms (by December 31, 1993) 309
Table 7: Privatization Sales to Foreign Investors (by December 31, 1993) 310

Chapter O

Table 1: Absolute and Relative Price Changes in the GDR from July 1989 to July 1990 (percent) 325
Table 2: Index of Industrial Production in the GDR (1989 = 100) 326
Table 3: Registered Openings and Closings of Enterprises in the GDR 1990 330
Table A1: Unemployment and Short-Time Work in the (Former) GDR 338
Table A2: Selected Measures for Promoting Fixes Capital Formation in the Five New States 339
Table A3: Selected Measures for Promoting the Employment of Labor in the Five New States 342

Figure 1: Unemployment, Short-Time Work and Industrial Production in in the (Former) GDR 1990 323
Figure 2: Evaluation of Inventories in Wholesale and Retail Trade of the GDR, July 1990 (percent of reviewed enterprises) 328
Figure 3: Production Function, Factor Prices and Subsidies 332

Chapter Q

Table 1: Physical Productivity and Gross Value-Added per Employee in Small Firms in Eastern Germany 364
Table 2: Employment and Unemployment in Eastern Germany, 1989 - 93 (in 1000) 365
Table 3: Sectoral Shares in Gross Value-Added in Eastern Germany, 1990.2 (second half) and 1993 369
Table 4: Voter Turnout in EC Parliamentary Elections (ranked according to 1994 turnout) 380
Table 5: Prospective Enlargements of the EU (figures refer to 1992) 382
Table 6: Bhanzaf Index for EU Countries/Candidates 383
Table 7: Twelve Most Active 3rd Countries in Number of M & As Concerning EC Enterprise, 1990 - 92 384
Table 8: Competitive Position of Eastern Europe in Trade with Germany 385

Figure 1: Labor Market Disequilibria 376

Chapter R

Table 1: Structure of Polish Foreign Trade with Germany in 1989 399
Table 2: Structure of Polish Foreign Trade with Selected Countries in 1989 400

Chapter T

Table 1: Foreign Exchange Between USSR and West Germany (Billions of Foreign Exchange Rubles) 414
Table 2: Foreign Exchange Between USSR and East Germany (Billions of Transferable Rubles) 415
Table 3: West German Share in USSR Total Trade (Percentages) 415
Table 4: East German Share in USSR Total Trade (Percentages) 415
Table 5: Structure of Bilateral Trade Between USSR and East Germany by Commodity Groups (in Percentages) 416
Table 6: Structure of Bilateral Trade Between USSR and West Germany by Commodity Groups (in Percentages) 417
Table 7: Annual Percentage Changes in Bilateral Trade Between USSR-East Germany and USSR-West Germany 418

Chapter Y

Table 1: Key Indicators for West and East Germany in 1989 479
Table 2: Trade and Investment Links with West Germany 1989/90 484
Table 3: Imports and Exports from the USSR and Central Europe in 1989 (bill. US-$) 489
Table 4: German Trade Orientations in 1913 and 1989 491
Table 5: Trade Patterns of the CMEA Countries in 1988 (imports/exports in percent) 493
Table A1: Key Economic Data for Eastern Germany and Western Germany 1990/91 506
Table A2: Exports to European CMEA Partners as a Percentage of Total Exports 506

Map of Western and Eastern Germany 514

Table 1: Origin, Distribution and Expenditure of National Product 516
Table 2: Index of Net Output in the Producing Sector 517
Table 3: Prices 518
Table 4: Selected Economic Data for Eastern Germany 519

Springer-Verlag and the Environment

We at Springer-Verlag firmly believe that an international science publisher has a special obligation to the environment, and our corporate policies consistently reflect this conviction.

We also expect our business partners – paper mills, printers, packaging manufacturers, etc. – to commit themselves to using environmentally friendly materials and production processes.

The paper in this book is made from low- or no-chlorine pulp and is acid free, in conformance with international standards for paper permanency.

MIX
Papier aus verantwortungsvollen Quellen
Paper from responsible sources
FSC® C105338

If you have any concerns about our products,
you can contact us on
ProductSafety@springernature.com

In case Publisher is established outside the EU,
the EU authorized representative is:
Springer Nature Customer Service Center GmbH
Europaplatz 3, 69115 Heidelberg, Germany

Printed by Libri Plureos GmbH
in Hamburg, Germany